Logistics Management and Strategy

Logistics Management and Strategy

Competing through the supply chain

Seventh edition

Heather Skipworth

Remko van Hoek

James Aitken

Alan Harrison

Pearson

Harlow, England • London • New York • Boston • San Francisco • Toronto • Sydney • Dubai • Singapore • Hong Kong
Tokyo • Seoul • Taipei • New Delhi • Cape Town • São Paulo • Mexico City • Madrid • Amsterdam • Munich • Paris • Milan

Pearson Education Limited
KAO Two
KAO Park
Harlow CM17 9NA
United Kingdom
Tel: +44 (0)1279 623623
Web: www.pearson.com

First published 2002 (print)
Second edition published 2005 (print)
Third edition published 2008 (print)
Fourth edition published 2011 (print)
Fifth edition published 2014 (print and electronic)
Sixth edition published 2019 (print and electronic)
Seventh edition published [2025] [print and electronic]

ISBN: 9781292465340 (print)
9781292733463 (ePub)
9781292479897 (eTextbook)

British Library Cataloguing-in-Publication Data
A catalogue record for the print edition is available from the British Library

Library of Congress Cataloging-in-Publication Data
A catalog record for the print edition is available from the Library of Congress

10 9 8 7 6 5 4 3 2 1
23 22 21 20 19
29 28 27 26 25

NOTE THAT ANY PAGE CROSS REFERENCES REFER TO THE PRINT EDITION

To Cathi, Nick, Katie, Maryl, Ticho, Dylan, Jason, Rade, Luka, Daniel, Jacqueline, Garrie and James, with love.

Contents

Part Two LEVERAGING LOGISTICS OPERATIONS

Personal foreword

I am honoured to be asked to write a personal foreword to the latest edition of *Logistics Management and Strategy*. Alan, my husband until his death in October 2012, was justifiably proud of this book; it epitomises his approach to teaching and training, delivering applied theory and research to satisfy rigorous academic enquiry, in a format attractive and useful to busy practitioners and new recruits to the industry. He would be delighted to see his work reach a seventh edition; he relished the challenge of developing a popular and trusted resource, ever seeking to progress in the light of latest thinking and innovation.

Alan's good friends and close academic colleagues Heather, Remko and Jim bring their expertise and passion into the authorship of this book, building on the foundation of Alan's achievement and taking his work into the future. I salute all three, and wish them, this book and all its readers every success.

Catherine Maryon,
October 2024

Professional foreword

I am delighted to introduce *Logistics Management and Strategy*, now in its seventh edition, a further aid in our ability to drive our understanding of such a critical part of the business environment. In my 45 years of operational experience in global supply chains, within Bausch & Lomb, Johnson Matthey and, most recently, as an independent consultant in supply chain management, logistics remains a key area of management attention, given its central role in customer service and the opportunities it provides for cost control, two fundamental essentials for any global business today.

Whilst I was at Bausch & Lomb, the focus was committed to producing state-of-the-art optical products, from contact lenses to cataract surgery and the fast-growing optical pharmaceutical markets. These complex supply chains cover five continents and serve varying types of customers including hospitals, opticians and multiple retailers. They involved stock-keeping units (SKUs) requiring temperature control, serial traceability and sterility, and made for a diverse and challenging set of logistics demands.

When you then add these challenges to a range of over 100,000 SKUs – with some products being offered in over 7,000 different refractive powers/pack sizes – then you can understand why utilising the very latest approaches to logistics management and strategy is absolutely crucial.

During my 23 years at Bausch & Lomb we invested heavily in automated warehouses, such as at our site in Amsterdam, recognised as one of the 'top 10' logistics facilities in the Netherlands. We also developed our utilisation of agile logistics. This was addressed by reducing the number of base products produced in our 17 factories, whilst increasing customer responsiveness through postponement of labelling, bundling, promotional artwork and language compliance. In this regard, being a member of the Agile Supply Chain Research Club at Cranfield University, originally working with Alan and more recently with Heather, has been a rewarding and beneficial experience. I note that some of our experience has been invested in Chapter 7.

My next career move was to work for three years at Johnson Matthey, an FTSE100 company in the automotive sector. Here again the logistics and supply chain management went hand in hand with a global environment, and featured a strong emphasis on a customer-focused supply chain, aggressive cost controls and the use of tools such as sales and operations planning (S&OP), risk analysis and an end-to-end supply chain view from raw materials supply to final customer delivery.

More recently, I have worked for multiple global organisations in supply chain consultancy, and many of the key areas in this publication have been the focus of the needs of those customers time and time again, proving its relevance and timeliness. Indeed, in my career I have found that across multiple industry sectors – pharmaceuticals, healthcare, FMCG and automotive – the fundamentals of supply chain and logistics management are consistent, and therefore the value of this publication is accordingly high across all sectors of industry and commerce.

With the addition of many important supply chain aspects in this latest edition, it is with texts such as *Logistics Management and Strategy* in your armoury that you can continue to drive further improvements in your supply chain. The great aspect of this text is its readability; it does not seek to lecture the reader, but imparts its wisdom in a straightforward and practical manner. Fundamentally, I believe that is the essence of the science of logistics. Every element of our complex logistical environment is captured in this book with new sections including integrated supply chain strategy; supply chain risk assessment and mitigation, (with the recent issues impacting shipping through the Suez canal as a great example of such supply chain risks); global perspectives and coverage; the use of big data including the potential applications of AI; approaches to automation, and of course the impact of environmental considerations to our supply chains – all adding to the rich content.

In introducing this collaboration between Alan, Remko, Heather and James, my parentage springs to mind. This was another Anglo-Dutch partnership, albeit with different outcomes! I have spent the last 45 years in logistics, working in British, American and Dutch environments. The last 30 of these have been in a global role.

It was a personal tragedy when I learned of Alan's illness and eventual passing. As mentioned elsewhere, he was a fantastic contributor to the Agile Supply Chain Research Club and an inspiration to all of us who worked with him. I was fortunate to work with Alan for many years and it was a terrible loss to the world of supply chain when he sadly passed away, but this book is part of a tremendous legacy which he left to us all.

The output of the collaboration between Alan, Remko, Heather and now James rings true in so many areas and offers methods and approaches that will continue to drive our improvements in the coming years.

Paul Mayhew MSc, FCILT
Global Supply Chain Consultant

Preface

Logistics has been emerging from Peter Drucker's shadowy description as 'the economy's last dark continent' for some years. From its largely military origins, logistics has accelerated into becoming one of the key business issues of the day, presenting formidable challenges for managers and occupying some of the best minds. Its relatively slow route to this exalted position can be attributed to two causes. First, logistics is a cross-functional subject. In the past, it has, rightly, drawn on contributions from marketing, finance, operations and corporate strategy. Within the organisation, a more appropriate description would be a *business process*, cutting across functional boundaries yet with a contribution from each. Second, logistics extends beyond the boundaries of the organisation into the supply chain. Here, it engages with the complexities of synchronising the movement of materials and information between many businesses. The *systems nature* of logistics has proved a particularly difficult lesson to learn, and individual organisations still often think that they can optimise profit conditions for themselves by exploiting their partners in the supply chain. Often, they can - in the short term. But winners in one area are matched by losers in another, and the losers are unable to invest or develop the capabilities needed to keep the chain healthy in the long term. Thus, the supply chain as whole loses its competitiveness from this short-term exploitative approach. The emergence of logistics has, therefore, been dependent on the development of a cross-functional model of the organisation, and on an understanding of the need to integrate business processes across the supply network.

Whilst its maturity as a discipline in its own right is still not complete, we believe that it is important to further develop logistics management and strategy. Tools and concepts to enable integration of the supply chain are starting to work well. Competitive advantage in tomorrow's world will come from responding to end-customers better than competition and, to this end, understanding how to exploit the latest advances in technology that are developing at an increasing rate. Logistics and supply chain management play a vital role in this response, and it is this role that we seek to describe in this book.

The globalisation of logistics assumes that quality can be duplicated anywhere, that risks are relatively small, and that sustainability does not really matter. The reality is that twenty-first-century supply chains are developing very different profiles from those developed by the mindsets of 20 or 30 years ago. Risk is growing in its importance. Plans will need to be in place to prevent or mitigate the impact of financial, operational, natural and political uncertainty. It is both environmentally and economically right to focus on sustainability. Logistics stands at the heart of this debate.

This text has a clear European foundation and an international appeal. In line with the globalisation of logistics, we have included cases from other parts of the world than Europe - diverse though European logistics solutions are - including South Africa, the United States, Japan, China and Australia.

Accordingly, we start in Part One with the strategic role of logistics in the supply chain. We continue by developing the marketing perspective by explaining our view of 'putting the end-customer first'. Part One finishes by exploring the concept of value and logistics costs. In Part Two, we review leveraging logistics operations in terms of their global dimensions, and of the lead-time frontier. Part Two continues by examining the challenges of coordinating manufacturing and retail processes, and the impact on logistics of just-in-time and the agile supply chain. Part Three reviews working together, first in terms of integrating the supply chain and second in terms of sourcing and supply management. Our book ends with Part Four, in which we outline the logistics future challenge.

This text is intended for MSc students on logistics courses, and as an accompanying text for open learning courses such as global MSc degrees and virtual universities. It will also be attractive as a management textbook and as recommended reading on MBA options in logistics and supply chain management.

Changes made for past editions

In the second edition, we listened carefully to students and to reviewers alike and set out to build on the foundation of our initial offering. We updated much of the material whilst keeping the clear structure and presentation of the first edition. There were lots of new cases and we updated others. We attempted to touch on many of the exciting developments in this rapidly expanding body of knowledge, such as governance councils, the prospects for a radio frequency identification device (RFID) and the future of exchanges.

The third edition retained the clarity and up-to-date content that had become hallmarks of the previous editions. It continued to provide further new and updated cases to illustrate developments in the subject. Chapters 6, 7 and 10 were largely reconstructed, but we also made many improvements to other chapters resulting from our research and work with industrial partners.

The fourth edition built on the foundations we had developed so far, whilst continuing to update the content and keep it abreast of the rapidly developing logistics body of knowledge. Many of the cases were updated too and new ones introduced. Chapters 6 and 7 were again largely reconstructed, and we refocused Chapter 9 around sourcing and supply management. We continued to develop the theme of sustainable logistics, which we classify as a competitive priority right from the start.

We worked with Alan on the fifth edition before his death, after which we continued without his direct intervention, but very much within his guidance. That edition carried forward the healthy tradition established for this book by further developing areas on the basis of the latest research and providing cases to illustrate practice. In response to reviewers we further developed the alignment between marketing and supply chain, culminating in a new expanded section on segmented supply chain strategy in Chapter 2. We also took the opportunity to reconstruct and expand Chapter 3 on value and logistics costs, equipping the reader with the latest thinking on improving liquidity through supply chain management and approaches to making capital investment decisions. Risk readiness in Chapter 4 was also updated in the light of food scares such as the horsemeat scandal. Related to this, a new section was also added to Chapter 4 to address the global governance of supply chains.

Agility is not new but the concept has developed across organisational and relational practices. Chapter 7 was therefore reconstructed and expanded to reflect the body of knowledge now available on supply chains able to respond to unpredictable demand. Chapter 10 was revised to reflect the changing future and revisited corporate social responsibility from the perspective of supply chain trade-offs. Humanitarian logistics was also a new section, created in response to the growing number of humanitarian crises - both political and natural - and the need for existing supply chain strategies to be applied to save lives. As with all previous editions, many of the cases were updated and new ones introduced. In response to reviewers, we introduced more global cases, such as the Li & Fung case and also food supply chain cases.

For the sixth edition we were fortunate to welcome Professor James Aitken as a third active author. He brings with him a wealth of experience both in industry and academia and has greatly contributed to this edition. We felt it important to ensure that technological advances under the banner of Industry 4.0 were covered, so you will find such additions as big data and the Internet of Things covered in Chapters 2 and 10; the use of industrial robots and augmented reality in Chapter 5; 3D printing, adaptable distribution networks and drones in Chapter 7; an updated review of the use of radio frequency identification devices (RFID) and an entirely new section on blockchain in Chapter 8.

In response to reviewers' comments we have improved and expanded the explanations of the balanced scorecard and the SCOR model in Chapter 3; covered in depth the changing role of logistics service providers, expanded risk management and added a section on tax efficient supply chains in Chapter 4; created a new section on the transaction cost economics (TCE) perspective of relationships in Chapter 8; and expanded the existing section on corporate social responsibility (CSR) in Chapter 10.

We also took the opportunity to improve Chapter 5 to focus more clearly on the various speed trade-offs and how they can be overcome, such as cost versus speed and variety versus speed. We also raise an interesting debate about managing time in a high process variety environment by being mindful of how that time is used. Finally, the section on strategies and practices for the situation where total logistics time (cycle time) is greater than the time the customer is willing to wait has been expanded. Chapter 6 also underwent significant improvement, including a new section on sales and operations planning, incorporating a new case study with a basic simulation tool, and an improved section on efficient consumer response (ECR). Finally Chapter 8 has been expanded to reflect its increasing importance; we have further developed the sections on external integration between companies and electronic integration.

Changes made for the seventh edition

The seventh edition was needed to respond to three areas that are a particular challenge for supply chain management and undergoing rapid development: supply chain risk and resilience; social and environmental sustainability; and the role of technology within the supply chain. So, what have we done to address this?

Over the last few decades supply chains have been extended globally through outsourcing and offshoring and simultaneously leaned out reducing the buffers, such as inventory and capacity, available to respond to supply or demand disruptions. This has left supply chains exposed and vulnerable to risk events, and we have seen many of these over the last few years; to name a few examples, Brexit, US-China trade war, COVID-19, Ukraine-Russian war and Israel-Palestinian war. These have disrupted supply and demand with COVID-19 testing supply chains to breaking point generating global supply and demand shocks simultaneously. To provide relevant knowledge and practices to combat these challenges, we have developed an entirely new Chapter 4 devoted to supply chain risk and resilience, drawing on the latest research, more established enduring knowledge and providing six new case studies. This chapter categorises and explains the many supply chain risks in a newly developed framework. It also describes how international supply chains can be redesigned, at a more structural level, to mitigate risk. The supply chain risk management process is broken down into four clear stages, each of which is explained in depth, including supply chain mapping, risk identification, risk evaluation and risk mitigation. Finally, supply chain resilience is explained in terms of its chronological phases and the required capabilities in response to risk events.

Supply chain sustainability has been of growing importance over the last few years, often topping company's agendas. Environmentally, it is now commonplace for companies to have a next zero carbon emission target, typically 2050, in line with the Paris Agreement. Societally, companies are keen to avoid negative societal impacts in their supply chains, such as modern slavery, forced and/or child labour and dangerous working conditions, and subsequently are signing up to, and aiming to comply with, industry codes of conduct. To address sustainability challenges, we have added new sections in Chapter 1. The first (Section 1.3.3) focuses on the triple bottom line including carbon emission targets and how emissions are measured against these targets across the whole supply chain, using a Nestle case to exemplify. The second new section (1.3.4) covers green logistics describing relevant practices, their influencing factors and alignment of corporate strategy, culminating with a new case at an Italian logistics provider to illustrate these approaches. We've also added a new section (3.5) to Chapter 3 on carbon costing for more sustainable supply chains covering external and internal carbon pricing approaches, and how they incentivise polluting companies to reduce carbon emissions. A case on Volvo illustrates a carbon pricing approach. In Chapter 9 the role of procurement in improving social and environmental sustainability (Section 9.4) has been updated and improved. Finally, in Chapter 10 innovation practices are provided which enable environmentally and socially responsible organisations to gain advantage.

Technology has an ever-stronger role to play in supply chains whether we are considering physical automation and robotics or machine learning and artificial intelligence. We've updated the technological aspects of the book around 3D printing, blockchains, RFID and robotics and added some new sections. For instance, a new section within 5.4.3 on demand forecasting using Artificial Intelligence (AI). We've also added a new section (10.1) in Chapter 10 explaining the latest technological advancements and how they enable new supply chain capability and performance levels. We've also added some new cases on using technologies, such as a case on Altana's unified global supply chain map generated using AI (Case 4.3), Flex Pulse supply chain risk data visualisation (Case 4.5) and Improving information flow and S&OP through Massive IoT sensor technology (Case 6.5).

As with all previous editions, many of the cases have been updated and new ones introduced, such as supplier segmentation at Ford Motor Company, Flex's supply chain resilience levers and Walmart automates supplier negotiations and many more. In response to reviewers' comments, the 19 new cases relate to different sectors and countries to improve the balance of cases.

We are grateful to Paul Mayhew, formerly of Bausch & Lomb and later Johnson Matthey and now a Global Supply Chain Consultant, who has once again written the foreword. We are also indebted to Catherine Maryon, who has provided a personal foreword for this book to pay tribute to our beloved colleague and friend Professor Alan Harrison, who passed away in 2012. We will always miss Alan, and we are proud to take the book to a seventh edition as if he were still by our side.

We hope that our book will offer support to further professional development in logistics and supply chain management, which is needed today more than ever before. In particular, we hope that it encourages you to challenge existing thinking and to break old mindsets by creating a new and more innovative future. Transformation of supply chains is a focus for everyone in the twenty-first century. Since we first launched this textbook in 2001, it has been adopted in the US, Australia, Singapore and South Africa. Our book has also been published in other languages including Greek, Lithuanian and Simplified Chinese.

Authors' acknowledgements

We should like to acknowledge our many friends and colleagues who have contributed to our thinking and to our book. Cranfield colleagues deserve a special mention: Prof Janet Godsell (now Dean at Loughborough Business School), Prof Carlos Mena (now at Portland State University), Dr Simon Templar, Dr Silvia Rossi, Dr Paul Chapman (now at Saïd Business School), Prof Paul Baines and Professor Richard Wilding have all made important contributions. Sri Srikanthan helped us with the financial concepts in Chapter 3. Members of the Agile Supply Chain Research Club at Cranfield also deserve special mention, notably Stuart Bailey of Brakes Group (formerly of Kimberley-Clark), Simon Marshall and Paul Horton of Travis Perkins, Paul Mayhew (formerly of Johnson Matthey and now a Global Supply Chain Consultant), who provides the foreword for the new edition, Ian Shellard and David Evans of Rolls-Royce, Mark Baker of Pentland Brands (who updated Case study 8.6), Joe Thomas of Tesco (who updated Case study 1.1), Martyn Walker of Agility Science and Jody Cleworth of Marine Transport International (who provided Case study 8.8 on blockchains), Jon Hinton and Shane Artiss of DHL (who supported Case study 5.4 on vision picking) and Nicky McGroarty of O2 (for supporting development of Case study 8.4), Matt Ryan of Nestle (who supported development of Case study 1.5). Other individuals who have provided information for cases include Jeremy Roberts of Tilda Limited (Case study 2.3), Ewan McAsh of Oceanfarmr (Case study 6.3), Michael Burton of BinaryBeer who supported Case study 6.5, William Medcalf of Vintage Bentley (Case 7.5), Chris Guacci of DW Windsor Lighting Limited (Case study 7.6), Mohammed Zameer of GKN Driveline who provided material for Case study 5.3, Richard Renshaw of KPMG (also a Cranfield Visiting Fellow), who created an excellent teaching case on Sales and Operations Planning (Case study 6.2), Hasan Khan, a Doctorate student at Cranfield School of Management, who wrote much of Section 4.1, based on his Doctoral Systemic Literature Review and wrote a case on supply chain risk categorisation and prioritisation (Case study 4.1) and Tom Morrison of Altana who provided information for a case on their unified global supply chain map generated using AI (Case study 4.3). We have picked the brains of several who have retired from the industry, including David Aldridge (formerly of Cussons UK) and Philip Matthews (formerly of Boots the Chemist). A number of academics from other universities have contributed ideas and cases, including Prof Corrado Ceruti (University of Roma), Tor Vergata, Prof Marie Koulikoff-Souviron (SKEMA Business School, Nice), Jacques Colin (CretLog, Aix-en-Provence), Prof Konstantinos Zographos (Athens University of Economics and Business), Prof Huo Yanfang (University of Tianjin), Prof Thomas Choi (Arizona State University), Prof David Bennett (Newcastle Business School) and Dr Lorenzo Prataviera (Verona university) who wrote a case on developing a comprehensive approach for Green Logistics in Italy (Case study 1.6) and wrote much of the green logistics section. Iana Shaheen (University of Arkansas) contributed a section on humanitarian logistics in Chapter 10. Multiple industry collaborators and professional friends feature with cases in Chapters 9 and 10, including Dominique Lebigot (Moet Hennessy), Thomas Udesen (Bayer) and Michael deWitt (Walmart). Many of our MSc graduates, such as Steve Walker and Alexander Oliveira, also made important contributions. Prof Yemisi Bolumole (University of Tennessee) helped us to redraft earlier versions of the first edition. Also, we thank the reviewers who made many valuable comments on earlier editions of this book. We are very grateful to all of these, and to the many others who made smaller contributions to making this book possible. Cathi Maryon helped to research several of the cases. Finally, we thank Lynne Wall for helping wherever she could – in addition to helping to run our Centre for Logistics, Procurement and Supply Chain Management at Cranfield!

How to use this book

This book is divided into four parts, centred on a model for logistics. The model for logistics is introduced in the first chapter of Part One, which places logistics in terms of its contribution to competitiveness, customer service and the creation of value. Part Two of the book focuses on leveraging logistics operations within the context of quality of service and cost performance objectives. Part Three focuses on working together, and Part Four pulls together four elements of leading-edge thinking in logistics, homing in on future challenges for the subject.

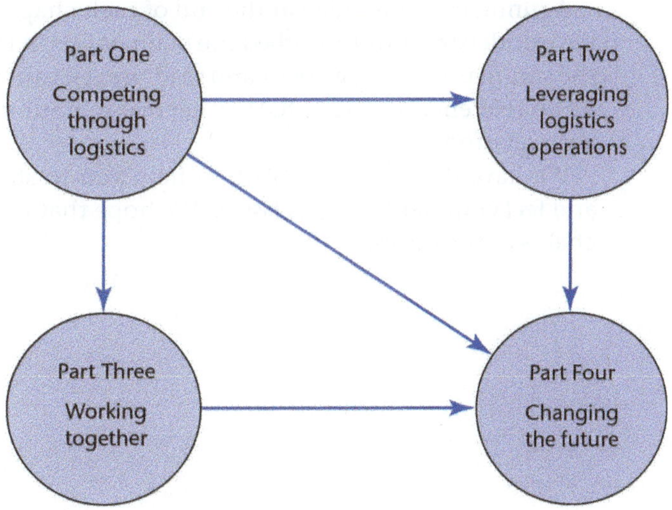

The book has been arranged to take you through the subject in logical stages. The limitation of a text presentation is that the subjects are then arranged in sequence, and links between stages have to be made by the reader. We have set out to facilitate cross-linkages by including:

- *activities* at the end of many of the sections, which are aimed at helping you to think about the issues raised and how they could be applied;
- *discussion questions* at the end of each chapter to help you assess your understanding of the issues raised, and give you practice in using them;
- *case studies*, which draw together a number of issues and help you to think about how those issues are linked together in a practical setting. Use the study questions at the end of each case to guide your thinking.

We have sought to break up the text with figures, tables, activities and case studies, so rarely will you find two successive pages of continuous text. You should, therefore, regard the activities and case studies as an integral part of the method used in this book to help you to learn.

Where possible, discuss the activities and case study questions in groups after you have prepared them individually. Discussion helps to broaden the agenda and create confidence in handling the issues. Whilst you are studying this book, think about the logistics issues it raises – in your own firm or ones that you know well, and in articles in newspapers such as the *Financial Times* and magazines such as *Business Week*. Follow up the website addresses we have included in the text and again link them with the issues raised in the book.

A few words on terminology are appropriate here. We have taken the view that logistics and supply chain management (SCM) are sufficiently different for separate definitions to be needed. We have included these definitions in Chapter 1: logistics is a subset of SCM. 'Supply chain' and 'supply network' are used interchangeably, although we favour 'chain' for a few organisations linked in series and 'network' to describe the more complex inter-linkages found in most situations. Again, our position is explained in Chapter 1.

A summary is provided at the end of each chapter to help you to check that you have understood and absorbed the main points in that chapter. If you do not follow the summary points, go back and read the relevant section again. If need be, follow up on references or suggested further reading. Summaries are also there to help you with revision.

We have designed this book to help you to start out on the logistics journey and feel confident with its issues. We hope that it will help you to improve supply chains of the future.

Plan of the book

Part One COMPETING THROUGH LOGISTICS

Chapter 1
Logistics and the supply chain

Chapter 2
Putting the end-customer first

Chapter 3
Value and logistics costs

Part Two LEVERAGING LOGISTICS OPERATIONS

Chapter 4
Supply chain risk and resilience

Chapter 5
Managing the lead-time frontier

Chapter 6
Supply chain planning and control

Chapter 7
Lean thinking and agile supply chains

Part Three WORKING TOGETHER

Chapter 8
Integrating the supply chain

Chapter 9
Sourcing and procurement

Part Four CHANGING THE FUTURE

Chapter 10
Logistics future challenges and opportunities

Part One

COMPETING THROUGH LOGISTICS

Our model of logistics structures the supply network around three main factors: the flow of materials, the flow of information and the time taken to respond to demand from source of supply. The scope of the network extends from the 'focal firm' at the centre across supplier and customer interfaces, and therefore typically stretches across functions, organisations and their borders. The network is best seen as a system of interdependent processes, where actions in one part affect those of all others. The key 'initiator' of the network is end-customer demand on the right: only the end-customers are free to make up their mind when to place an order. After that, the system takes over.

Chapter 1 explains how networks are structured, the different ways in which they may choose to compete and how their capabilities have to be aligned with the needs of the end-customer. Chapter 2 places the end-customer first in logistics thinking and develops the theme of aligning logistics strategy with marketing strategy. Chapter 3 considers how value is created in a supply network, how logistics costs can be managed and how a balanced measurement portfolio can be designed.

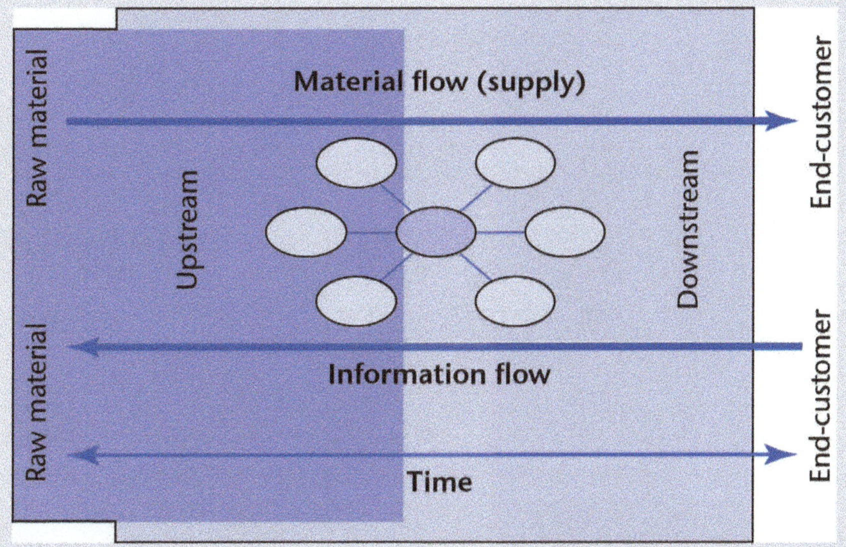

CHAPTER 1

Logistics and the supply chain

Objectives

The intended objectives of this chapter are to:

- **identify and explain logistics definitions and concepts that are relevant to managing the supply chain;**
- **identify how supply chains compete in terms of hard objectives, time, cost and quality and supporting capabilities, dependability, agility and sustainability;**
- **understand supply chain sustainability in terms of the triple bottom line, environmental, societal, and economic values;**
- **examine green logistics, the wide ranging green practices, what influences their application and how to align corporate strategy;**
- **show how different supply chains may adopt different and distinctive strategies for competing in the marketplace.**

By the end of this chapter you should be able to understand:

- **how supply chains are structured;**
- **different ways in which supply chains may choose to compete in the marketplace;**
- **the need to align supply chain capabilities with competitive priorities.**

Introduction

It takes only 17 hours or so to assemble a car, and a couple more days are needed to ship it to the customer via the dealer. So why does it take more than a month for a manufacturer to make and deliver the car I want? And why are the products I want to buy so often unavailable on the shelf at the local supermarket? These are questions that go to the heart of **logistics** management and strategy. **Supply chains** today are slow and costly in relation to what they will be like in the future. But let us start at the beginning, by thinking about logistics and the supply chain in terms of what they are trying to do. It is easy to get bogged down in the complexities of how a supply chain actually works (and very few people actually know how a whole supply chain works!). We shall address many of these details later in this book. First, let us focus on how a supply chain competes, and on what the implications are for logistics management and strategy.

The overall aim of this chapter is to provide an introduction to logistics and to set the scene for the book as a whole. The need is to look outside the individual organisation and to consider how it aligns with other organisations in a given supply chain. This is both a strategic and a managerial task: strategic, because it requires long-term decisions about how logistics will be structured and the systems it will use; managerial, because it encompasses decisions about sourcing, making and delivering products and services within an overall 'game plan'.

Key issues

This chapter addresses four key issues:

1. **Logistics and the supply chain:** definitions, structure, tiering.
2. **Material flow and information flow:** the supply chain and the demand chain.
3. **Competing through logistics:** competitive criteria in the marketplace.
4. **Logistics strategies:** aligning capabilities across the supply chain.

1.1 Logistics and the supply chain

Key issues: **What is the supply chain, and how is it structured? What is the purpose of a supply chain?**

Logistics is a big word for a big challenge. Let us begin by giving an example of that challenge in practice, because that is where logistics starts and ends.

CASE STUDY 1.1

Tesco PLC

Tesco PLC is the UK's largest food retailer, with a revenue of about £61.5 billion and more than 330,000 employees in 2023, operating 4,506 stores across the UK, Republic of Ireland, Czech Republic, Slovakia and Hungary. The UK business dominates with 3,786 stores (by the end of 2023); therefore, the remainder of this case focuses on operations in Tesco UK.

Stores and sales channels

Between 2010 and 2013 the number of stores in the UK rose quickly from 2,300 to 3,146, and this was partially due to the opening of further Tesco Express stores (smaller convenience stores, which are now by far the most numerous). Since 2013 the rate of increase in the number of stores has slowed, reaching 3,433 in 2017 and 3,786 in 2023 (see Table 1.1 for a breakdown of the different store formats). The slowing rate of new store openings is mainly due to the increase in online sales, in common with most other retailers. Consistent with the multi-channel approach (discussed in Section 2.1.3), Tesco UK operates an online Tesco store (Tesco.com), where its full range of products, estimated at around 90,000, is available. This channel offers delivery of products direct to the customer's home or, by using 'Click and Collect', the customer can choose a convenient Tesco store (or other location) from which to pick up their order.

Tesco online

When Tesco.com was first opened, Tesco online orders were 'picked' from stores open to the public (rather than distribution centres). However, since 2009 Tesco UK has operated a number of 'dark' stores dedicated to the fulfilment of online orders, now known as 'Dotcom' stores. As shown in Table 1.1 there are now six **Dotcom stores**, which are distribution centres (DC) that exclusively process online orders and are not open to consumers from the general public. They may be similar to conventional supermarkets laid out with aisles of shelves but, dissimilar to retail stores – there are no shop assistants or check-outs. Online orders are processed and optimised picking routes are created using the store layout. The online orders are then picked 24 hours a day, 7 days a week, by employees, known as 'personal shoppers', who normally are processing multiple orders at the same time. Online sales remains strong accounting for approximately 34 per cent of revenue. Online availability has been increased to 98.1 per cent, and the rapid delivery service, Whoosh, has been rolled out to 1,424 stores, with 74 per cent of deliveries arriving within 30 minutes!

Table 1.1 Tesco's UK stores as of April 2023.

Format	Number	Total area (m^2)	Percentage of space	Changes in number of stores through 2023
Large Store (Extra and Superstore)	805	2,919,663	67.1 per cent	+7
Convenience (Express)	1,998	496,473	11.4 per cent	+60
One Stop	712	108,603	2.5 per cent	+27
Dotcom only (online fulfilment)	6	66,518	2.3 per cent	
Booker	191	760,039	17.5 per cent	
Total	3,712	4,351,299	100 per cent	

Product range

The product range offered by Tesco has expanded quickly, establishing a presence in the non-food market for such items as entertainment, toys, electrical goods, clothing, gardening and the like. This extensive range is supplied by thousands of suppliers, who are contracted to meet specified service levels (in terms of both timing and quantities) by delivering to Tesco within specific time 'windows'. Considering just England 270 suppliers are each supplying more than 1,250 products. The annual quantities delivered to Tesco stores by suppliers are staggering at around 2 billion cases of product. This is part of a virtuous circle where Tesco develops economies of scale with its suppliers, allowing it to provide attractive offers for consumers, which results in Tesco selling more, and increased economies of scale and this cycle continues. This is an important element of the Tesco business model.

Material flow from suppliers to stores

An early improvement for supermarket operation was to ensure suppliers delivered to depots rather than to every store. During the 1980s, 26 depots distributed to retail stores and these depots were small and not so efficient with just a single-temperature operation – no chiller or freezer areas. It was not economically viable to deliver to each store every day, because delivery volumes were relatively low. Any products that needed temperature-controlled conditions were transported on special separate vehicles. Ordering systems were not common across product groups but instead differed leading to further inefficiencies and complexities. This depot network was unable to process the volume growth and the more demanding standards for temperature control; therefore, an improved distribution strategy was required.

Fresh food depots, which provided a number of different storage temperature environments, replaced many of the existing small depots which had insufficient temperature control facilities. The opportunity was to provide a cost-effective daily delivery service of fresh product to all stores, based on the idea that commonly, a fresh food depot can process over 80 million cases per year with a 40-acre site. The depot building provides three temperature zones: –25°C (frozen), 1°C (chilled) and 12°C (semi-ambient). Each depot serves a group of between 50 and 500 retail stores. To enable fresh food delivery vehicles to not only operate at different temperatures, but be able to vary the space available at each temperature, insulated trailers were used which were divided into chambers by means of movable bulkheads. Using both in-house and outsourced logistics, deliveries to stores are made within scheduled time windows. Long shelf-life food and non-food products, such as dried food and electrical items, are delivered separately.

Tesco has introduced different retail store formats (as shown in Table 1.1) – Extra, Superstore, Metro, Express and One Stop – which vary considerably in size from 6,500 square metres (Extra) to 150 square metres (One Stop). They also stock different product ranges and are strategically positioned in different locations from out of town (Extra) to city centre (Express). The resulting variety in terms of product ranges, location and size and design of store presents major challenges to supply chain management. For instance, delivering to a Tesco Express in the middle of London will require frequent small deliveries using small vans facing strict restrictions in delivery times and Ultra Low Emission Zones. On the other hand, a Tesco Extra will require lorry load deliveries of a much wider product range.

Jack's stores

In September 2018 Tesco announced its plans to launch a chain of discount stores. Chief executive Dave Lewis claimed that Jack's – named after Tesco founder Sir Jack Cohen – would be cheaper than Aldi or Lidl. Jack's stores will sell 2,600 products – far fewer than the 35,000 carried by a Tesco Superstore – with 1,800 branded 'Jack's'. This compares to the reduced variety offered by Lidl and Aldi. It was a strategy to drive lower prices through aggregating demand onto fewer suppliers and improving distribution and retailing efficiencies through the simplicity, and reduced volatility in demand, enabled by lower variety. However, in January 2022 Tesco announced it will close down seven of its Jack's stores, while the remaining six branches will be converted into Tesco Superstores. Jason Tarry, chief executive of Tesco UK and Ireland, said:

"We have learnt a huge amount from Jack's and this has helped Tesco become more competitive, more efficient and strengthened our value proposition, including through the launch of Aldi price match (BBC, 2022)."

But, according to *Forbes* (Faithfull, 2022) Tesco's real problem was that Aldi and Lidl had already become very well established in the UK, with their success driven through the aggregation of huge volumes across their *European* estate, enabling enormous buying power to deliver both quality and value. Jack's could never match that buying power. Plus Aldi and Lidl have both created reasons, beyond low prices, to drive loyalty, such as expanded homewares, and the cult following of their ever-changing central aisle concept.

Information flow

So much for the method of transporting goods from supplier through to the stores, but how much should be sent to each store? With such a huge product range today, it is impossible for the individual store to reorder across the whole range (store-based ordering). Instead, sales of each product line are tracked continuously through the till by means of electronic point of sale (EPOS) systems. As a customer's purchases are scanned through the barcode reader at the till, the sale is recorded automatically for each stock-keeping unit (SKU). Cumulative sales by store are updated frequently on Tesco Information Exchange (TIE), a system based on the Internet. TIE enables Tesco and its suppliers to more effectively communicate trading information to reduce lead times from manufacturer to stores and to maintain high product availability on Tesco's shelves. TIE enables many improvement initiatives, such as improving the introduction of new products, running promotions and monitoring service levels.

Using sales information on TIE Tesco places orders with its suppliers by means of electronic data interchange (EDI). Tesco reduce stock in their depots by ordering only what is required to meet the next day's forecast sales. For fast-moving products such as washing powders and certain types of cheese, the aim is *day 1 for day 2*: that is, to order today what is needed for tomorrow. The target is to *pick to zero* in the depot so no stock is left after the store orders have been fulfilled. This way the same space in the depot can be used many times over. To improve product availability at stores during a given day, and meet fluctuations in demand through the day, deliveries to stores are made in two *waves*, at specific times and within defined windows. Finally, to meet customers' need for fast and convenient shopping Tesco are piloting new tills at their Express store in Fulham Reach, giving customers the option to checkout their products without scanning them.

(Source: Updated by Joe Thomas (Tesco), 2010, through access to the Tesco PLC website (www.tescoplc.com) October 2013, and from the Tesco Annual Report 2018 and 2024.)

Questions

1. Describe the key logistics processes at Tesco UK.
2. What do you think are the main logistics challenges in running Tesco UK?
3. Why do you think the Jack's stores failed?

So why has Tesco grown in an intensely competitive market? Tesco has to understand customer needs and how they can be served. Its products must be recognised by its customers as representing outstanding value for money. To support such goals, it must ensure that the products that its customers want are available on the shelf at each of its stores, and online, at all times, day and night. Logistics is the task of planning and controlling the purchase and distribution of Tesco's massive product range from suppliers to stores. Logistics is concerned with managing two key flows:

- *material flow* of the physical goods from suppliers through the distribution centres to stores and for the online business through to the end-customer;
- *information flow* of demand data from the end-customer back to purchasing and to suppliers, and supply data from suppliers to the retailer, so that material flow can be planned and controlled accurately.

The logistics task of managing material flow and information flow is a key part of the overall task of *supply chain management.* Supply chain management is concerned with managing the entire chain of processes, including raw material supply, manufacture, packaging and distribution to the end-customer. The Tesco UK supply chain comprises three main functions:

- *distribution:* the operations and support task of managing Tesco's distribution centres (DCs), the distribution of products from the DCs to the associated stores and, in the case of the online offering, delivery to the end-customer;
- *network and capacity planning:* the task of planning and implementing sufficient capacity in the supply chain to ensure that the right products can be procured in the right quantities now and in the future;
- *supply chain development:* the task of improving Tesco's supply chain so that its processes are stable and in control, it is efficient, and it is correctly structured to meet the logistics needs of material flow and information flow.

Thus, logistics can be seen as part of the overall supply chain challenge. Whilst the terms 'logistics' and 'supply chain management' are often used interchangeably, logistics is actually a subset of supply chain management. It is time for some definitions.

1.1.1 Definitions and concepts

A supply chain as a whole ranges from basic commodities (what is in the ground, sea or air) to selling the final product to the end-customer, to recycling the used product. Material flows from raw materials (such as a bauxite mine as a source of aluminium ore) to the finished product (such as a can of cola). The can is recycled after use. The analogy to the flow of water in a river is often used to describe organisations near the source as *upstream* and those near the end-customer as *downstream.* We refer to firms that are involved in supply chains as *partners,* because that is what they are. There is a collective as well as an individual role to play in the conversion of basic commodity into finished product. At each stage of the conversion, there may be *returns,* which could be reject material from the preceding firm, or waste such as the finished can that needs to be recycled. Sometimes, the whole product is wasted because the consumer throws it away.

A supply chain is a network of partners who collectively convert a basic commodity (upstream) into a finished product (downstream) that is valued by end-customers, and who manage returns at each stage.

Each partner in a supply chain is responsible directly for a process that *adds value* to a product.

A process transforms *inputs* in the form of materials and information into *outputs* in the form of goods and services.

In the case of the cola can, partners carry out processes such as mining, transportation, refining and hot rolling. The cola can has *greater value* than the bauxite (per kilogram of aluminium).

Supply chain management (SCM) involves *planning and controlling* all of the processes from raw material production to purchase by the end-user to recycling of the used cans. Planning refers to making a plan that defines how much of each product should be bought, made, distributed and sold each day, week or month. Controlling means keeping to plan – in spite of the many problems that may get in the way. The aim is to coordinate planning and control of each process so that the needs of the end-customer are met correctly. The definition of SCM used in this book is adapted from the Council of SCM Professionals (CSCMP, 2010):

SCM encompasses the planning and controlling of all processes involved in procurement, conversion, transportation and distribution across a supply chain. SCM includes coordination and collaboration between partners, which can be suppliers, intermediaries, third-party service providers or customers. In essence, SCM integrates supply and demand management within and between companies in order to serve the needs of the end-customer.

'Serve the needs of the end-customer' has different implications in different contexts. In not-for-profit environments, such as public health and local government, serving implies 'continuously improving', 'better than other regions/countries', 'best value', and the like. In the commercial sector, serving implies 'better than competition', 'better value for money', and so on. In either situation, the focus of managing the supply chain as a whole is on *integrating* the processes of supply chain partners, of which the end-customer is the key one. In effect, the end-customer starts the whole process by buying finished products. It is the buying behaviour of the end-customer that causes materials to flow through the supply chain. This shall be explored later in Chapter 2.

The degree to which the end-customer is satisfied with the finished product depends crucially on the management of material flow and information flow along the supply chain. If delivery is late, or the product has bits missing, the whole supply chain is at risk from competitors who can perform the logistics task better. Logistics is a vital enabler for supply chain management. We use the following definition of logistics in this book:

Logistics is the task of coordinating material flow and information flow across the supply chain to meet end-customer needs.

Logistics has both *strategic* (long-term planning) and *managerial* (short- and medium-term planning and control) aspects. A breakdown of costs in a supermarket's supply chain is as follows:

- Supplier delivery to supermarket's distribution centre (DC) — 18 per cent
- DC operations and deliver to store — 28 per cent
- Store replenishment — 46 per cent
- Supplier replenishment systems — 8 per cent

Nearly half of the supply chain costs were incurred in in-store replenishment. In order to reduce these in-store costs, the supermarket realised that the solution is 'to spend more upstream and downstream to secure viable trade-offs for in-store replenishment'. If a product is not available on the shelf, the sale is potentially lost. By integrating external manufacturing and distribution processes with its own, the supermarket seeks to serve the needs of its customers better than its competitors. This might include, for instance, ensuring all products are supplied in retail-ready packaging (RRP) and merchandisable units (MUs) to simplify and improve the speed of shelf replenishment and reduce costs.

1.1.2 Supply chain: structure and tiering

The concept of a supply chain suggests a series of processes linked together to form a chain. In Figure 1.1 milk is produced by a dairy cooperative and shipped to a cheese factory. Once made, the cheese is shipped to the manufacturer's national distribution centre (NDC), where it is stored and matured for nine months. It can then be shipped in response to an order from the retailer and is transported first to the retailer's regional distribution centre (RDC). From there, it is shipped to the store. Looking at the arrows in Figure 1.1, we can see that material flows from left to right. Information is shared across the chain: it is demand from the end-customer that makes the whole chain work.

If we look more closely at what happens in practice, the term 'supply chain' is somewhat misleading in that the 'chain' represents a simple series of links between a basic commodity (milk in this case) and a final product (cheese). Thus, the cheese

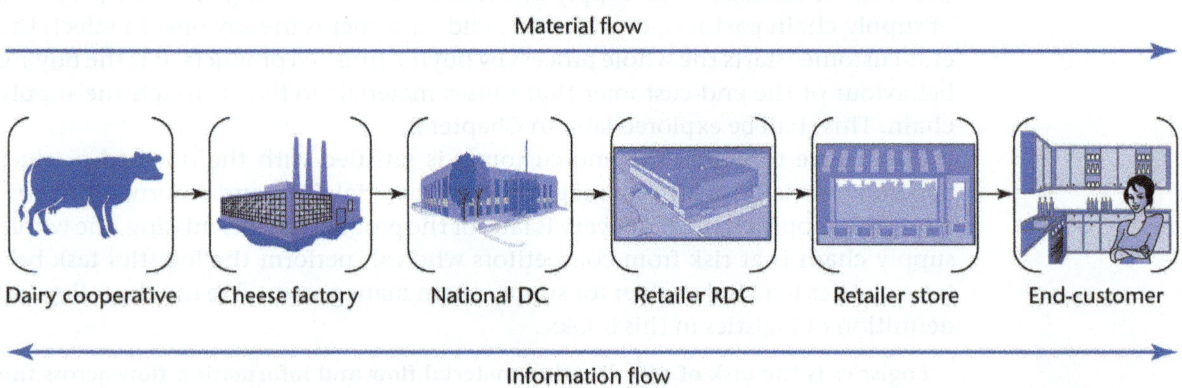

Figure 1.1 **From cow to customer.**

manufacturer will need packaging materials such as film, labels and cases. Cheese requires materials additional to milk in the manufacturing process. So the manufacturer deals with suppliers other than the milk cooperative alone. Once made, the cheese is dispatched for maturation to the supplier's NDC and then dispatched to many customers in addition to Tesco. Once at a Tesco RDC, the 'chain' spreads again because up to 100 stores are served by a given RDC. The additional complexity prompts many authors to refer to *supply networks* rather than supply chains, a point we return to shortly. Logistics today is also concerned with what happens *after* a product has been sold. Two major concerns are:

- *Reverse logistics:* the return of unwanted goods and packaging in the opposite direction (from right to left) to the normal flow shown in Figure 1.1.
- *Waste:* the discarding of product at any stage in the supply chain due to quality problems – for example, the disposal of out-of-date or damaged stock by a retailer or by an end-customer. We consider waste more generally in Chapter 6 under 'just-in-time' scheduling and in Chapter 7 under 'lean' supply chain strategies.

A more realistic representation of the supply chain is shown in Figure 1.2, where each link can connect with several others. A *focal firm* is shown at the centre of many possible connections with other supplier and customer companies.

The supply chain can be seen in this diagram as a number of processes that extend across organisational boundaries. The focal firm is embedded within the chain, and its internal processes must coordinate with others that are part of the same chain. Materials flow from left (upstream) to right (downstream). If everything is as orderly as it seems, only then the end-customer (to the extreme right of the chain) is free to place orders when he or she likes: after that, the system takes over.

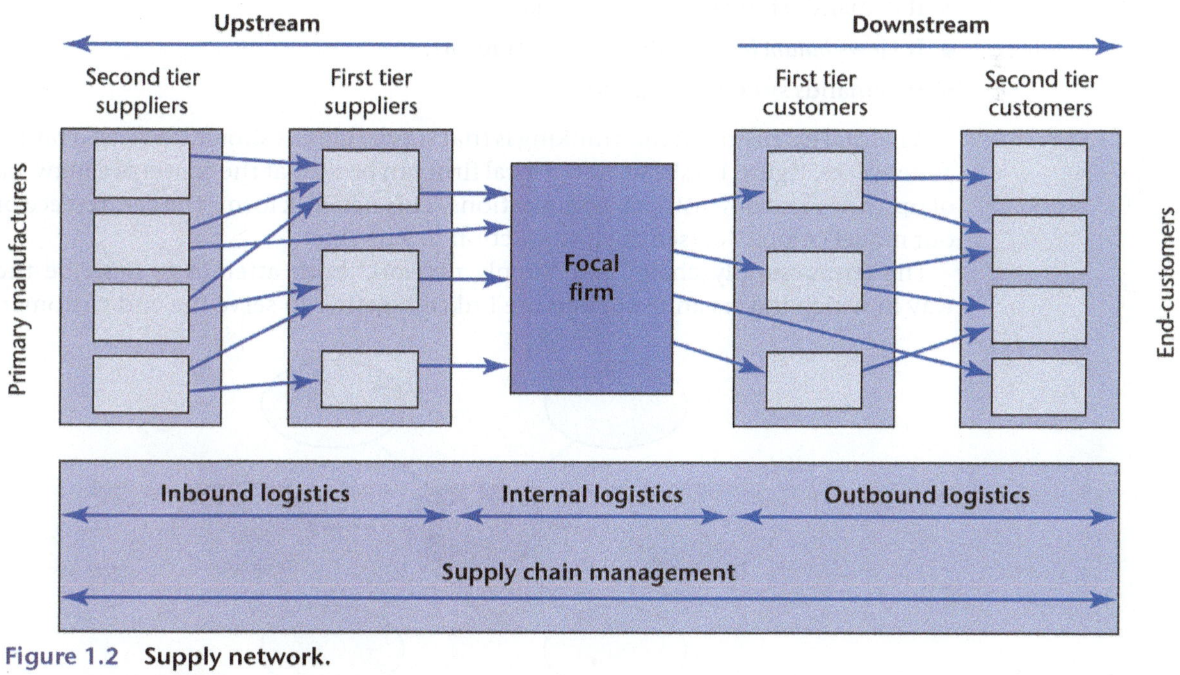

Figure 1.2 Supply network.
(Source: Adapted from Slack et al., 1997.)

The supply chain is *tiered,* in that inbound and outbound can be organised into groups of partners with which we deal. Thus, if we place an assembler such as the Ford plant at Valencia as the focal firm, *inbound logistics* comprises tier 1 suppliers of major parts and subassemblies that deliver directly to Ford, whilst tier 2 suppliers deliver to the tier 1s, and so on. *Outbound logistics* covers the supply by the Ford Valencia plant to national sales companies as tier 1 customers, which in turn supply to main dealers at tier 2, and so on. *Internal logistics* covers the planning and control of parts movements within the Ford Valencia plant. The ultimate aim of supply chain management is to *integrate* inbound, outbound and internal logistics into a seamless whole, focused on meeting end-customer needs with no waste.

Other terms that are used to describe aspects of managing the supply chain are:

- *Purchasing and supply* deals with a focal firm's immediate suppliers (upstream).
- *Physical distribution:* the task of distributing products to tier 1 customers (downstream).
- *Logistics* refers to management of materials and information flows (as defined in Section 1.1.1). *Inbound logistics* deals with links between the focal firm and its upstream suppliers, whilst *outbound logistics* refers to the links between the focal firm and its downstream customers. *Internal logistics* deals with planning and control of material flow within the boundaries of the focal firm.

Supply chain management thus appears as the 'end-to-end' (or 'cow to customer' as we have expressed it in Figure 1.1) management of the network as a whole and of the relationships between the various links. The essential points were summarised long ago by Oliver and Webber (1982):

- Supply chain management views the supply chain as a *single entity.*
- It demands strategic decision making.
- It views *balancing inventories* as a last resort.
- It demands system integration.

A natural extension of this thinking is that supply chains should be viewed rather as networks. Figure 1.3 shows how a focal firm can be seen at the centre of a network of upstream and downstream organisations. This network forms the centrepiece of our model of logistics (see the introduction to Part One).

The terms 'supply chain' and 'supply network' both attempt to describe the way in which buyers and suppliers are linked together to serve the end-customer.

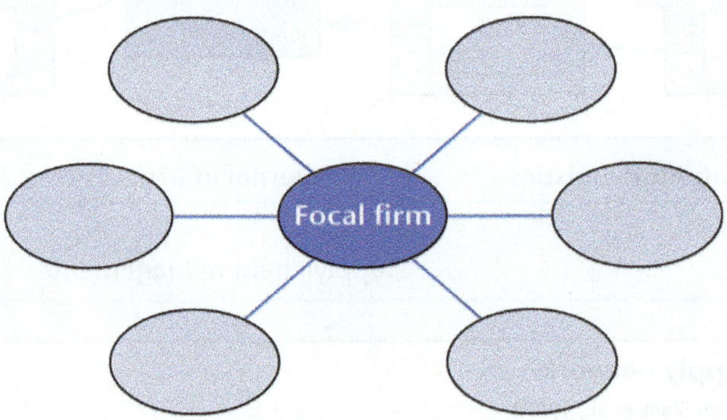

Figure 1.3 A network of organisations.

'Network' describes a more complex structure, where organisations can be cross-linked and there are two-way exchanges between them; 'chain' describes a simpler, sequential set of links (Harland et al., 2001). We have used the terms interchangeably in this book, preferring 'chain' to describe simpler linear sequences of a few organisations and 'network' where there are many organisations linked in a more complex way.

Figure 1.3 takes a basic view of the network, with a focal firm linked to three upstream suppliers and three downstream customers. If we then add material flow and information flow to this basic model, and place a boundary around the network, Figure 1.4 shows the network in context. Here, we have added arrows showing the logistics contribution of material and information flows, together with the time dimension. Material flows from primary manufacture (for example, farming, mining or forestry) through various stages of the network to the end-customer. Material flow represents the *supply* of product through the network in response to demand from the next (succeeding) organisation. Information flow broadcasts *demand* from the end-customer to preceding organisations in the network. The time dimension addresses the question 'How long does it take to get from primary source to the end-customer?' That is, how long does it take to get the product through the various stages from one end of the supply chain to the other? Time is important because it measures the speed with which a given network can respond to demand from the end-customer. In fact, the concept of flow is based on time:

Flow measures the quantity of material (measured in input terms such as numbers of components, tonnes or litres) that passes through a given network per unit of time.

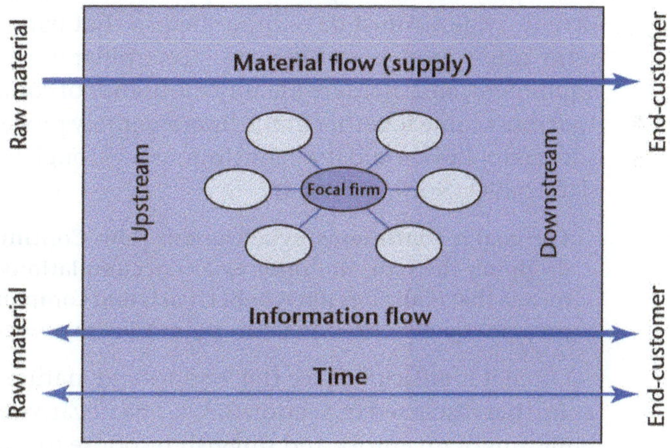

Figure 1.4 The network in context.

Activity 1.1

Draw a network map showing how your organisation, or one that you know well, links with other organisations. Explain the upstream, downstream and internal processes as far as you can. We expect you to address at least the first tiers of demand and supply. You will derive further benefit from researching additional tiers and by developing the linkage of relationships that is involved. Explain how these work in practice and how materials flow between the different tiers.

An important point here is that the supply network should be viewed as a *system*. All processes within the network need to be understood in terms of how they interact with other processes. No organisation is an island: its inputs and outputs are affected by the behaviour of other players in the network. One powerful, disruptive player can make life very difficult for everyone else. For example, several auto assemblers optimise their own processes, but disrupt those of upstream suppliers and downstream distributors. The effect is to increase total system costs *and* reduce responsiveness to **end-customer demand**.

1.2 Material flow and information flow

***Key issue:* What is the relationship between material flow and information flow?**

As we have already seen, logistics is about managing material flow and information flow. In this section, we examine material flow and information flow in more detail.

1.2.1 Material flow

The aim within a supply chain is to keep materials flowing from source to end-customer. The time dimension in Figure 1.4 suggests that parts are moved through the supply chain as quickly as possible. In order to prevent local build-ups of inventory, flow must be orchestrated so that parts movement is coordinated. The term often used is *synchronous*. Caterpillar Inc. makes complex earth-moving equipment, and there are literally thousands of component parts and subassemblies that must come together in the final assembly processes. The vision is that parts and subassemblies should flow continuously through the supply chain, all orchestrated like a ballet (Knill, 1992: 54):

> **The goal is continuous, synchronous flow. Continuous means no interruptions, no dropping the ball, no unnecessary accumulations of inventory. And synchronous means that it all runs like a ballet. Parts and components are delivered on time, in the proper sequence, exactly to the point they're needed.**

Often it is difficult to see the 'end-to-end' nature of flow in a given supply chain, as further discussed in Section 2.3.4. The negative effects of such difficulty include build-ups of inventory and sluggish response to end-customer demand. And sheer greed by the most powerful members of a supply chain often means that it is weaker partners (notably small- to medium-sized enterprises – SMEs) who end up holding the inventories. So management strategies for the supply chain require a more holistic look at the links and an understanding that organisational boundaries easily create barriers to flow.

Case study 1.2 describes how one company – Xerox in this case – re-engineered material flow in its distribution system.

CASE STUDY 1.2

Xerox

Once the problems of introducing 'just-in-time' production systems (internal logistics) had been solved at the Xerox plant making photocopiers at Venray in Holland, attention shifted towards the finished product inventory (outbound logistics). Historically, stocks of finished products had been 'managed' by trying to turn the sales 'tap' on or off as stocks developed. This was characterised by the familiar 'feast or famine' situations. The objective of the next move for Xerox became clear: making only what you need when you need it, then shipping direct to the customer. But the key question had to be answered: just-in-time for what? The answer is – the end-customer. And customer surveys showed that three types of delivery were needed:

- Commodity products should be delivered 'off the shelf'.
- Middle-range products were required in five days.
- Larger products that had to be integrated into existing customer processes and systems had to be planned months ahead, but the quoted delivery date had to be met 100 per cent.

It was envisaged that this would lead to a radically different inventory 'profile' in the supply chain. Figure 1.5 shows a traditional inventory profile on the left. Most of the stock was held in local depots waiting for customer orders. If the mix had been incorrectly forecast, too many of the wrong products were in plentiful supply, whilst needed products were unavailable. Further, a batch of replacement products would take a long time to fight their way through the pipeline. A new 'just-in-time' strategy was conceived to make the supply chain much more responsive. This strategy had a profound effect on the inventory profile, pushing much of the inventory upstream. The closer that inventory is located towards the end-customer, the higher the value added – and the more that it is committed to a given finished product specification. Instead, inventory was held mostly further upstream. This was a more flexible solution, where product could be assembled finally to known orders and where it had lower value. Of course, it has since been possible to remove several stages of the distribution process, thereby eliminating some of the sources of inventory altogether.

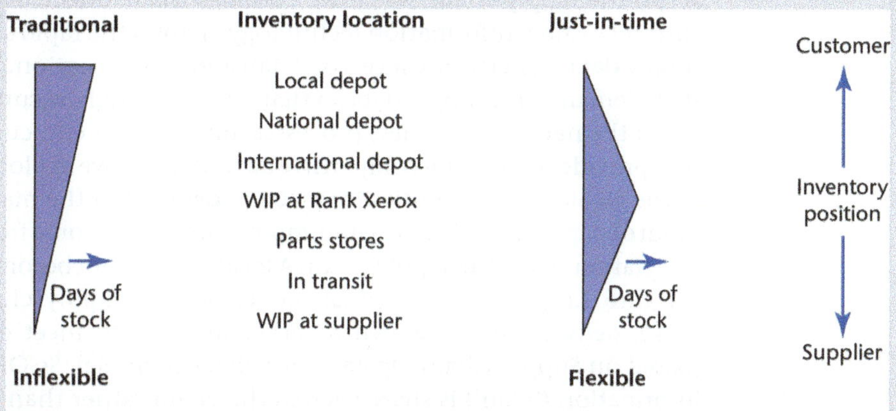

Notes: WIP = work in progress, i.e. products being worked on, but not yet ready for sale.
Shaded areas indicate days of stock: the wider the area, the more days of stock in that position.

Figure 1.5 Xerox: the impact on inventories.

For commodity products, Xerox coined the term *deliver JIT*: that is, the product had to be delivered out of stock. Where sales forecasts are traditionally poor, the challenge was one of flexibility, simplicity and speed of manufacture. For mid-range products, it was unrealistic to hold 'just-in-case' inventories of products that are too complex to be assembled quickly. Instead, *finish JIT* was the term coined to describe the new policy of building semi-finished products with the minimum of added value, consistent with being able to complete and deliver the product in the five-day target. Finally, *build JIT* was the term used to describe the new philosophy of building larger products quickly within a defined lead time.

The impact of the new build philosophies on the downstream supply chain processes can be judged from Figure 1.6. Whilst the traditional inventory profile shows a maximum number of days of stock (shown in the shaded area) at finished product level, this is risky. It always seems that demand is greatest for the very items that are not available! *Postponing* the decision on exact specification until as late as possible in the process, when we are more likely to know precisely what the end-customer wants, helps to create the much flattened inventory profile to the right of the diagram. These are issues to which we return in Chapter 7 under agile practices.

(Source: Based on Eggleton, (1990).)

Question

1. How did inventory reduction in the supply chain lead to improved competitiveness at Xerox?

1.2.2 Information flow

As asked in the Xerox Case study, just-in-time *for what*? It is all well and good to get materials flowing and movements synchronised, but the 'supply orchestra' needs to respond in unison to a specific 'conductor'. The 'conductor' in this analogy is actually the end-customer, and it is the end-customer's demand signals that trigger the supply chain to respond. By sharing the end-customer demand information across the supply chain, we create a *demand chain,* directed at providing enhanced customer value. Information technology enables the rapid sharing of demand and supply data at increasing levels of detail and sophistication. The aim is to integrate such demand and supply data so that an increasingly accurate picture is obtained about the nature of business processes, markets and end-customers. Such integration provides increasing competitive advantage, as we explore further in Chapter 8.

The greatest opportunities for meeting demand in the marketplace with a maximum of **dependability** and a minimum of inventory come from implementing such integration across the supply chain. A focal firm cannot become 'world class' by itself!

Figure 1.6 gives a conceptual model of how supply chain processes (source, make, deliver) are integrated together in order to meet end-customer demand (based on Supply Chain Operations Reference model, SCOR®). Demand planning information ('plan') is shared across the chain rather than being interpreted and then changed by the 'sell' process next to the market. Demand fulfilment is also envisaged as an integrated process, as materials are moved from one process to the next in a seamless flow. Information is the 'glue' that binds supply chain processes together, and which coordinates planning and fulfilment. (We explain the SCOR model in more detail in Section 3.7.)

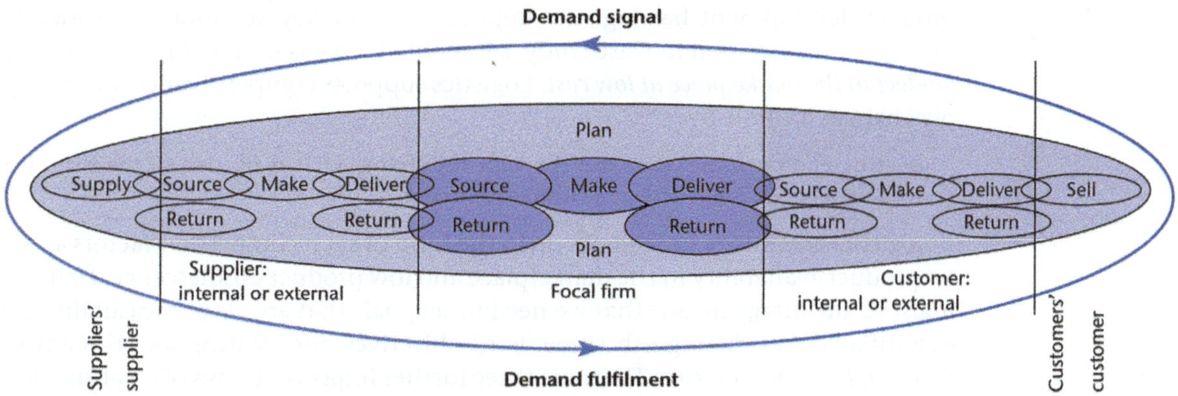

Figure 1.6 **Integrating demand and supply chains.**

Activity 1.2

Write a brief (200 words) appraisal of material and information flow in the supply network affecting one of the major products in the response you gave in Activity 1.1. Perhaps the current situation is different from the above ideals?

1.3 Competing through logistics

***Key issues:* How do products win orders in the marketplace? How does logistics contribute to competitive advantage?**

There are many potentially conflicting demands on an organisation today. All those unreasonable customers seem to want it yesterday, at lower prices and to be compensated if it goes wrong! Within a given supply chain, it is important that each organisation understands how each group of products competes in the marketplace and that it aligns its capabilities with those of its partners.

A 'product' is actually a combination of the *physical product* (for example, a 200 g pack of Camembert cheese) and its accompanying *service* (for example, how it is merchandised in the store – easy to find, always available, attractive presentation, lighting, temperature). Whilst the physical product is determined by marketing and research and development (R&D), service is influenced heavily by logistics.

It is impossible to be outstanding at everything, and supply chain partners need to give priority to capabilities that give each product group its competitive edge. These are the advantages where supply chain partners 'dig in deep' by giving priority to investment and training, and by focusing on product development and marketing efforts. They need only match industry average performance on other criteria. Let us now look at the competitive priorities that can be delivered by logistics in the supply chain.

There are various ways in which products compete in the marketplace. Perhaps a given product is something that no one else can match in terms of price. Or maybe you offer a product that is technically superior, such as Gillette razors. Whilst new product development has logistics implications, the key advantage provided by logistics – as suggested in Case study 1.1 about Tesco – is *availability of conforming product in the marketplace at low cost.* Logistics supports competitiveness of the supply chain as a whole by:

> **meeting end-customer demand through supplying what is needed in the form it is needed, when it is needed, at a competitive cost.**

Logistics advantage thus shows up in the form of such competitive factors as better product availability in the marketplace and low product obsolescence. Defining logistics advantage means that we need to set goals that are clear, measurable and quantifiable. We distinguish three 'hard objectives' for creating logistics advantage: *quality, time* and *cost.* There are three further important ways of creating logistics advantage: *controlling variability* in logistics processes, *dealing with uncertainty* and *sustainability.* We have called these 'supportive capabilities', and they can be just as important as hard objectives. Finally, there are 'soft objectives', which relate to service aspects such as the confidence customers develop in the way the logistics operation is performed. Let us look at each of these ways of creating advantage in turn.

1.3.1 Hard objectives

Traditional ways of competing are to offer the end-customer advantages related to product quality, the speed with which it is delivered, and/or the price at which it is offered. We refer to quality, time and cost as 'hard objectives' because they are easy to measure and relatively obvious to the end-customer.

The quality advantage

The most fundamental objective – in that it is a foundation for the others – is to carry out all processes across the supply chain so that the end product does what it is supposed to do. Quality is the most visible aspect of supply chain performance. Defects, incorrect quantities and wrong items delivered are symptoms of quality problems in supply chain processes that are all too apparent to the end-customer. Such problems negatively influence customer loyalty. Robust processes are at the heart of supply chain performance. Internally, robust processes help to reduce costs by eliminating errors and help to increase dependability by making processes more certain. When quality was positioned second to sales growth and cost, even the iconic Toyota Motor Corporation's brand suffered – as a string of recalls and safety concerns in recent years has shown. For example, Toyota recalled 1 million cars over defects that could cause airbags not to deploy (The Guardian, 2023).

Whilst conformance quality in the factory may be controlled to defect levels that are below 25 parts per million (ppm), a product may end up on the retailer's shelf with between 2 and 5 per cent defects, which is 10,000 to 20,000 ppm. This huge escalation takes place as the result of cumulative problems in successive supply chain processes. Cases may be crushed when shrink-wrapped at the manufacturer's NDC. In the back of the retail store, cases may be cut open with a sharp knife – despite instructions to the contrary. The end-customer sees the product on the retail shelf at its *worst* state of quality performance, and that is where the buying decision is made that drives the supply chain as a whole.

In many logistics situations, 'quality of service' is concerned with selecting the right quantity of the right product in the right sequence in response to customer orders. For example, store orders must be picked from a range of thousands of SKUs (stock keeping units) at a Tesco RDC. This must be carried out accurately (correct SKU, correct quantity) against tight delivery schedules day in and day out. *Pick accuracy* (for example, 99.5 per cent correct SKU and correct quantity) is used widely to measure the quality of this operation. And increasing requirements for in-store efficiencies mean that categories of product (for example, shampoos and toothpastes) need to be picked in a set sequence to facilitate direct-to-shelf delivery at the store. Logistics service providers who can implement and maintain the highest standards of service quality place themselves at an advantage over those who cannot.

The time advantage

Time measures how long a customer has to wait in order to receive a given product or service. Volkswagen calls this time the *customer to customer* lead time: that is, the time it takes from the moment a customer places an order to the moment that customer receives the car he or she specified. Such lead times can vary from zero (the product is immediately available, such as goods on a supermarket shelf) to months or years (such as the construction of a new building). Competing on time is about survival of the fastest!

Time can be used to win orders by companies who have learnt that some customers do not want to wait – and are prepared to pay a premium to get what they want quickly. An example is Vision Express, which offers prescription spectacles 'in about one hour'.

Technicians machine lenses from blanks on the premises. Staff are given incentives to maintain a 95 per cent service level against the one-hour target. Vision Express has been successful in the marketplace by re-engineering the supply chain so that parts and information can flow rapidly from one process to the next. Compare this with other opticians on the high street, who must send customer orders to a central factory. Under the 'remote factory' system, orders typically take about 10 days to process. An individual customer order is first dispatched to the factory. It then has to join a queue with orders from all the other high street branches around the country. Once the order has been processed, it must return to the branch that raised the order. Whilst this may be cheaper to do (a central, highly productive factory serves all of the branches), it takes much longer to process an order.

Time can equally lose orders if competitors are able to offer faster deliveries. Whilst online shopping *cannot* give the immediate availability of a store, it can still provide a fast service. Online shoppers often expect next-day, or same-day, delivery and when retailers like M&S can't match their competitors on speed, sales are lost (as described in Section 7.2.5).

The time advantage is described variously as *speed* or *responsiveness* in practice. Speeding up supply chain processes may help to reduce the risk of obsolete or overaged stock in the system or to improve freshness of the end product. Indeed, some food products are not only perishable, but the quality is also highly time dependent. For example, watercress has a shelf life of five to six days from packing, and retailer requirements are such that no packed stock can be held by the supplier, Vitacress. To ensure high levels of freshness in store, the retailers require a six-hour lead time from placing the order to receipt of the packed watercress in the retailers' DCs.

Time is an *absolute* measure, that is, it is not open to interpretation as quality and cost are. By following a product through a supply chain, we can discover which processes add value and which add time and cost but no value. We explore this further in Chapter 5, which is about managing time for advantage in the supply chain.

The cost advantage

Cost is important for all supply chain processes – that goes without saying – and we address logistics costs in detail in Chapter 3. Low costs translate into advantages in the marketplace in terms of low prices or high margins, or a bit of each. Many products compete specifically on the basis of low price. This is supported from a supply chain point of view by low-cost manufacture, distribution, servicing and the like. Examples of products that compete on low price are 'own-brand' supermarket goods that reduce the high margins and heavy advertising spend of major brands. They also perhaps cut some of the corners in terms of product specification in the hope that the customer will consider low price to be more important than minor differences in product quality.

The pressure to reduce prices at automotive component suppliers, and hence costs to the assemblers, is intense. The assemblers have been setting annual price reduction targets for their inbound supply chains for some years. Toyota announced demands for a 30 per cent reduction in prices on many components by the time that new models were launched in 2013. But unless a supplier can match reduced prices at which products are being sold by means of reduced costs, that supplier will gradually go out of business. As a result, many suppliers are cynical about the 'price down' policies of the assemblers. Reduced prices are the reward of cost cutting, and that is most often a collaborative effort by several partners in the supply chain. So suppliers are unlikely to meet Toyota's demands on their own: 'Toyota will need to consider moving to global platforms and increasing the proportion of common parts across its product range' (Soble, 2009). As indicated in Section 1.1, supermarkets can make only limited inroads into their in-store costs without the help of their supply chain partners.

1.3.2 Supportive capabilities

Whilst the hard objectives listed above are always important to competitive advantage, supportive capabilities can also be key to creating logistics advantage in the marketplace. When there is little to choose from in terms of quality, time or cost, supportive capabilities can make all the difference to the end-customer. Variability refers to real and identifiable differences within a population, such as the differences in time each patient at an optician has to wait for his or her eyes to be tested. Uncertainty refers to our lack of knowledge: in logistics terms, uncertainty results in us having to deal with changes that are either not known in advance or cannot be forecast with accuracy. Sustainability addresses the improvement of environmental, social and economic values in the design of logistics systems.

Controlling variability: the dependability advantage

Time is not just about speed. Quality is not just about meeting defect targets. Behind both 'hard' objectives is the need to *control variability* in logistics processes. Variability undermines the *dependability* with which a product or service meets target. Whilst Vision Express offers a one-hour service for prescription glasses, the 95 per cent service level is a measure of the dependability of that service against the one-hour target. Firms that do not offer instantaneous availability need to tell the customer – in other words to 'promise' – *when* the product or service will be delivered. Delivery dependability measures how successful the firm has been in meeting those promises. For example, the UK's Royal Mail quality of service target, for letters posted with a 'first-class' stamp, is that 93 per cent will arrive the next working day and, in the first quarter of 2018, they missed that target, delivering only 91.6 per cent (Royal Mail, 2018). Royal Mail reported that their service was significantly impacted by a number of exceptional events, including 'a very challenging industrial relations environment, some very severe weather, Cyber Week falling outside the exemption period and significantly reduced staffing levels caused by the Australian flu outbreak' (Royal Mail, 2018 press release). It is important to measure dependability in the same 'end-to-end' way that speed is measured. Dependability measures are used widely in industries such as train and air travel services to monitor how well published timetables are met. And in manufacturing firms, dependability is used to monitor a supplier's performance in such terms as:

- *on time* (percentage of orders delivered on time and the variability against target);
- *in full* (percentage of orders delivered complete and the variability against target);
- *on quality* (percentage of defects and the variability against target).

So logistics is concerned not just with the *average* percentage of orders delivered on time but also with the *variability*. For example, a manufacturer has to cope with the day-to-day variability of orders placed. In practice, this is more important than the average orders placed because of the resource implications of the peaks and troughs of demand. Case study 1.3 explores the impact of variability on a supplier's processes.

CASE STUDY 1.3

Measuring schedule variability

A problem that is all too familiar to suppliers in the automotive industry is that of schedule variability. A vehicle assembler issues delivery schedules to specify how many parts of each type are required each day for the following month. And each day a 'call-off' quantity is issued, which specifies how many the vehicle assembler actually wants. The two sets of figures are not necessarily the same, although usually they add up to the same cumulative numbers for the month as a whole. In other words, the total scheduled quantities and the total call-off quantities are the same. So what is the problem?

The problem is that the supplier has to cope with the variability of call-off quantities that create huge problems for the supplier's process. Let S = Scheduled demand and A = Actual call – off quantity. Then the difference D between schedule and actual is given by $D = S - A$. If the supplier produces to schedule, there are two possible scenarios that follow:

- $S > A$, so the supplier will over-produce the part and end up with excess stock; or
- $S > A$, so there is a shortfall $(S - A)$ of parts from the supplier, unless the supplier holds a stock of the parts, in which case it is an opportunity to reduce them.

The two conditions $(S > A$ and $S < A)$ therefore have different logistics implications. Figure 1.7 shows that actual demand, totalled across four different parts at PressCo (a supplier of pressed metal components), may be up to 1,600 units above schedule or 2,200 below schedule when supplying the vehicle assembler WestCo. This range has been divided up into intervals of 100 units. The mode (0–99) indicates that $S = A$ for a frequency of 18 per cent of the observations.

Assuming that the distribution is roughly normal, the standard deviation (SD) is 573, which is characteristic of the flat, wide spread of data. Figure 1.8 shows the distribution of $S - A$ for four similar parts from the same supplier, PressCo, but for a different vehicle assembler, EastCo. This time, the SD for the distribution is 95, representing a much narrower spread of differences than for the assembler, WestCo.

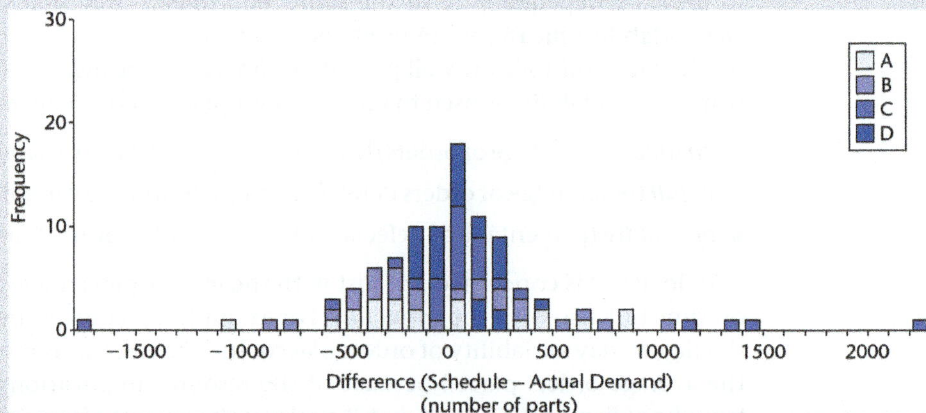

Figure 1.7 Distribution of differences between scheduled and actual demand for WestCo.

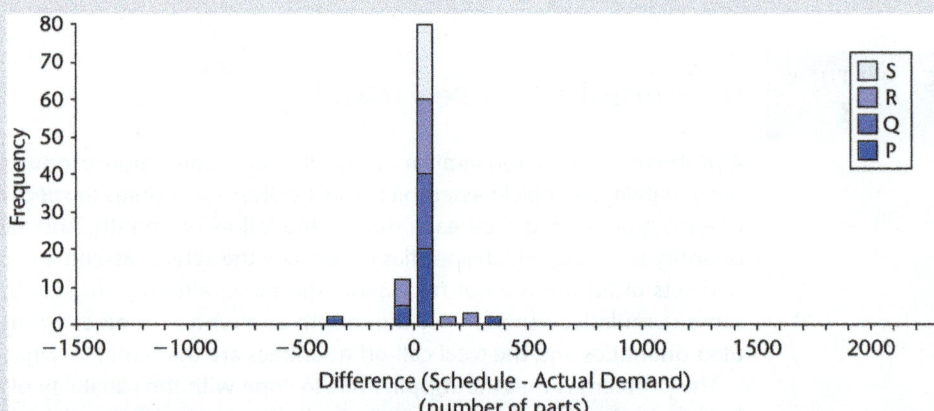

Figure 1.8 Distribution of differences between scheduled and actual demand for EastCo.

Questions

1. What are the logistics implications for PressCo to ensure high delivery reliability to customers WestCo and EastCo?
2. What steps will the supplier need to take in order to satisfy call-off orders from WestCo?
3. If separate parts of the PressCo factory were dedicated to production for WestCo and for EastCo, which would be the more efficient in terms of labour costs and inventory holding?

Quality is not just about meeting target pick accuracy or target defect levels. It is also about controlling variability. The same argument can be made about costs. The implication of dependability for logistics is that supply chain processes need to be robust and predictable. In Chapter 6 we develop the case for dependability in supply chains under the themes of planning and control and just-in-time pull scheduling.

Dealing with uncertainty: the agility advantage

Dealing with uncertainty means responding rapidly to changes that affect logistics processes. These changes may be unanticipated or anticipated but not with a high degree of accuracy. Sometimes, problems can be foreseen – even if their timing cannot. Toyota UK manages inbound deliveries of parts from suppliers in southern Europe by a process called *chain logistics*. Trailers of parts are moved in four-hour cycles, after which they are exchanged for the returning empty trailer on its way back from the UK. One hitch in this highly orchestrated process means that incoming parts do not arrive just-in-time at the assembly plant. Toyota demands that its suppliers, and logistics partner, plan *countermeasures*. This means that alternative routes for suppliers to deliver to its Burnaston assembly plant in the UK have been planned in advance to deal, for example, with a French channel ferry strike at Calais. The weather is also a cause of uncertainty in logistics – for example, it may mean that Tesco has to switch between salads and soups as the result of a cold snap. More seriously, natural disasters, such as earthquakes, can be devastating to supply chains but are difficult to predict in terms of either timing or scale. Other forms of uncertainty concern events where neither the problem nor its timing can be foreseen. Case study 1.4 provides an example of such an event and how the manufacturer and its suppliers responded.

CASE STUDY 1.4

P&G's supply chain keeping babies dry

Consumer products giant P&G has its share of supply chain scope. In 2012 the company realised $84 billion in sales and 25 of its brands generated $1 billion or more revenue. In order to realise this revenue, the company procures inputs worth over $51 billion from over 75,000 suppliers, operates 140 plants around the world and over 250 shipping locations, and transports products a total distance of over 1.5 billion kilometres per year to reach 4.6 billion consumers daily.

▶

Needless to say, this scale and scope of the supply chain does not come without risks, and supply chain disruptions can happen anywhere, any time. For example, in the last week of September 2012, an explosion at a Japanese chemical plant threatened to cause a global nappy shortage. The plant in the coastal city of Himeji, operated by Nippon Shokubai Co., is one of the world's largest producers of acrylic acid, a primary ingredient used in disposable nappies. Powerful blasts rocked the facility as firefighters tried to control a blaze at one of the tanks containing the chemical. One firefighter died and 34 employees and first responders were injured in the blast.

Acrylic acid is a key component of superabsorbent polymers (SAP), which absorb large amounts of liquid. Nippon Shokubai makes roughly 20 per cent of the world's SAP and maintains a 10 per cent global market share of acrylic acid. The plant had been ramping up production to meet increasing global demand, especially from China, according to Japanese media reports. Prior to the accident, the plant manufactured 460,000 tonnes of acrylic acid annually and P&G relied on Nippon Shokubai Co. for products sold in Asia.

In the face of this disaster, P&G supply chain teams had to move quickly and consider their options. There were two alternative suppliers, but these did not have sufficient idle capacity to compensate for the productivity lost from the Nippon Shokubai plant. Supply chain leadership connected to Nippon Shokubai immediately offered its assistance. The company's Chief Procurement Officer flew to Japan to work with the P&G crisis team to consider options and solutions. As an emergency response, a Nippon Shokubai plant in the USA, which previously had been shut down, was restarted with P&G assistance and shipments were rerouted. Adjustments were required to the supply chain plan, including the delay of some new product introductions. But, in the end, zero shipments to customers were missed and no nappy scarcity was experienced at the retail level, whilst relationships between P&G and Nippon Shokubai improved and strengthened.

(Source: Based on Rick Hughes, P&G's CPO, at the Procurement Leaders Conference, May 2013.)

Question

1. What are the key lessons from this case for dealing effectively with disruptions to the supply chain?

The implication of uncertainty for supply chain processes is that they need to be *flexible* to respond to both anticipated and unanticipated changes. Flexibility is defined as the 'ability to react or transform [supply chain processes] with minimum penalties in time, cost and performance' (Upton, 1995). More recently, Christopher and Holweg (2011) defined two types of flexibility:

- *Dynamic flexibility:* allows firms to cope with certain shifts in demand and technology, but only within the set structure of their existing supply chain design. Mix flexibility and volume flexibility (Slack, 1987) are key types of dynamic flexibility.
- *Structural flexibility:* builds flexible options into the design of the supply chain, such as dual sourcing, sharing assets, postponement, rapid manufacture, flexible labour arrangements and outsourcing.

Agility is a strategy for providing both these types of flexibility (and therefore dealing with uncertainty) and is discussed in detail, together with specific agile practices, in Chapter 7.

Acting responsibly: the sustainability advantage

Sustainability has been defined as 'development that meets the needs of the present without compromising the ability of future generations to meet their needs' (UNWCED, 1987). Logistics has been increasingly turned to in recent years because it offers enormous potential to mitigate damage to the environment in which we live. Many logistics decisions impact the environment – for example, sourcing from suppliers who use renewable raw materials and who practise ethical labour standards, and transportation modes that minimise carbon dioxide emissions (CO_2e). Sustainability emerges as a way of considering the environmental and social values of business decisions alongside their economic value. This thinking gave rise to the term '**triple bottom line**' (TBL) (Elkington, 1997, 2004), which considers these three values simultaneously. It is now commonplace for companies to apply these values to their supply network through supplier Codes of Conduct (such as Cisco Systems, 2024 and Hewlett Packard Enterprise, 2023), which give preference to suppliers who are socially and environmentally progressive. In other words, sustainability has become a competitive advantage in its own right!

There are industry wide supplier codes of conduct. For example, Cisco has adopted the Responsible Business Alliance (RBA) Code of Conduct designed for industries where electronics are a key component to ensure that working conditions in the industry and its supply chains are safe, that workers are treated with dignity and respect, and that business operations are conducted in an environmentally responsible and ethical way. Hewlett Packard Enterprise (HPE) Supplier Code of Conduct is based on the RBA but reflects additional HPE standards and expectations, such as those related to the employment of foreign migrant workers or dispatch workers in China.

1.3.3 Supply chain sustainability

The Triple Bottom Line (TBL) is at the heart of **supply chain sustainability** initiatives, so let's take the three 'values' in turn.

Environmental value

A focal firm such as Tesco is concerned with reducing consumption of non-renewable resources such as energy and materials. It is also concerned with measuring and reducing the environmental impact of processes across the end-to-end supply chain (SC) – from cow to customer (Figure 1.1), including collection and disposal by the end-user. The environmental impact is typically in terms of waste materials and different forms of pollution, the most prominent of which is Green House Gas (GHG) emissions normally measured in terms of kilograms of CO_2 equivalent. What can be done to reduce the environmental impact of supply chain activities such as transportation and/or waste packaging?

TBL thinking states that environmental polluters should not be given a free ride anymore – they should be made to pay. According to the International Monetary Fund (Black et al., 2022) 46 countries are pricing emissions through carbon taxes or emissions trading schemes (ETS) and others are considering it. Globally, ETSs and carbon taxes cover 30 per cent of emissions, with prices rising as high as $90 per ton (in the European Union). For more in-depth explanation of carbon costing, see Section 3.5. Further, the United Nations (2024) state that to keep global warming to no more than 1.5°C – as called for in the Paris Agreement – emissions need to be reduced by 45 per cent by 2030 and reach net zero by 2050. The good news is that more than 140 countries, including the biggest polluters – China, the United States, India and the European Union – have set a net-zero target, covering about 88 per cent of global emissions. Many large companies have followed suit and have a net zero carbon emissions target of 2050, which is publicised such that they can be held accountable. For example, Nestle have such a target and Case study 1.5 explains how they are achieving this. For a country or company to achieve net zero carbon emission it means it must absorb the same amount of Green House Gases as it emits in a given time period. For companies these are measured across three different scopes as described by the World Economic Forum (Read and Shine, 2022) and shown in Figure 1.9:

- **Scope 1 emissions**: 'Direct' emissions that a company causes by operating the things that it owns or controls. These can be a result of running machinery to make products, driving vehicles, or just heating buildings and powering computers.
- **Scope 2 emissions**: 'Indirect' emissions created by the production of the energy that an organisation buys. Installing solar panels or sourcing renewable energy rather than using electricity generated using fossil fuels would cut a company's Scope 2 emissions.

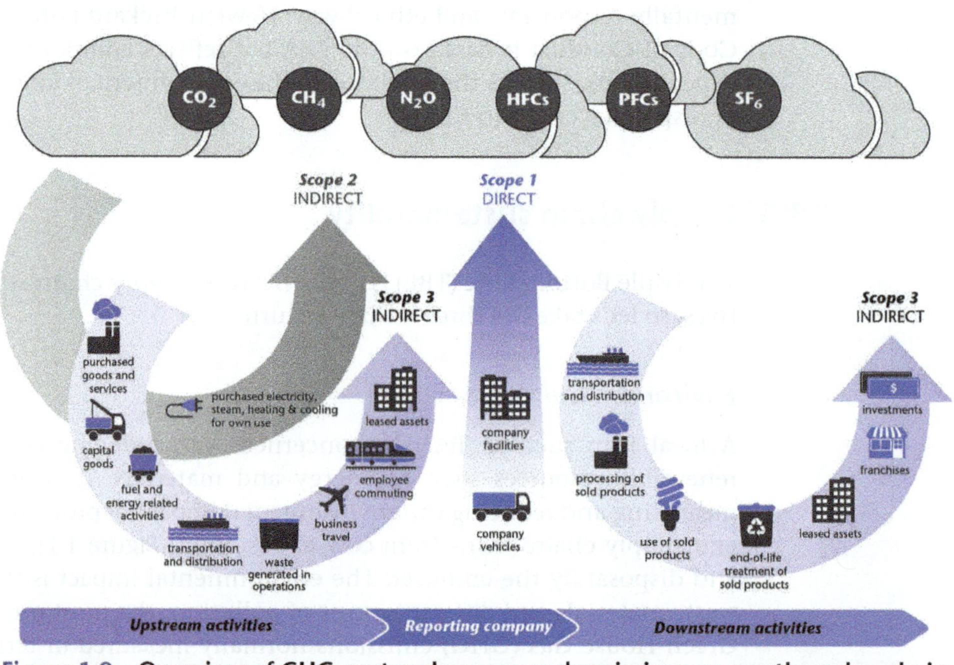

Figure 1.9 Overview of GHG protocol scopes and emissions across the value chain.

(Source: Corporate Value Chain (Scope 3) Accounting and Reporting Standard, Supplement to the GHG Protocol Corporate Accounting and Reporting Standard, GHG Protocol.)

- **Scope 3 emissions**: These are also indirect emissions – meaning those not produced by the company itself – but they differ from Scope 2 as they cover those produced by customers using the company's products or those produced by suppliers making products that the company uses.

As would be expected the Scope 3 emissions are not only far more difficult to measure and control, but also account for the vast majority of a company's emissions, typically more than 70 per cent. The Nestle Case study 1.5 focuses on managing these more challenging emissions and achieving net zero carbon emissions across its ingredient suppliers.

CASE STUDY 1.5

Achieving net zero emissions at Nestlé through Ingredients Sourcing

Introduction

Nestlé is the world's largest food and beverage company and have been providing safe, quality nutrition for more than 155 years. They employ around 270,000 people, have more than 2,000 brands sold into 188 countries produced in 354 factories around the world. Nestlé works with a supply network of more than 500,000 farmers, so there is a big potential for a positive impact on sustainable agriculture.

The idea of going beyond sustainability from degeneration to regeneration

Sustainability is at the top of Nestlé's agenda. Indeed, they're aiming to go beyond sustainability to regeneration. According to Nestlé regenerative agriculture is an approach to farming that aims to conserve and restore farmland and its ecosystem, to improve soil health and soil fertility, so it goes beyond just sustaining farmland, and its ecosystem, and instead aims to improve it!

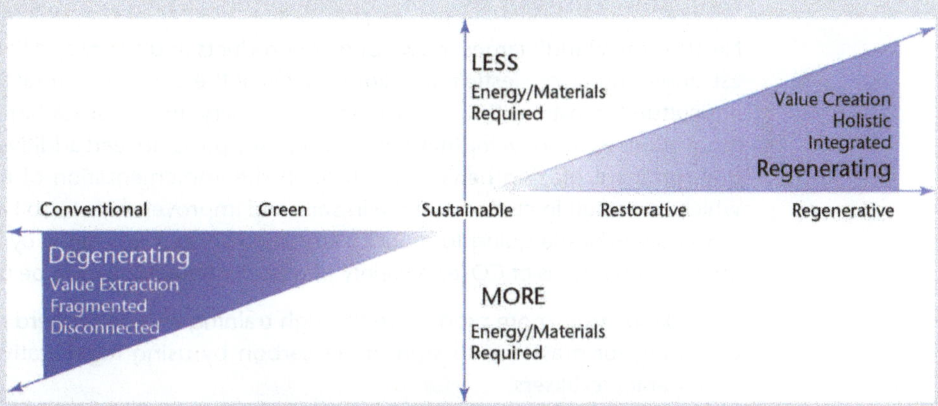

Figure 1.10 The relationship between degenerative, sustainability and regenerative approaches.

(Source: Adapted from Reed, 2007.)

Restoring soil health helps draw down and capture increased levels of carbon in soils and plant biomass, thus contributing to reduce and remove carbon emissions from the atmosphere. The techniques associated with regenerative agriculture also improve the resilience of farmland to climate change and can contribute to improved farmers' livelihoods. This is why, as part of Nestlé's Net Zero Roadmap, they have committed to source 20% of their key ingredients from regenerative agriculture methods by 2025, and 50% by 2030.

Net zero carbon emission targets

Nestlé are committed to halve their Green House Gas (GHG) emissions by 2030 and achieve net zero by 2050, despite continuing to grow. Progress toward net zero will be measured against Nestlé's 2018 GHG emissions baseline. Back then emissions from their direct operations, known as Scope 1 and Scope 2, accounted for just 5% of their GHG emissions. While the vast majority of their GHG emissions (95%) came from activities in their supply chain, both upstream across the supply base and downstream where the products are used by customers. As a result, that is where Nestlé focus most of their efforts.

Scope 3 emissions for sourcing ingredients

The majority of the Scope 3 emissions (65.6 million tonnes of CO_2e, 71.4%) come from sourcing the ingredients and Nestlé plan to reduce this by 32% to 44.3 million tonnes of CO_2e by 2030, which is less than half of the estimated business as usual level, if nothing was done of 97.1 million tonnes. The vast majority of these emissions come from two sources, 'dairy and livestock' and 'soil and forests', as classified by Nestlé, therefore the rest of this case will focus on these source types.

Incidentally, Nestlé also plan to remove CO_2 from the atmosphere (scope 3 removals) and this includes Natural Climate Solutions (NCS), such as agroforestry, silvopasture and the restoration of forests and peatland.

Dairy and livestock sources

Nestlé is the world's largest buyer of dairy products and 'dairy and livestock' is the largest single source of Nestlé's emissions – 23% of the company's total footprint. Many of agriculture's most exciting innovations are in dairy and livestock farming. For example innovations in the development of methane-suppressing feed additives; mimicking natural ruminant grazing behaviours through the implementation of rotational grazing, which can result in carbon storage in soils and improvements to soil and forage health.

So how is Nestlé going to reduce dairy and livestock emissions by 14% from 34.2 to 29.3 million tonnes of CO_2e? A variety of global interventions will be used for:

- Making farms more productive through training and better herd management.
- Caring for grassland to store more carbon by using regenerative agriculture and organics fertilisers.
- Cutting the methane produced by animals during digestion through nutrition changes.
- Feeding livestock with more sustainable feed.

- Other livestock actions.
- Helping suppliers become more energy efficient.
- Making the most of manure and using biogas digesters.

Soils and forest sources

27% of Nestlé's carbon footprint is linked to agricultural crops, which includes cocoa, coffee and cereals. Protecting ecosystems where ingredients are grown is vital to Nestlé's long-term success and they classify this as 'Soils and forests'. But how is Nestlé going to reduce soils and forest emissions by 44% from 25 to 14 million tonnes of CO_2e? A variety of global interventions will be used for:

- Preventing deforestation in our supply chain.
- On-farm agroforestry planting trees and other plants around and among crops.
- Improved agricultural practices like cover cropping, using organic fertilisers and multiple crop rotation.
- Agroforestry off-farm.
- Restoring degraded forests and peatlands.
- Installing palm oil mill effluent methane capture systems.

Progress so far

So by 2023, since their benchmark year of 2018, how are Nestlé progressing:

- One objective was to achieve 100% deforestation-free supply chains for meat, palm oil, pulp and paper, soy and sugar by 2022 and they achieved 99.1% for these raw materials by this date.
- Another objective was to source 20% of their key ingredients from regenerative agriculture methods by 2025, and 50% by 2030. By the end of 2023, they had sourced 15.2% of fresh milk, dairy derivatives, cocoa, green coffee, cereals, soy and vegetables from selected suppliers and farmers adopting regenerative agricultural practices. Reached more than 148 000 coffee farmers in 16 countries via the Nescafé Plan 2030 (espresso AAA Sustainable Quality™ Program) with trainings on regenerative agricultural practices.
- Supported regenerative landscape initiatives in Brazil,Chile, Côte d'Ivoire, Indonesia, Malaysia, Mexico, Peru and the United Kingdom which aim to restore 60,000 hectares of land and support 60,000 local people.
- Secured plans to plant and grow 14.7 million trees via Nestlé's Global Reforestation Program.

(Source: written with assistance from Matt Ryan of Nestlé, using Nestlé website, Nestlé Net Zero Roadmap (March 2023), the Regenerative Agriculture at Nestlé (January 2024) and Nestlé Creating Shared Value and Sustainability Report (2023).)

Questions

1. How do you evaluate the triple bottom line impacts of Nestlé's sustainability initiatives and targets? How do you think efficiencies and the economic performance will be impacted?
2. What might the challenges be for Nestlé's agricultural suppliers?

In company's efforts to reduce environmental impacts, accreditation to the ISO 14001 series on Environmental Management Systems is becoming increasingly influential with more than 500,000 certifications for ISO 14001 in over 180 countries around the world (ISO, 2024).

Social value

Large focal firms such as Nike and Walmart have been forced to consider the social contexts of the suppliers with whom they deal. Often, suppliers are based on the other side of the world, but consumer pressure, created by adverse publicity, has forced such firms to recognise their responsibility in ensuring that goods are manufactured in socially responsible conditions. Nike came under heavy scrutiny from customers in the 1990s for its use of low-cost labour, predominantly in Asia. There were suspicions of use of child labour, and other unethical labour practices amongst Nike suppliers. Nike launched a comprehensive Corporate social responsibility (CSR) effort – including the appointment of a vice-president for CSR – and now is a leader for improving supplier practices and for responsible behaviour along the supply chain.

Companies, like Nike, are subscribing to codes of conduct to ensure they operate in a socially responsible manner and are expecting their suppliers to sign up to the same codes, such as the Responsible Business Alliance (RBA) Code of Conduct for the electronics industry, mentioned earlier. Like similar codes, this covers the following, as well as ethics, management systems and the environment:

- **Labour:** freely chosen employment; humane treatment; young workers; non-discrimination/non-harassment; working hours; freedom of association (right to be in a Union); and wages and benefits.
- **Health and safety:** Occupational safety; physically demanding work; emergency preparedness; machine safeguarding; occupational injury and illness; sanitation, food and housing; industrial hygiene; and health and safety communication.

Companies such as Nike and Hewlett Packard visit suppliers, conduct audits to identify improvement opportunities and proactively carve out opportunities to collaborate on achieving improvements against their code of conduct.

Non-governmental not for profit trade organisations aim to ensure fair treatment of workers in developing countries. A good example of this is the Fairtrade Foundation (2024), which works with farming co-operatives, businesses and governments to make trade fairer, so that producers, typically in developing countries, earn secure and sustainable livelihoods. Fairtrade sets social, economic and environmental standards for the companies and farmers involved in the supply chain:

> **For farmers and workers the standards include protection of workers' rights and the environment, for companies they include the payment of the Fairtrade Minimum Price safety net and an additional Fairtrade Premium**

To reassure consumers that the Fairtrade standards have been met, a FAIRTRADE Mark (shown in Figure 1.16) is used on products when all the ingredients, that could be assessed by Fairtrade, are deemed to meet the Fairtrade standards

Economic value

This is the net value that a firm generates after social and environmental values have been taken into account. This implies making the connection between TBL values and financial performance. The organisational changes involved in recognising economic value can be wrenching and can take years to implement. Nike – along with other premium brand companies – came under enormous pressure from labour activists in the 1990s to adopt more sustainable codes of conduct in their global supply chains. For example, purchasing teams had to be constrained from going for lowest prices from suppliers, which threatened short-term profitability. Now, sustainability is about not just complying with codes of conduct, but going beyond and generating business value from protecting the environment and enabling economic inclusion of people and communities, as described in Section 10.2 and later in this section.

Environmental, social and governance (ESG)

In the last two decades, the term environmental, social and governance (ESG) has grown in importance as a way of capturing sustainability performance. Porter and Van Der Linde (1995), proposed that investments in ESG practices should be considered competitive opportunities, rather than costs or threats. They stated that adequate environmental standards and regulations may encourage firms to innovate, increase the productivity of their resources and consequently, improve its competitiveness – Porter's Hypothesis, as it has been known. The 'pays to be green' debate (Berchicci & King, 2007) emerged from this research. More recently, in a survey with chief executive officers (CEOs) by the United Nations Global Compact-Accenture (2019), 99 per cent of CEOs from companies with more than $1 billion in annual revenues considered sustainability as at least 'important' to the success of their business and a considerable percentage indicated it was 'very important'. Further, the percentage of CEOs citing 'no clear link to business value' as a barrier to sustainability has consistently dropped from 37 per cent in 2013 to 31 per cent in 2016 and to 26 per cent in 2019, showing that the 'pays to be green debate' has gained traction!

1.3.4 Green logistics

Logistics contributes considerably to greenhouse gas (GHG) emissions, with some scholars suggesting it is responsible for 13 per cent of all such emissions (Perotti et al., 2022). As logistics environmental impacts are expected to increase, in step with rising levels of pollution, addressing logistics environmental sustainability is a big concern for managers and policymakers. Principles of sustainable logistics, and related actions that companies can undertake, have been described (e.g. Carter and Rogers, 2008), and the term 'Green Logistics Practices' (GLPs) indicates many logistics-related initiatives to reduce the impact on the natural environment (e.g. Evangelista et al., 2017).

Many GLPs have been developed in recent years to reduce the carbon footprint left by supply chains, and these have generally considered GLPs in transportation, warehousing and inventory management, in terms of either intra-organisational (internal) practices or inter-organisational (external) practices involving multiple supply chain partners (Huge-Brodin et al., 2020). In recent years, redesigning the transport fleet to replace internal combustion engines vehicles with electric vehicles has been gaining significant traction; however, GLPs affect many aspects of logistics (Perotti et al., 2012). Overall, GLPs can be clustered into nine major categories under 'internal' and 'external', where internal includes:

- Distribution Network Design
- Distribution Planning and Transportation Execution
- Green Warehousing
- Reverse Logistics
- Packaging Design and Management
- Internal Management.

External GLPs require commitment and joint goal setting among different players of the same supply chain (Colicchia et al., 2013) and cover:

- Green Purchasing
- Collaboration with Customers
- Other Collaborations have been defined as inter-organisational (i.e. 'external') GLPs.

Table 1.2 shows each of these major GLP categories, sub-categories and associated examples of practices. Case study 1.6 further illustrates the use of GLPs in an Italian Logistics Provider.

Table 1.2 GLP categories and related example.

Type of GLPs	Category	Sub-category	Green logistics practices
Internal	Distribution network design	Network nodes	Facility location to reduce transport intensity
			Operationalisation of urban consolidation centres
		Transportation mode selection	Use of alternative transportation modes (e.g. intermodal, combined) and modal shift
	Distribution planning and transport execution	Fleet design	Use of alternative green fuels (e.g. biofuels) and green vehicles (e.g. electric)
			Vehicle maintenance and disposal
		Eco-driving	Limiting the speeds at which company equipment is operated
		Transportation routing and scheduling	Route planning optimisation and increase of vehicle utilisation rate (FTL)
			Shipment/freight consolidation
			Vehicle idle time reduction
			Empty backhauling reduction

Type of GLPs	Category	Sub-category	Green logistics practices
	Green Warehousing	Land use reduction	Efficient land use (e.g. brownfield redevelopment, retrofitting)
		Warehouse energy-efficiency	Thermal insulation (e.g. loading docks with insulated doors)
			Energy consumption reduction through energy efficient heating/lighting systems that use alternative energy sources and sensors/smart metering
			Water usage minimisation
			Adoption of green/energy-efficient material handling equipment
			Operational practices (e.g. optimal scheduling of material handling activities)
		Green IT	Adoption of IT systems to monitor the environmental performance and guide actions for improvement
Internal	Reverse logistics	Product reverse logistics	Design for recycling
			Improve visibility to allow material separation and more efficient recovery
			Reconditioning or refurbishing used products for logistics
		Transportation	Development of synergies between direct flows and reverse flows
	Packaging design and management	Material usage	Packaging design to reduce waste
			Packaging reuse and recycling
			Use of sustainable materials
		Freight load optimisation	Reduction of packaging weight and volume
			Shape optimisation for shipment
	Internal management	Environmental sustainability monitoring	Reporting systems to monitor achievement of sustainability goals
			Definition of sustainable KPIs, environmental targets and priorities
			Research activities and investments for green innovation
		Offices and employees	Employee incentive programmes for environmental suggestions
			Personnel training to increase awareness
		Supply chain traceability	Tracing of purchased goods through the entire supply chain
			Environmental performance measurement at a supply chain level
		Publicise environmental efforts	Achieving green certifications
			Eco-branding and labelling
		Alignment with company's sustainability strategy	Incorporating sustainability in the company's vision and mission

Type of GLPs	Category	Sub-category	Green logistics practices
External	Green purchasing	Green sourcing	Use green KPIs in supplier selection processes (e.g. contractual environmental goals)
			Controlling suppliers' certifications
			Formalised long-term supplier cooperation towards environmental objectives (e.g. by sharing investments)
		Green monitoring	Adoption of green KPIs in suppliers' monitoring and rating
	Collaboration with customers	Customers' engagement in GLPs development	Recovery policies for end products
			Awareness campaigns
			Customer's involvement in green product design
		Data sharing	Cooperation with customers for route planning optimisation
			Web portals to calculate energy and CO_2 emissions
	Other collaborations	Collaboration with other stakeholders	Collaboration with product designers, OEMs and competitors
			Collaborations with public institutions, universities and research centres
			Membership in environmental programmes with NGOs
			Investment sharing

(Source: Prataviera et al., 2024.)

There are many factors that may accelerate (enablers) or jeopardise (barriers) the adoption of GLPs (Marchet et al., 2014). Internal factors affect processes within the company boundaries, while external factors tackle the decisions made by companies within their supply chain and the network of relationships with customers, suppliers, governments and institutional bodies. Table 1.3 offers an overview of the influencing factors organised into five categories: economic and financial, organisational, technological, collaboration and external.

Recent studies acknowledge that economic (and external) factors are the most important influencers of GLPs adoption (Huge-Brodin et al., 2020; Prataviera et al., 2024). However, it's not that simple, as the influencing factors impact each other. For example, key economic factors are affected by external factors which also influence organisational and collaboration factors. This makes GLPs adoption complex, and it involves many stakeholders. These include indirect stakeholders, such as governments and final consumers, which are increasingly important to explain and motivate GLPs adoption. As a matter of fact, firms can no longer address the adoption of GLPs as 'focal companies', but only as part of a 'focal network of interconnected stakeholders', all of them influencing GLPs adoption (Prataviera et al., 2024).

To encourage GLPs adoption and enhance their effectiveness, some scholars (e.g. Etzion, 2007) suggest improving the alignment between corporate strategies and logistics environmental sustainability. This can not only improve organisations' sustainability but also lead to better firm performance (Golicic and Smith, 2013), enhanced sustainable competitive advantage, and long-term business

Table 1.3 Influencing factors for GLPs.

Category	Influencing factors
Economic and financial	Profitability
	Investments
	Incentives
Organisational	Performance measurement (e.g. control and monitoring activities)
	Competence/knowledge/awareness
	Change management approach (e.g. internal resistance/support to changes)
	Reputation/image
Technological	Infrastructure development (e.g. charging infrastructure)
	Implementation process
	Technological maturity
	Technological complexity
Collaboration	Availability of collaborations along the supply chain
	Mutual acknowledgement of efforts and investments
External	Pressure from suppliers
	Pressure from customers and their awareness
	Pressure from competitors
	Pressure from the government and institutions

(Source: Prataviera et al., 2024.)

development of firms (Schrettle et al., 2014). Practical advice on how to achieve this is given in Table 1.4, which provides a maturity framework for the alignment of corporate strategy with logistics environmental sustainability (Prataviera et al., 2023).

Companies, especially Logistics Service Providers, are increasingly making efforts to integrate logistics environmental sustainability into corporate strategy. Many firms currently acknowledge the importance of drafting sustainability reports, to legitimise themselves before society, by raising awareness of their environmental performance. Releasing sustainability reports is often a first step which helps define targets and identify appropriate measurement systems. Developing specific KPIs to evaluate the achievement of well-defined objectives is widely considered a powerful leverage to consider, but collecting the right data can be critical. To increase impact, companies are improving their organisational structure and accountability, appointing managers to deal with environmental issues and creating cross-functional teams with increasing commitment. However, typically, this is not reflected by the allocation of specific budgets to sustainability initiatives, which limits the feasibility of a quick change in the logistics operations (Prataviera et al., 2023).

Table 1.4 A maturity framework for the alignment of corporate strategy with logistics environmental sustainability.

Dimension	Stage of alignment		
	Early stage of alignment	**Medium stage of alignment**	**Advanced stage of alignment**
Degree of awareness	Logistics environmental sustainability is not included in the corporate strategy	Logistics environmental sustainability is deemed supportive to the corporate strategy	Logistics environmental sustainability is core to the corporate strategy
Degree of formalisation	Targets are defined in a qualitative way	Targets are defined in a quantitative way	Targets are granularly defined in quantitative and qualitative ways for each business unit
Measurement systems	There are no measurement systems adopted	Measurement occurs at a high-level	Specific KPIs are developed to evaluate the target achievement
Governance and accountability	There is an individual adding accountability for environmental sustainability to normal work responsibilities	There is a cross-functional team that adds collective accountability for environmental sustainability to normal work	There is a cross-functional team that is fully committed to developing environmental sustainability
Budget allocation	There is no defined budget dedicated to environmental sustainability	There is a specific budget dedicated to environmental sustainability, which is shared across business units	Every business unit has its budget dedicated to environmental sustainability

(Source: Prataviera et al., 2023.)

Case study 1.6 provides an illustration of how Logistics Service Providers are adopting GLPs, the factors that influence this and how alignment with corporate strategy may be achieved.

CASE STUDY 1.6

ItalyLog: Developing a comprehensive approach for Green Logistics

ItalyLog is a leading logistics service provider in the grocery industry, achieving an annual revenue of around € 250 million in 2022. It serves more than 70 customers across Italy, using 54 logistics sites (including 9 distribution centres) and over 120,000 delivery points. Over the years, ItalyLog has been developing several Green Logistics Practices (GLPs) related to many of the categories proposed in Table 1.2.

Distribution planning and transport execution

'Project Synchro' involved developing a fixed delivery schedule to aggregate delivery volumes and reduce the empty mileage and the overall number of trips, leading to both environmental and economic benefits. Beyond 'Project Synchro' the firm operated a significant fleet redesign in recent years. For longer distances, they currently use only EURO 6 class vehicles (characterised by lower GHG emissions than older vehicles) and liquified natural gas (LNG) vehicles, which further reduces NOx emissions. In many instances, ItalyLog did not purchase the new vehicles but relied on collaborations with smaller transport providers which could satisfy the company's requirements concerning GHG and NOx emissions. Recently, for last mile delivery they also started using medium-size electric vehicles, through a partnership with an OEM which offered the opportunity to test state-of-the-art vehicles. This latter initiative is planned to reduce the annual GHG emissions by 50,000 CO_2 tons.

Green warehousing

Solar panels and LED sensors are adopted in every logistics facility: when buildings are not owned but rented, environmentally oriented improvements are negotiated with the other stakeholders involved. These negotiations also included the creation of recharging plants for electric vehicles at every logistics facility included in the network. A measurement system to monitor emissions and consumptions at every logistics node across the network was developed at the beginning of 2023.

Packaging design and management

The firm is aiming to reduce plastics usage by using corrugated cardboard packaging whenever possible. This led to a 78 per cent reduction of the overall plastics items since 2005.

Internal management

The company is committed to increase internal awareness about the urgency of the problem by promoting volunteering programmes as well as fostering bottom-up suggestions which are collected through platforms specifically aimed to share information and knowledge about sustainability. Incentives are provided to the whole workforce to create a greener community (e.g. creating bike stations or offering discounts to support fossil-free local mobility).

Green purchasing

ItalyLog has been developing agreements with OEMs and smaller suppliers. Surveys are regularly conducted with the supplier's base to ensure information sharing and suggestions for possible practices. The firm is liaising with different OEMs to test electric vehicles opportunities (and overcome the ongoing challenges). With smaller suppliers, the firm discusses incentives and rewards mechanisms to support their fleet renewal. However, governance clauses are included to guarantee that suppliers carry out a given amount of transport activities for ItalyLog, in return for the support on the investment.

Collaboration with customers

Although this is still limited, ItalyLog started collaborating with various indirect stakeholders (including NGOs) to increase its impact over local communities and commit to fostering, not only environmental, but also social sustainability in the logistics industry.

Various influencing factors could encourage ItalyLog to adopt GLPs. Although economic factors are widely acknowledged as important, ItalyLog highlighted how investment costs should be carefully traded off against the potential economic benefits, which often allow for payback times shorter than 5 years. This also depends on the individual GLPs, as investments related to fleet redesign are usually higher than those required for Packaging Management or Internal Management (from an organisational perspective). Concerning technological factors, the lack of measurement systems and precise KPIs is not considered as a constraint, since measurement tools can be developed after developing GLPs. However, technological complexity has been pointed out as a relevant constraint, since it is considered difficult to obtain the knowledge on technologies at sufficient scale. Moreover, customers usually do not acknowledge the economic benefits linked to ItalyLog's improved green footprint, making it harder to justify the return on the investments needed to implement GLPs. On the other hand, the collaboration with suppliers is somewhat developed, even though it seems more driven by compliance (especially for vehicles specifications) and efficiency rewards than by the genuine understanding of the urgency to reduce GHG emissions. However, it is also pointed out that a green-oriented culture represents a strong enabler to develop GLPs, within and across firms.

In fact, ItalyLog's approach towards sustainability is defined at corporate level and then shared across business units through three pillars, namely 'community', 'planet' and 'ecosystem'. The first pillar focuses on people: 'Project Next' is an example of a community-support initiative, which aims at providing work to people who are victims of discriminations. Secondly, 'planet' oriented GLPs aim to reduce the environmental impact by eliminating polluting materials from the operations and by greening the processes. Finally, 'ecosystem' refers to collaborations with business partners to extend the scopes of planet and community initiatives. ItalyLog's sustainability report includes corporate-level targets and progress, where plans and expected outcomes are aligned with the United Nations Sustainability Development Goals (SDGs). Their sustainability report includes a Benefit Impact Assessment (BIA), needed to become a certified B-Corp organisation. From an organisational viewpoint dissemination and training activities take place to increase people's awareness and commitment. Each business unit has a Sustainability Manager, and the company created a cross functional impact team to monitor environmental performance. Although no fixed budget is allocated to sustainability actions, the firm created a 'flexible' budget which could be used according to the claims associated with the individual GLPs.

(Source: Written by Dr Lorenzo Prataviera, 2024.)

Study questions

1. How can the company improve certain aspects of their green logistics?
2. How might this be enabled?
3. What might the barriers be?

1.3.5 Order winners and qualifiers

The relative importance of logistics performance objectives, discussed in Section 1.3.1, is usually different for a given market segment. A helpful distinction is that between order winners and order qualifiers (Hill, 2000):

Order winners are factors that directly and significantly help products to win orders in the marketplace. Customers regard such factors as key reasons for buying that product or service. If a firm raises its performance on those factors, it will increase its chances of getting more business. Thus, a product that competes mainly on price would benefit in the marketplace if productivity improvements enabled further price reductions.

Order qualifiers are factors that are regarded by the market as an 'entry ticket'. Unless the product or service meets basic performance standards, it will not be taken seriously. An example is quality accreditation: a possible supplier to major utilities such as PowerGen in Britain and EDF in France would not be considered seriously without ISO 9000 certification. And delivery reliability is a must for automotive assemblers – cars can't be assembled without all components! Note that, in both examples, order qualifiers are *order-losing sensitive*: loss of ISO 9000 accreditation would make it impossible to supply to major utilities, and late delivery of automotive components would cause late deliveries and incur high fines for the suppliers.

Order winners and qualifiers are *specific to individual segments,* a point we develop in the next chapter. Table 1.5 provides an example of how two different products made by the same manufacturer and passing through the same distribution channel have different performance objectives. The first product group comprises standard shirts that are sold in a limited range of 'classic' colours and sizes. The second product group comprises fashion blouses that are designed specially for each season in many colours and a choice of styles with associated designer labels.

Table 1.5 Different product ranges have different logistics performance objectives.

	Classic shirts	Fashion blouses
Product range	Narrow: few colours, standard sizes	Wide: many colours, choice of styles, designer labels
Design changes	Occasional	Frequent (at least every season)
Price	Everyday low price	Premium prices
Quality	Consistency, conformance to (basic) spec	High grades of material, high standards of workmanship
Sales volumes	Consistent sales over time	Sales peak for given fashion season
Order winners	Price	Time-to-market Brand/label Quality
Order qualifiers	Quality Availability Cost	Price Availability Speed
Logistics priorities	Dependability Quality	Flexibility Quality

Analysis of the order winners and qualifiers shows that the two product ranges have very different performance criteria in the marketplace. Of the two, the range of fashion blouses presents more logistics challenges because demand for individual SKUs is much more difficult to forecast. It is not until the season is underway that a picture begins to emerge about which colours are selling most in which region of the market. The logistics challenge, therefore, is concerned with speed of response and flexibility to changing demand. The logistics challenges between the two ranges are quite distinctive.

Not only can order winners and qualifiers be different for different products and services, but they can also *change over time*. Thus, in the early phase of a new product lifecycle, such as the launch of a new integrated circuit, the order winners are availability and design performance. Price often would be a qualifier: provided the price is not so exorbitant that no one can afford it, there is a market for innovators who want the best-performing chip that is available. But, by the maturity phase of the lifecycle, competitors have emerged, the next generation is already on the stocks and the order winners have changed to price and product reliability. The former order winners (availability and design performance) have changed to become order qualifiers. The logistics challenge is to understand the market dynamics and to adjust capabilities accordingly.

The *actions of competitors* are, therefore, a further influence on logistics performance objectives. For example, low-price competitors are a feature of most markets, and they attempt to differentiate themselves from the perhaps higher-grade but pricier incumbents. Thus competitors such as Matalan have sparked fundamental changes in **logistics strategy** at Marks and Spencer (M&S). In response to loss of sales to cheaper new entrants, M&S ditched long-standing agreements with local UK suppliers and sourced garments from new, lower-priced suppliers in Asia.

Whilst the above helps to show some of the thinking in setting logistics strategy, there are limitations to the use of order winners and qualifiers. They are subjective and so provide *perceived* relative priorities. Whilst this creates useful debate between marketing and logistics, it lays the foundation for more informed strategy setting in the context of the values of other variables in Table 1.5, such as volumes. It is also important to share understanding of these priorities with partners, a point that we develop next.

1.4 Logistics strategies

Key issues: **What is 'strategy'? How can competitive criteria be aligned within a supply chain? How can logistics strategies be tuned to different product needs?**

1.4.1 Defining 'strategy'

Strategy is about planning as distinct from doing. It is about formulating a long-term plan for the supply chain, as distinct from solving the day-to-day issues and problems that inevitably occur. Extending the concept of 'strategy' from Hayes and Wheelwright (1984):

Logistics strategy is the set of guiding principles, driving forces and ingrained attitudes that help to coordinate goals, plans and policies, and which are reinforced through conscious and subconscious behaviour within and between partners across a network.

All too often, logistics 'strategy' is set using few such characteristics: decisions are made piecemeal by accident, muddle or inertia. We need, however, to recognise that strategic decisions may, indeed, be made by such means.

Whittington (2000) proposes four approaches to setting strategy. He starts by suggesting different motivations for setting strategy:

- *How deliberate are the processes of strategy setting?* These can range from clearly and carefully planned to a series of ad hoc decisions taken on a day-to-day basis.
- *What are the goals of strategy setting?* These can range from a focus on maximising profit to allowing other business priorities such as sales growth to be included.

If we make these two considerations the axes of a matrix, Figure 1.11 suggests four options for crafting strategy.

What are the implications for the way in which supply chain strategy is approached in different organisations? Following is a brief description of the four options:

- *Evolve.* 'Strategy' is not something that is undertaken formally at all. 'Our strategy is not to have a strategy' is a typical viewpoint. Operating decisions are taken in relation to the needs of the moment, with financial goals as the main guiding principle.
- *Classical.* Whilst financial goals are again the main guiding principle, these are achieved through a formal planning process. This is called 'classical' because it is the oldest and most influential option.

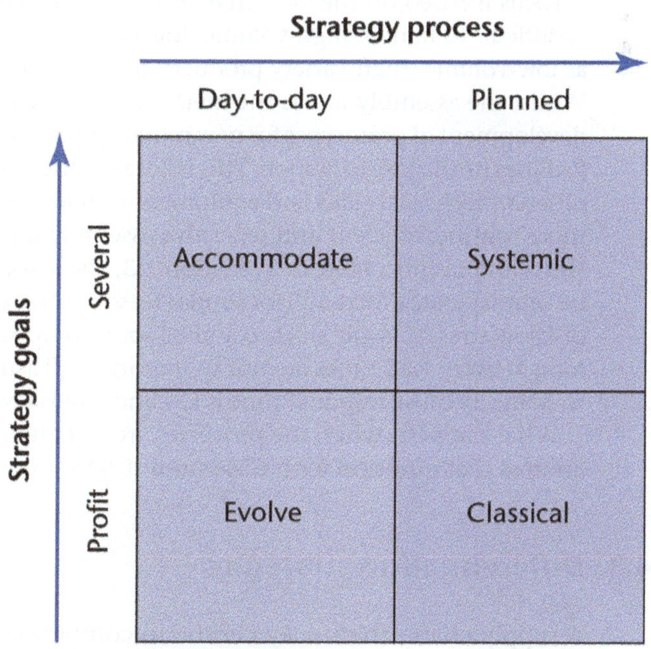

Figure 1.11 **Four options for crafting strategy.**

- *Accommodate.* Here, decisions are back to the day-to-day mode, but financial objectives are no longer the primary concern. Strategy is accommodated instead to the realities of the focal firm and the markets in which it operates.
- *Systemic.* This option for strategy setting sees no conflict between the ends and means of realising business goals. Whilst goal setting takes place across all major aspects of the business (including human resources, marketing and manufacturing policies), these are linked to the means by which they will be achieved in practice.

Logistics strategy usually demands systemic strategy setting between network partners, who may have to coordinate order winners and qualifiers across different market segments.

1.4.2 Aligning strategies

In Section 1.1 we showed the supply chain as a network of operating processes. In Section 1.2 we emphasised the need to 'integrate' these processes to maximise flow and focus on the end-customer. And in Section 1.3 we saw how supply chains can choose to compete on a range of different competitive priorities. Now it is time to put these ideas together and show how strategies need to be *aligned* across the supply chain.

If different links in the supply chain are directed towards different competitive priorities, then the chain will not be able to serve the end-customer as well as a supply chain in which the links are directed towards the same priorities. That is the basic argument for alignment in the supply chain (Cousins, 2005). Where the links are directed by a common and consistent set of **competitive criteria**, that supply chain will compete better in the marketplace than one in which the links have different, conflicting priorities. This is the concept of 'focus'.

Focus is based on the view that you cannot be good at everything. For example, it is difficult to handle high-volume, low-cost products in the same channel to market as low-volume, high-variety products, for which flexibility is the name of the game. Whilst the assembly line is the method of choice for manufacturing cars in volume, development of prototypes for new models is kept well away from the factory in special facilities until close to launch. This is because the development process demands quite different technical skills and equipment that are better physically separated from the more routine, efficient and repetitive assembly line. In the example of the standard shirts and fashion blouses in Section 1.3, the associated operations processes would be kept separate ('focused') for similar reasons. And the separation could be thousands of kilometres. 'Classic' shirts could be sourced from China, where prices are low, and long delivery lead times are not so important. 'Fashion' shirts may be sourced nearer to home, because response time is key and cost is less important (see Case study 8.6).

What happens when the processes are not aligned within a supply chain? Let us address that question with Case study 1.6 to show the problems that can arise.

1.4.3 Differentiating strategies

A supply chain, then, may choose to compete on different criteria. Such criteria in turn need to be recognised and form part of the business strategies of all the members of a given network. The choices so made have major implications for the operation of each member. Failure to recognise competitive criteria and their implications for a given product or service *by any member* means that the supply chain will compete less effectively. It is like playing football when the goalkeeper makes an error and lets in a goal that should not have happened – he or she lets the whole side down.

CASE STUDY 1.7

Auto Roadside Recovery

Auto Roadside Recovery (ARR) is a medium sized company operating around Madrid. ARR provides a vehicle breakdown service offering roadside repair and recovery of the vehicle. Frequently used parts include starters and alternators, which are sourced from a Local Distributor, who in turn procures from a National Distributor. Starters and alternators are remanufactured by replacing the windings and conducting performance tests, which require parts bought from another supplier, as shown in the schematic of the supply chain in Figure 1.12.

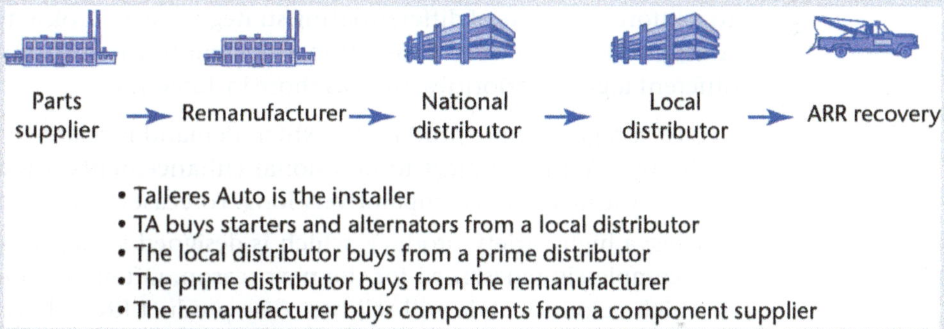

Figure 1.12 Auto Roadside Recovery.

Typically, ARR's customers make 'distress purchases' where their car has broken down and they are desperate for it to be repaired quickly. Therefore, it is essential that ARR receives a rapid delivery of the starters and alternators, which in turn require fast replacements by both the Local and National Distributors. However, while both the Distributors appreciate the need for a highly responsive service, the Remanufacturer has prioritised cost and in particular measures the performance of its purchasing department on the basis of minimised parts costs. This leads to the Parts Supplier believing that low cost is the priority.

Questions

1. What are the order winners and order qualifiers at ARR?
2. What are the order winners and order qualifiers at the Parts supplier?
3. What impact on customer service is this lack of alignment likely to cause?

What makes a successful strategy? Five principles of strategic positioning, related to logistics strategy, are as follows (after Porter, 1984):

- *A unique value proposition:* determining what makes the product/service different from its competitors.
- *A tailored supply chain:* governed by consistent order winning and qualifying criteria.
- *Identify the trade-offs:* by choosing not just the priorities but also what not to do. A responsive supply chain is not compatible with an efficient supply chain (Fisher, 1997).
- *Align logistics processes:* so that processes are mutually reinforcing.
- *Continuity:* logistics processes are improved continually and consistently over time.

1.4.4 Trade-offs in logistics

To reinforce the issue of differentiating strategies, let us look at two commonly used strategies that have very different logistics implications. Consider products with different logistics priorities, such as those in Table 1.5:

- *Cost:* a high-volume product for which demand is relatively stable throughout the year. Whilst subject to occasional enhancements, these are usually small scale: the lifecycle is comparatively long. Forecast error is relatively low.
- *Time:* a high-variety product, which is designed for a given season and which is completely redesigned for the next season. Often, it is impossible to predict which colour or style will sell best. The product lifecycle is short, and forecast error is relatively high.

Cost and time have quite different logistics implications. The very actions that help to reduce costs, such as Far East sourcing, are completely the wrong strategy when speed and responsiveness are top of the agenda. Similarly, investing in high-volume, low-variety equipment in the factory may create efficiency and low cost, but limit a firm's ability to offer variety and fast response times. Developing the capability to support more of one priority (cost) hobbles the capability to support another (time). This is the principle of *trade-off* in logistics: more of one thing means less of another.

Ideally, we want two separate supply chains, one focused on cost, the other on time. This may not be fully practical because of the need to maintain a single European distribution centre. But logistics operations within the DC may well be kept separate to avoid product lines where the priority is low cost from interfering with time sensitive product lines. The same thinking may also apply *within* a given product range, when everyday ('base') demand may need to be kept separate from promotional demand. These are two examples of the various ways in which trade-offs may apply in practice. We return to these concepts in the next chapter.

Activity 1.3

1 Using the concepts from this section, analyse the supply chain support for both of the products you analysed in Activity 1.2. What should the supply chain be (*functional-efficient or innovative-responsive*)? What is the reality, and why are the two different?
2 To what extent is there alignment of strategy in the supply chains for these two products?

Summary

How does logistics work within the supply chain?

Supply chain management is defined as 'encompassing the planning and controlling of all processes involved in procurement, conversion, transportation and distribution across a supply chain. SCM includes coordination and collaboration between partners, which can be suppliers, intermediaries, third party service providers and customers. In essence, SCM integrates supply and demand management within and between companies in order to serve the needs of the end-customer.'

Logistics is defined as 'the task of coordinating material flow and information flow across the supply chain to meet end-customer needs'.

In a supply chain, materials flow from upstream to downstream. Demand information from the end-customer flows in the opposite direction. A focal firm is positioned within a supply 'network', with tier 1 suppliers and tier 1 customers as its immediate neighbours. Material flow measures the quantity of material that passes through a given network per unit of time.

A supply network is a system in which each organisation is linked to its immediate neighbours. Therefore, the overall performance of the network results from the combined performance of the individual partners.

Logistics supports competitiveness of the supply chain as a whole by meeting end-customer demand through supplying what is needed, when it is needed, at low cost.

What are the performance objectives of the supply chain, and how does logistics support those objectives?

'Hard objectives' are quality, speed and cost because they are easy to measure and relatively obvious to the end-customer. Briefly, quality is about doing things right, speed is about doing things fast, and cost is about doing things cheaply. Supporting capabilities are concerned with controlling variability (the dependability advantage), dealing with uncertainty (the rapid response advantage) and acting responsibly (the sustainability advantage). Uncertainty can be addressed by flexibility in logistics processes – either proactively or reactively. Sustainability is concerned with addressing the 'triple bottom line' – social, environmental and economic values. 'Soft objectives' are service-orientated, such as security and confidence. They are less easily measurable than hard objectives.

Such performance objectives can be, and often are, augmented by other objectives that are outside logistics. These include product superiority, innovation and brand. Here, the logistics task is to support such performance objectives in the marketplace.

The relative importance of logistics performance objectives varies from one situation to another. It can also vary over time. The concept of order winners and qualifiers helps to prioritise the logistics task. Key influences on relative importance are individual product needs in the marketplace, position in the product lifecycle and competitor activity.

Logistics strategy is the set of guiding principles, driving forces and ingrained attitudes that help to communicate goals, plans and policies, and that are reinforced through conscious and subconscious behaviour within and between partners across a network.

Discussion questions

1. Bill Gates of Microsoft describes the 2000s as 'business @ the speed of thought'. Discuss the importance of speed in the supply chain. How can speed be increased within the supply chain?
2. Suggest logistics performance priorities for the following, explaining why you have come to your conclusions:
   a. a low-fare airline such as Ryanair
   b. a fast-food chain such as McDonald's
   c. an overnight parcels service such as DHL.
3. What is meant by the term alignment in relation to supply chain processes? Why is alignment important in setting a strategy for a given supply chain?
4. What does flow mean in a supply chain context? Explain how material flow relates to information flow in a supply network.

References

APICS SCOR Model (2010) https://www.apics.org/about/overview/about-apics-scch

Barry, M. and Calver, L. (2009) 'Backing the future', *Marketing,* 28th October 2009, pp. 16–7.

BBC (2022) Tesco to shut down its Jack's discount stores, 31st January 2022 https://www.bbc.co.uk/news/business-60208462

Berchicci, L. and King, A. (2007) Postcards from the edge: A review of the business and environment literature. *The Academy of Management Annals*, vol. 1, no. 1, pp. 513–47. https://doi.org/10.5465/078559816

Black, S., Parry, I and Zhunussova, K. (2022) 'More Countries Are Pricing Carbon, but Emissions Are Still Too Cheap', International Monetary Fund Blog, 21st July, 2022.

Carter, C.R. and Rogers, D.S (2008) 'A framework of sustainable supply chain management: Moving toward new theory', *International Journal of Physical Distribution and Logistics Management*, vol. 38, no. 5, pp. 360–87.

Christopher, C. and Holweg, M. (2011) 'Supply chain 2.0: Managing supply chains in the era of turbulence', *International Journal of Physical Distribution & Logistics Management,* vol. 41, no. 1, pp. 63–82.

Cisco Systems (2024) 'Cisco supplier code of conduct', 25th June, at https://www.cisco.com/c/en/us/about/csr/impact/environment/supplier-code-of-conduct.html

Colicchia, C., Marchet, G., Melacini, M. and Perotti, S. (2013) 'Building environmental sustainability: Empirical evidence from Logistics Service Providers', *Journal of Cleaner Production*, vol. 59, pp. 197–209.

Cousins, P. (2005) 'The alignment of appropriate firm and supply strategies for competitive advantage', *International Journal of Production and Operations Management,* vol. 25, no. 5, pp. 403–28.

CSCMP (2010) http://cscmp.org/aboutcsmp/definitions.asp

Eggleton, D.J. (1990) 'JIT in a distribution environment', *International Journal of Logistics and Distribution Management,* vol. 9, no. 1, pp. 32–4.

Elkington, J. (1997) *Cannibals with Forks: the triple bottom line of 21st century business.* Oxford: Capstone.

Elkington, J. (2004) in Henriques, A. and Richardson, J. (eds) *The Triple Bottom Line – does it all add up?.* London: Earthscan.

EPA (2010) http://www.epa.gov/sustainability/basicinfo.htm

Etzion, D. (2007) 'Research on organizations and the natural environment, 1992-present: A review', *Journal of Management*, vol. 33, pp. 637–64.

Evangelista, P., Colicchia, C. and Creazza, A. (2017) 'Is environmental sustainability a strategic priority for logistics service providers?', *Journal of Environmental Management*, vol. 198, pp. 353–62.

Faithfull, M. (2022) 'Tesco ditches Jack's as discounter flops amid strong grocery sales', Forbes, 1st February 2022.

Fairtrade Foundation (2024) https://www.fairtrade.org.uk/what-is-fairtrade/what-fairtrade-does/

Fisher, M. (1997) 'What is the right supply chain for your product?', *Harvard Business Review,* March/April, pp. 105–16.

Golicic, S.L. and Smith, C.D. (2013) 'A meta-analysis of environmentally sustainable supply chain management practices and firm performance". *Journal of Supply Chain Management*, vol. 49, pp.78–95.

The Guardian (2023) 'Toyota recalls 1m cars over defect that could cause airbags not to deploy', 21st December, 2023. Accessed at https://www.theguardian.com/business/2023/dec/20/toyota-vehicle-recall-lexus-camry-corolla-rav4

Harland, C. (1997) 'Talleres Auto', in Johnston, R., Chambers, S., Harland, C., Harrison, A. and Chambers, S. (eds) (1997) *Cases in Operations Management,* 2nd edn., pp. 420–8. London: Pitman.

Harland, C., Lamming, R., Zheng, J. and Johnsen, T. (2001) 'A taxonomy of supply networks', *Journal of Supply Management,* September, pp. 21–7.

Hayes, R.H. and Wheelwright, S.C. (1984) *Restoring Our Competitive Edge.* New York: John Wiley.

Hewlett Packard (2023) 'Hewlett Packard Enterprise Supplier Code of Conduct' Version 6.0, effective 26th June.

Hill, T. (2000) *Manufacturing Strategy,* 2nd edn. London: Macmillan.

Huge-Brodin, M., Sweeney, E. and Evangelista, P. (2020) 'Environmental alignment between logistics service providers and shippers – a supply chain perspective', *The International Journal of Logistics Management*, vol. 31, no. 3, pp. 575–605.

ISO (2024) 'ISO 14000 family' https://www.iso.org/standards/popular/iso-14000-family#:~:text=There%20are%20more%20than%20500%2C000,the%20ISO%20Survey%20of%20certifications.

Jonathan Soble, (2009), "Toyota presses suppliers to slash prices", The Financial times limited. Retrieved from https://www.ft.com/content/1b771bee-eed5-11de-92d8-00144feab49a.

Knill, B. (1992) 'Continuous flow manufacturing', *Material Handling Engineering,* May, pp. 54–7.

Marchet, G., Melacini, M. and Perotti, S. (2014) 'Environmental sustainability in logistics and freight transportation: A literature review and research agenda', *Journal of Manufacturing Technology Management*, vol. 25, no. 6, pp.775–811.

Nestlé (2023) Creating Shared Value and Sustainability Report.

Nestlé (2024) Regenerative Agriculture at Nestlé, January 2024.

Oliver, R.K. and Webber, M.D. (1982) 'Supply chain management: Logistics catches up with strategy', *Outlook,* vol. 5, no. 1, pp. 42–7.

Perotti, S., Zorzini, M., Cagno, E. and Micheli, G.J.L. (2012) 'Green supply chain practices and company performance: The case of 3PLs in Italy', *International Journal of Physical Distribution and Logistics Management*, vol. 42, no. 7, pp. 640–72.

Perotti, S., Prataviera, L.B. and Melacini, M. (2022) 'Assessing the environmental impact of logistics sites through CO_2eq footprint computation', *Business Strategy and the Environment*, vol. 31, no. 4, pp. 1679–94.

Porter, M. (1984) *Competitive Advantage.* New York: Free Press.

Porter, M. and Van Der Linde, C. (1995) 'Green and competitive: Ending the stalemate', *The Harvard Business Review*, vol. 73, pp. 120–34.

Prataviera, L.B., Creazza, A., Perotti, S. and Rodrigues, V.S. (2023) 'How to align logistics environmental sustainability with corporate strategy? An Italian perspective', *International Journal of Logistics Research and Applications*, pp. 1–23. https://www.tandfonline.com/doi/full/10.1080/13675567.2023.2230916.

Prataviera, L.B., Creazza, A. and Perotti, S. (2024) 'A call to action: A stakeholder analysis of green logistics practices', *The International Journal of Logistics Management*, vol. 35, no. 3, pp. 979–1008.

Reed, B. (2007) 'Shifting from "sustainability" to regeneration', *Building Research & Information,* vol. 35, no. 6, pp. 674–80.

Read, S. and Shine, I. (2022) 'You've probably heard of Scope 1, 2 and 3 emissions, but what are Scope 4 emissions?', World Economic Forum, 20th September 2020.

Royal Mail (2018) 'Royal Mail Quality of Service 2017/18', Press Release, 11 May, at https://www.royalmailgroup.com/en/press-centre/press-releases/royal-mail-group/royal-mail-quality-of-service-201718/

Schrettle, S., Hinz, A., Scherrer-Rathje, M. and Friedli, T. (2014) 'Turning sustainability into action: Explaining firms' sustainability efforts and their impact on firm performance'. *International Journal of Production Economics*, vol. 147, pp.73–84.

Slack, N. (1987) 'Manufacturing systems flexibility: Ten empirical observations', *Management Research Papers,* Templeton College, The Oxford Centre for Management Studies, MRP/87–9.

Slack, N., Chambers, S., Harland, C., Harrison, A. and Johnston, R. (1997) *Operations Management,* 2nd edn. Harlow: Financial Times Prentice Hall.

United Nations Global Compact-Accenture. (2019) 'The UN Global Compact-Accenture Strategy CEO Study on Sustainability 2019'. September/2019.

United Nations (2024) 'For a livable climate: Net-zero commitments must be backed by credible action', https://www.un.org/en/climatechange/net-zero-coalition#:~:text=zero%20by%202050.-,2030,cent%20compared%20to%202010%20levels

UNWCED (1987) *Our Common Future* (the Brundtland Report). Oxford: Oxford University Press.

Upton, D.M. (1995) 'What makes factories flexible?', *Harvard Business Review,* July/August, pp. 74–84.

Whittington, R. (2000) *What is Strategy and Does it Matter?* London: International Thomson Business Press.

Zadek, S. (2004) 'The path to corporate responsibility', *Harvard Business Review,* December, pp. 125–32.

Zheng, J., Harland, C., Johnsen, T. and Lamming, R. (1998) 'Initial conceptual framework for creation and operation of supply networks', Proceedings of the 14th AMP Conference, Turku, 3–5 September, vol. 3, pp. 591–613.

Suggested further reading

Chopra, S. and Meindl, P.S. (2010) *Supply Chain Management,* 4th edn. (global). Upper Saddle River, NJ: Pearson.

Harrison, A. (1996) 'An investigation of the impact of schedule stability on supplier responsiveness', *International Journal of Logistics Management,* vol. 7, no. 1, pp. 83–91.

Stock, J.R. and Lambert, M. (2001) *Strategic Logistics Management,* 4th edn. Boston, MA: McGraw-Hill/Irwin.

Willard, R. (2002) *The Sustainability Advantage.* Gabriola Island, BC: New Society Publishers.

CHAPTER 2

Putting the end-customer first

Objectives

The intended objectives of this chapter are to:

- **develop the marketing perspective on supply chain management and the need for close coordination between the two functions;**
- **outline the importance of understanding customer value in designing supply chains;**
- **explain how customer segmentation works, and to emphasise its implications for supply chain management and why it is important;**
- **outline the role of demand forecasting and the links with marketing;**
- **explain current approaches to supply chain segmentation and how they can be used to align marketing and supply chain activities, whilst improving customer service and efficiencies.**

By the end of this chapter you should be able to understand:

- **what is meant by customer value and its critical role in operating the supply chain;**
- **the growing importance of the information revolution through the Internet of Things (IoT) and Big Data;**
- **how supply chains should compete by aligning supply chain strategy with marketing strategy;**
- **how to use logistics strategy drivers – demand, competitive and product – to help redefine segments to achieve alignment between marketing and supply chain management.**

Introduction

In Chapter 1 we looked at the logistics task from the perspective of material flow and information flow. We also saw how logistics contributes to competitive strategy and the performance objectives by which we can measure this contribution. But what is it that drives the need for flow in the first place? The key point to recognise here is that it is the behaviour of the **end-customer** and what they value that should dictate what happens. The end-customer starts the logistics response by buying finished products. It is this behaviour that causes materials to flow through the supply chain. Only end-customers should be free to make up their minds about when they want to place an order on the network – after that, the system takes over.

Understanding the value that customers place upon the product and its supporting services requires organisations to comprehend the needs of the market in which they trade. Each individual has his or her own specific sets of requirements; however, it is the role of marketing to develop a strategy that can recognise and segment these into a format that the supply chain can deliver in a profitable manner.

This chapter explores the link between **marketing strategy** and supply chain strategy. There naturally exists a tension between the demand creation objectives of marketing and the demand fulfilment objectives of supply chain management. For instance, marketing has a tendency to proliferate product ranges in order to gain market share. We see this with almost any consumer product we care to think of – toothpaste, for instance, appears in many brands, flavours, formulas, types of packaging and sizes. From a marketing perspective, this increases visibility of the product range whether on the store shelf or online; it also increases the likelihood that the products will fulfil customer needs in all the many market segments. However, from a supply chain management perspective, variety results in an increasing number of SKUs introducing greater complexity and costs, such as an increased number of suppliers and increased inventory levels, in part due to a higher number of SKUs and higher **demand variability** at SKU level. And product range is just one area of tension between marketing and logistics.

Segmented supply chain strategy offers an approach to aligning logistics strategy with marketing and, most importantly, the changing needs of the customers and market. By having multiple supply chain strategies determined by drivers – demand, competitive and product – our research suggests that efficiencies and customer service levels can be improved simultaneously.

Key issues

This chapter addresses three key issues:

1. **The marketing perspective**: the impact of rising **customer value** expectations and the information revolution. The existing marketing approaches to segmentation and their implications for supply chain strategy.
2. **Demand profiling:** different approaches to demand forecasting and the implications for supply chain strategy.
3. **Segmented supply chain strategy:** how we can develop multiple supply chain strategies that simultaneously improve efficiencies and service levels. We acknowledge the assistance of our colleague at Cranfield University, Janet Godsell (now of Loughborough University), in sharing her extensive knowledge on segmented supply chain strategy and her assistance with Section 2.3.

2.1 The marketing perspective

Key issue: What are the marketing implications for logistics strategy?

'Marketing' traditionally has been associated with anticipating, identifying and satisfying customer requirements profitably. In our terms, such a definition emphasises the focal firm and outbound logistics. But a more current definition emphasises value in the context of the broader supply chain – and that includes partners rather than just customers:

> **Marketing is the activity, set of institutions, and processes for creating, communicating, delivering, and exchanging offerings that have value for customers, clients, partners, and society at large.**
>
> **(Source: American Marketing Association, 2023a.)**

Marketing in practice comprises the plans and decisions that determine how these processes will be carried out.

Ultimately, satisfied end-customers are seen as the only source of profit, growth and security. According to the chief executive of Amazon, Jeff Bezos (2020):

> **The balance of power is shifting toward consumers and away from companies . . . The right way to respond to this if you are a company is to put the vast majority of your energy, attention and dollars into building a great product or service and put a smaller amount into shouting about it, marketing it.**

In Chapter 1, we referred to '**tier 1 customers**' with whom a focal firm deals directly and to 'end-customers' who are the individuals or businesses that buy the finished 'product' at the downstream end of the supply network (as illustrated in Figure 1.2). It is therefore usual to refer to two types of customers:

- *1st tier customers:* who represent the focal firm's immediate trading environment and are businesses (unless the 1st tier is also the end-customer, in which case they might be individual consumers);
- *end-customers:* who represent the ultimate customer for the network as a whole and may be businesses or individual consumers.

We also need to distinguish here between different types of customers. Customers are individuals or businesses who buy the product, meaning that they acquire it and pay for it. It is usual in business today to refer to 'customers' as the next echelon downstream in a supply chain. This includes 'all types of marketing intermediaries or channel members who buy for resale to their customers' (Webster, 2000). Consumers are a particular type of end-customer – people who use or consume the product or service and derive value from the experiences and perceptions they develop (Zeithaml et al., 2020).

Different types of customers give rise to different types of relationships, commonly referred to as '**business to business**' (B2B) and '**business to consumer**' (B2C). In Section 1.2.2 of Chapter 1, we referred to the need to integrate supply chain processes so that they are aligned towards end-customer needs. In this sense, B2B integration should be aligned towards the ultimate B2C process or, in the case of an industrial product, B2B process.

But 'satisfied customers' are increasingly hard to find. In order to win and retain customers it is critical that businesses understand what customers value. We expand on this in the next section.

2.1.1 Customer value

Understanding what customers value is critical in the design and operation of any supply chain. Without comprehending the value that customers derive from a product it is possible for businesses to develop processes and procedures which fail to deliver satisfaction, potentially optimising what is good, economically, for the manufacturer but not necessarily what is desired by the customer. Bicheno and Holweg (2016) define customer value as follows:

Value must be defined in the eyes of the customer, in terms that are meaningful to the customer.

The automotive sector has recognised the importance of understanding what is meaningful to customers. Vehicle manufacturers have altered their perspectives from being car producers to being more concerned about the mobility of the customer. This change in emphasis has been driven by changing customer needs, such as:

- reduced desire to own a car (more people are switching to leasing a vehicle instead);
- increased parking restrictions (particularly in major cities);
- increased operating costs (fuel, taxation, maintenance, and so on)
- technological advances (self-driving cars);
- quick and easy access to alternative modes of travel (e.g. Uber).

The customer's focus on mobility and not car ownership has led to car manufacturers investing in driverless technology, smaller cars, leasing services and increased fuel efficiencies. The change in ethos of the sector is exemplified by BMW's mission statement (2024):

to move people with products that evoke emotions.

Delivering greater value to customers cannot be done in isolation. Businesses have to consider the needs and expectation of shareholders (see Chapter 3). Delivering value to both shareholders and customers can result in tension if the objectives of each group are not aligned. One approach to managing the tension is lean thinking (see Chapter 7) where the concept is expected to deliver value for both groups through minimising waste in processes. Through working in partnership with suppliers, improving internal operations and enhancing customer relationships businesses can work on reducing waste and maximising value for all members of the supply chain (Christopher and Ryals, 1999). In addition to balancing value requirements, supply chain professionals are also facing the challenges presented by increasing customer expectations and the information revolution (Doyle, 2000). We expand on these next.

2.1.2 Rising customer expectations

Recognising current needs, however, is only the starting point: customer expectations continue to increase as consumers demand more for their cash. For manufacturers this is not a new phenomenon, but the pace of change is becoming more challenging. These pressures are leading to shorter order-to-delivery cycle times, product range growth and greater uncertainty in demand, all of which increase pressure on businesses to respond quickly in terms of product development and supply chain delivery in order to satisfy customer expectations.

Activity 2.1

The images in Figure 2.1 show televisions that were manufactured ten years apart. The difference in functionality and appearance is quite significant. What level of functionality would you have got ten years ago if you spent €1,000? What would you get today for the same price? And what functionality will you get for €1,000 ten years from now, assuming inflation remains low? What will this mean in terms of the supply chain for television manufacturers?

Figure 2.1 Changing value of televisions.
(Sources: pockygallery/Shutterstock; cobalt88/Shutterstock.)

These expectations have not only led to consumers aspiring to more desirable products; in addition, they are also demanding much better levels of service associated with those products. Businesses are also expecting more from their suppliers. Suppliers need to pay increasing attention to the service aspects of their dealings with business customers. This is especially true when the customer has implemented more customer-centric management systems such as just-in-time or vendor managed inventory (Chapters 7 and 8).

2.1.3 The information revolution

The explosion in applications of internet technology continues to have sweeping effects on the way that business is transacted today. Applications that have sprung from the world wide web have impacted both B2C and B2B relationships.

Business to consumer (B2C)

Online retailing has become an established distribution channel with organisations such as Amazon and Alibaba continuing to extend the range and breadth of products they offer. Many retail firms based on the traditional 'bricks and mortar' model have fought back by launching their own websites, online catalogues and delivery-to-home services. The internet has become another channel to market for the retail industry, as home shopping accelerates in industry sectors as diverse as books, music and furniture. This has resulted in *multi-channel retailing:*

> **The improvement of retail activities in such a way, to the point that empowers the client to execute with the business (pursue, purchase or return) through autonomously overseen mediums, including retail locations, online stores, mobile stores, portable application stores and phone deals.**

However, this has led to numerous logistics challenges as retailers struggle to apportion and control inventories across the different channels and at the same time provide the customer with high availability and stock visibility. The majority of retailers have now transitioned to an *omnichannel* structure to service the varied market segments which they now face in order to deliver value to customers highlighting the pivotal role of data management and integration (Mirzabeiki, and Saghiri, 2020). According to a survey of retail boards in the UK and USA conducted by LCP Consulting, which specialises in the retail sector (Lockton et al., 2013):

> **A really coordinated methodology over the entire retail activity that conveys a consistent response to the consumer encounters through all accessible shopping stations, regardless of whether on versatile web gadgets, PCs, in store on TV and in catalog.**

Regardless of the channel, the experience in terms of assortment, ease of use, availability and delivery should be uniform with a focus on fulfilment excellence (in terms of speed and reliability) enabled by integrated IT systems.

Retailers are investing heavily in the development of the Internet of Things (IoT) to capture and analyse large volumes of data. The possibility of IoT products, such as fridges, which can notify both you and the supermarket of the need to replenish stocks of a particular item, are becoming available. Through the interconnectivity of IoT devices, populated with electronics, sensors and software, large volumes of data can be transferred between people and businesses. In addition to IoT, data retailers are also gathering and harvesting information from social media and loyalty cards. This large volume of data is complex in nature and includes text, photos and sound, allowing organisations to visualise customers' preferences and demands in terms of simulations and graphic representations to aid decision making and forecasting.

These large data sets are commonly known as **Big Data** (BD) and have the potential to support and develop greater understanding of what consumers value. BD can be characterised by what are known as the three Vs:

- Volume: the quantity of data collected;
- Variety: the form and nature of the data collected;
- Velocity: the pace at which the data is collected and processed.

Obtaining large volumes of complex data sets is not a major challenge for businesses. Making sense of the data through analytics and utilising its outputs to strengthen and quicken the decision-making process are the obstacles that must be addressed for businesses and consumers. Data analytics provides the opportunity for retailers to develop a fuller and more robust understanding of what the likes and dislikes of individual consumers are. Advanced algorithms can support machine learning and predictive analytics, allowing marketing to visualise trends and the impact of new product introductions with more accuracy and speed. Predictive analytics can also enable supply chain professionals to improve the accuracy of demand forecasting, which underpins improved on-shelf availability and the lowering of obsolescence for retailers.

Within transportation the power of analytics is disrupting traditional business models, based on vehicle ownership and warehouses, leading to innovative and service-driven solutions. For example, personal mobility and choice have increased for consumers through the use of taxi service apps such as Uber. Through predictive analytics these data-driven businesses have improved the availability and responsiveness of the service provided without investing in capital costs such as vehicles. Similarly, within distribution we have new companies which deliver parcels, through utilising self-employed drivers and transshipment centres, without owning vehicles or warehouse assets.

Business to business (B2B)

Here, the impact has been just as great as in B2C, but perhaps less visible. Businesses increasingly use web portals, online marketplaces and other collaborative online applications to exchange information, undertake transactions (such as buying and selling) and organise delivery and payment. These forms of inter-firm collaboration are leading to closer integration of processes between businesses and are helping to break down some of the traditional barriers in buyer–supplier relationships, as discussed further in Section 8.2 on electronic integration. Equally, e-auctions, where a tender is put online and suppliers are invited to bid over a short period of time (e.g. three hours), can increase competition amongst suppliers. Suppliers have sight of competitors' bids, thereby intensifying the competition and further reducing suppliers' prices and/or improving the service or product quality.

Other supply chain implications

Developments in B2B and B2C exchanges also have an impact on how the supply chain operates. The ability to exchange information more effectively and accurately should enable more reliability in supply chain operations, as well as lowering the costs of ordering. The availability of shared information also facilitates improved management of inventory, forecasts and use of assets. Web-enabled data exchange facilitates replacement of inventory with information, resulting in lower working capital.

Faced with rising customer expectations and the information revolution, supply chain partners are looking increasingly at how they can be more demand-led and respond more rapidly to market requirements. The starting point is to put the end-customer first by analysing what they value and want. The marketing perspective has a well-known way to help in this analysis – marketing segmentation.

2.1.4 Marketing segmentation

Segmentation describes how a given market might be broken up into different groups of customers with similar needs. It provides a 'direction fora firm's marketing strategy and resource allocation. The value of market segmentation lies in helping firms to adopt a position somewhere between the overgeneralized and over customized' (Cortez et al., 2021). We start by considering market segmentation from a *customer* perspective in what are usually described as 'fast-moving consumer goods (FMCG)' markets. For example, segmentation of the market for sun creams would begin with an understanding of:

- the benefits wanted (e.g. water resistance, oil/non-oil, SPF);
- the price consumers are prepared to pay;
- the media to which they are exposed (television programmes, magazines, Google ads, etc.);
- the amount and timing of their purchases.

Profiles of the segments and evaluation of their relative attractiveness to a focal firm can then be developed.

There are many possible ways in which markets can be segmented, including:

- *demographic:* such as age, sex and education;
- *geographic:* such as urban versus country, type of house and region;
- *technical:* the use that customers are going to make of a product;
- *behavioural:* such as spending pattern and frequency of purchase.

Of the various ways to segment markets, we have found that behavioural segmentation, which 'divides buyers into groups based on their knowledge of, attitude towards, and use of or response to a product' (Kotler and Keller, 2009), is a powerful way to bridge marketing and logistics, largely because behaviour typically impacts on the demand and competitive profiles (described later in this chapter in Section 2.3.2). For example, Finne and Sivonen (2009) describe a study of behavioural segments in convenience stores in Europe. Six segments were identified – main, top-up, impulse, distress, grab-and-go and habitual shoppers. 'Top-up' shoppers may value only bread, milk and convenience foods, whilst an 'impulse' shopper is attracted by special offers and displays.

It is vital that the definition of segments is not a marketing-only task, but that logistics is involved. The key point is that defining segments that cannot be served because logistics capability does not exist is unlikely to work. For example, if most of the spending pattern is around Christmas, then logistics must be capable of supporting the huge surge in demand at that time.

The important characteristics of segments (McGoldrick, 2002) are that they must be:

- *measurable:* variables that can be identified and measured easily;
- *economically viable:* capable of producing the contribution that justifies the effort and cost of marketing;
- *accessible:* geographically or in terms of media communications;
- *actionable:* can be attracted and served effectively.

The next step is to select target segments and identify how a focal firm is going to win orders in each. In other words, to define *differential advantage* that distinguishes our offerings from those of our competitors. In logistics terms, the important issues here are the order winning criteria (OWC), and qualifying criteria (QC) for the target segments. These help in turn to define the *marketing mix*.

The marketing mix is the set of marketing decisions that is made to implement positioning strategy (target market segments and differential advantage) and to achieve the associated marketing and financial goals. The marketing mix has been popularly termed the '4 Ps' (American Marketing Association (AMA), 2023b):

Activity 2.2

Figure 2.2 shows a Pareto analysis of the annual sales to 886 customers in the portfolio of a book stockist. What actions could the stockist take to segment its market? How could each segment best be served? What are the operational implications for the stockist? (Check out Brynjolfsson et al., 2010, The Longer Tail: The Changing Shape of Amazon's Sales Distribution Curve).

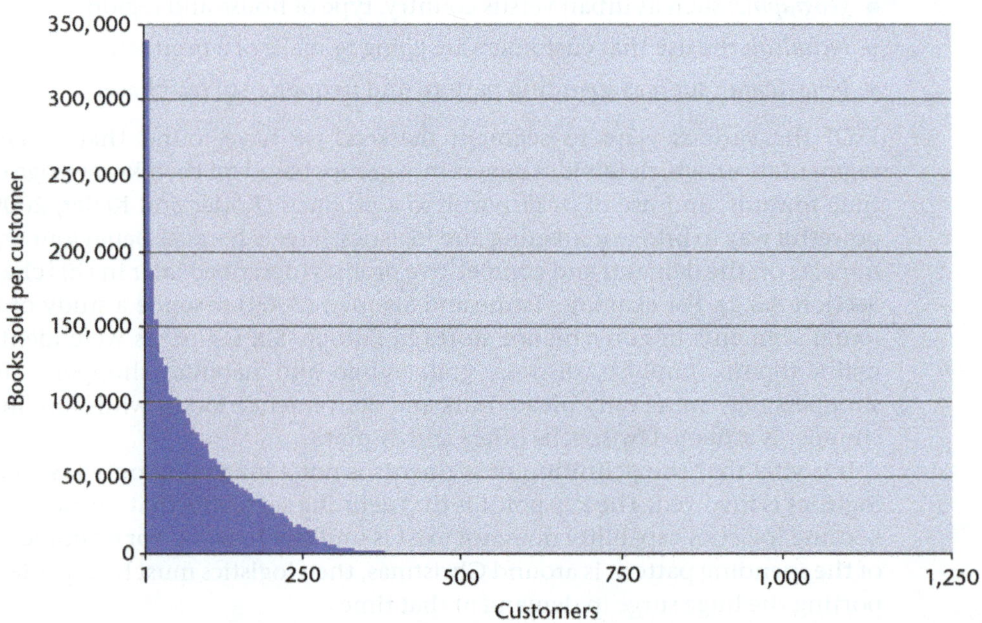

Figure 2.2 Annual sales per customer for a book distributor, shown as a Pareto diagram.

- *product:* range, sizes, presentation and packaging, design and performance;
- *price:* list price, discounts, geographical pricing, payment terms;
- *promotion:* salesforce, advertising, consumer promotion, trade promotion, direct marketing;
- *place:* channel selection, market coverage, distribution systems, dealer support.

Logistics contributes fundamentally to the 'place' decisions, as well as supporting 'product' and 'promotion' decisions and, arguably, enables more competitive pricing by controlling logistics costs. All too often, 'place' activities are viewed as the bit bolted to the back of production that gets inventory away from the factory and into stock-holding points such as warehouses. In order to achieve the goal of 'the right product in the right place at the right time', logistics systems and processes need to be designed to support products in the marketplace.

Segmentation principles can also be applied to industrial marketing. But 'there are distinct differences between the marketing of industrial products and consumer goods' (Millier and Palmer, 2000: 60), as summarised in Table 2.1.

Table 2.1 Comparison between consumer and industrial marketing.

	Consumer	Industrial
Customers	Many, widely dispersed	Few, concentrated
Market	Consumers directly served by retailers and distributors	Derived demand Industrial chain, long and complex
Buying behaviour	Individual and family decision	Group decision Formal procedures High buyer power
Relationships	Low individual buying power	Formal procedures High buyer power
Product	Standard Positioned on emotional and perceptual factors	Technical complexity Specification important Bespoke and customised
Price	Low unit price Take it or leave it No negotiation	High unit price Tender and negotiation Standard items from price list
Promotion	Mass media advertising Role of the brand	Emphasis on personal selling Reputation important
Place	Established retail chain Stock availability Seasonality	Direct made to order Standard items in stock

Let us turn to an industrial marketing example (Case study 2.1) to illustrate how a new marketing mix can impact on logistics capability and, ultimately, the fulfilment of different market segments.

CASE STUDY 2.1

Powerdrive Motors

At the time Tom Cross took over as managing director at Powerdrive Motors in South Africa, the company was an established manufacturer of small electric motors with a strong reputation for product reliability and technical leadership. On the downside, it was also regarded in the trade as having high prices and variable delivery. Tom's first task was to tackle the huge product variety on offer. He saw this as the major problem in addressing the negative views in the marketplace, and also saw opportunities in streamlining design and production. The product range was replaced with a new generation of designs based on a few hundred 'modules', which could be assembled in many different combinations to give variety at low cost. This meant the loss of some customers who had gone to Powerdrive because they could rely on the company's technical leadership to produce designs that suited their particular needs. This was not considered important because the combined sales volume of such customers was under 5 per cent.

Using the new designs, Tom was now able to reorganise the factory into cells that produced major subassemblies such as rotors and stators. The workflow was transformed, and manufacturing throughput time was reduced from six weeks to just four days. Cost improvements meant that average price reductions of between 10 and 15 per cent could be offered.

Powerdrive's customer service policy was redrafted to offer quotations within a maximum of one hour of any enquiry, and for deliveries of finished product to be made within one week 'anywhere in northern Europe'. This new policy was explained to internal sales staff, and to sales representatives and agents employed by the organisation. If 'old' customers wanted special designs that were no longer in the range, the sales staff were instructed to explain Powerdrive's new policy and politely decline the order.

At first, business soared. Impressed by the lower prices and short delivery times, customers flocked to Powerdrive and sales jumped by 50 per cent. But then things began to go sour. First, the factory could no longer cope with the demands being placed on it. The addition of a large order for lawnmower motors blocked out a lot of production capacity from January to June. Order lead times during this period in particular slid back to former levels. Second, a Brazilian supplier spotted the opportunity to enter the market with prices that undercut Powerdrive by 20 per cent. Whilst only half of the product range was covered by this new entrant, it was the high-volume products that were especially threatened. Further, the new competitor offered three-day lead times from stock that had been established in the country. Third, some of the former customers, who could no longer obtain their bespoke designs from Powerdrive, were complaining within the industry that Powerdrive's technical leadership had been sacrificed. Although small in number, such customers were influential at trade fairs and conferences.

Questions

1. Characterise the changes in the market segments using the concept of order winners and qualifiers.
2. Evaluate the changes that took place in the marketing mix and how this impacted on the fulfilment of different market segments' needs (in terms of OWC and QC) by logistics.

Segmentation is often undertaken by adopting the easy way to group customers – by account size. Whilst this is easily measurable, it fails on the fourth of McGoldrick's criteria listed above: it is not actionable in supply chain terms. Indeed, when we review conventional approaches to market segmentation and their implications for marketing and supply chain strategy (as summarised in Table 2.2), it can be seen that there are limited implications for supply chain strategy.

- *Product and service segmentation:* this involves dividing customers into groups, depending on the products or services they buy. From a marketing perspective, this does not provide any information about the customer in terms of their motivations for buying the products or the benefits they seek. Therefore this method of segmentation cannot be used to drive marketing activities. From the supply chain strategy perspective, different products can often be distinguished by their demand characteristics and service requirements, which drive supply chain strategy (as described in Section 2.3.2). However, this is not always the case, and different customers buying the same product may exhibit different buying behaviours depending on other factors (as discussed in Section 2.3.3).

Table 2.2 Summary of marketing and supply chain strategy implications of conventional market segmentation.

Segmentation approach	Marketing implications	Supply chain strategy implications
Product and service	No information about the customer	Limited differentiation of supply chain strategy
Demographics *Consumer:* age, lifestyle, life cycle stage *Business:* sector turnover	Provide important profiling information that can be used in determining the appropriate marketing mix	When linked to product type can be used for limited differentiation of supply chain strategy
Geography		Differentiate distribution strategy
Channel		

- *Demographic segmentation:* a market can be segmented on the basis of demographics – such as age and lifestyle for consumers, and sector and turnover for industrial customers. From a marketing perspective, this provides important profiling information, which can be used for promotional and pricing activities. Demographics have no implications for supply chain strategy except when products can be linked to specific demographic segments.
- *Geography:* this requires segmenting customers on the basis of their geographical location, for instance rural versus urban. As with demographics, this can provide marketing with important profiling information. From a supply chain perspective, geographical location can be used to differentiate distribution strategy.
- *Channel:* routes to market are becoming more sophisticated and complex and are an increasingly important component of many winning value propositions. For instance, in the past, pet foods tended to be cheap, low quality and sold

exclusively through supermarkets. But now premium pet foods are sold through veterinarians, breeders and pet stores. Like geographical location, channels help profile customers for marketing activities and can be used to differentiate distribution strategy.

In practice, market segmentation is typically implemented by the marketing function in order to determine segment-specific marketing mix and value propositions. Thus, segmentation tends to be actionable by marketing and drives marketing strategies and processes, but does not drive supply chain strategies and processes. An example from our research in the fast-moving consumer goods (FMCG) sector (in Case study 2.2) illustrates the problems of poor alignment between market segmentation and supply chain strategy and processes.

The question arises - what approach to market segmentation can be used to determine supply chain strategy? It is widely acknowledged by scholars developing multiple supply chain strategies, as discussed in Section 2.3, that the demand profile is a key determinant of the appropriate strategy, so let's start by understanding how demand is forecast.

CASE STUDY 2.2

Segmentation at Electrical Co

Electrical Co is a manufacturer of electrical and electronic products that serves the European market. Electrical Co currently segments its customers on the value of customer accounts. The primary division is between *national accounts*, for which 50 accounts constitute 60 per cent of sales by value, 30 *retail* accounts which provide 25 per cent of sales and *field sales*, which comprise of a long 'tail' of more than 350 accounts that together make up only 15 per cent of sales. Due to the size of the field sales structure, a secondary classification groups accounts by channel type: OEMs (Other Equipment Manufacturers), government agencies and specialist distributors as summarised in Table 2.3.

Table 2.3 Electrical Co – current 'account size' approach to market segmentation.

	National accounts	Retail sales	Field sales		
% Sales	60	25	15		
Number of accounts	50	30	350+		
Channel	Distributors	Grocers	OEM	Government agencies	Specialist distributors

Whilst Electrical Co currently segments its customers by account classification, its sales organisation has identified two significant types of buying behaviour displayed by the customer base, shown in Table 2.4:

- *volume-driven* buying behaviour
- *margin-driven* buying behaviour.

Volume-driven customers are keen to capitalise on both product and supply chain cost savings to pass them on to their customers to drive volume sales. There are three variants of the volume-driven behaviour:

- own brand
- everyday low price (EDLP)
- discount.

Customers with own brand expect a 'no frills' low-cost product range that can be priced at a level below EDLP. Customers pursuing an EDLP strategy strive for continuous price reduction from suppliers such as Electrical Co to drive a consistent, high volume of sales. EDLP strategy recognises the value of the supplier brand. This should result in a relatively stable pattern of demand, excluding promotions, in the electrical sector. Discounters, on the other hand, are looking for bargains so they can 'stack 'em high and sell 'em cheap', a strategy more likely to result in a volatile demand pattern. Margin-driven customers are keen to add value for their customers by offering a wide selection of products, customised solutions and value-adding services. This strategy also results in a relatively stable demand pattern in this sector.

Table 2.4 Electrical Co – potential approach to behavioural segmentation.

Behavioural Segments	Volume-driven			Margin-driven
	Own brand	EDLP	Discount	
Order winner	'no-frills'	Continuous price reductions	Bargains – stack 'em high, sell 'em cheap	Value-adding services and wide selection of products and customised solutions
Demand variability (excluding promotions)	Low	Low	High	Low

However, a complicating factor when trying to deconstruct the buying behaviour of Electrical Co's retailer customers is that several secondary factors are used to support products in the marketplace. Such factors include product types (e.g. premium, basic, own brand), product range (e.g. current products, customised, promotional), and promotions strategy (e.g. seasonal, responsive, monthly). Promotions are by far the most disruptive of these factors and occur in all volume-driven behavioural segments. Although the promotions are generally planned well in advance, they cause significant disruption to the supply chain operations due to the peaks and troughs in labour and material demands that they create. Furthermore, the deeper the promotional activity, the greater the volatility created and the greater the disruption to the supply chain. This has the effect of masking what is fundamentally a stable demand pattern with somewhat artificial volatile demand (see Chapter 6 for more details on the impact of promotions).

Consequently, neither the current sales account segmentation nor the potential behavioural segmentation can be used to determine different supply chain strategies for each segment. Instead, each operation within the supply chain makes decisions based on the functional criteria that affect its part of the supply chain – decisions which bear no relation to either of the segmentation approaches. Thus, there is a misalignment between marketing segmentation and supply chain strategy, as illustrated in Table 2.5.

Table 2.5 Supply chain segmentation criteria.

Management process	Supply chain decision	Determined by
Source	Which suppliers?	Raw material commodity type
Make	Which European manufacturing site?	Product family type
Deliver	Which national Electrical Co RDC?	Product type, lead-time and location of customer to be served
	Which transport method?	Volume and delivery window. Several customers state fixed times and full loads, some stipulate days of the week with mixed deliveries on a pallet, and others demand JIT.

(Source: Based on James M Aitken 2023; Godsell, J. and Harrison, A. (2002).)

We develop the management processes 'source', 'make' and 'deliver' in the next chapter.

Questions

1. How could Electrical Co deal with promotions when using the behavioural segmentation approach?
2. Could this be used to drive different supply chain strategies and why?
3. Electrical Co are considering leasing products to government agencies rather than selling. Through harnessing the power of IoT and providing the benefit of the product without concerns about maintenance and end-of-life replacement. What impact could this have on the supply chain strategy?

2.2 Demand profiling

Marketing people want to forecast demand in order to plan broad goals such as allocating the salesforce, setting sales goals, promotions planning and advertising campaigns. But logistics people need to know how many to deliver, where and when to do so, for each SKU in the product range and for each channel – not just for the range as a whole. This leads to a common perception of the two functions – marketing dealing in the abstract and logistics dealing in the day-to-day realities. The two business functions must be careful not to talk past each other, for both have important insights into what the end-customer wants. For many firms, of course, this is not an issue, and the two functions collaborate extensively. The aim is to combine forces and produce the most accurate profile of future demand.

It is impossible to predict the future with certainty, so it is necessary to forecast what will happen. Accurate forecasts of demand are one of the key starting points for achieving competitive supply chains, reflected in such measures as high on-shelf availability (the percentage of a trading day for which a given SKU is available 'on the shelf' to be purchased by an end-customer) and low inventories. The key approaches to forecasting demand are explained at length in such texts as Wild (2017) and Waters (2008). Here, we will stick to some of the broad principles that apply to demand forecasting: first when there are limited or no historical data available, and second when such data is available.

First, consider the demand profiles in Figure 2.3 when forecasting demand for a new product during the early stages of its lifecycle (introduction and growth).

A forecast that over-estimates the way that demand takes off results in too much inventory too early in the product lifecycle. If this situation is allowed to continue, it will result in the need to get rid of the surplus unsold stock by mark-downs or by disposal. On the other hand, a forecast that under-estimates actual demand results in insufficient stock to meet what the end-customer wants. If allowed to continue, this results in lost sales opportunities and hence loss of market share to competitors who can better meet demand. Both scenarios are familiar challenges for grocery (such as managing promotions) and planning fashion goods for a new season when there is no directly usable history of demand, and forecasting relies on *judgemental* methods such as historical analogy, perhaps augmented by market research. Demand forecasting of new drugs (called 'new pharmaceutical entities' – NPEs) is especially problematic because of the uncertainties of approval from the Food and Drug Administration (FDA) – which takes five years on average – and the take-up by physicians after launch. Lifecycle curves and growth functions can be used to model demand by incorporating 'market based evidence, uncertainty and judgements about what might happen during the drug's lifetime' (Latta, 2007).

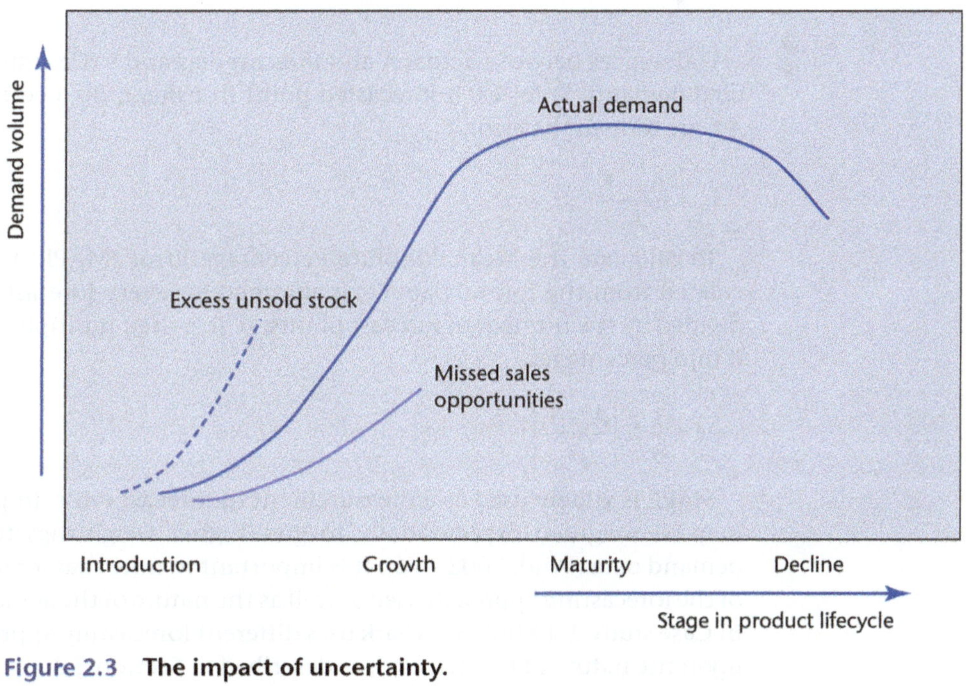

Figure 2.3 The impact of uncertainty.

When historical demand data such as point of sale (POS) are available, various modelling techniques can be used to produce *projective forecasts*. Consider the demand profile in Figure 2.4a, which shows actual demand for years 1–3, and forecast demand for years 1–4. It is based on the profile of sales of a product called 'barbecue sauce', which is produced in many flavours and is sold mainly in the summer.

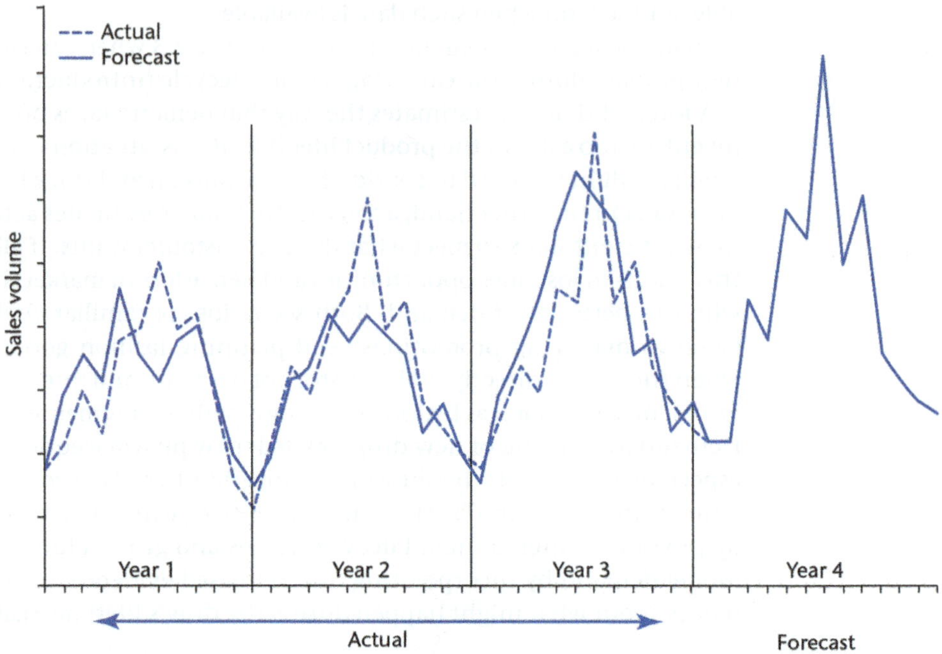

Figure 2.4a Modelling trend and seasonality.

Differences between actual A and forecast demand F (Case study 1.3 uses scheduled demand, S) for each forecasted point in time, *t*, divided by the actual value *A t*, are termed the error, *E*:

$$E_t = \frac{A_t - F_t}{A_t}$$

To calculate the Mean Absolute Percentage Error (MAPE) the error value, calculated from the formula above, is summed for every forecast point in time and divided by the number of forecast points, *n*. It is then multiplied by 100 to convert it into percentage:

$$M = \frac{1}{n}\sum_{t=1}^{n}\left|\frac{A_t - F_t}{A_t}\right|$$

MAPE is widely used as a measurement of forecast error. In practice, the MAPE may be weighted exponentially to give higher weightings to the most recent demand data (Wild, 2002: 176). It is important to note that forecast error is a result of the forecasting approach used as well as the nature of the actual demand. Indeed, in Case study 2.4 Kimberly-Clark uses different forecasting approaches, depending upon the nature of the demand, as described in Section 2.3.

Figure 2.4b shows how the total (aggregate) demand for this product can be broken down into four components:

- *Base:* the level demand that needs to be adjusted for trend and seasonality.
- *Trend:* the long-term trend, which in this case shows a healthy increase year-on-year from base.
- *Seasonality:* the periodic increase and reduction in demand as a result of consumer behaviour – in this case between summer and winter. This can be measured by means of a *seasonal index* – which is the seasonal value divided by the trend, calculated for each period.
- *Uncertainty:* sometimes called 'randomness', this is the balance of demand due to effects we cannot predict with accuracy. These effects may include short-term weather variations, which mean that the consumer is put off barbecuing because it is too cold, wet or windy. Other demand 'spikes' may be due to special causes like the promotion of a particular flavour of sauce by a chef in a popular television programme.

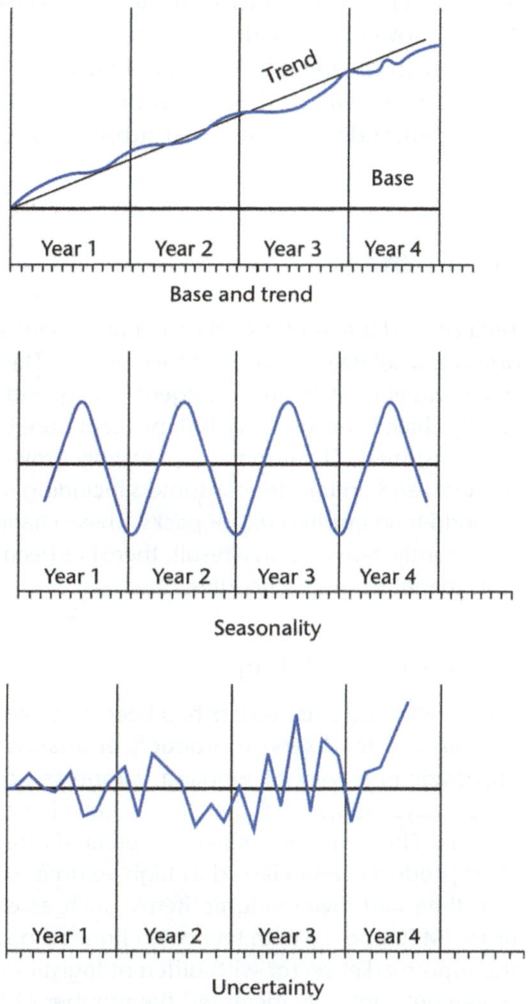

Figure 2.4b Modelling trend and seasonality.

Base and trend demands can be found by linear regression analysis, and a seasonality index can be found by dividing the original data by the trend for each period. Uncertainty is usually allowed for by *increasing* the forecast to provide a safety margin to make it unlikely that there are missed sales opportunities (see Figure 2.3). Forecast demand for a future period n is then calculated from:

$$F_n = (\text{base} + \text{trend}_n) \times \text{seasonality index}_n + \text{uncertainty}_n$$

So forecast demand for year 4 was based on projecting historical data for these four components into the future.

So far, the forecast has been carried out at the aggregate level, 'barbecue sauce'. And this is what forecasting professionals often encourage you to do – forecast accuracy is best at aggregate level and worst at SKU level. But there are many flavours in the range – such as sweet hickory, Cajun and peri-peri. And there are different pack sizes and territories that are supplied. So the aggregate plan has to be *disaggregated* into individual SKUs. Often, this is achieved by calculating the percentage of the total demand for each SKU from historical data and then applying a seasonality index to refine the forecast for each period (see, for example, Ogrodowczyk, 2008). An even lower level of disaggregation maybe required if promotions play a significant role in the overall demand of SKUs. Case study 2.3 provides an example from Tilda Limited where the operations team were required to split base and promotional demand to operate their supply chain.

CASE STUDY 2.3

Tilda Limited

Tilda Limited is a food manufacturer and major supplier of pure basmati rice to the UK grocery, wholesale and food service sectors. The rice is sourced from the foothills of the Himalayas and undergoes stringent quality and DNA verification tests across its entire supply chain to ensure only 100 per cent pure basmati rice is supplied to its customers and consumers. The firm has successfully grown its business through developing new products and options for consumers including microwavable steamed rice and a range of world food inspired recipe packs. These changes have helped the company to grow significantly; however, as a result, there has been an increase in pressure on the stability of its manufacturing schedules.

Increase in scheduling challenges

Historically, customer orders had been received against an agreed lead time of 7 days for standard food service products or against a schedule for export-specific items. This traditional way of working, supported by finished goods inventory levels of 14–21 days, supported the generation of manufacturing schedules with a 14-day horizon. The firm predominantly operated through a make-to-stock (MTS) process as most products were classed as high volume with low demand variability. For longer lead time and lower-volume items, such as export, the firm employed a make-to-order (MTO) policy with few or no finished goods inventories being held. Entry into the supermarket sector with different logistics needs, pack sizes and promotional requirements not only increased the number of SKUs but also compressed lead times.

An increase in customer demand variation placed pressure on operations in terms of fluctuating inventories and lower schedule stability. The shortening of lead times, expanded product offering and the variability of demand forced operations management to reconsider the principle of a two-week window for manufacturing and their MTO/MTS product classification.

Responding to schedule instability

In order to consider possible changes to the scheduling procedures Tilda Limited developed a thorough understanding of (1) the decisions and control systems that were used to transfer and produce customer orders; and (2) variability of customer demand. The analysis highlighted that the management of changeovers would have to be improved (though lean manufacturing techniques) and that customer demand would have to be segmented further. One of the most significant impacts of working with major supermarkets was the increase in promotional activity. An analysis of one of Tilda's main MTS products highlighted the impact that promotional activity had on the demand (see Figure 2.5a, where the dotted red line represents the level of variation caused by promotions while the full red line shows average demand). Removing promotions from the demand profile demonstrated that the MTS classified product was relatively stable (see Figure 2.5b). The production planning manager, having identified the impact of promotional items on schedule stability, worked with sales and marketing to improve the management of promotions and its associated lead times. This resulted in a classification change to an MTO status for products subject to promotions, which in turn led to the normal demand item being managed under an MTS process while promotions were planned through MTO.

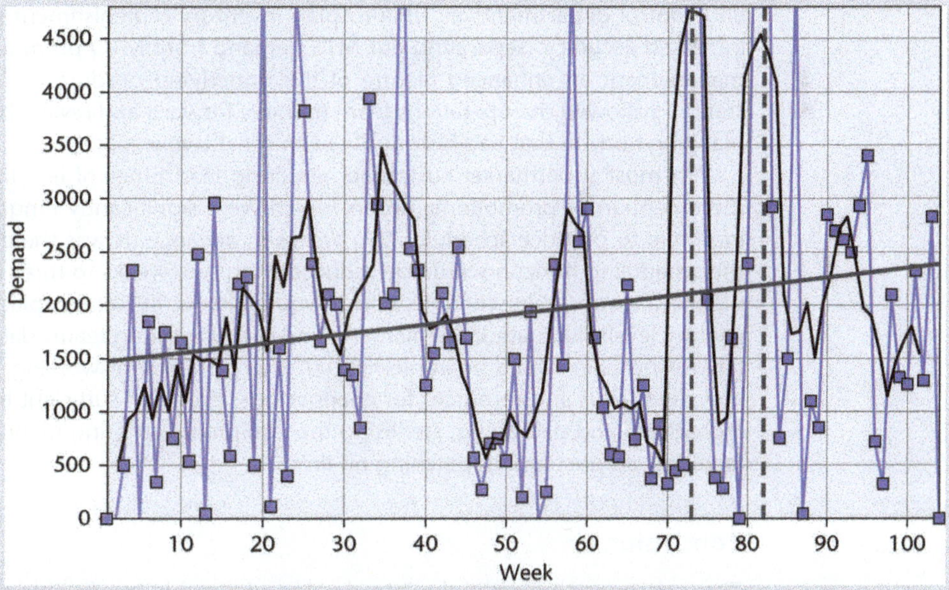

Figure 2.5a Demand comparison showing impact of promotions on demand variability.

(Source: Garn. W and Aitken, J. reference is Garn, W. and Aitken, J., 2015. 'Agile factorial production for a single manufacturing line with multiple products', European Journal of Operational Research, 245(3), pp. 754–766.)

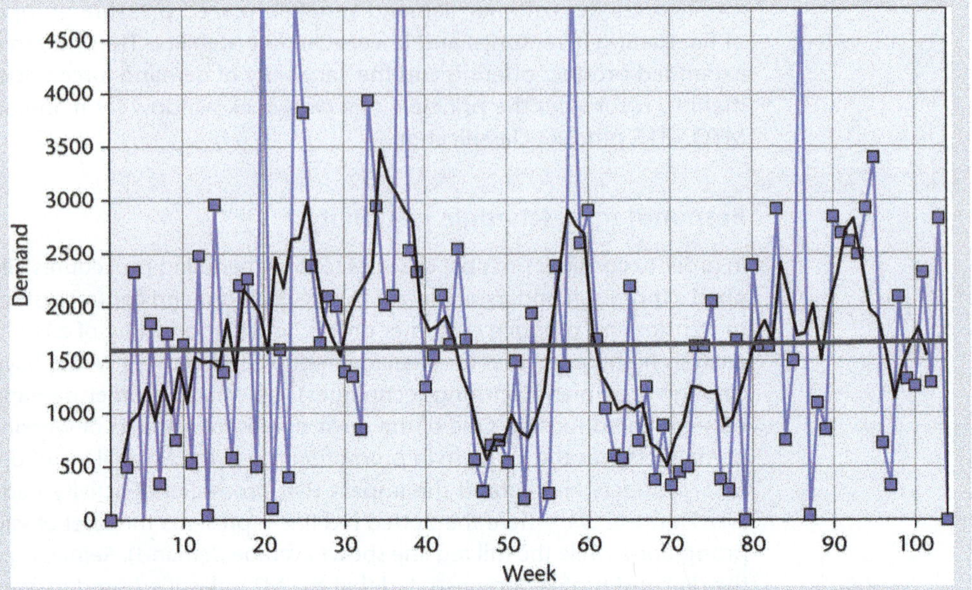

Figure 2.5b Demand comparison showing impact of promotions on demand variability.

(Source: Garn., W. and Aitken, J., 2015. 'Agile factorial production for a single manufacturing line with multiple products', *European Journal of Operational Research*, 245(3), pp. 754–766.)

Managing variability

Segmenting products in terms of demand profile and lead time allowed the planning and control departments at Tilda to plan inventory replenishment (MTS items) with increased accuracy. Separating out MTS demand from MTO promotional orders gave management an enhanced picture of the underlying product demand. This understanding allowed the operations team to move forward and review how they used the planning horizon that had historically been set at two weeks.

With most supermarket customers requiring lead times of less than a week (with the exception of promotional orders which were significantly longer) it was becoming futile to produce schedules two weeks in advance. It was therefore decided that the scheduling horizon would be reduced from two weeks to three days. Rather than planning an unstable schedule, which would alter as customers placed orders and inventory levels fluctuated, the planning and manufacturing teams decided that a three-day rolling plan would be implemented. This new way of working, supported by an increased focus and resources for changeovers, provided sufficient time for preparing ingredients and packaging, sterilising the equipment, altering manning levels, manufacturing product and dispatching on time.

Conclusion

These changes supported the introduction of a stable but flexible production schedule. Understanding customer demand and aligning scheduling procedures and processes supported Tilda's operations team in meeting market needs and shareholder requirements.

Questions

1. What are the likely effects of the changes to Tilda's scheduling horizon on its suppliers?
2. Increasing demand variation and product variety is an ongoing challenge for most businesses to manage. What other steps could Tilda take to buffer production against these growing issues?

Activity 2.3

Explain how marketing and logistics functions should work together to create more accurate forecasts of demand.

We return to the issue of disaggregation in Section 2.3, when we address demand profiling for segmented supply chain strategy. Disaggregation is also covered in Section 6.1.1 from the point of view of planning and control in manufacturing.

Forecasting is a major factor in logistics today, and we have touched on only some of the key issues in this section. We address further issues in other sections of this book as follows:

- Because of uncertainty, it is better to rely less on forecasting by shrinking lead times and engaging more closely with actual demand (Section 5.1.4).
- Several management approaches can be used to improve forecast accuracy (Section 6.1.1).
- Poor internal coordination compounds forecasting problems (Section 6.1.5).
- External coordination with partners in a supply chain can be used to develop better forecasts through collaborative planning, forecasting and replenishment (CPFR, Section 8.1.2).

Demand profiling has been shown to be the most appropriate approach to segmentation (see Section 2.3.4) as it supports the development of supply chain drivers and the resultant strategy.

2.3 Segmented supply chain strategy

Key issues: **How can we develop multiple supply chain strategies that simultaneously improve efficiencies and service levels?**

In a highly competitive global market, businesses face the apparently conflicting challenges of driving growth through innovation by 'product leadership', whilst simultaneously reducing costs via 'operational excellence' (Treacy and Wiersema, 1997). This business challenge has a direct impact on the supply chain. Further to Section 1.4.3 on differentiating strategies, Shewchuk (1998) suggested 'one size does not fit all'; in other words, it is unlikely that markets can be represented by one segment and fulfilled by one supply chain strategy. Whilst this has been long recognised, businesses have been slow to segment supply chain strategy, which implies the development of multiple supply chain strategies aligned with the needs of different market segments. This concept is now gaining support and has been a feature of the Gartner AMR Research Supply Chain Executive conferences in 2010 and 2011.

The idea of **segmented supply chain strategy** emerged with Fisher's seminal *Harvard Business Review* (HBR) article in 1997, when he proposed that different supply chain strategies are required for different product types. He proposed that there is a match between efficient supply chains and functional products and responsive supply chains and innovative products. Other supply chain-product combinations are deemed a mismatch, as shown in Figure 2.6.

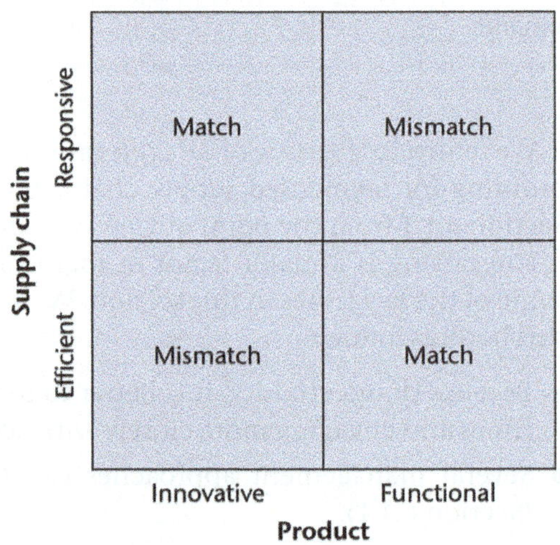

Figure 2.6 Matching supply chains with products.
(Source: Adapted from Fisher, 1997.)

Whilst Fisher's article represented the emergence of the idea of differentiated and multiple supply chain strategies, it had a number of shortcomings:

- It is highly simplistic, suggesting that all products can be categorised into either functional or innovative and that this could be used to determine which of two supply chain strategies should be adopted.
- It ignores the reality that the demand profile for a product depends on many factors, other than the product type, including marketing promotions and the context in which the product is purchased, e.g. bathing products may be bought occasionally as presents or routinely.
- Few products now fit the ideal of a functional product, satisfying a basic need with little change over time and subject to stable demand.
- Finally, the whole approach is orientated around products rather than customers, whose buying behaviour may be quite different for the same product.

Following Fisher's product-matched supply chain strategies, a series of papers were published by scholars examining the combination of lean and agile strategies (see, for example, Christopher and Towill, 2001; Childerhouse et al., 2002; and

Piotrowicz et al., 2021 as discussed in detail in Chapter 7). The use of the demand profile – such as volume, variety, variability and uncertainty – as a determinant of the appropriate supply chain strategy was a common thread in this research.

In parallel to the development of the lean, agile approaches, the 'strategic alignment' approach sought to establish a formal link between marketing and supply chain strategy. As its name suggests, it took a more strategic approach. Gattorna and Walters (1996) introduced a four-stage framework for strategic alignment, proposing that strategy is developed in response to the competitive environment, supported by the right culture and leadership style. Although this was customer-, rather than product-, orientated it was highly prescriptive, depending on customers fitting one of four pre-defined types.

We present in Section 2.3.4 a simplified four-step approach to developing segmented supply chain strategy. However, first it is important to understand the following, as covered in the next three subsections:

- supply chain and marketing alignment;
- the supply chain strategy drivers;
- how to select drivers for segmentation.

2.3.1 Supply chain and marketing alignment

In Section 1.4.2 we addressed the issue of alignment of logistics processes within the supply chain, whereas here we consider alignment of supply chain strategy with marketing strategy. The ultimate goal of a publicly listed company is to deliver a sustainable return to its shareholders. It does so through its business strategy, which is typically a mix of sales growth and cost reduction targets. The traditional cascade of strategy typically assigns the sales growth targets to the domain of marketing, and cost reduction targets to the supply chain (Smith, 1956). Such approaches tend to lead to the pursuit of marketing and supply chain targets in isolation and the long-term erosion of shareholder value (Christopher and Ryals, 1999). Further, this typically leads to tension, as shown in Figure 2.7.

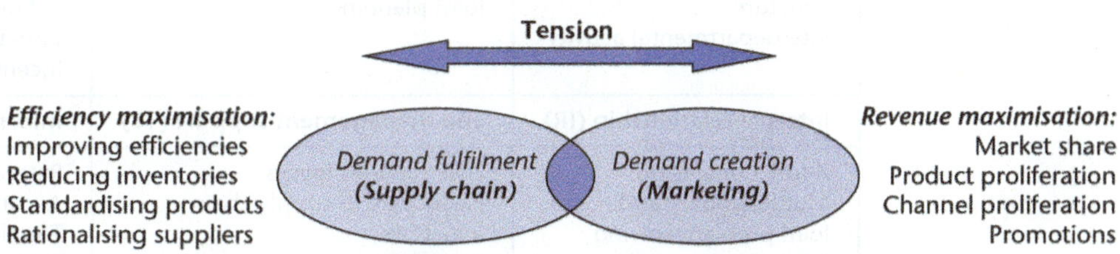

Figure 2.7 Tension between supply chain and marketing objectives.

On the one hand, marketing is about creating demand, and its objectives tend to be around maximising revenue through changes to the marketing mix, for example, introducing new product variants, selling through new distribution channels and running promotions to boost demand. On the other hand, supply chain is about fulfilling demand, and its objectives are often around cost minimisation, for example improving efficiencies and quality, reducing inventories and increasing the number of turns, standardising products where possible and rationalising suppliers. Many of these objectives can be conflicting; for instance if marketing proliferate the number of products or variants, this both increases the number of SKUs, and the demand variability to which they're subjected, increasing the safety stock, and thus inventory, required. Further, promotions employed by marketing dramatically increase demand variability and uncertainty, again requiring increases in safety stock, if product availability is to be maintained.

Whilst there will always be a natural tension between marketing and supply chain, it is vital to business competitiveness that conflicting objectives are resolved, leading to congruence between supply chain strategy (spanning plan, source, make and deliver processes) and marketing strategy (encapsulating the marketing mix in terms of product, place, promotion and price). There are a number of approaches to this, which are complementary to each other:

- Promote integrative behaviours between marketing and supply chain, as described in Section 8.1.1 on internal integration. Employ enablers of customer alignment as identified in our systematic review of the disparate and multidisciplinary literature (Wong et al., 2012): process orientated organisational structure, internal relational behaviour, customer relational behaviour, top management support, information sharing and business performance measurement system (illustrated in Table 2.6).
- Employ a sales and operations planning (S&OP) process, as described in Chapter 6, which has been shown to improve alignment and integration across all functions involved.
- Develop and implement segmented supply chain strategy.

Table 2.6 Enablers to customer and shareholder alignment.

Firm structures (OS)	Customer relationship (CR)	Business performance measurement (PMS)
SC director control spans SC process ownerships X-functional knowledge Process-orientated firm structure Interdepartmental activity	Goal sharing Cost sharing Profit sharing Joint problem-solving Joint planning	Performance targets linked to goals Report at agreed intervals Targets reviewed Action taken to achieve targets Incentive
Internal relationship (IR)	**Top management support (TS)**	**Information sharing (IS)**
X-functional team Mutual understanding Joint problem-solving Joint planning	Listen to employees Participate in supply chain initiatives Provide resources Provide finance SCM at corporate agenda Aware of required SC capability	Relevant information Accurate information Timely information Sufficient information Knowledge to use information

(Source: Adapted from Wong et al., 2012.)

To develop segmented supply chain strategy it is necessary that supply chain strategy is developed to meet different market needs. But what are the market needs that drive supply chain strategy and can be used to segment the market? As discussed earlier in this chapter, approaches to segmentation used by marketing are not actionable by the supply chain (see Section 2.1.4).

2.3.2 The supply chain strategy drivers

From a synthesis of the previous work on lean and agile supply chains and research at Cranfield University, three profiles have been identified which drive supply chain strategy and can be used to segment the market, as illustrated in Figure 2.8.

Whilst there are three types of profiles that can be used to determine segmented supply chain strategy, it should be stressed that they represent a suite of profiles and measures which may be used, rather than a fixed set that are mandatory. Moreover, the use of the demand profile has been found to be the most powerful approach to segmentation (as illustrated by the four-step segmentation approach described in Section 2.3.4). This is due largely to the high costs associated with fulfilling unpredictable and variable demand, either in reduced customer service (as orders are not fulfilled) or through increased supply chain costs, such as inventory (as discussed under demand profiling in Section 2.1.4). The reality is that for many products consumer demand is actually stable. Research into consumer packaged goods companies has identified that typically 60–70 per cent demand is actually stable (Godsell, 2012). The key to success for the supply chain is to find the stable, or base, demand. If you can identify and isolate the stable demand, you can maintain or increase customer service whilst removing the costly buffers (inventory, spare capacity, work in progress, etc.) against uncertainty. You create a stable supply chain process that may account for 70 per cent of demand, but requires less than 30 per cent of management effort. It creates the management headroom to focus on the truly variable or unpredictable products: the promotions, brand extensions and new product introductions critical to driving growth through innovation.

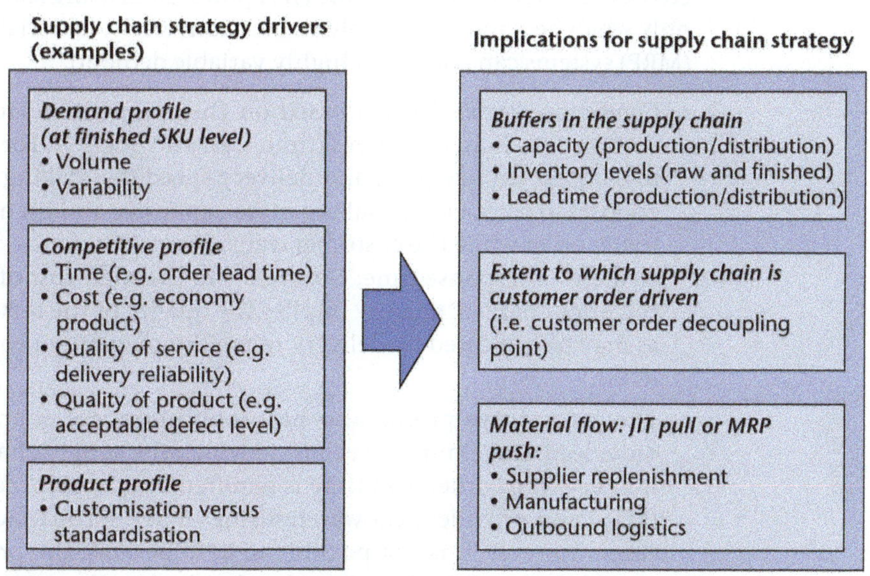

Figure 2.8 **Strategy drivers and their implications for supply chain strategy.**

First, however, let us understand the three profiles and their implications for supply chain strategy: demand profile, competitive profile and product profile.

- *Demand profile.* Demand profiling (discussed in Section 2.2) requires an understanding of base, trend, seasonality and uncertainty of demand, promoting an understanding of the causes of variable demand. Further, what's important for segmented supply chain strategy is to separate out base demand from the variable and uncertain demand. Consistent with this, the demand profile is characterised by demand volume and variability measured at SKU level:
  - *Demand volume* is the number of units of an SKU ordered as used by a number of authors (Childerhouse et al., 2002; Christopher and Towill, 2001) to drive segmented supply chain strategy.
  - *Demand variability* is the change in demand over a sequence of time buckets for a particular SKU (Bhattacharya and Jina, 1995) and is indicated by the coefficient of variation (CV) – the ratio of standard deviation to the average over a given time period. It has been used by a number of authors (Naylor et al., 1999; Childerhouse et al., 2002; Christopher and Towill, 2002) to determine segmented supply chain strategy. Quite often, if demand variability is high, so is demand uncertainty, indicated by forecast error. However, as we have seen in Section 2.2, some components of demand variability, such as those due to trends or seasonality, can be predicted or forecast (at least in part) and therefore are not classed as uncertain demand.

Demand profile has implications for supply chain strategy, as shown in Figure 2.8. For example, high levels of demand variability and uncertainty imply the need for larger buffers to enable the supply chain to respond whilst still providing high levels of service. Buffers can be in the form of excess capacity in manufacturing or transport, inventory levels and extended quoted lead times. Also, the level of demand variability has important implications for the control of material flow covered in Chapter 6. A just-in-time (JIT) pull system using *kanban* operates effectively only when demand is relatively stable. Conversely, material requirement planning (MRP) systems can cope with highly variable demand.

- *Competitive profile.* This is based on the competitive factors we introduced in Section 1.3 – hard objectives (time, cost and quality). For example, Ford chooses to compete on low price and delivery speed (by making to stock), whilst BMW chooses to compete by making more expensive and highly specified cars to customer order while the customer waits. Time refers to the order lead time or some element of response time. Cost refers to the total cost of supply and underpins the price charged. Quality implies the quality of the service and products, such as may be indicated by delivery reliability of quality products (at an acceptable level).

  The competitive profile also has implications for supply chain strategy. The order lead time limits the extent to which the supply chain can be order-driven. If a very short order lead time is required, it may be necessary to make-to-stock (MTS) and provide local warehousing or vendor managed inventory. In some cases, however, it is not possible to MTS because the product is customised or provided in such high variety that finished stocks are not economically viable.

In this case the product is made-to-order (MTO), and the manufacturing process may require buffers in terms of excess manufacturing capacity and raw material stocks to support a short order lead time.

- *Product profile*. The level of product standardisation, or conversely the level of customisation where the product specification is specific to a certain customer, is the product profile dimension. It is an important determinant as all customised operations must be order driven and therefore may extend lead times, or alternatively require excess capacity, to be responsive. The customisation level requires analysis at SKU level in terms of the proportion of internal manufacturing activities, and sourced components, that are customised. This analysis can result in the categorisation of SKUs on the basis of customisation levels: high, medium and low. For high levels of customisation, particularly where the customisation occurs early in the manufacturing process and therefore necessitates a long lead time, there may be the potential to reduce customisation levels in two ways. First, the relevance to customers may be questioned – is this aspect of customisation providing value to the customer? Second, the possibility of different options being built in as standard could be explored, resulting in a certain level of redundancy, but allowing greater standardisation of the manufacturing process and a shorter lead time.

Now that the three profiles of supply chain strategy drivers are understood, how may they be used for market segmentation and the development of segmented supply chain strategy?

2.3.3 Selecting drivers for segmentation

In practice it is not possible, nor desirable, to segment the market using the full suite of profiles and drivers of supply chain strategy. Instead, the selection should be viewed as being specific to the context – company and market served. Appropriate drivers can be selected in various ways and here we propose two selection criteria:

- the extent to which the drivers vary across the SKUs – select those that vary the most;
- the value delivered by the focal firm, from the customer's perspective, compared to that delivered by competitors – customer value gap analysis.

Driver selection using variation of drivers

One approach to examining the extent to which drivers vary across customers is to develop supply chain strategy profiles, as shown in Figure 2.9, for two contrasting customers (A and B) of AutoCo (an automotive seat manufacturer). The profiles show that both customers want 100 per cent on time, in full, delivery performance and the same high level of product quality. However, they differ in that customer A demands relatively high volume on a shorter lead time with a higher delivery frequency and customer B exhibits relatively unpredictable demand and the products are generally more customised (i.e. a greater proportion of the product is unique to that customer). This indicates possible drivers for segmenting customers.

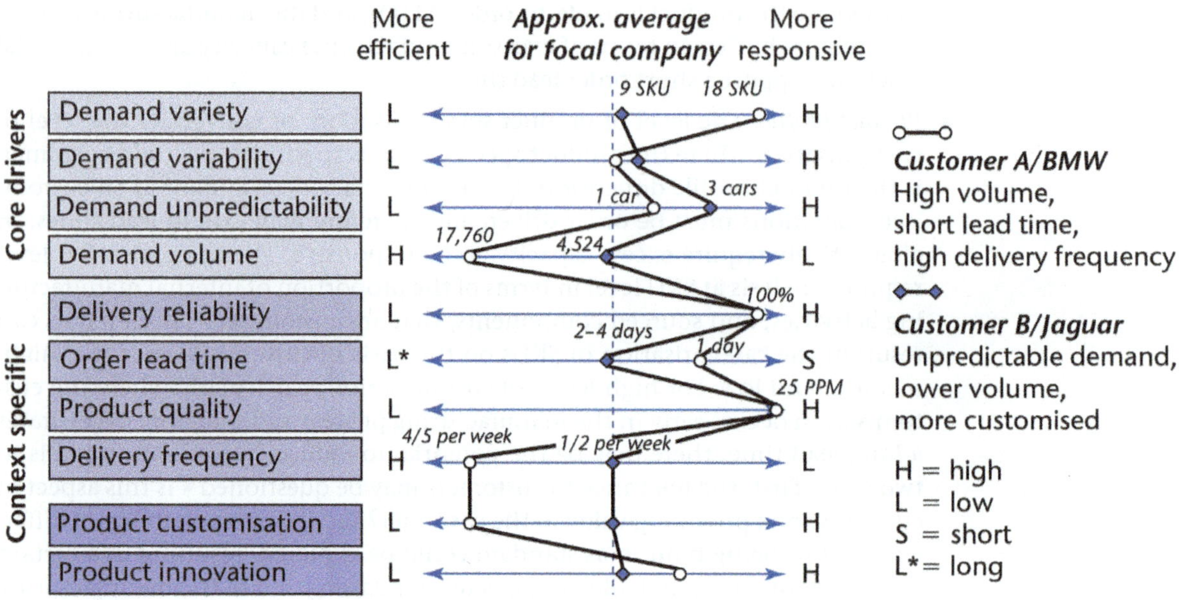

Figure 2.9 Supply chain strategy driver profiles for two customers of AutoCo.
(Source: Harrison et al., 2007.)

Selecting the most appropriate drivers to segment the market, and thus drive segmented supply chain strategy, is particularly challenging because they vary with many factors, not just customers. Equally, the demand profile varies across a given product range with typically a small proportion of the SKUs accounting for a large proportion of the demand. Moreover, the drivers vary with other important factors:

- *Marketing activity*. Promotions introduce artificial fluctuations in demand with an initial peak in demand followed by a series of peaks and troughs, increasing demand variability and, typically, uncertainty as well. Related to promotion can be the introduction of new variants or products, which affect demand for other variants.
- *Context of purchase*. The context of purchase tends to affect competitive profile. For example, a direct current motor can be bought as a breakdown replacement, where the order winner (OW) is short lead time, or as part of a planned installation where the OW is price.
- *Product life cycle stage*. The competitive and demand profiles vary with the stage in the product life cycle as shown in Figure 2.10. The diagram presents the supply chain strategies used by an electrical product manufacturer at each stage in the life cycle. During the uncertain launch phase, the supply chain operated through a MTO (make-to-order) approach however, as volumes increased in the growth stage, service level in terms of availability became the OW and MTS (Make-to-stock) became the mode of operation. Through the maturity phase, as volumes peak, price was the priority (OW) leading to the company deploying form-postponement to maintain low costs while achieving the high service levels provided by agility (see Chapter 7). During the decline stage, the company switched to a hybrid approach with some higher volume products being made through form-postponement while low volume items returned to an MTO approach.

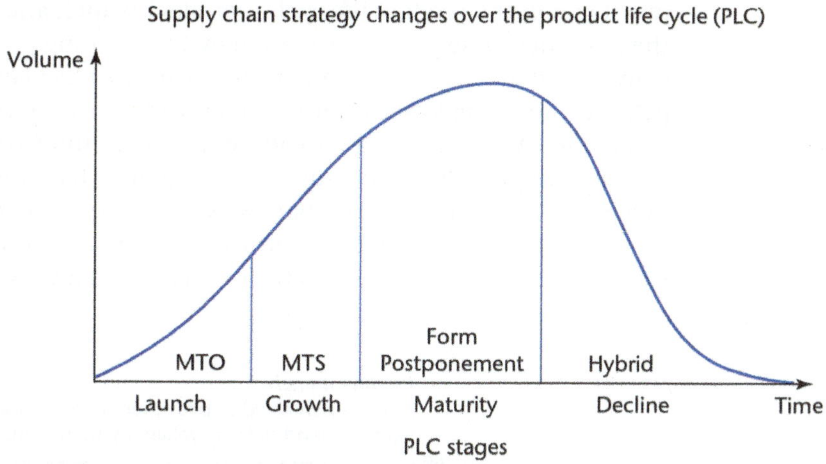

Figure 2.10 Demand and competitive profile vary with product life cycle stage.
(Source: Adapted from Childerhouse et al., 2002.)

Activity 2.4

Develop a supply chain driver profile of a small organic baker currently supplying local delicatessens. The company has been identified by a large supermarket as a potential supplier for its regional stores. Sourcing from the baker will assist the supermarket in promoting its sustainability agenda. Map the delicatessens and supermarket profiles and compare them to explain the potential supply chain challenges for the baker if they accept the new opportunity.

Driver selection using customer value gap analysis

Customer value is the customer-perceived benefit gained from a product/service compared with the cost of purchase. In order to measure customer value, we need to understand what *aspects* of a product or service a customer values (Johnson and Scholes, 2005). Here, we are interested primarily in aspects of customer value that impact on logistics strategy – in other words the three profiles described earlier:

- *demand profile:* the characteristics of demand in terms of volume and variability;
- *competitive profile:* how the focal firm chooses to compete in the marketplace, with regards to cost, time and quality;
- *product profile:* the extent to which the product is customised to specific customer requirements.

Customer value is assessed by means of an administered questionnaire to measure customer views of the three profiles (specifically drivers that are relevant to the focal firm) in terms of:

- *relative importance* (by apportioning 100 points across the drivers);
- *performance* of the focal firm and a key competitor identified by the customer (measured on a 0–5 Likert scale).

The charts in Figure 2.11 show the value (relative importance multiplied by performance) plotted across the drivers for both AutoCo and its key competitor for two stages in the product life cycle – product launch and steady state. This reveals the customer value gaps, as perceived by the customer, between the value AutoCo delivers and that of its key competitor. During product launch, AutoCo is less competitive, providing lower value on order lead time and delivery reliability than its competitor. Whereas, during steady state, when AutoCo is more competitive, it is perceived as providing value superior, or equal, to its competitor on all dimensions except quality. This suggests that SKUs might be segmented in terms of stage in product life cycle, although to confirm this, other customers' perceptions of value would be required. We return to the concept of 'value' in Chapter 3.

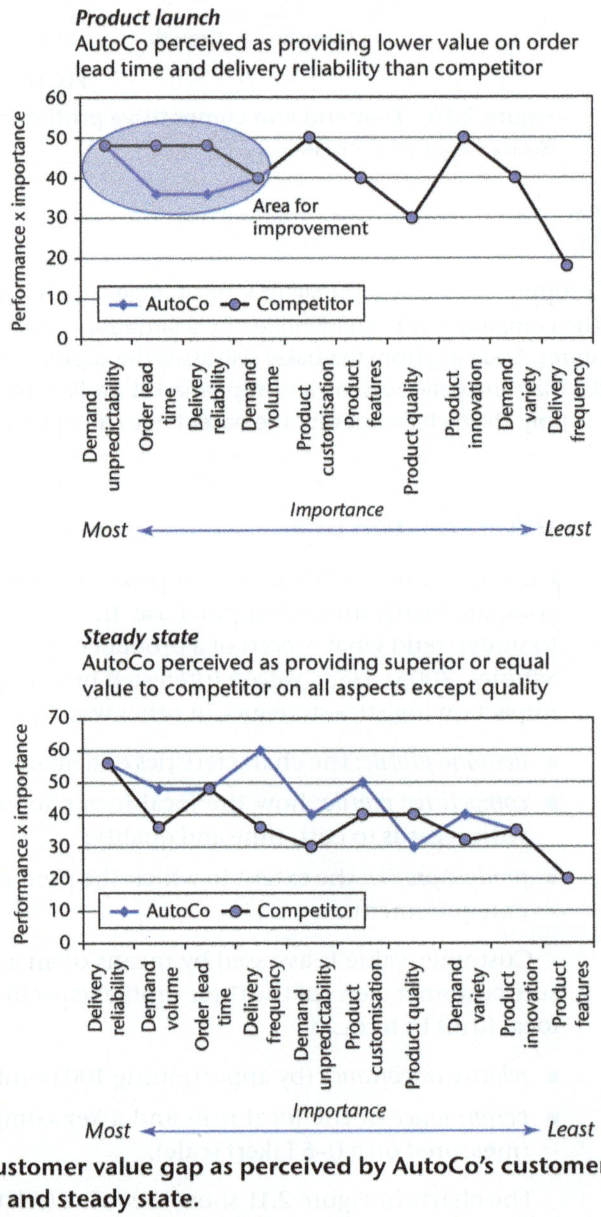

Figure 2.11 Customer value gap as perceived by AutoCo's customer during product launch and steady state.

Once appropriate supply chain strategy drivers have been selected, a driver matrix can be developed like that used by Kimberly-Clark (K-C) in Case study 2.4, where specific elements of profiles (in the K-C case, demand variability and demand volume) are used to segment the SKUs and tailored supply chain strategies are developed for each quadrant. Another driver matrix is presented in Chapter 7 (Section 7.3) where specific elements of the competitive profile (lead time and delivery frequency) and demand profile (demand variability) are used to segment the SKUs and drive segmented supply chain strategy.

2.3.4 The four-step approach to developing segmented supply chain strategy

After studying segmented supply chain strategy with many companies over more than a decade, Godsell (2012) claims:

> **A major inhibitor to the more widespread adoption of SC segmentation is the confusion caused by the vast array of complicated models presented by consultants and academics to address the issue. A problem exacerbated by confusion as to who the customer actually is? Is it the consumer, the store, the regional warehouse or end market? The problem becomes so complicated that organisations don't know where to begin. The key is to start simple and only get more complex if required. As obvious as it may sound this has been a major enabler in the organisations where segmentation has been successfully implemented.**

There are four steps proposed:

- *Step 1:* Identify the customer demand signal to which the supply chain will respond.
- *Step 2:* Conduct a demand profiling analysis using demand volume and variability.
- *Step 3:* Identify the key supply chain segments.
- *Step 4:* Develop tailored practices for each of the supply chain functions involved.

The four steps are illustrated in the Kimberly-Clark (K-C) Europe Case study 2.4.

CASE STUDY 2.4

Segmented supply chain strategy process at Kimberly-Clark Europe

For more than a century, Kimberly-Clark (K-C) has supplied personal care products and now can claim that nearly a quarter of the world's population, across 175 countries, use their products.

The K-C product range spans personal care, healthcare and professional ranges and includes household brands such as Huggies nappies, Kleenex tissues and Kotex sanitary towels. This case concerns the consumer K-C products sold through K-C Europe and illustrates how K-C followed the four-step approach to developing segmented supply chain strategy.

Step 1: Identify the customer demand signal

First it is necessary to map out the end-to-end supply chain to provide visibility across the business. Galbraith (1983) conceptualised the extended supply chain from raw materials through to the retailer (end-to-end), and this is echoed by many organisations who talk of 'seed to smoke' (tobacco) or 'farm to fork' (food) strategies. However, such a broad scope or wide 'arc of integration' (Frohlich and Westbrook, 2001), as described in Section 8.1, is difficult to manage.

We propose that it is desirable to understand the end-to-end supply chain but, in the development of segmented SC strategy, it is important to identify a set of primary customers to which the supply chain responds, and these, it could be argued, are the customers for the supply chain. Unfortunately, the real world is complex, particularly in the field of SCM, where an SC has many different customers.

The simplified end-to-end supply chain for K-C Europe is shown in Figure 2.12. The primary customers for K-C Europe are the retailers and this is the demand signal for the supply chain. The point at which demand is decoupled from supply is referred to as the 'decoupling point'. This is where a strategic stock is maintained speculatively in order to respond quickly (and with potentially lower inventory levels) to changes in retailer demand. Ideally, the retailer shares the point of sale (POS) data representing consumer demand, but typically this isn't the case and K-C is reliant on the retailers' inventory management, which can induce the bullwhip effect, sometimes referred to as demand amplification. The position of the decoupling point, for each SKU, depends on the location of K-C manufacturing relative to the market served. Where K-C manufacturing is local to the market (typically for the high-volume, commoditised manufacture that generates economies of scale), it is possible for the decoupling point to be further up the supply chain, at the inbound pulp for the K-C factory, thus enabling a considerable reduction in the value of inventory. If K-C manufacturing is remote to the market (as is often the case for the specialised products, which are manufactured in relatively low volumes and therefore manufactured centrally), the decoupling point is in the distribution centres local to the market served.

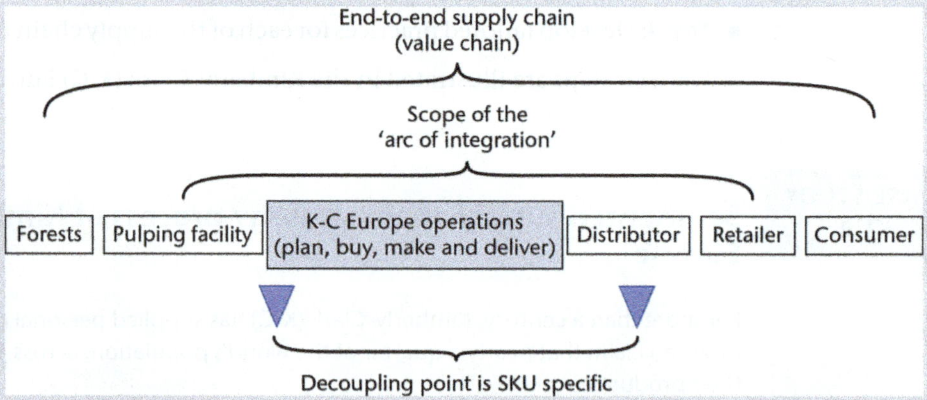

Figure 2.12 The simplified end-to-end supply chain for Kimberley-Clark Europe.

Tip: Leading practice has shown that organisations with a track record in implementing segmented supply chains have just started with the actual demand signal that they receive from the customer (it is the one they need to respond to) and accept that it is likely to be subject to the bullwhip effect, which is the phenomenon where variations in end-customer demand are amplified as you move upstream.

Step 2: Conduct a demand profiling analysis

Once the correct demand signal has been identified, it is then possible to do the demand profiling analysis. Experience has shown that it is best to start simple, with an analysis of demand volume and demand variability (indicated by the coefficient of variation, CV) for the SKUs in a given region, end-market or category, as illustrated in Figure 2.13 for K-C Europe. K-C identified the category level within a region as the most appropriate level at which to begin the analysis.

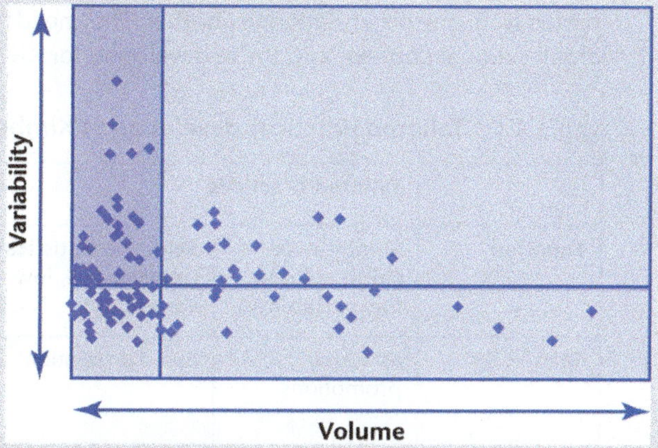

Figure 2.13 Analysis of demand volume and variability for SKUs in Kimberley-Clark Europe, Consumer Products.

Step 3: Identify the key supply chain segments

Where to 'draw the lines' to determine the segments is a decision specific to each organisation. The most important thing is that the 'lines are drawn' in a way that is meaningful to the organisation. In K-C Europe it was based initially on a simple 80:20 Pareto on volume (high:low) and 50:50 split on variability, which gave the four segments illustrated in Figure 2.14.

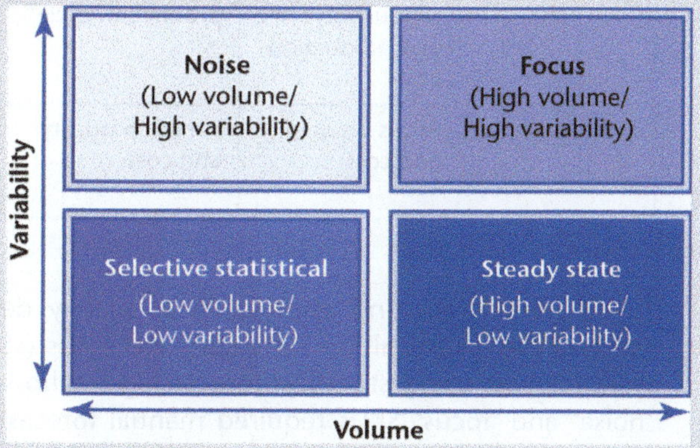

Figure 2.14 Four SKU segments defined by Kimberley-Clark Europe.

These segments were particularly informative in terms of communications between supply chain function and marketing. For instance, in terms of managing the product range it was clear that SKUs categorised as 'noise', subject to low volume yet highly variable demand, were not desirable and should be eliminated or rationalised where possible.

Step 4: Develop tailored practices for each of the supply chain functions involved

The final step is to develop the tailored practices for each of the identified segments, which involves identifying what each function needs to do to align supply with the demand for the respective SKU segments. Tailored practices cannot be copied and pasted from one organisation to another. They need to be developed to meet the specific organisational context, and those developed for K-C Europe are shown in Table 2.7.

Table 2.7 Tailored practices developed at Kimberley-Clark Europe.

	Tailored practices			
Function	**Steady state (high volume, low variability)**	**Selective statistical (low volume, low variability)**	**Focus (high volume, high variability)**	**Noise (low volume, high variability)**
Sales	Minimise promotions	Avoid promotions	Drive volume through promotion in close collaboration with customer	Avoid promotions and validate why an SKU is in the portfolio
Marketing	Build SKU base	Increase volume base and consolidate SKUs	Build flexibility into the portfolio	Reduce SKU complexity
Planning	Statistically forecast	Statistically forecast	Manual forecast based on past history	Collaborative forecast with customer and commercial teams
Manufacturing	Minimise production cycle and production costs	Minimise/maintain production cycle	Maximise agility with a must respond mentality	Make to order
Procurement	Focus on quality and cost	Focus on quality and cost	Minimise order lead time	Cover variability with inventory

The sales forecasting approach was mainly dependent on demand variability, so 'selective statistical' and 'steady state' SKUs (subject to low demand variability) were forecast using statistical forecasting methods based on past sales, whilst the 'noise' and 'focus' SKUs required manual forecasting involving collaboration with the retailers.

Identifying the segments and implementing tailored practices was not straightforward. Case study 10.6 in Chapter 10 describes the five enablers identified by K-C Europe for the organisational change required.

(Source: Dr Janet Godsell and Stuart Bailey, Brakes Group, formerly of K-C Europe, 2011.)

Questions

1. As mentioned, the K-C segments were particularly useful for communications between supply chain and marketing. Discuss how else they might be useful.
2. Marketing encountered difficulties implementing the tailored practices at SKU level. Discuss what the difficulties might have been.
3. What difficulties might the decoupling points in the K-C supply chain present to the implementation of the manufacturing tailored practices?

Summary

What is putting the end-customer first in the context of logistics?

- Marketing is defined as 'the activity, set of institutions and processes for creating, communicating, delivering and exchanging offerings that have value for customers, partners and society at large'. Marketing, in practice, starts with understanding customer value and identifying segments, evaluating those segments and targeting them. Segments need to be measurable, economically viable, accessible and actionable. Marketing, in practice, continues by market positioning, which requires differential advantage to be defined, and the marketing mix to be formulated.
- The key logistics contribution to the marketing mix is in the 'fourth P': place. This includes decisions about factors such as channel selection, market coverage, distribution systems and dealer support. Logistics also supports product decisions (for example, product range) and promotion activity.
- An important logistics contribution to putting the end-customer first is to forecast demand. This can be undertaken using judgemental forecasting (where no demand history exists) or by causal forecasting (where historical data is available).

Business to business (B2B) refers to relationships between businesses. Business to consumer (B2C) refers to relationships between businesses and consumers, and these are always the end-customers in a supply chain, although the end-customer can be a business, as is the case for industrial products, e.g. aero engines.

How do we win and retain customers through supply chain management?

- Gaining an understanding of what customers value and recognising how to meet or exceed these rising expectations through the supply chain.
- Marketing through the use of IoT, Big Data, social media and other forms of data is developing analytic tools to inform and refine the segmentation of the market

in order to define the differential advantage which makes the focal firm different from its competitors.

- There naturally exists a tension between the demand creation objectives of marketing and the demand fulfilment objectives of supply chain management; what matters is how the conflict can be resolved to meet customer needs efficiently. Segmented supply chain strategy offers one of a number of approaches to achieving this.
- The segmented approach is based on the idea that 'one size does not fit all' when it comes to supply chain strategy and that developing multiple strategies determined by drivers – demand, competitive and product – can simultaneously improve customer service and efficiencies.
- Selecting the appropriate supply chain strategy drivers is not easy and we present two approaches: one based on the extent to which the driver varies across the range of SKUs; and the other using the value delivered by the focal firm, from the customer's perspective, compared to that delivered by competitors – customer value gap analysis.
- We present a four-step approach to developing segmented supply chain strategy, which involves: identifying the demand signal to which the supply chain will respond; demand profiling on the basis of demand volume and variability; identifying the key supply chain segments; and developing tailored practices for each supply chain function.

Discussion questions

1. Suggest ways in which logistics can play a part in the marketing mix for:
   a. a manufacturer of electrical and electronic products like Electrical Co (Case study 2.2)
   b. a retailer such as Tesco (Case study 1.1)
   c. an automotive repair and recovery firm such as Talleres Auto (Case study 1.6).
2. In each case, specify the organisation you have in mind and explain the reasons for your suggestions.
3. Whilst top companies such as IBM and Tesco say that the customer is king, will customer choice continue to be unrestrained in (a) 2025 and (b) 2050? Explain your thinking in each future state scenario.
4. Explain what is meant by uncertainty in demand forecasting.
5. The barbecue sauce focal firm described in Section 2.2 has manufacturing facilities in the Netherlands, which are described as 'high on quality and reliability, but low on responsiveness'. In order to maximise production efficiency, large batches of each flavour are made so that process cleanouts (each lasting greater than four hours) are kept to a minimum. After manufacturing, each batch of a given flavour is transported to an off-site finishing operation, where bottles of the different flavours are packed into a display box for attractive presentation to the end-customer at the retail customer outlets customers. This process takes an average of two weeks because of the need to ensure that all flavours are available.

Finally, the display boxes are distributed through warehousing operations which have been situated in six carefully selected locations around the product's major European market in Germany.

Management of the focal firm is under pressure to reduce inventories and stock write-offs (the sauce has a shelf life of three months). Propose what actions could be taken to improve the supply chain to permit improved responsiveness to end-customer demand.

References

American Marketing Association (AMA) (2023a) 'Definition of Marketing', at https://www.ama.org/the-definition-of-marketing-what-is-marketing/

American Marketing Association (AMA) (2023b) https://www.ama.org/marketing-news/the-four-ps-of-marketing/

Bezos, J. (2020) https://www.supplychaintoday.com/amazon-ceo-jeff-bezos-quotes/#:~:text=%E2%80%9Cthe%20balance%20of,it.%E2%80%9D%20~Jeff%20Bezos

Bhattacharya, A.K., Jina, J. and Walton, A.D. (1995) 'Turbulence in Manufacturing Systems: its identification and management', Proceedings of Irish Manufacturing Committee 12th Conference, September, University College Cork.

Bicheno, J. and Holweg, M. (2016) *The Lean Toolbox – the Essential Guide to Lean Transformation*, 5th edn. Buckingham: Picsie Books.

Brynjolfsson, E., Hu, Y.J. and Smith, M.D. (2010) The longer tail: The changing shape of Amazon's sales distribution curve. *Available at SSRN 1679991*.

Childerhouse, P., Aitken, J. and Towill, D.R. (2002) 'Analysis and design of focussed demand chains', *Journal of Operations Management*, vol. 20, no. 6, pp. 675–89.

Christopher, M. and Ryals, L. (1999) 'Supply chain strategy: its impact on shareholder value', *International Journal of Logistics Management*, vol. 10, iss. 1, pp. 1–10.

Christopher, M. and Towill, D. (2001) 'An integrated model for the design of agile supply chains', *International Journal of Physical Distribution & Logistics Management*, vol. 31, no. 4, pp. 235–46.

Cortez, R.M., Clarke, A.H. and Freytag, P.V. (2021) 'B2B market segmentation: A systematic review and research agenda. *Journal of Business Research*', vol. 126, pp. 415–28.

Doyle, P. (2000) *Value-based Marketing: Marketing Strategies for Corporate Growth and Shareholder Value*. Chichester: Wiley.

Finne, S. and Sivonen, H. (2009) *The Retail Value Chain*, London: Kogan Press.

Fisher, M.L. (1997) 'What is the right supply chain for your product?', *Harvard Business Review*, vol. 75, no. 2, pp. 105–16.

Frohlich, M.T. and Westbrook, R. (2001) 'Arcs of integration: An international study of supply chain strategies', *Journal of Operations Management*, vol. 19, no. 2, pp. 185–200.

Galbraith, J.R. (1983) 'Strategy and organisation planning', *Human Resource Management*, vol. 22, nos 1/2, pp. 63–77.

Gattorna, J.L. and Walters, D.W. (1996) *Managing the Supply Chain: A Strategic Perspective*. Basingstoke: Macmillan.

Godsell, J. (2012) *Thriving in a Turbulent World: The Power of Supply Chain Segmentation*. Bedford: Cranfield School of Management.

Godsell, J. and Harrison, A. (2002) 'Strategy formulation in an FMCG supply chain', Proceedings of the EurOMA Conference, Copenhagen.

Harrison, A., Godsell, J., Skipworth, H., Wong, C. and Achimugu, N. (2007) *Developing Supply Chain Strategy: Balancing Shareholder and Customer Value*. Bedford: Cranfield School of Management.

Johnson, G. and Scholes, K. (2005) *Exploring Corporate Strategy*, 7th edn. London: Financial Times Prentice Hall.

Kotler, P. and Keller, K.L. (2009) *Marketing Management*, 13th edn. Harlow: Pearson Education.

Latta, M. (2007) 'How to forecast the demand for a new drug in the pharmaceutical industry', *The Journal of Business Forecasting*, vol. 26, no. 3, pp. 21–8.

Lockton, J., Higgins, S. and Streatfield, P. (2013) 'Retail supply chain management: The omni-channel revolution'. Technical report, LCP Consulting, UK, 2013. URL www. lcpconsulting. com.

McGoldrick, P. (2002) *Retail Marketing*, 2nd edn. Maidenhead: McGraw-Hill Education Europe.

Millier, P. and Palmer, R. (2000) *Nuts, Bolts and Magnetrons: A Practical Guide for Industrial Marketers*. Chichester: Wiley.

Mirzabeiki, V. and Saghiri, S.S. (2020) 'From ambition to action: How to achieve integration in omni-channel?', *Journal of Business Research*, vol. 110, pp.1–11.

Naylor, J.B., Naim, M.M. and Berry, D. (1999) 'Leagility: integrating the lean and agile manufacturing paradigms in the total supply chain', *International Journal of Production Economics*, vol. 62, no. 1, pp. 107–18.

Ogrodowczyk, J. (2008) 'Disaggregating forecasts: Fairchild semiconductor's experience', *Journal of Business Forecasting*, Spring, pp. 34–43.

Piotrowicz, W.D., Ryciuk, U. and Szymczak, M. (2021) 'Lean and agile metrics. Literature review and framework for measuring leagile supply chain', *International Journal of Productivity and Performance Management*, vol. 72, no. 6, pp. 1560–83.

Shewchuk, J.P. (1998) 'Agile manufacturing: One size does not fit all', in Bititci, U.S. and Carrie, A.S. (eds), *Strategic Management of the Manufacturing Value Chain*. IFIP International Federation for Information Processing, vol. 2, pp. 143–50. Boston, MA: Springer.

Smith, W.R. (1956) 'Product differentiation and market segmentation as alternative marketing strategies', *Journal of Marketing*, vol. 21, no. 1, pp. 3–8.

Waters, D. (2008) *Inventory control and management*. John Wiley & Sons.

Webster, F. (2000) 'Understanding the relationships among brands, consumers and retailers', *Journal of the Academy of Marketing Science*, vol. 28, pp. 17–23.

Wild, A. (2002) *Best Practice in Inventory Management*, 2nd edn. Oxford: Elsevier.

Wild, T. (2017) *Best Practice in Inventory Management*. Third edition, Routledge.

Wong, C., Skipworth, H., Godsell, J. and Achimugu, A. (2012) 'Towards a theory of supply chain alignment enablers: a systematic literature review', *Supply Chain Management: an International Journal*, vol. 17, iss. 4, pp. 419–37.

Zeithaml, V.A., Verleye, K., Hatak, I., Koller, M. and Zauner, A. (2020) 'Three decades of customer value research: Paradigmatic roots and future research avenues', *Journal of Service Research*, vol. *23*, No.4, pp. 409–32.

Suggested further reading

Christopher, M. and Peck, H. (2012) *Marketing Logistics*, 2nd edn. Routledge.

Doyle, P. and Stern P. (2006) *Marketing Management and Strategy*, 4th edn. Harlow: Pearson Education.

McDonald, M. and Dunbar, I. (2012) *Market Segmentation: How to do it and how to profit from it*, 4th edn. John Wiley & Sons.

CHAPTER 3

Value and logistics costs

Objectives

The planned objectives of this chapter are to:

- **explain the concept of shareholder value and how it relates to customer value;**
- **describe how return on capital employed (ROCE) can be measured and how supply chain management can affect it;**
- **discuss why cash flow, known as liquidity, is important and how supply chain management might improve it;**
- **explain how total logistics costs can be divided up in different ways, and how they can be applied to managing the supply chain;**
- **appreciate carbon pricing, how it is used to incentivise polluters to reduce their carbon footprint, internal carbon pricing and the different methods available;**
- **understand how activity-based costing allocates costs to processes so that better decisions can be made;**
- **examine and compare the key approaches to capital investment decisions in the supply chain;**
- **describe a balanced measurement portfolio, which addresses all stakeholders and measures across the supply chain.**

By the end of this chapter you should be able to understand:

- **what is meant by the term 'shareholder value';**
- **how supply chains can be managed for better shareholder value;**
- **how carbon can be costed to drive improvements in environmental sustainability;**
- **how activity-based management can be used to identify the cost drivers in your business;**
- **how to make capital investment decisions;**
- **how a balanced measurement portfolio can be applied across the supply chain.**

Introduction

In Section 1.4 we reviewed the way in which different products may have different logistics strategies. Whilst the range of classic shirts compete on price and brand, and demand is relatively stable over the year, fashion blouses compete on style, responsiveness to market and brand. For a fashion product, the logistics challenge is to be able to support highly uncertain demand in the marketplace.

The logistics task for the two supply chains is essentially different, and some companies refer to a 'supply chain for every product' to emphasise this difference. In Chapter 2, we stated the need for compromise here – between 'one size fits all' on the one hand, and endless customisation of the supply chain on the other, proposing an approach to segmenting supply chain strategy.

Here, we develop the information flow aspects of our model in Figure 1.4. We also show how there is another flow in supply chains – *funds flow*. Funds flow in the opposite direction to materials. Funds – in the form of cash – originate from the end-customer and are used to pay the bills progressively from one supply chain partner to the next upstream.

Whilst funds flow has not yet been formally included in the logistics domain, the integration of finance and logistics is an increasingly important aspect of logistics in the twenty-first century. The acquisition of Vastera (a third-party logistics company) by JP Morgan Chase Bank (a financial institution), to form JP Morgan Chase Vastera, is aimed at 'driving cost savings and global supply chain efficiencies whilst providing best-in-class compliance with government regulations'.

This chapter probes the financial implications of different logistics strategies. Whilst it may be clear that cost must form a central plank of supply chain strategy for classic shirts, the product team for fashion blouses cannot ignore the cost implications of their actions (see Table 1.2). The common theme is the concept of *value*, and the extent to which both management teams are creating value for the end-customer. In this chapter, we advance the concept of 'value' beyond the mainly end-customer view that we took in Chapter 2 and extend it to other stakeholders in the supply chain.

Whilst value is based on *cost* from the point of view of the company accountant, the concept of value may have different interpretations outside the company. In Section 2.3.3, we stated that value from the end-customer's point of view is the *perceived benefit* gained from a product/service compared with the cost of purchase. From the shareholder's point of view, value is determined by the *best alternative use* of a given investment. In other words, value is greatest where the return on investment is highest.

The chapter assumes a basic knowledge of a profit/loss account and balance sheet. If finance is not your long suit, then a helpful accompanying financial text is *Accounting and Finance for Non-specialists* (Atrill and McLaney, 2018). We acknowledge the assistance from our colleague at Cranfield School of Management, Dr Simon Templar, for his help with Sections 3.3 and 3.6 on liquidity and capital investment decisions, respectively and also for sharing his wealth of knowledge on accounting and finance for the supply chain. We also acknowledge Sri Srikanthan for his help with Sections 3.2 and 3.4.

Key issues

This chapter addresses seven key issues:

1. **Where does value come from?** Customer and shareholder views of value and the relationship between them.
2. **How can conventional return on capital employed (ROCE) be measured?** ROCE is an internal measure of shareholder value but what is it and how can supply chain management affect it?
3. **Why is liquidity important and what are the implications for supply chain management?** Supply chain management is required to balance the objectives of profitability, liquidity and asset utilisation.
4. **How can logistics costs be represented?** Three different ways to divide up total costs.
5. **How can carbon be costed to drive more sustainable supply chains?** Carbon pricing approaches including three methods for Internal Carbon Pricing.
6. **Activity-based costing (ABC):** a process-based alternative to allocating overheads, which allows better decisions to be made.
7. **How can capital investment decisions be made?** Four approaches to investment appraisal, which take into account the subsequent cash flows that dictate the future liquidity of the company.
8. **A balanced measurement portfolio:** balancing the needs of all stakeholders using process thinking, as embodied by the supply chain operations reference model (SCOR).

3.1 Where does value come from?

Key issues: **How can shareholder value be defined and what is its relationship with customer value? How can shareholder value be measured?**

Creating shareholder value is used widely today to describe the main objective of a business. Shareholder value is the financial value created for shareholders by the companies in which they invest. In its simplest form, shareholder value is created when the shareholder gets a better return by investing in your business than from a comparable investment. A *comparable investment* is one that has a similar level of risk. You might make the same return on €100,000 from playing roulette as you do from buying a house, but the risk profiles are very different! In order for a business to create superior shareholder value, it must have a competitive advantage.

Customer value is determined from the customer's point of view and is the *perceived benefit* gained from a product/service compared with the cost of purchase (as described in Section 2.3.3). In effect, the customer evaluates the benefit derived from the product in the light of the cost (not just price) of purchase, so a low-cost product may not be perceived as high value if the benefits are proportionally lower than that of a more expensive product.

You should be aware that there has been a debate in the literature over which of these values, shareholder or customer, should take priority. Some argued that organisations are in business primarily to maximise shareholder value (Cornelius and Davies, 1997; Rappaport, 1987) and can do so by also delivering customer value and therefore maintaining competitiveness. Others have argued that alignment with customer needs comes first because a business is more likely to achieve its goals when it organises itself to meet the current, and potential, needs of customers more effectively than its competitors (Doyle, 1994; Drucker, 2001; Copulsky, 1991; Laitamäki and Kordupleski, 1997).

An alternative to this trade-off perspective is that organisations need to be able to balance between the two (Feurer and Chaharbaghi, 1994; Cleland and Bruno, 1997) as shareholder and customer value can be conflicting and can destroy each other. For instance Frohlich (2002) argued that the lack of alignment between business practices and customer needs will have an adverse effect on shareholder value.

In a way, customer value ensures customer loyalty and thus promises continuous revenue and contributing to shareholder value, and shareholder value promises continuous investment that supports the implementation of the business unit and supply chain strategies to meet customer need (Slater and Narver, 1994; Kaplan and Norton, 2004). From this perspective, shareholder value and customer value appear to reinforce each other, meaning that shareholder value positively affects customer value and vice versa.

However, a later study (Skipworth et al., 2015), a survey of 151 medium-to-large UK manufacturing companies, showed that:

> **only customer alignment has a direct positive impact on business performance, while shareholder alignment is an antecedent of customer alignment**

This is not as surprising as it first seems. Customer alignment requires the development of supply chain strategy that, first, ensures that customer needs are met; flexes to ensure key customer needs continue to be met; and is willing to take corrective action to both key processes and organisational structure if needs are not met. In other words, and supporting the argument of Drucker (1974), customer alignment is focused on effectiveness, or 'doing the right things', which is the foundation for success. In contrast, shareholder alignment is internally ('efficiency') focused and not externally ('effectiveness') focused, considering the internal alignment of the organisation to the company strategy and its shareholder objectives.

In this chapter we will be concerned mainly with shareholder value and how supply chain management affects it, but it is clear that customer value (as discussed in Chapter 2) is inextricably linked to shareholder value. There are two ways to measure shareholder value – market-based external measures and internal measures. We shall focus on the internal measures by first considering conventional return on capital employed (ROCE), which is used widely to assess shareholder value.

3.2 How can conventional return on capital employed (ROCE) be measured?

***Key issue*: What is return on capital employed and how can supply chain management affect it?**

One way of looking at the creation of shareholder value is to think about ending the year with a lot more money than at the start. If this extra money results from profitable trading, then management has been successful in *improving the productivity of capital*. Return on capital employed (ROCE) is measured as profit before interest and tax as a percentage of capital employed:

$$\text{ROCE} = 100 \times \text{Profit/Capital employed}$$

Capital employed is equivalent to the money invested in the business. ROCE can also be seen as the outcome of profitability and asset utilisation:

$$\%\text{ROCE} = 100\ \frac{\text{Profit}}{\text{Sales}} \times \frac{\text{Sales}}{\text{Capital employed}}$$

3.2.1 ROCE and implications for supply chain management

Let us look at the detail behind each of these ratios and the way they fit in with each other. Figure 3.1 provides a family tree of the way ROCE is made up. Let us look at the potential for improving each from a point of view of managing the supply chain better.

Sales

Superior customer service improves sales and makes a focal firm more valued by the customer in the long term.

- Improving customer responsiveness is a key goal for managing the supply chain, as discussed in Chapter 2.

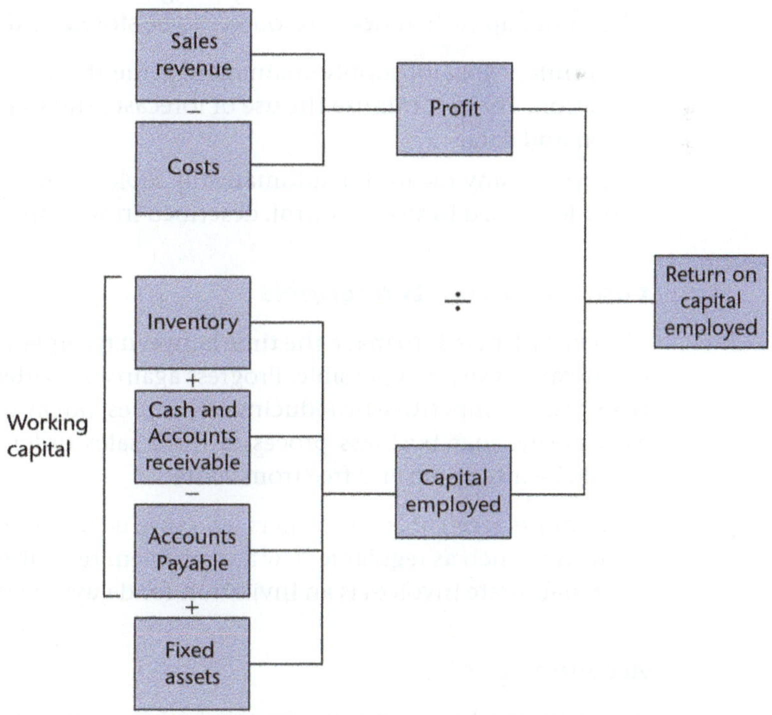

Figure 3.1 The make-up of return on capital employed (investment).

Costs

The supply chain is a potential gold mine for making bottom-line improvements to business performance. But directors of many businesses are impatient for cost improvement and consider that cutting stocks and headcount is the primary task – as in the 'evolution' strategy in Figure 1.10. This may achieve short-term margin improvement, but strategic supply chain management is, more importantly, concerned with process improvement over the long term.

- Supply chain modelling shows that manufacturing and distribution costs, together with inventories, can be optimised whilst customer service is maximised.
- Studies in efficient consumer response (ECR) have shown that cutting out non-value-added products and inefficient promotional activity can reduce overall costs by 6 per cent. (ECR is discussed in Chapter 6.)

Working capital

Note that the sum of inventory, cash and accounts receivable *less* accounts payable is called working capital. Each of the elements of working capital is considered in turn.

Inventory

This is a major asset in many businesses. It is there to buffer uncertainty of supply and demand, and to permit immediate availability when replenishment times are too lengthy. However, inventory is regarded often as a hindrance rather than a help: it ties up cash, it needs resources to be stored, and it becomes obsolete.

- A primary goal for supply chain management is to replace inventory with information. Try to minimise the use of forecasts and to increase the use of real-time demand data.
- Question any means for automatically replenishing inventory (such as the reorder level used in stock control, described in Section 6.1.3).

Cash and accounts receivable

The key task here is to make the time between receipt of customer order and receipt of the cash as short as possible. Progress against this ideal not only makes the company more competitive by reducing lead times, but also improves its cash position. This means that business processes from sales order processing to distribution should be integrated and free from waste.

- Accounts receivable (customers who owe us money) can be minimised by basic controls such as regular review and problem resolution. Sending out incomplete or inaccurate invoices is an invitation for delays or even non-payment!

Accounts payable

Accounts payable are companies to whom we owe money. In supply chain terms, this term applies mainly to our suppliers. Many organisations think that lengthy payment terms to suppliers maximise credit and therefore improve the balance sheet. The downside of this thinking is that suppliers factor in the credit terms to their prices, as their own balance sheets become saddled with debt.

- Plan material requirements and distribution requirements to maximise flow of parts through the supply chain as needed.
- Discipline goods inwards to check delivery date, quality and correct prices. There is no point in starting the credit cycle early by accepting goods before they are due.
- If the supplier is a smaller company, it may be that the cost of capital is higher than it is for your company. It may then be worthwhile to consider negotiating with the supplier to pay early, and therefore getting a share of the money that the supplier is paying in interest to the bank.

Fixed assets (now known as non-current assets)

The value-generating assets of a business that form the focus of supply chain management are a heavy drain on capital. They include manufacturing facilities, warehousing and distribution. They contribute to high *fixed costs* for an operation: that is, costs that do not change much with throughput. Such costs are therefore highly volume sensitive, as we shall see.

- Many organisations respond by a 'maximum variable, minimum fixed' policy. This refers to keeping fixed costs to a minimum and is helped by outsourcing all but the core capabilities, which are retained inhouse. Outsourced processes can then be cut more easily in the event of a downturn, such as the recession of 2009/10. Thus, transport and warehousing today often are outsourced to specialist 'third party logistics providers' such as DHL, Exel and UPS.

Activity 3.1

1. Review the categories in Figure 3.1 and compile your own list of the way in which these categories can be influenced (made better or worse) in an organisation.
2. What are the implications for logistics strategy?

3.2.2 Financial ratios and ROCE drivers

ROCE is an important measure for assessing shareholder value and is underpinned by two main drivers:

- increased profitability;
- increased asset utilisation.

As discussed at the beginning of Section 3.2, these two supporting drivers are the key determinants for increasing ROCE and hence shareholder value. An understanding of the financial ratios that affect these two drivers is essential when formulating a focal firm's supply chain strategy. Whilst financial ratios are based on historical information, and therefore have limitations, they have a number of advantages for an organisation. They can be:

- a benchmark for comparing one organisation with another;
- used as a comparator for a particular industrial sector;
- used to track past performance;
- a motivator for setting performance targets;
- an early warning indicator if the organisation's performance starts to decline.

Table 3.1 provides a guide to linking ROCE and its drivers with the financial ratios for a manufacturing company (CIMA, 2005).

We now turn to the criticality of cash flow, its impact on shareholder value and the implications for supply chain management.

Table 3.1 ROCE and its key drivers.

Level 1	Level 2	Level 3	Level 4
Return on capital employed	$\frac{\text{Profit before tax and interest}}{\text{Sales}}$	Production costs as % of sales	Labour costs as % of sales Materials as % of sales
		Selling costs as % of sales	Labour costs as % of sales
		Administration costs as % of sales	Labour costs as % of sales
	$\frac{\text{Sales}}{\text{Total net assests}^{*}}$	Non-current assets as % of sales	Property as % of sales Plant as % of sales Vehicles as % of sales
		Current assets as % of sales	Inventory as % of sales Accounts receivable as % of sales Cash as % of sales
		Current liabilities	Accounts payable

*Note: Total net assets = non-current assets + current assets − current liabilities

(Source: CIMA, 2005.)

3.3 Why is liquidity important and what are the implications for supply chain management?

Key issue: **Why is liquidity important and how can supply chain management balance the objectives of profitability, liquidity and asset utilisation?**

There are three key areas where supply chain management can affect an organisation's financial performance: profitability, liquidity and productivity or asset utilisation (Christopher, 2022). Profitability and asset utilisation are covered by ROCE (see the previous section) but liquidity (cash to cash cycle times) is not considered by ROCE. Yet the widely held view of Warren Buffett is that, ultimately, the value of a business to its owners (shareholders) is determined by the net present value (NPV, described in Section 3.6) of the cash flows occurring from the business's operations over its lifetime.

In response to the importance of liquidity, Johnson and Templar (2011) developed a proxy for supply chain performance (called the 'supply chain ratio') to explain the relationship between supply chain and firm performance. The supply chain proxy (a model for which is shown in Figure 3.2) is closely related to ROCE. However, rather than considering operating profit, it uses 'net cash inflow from operations':

$$\text{Supply chain ratio} = \frac{\text{Net cash inflow from operations}}{\text{Total assets less current liabilities}}$$

The model (shown in Figure 3.2) shows examples of potential tactical decisions that could impact the strategic imperatives that drive the proxy and the

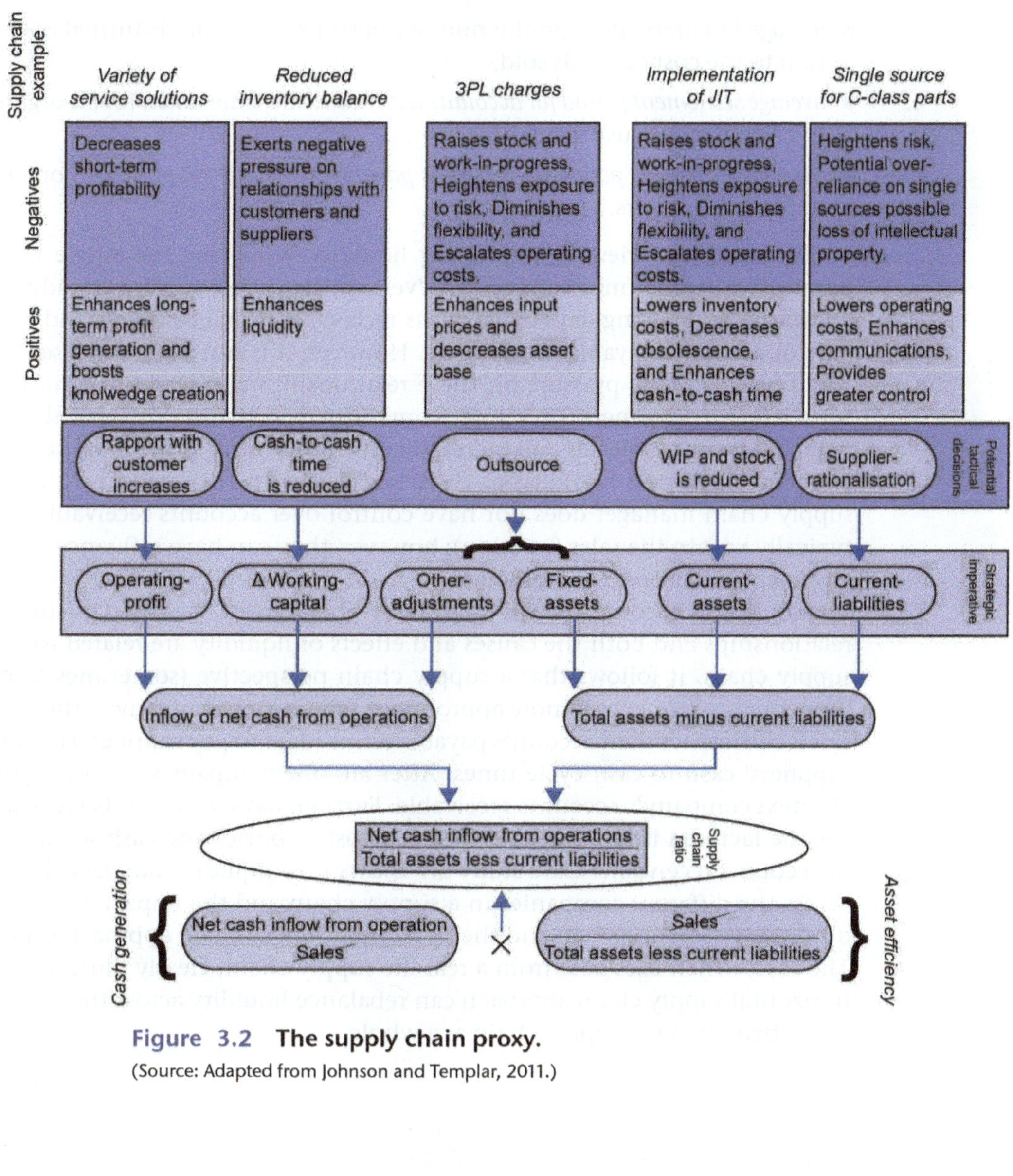

Figure 3.2 The supply chain proxy.
(Source: Adapted from Johnson and Templar, 2011.)

potential positive and negative trade-offs that should be quantified before implementing an initiative. The challenge for the supply chain manager is to develop a combination of initiatives that will lead to an increase in the supply chain ratio.

Reductions in working capital have a beneficial effect on an organisation's supply chain ratio (and its ROCE). For example, inventory reductions increase both profitability (by reducing costs) and asset utilisation (by reducing current assets, as well as reducing cash to cash cycle times (or liquidity). The supply chain ratio emphasises the importance of reducing working capital, such as inventory, on cash-to-cash cycle times to improve liquidity.

Liquidity is the ability of an organisation to meet its obligations as and when they fall due (Johnson and Templar, 2011). The use of time-related financial ratios is key to monitoring the cash-to-cash cycle and liquidity. Key ratios, which reflect the three key levers of liquidity, are:

- *average inventory turnover*: the number of times inventory is turned over in relation to the cost of goods sold;
- *average settlement period for accounts receivable*: the time taken for an organisation to be paid by its customers;
- *average settlement period for accounts payable*: the time taken for an organisation to pay its suppliers.

The traditional view to improving liquidity is to take the single company's perspective (sometimes termed the 'vertical' approach). Here liquidity can be improved by reducing days of accounts receivable from customers and increasing days of accounts payable to suppliers. However, it is not difficult to see how this could place adverse pressure on these relationships and lead to both dissatisfied suppliers and customers. Therefore, from the perspective of the 'vertical' approach, reducing inventory levels and increasing inventory turns is the main supply chain lever for improving liquidity, as discussed earlier in this section. In any case, a supply chain manager does not have control over accounts receivable (as this is typically within the sales function); however, they can have influence of accounts payable, in relation to procurement.

Liquidity, as accounts payable and receivable suggest, is related to supply chain relationships and both the causes and effects of liquidity are related to the wider supply chain. It follows that a supply chain perspective (sometimes termed the 'horizontal' approach) is more appropriate, where each company in the chain considers the impact their accounts payable terms (days to pay suppliers) have on their suppliers' cash-to-cash cycle times. After all, one company's accounts payable is the next company's accounts receivable. Further, days of accounts receivable may well be factored into prices, as there is a cost of borrowing cash to support days of accounts receivable. Case study 3.1 shows how liquidity can vary dramatically across the different companies in a supply chain and the impact of both the traditional vertical approach and the horizontal supply chain approach on liquidity. The case, which uses data from a real-life supply chain, clearly illustrates how the horizontal supply chain approach can rebalance liquidity across the supply chain to the benefit of the supply chain as a whole.

CASE STUDY 3.1

Improving liquidity across an FMCG food supply chain

Food supply chains are driven often by retailers and this holds for this case, which features a food sold in supermarkets that can be classed as a fast-moving consumer good (FMCG). Table 3.2 illustrates the cash-to-cash cycle times for three companies in the supply chain: the retailer, the food processor and the main raw material supplier.

Table 3.2 Cash-to-cash cycle times for the FMCG food supply chain.

Financial measure (number of days)	Supermarket chain	Food processor	Key raw material supplier
Days of inventory (Average inventory/annual cost of sales) × 365	16	34	35
+ Days of accounts receivable (Average receivables/annual sales turnover) × 365	2	29	30
−Days of accounts payable (Average payable/annual credit purchases) × 365	26	34	23
Average operating cash cycle	**−8**	**29**	**42**

The supermarket chain has good cash flow with, on average, eight days of credit. Therefore, no borrowing is required to support cash flow. However, both the food processor and the raw material suppliers require borrowing, where they each have more than double the days of inventory held by the retailer and days of accounts receivable is also around the more typical level of 30 days. The retailers typically have about two days of accounts receivable, because the consumers pay almost immediately with debit or credit cards.

The arrows indicate that the days of accounts payable by the supermarket impact on the days of accounts receivable by the food processor. However, these two figures are not the same (and neither are the subsequent changes as described) because the retailer has many suppliers, but here we are illustrating a single chain from a more complex supply network.

Traditional 'vertical' approach to improving liquidity

If each organisation takes the 'vertical' approach and attempts to improve the liquidity of their company alone by increasing the days of accounts payable to suppliers, without consideration for the effects on the supply chain, the possible impact is shown in Table 3.3. This is a simplified and hypothetical response because it ignores the possibility of reducing inventory, which each company may pursue.

The retailer increases days of accounts payable by six days, improving their liquidity further to 14 days of credit without borrowing. This results in an increase of four days of accounts receivable for the food processor, who passes this on to its suppliers as an increase in days of accounts payable, resulting in no change in the liquidity of the food processor. Finally, this results in an increase of three days in the accounts payable for

Table 3.3 Hypothetical cash-to-cash cycle times for the FMCG food supply chain following the traditional 'vertical' approach to liquidity improvement.

Financial measure (number of days)	Retail multiple	Food processor	Raw material supplier
Days of inventory (Average inventory/annual cost of sales) × 365	16	34	35
+ Days of accounts receivable (Average receivables/annual sales turnover) × 365	2	~~29~~ 33 (↑4)	~~30~~ 33 (↑3)
− Days of accounts payable (Average payable/annual credit purchases) × 365	~~26~~ 32 (↑6)	~~34~~ 38 (↑4)	23
Average operating cash cycle	**−8 −14 (↓6)**	**29**	**~~42~~ 45 (↑3)**

the raw material supplier, which they find difficult to pass on to their suppliers. So the raw material supplier's liquidity deteriorates further to 45 days of borrowing, leaving this supplier at increased risk of liquidation. Viewing the supply chain holistically, the 'vertical' approach has led to a further imbalance in liquidity across the supply chain, with the supermarket enjoying yet greater credit and the raw material supplier requiring even higher levels of borrowing.

'Horizontal' supply chain approach to improving liquidity

If each organisation takes the 'horizontal' approach and aims to rebalance liquidity across the supply chain by reducing the days of accounts payable to suppliers, the hypothetical impact is shown in Table 3.4.

Table 3.4 Cash-to-cash cycle times for the FMCG food supply chain.

Financial measure (number of days)	Retail multiple	Food processor	Raw material supplier
Days of inventory (Average inventory/annual cost of sales) × 365	16	34	35
+ Days of accounts receivable (Average receivables/annual sales turnover) × 365	2	~~29~~ 25 (↓ 4)	~~30~~ 27 (↓ 3)
− Days of accounts payable (Average payable/annual credit purchases) × 365	~~26~~ 20 (↓ 6)	~~34~~ 30 (↓ 4)	23
Average operating cash cycle	**−8 −2 (↑6)**	**29**	**~~42~~ 39 (↓ 3)**

The retailer shares its liquidity with its suppliers by reducing the days of accounts payable by six days, reducing its own liquidity to −2 days of credit without borrowing. This results in a reduction of four days of accounts receivable for the food processor, who passes this on to its suppliers as a reduction in days of accounts payable, resulting once again in no change in the liquidity for the food processor. Finally, this results in a reduction of three days in the accounts payable for the raw material supplier, which they decide not to pass on to their suppliers because they need to improve their liquidity. So the raw material supplier's liquidity reduces to 39 days of borrowing, reducing the risk that this supplier will go into liquidation. Viewing the supply chain holistically the 'horizontal' approach has led to a rebalancing of liquidity across the supply chain, reduced credit (whilst still not borrowing) and the raw material supplier being able to reduce its levels of borrowing.

(Source: Dr Simon Templar, Cranfield School of Management.)

Questions

1. Considering the 'horizontal' approach, argue why the retailer should reduce further the days of accounts payable. What will be the impact on the relationship between all three members of the supply chain?
2. Considering the 'horizontal' approach, how will the changes impact the supply chain ratio for the retailer?
3. Try building in plausible inventory reductions across the supply chain for the 'horizontal' approach. What is the effect on the cash cycle times?

The supply chain ratio allows the trade-offs across profitability, liquidity and asset utilisation to be managed. This is important for maintaining liquidity, as it can suffer as a result of pursuing either profitability or asset utilisation improvements. For example, chasing profitability by extending payment terms to customers may increase sales revenue, but can cause liquidity problems by increasing cash-to-cash cycle times. Alternatively, seeking higher utilisation levels of manufacturing assets can lead to lower costs per unit but also can result in excessive finished stock. This results in cash being tied up for longer and higher inventory management costs (e.g. storage, insurance, obsolescence).

Perhaps most important of all is that the supply chain ratio allows supply chain directors and managers to have a dialogue at board level by acknowledging that supply chains are an enabler, not an impediment, to superior firm performance.

3.3.1 Supply Chain Finance (SCF)

It is essential for everyone involved with an organisation not to underestimate the importance of cash flow management and its link to financial performance, in particular the three components of the cash-to-cash cycle as illustrated in the previous case study. However, when the economic climate goes into recession and access to credit is difficult to obtain, then excellent cash flow management becomes essential for any business to survive. Unfortunately, not all organisations have extensive reserves of cash on their balance sheet or are able to optimise their cash flows. There are a number of variables that can impact on a business's liquidity, including the relationships between buyer and seller, their ability to obtain credit, the cost of credit and their capability of converting current assets (inventory and accounts receivables) into cash. The financial crisis of 2008 highlighted the importance of access to credit, especially for those organisations where cash flow was critical. In 2012 the then Prime Minister David Cameron's government recognised the significance of cash flow, not only for financial sustainability of organisations but as an agent of economic growth for the country as a whole:

> **This Government is determined to back all those businesses who aspire to get ahead and take on more people. In the current climate, viable businesses can struggle to get the finance they need to grow – this scheme will not only help them secure finance and support cash flow but will help secure supply chains for some of our biggest companies and protect thousands of jobs. It can be a win-win, with large companies and small suppliers both benefiting from this innovative scheme.**
>
> **(Quotes by Prime Minister David Cameron, 2012.)**

The scheme in question was a Supply Chain Finance (SCF) initiative, which would help the organisations improve their cash flow. SCF is a set of financial instruments that can be deployed by an organisation to improve the three components (inventory days, accounts receivable days and accounts payable days) of its cash-to-cash cycle. The Global Supply Chain Finance Forum (2016: 8) defines SCF as:

> **the use of financing and risk mitigation practices and techniques to optimize the management of the working capital and liquidity invested in supply chain processes and transactions. SCF is typically applied to open account trade and is triggered by supply chain events. Visibility of underlying trade flows by the finance provider(s) is a necessary component of such financing arrangements which can be enabled by a technology platform.**

An array of SCF instruments is mapped to the three components of the cash-to-cash cycle, providing a useful framework for the identification of financial approaches to reduce cash-to-cash cycle time.

1. Reducing inventory days
   - Warehouse finance
   - Goods-in-transit finance
   - Vendor-managed inventory
   - Financing of supplier's inventory
   - Trade acceptance discounting
2. Reducing accounts receivables
   - Forfaiting/discounting
   - Factoring
   - Distributor finance

  - Trade receivable backed financing
  - Pre-shipment financing
  - Post-shipment financing
  - Early payment discount programme
  - Collateral management

3. Increasing accounts payables
   - Reverse factoring/confirming
   - Extended payment terms
   - Purchasing card

(Cosse, 2011)

Templar et al. (2012) identified both tangible and intangible benefits of SCF.

- Tangible
  - Concrete improvements in working capital
  - Effective cash flow management
  - Enhanced value on the balance sheet
  - Potential investment opportunities
  - Lowered cost of goods sold
  - Decreased processing costs
- Intangible
  - Limited factoring of receivables
  - Established goodwill with suppliers
  - Strengthened relationships with key suppliers
  - Financial support for strategic suppliers
  - Enhanced discipline and visibility in transactions
  - Effective negotiation tool for extended payment terms
  - Streamlined settlement process
  - Increased risk awareness in the supply chain
  - Improved financial knowledge among purchasers
  - Harmonised business practices through supply base review

SCF benefits are not only financial, such as working capital improvements and lower cost of goods sold, but can also be non-financial, including improved relationships with key suppliers and purchasers' greater financial knowledge.

If you would like to explore SCF further there are a number of relevant publications (Hofmann and Belin, 2011 and Templar et al., 2016), definitions (Global Supply Chain Finance Forum, 2016), a literature review (Gelsomino et al., 2016) and the Supply Chain Finance Community (www.scfcommunity.org), a not-for-profit association which focuses on SCF knowledge transfer and research.

We now turn to issues concerning the visibility of costing information, which is important for evaluating the financial performance of a supply chain, whether seeking ways to improve it or making capital investment decisions, as later described in Section 3.6.

3.4 How can logistics costs be represented?

***Key issue:* What are the various ways of cutting up the total cost 'cake', and what are the relative merits of each?**

We all have a pretty good idea of what the total costs of a business are in practice. The costs of items such as materials used, power and wages all lead to bills that have to be paid. What is not so clear is how these costs should be allocated to supply chain processes – or even to products, for that matter. Figure 3.3 shows a breakdown of the costs of producing a bottle of mineral water against its total sales price, showing the approximate proportions of each. Starting at the bottom:

- *Manufacturing costs:* of extracting the water from source, testing, purifying and bottling. Add on the costs of plastic and labels for the bottles.
- *Transport costs:* from bottling plant to the supplier's national distribution centre (NDC) in a given territory.
- *Processing costs:* in the supplier's NDC.
- *Transport costs:* from the supplier's NDC to the retailer's regional distribution centre (RDC).
- *Processing costs:* in the retailer's RDC.
- *Processing costs:* in the retailer's store.

The balance of the sales revenue, less costs, is shared between supplier and retailer as profit (or 'margin'). But how are costs allocated to product lines (for example, plastic bottles, glass bottles, facial spray) and individual SKUs (for example, 1.5 litre, 500 ml)?

This section reviews three commonly used ways of representing costs: fixed and variable, direct and indirect, and engineered and discretionary. Bear in mind that the *total cost* picture is the same: the three different ways of allocating them to products are simply different ways of 'cutting the cake'. Let us look at total cost as a cube instead of a cake. Then the three different ways of representing costs can be shown as different ways of cutting up the cube.

The important point here is that the total cost is constant: it is the ways we *analyse* that cost that are different. Why analyse it in different ways? To gain better information about our cost basis so that we can manage the business better. Let us look in turn at each of these ways to cut the total cost cube.

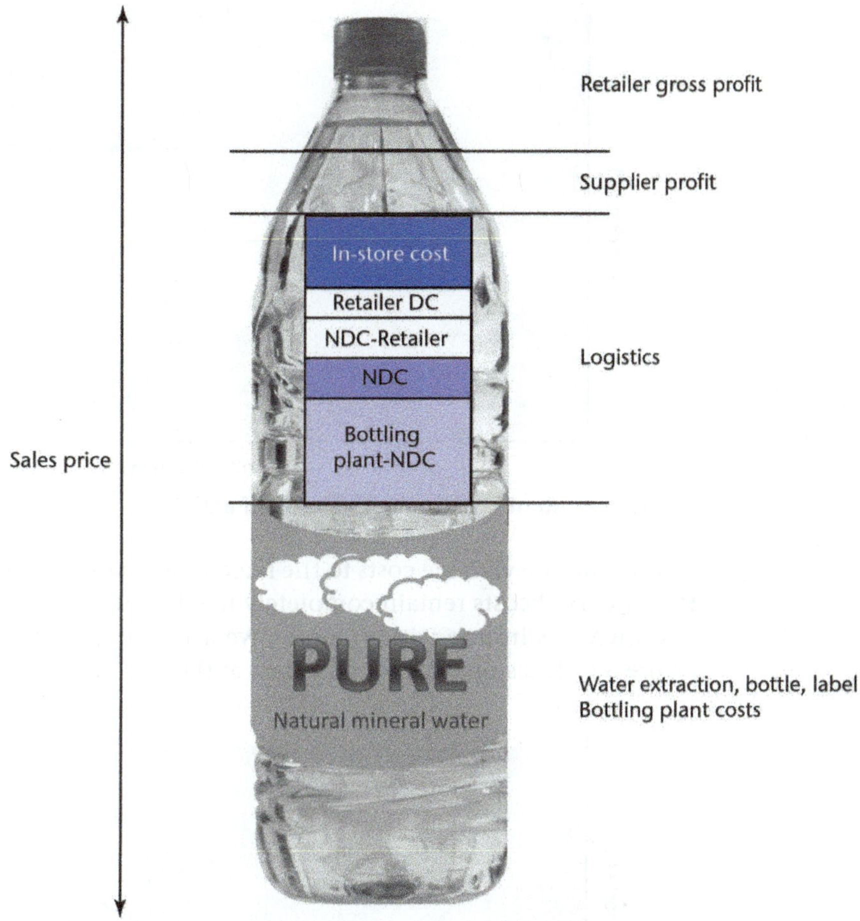

Figure 3.3 **Cost breakdown of a bottle of mineral water.**

3.4.1 Fixed/variable

One popular way of analysing costs is to consider the effect of *volume of activity* on them. Costs tend to respond differently as the volume changes:

- *fixed costs* tend to stay the same as volume of activity changes, or at least within a given volume range;
- *variable costs* change as the volume of activity changes.

Fixed costs include items such as warehouse rental, which is charged on a time basis (€/month). As volume of activity increases, additional warehouses may be added around Europe, and we get the familiar *stepped fixed costs*, as shown in Figure 3.4. The same relationship would apply if volumes were reduced and a warehouse closed.

Variable costs include things such as direct materials, which are ordered in line with demand. If demand increases, we buy more. Starting with zero cost at zero activity, variable costs increase roughly in line with volume, as shown in Figure 3.5.

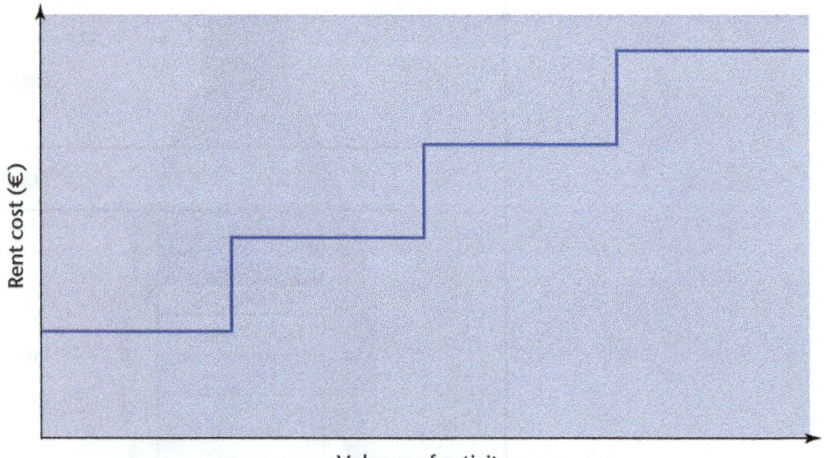

Figure 3.4 Rent cost against volume of activity.

If we add the variable costs to the fixed costs against a given range of volume (so that the fixed costs remain completely fixed) and add in the sales revenue (which also increases in line with volume), we arrive at the break-even chart shown in Figure 3.6. The sloping line that starts at 0 is the sales revenue. The total cost line

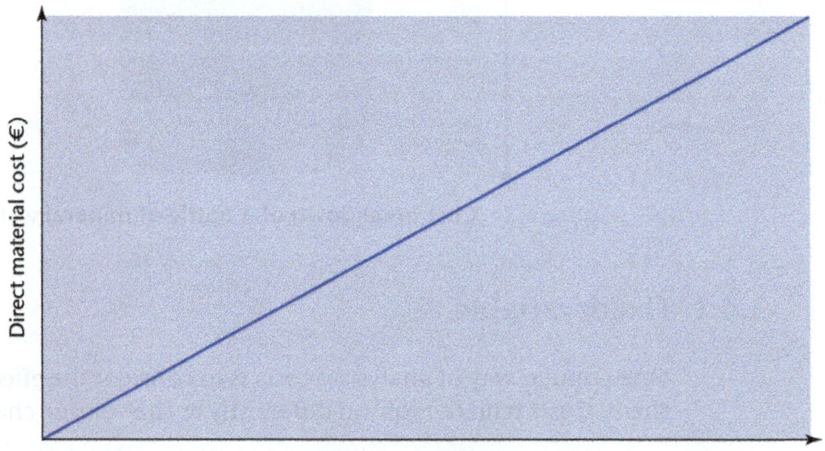

Figure 3.5 Direct material costs against volume of activity.

starts at F and represents the sum of fixed and variable costs. The point at which the sales revenue line crosses the total cost line is the break-even point. Below this point, a loss will be incurred; above it a profit will be made.

A helpful concept in evaluating break-even charts is that of contribution:

Contribution = Sales less variable costs

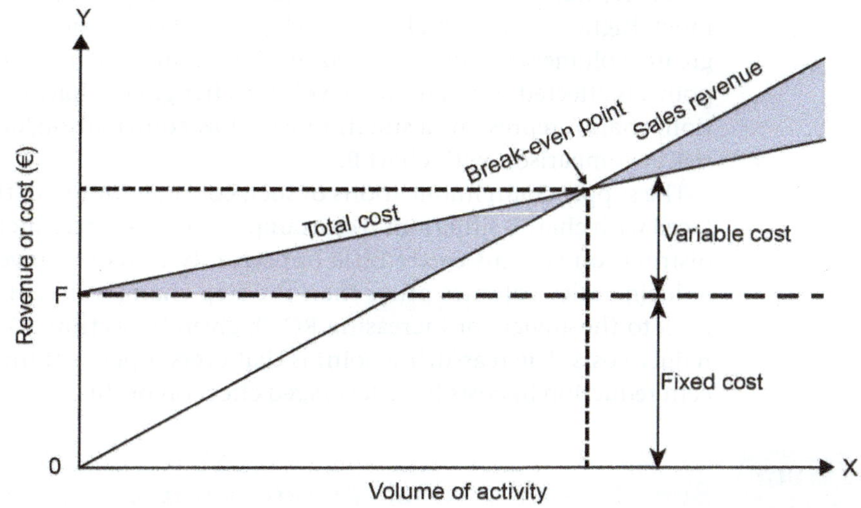

Figure 3.6 Break-even chart.

Therefore, contribution is the fixed costs plus the profit. Contribution is useful in decision making. High contribution per unit indicates a more volatile business: that is, one that is more risky. Therefore, we should expect a business with high contribution/unit to provide a higher return on investment in the longer term. Look at the two break-even charts in Figures 3.7 and 3.9. What are the differences between the two situations? What has happened to the break-even point and why?

Chart A shows a situation with high variable costs and low fixed costs. In chart B (Figure 3.9), the situation is reversed. The break-even point has moved well to the right: that is, chart B requires a higher volume to break-even than A. This is because a much higher volume of sales is needed to cover the high level of fixed costs.

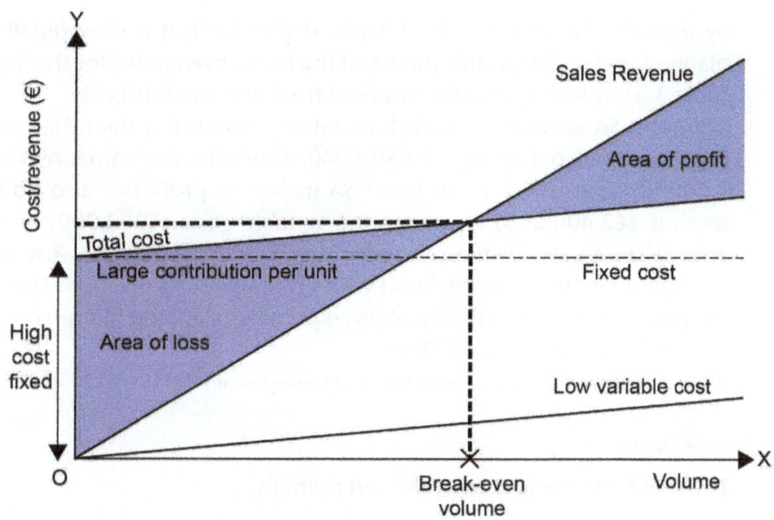

Figure 3.7 Break-even chart B.

Furthermore, additional volume has a small impact on chart A, whereas it has a much higher impact on chart B. So high fixed costs and low variable costs lead to greater volume sensitivity. Accordingly, profitability (the area above the break-even point) is affected much more by volume changes in chart B. In terms of contribution, chart A represents a situation with low contribution/unit, and therefore low risk in comparison with chart B.

The supply chain implications of such considerations are that most often we are faced with chart B situations. For example, core resources such as warehousing and distribution systems create little opportunity to reduce investments in line with reducing sales volumes other than the step changes shown in Figure 3.5. We are back to the advice for increasing ROCE given in Section 3.2 to increase sales and reduce costs. The reassuring point is that every 1 per cent increase in sales or 1 per cent reduction in costs has a leveraged effect on profits.

CASE STUDY 3.2

Bond SA – a marginal costing example

Bond SA is planning to manufacture a new product with an initial sales forecast of 3,600 units in the first year at a selling price of €800 each. The finance department has calculated that the variable cost for each truck will be €300. The fixed costs for the manufacturing facility for the year are €1,500,000. Using the information provided by the sales forecast and the finance department, it is now possible to calculate the planned profit, the contribution and the break-even point for this venture (as shown in Table 3.5) by leveraging the nature of fixed and variable costs.

Table 3.5 Planned profit and break-even point for Bond's new product.

Planned profit	€	Planned break-even point	€
Sales revenue Less variable costs Contribution Less fixed costs Profit	2,880,000 1,080,000 1,800,000 1,500,000 300,000	Fixed costs Contribution per unit = Sales value – variable cost Break-even point (units) = Fixed cost/contribution per unit	1,500,000 500 3,000

If Bond SA achieves its sales forecast of 3,600 units, then the company will make a planned profit before tax of €300,000. Crucially, the company's break-even point is 3,000 units, at which point Bond SA makes no profit but also no loss, because sales revenue (€2,400,000) equals all the variable costs (€900,000) and all the total fixed costs associated with the production process (€1,500,000). Any additional unit sold after this point will provide Bond with profitable sales revenue. The difference between the planned profit and the break-even point is called the margin of safety. In the case of Bond SA, this equates to 600 units.

(Source: Dr Simon Templar, Cranfield School of Management.)

Questions

1. What happens to the break-even point if:

   a. Fixed costs increase by 10 per cent?

   b. The sales price reduces by 5 per cent?

3.4.2 Direct/indirect

Another way to cut up the total cost 'cube' is to analyse costs in terms of whether or not they can be allocated directly to a given product. Two further categories emerge:

- *Direct costs* can be tied to specific products. The most obvious examples are direct labour and direct materials. Thus, we can allocate exactly the cost of bought-in parts to the products into which they are built.
- *Indirect costs* are whatever is left over after direct costs have been allocated. Indirect costs are also called 'overheads' and include everything from the managing director's salary to the rent rates paid for the distribution centre - anything that cannot be allocated directly to a given product.

Directness of costs is concerned with the extent to which costs can be allocated directly to given products. This is a completely different concept from that of fixed/variable costs. Whilst there is a tendency to associate fixed costs with indirect and variable with direct, there is no necessary relationship at all. Thus, direct labour costs tend to be fixed, at least in the short term.

As stated previously, the reason for analysing costs differently is *to gain better information about our cost basis so that we can manage the business better.* Direct and indirect costs help us to decide the full cost of a product or service when more than one is offered. If there were just a single product, life would be easy, because all of the costs could be allocated to that one product. Most businesses are much more complex than that and are faced with the issue of how indirect costs should be apportioned to products. The most popular way to spread indirect costs is on the basis of direct labour. This is not the 'correct way', nor is it the only way.

A closer view of how fixed costs behave by product is achieved by using a method called *direct product profitability* (DPP). This method has been used widely in the retail industry to understand the way in which logistics costs behave for each product. The understanding is achieved by allocating fixed costs, making assumptions about how these are incurred by a product as it moves through the logistics system.

A good DPP system should take account of all the significant differences in the ways products are developed, sourced, produced, sold and distributed. In order to make this analysis practical, products normally will need to be grouped together. Product groups need to recognise shared technologies, processes, fixed assets, raw material inputs and packaging methods. The key objective of product groupings is to remove the need for apportioning costs, and thereby not to apportion profit across the products.

DPP assumes that only those costs that can be allocated rationally may be deducted. Thus, DPP may be viewed as a development of direct/indirect costing in that it attempts to convert into direct costs logistics costs that otherwise would have been regarded as fixed. In this way, DPP seeks to provide more accurate information about which products are contributing most to profitability - and which are contributing least.

The principle at stake here is that good accounting and financial analysis force us to ask more questions about what is going on in our business. DPP can have a role to play here: it attempts to allocate logistics costs more specifically to products (and, in this case, orders as well) than is possible by spreading 'fixed' costs on the basis of an assumption such as direct labour. The assumption otherwise would be that direct labour actually 'drives' the overheads, which is highly doubtful.

CASE STUDY 3.3

Direct product profitability

Filmco makes two thin film (gauge = 12μm) products for packaging applications in the food industry. Product A is coated so that subsequently it can be printed on; product B is uncoated. There is no changeover time on the production line, because all that needs to happen is for the coating drum to be switched on or off. Once produced on the film-making lines, the film is slit to width and length to customer order. Roughly 40 per cent of Filmco's output is A, and 60 per cent B, and film-making takes place 360 days/year on a continuous basis because of the high capital cost of the process.

A DPP study was carried out at Filmco to determine the relative profitability of the two products A and B by major customer. The method was adapted from that shown in Table 3.1 because Filmco is a manufacturing environment. Here is how it was done:

a. *Invoice price:* this was the total sales value invoiced to the customer.
b. *Cost of placing orders:* the total cost of the sales office (salaries, etc.) was divided by the number of orders dispatched that month. This cost per order (€150) was allocated to each order placed by each customer.
c. *Manufacturing cost:* a variable cost for each product was found by collecting raw material, labour, power, packaging and waste costs. Manufacturing overheads (fixed costs) were allocated on the basis of direct labour. Because of the small difference in manufacturing methods, the manufacturing costs for the two products were similar. They were €2,107 for A and €2,032 for B.
d. *Storage costs:* the total cost of the warehousing operation is €800k/year. There are 8,300 pallet locations, and the cost/day for a pallet was calculated as €0.30, assuming 360 working days. The storage cost for a given order was calculated as the number of pallets × the number of days × €0.30.
e. *Opportunity costs:* orders must wait in the warehouse until the last reel has been produced. An order with a value of €3,000 that stays for seven days in the warehouse with an interest rate of 14 per cent is said to have an opportunity cost of €8.20.
f. *Transport cost:* this was based on a price per tonne delivered to a given customer.
g. *Total cost:* this was the sum of b to f for a given order.
h. *DPP:* this was sales price less total cost g.

Table 3.6 gives a sample of the DPPs for four orders for customer P. The average DPP for customer P over all orders shipped over a given month was 19.6 per cent, whilst that for customer Q was 23.1 per cent and customer R was 33 per cent.

Table 3.6 DPP for customer P for a sample of four orders in a given month.

Order no.	Film	Weight (t)	a	b	c	d	e	f	g	h (%)
186232	A	482	1,210	150	876	1.08	1.88	79	1,108	8.4
185525	A	2,418	5,997	150	4,344	7.83	9.33	190	4,702	21.6
185187	B	4,538	13,000	150	8,402	20.8	30.33	343	8,946	31.2
185351	B	2,615	7,576	150	4,897	14.58	17.68	198	5,277	30.3

Question

1. What can we tell from the above analysis in Table 3.6 and the average DPPs per customer? (Consider in particular the differences in DPP between the four orders shown, and between the three customers P, Q and R.)

3.4.3 Engineered/discretionary

A third way of analysing costs is to consider *the ease of allocating* them. Some things are easy to cost; others may require considerable thought and analysis because they are difficult to cost under current methods. This line of thinking creates a third way of cutting the total cost cube:

- *Engineered costs* have a clear input–output relationship. In other words, the benefit of a given cost is measurable. For example, if it takes 10 hours to produce 10 boxes of product A in the factory, then we have a clear output benefit (1 box) for the cost of each hour of input.
- *Discretionary costs* do not have a clear input–output relationship. Here, the input cost is clear but the output benefit is unclear. For example, the cost of the contract cleaners who clean the factory is clear, but the benefit they produce is not easily quantifiable.

The challenge is to convert discretionary costs into engineered costs, so that we can better quantify the competitive impact of a given course of action. A classic example of converting discretionary costs into engineered costs has been the conversion of 'quality' as a discretionary concept into engineered 'quality costs' (Dale and Plunkett, 1995). This was achieved by breaking down the concept of quality into three cost drivers:

- *Prevention*. This comprises the costs of measures to prevent defects from taking place, such as training and process capability studies.

- *Appraisal*. This comprises the costs incurred in detecting defects, which would include testing and inspection.
- *Internal and external failure*. Internal costs are scrap, rework and the associated costs of not getting it right the first time. External failure costs are rectification after products have reached the final customer, such as warranty claims, returns and repairs.

In this case, it was argued, greater investment in prevention would result in the overall cost of quality being reduced over time.

The principle is to convert discretionary costs into engineered costs where possible. As indicated in the above examples, it is usually possible to make an estimate of what the engineered costs are, perhaps accompanied by a sensitivity or risk analysis. Without such guidelines, decisions would have to be taken on 'gut feel' – or, as usually happens, not taken at all! In other words, the logistics team may have an excellent project for increased flexibility in the distribution centre but, because they have not quantified the outputs (for example, the cost savings), the application for funding is rejected.

CASE STUDY 3.4

Glup SA

Glup SA supplies a range of household soaps to supermarkets in northern Europe. There are 12 stock-keeping units (SKUs) in the range. The logistics manager has determined that an investment of €0.5 million on improved material handling equipment would convert the main distribution centre into a more flexible facility. A number of benefits in improved product availability have been identified – but current information is largely in the form of discretionary costs. Glup's assessment of the benefits and its plans to convert the justification into engineered costs are outlined next.

Improved in-store availability

This is the percentage of time for which a product is available on the shelf. If the product is not available on the shelf, then it will lose sales to competitive products that are available, such as supermarket own brands. (Availability is a classic 'order losing sensitive' qualifying criterion, as described in Section 1.3.) Current available data at Glup are scant, but suggest that average in-store availability is as low as 85 per cent for a given SKU. In order to convert this discretionary benefit into an engineered cost, Glup intends to measure the time for which each of the 12 product lines is unavailable each week. One way to do this is to use a market research agency to conduct sample studies of product availability in selected stores at random times across the working week. This will yield an availability guide, such as the 85 per cent figure referred to. The new system will, it is believed, reduce this unavailable time. Glup then plans to model the new material-handling equipment methods using simulation, and to calculate the new in-store availability. The reduced non-availability time could then be converted into additional contribution for each SKU to give an engineered cost saving.

Reduced transportation costs

The new equipment would also allow lower transportation costs, because trays of different SKUs could be mixed together on the same pallet. Glup again intends to use simulation modelling to identify the opportunities for savings using this method. It is considered that this will offer the opportunity to reduce overall transport costs by more flexible loading of the trailers used to distribute the products to Glup's customers.

Promotions and new product launches

It is considered that the new equipment will enable promotions and new product launches to be delivered to selected stores more accurately and more quickly. Demand uncertainty in such situations is very high: for example, a recent 'three for the price of two' promotion created a fivefold increase in sales. In order to launch a new product, it is first necessary to drain the pipeline of the old product, or to 'write it off' as obsolete stock. If the more flexible warehouse system can reduce the length of the pipeline from factory to supermarket, it is argued, then a real saving in time or obsolete stock is possible. Glup again intends to measure this by simulation. It will then be necessary to determine by how much sales will increase as a result of the new product advantages. This will be estimated by Glup marketing people, who will use experience of previous promotions and new product launches. The engineered cost will be the additional time for which the new product is available multiplied by the additional estimated sales volume multiplied by the contribution per unit. Alternatively, it will be the reduction in obsolete stocks multiplied by the total cost per product plus any costs of double handling and scrapping.

Question

1. Comment on Glup's plans to create engineered costs from the perceived benefits of the new material-handling equipment.

3.5 Carbon costing for more sustainable supply chains

Key issues: **How can carbon emissions be costed to incentivise polluting companies to become more environmentally sustainable? What are the approaches companies can use for setting their own Internal Carbon Prices?**

Companies are striving to reduce their carbon emissions to meet their net zero carbon emission targets, typically set at 2050, as described in section 1.3.3. Carbon costing, or pricing, is a cost applied to carbon pollution to encourage polluters to reduce the amount of Green House Gas (GHGs) emissions they emit into the atmosphere – it's a way of shifting the cost of damage back to those who are responsible! This will incentivise polluters to reduce their carbon footprint and seek alternative methods that are more environmentally friendly. Addressing an audience at the COP28 climate summit in Dubai, European Commission President Ursula von der Leyen made the case for carbon pricing:

> **If you pollute, you have to pay a price for that. If you want to avoid paying that price, you innovate and invest in clean technologies.**

Carbon costing is especially important for an organisation carrying out sustainable capital expenditure projects, which may have a longer payback time (see section 3.7) compared to other projects. Savings in carbon costs can result in a higher return on investment (ROI) and a better business case compared to alternative projects. This approach can also be used in supplier selection and evaluation by rating a supplier higher depending on their sustainability and carbon emission business policy, including their carbon footprint. This will assist an organisation to target upstream emissions, part of scope 3 emissions, which account for the majority of emissions and can be difficult to manage as they are generated outside the company.

According to the World Bank (2024) there are two main methods of carbon pricing external to companies:

1. ***Cap-and-trade scheme (or emissions trading system, ETS),*** caps the total level of greenhouse gas emissions and allows those industries with low emissions to sell their extra allowances to larger emitters. By creating supply and demand for emissions allowances, an ETS establishes a market price for greenhouse gas emissions. The cap helps ensure that the required emission reductions will take place to keep the emitters (in aggregate) within their pre-allocated carbon budget.
2. ***Carbon tax***, where governments directly set a price on carbon by defining a tax rate on GHG emissions or – more commonly – on the carbon content of fossil fuels. It is different from an ETS in that the emission reduction outcome of a carbon tax is not predefined, but the carbon price is.

According to the World Bank (2024), 110 carbon pricing initiatives have been implemented (36 ETS, 39 taxes and 35 government crediting mechanisms) covering 53 countries in 2024. This covers approximately 24 per cent of global GHG emissions and the carbon price ranged widely from US$0.46 to US$167 per tonne of CO_2e, which raised $104 billion in carbon pricing revenue in 2023. However, only 1 per cent of global emissions were priced above the recommended level and the current global average carbon price, is a meagre US$2.79 per tonne according to the Institute of Sustainable Finance (Cleary and Willcott, 2023). Further, they argue that carbon pricing can be a powerful tool to combat climate change and reduce emissions, but not on its own – carbon pricing in isolation will not allow us to meet the Paris Agreement target 1.5 C or 2 C warming scenarios! Their models suggest that:

> **Carbon pricing on its own could limit global warming to 2.4 C, but the global price would have to rise dramatically and rapidly to accomplish this. The price would have to start at $223.31 per tonne in 2023 and increase to $435.55 per tonne by 2045.**

The Bank of England has warned banks and businesses to start assessing the risks they face from climate change and be braced to pay more in taxation.

3.5.1 Internal Carbon Pricing (ICP)

Internal Carbon Pricing (ICP) is adopted by an organisation as a tool to internalise negative external effects caused by their carbon emissions and to prepare themselves for a low-carbon economy (Riedel et al., 2021). Legislation is ever-changing to meet 2050 net-zero targets set by The Paris Agreement and more rigorous government taxation on carbon emissions is likely. Hence, an ICP protects an organisation from any additional emission taxation. There are three main methods for ICP:

1. ***Shadow price:*** this is a theoretical price as a risk assessment tool to evaluate investments, test assumptions, and guide business strategy in anticipation of future carbon constraints. This is usually based on forecasted price of carbon based on regulations such as the European Union Emissions Trading Scheme (EU ETS) and prices can be set or vary by location/type of activity (Ahluwalia, 2017). It is a means to make carbon-intensive projects more expensive or uneconomical. For example BP have a shadow ICP of $40 per tonne to guide decision making and apply a higher rate of $80 per tonne to stress test robustness of its portfolio in jurisdictions highly exposed to carbon taxation such as the EU (Ahluwalia, 2017). Unilever's (2024) internal carbon price – which is used to inform investment decision-making – is currently set at €70 per tonne of CO_2 and they claim it is aligned with their ambition to limit the global temperature rise to 1.5°C.
2. ***Internal carbon tax:*** this assigns a monetary value to emissions that result from normal business activities as a price per tonne of CO_2. This would generate an income stream that can be used to meet a company's sustainability goals where the price is fixed but the amount of emitted carbon is not predefined (Riedel et al., 2021). For example Microsoft have an internal carbon tax since 2012 where the money generated is invested into energy efficiency projects, renewable energy purchases and carbon offset projects to meet their carbon neutral commitments. Indeed since 2020 Microsoft extended this beyond scope 1 and 2 emissions and began charging their internal business groups for all scope 3 emissions (Microsoft, 2022).
3. ***Implicit price:*** this is based on how much a company spends to reduce GHG emissions and/or the cost of complying with government regulations. This includes using the amount spent on renewable energy purchases, carbon offsets, energy efficiency projects or compliance with fuel economy standards (Ben-Amar et al., 2022). This price is not used to assess implications for the future, but instead it can help a company understand its current carbon footprint, improve external communication, and evaluate economic cost of regulations. This can be used as a benchmark before launching other ICP approaches such as shadow pricing.

ICP approaches are not mutually exclusive and can be used in combination to meet an organisation's GHG emission targets. This is known as Hybrid Carbon Pricing where companies can use an internal carbon tax to meet their GHG reduction targets but also implement a shadow price to guide future investment decisions.

CASE STUDY 3.5

Sustainability and carbon pricing at Volvo

Volvo are a Swedish automotive manufacturer of luxury vehicles with a revenue of €48.8 billion in 2023 representing around a €7 billion increase on the previous fiscal year. They have ambitious environmental sustainability targets where they aim for net zero carbon emissions by 2040 (Volvo, 2024) and a step towards this their sustainability ambitions for 2030 are:

1. Reduce CO_2 emissions per car by 75 per cent compared to 2018 levels.
2. Reduce energy usage in their operations per average car by 40 per cent compared to 2018 levels.

3. Reach 30 per cent average recycled content across the fleet, with new car models having at least 35 per cent recycled content.
4. Reduce water use in internal operations by 50 per cent average per car, compared to 2018 levels.
5. At least 99 per cent of all waste from internal operations to be either reused or recycled

Outstanding supplier collaborations which will contribute to the net zero carbon target include:

- ***Working with SSAB steel manufacturer*** (SSAB, 2021) to use ground-breaking technology and be the first automotive manufacturer to use fossil-free steel. This is critical as steel is responsible for 35 per cent of CO_2 emissions for the material and components in a new Volvo car.
- ***Partnering with battery suppliers,*** Northvolt, that uses 100 per cent carbon neutral energy in electric battery production, which is normally carbon intensive, and is making the battery circular through end-of-life recycling (Volvo, 2022).

To further accelerate its carbon footprint reduction, Volvo Cars announced the introduction of an internal carbon price of 1,000 SEK (approximately 100 US$) for every tonne of carbon emissions from across its entire business, in line with its ambition to become a climate neutral company by 2040 (Volvo, 2021). This made Volvo the first car manufacturer to implement a carbon pricing mechanism across its complete operations. Further, the price is set at a significantly higher level than what is being recommended by organisations such as the International Energy Agency. Effectively, the company is aiming to future-proof its organisation and be ahead of the regulatory curve, as it anticipates, and is even in favour of, more governments implementing carbon pricing in coming years.

Under the carbon pricing scheme, every future car project will undergo a 'sustainability sense-check' and a CO_2 cost will be used for every anticipated tonne of carbon emissions throughout the car's full life cycle. The aim is to ensure that each car model would be profitable even under a strict carbon pricing scheme, steering project-, sourcing- and manufacturing-related decisions towards the most sustainable option on the table. According to Björn Annwall, the Chief Financial Officer (CFO):

> **A global and fair price on CO_2 is critical for the world to meet its climate ambitions, and we all need to do more. We strongly believe progressive companies should take the lead by setting an internal carbon price. By evaluating future cars on their CO_2-adjusted profitability, we expect to accelerate actions that will help us identify and reduce carbon emissions already today.**

In a Bloomberg interview with the Volvo CFO (Lindeberg, 2021) he said:

> **People speak in USD rather than tonnes of CO_2 and by placing a value on CO_2 in USD will give a clear cost on the CO_2 footprint you create when making decisions. The cost of abatement, e.g., carbon capture, will be around $100 per tonne in 2040 so it is better to add it in now as a cost. There will definitely be legislation in the future which will put a tax on carbon, so it is better to start planning ahead. A key point is to put a USD value on carbon and get a discussion on sustainability in the same context as you make your business decisions.**

(Source: Volvo (2021, 2022 and 2024.)

Questions

1. What is the method of Internal Carbon Pricing (ICP) being used by Volvo and explain why you think this?
2. What should Volvo do, if a good performing supplier they have partnered with for years, is not an economically viable supplier when using Volvo's internal carbon costing (CO_2-adjusted profitability)?

3.6 Activity-based costing (ABC)

Key issues: **What are the shortcomings of traditional cost accounting from a logistics point of view? How can costs be allocated to processes so that better decisions can be made?**

The driving force behind **activity-based costing (ABC)** is that the traditional way of allocating indirect costs by spreading them to products on the basis of direct labour is becoming difficult to manage. Whilst direct labour used to constitute a substantial portion of product costs, today that rarely applies. Therefore, overhead rates of 500 per cent or more on direct labour are not uncommon. Just a small change in direct labour content would lead to a massive change in product cost.

Cooper and Kaplan (1988) explain the problem by referring to two factories, which we here refer to as Simple and Komplex. Both factories produce 1 million ballpoint pens each year; they are the same size and have the same capital equipment. But whilst Simple produces only blue pens, Komplex produces hundreds of colour and style variations in volumes that range from 500 (lavender) to 100,000 (blue) units per year. A visitor would notice many differences between the factories. Komplex has far more production support staff to handle the numerous production loading and scheduling challenges, changeovers between colours and styles, and so on. Komplex would also have more design change issues, supplier scheduling problems, and outbound warehousing, picking and distribution challenges. There would be much higher levels of idle time, overtime, inventory, rework and scrap because of the difficulty of balancing production and demand across a much wider product range. Because overheads are allocated on the basis of direct labour, blue pens are clobbered with 10 per cent of the much higher Komplex overheads. The market price of blue pens is determined by focused factories such as Simple, so the blue pens from Komplex appear to be unprofitable. As a result, the management of Komplex considers that specialist products such as lavender - which sell at a premium - are the future of the business, and that blue pens are low priority. This strategy further increases overheads and costs, and perpetuates the myth that the unit cost of each pen is the same. Traditional cost systems often understate profits on high-volume products and overstate profits on low-volume, high-variety products. ABC principles would help the management of Komplex to make more informed product decisions on the basis of realistic costs, as illustrated by Case study 3.5. The management of Simple has no need for another costing system; the current one works well for them.

ABC recognises that overhead costs do not just happen, but are caused by activities, such as holding products in store. ABC therefore seeks to break the business down into major processes – such as manufacture, storage and distribution – and then break each process into activities. For example, the distribution process would include such activities as picking, loading, transport and delivery. For each of these activities, there must be one cost driver: what is it that drives cost for that activity? For example, the cost driver for the storage activity may be the volume of a case, whereas the transport activity may be driven by weight. Once we know the cost driver, we need to know how many units of that cost driver are incurred for that activity, and the cost per unit for the cost driver. For example, the cost driver for the transportation activity may be the number of kilometres driven, and therefore cost per kilometre would be the cost per unit of the cost driver. This yields the cost of the activity and, when summed across all the activities in a process, the total cost of that process.

ABC is difficult to implement because we need first to understand what the discrete processes are in a business where the existing links between functions are not well understood. There is then the issue of identifying the cost driver, which requires a fresh way of looking at each activity. For example, the cost driver for a warehouse fork-lift operator would be the number of pallets moved. The cost driver for stocking shelves would be the number of pieces that must be stacked in a given time period. A further problem occurs if there is more than one cost driver for a given activity. You are then faced with the same problem as with overhead allocation: on what basis should the cost drivers be weighted? Usually, this problem shows that activities have not been broken down into sufficient detail, and that more analysis is needed. ABC can therefore become resource-intensive to implement.

In spite of the implementation challenges, logistics and ABC go hand in hand (van Damme and van der Zon, 1999). It is a very rational way to analyse costs, and logistics practitioners recognise that providing a service is about managing a sequence of processes. Logistics or supply chain managers are particularly well placed to understand, analyse and apply ABC. They understand business processes and the activities that go with them. Theirs is a cross-functional task. The value chain stares them in the face.

The procedure of determining cost drivers is often considered to be more valuable than the ABC system itself. Activity-based management enables the cost structure of a business to be examined in a new light (as illustrated by Case study 3.5), allowing anomalies to be resolved and sources of waste highlighted. It may also help in better targeting investment decisions.

CASE STUDY 3.6

ABC costing at Komplex GmbH

Komplex GmbH has four production lines, each of which operates for 8,000 hours a year. Each line makes a number of products, which are based on size and colour. Therefore, many changeovers are required, each incurring set-up and maintenance costs. Traditionally, the maintenance costs have been allocated on the basis of machine hours, so each production line is charged equally. This year, the maintenance budget of €1 million has been divided into four, so each line is charged with €250,000.

Sales and marketing are concerned that certain products are losing market share, and this is due to prices relative to the competition. All departments have been instructed to investigate costs and suggest improvements. How can activity-based costing improve this situation? By identifying the cost driver for maintenance, in this case the number of changeovers, costs can be allocated to each production line on this basis. Costs are then matched to the activity that generates them, so avoiding cross-subsidies.

The results are illustrated in Table 3.7. Maintenance costs have now been transferred to the production lines that incur the activity. For example, costs on line.

A have doubled to €500,000, whilst costs on line D have reduced to €50,000. ABC in this example has not taken cost out of the process, but has reallocated the costs to give a better understanding of the cost base. Komplex is now in a better position to make decisions that affect the cost competitiveness of the product range.

Table 3.7 Different ways of allocating maintenance costs.

Production lines	A	B	C	D	Total
Machine hours	8,000	8,000	8,000	8,000	32,000
No. of changeovers	50	30	15	5	100
Equal allocation	250,000	250,000	250,000	250,000	1,000,000
Allocation by activity	500,000	300,000	150,000	50,000	1,000,000
Difference	250,000	50,000	−100,000	−200,000	0

(Source: Dr Simon Templar, Cranfield School of Management.)

Questions

1. For which other activities could the number of changeovers be a cost driver? Explain your answer.
2. What is the likely effect on the costs for each production line compared to the equal allocation?

We will now consider two costing approaches that are based on ABC costing: cost–time profile (CTP) and cost to serve (CTS). Later in the book (in Chapter 9), 'total cost of ownership' (TCO), another ABC costing approach used by the procurement function, is described.

3.6.1 Cost–time profile (CTP)

A key benefit of being able to cost logistics processes is that cost information can be used in conjunction with time information. The synergies of the two can then provide opportunities for identifying activities that create either value or waste.

The cost–time profile (CTP) (Bicheno, 2005) is a graph that plots cumulative time against cumulative cost for a set of discrete activities, which together form a process or a supply chain. The CTP utilises outputs from two sources:

- *activity times*: from the time-based process mapping (TBPM) process time recording system (see Chapter 5);
- *activity costs*: from a process costing system that is underpinned by activity-based costing.

As discussed earlier, ABC strives to achieve an equitable distribution of overhead costs to activities. Table 3.8 illustrates cumulative time and cost for a process comprising six activities.

Table 3.8 Cumulative time and cost data by activity.

Activity	A	B	C	D	E	F
Cumulative time (%)	14	64	65	67	97	100
Cumulative cost (%)	25	45	83	85	95	100

Such data can be used to construct a cost–time profile like that displayed in Figure 3.8, which records the process in terms of time and cost for a metal product from receipt of raw metal to delivery of finished product to the retailer. Overall, the process takes an average of 93 hours to complete. The profile shows the extent to which different processes consume time and cost within the supply chain, highlighting those for future investigation that could yield savings. For example, distribution accounts for 50 per cent of process time, but only 5 per cent of total cost. Etching and plating are more in line, since they account for 22 per cent of process time and are responsible for 32 per cent of the total cost.

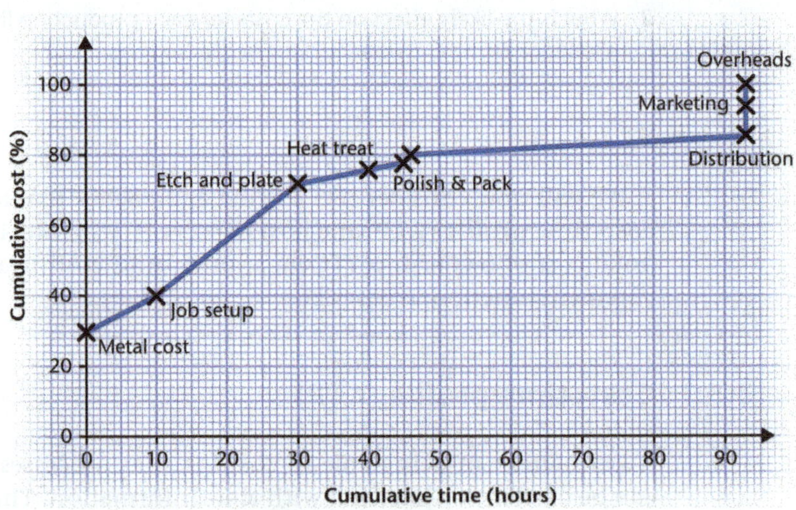

Figure 3.8 Cost–time profile for Metal product.

(Source: Adapted From a study by Dr Paul Chapman and Professor Richard Wilding, Cranfield Centre for Logistics and Supply Chain Management.)

The profile shows that time and cost are *not related linearly*. Bicheno and Holweg (2008) stress the importance of interpreting both the horizontal and vertical lines of the CTP:

- *Long, horizontal lines* tend to occur when there is a relatively small increase in total cost as a result of an activity that runs over a relatively long period of time. An example is distribution of finished product after slicing and packing.
- *Steep, vertical lines* tend to occur when costs are consumed over a relatively short period of processing time. An example is deboning, where the cumulative cost rises sharply.

A focus on the long, horizontal sections of the CTP graph may help reduce cumulative time (see Chapter 5). A focus on steep, vertical lines may help reduce cumulative cost. The CTP can be used to prioritise improvement processes, as shown by the cost–time grid in Figure 3.9 for a herb and spice manufacturer, which was developed as part of a Cranfield study (SUCCESS project at Cranfield School of Management, 2003).

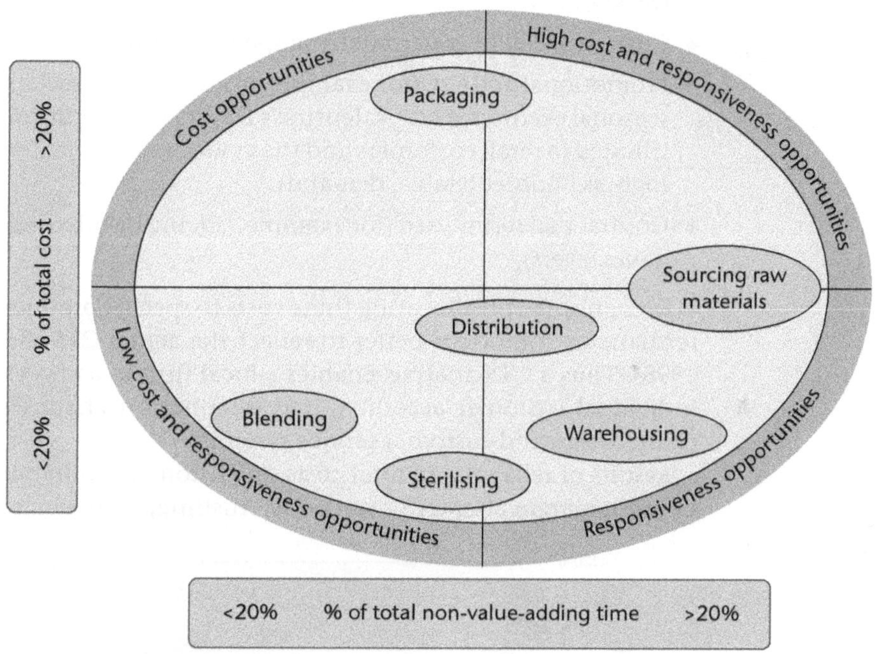

Figure 3.9 Cost–time grid.

(Source: Adapted from Cranfield School of Management (2003) The route to SUCCESS: Project managers Handbook. Bedfordshire: Cranfield University.)

Processes in the top right-hand box are prime candidates for savings in both time *and* cost. Processes in the bottom left-hand box are low on the list of priorities.

A further Cranfield study, this time of a food sector FMCG in the confectionery business, concluded that decisions to optimise cost in one area could have a detrimental effect downstream (Whicker et al., 2009). Large batch sizes reduced the need for machine changeovers in manufacturing. But this meant that the national distribution centre was often supplied with excess stock, and the resulting inventory overspill had to be extracted and sent to third party warehouses. Savings in manufacturing efficiency were causing extra costs and lead times in distribution.

3.6.2 Cost-to-serve (CTS)

So far, we have focused on manufacturing costs, but what about the cost of distributing products to customers? 'Putting the end-customer first' (Chapter 2) includes both the need to understand what aspects of service a particular customer values and the need to serve customers in different ways. *Cost-to-serve* (CTS) is defined (Guerreiro et al., 2008) as:

the cost of the administrative, commercial and logistics activities related to customer service delivery, as measured through ABC methodology.

Identical manufactured products may be distributed in many different ways, each of which affects CTS. Examples of factors that may influence CTS are:

- Distribution channel used (for example, wholesalers, supermarkets, hypermarkets - see Case study 2.2).
- Delivery frequency (for routinely planned replenishment deliveries - daily, weekly, etc.).
- Customised deliveries (requiring special planning).
- Promotional activity (for example promotions, especially those associated with seasonal events, such as Valentine's Day, require additional display aids to be distributed to retail customers and the associated seasonal products are subjected to high, yet unpredictable, demand).
- Contractual terms used (for example, pricing by full truck loads, full pallet loads, pallet layers).

Recognising and allocating these costs to specific products and customers means rebalancing total costs better to reflect the actual CTS (Braithwaite and Samakh, 1998). Thus a CTS analysis enables a focal firm to assess the profitably of serving individual customer accounts, and distribution channels, with current supply chain design and customer service systems.

Results of rebalancing total costs on customer profitability - made on the basis of profit margin after CTS - can be astonishing, as shown by Figure 3.10. In place of

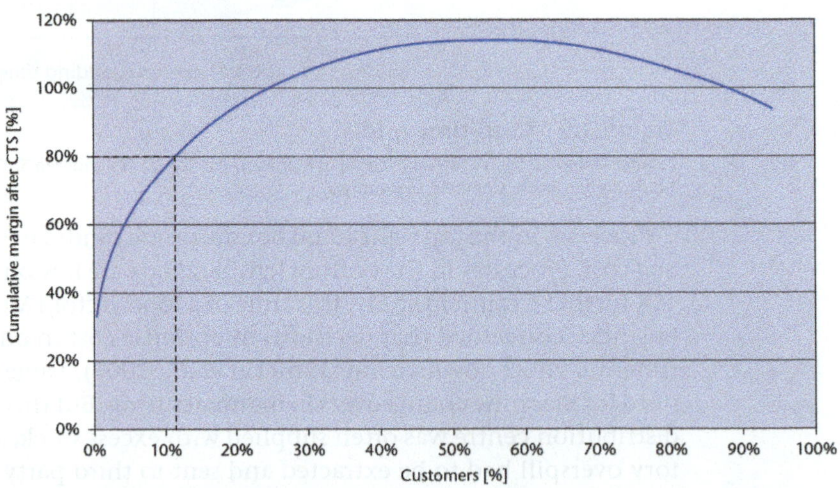

Figure 3.10 Customer profitability curve.

(Source: Adapted from Guerreiro et al., 2008.)

the traditional Pareto curve, a 'whale curve' may result, where profits are generated by 50 per cent of the customer base, and the other 50 per cent of customers are currently unprofitable. Further, a shocking 80 per cent of the final cumulative margin (shown as 100 per cent on the chart) comes from only 12 per cent of customers (Cooper and Kaplan, 1988; Guerreiro et al., 2008).

This reveals a large proportion of loss-making customers for this Brazilian food business. Axing the loss-making customers needs to be undertaken with great care, because 'a significant proportion of service activity costs are fixed costs' (Guerreiro et al., 2008). Such action would remove the contribution that these customers provide, thus reducing the profit margins of the remaining customers. Rather, knowledge of the causes of higher and lower margins and of relatively high CTS costs for certain customers has implications including:

- service terms and conditions for unprofitable accounts need to be changed, and converted into profitable alternatives;
- if this is not possible, prices should be increased for unprofitable customers, or they should be removed gradually from the focal firm's sales portfolio altogether;
- the most valuable customers may need more attention, by focusing more customer service efforts on these customers. After all, it would be profitable to grow sales with these customers.

Most importantly, CTS enables focal firms to link supply chain efforts to customer value and market opportunity in a way that improves customer relations and revenues in a profitable manner. CTS shows that outbound logistics contribute significantly to profitability, and it enables a firm to identify the most profitable growth opportunities and, equally, where rationalisation of product mix might be required.

Commonly companies generate growth in revenue through the introduction of new products. This leads to a broadening and proliferation of the product range with more variants being added. The marketing function argue that this will meet the needs of more customers and thus lead to growth in the market share. However, from a supply chain perspective, increasing the number of variants leads to an increase in CTS and a reduction in profit margins for many of the products. Cost increases are often in purchasing, inventory, manufacturing and distribution, driven by increased variety at every stage. Indeed companies can find that large proportions of their products can become unprofitable. One such company found that the bottom 40 per cent of its products generated less than 5 per cent of revenue, and the bottom 20 per cent of its products were highly unprofitable. One approach to addressing this is to measure CTS and revenue by SKU and establish a cross functional team (sales, marketing, finance and supply chain) to review the SKU profitability against targets. Where SKUs are underperforming, specific actions are determined such as discontinuation, substitution or increasing distribution to drive higher sales. However, discontinuation and rationalising the product range is an approach to be used with caution, as key customers accounting for high proportions of revenue may care about these products and eliminating them from the range will damage the customer relationship.

An understanding of activity-based costing approaches and ROCE (Section 3.2) is necessary before addressing the important subject of capital investment decisions. This is critical to a company's long-term financial performance and is addressed in the next section.

3.7 How can capital investment decisions be made?

***Key issue:* How can capital investment decisions be made by taking into account the subsequent cash flows, which dictate future liquidity of the company?**

Supply chains typically require high capital investment in fixed assets, now known as non-current assets, such as manufacturing facilities and equipment, distribution centres and vehicle fleets. These non-current assets are distinct from current assets in that they are 'tangible or intangible assets, acquired for retention by an entity [such as a company] for the purpose of providing a service to the entity and not held for resale in the normal course of trading' (CIMA, 2005). In other words, unlike current assets, they are retained by the company and are not sold. Typically, companies aim to minimise investment in non-current assets (possibly by outsourcing non-core activities) as a way to improve ROCE (as discussed in Section 3.2). Yet the key point is making the right investment decisions that ensure that non-current assets generate good rates of returns to the company and improve its profitability. In the words of Hussey (1989, p. 196):

> **When management is considering the investment of a large sum of money over a number of years, the fundamental objective is to ensure that the total monies received over time are higher than the amount of the original investment.**

Moreover, as a supply chain manager it is important to be able to influence the board of directors' investment decisions using investment appraisal methods, which show the likely impact on profitability and liquidity of the company. Typically, there are three factors that need to be considered when conducting an investment appraisal (Lucey 1990, 302):

- the investor's beliefs about the future;
- the alternatives available in which to invest;
- the investor's attitude to risk.

3.7.1 Four investment appraisal approaches

There are a number of investment appraisal approaches, and four key approaches are listed in Table 3.9. They are all focused on profitability, except for payback period, which is concerned with liquidity (or cash flow). Also, it is important to understand that, whilst the first two approaches (cost benefit analysis and payback period) do *not* take into account the 'time value' of money, the latter two approaches *do*, using the idea of 'discounted cash flows', which we will address in the next subsection. This is an important concept because we all know that cash can earn interest in the bank, which is not possible if it is invested in fixed assets.

A definition of each approach quoted from the Chartered Institute of Management Accountancy (CIMA, 2005) is provided in Table 3.10 and an illustration of their application to a supply chain investment appraisal is in Case study 3.6. The

Table 3.9 **Four investment appraisal approaches.**

Investment appraisal approach	Definitions (CIMA, 2005)*	Focus	Time value of money
Cost benefit analysis	Comparison between the cost of the resources used plus any other costs imposed by an activity (for example, pollution, environmental damage) and the value of the financial and non-financial benefits	Profitability	Not taken into account
Payback period	Time required for the cash inflows from a capital investment project to equal the cash outflows	Liquidity (cash flow)	Not taken into account
Net present value (NPV)	Difference between the sum of the projected discounted cash inflows and outflows attributable to a capital investment or other long-term project	Profitability over time	Discounted cash flows used
Internal rate of return (IRR)	Annual percentage return achieved by a project, at which the sum of the discounted cash inflows over the life of the project is equal to the sum of the discounted cash outflows	Profitability	Discounted cash flows used

*Based on CIMA (2005) Management Accounting, Official Terminology. London: CIMA

cost benefit analysis is often the initial assessment of an investment and simply involves collecting all the costs of a proposed investment and comparing them to all the benefits (in terms of cash inflows or savings) and, if the benefits are greater than the costs, it is considered to be a good investment.

The payback period measures the time it takes for a proposed investment to generate cash that equates to the original cost, and the proposal with the shortest payback period is normally the one that is accepted. This approach is concerned with liquidity (cash flows) and minimising risk, rather than profitability because, after the payback period, the cash flows (and their timing) are not taken into consideration.

3.7.2 What are discounted cash flows?

As mentioned earlier, both net present value (NPV) and internal rate of return (IRR) take into account the time value of money by using discounted cash flows. According to Hussey (1989, p. 199) 'this is done by converting future cash flows from the project into equivalent values as at the present time, usually by using discount tables'. This is taking into account the so-called 'opportunity cost', which is the lost cash inflow, that could have been gained from simply investing the capital in a bank and generating interest of say 5 per cent, as illustrated in Figure 3.11. According to Drury (2004, p. 496), 'a firm should invest in capital projects only if they yield a return in excess of the opportunity cost of the investment', in other words, if they generate a greater return than simply putting the cash in a bank.

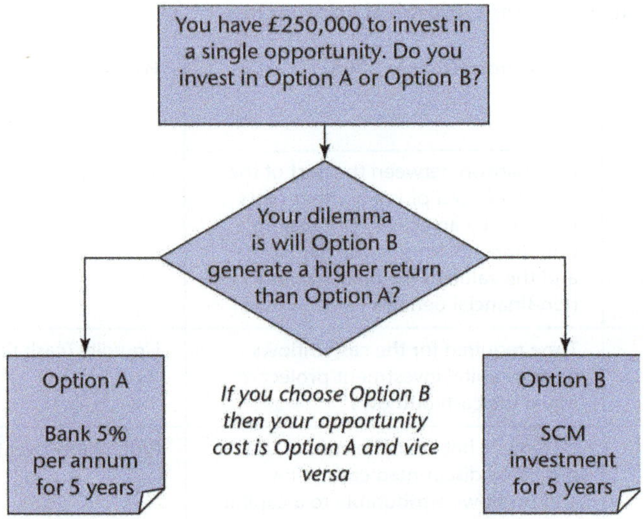

Figure 3.11 Investment decision considerations taking into account opportunity cost.
(Source: Dr Simon Templar, Cranfield School of Management.)

Net present value (NPV) is 'a method of evaluating capital projects by selecting a discount rate to express future cash flows in present-day monetary terms' (Hussey, 1989, p. 209). The discount rate is the rate of interest you could be expected to earn if you did not invest in the project and is called the 'test discount rate' because it tests if this is a good investment. There are three main factors that affect the discount rate (Atrill and McLaney, 2018):

- *interest forgone*: the interest the capital won't earn from, say being deposited in a bank;
- *risk premium*: some investments are higher risk than others. For instance, investing in manufacturing equipment to produce a new range of products, where the demand is highly uncertain, is a greater risk than the case where the products produced are mature with far more accurate sales forecasts. Where the risk is higher, a higher rate of return would be expected to compensate for the increased risk of not getting the expected returns;
- *inflation*: due to inflation in a given country, money devalues each year. However, if both the capital investment (cash outflow) and the returns (cash inflow) are subject to the same rate of inflation, this can be ignored.

Present value curves are available that apply discount rates, in a compound fashion (year on year), examples of which are shown in Figure 3.14. The present value curves for 10 per cent, 30 per cent and 50 per cent discount rates show that, the longer the period of the investment, and/or the higher the discount rate, the lower the present value.

Using the present value curves in Figure 3.12 we can determine how much £1,000 is worth in five years' time by drawing a vertical line up from five years and reading off the present value, which gives a discount factor. We have done this for 10 per cent and 30 per cent in Table 3.10.

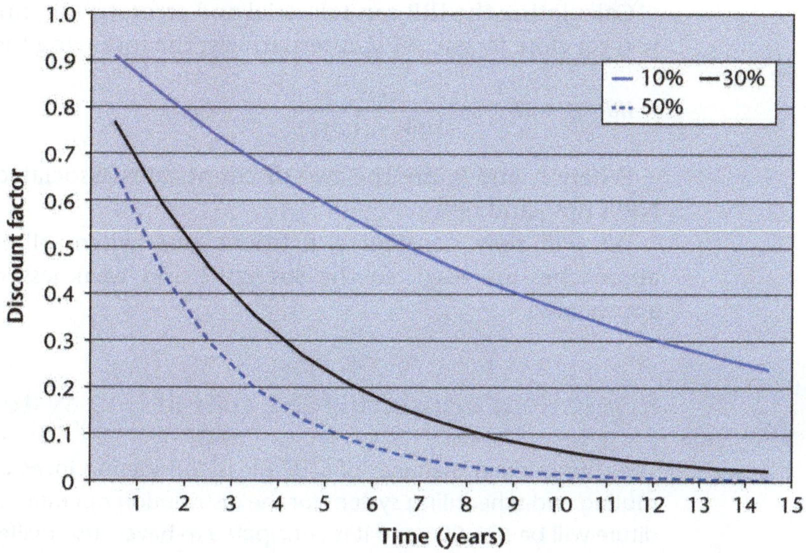

Figure 3.12 Present value curves for 10 per cent, 30 per cent and 50 per cent discount rates.

(Source: Dr Simon Templar, Cranfield School of Management.)

Table 3.10 The present value of £1,000 in five years using 10 per cent and 30 per cent discount rates.

Discount rate	Discount factor	Present value
10%	0.621	£621
30%	0.269	£269

To calculate net present value, both the initial cash outflow for the investment, and the subsequent cash inflows of the returns, must be at present value to enable the calculation of the net present value of cash flows over the life of the asset, as shown in Case study 3.6.

There are three outcomes for net present value (Francis, 1986, p. 302):

- If the NPV is positive it should be accepted.
- If it is zero the investment breaks even.
- If the NPV is negative then the investment should be rejected.

However, where the risk level is difficult to judge, as in Case study 3.6, then it is useful to determine at what discount rate the NPV is zero and therefore the investment is break-even. This is exactly what the internal rate of return (IRR) is, according to Atrill and McLaney (2012, p. 368):

> **The IRR of a particular investment is the discount rate that, when applied to its future cash flows, will produce a NPV of zero. In essence, it represents the yield from an investment opportunity.**

Calculating the IRR can take trial and error, trying different discount rates until you get close to zero NPV. Alternatively, the following formula can be used:

$$IRR = i_1 + \left[(i_2 - i_1) * \frac{npv_1}{npv_1 - (npv_2)} \right]$$

Where i_1 and i_2 are the two discount rates associated with the corresponding NPVs npv_1 and npv_2.

We will now consider a fictitious case where all four investment appraisal approaches are used, so the strengths and weakness of each approach can be appreciated.

CASE STUDY 3.7

Investment appraisal for a scheduling system at OTIF plc

The supply chain manager of OTIF plc is considering investment into a computerised routing and scheduling system for the distribution operation. The initial capital expenditure will be £25,000 and it is anticipated to have a useful life of five years. Four investment appraisal approaches are used to determine if this is a good investment.

Cost benefit analysis

It is anticipated that the new system will generate the cash savings shown in Table 3.11 by reducing distribution operating costs, associated with fuel consumption, tyre replacement and vehicle maintenance.

Table 3.11 Cash flows associated with the system investment over its five-year life.

Year	0	1	2	3	4	5	Total
Cash flows (£)	(25,000)	8,750	8,250	8,000	7,500	7,000	14,500
Cumulative cash flows (£)	(25,000)	(16,250)	(8,000)	0	7,500	14,500	

Note: the brackets indicate a negative cash outflow from the company

Payback period

The cumulative cash flows shown in Table 3.12 demonstrate that after three years the initial capital investment has been paid back by the cash savings each year.

Net present value

First OTIF plc needs to determine the discount rate appropriate for the £25,000 investment in the routing and scheduling system. Inflation was ignored because the same rate applied to both the investment and the returns, so the inflation effect is cancelled out. The company's cost of capital (equivalent to the bank rate) was 10 per cent, therefore it was decided to try discount rates of both 10 per cent and 20 per cent. These are applied to the cash flows for the system investment to give the net present values shown in Table 3.12.

Table 3.12 The NPV for the system investment based on 10 per cent and 20 per cent discount rates.

Year	Cash flows (£)	Discount factor based on 10%	PV for 10% discount rate (£)	Discount factor based on 20%	PV for 20% discount rate (£)
0	(25,000)	1.0000	−25,000	1.0000	−25,000
1	8,750	0.9091	7,955	0.8333	7,291
2	8,250	0.8264	6,818	0.6944	5,729
3	8,000	0.7513	6,010	0.5787	4,630
4	7,500	0.6830	5,123	0.4823	3,617
5	7,000	0.6209	4,346	0.4019	2,813
Total	14,500		5,252		(920)

The cost benefit analysis shows that the total cash benefit is £14,500, so it would appear to be a good investment.

The discount rate of 10 per cent gives a positive NPV of £5,252, whilst the 20 per cent discount rate produces a negative NPV of £920. The question arises at what discount rate the NPV zero is and therefore when the investment is break-even. The internal rate of return is the answer.

Internal rate of return (IRR)

The IRR can be approximated by plotting the graph shown in Figure 3.13.

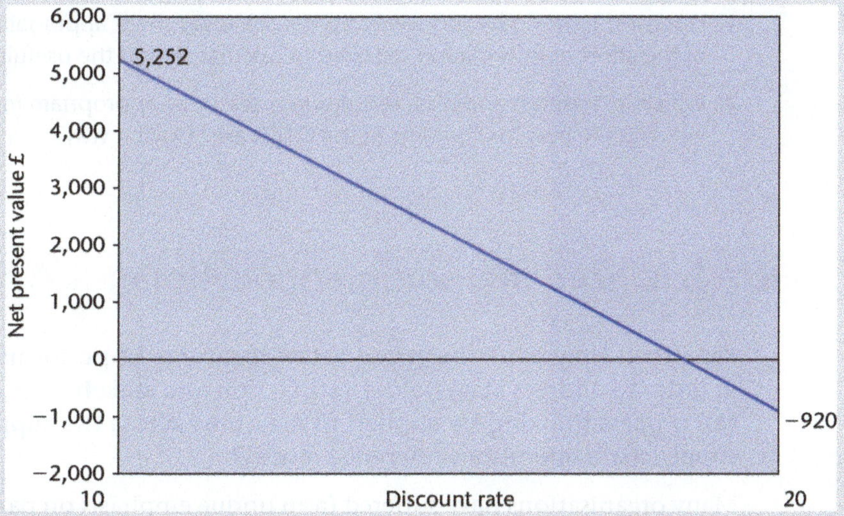

Figure 3.13 Graphical approach to calculating IRR for the OTIF investment.

However, this graph assumes a linear relationship between discount rate and NPV, which isn't the case; hence this gives only an approximate IRR. To calculate the IRR, the formula previously stated can be used:

$$\text{IRR} = 10 + [10 * (5,252/(5,2522 - -920))$$
$$= 18.51\%$$

Note: Two minuses make a plus

This produces a similar result to the graphical approach.

Summary of results

The results from the four investment appraisal approaches, see Table 3.13, suggest that the proposed investment in a routeing and scheduling system is a good investment. However, these figures do depend on the accuracy of the forecast cash savings that the system is expected to bring.

Table 3.13 Summary of the results from the four investment appraisal approaches.

Investment appraisal method	OTIF results
Cost benefit analysis	£14,500
Payback period	3 years
Net present value at 10% discounted rate	£5,252
Internal rate of return	18.51%

(Source: Dr Simon Templar, Cranfield School of Management.)

Questions

1. Discuss the strengths and weakness of each investment appraisal approach in terms of the effort or information required to calculate it and the usefulness of the results.
2. Which investment appraisal technique is the most appropriate for profitability, and which is the best for liquidity, in the OTIF case? Explain why.

3.8 A balanced measurement portfolio

Key issues: **How can a balanced set of measures of performance be developed in order to address stakeholder satisfaction and stakeholder contribution? How can process thinking be applied to measures across the supply chain using the supply chain operations reference model?**

Many organisations have suffered from undue emphasis on particular measures of performance within the firm. For example, a preoccupation with labour productivity may lead to excessive stocks of inbound parts ('do not run out of raw materials otherwise bonuses will suffer'). Such a preoccupation may also lead to excessive stocks of outbound products, because the most important priority is to keep workers busy, whether the product can be sold or not. Whilst this priority may be good for productivity, it may well disrupt flow in the supply network: inbound parts are ordered too early, and outbound products are made too early. What is good for one measure (productivity in this case) is bad for others (inventories and material flow).

In reality, management today is faced with the challenge of performing across a whole range of objectives. Different groups of stakeholders in a firm include shareholders, employees, customers, suppliers, the local community and government. This is not a comprehensive list, and industries such as pharmaceuticals have other important stakeholders, including regulators, such as the Drug Enforcement Agency. The challenge for the directors of a firm is to *balance* the diverse interests of these groups of stakeholders. We review the interests of each group in turn:

- *Shareholders* typically have a passing interest in a firm in which they invest. They will keep their shareholding as long as it provides a return that is competitive with other investments. Shareholders are impressed by high dividends and share appreciation resulting from profitability and growth of the business. Failure to deliver adequate returns often turns shareholders against the management of the day.
- *Employees* often have a long-term commitment to a firm, and are concerned with employment stability, competitive wages and job satisfaction. Failure to deliver on such goals may create negative reactions, such as loss of motivation and loyalty, difficulty in recruitment, and various forms of industrial action.
- *Customers* are, in theory, the most important stakeholders in a free market economy. It is their demand that draws material through the supply network. Customers can choose from whom they buy, and failure to keep them satisfied creates the risk of loss of business.
- *Suppliers* are interested in such benefits as long-term business, involvement in new product development and, of course, payment on time. Failure to meet such benefits leads to sanctions such as disruption of supply and higher prices.
- *Local community*. Here, the interests are in the firm as a local employer, with a reputation for civic responsibility and long-term commitment to the region as an employer and as a ratepayer. Failure to deliver against such interests may lead to environmental disputes and difficulty in obtaining planning permission.
- *Government* is interested in the firm as a contributor to employment and value creation in the economy, and as a source of revenues. Failure to meet government laws, on the other hand, may lead to prosecution or even closure of the business.

Thus, the directors of a business are faced with the need to manage the potentially conflicting interests of the stakeholders, keeping each within what Doyle (1994) refers to as a *tolerance zone*. Each stakeholder has a limit beyond which the risk of disruption to the business increases rapidly. An upper limit exists as well. For example, a preoccupation with profits may please shareholders for the time being, but may result in negatives from labour exploitation and low levels of investment. Whilst bumper profits appear in year one, these are rapidly eroded as the negatives cut in during later years. In the end, the whole business suffers. And customers can disrupt the business too: a preoccupation with customers at the expense of everything else can lead to shrinking margins and loss of focus. The challenge for the directors is to keep all stakeholders just satisfied, keeping each within the tolerance zone.

3.8.1 Balanced scorecard

Whilst balance between stakeholders is one issue, another is the balance between financial and non-financial (or operational) measures of performance, and between history and the future. Kaplan and Norton (1996) point to the shortcomings of traditional cost accounting systems. Traditional systems are geared to the needs of the stock market, and essentially are historical and financial in emphasis. Modern systems, they argue, need to balance performance measures across four perspectives: financial, customer, internal business and learning and growth, defining objectives, measures, targets and initiatives as shown in Figure 3.14.

Kaplan and Norton also suggest that the scorecard should be informed by the company's strategy using a four-stage strategy process:

Stage 1: Translating the vision: Clarifying the vision and gaining consensus

Stage 2: Communicating and Linking: Educating, setting goals and linking rewards to performance measures

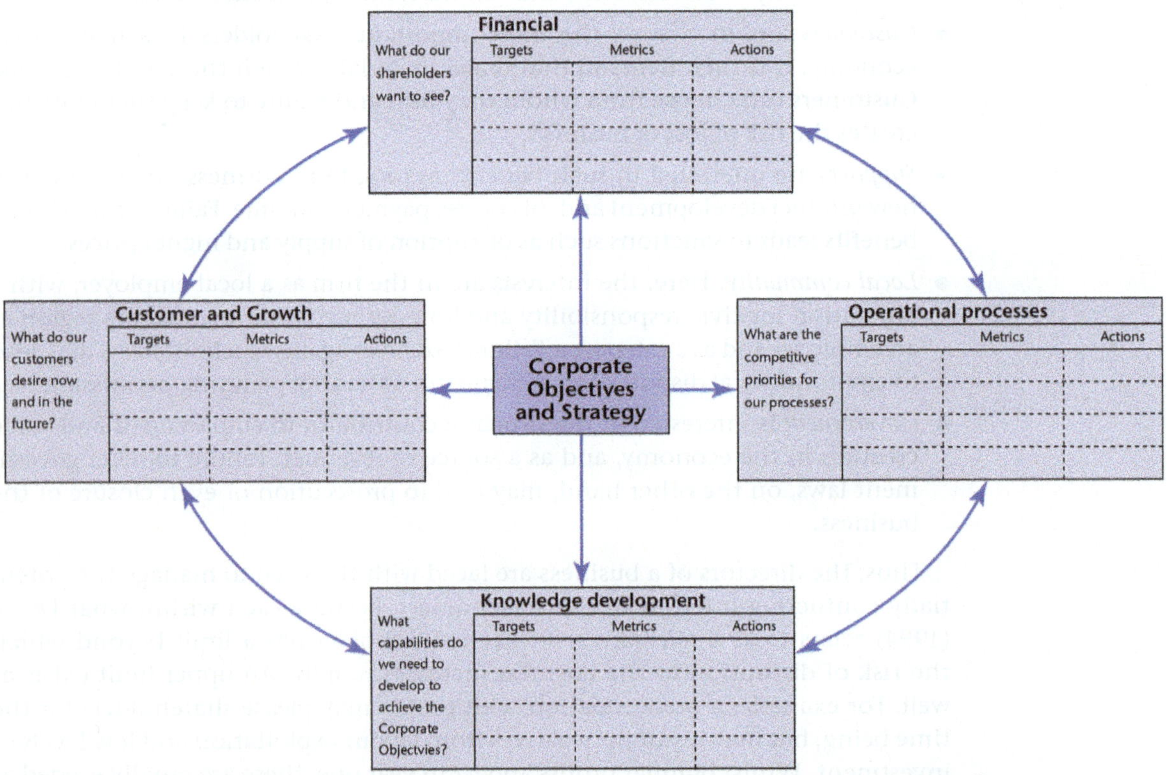

Figure 3.14 Balanced scorecard as a strategic management system.

Stage 3: Business Planning: Setting targets, aligning strategic initiatives, allocating resources and establishing milestones

Stage 4: Feedback and learning: Articulating the shared vision, supplying strategic feedback and facilitating strategy review and learning.

Used in this way the scorecard addresses a serious deficiency in traditional management system: their inability to link a company's long-term strategy with its short term actions.

While the scorecard has been widely embraced by organisations and remains largely unchanged today, it has received criticism that it is focused on commercial organisations concerned with return on investment. Non-profit organisations may therefore consider other approaches. This may include the UN's (2024) Results Based Budgets (RBB), a performance framework first introduced in 2017/18 for peacekeeping missions and service centres, which is a scorecard based on 15 performance indicators.

3.8.2 Supply chain management and the balanced scorecard

Extending the balanced scorecard into the context of the supply chain, Brewer and Speh (2000) consider that performance measurement systems must be aligned to supply chain practices:

> **If firms talk about the importance of supply chain concepts, but continue to evaluate employees using performance measures that are . . . unaffected by supply chain improvements, then they will fail in their supply chain endeavours.**

Traditional performance measurements within a focal firm have a number of significant deficiencies. They track individual activities often within functions: this can promote the optimisation of the function rather than of the supply network as a whole.

As a general rule, effective cross-supply chain measures should have the following characteristics (Derocher and Kilpatrick, 2000):

- be simple to understand;
- total no more than 10;
- be representative of a significant causal relationship;
- have an associated target;
- be capable of being shared across the supply chain.

The following are eight such measures, which can be adapted to focus on specific sectors:

- *on time in full, outbound:* a measure of customer orders fulfilled, complete and on time, conforming to specification;
- *on time in full, inbound:* a measure of supplier deliveries received, complete and on time, conforming to specification;
- *internal defect rates:* a measure of process conformance and control (rather than inspection);
- *new product introduction rate:* a measure of supply chain responsiveness to new product introduction;

- *cost reduction:* a measure of sustainable product and process improvement;
- *stock turns:* a measure of supply chain goods flow. This measure is useful when applied to supply chains focused on segments: as a 'blanket' measure, it can be misleading;
- *order to delivery lead time:* a measure of supply chain process responsiveness;
- *financial flexibility:* a measure of how easy it is to structure the supply chain for financial advantage (with international supply chains, channelling operations through low-tax locations for purposes of gaining supply chain cost benefits should be considered).

The main benefits of these measures are that they can be applied to all partners in a supply chain, and thereby can help to improve visibility and control *between* partners, as well as *within* a focal firm. The challenge is especially tough when there are many operating units in a large, decentralised organisation. ***Tesco*** provides an example of the communication needed by means of its 'corporate store steering wheel' (shown in Figure 3.15). Case study 1.1 describes the sheer scale of the Tesco operation – manned by some 330,000 employees across around 4,500 stores. How

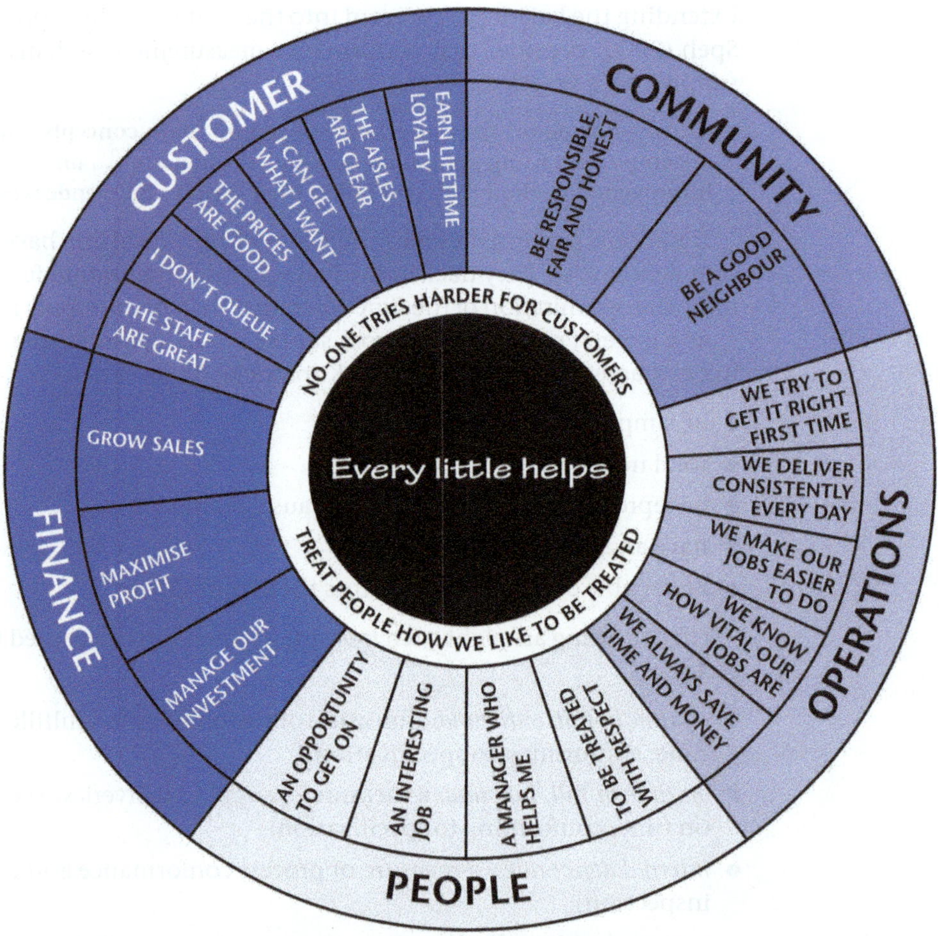

Figure 3.15 Tesco's corporate store steering wheel.

do you keep so many people in such a large organisation 'facing the same direction' – that is, pursuing corporate strategy consistently? Tesco's answer had been to focus on 20 measures across 5 key stakeholders – customer, finance, people, operations and community. The then CEO Sir Terry Leahy said at the time, 'The Steering Wheel creates a shared language, a shared way of thinking and a common blue print for action.' The Steering Wheel was used to measure performance right across the organisation, from leaders in the head office to shop floor workers. Stores also had their own 'local' Steering Wheels, designed to help engage frontline workers in corporate objectives.

However, after almost 20 years of using the Steering Wheel, in 2015 ***Tesco*** CEO Dave Lewis found the old Balanced Scorecard, (The Steering Wheel), too complex for staff to handle, with more than 40 different metrics and instead launching 'The Big Six', a new set of principles he believes are more focused for staff – a more simplified and focused scorecard (Quinn, 2015). Keeping the right balance between perfect balanced measures and clarity of purpose is at the heart of the challenge of implementing a good Balanced Scorecard. 'The Big Six' measures are:

- ***Sales:*** increasing volume is key to the success of the business model.
- ***Operating profit:*** this depends on building more value into the Tesco offer.
- ***Operating cash flow:*** strong cash flow is needed to keep the business running and for reinvestment.
- ***Customers recommend us and come back time and again:*** by putting customers first and making them the main focus, more shoppers will choose to shop at Tesco.
- ***Colleagues recommend us as a great place to work and shop:*** colleagues are focused on serving shoppers a little better every day.
- ***We build trusted partnerships:*** simplified relationships with suppliers aiming for improved supplier satisfaction.

So, the idea is to drive greater focus on what needs to be done, but leave colleagues more freedom on how they contribute to those goals.

3.8.3 Supply chain operations reference model (SCOR)

The previous two sections consider the balanced scorecard which can be used within any organisation. This section reviews a model that places a focal firm in the context of the supply chain. In order to help companies to understand their supply chain performance and opportunities for improvement, a cross-industry framework has been developed by the APICS Supply Chain Council (SCC, 2018).

This section gives an introduction to the Supply Chain Operations Reference (SCOR) model based on publicly available material. To obtain detailed benchmarking data from the model, your organisation would need to become an affiliate of the APICS SCC.

SCOR is founded on five distinct management processes. The supply chain is viewed in terms of overlapping management processes – source, make, deliver and return – within an integrated planning framework that encompasses all of the organisations in the chain, as shown in Figure 3.16. It is a process-based version of Figure 1.1 in Chapter 1. The management processes of the 'focal firm' are seen as linked with corresponding processes within supplier and customer organisations. However, SCOR does not describe every business process or activity. It does not address sales and marketing, research and technology development, or product development and SCOR assumes, but does not specifically address, quality, information technology, or administration. The five distinct management processes covered by SCOR can be described as follows:

- *Plan:* the tasks of planning demand and supply set within an overall planning system that covers activities such as long-term capacity and resource planning.
- *Source:* the task of material acquisition, set within an overall sourcing system that includes activities such as vendor certification and vendor contracting.
- *Make:* the task of production execution, set within an overall production system that includes activities such as shop scheduling. Any added value activity (e.g. material repackaging at a distribution centre; quality control at a production line) falls under this process type as well.
- *Deliver:* the day-to-day tasks of managing demand, orders, warehouse and transportation, and installation and commissioning. These tasks are set within an overall delivery management system that includes order rules and management of delivery quantities.
- *Return:* the return of non-conforming goods for replacement or rectification, and the recycling of materials no longer needed by the customer.

There are three levels to the SCOR model and at each level both processes and metrics are defined with each level providing a breakdown of the level immediately above:

- *Level 1:* a broad definition of the plan, source, make, deliver and return management processes, which is used to set competitive objectives.
- *Level 2:* defines core process categories that are possible scenarios of a supply chain (e.g. make to stock, make to order, engineer to order).

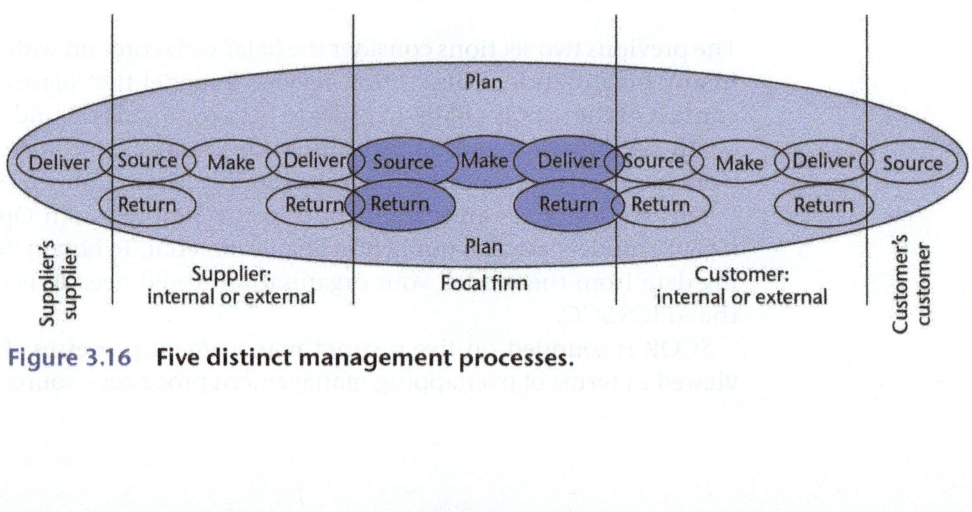

Figure 3.16 Five distinct management processes.

- *Level 3:* provides the process breakdown needed to describe each element that comprises the level 2 categories. Detailed performance metrics are set at this level.

At level 1 there are 10 metrics which contribute to delivering 5 attributes, three of which are customer facing (reliability, responsiveness and agility) and two are internally facing (cost and assets). An attribute itself cannot be measured; it is used to set strategic direction. The 10 level 1 metrics are as follows:

1. Perfect order fulfilment contributing to RELIABILITY
2. Order fulfilment cycle time contributing to RESPONSIVENESS
3. Upside supply chain flexibility contributing to AGILITY
4. Upside supply chain adaptability contributing to AGILITY
5. Downside supply chain adaptability contributing to AGILITY
6. Overall value at risk (VAR) contributing to AGILITY
7. Total cost to serve contributing to COST
8. Cash-to-cash cycle time contributing to ASSETS
9. Return on supply chain fixed assets contributing to ASSETS
10. Return on working capital contributing to ASSETS

The intention is that an individual company should not attempt to be 'best in class' in all areas. Rather, a given company should target its strength to create differentiation in the marketplace. For example, one product may need to be best in class for reliability, while another may need to be best in class for responsiveness. Metrics measure the ability of a supply chain to achieve these strategic attributes.

SCOR identifies five core supply chain performance attributes: reliability, responsiveness, agility, costs and asset management. Consideration of these attributes makes it possible to compare an organisation that strategically chooses to be the low-cost provider against one that chooses to compete on reliability:

- *The reliability attribute* addresses the ability to perform tasks as expected. Reliability focuses on the predictability of the outcome of a process.
- *The responsiveness attribute* describes the speed at which tasks are performed.
- *The agility attribute* describes the ability to respond to external influences and the ability to change. External influences include: Non-forecasted increases or decreases in demand; suppliers or partners going out of business; natural disasters; acts of (cyber) terrorism; availability of financial tools (the economy); or labour issues.
- *The cost attribute* describes the cost of operating the process. It includes labour costs, material costs, and transportation costs.
- *The asset management efficiency ('assets') attribute* describes an organisation's ability to utilise assets efficiently. Asset management strategies in a supply chain include inventory reduction and in-sourcing v. outsourcing.

A metric is a standard for measurement of the performance of a process. SCOR recognises three levels of predefined metrics and their function to diagnose low performance:

- *Level 1 metrics* are diagnostics for the overall health of the supply chain and are known as key performance indicators (KPIs). Benchmarking level 1 metrics helps establish realistic targets that support strategic objectives.
- *Level 2 metrics* serve as diagnostics for the level 1 metrics and therefore help to identify the root cause or causes of a performance gap for a level 1 metric.
- *Level 3 metrics* serve as diagnostics for level 2 metrics.

To illustrate the hierarchical and diagnostic nature of the SCOR metrics, the three levels of metrics for Supply Chain Reliability are as follows:

RL.1.1 – Perfect Order Fulfilment

RL2.1 – Percentage of Orders Delivered in Full

RL.3.33 – Delivery Item Accuracy

RL.3.35 – Delivery Quantity Accuracy

RL.2.2 – Delivery Performance to Customer Commit Date

RL.3.32 – Customer Commit Date Achievement Time Customer Receiving

RL.3.34 – Delivery Location Accuracy

RL.2.3 – Documentation Accuracy

RL.3.31 – Compliance Documentation Accuracy

RL.3.43 – Other Required Documentation Accuracy

RL.3.45 – Payment Documentation Accuracy

RL.3.50 – Shipping Documentation Accuracy

RL.2.4 – Perfect Condition

RL.3.12 – Percentage of Faultless Installations

RL.3.24 – Percentage of Orders/Lines Received Damage Free

RL.3.41 – Orders Delivered Damage Free Conformance

RL.3.42 – Orders Delivered Defect Free Conformance

RL.3.55 – Warranty and Returns

Participating companies in the Supply Chain Council may obtain benchmarking information on how their organisation's performance compares with others. In order to illustrate how such concepts could be applied in practice, Table 3.14 shows actual performance against the SCOR level 1 metrics for a given company. It also shows how those metrics compared with the SCOR database in terms of what was needed to achieve parity with the 'competitive population', what was needed to gain advantage and what was needed to show superior performance. Where is this supply chain positioned in terms of its competitive performance?

Table 3.14 **Supply chain performance evaluated within the context of the competitive environment.**

	Supply chain scorecard v. 3.0			Performance v. competitive population		
	Overview metrics	**SCOR level 1 metrics** Delivery performance to commit date	**Actual** 50%	**Parity** 85%	**Advantage** 90%	**Superior** 95%
CUSTOMER FACING	**Supply chain reliability**	Fill rates Perfect order fulfilment (on time in full) Order fulfilment lead times (customer to customer)	63% 0% 7 days	94% 80% 7 days	96% 85% 5 days	98% 90% 3 days
	Flexibility and responsiveness	Production flexibility (days master schedule fixed)	45 days	30 days	25 days	20 days
INTERNAL FACING	**Cost**	Total logistics management costs as % of revenues Warranty cost, returns and allowances Value-added per-employee productivity	19% NA $122K	13% NA $156K	8% NA $306K	3% NA $460K
	Assets	Inventory days of supply Cash-to-cash cycle time Net asset turns (working capital)	119 days 196 days 2.2 turns	55 days 80 days 8 turns	38 days 46 days 12 turns	22 days 19 turns 28 days

Not very well, it seems! *All* of the level 1 metrics are below parity, with the exception of order fulfilment lead times. External metrics, such as delivery performance and perfect order fulfilment, are seriously adrift. Production flexibility is way behind the competitive population, suggesting that the master schedule is 'fixed' for too long a period – and no doubt there will be underlying causes of that. Internal measures are not in good shape either, with a poor cost performance and a seriously uncompetitive asset utilisation record. The model associates level 2 and 3 process elements to the various metrics, so that, once the worst performing metrics have been identified, the user has an indication of what are the processes to look after in order to reduce the gap.

Summary

What is 'value' in the context of the supply chain?

- The delivery of customer and shareholder value needs to be balanced. They may each reinforce the other, but supply chain management must understand how it impacts these values.
- Return on capital employed (ROCE) is a widely used method for measuring shareholder value. ROCE encourages logistics management to control costs, working capital and fixed (non-current) assets.
- Logistics increasingly is concerned with funds flow as well as material flow and information flow (Chapter 1). Cash flow in terms of liquidity is important to the survival of any company and supply chain management should seek to balance the objectives of profitability, liquidity and asset utilisation.
- Traditional cost accounting is unhelpful in making logistics-related decisions because it is insensitive to processes and cost drivers. Traditional cost accounting tends to understate profits on high-volume products and overstate profits on low-volume/high-variety products.

How can logistics costs be better represented and capital investment decisions be made?

- Logistics costs can be better described by using a variety of methods of allocating costs to products. The purpose of such a variety of allocations is to gain better information about the cost base of logistics operations, and hence to take better decisions. For example, direct product profitability (DPP) attempts to allocate logistics costs more specifically to products by considering how they use fixed resources. Activity-based costing (ABC) seeks to understand what factors drive costs, and how costs are incurred by logistics processes that span the organisation – and the supply chain in general. It is, essentially, a process-based view of costing, and again seeks to enhance the quality of logistics decision making. Cost-to-serve (CTS) is an extension of ABC thinking that seeks to identify how distribution and service costs vary between customers.
- Supply chains typically require high capital investment in non-current (fixed) assets, such as manufacturing facilities and equipment, distribution centres and vehicle fleets. Typically, companies aim to minimise investment in non-current assets (possibly by outsourcing non-core activities) as a way to improve ROCE, yet the key point is making the right investment decisions that ensure that non-current assets generate good rates of returns to the company and improve its profitability. Approaches like net present value (NPV) allow the calculation of profitability over time, taking into account returns on alternative investment opportunities.
- Alone, financial measures that are rooted in the past are insufficient for taking logistics decisions in today's fast-moving environment. A balanced measurement portfolio is called for, one that takes into account the needs of different stakeholders in a business. A balanced measurement portfolio is extended into the supply chain by means of the supply chain operations reference model (SCOR).

Discussion questions

1. Explain what is meant by the term *value* in a supply chain. How can value best be measured in a supply chain context?
2. Discuss the ways in which a company might improve its ROCE.
3. What are the challenges and trade-offs for supply chain management in balancing the objectives of profitability, liquidity and asset utilisation?
4. Why are processes important in terms of managing logistics? Suggest how the processes of plan, source, make, deliver and return might differ in the case of the two factories Simple and Komplex, described in Section 3.5.
5. What are the advantages of cutting the 'total cost cube' in different ways? Summarise the different perspectives on logistics costs provided by fixed/variable, direct/indirect and engineered/discretionary costs, and by activity-based costing.
6. Suggest balanced measurement portfolios for the two factories Simple and Komplex, described in Section 3.5. In particular, suggest key performance measures in the areas of strategy, process and capability.

References

Ahluwalia, M.B. (2017) 'The business of pricing carbon', Center for Climate and Energy Solutions, accessed at https://www.c2es.org/wp-content/uploads/2017/09/business-pricing-carbon.pdf

APICS Case Study 'ExpressPoint adopts the SCOR model for strategic supply chain progress', at https://www.apics.org/apics-for-business/customer-stories/customer-profile-expresspoint

APICS Supply Chain Council (SCC, 2018), at http://www.apics.org/apics-for-business/frameworks/scor

Atrill, P. and McLaney, E. (2018) *Accounting and Finance for Non-Specialists*, 11th edn. Harlow: Pearson Education Ltd.

Ben-Amar, W., Gomes, M., Khursheed, H. and Marsat, S. (2022) 'Climate change exposure and internal carbon pricing adoption', *Business Strategy and the Environment*. https://doi.org/10.1002/BSE.3051

Bernon, M., Mena, C., Templar, S. and Whicker, L. (2003) 'Costing waste in supply chain processes: a European food drink industry case study', Proceedings of the 10th International EurOMA Conference, Cernobbio, Lake Como, June 2003, vol. 1, pp. 345–54.

Bicheno, J. (2005) *The New Lean Toolbox*. Buckingham: Picsie Books.

Bicheno, J. and Holweg, M. (2008) *The Lean Toolbox – The Essential Guide to Lean Transformation*, 4th edn. Buckingham: Picsie Books.

Braithwaite, A. and Samakh, E. (1998) 'The cost-to-serve method', *International Journal of Logistics Management*, vol. 9, no. 1, pp. 69–84.

Brewer, P.C. and Speh, T.W. (2000) 'Using the balanced scorecard to measure supply chain performance', *Journal of Business Logistics*, vol. 21, no. 1, pp. 75–93.

Buffet, W. (1994) 'Annual Report', Berkshire Hathaway Corporation.

Christopher, M. (2022) *Logistics and Supply Chain Management*, 6th edn. Harlow: Financial Times Prentice Hall.

CIMA (2005) *Management Accounting, Official Terminology*. London: CIMA.

Cleary, S and Willcott, N. (2023) 'Carbon pricing: necessary but not sufficient', Institute of Sustainable Finance, Smith School of Business, Queens University, Canada.

Cleland, A.S. and Bruno, A.V. (1997) 'Building customer and shareholder value', *Strategy & Leadership*, vol. 25, no. 3, pp. 22–8.

Cooper, R. and Kaplan, R.S. (1988) 'Measure costs right: make the right decisions', *Harvard Business Review*, September/October, pp. 96–105.

Copulsky, W. (1991) 'Balancing the needs of customers and shareholders', *Journal of Business Strategy*, vol. 12, no. 6, pp. 44–5.

Cornelius, I. and Davies, M. (1997) *Shareholder Value*. London: FT Financial Publishing.

Cosse, M. (2011) 'An Investigation into the Current Supply Chain Finance Practices in Business: A Case Study Approach'. Unpublished MSc thesis, Cranfield University.

Cranfield School of Management (2003) *The Route to SUCCESS: Project Managers Handbook*. Bedford: Cranfield University.

Dale, B.G. and Plunkett, J.J. (1995) *Quality Costing*, 2nd edn. London: Chapman & Hall.

van Damme, D.A. and van der Zon, F.L. (1999) 'Activity based costing and decision support', *International Journal of Logistics Management*, vol. 10, no. 1, pp. 71–82.

Derocher, R. and Kilpatrick, J. (2000) 'Six supply chain lessons for the new millennium', *Supply Chain Management Review*, vol. 3, no. 4, pp. 34–40.

Doyle, P. (1994) *Marketing Management and Strategy*. New York: Prentice Hall.

Drucker, P.F. (2001) 'What is our business?', *Executive Excellence*, vol. 18, no. 6, p. 3.

Drury, C. (2004) *Management and Cost Accounting*, 6th edn. London: Thomson Learning.

Feurer, R. and Chaharbaghi, K. (1994) 'Defining competitiveness: A holistic approach', *Management Decision*, vol. 32, no. 2, pp. 49–58.

Francis, A. (1986) *Business Mathematics and Statistics*. Eastleigh: DP Publications Ltd.

Frohlich, M.T. (2002) 'e-integration in the Supply Chain: Barriers and performance', *Decision Sciences*, vol. 33, no. 4, pp. 537–56.

Gelsomino, L.M., Mangiaracina, R., Perego, A. and Tumino, A. (2016) 'Supply chain finance: a literature review', *International Journal of Physical Distribution & Logistics Management*, vol. 46, iss. 4, pp. 348–66.

Global Supply Chain Finance Forum (2016) Standard Definitions for Techniques of Supply Chain Finance, at http://supplychainfinanceforum.org/ICC-Standard-Definitions-for-Techniques-of-Supply-Chain-Finance-Global-SCF-Forum-2016.pdf

Guerreiro, R., Rodrigues Bio, S. and Vasquez Villamor Merschmann, E. (2008) 'Cost-to-serve measurement and customer profitability analysis', *The International Journal of Logistics Management*, vol. 19, no. 3, pp. 389–407.

van Hoek, R. and Pegels, K. (2006) 'Growing by cutting SKUs at Clorox', *Harvard Business Review*, April.

Hofmann, E. and Belin, O. (2011) *Supply Chain Finance Solutions*, Springer Briefs in Business. Berlin: Springer.

Hussey, R. (1989) *Cost and Management Accounting*. Basingstoke: Macmillan Press.

Johnson, M. and Templar, S. (2011) 'The relationships between supply chain and firm performance: the development and testing of a unified proxy', *International Journal of Physical Distribution and Logistics Management*, vol. 41, no. 2, pp. 88–103.

Kaplan, R.S. and Norton, D.P. (1996) 'Using the balanced scorecard as a strategic management system', *Harvard Business Review*, January/February, pp. 75–85.

Kaplan, R.S. and Norton, D.P. (2004) 'The strategy map: guide to aligning intangible assets', *Strategy & Leadership*, vol. 32, no. 5, pp. 10–17.

Laitamäki, J. and Kordupleski, R. (1997) 'Building and deploying profitable growth strategies based on the waterfall of customer value added', *European Management Journal*, vol. 15, no. 2, pp. 158–66.Lindeberg, R. (2021) Volvo Cars CFO on Internal Carbon Pricing. YouTube. https://www.youtube.com/watch?v=O9T4oNpXKiU

Lucey, T. (1990) *Costing*, 3rd edn. London: DP Publications Ltd.

Microsoft (2022) 'How Microsoft is using an internal carbon fee to reach its carbon negative goal', 24th March 2022 accessed at https://www.microsoft.com/en-us/industry/blog/sustainability/2022/03/24/how-microsoft-is-using-an-internal-carbon-fee-to-reach-its-carbon-negative-goal/

Quinn, I. (2015) 'Dave Lewis ditches Tesco Steering Wheel in favour of Big Six', *The Grocer*, 17th April 2015.

Rappaport, A. (1987) 'Linking competitive strategy and shareholder value analysis', *Journal of Business Strategy*, vol. 7, no. 4, pp. 58–67.Riedel, F., Gorbach, G., & Kost, C. (2021) 'Barriers to internal carbon pricing in German companies', *Energy Policy*, 159, 112654. https://doi.org/10.1016/J.ENPOL.2021.112654

Skipworth, H, Godsell, J, Wong, C, Saghiri, S and Julien, D. (2015) 'Supply chain alignment for improved business performance: an empirical study', *Supply Chain Management: an International Journal*, vol. 20 no. 5, pp. 511–33.

SSAB (2021) 'Volvo Cars is first carmaker to explore fossil-free steel with SSAB', SSAB Newsroom, 16th June 2021, accessed at https://www.ssab.com/en-gb/news/2021/06/volvo-cars-is-first-carmaker-to-explore-fossilfree-steel-with-ssab

Slater, S.F. and Narver, J.C. (1994) 'Market orientation, customer value, and superior performance', *Business Horizons*, vol. 37, no. 2, pp. 22–8.

Templar, S., Cosse, M., Camerinelli, E. and Findlay, C. (2012) 'An investigation into current supply chain finance practices in business: a case study approach', Proceedings of the Logistics Research Network (LRN) Conference, Cranfield, September 2012.

Templar, S., Findlay, C. and Hofmann, E. (2016) *Financing the End to End Supply Chain: A Reference Guide to Supply Chain Finance*, 1st edn. London: Kogan Page.

UK Government (2012) 'Prime Minister announces Supply Chain Finance scheme', at https://www.gov.uk/government/news/prime-minister-announces-supply-chain-finance-scheme

Unilever (2024) 'Our position on carbon pricing', accessed on 6th July 2024 at https://www.unilever.com/sustainability/climate/using-our-voice-for-a-zero-carbon-future/#:~:text=Unilever's%20internal%20carbon%20price%20%E2%80%93%20which,rise%20to%201.5%C2%B0C

United Nations (2024) ' Performance Framework', Department of Operational Support, accessed on 8th July 2024 at https://operationalsupport.un.org/en/performance-framework

Volvo (2021) 'Volvo Cars signs zero emission road transport declaration at COP26, reveals groundbreaking internal carbon pricing mechanism', Volvo Cars Global Media Newsroom. https://www.media.volvocars.com/global/en-gb/media/pressreleases/290035/volvo-cars-signs-zero-emission-road-transport-declaration-at-cop26-reveals-groundbreaking-internal-c

Volvo (2022) 'Volvo Cars and Northvolt accelerate shift to electrification with new, 3,000-job battery plant in Gothenburg, Sweden', 4th February 2022 Press Release, accessed at https://www.media.volvocars.com/global/en-gb/media/pressreleases/294114/volvo-cars-and-northvolt-accelerate-shift-to-electrification-with-new-3000-job-battery-plant-in-goth

Volvo (2024) 'We're updating our sustainability strategy', 27th February 2024, accessed at https://www.volvocars.com/uk/news/sustainability/we-are-updating-our-sustainability-strategy/

Whicker, L., Bernon, M., Templar, S. and Mena, C. (2009) 'Understanding the relationships between time and cost to improve supply chain performance', *International Journal of Production Economics*, vol. 121, no. 2, pp. 641–50.

World Bank Group (2024) 'State and trends of carbon pricing dashboard' accessed 5th July 2024 at https://carbonpricingdashboard.worldbank.org/

Suggested further reading

Camerinelli, E. (2009) *Measuring the Value of the Supply Chain*. Farnham: Gower.

Ellram, L. (2002) 'Strategic cost management in the supply chain: a purchasing and supply management perspective', Centre for Advanced Purchasing Studies, Arizona State University.

Ellram, L.M. and Liu, B. (2002) 'The financial impact of supply management', *Supply Chain Management Review*, vol. 6, pp. 30–7.

Part Two

LEVERAGING LOGISTICS OPERATIONS

Part Two uses the foundation of logistics management and strategy developed in Part One to concentrate on key tasks for logistics operations. This covers the centre panel of our logistics model: the flow of materials, lead times and the network of operations in a global context.

Despite its role in corporate success, the logistics task ultimately boils down to orchestrating the flow of materials and information in the supply chain. The aim is to support products and services in the marketplace better than competitors. You could say that the logistics task is about making strategic objectives a reality by executing against demand and making value propositions to customers a reality. Logistics delivers value. Increasingly, this means improving sustainability (economic, societal and environmental), reducing supply chain risks in the international pipeline and planning and controlling the flows utilising lean and agile strategies as appropriate.

Chapter 4 considers how to manage and mitigate the plethora of supply chain risks to minimise costly disruptions and enable a resilient supply chain, while Chapter 5 examines the crucial strategic management of lead time. Chapters 6 and 7 then take that thinking a level higher by introducing key managerial concepts that support logistics operations. Chapter 6 addresses the immense amount of detail that is needed to plan and control material flow – both in the focal firm and more broadly in the supply chain. Chapter 7 reviews the role of lean thinking in reducing waste in the supply chain and explains the role of agility in enabling a quick response to unpredictable variations in supply and demand.

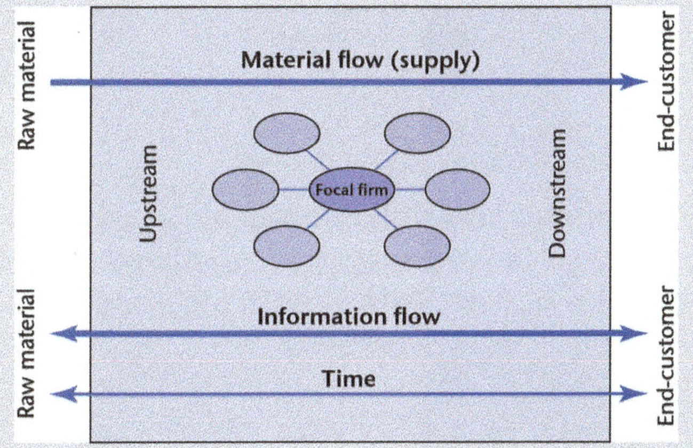

CHAPTER 4

Supply chain risk and resilience

Objectives

The intended objectives of this chapter are to:

- **explain supply chain risk, its sources, categories and types;**
- **illustrate how international supply chains can be redesigned to mitigate risk;**
- **describe and evaluate the supply chain risk management process including supply chain mapping, risk identification, risk evaluation and risk mitigation;**
- **understand resilient supply chains and the chronological phases and capabilities required in response to risk events.**

By the end of this chapter you should be able to understand:

- **how the many different types of supply chain risk manifests itself domestically and internationally across different sectors;**
- **how to redesign internal supply chains to mitigate the disruption caused by risk events;**
- **the supply chain risk management processes and how it can be applied;**
- **resilient supply chains and what capabilities distinguish them across the chronological phases of risk response.**

Introduction

Supply chains have become extended and complex spanning many tiers, through trends of outsourcing and offshoring. This has primarily been driven by companies seeking lower operational or manufacturing costs in low labour cost regions, with China the most popular destination. At the same time supply chains have been leaned out and stripped of 'waste' and this has led to the removal of buffers, in the form of excess inventories and excess capacity in manufacturing and distribution. While these buffers come at a cost, they provide a cushion against supply and demand disruptions and their removal has left extended complex international supply chains vulnerable and exposed to risk events.

In recent years there have been a series of international **geopolitical risk** events, for example Brexit, US–China trade war, COVID-19 and the Russia–Ukraine war, which have led to severe disruptions in supply chain material and product flows, and ultimately an erosion of supply chain financial and operational performance. The most severe, and in many ways unprecedented, event was COVID-19, which being a pandemic can be considered rare, but rapidly manifested at a global level, with lockdowns and social distancing causing large-scale disruption to supply chains, through factory and port closures and ultimately massive shortages of materials and products.

Aside from geopolitical risks there are many other categories of risk, such as sustainability compliance risks. For example, in June of 2022, the Uyghur Forced Labor Prevention Act (UFLPA) came into effect. This US legislation created a presumption that all goods imported into the US from Xinjiang, China - which includes massive shares of all the world's cotton, aluminium, food, chemicals and electronics - were produced through the forced labour of persecuted Uyghur minorities. Since then, US Customs has detained billions of dollars of US imports that contain raw materials or inputs sourced from Xinjiang in their upstream supply chains, which include apparel, automotive, electronics and other industries. These enforcement actions have impacted the world's most important brands, retailers and manufacturers.

The question arises how can a company's supply chains mitigate the effects of these risks and prevent the disruption and reputational damage that may follow? We will cover three schools of thought in this chapter:

- Redesigning international supply chains through changing the geographical location of operations (e.g. reshoring, offshoring, nearshoring and friend shoring), establishing focused factories (or not) and centralising or decentralising inventories.
- Supply chain risk management, which seeks to identify, evaluate and mitigate risks across the supply network with the aim of preventing (or at least reducing) the disruption.
- **Supply chain resilience** accepts that disruptions will happen and focuses on preparedness, response, recovery and ultimately adaptation to the disruption to improve the resilience of the supply chain.

We acknowledge the assistance from Hasan Khan, a Doctorate student at Cranfield School of Management, and his contribution to Section 4.1, based on his Doctoral Systemic Literature Review.

Key issues

This chapter addresses four key issues:

1. **Supply chain risk, sources and factors:** an understanding of **supply chain risk**, where it is sourced and the different categories and types;
2. **Redesigning international supply chains to mitigate risk:** how can international supply chains be redesigned in response to risk events and how does this mitigate risk;
3. **Supply risk management process:** what are the key steps to be followed to identify, evaluate and mitigate risk in the supply chain and how can supply chains be mapped and risk be measured and evaluated against a company's risk appetite;
4. **Supply chain resilience:** how does a resilient supply chain react to a disruptive risk event and what are the chronological phases and capabilities required.

4.1 Supply chain risk, sources and factors

***Key issues:* What is supply chain risk, where is it located and what are the risk categories and types?**

Risk in the supply chain is 'exposure to a premise, the outcome of which is uncertain' (Rao and Goldsby, 2009), so risk is all about uncertainty and unpredictability. Risks are evaluated across two dimensions: the probability of the risk event occurring and the negative consequences of the event (Christopher and Peck, 2004), which leads to disruptions and reductions in operational performance across quality, cost and speed (the hard supply chain objectives described in Chapter 1) and reputational damage. Some risks can be considered ***low profile*** where the probability of them happening is high, but the consequences are relatively low impact. For example, currency exchange rate fluctuations are highly likely, but their impact is not that disruptive to the supply chain, possibly increasing the cost of imported materials.

On the other hand, ***high-profile risk*** events are where the probability of them occurring is low, but when they do occur the consequences are highly disruptive to the supply chain. The most prominent recent example here are pandemics, which are considered to be rare, but as COVID-19 demonstrated, when they manifest at a global level, the consequences can be catastrophic, causing large-scale disruption to supply chains through factory and port closures and massive shortages of materials. What's interesting here is that COVID-19 didn't just cause massive disruptions in supply, but simultaneously caused volatile fluctuations in demand, largely as a result of social restrictions and lockdowns. Demand for some products dropped off a cliff, cars being the most notable example, while the demand for personal protective equipment (PPE) skyrocketed. These simultaneous impacts on supply and demand can be considered to the perfect storm, demand increasing for PPE, but supplies highly disrupted. But for some products disruptions in supply and demand were conveniently synchronised, from the point of view of the consumer, while automotive production lines ground to a halt through lack of components, so did demand, as consumers had little use for cars locked down in their homes.

This discussion highlights that risk events, and their consequences, can impact supply and demand. Indeed, risks are often categorised according to their location in the supply chain with respect to a focal company. Manuj and Mentzer (2008) provide a popular and enduring categorisation – supply, demand and operational risks – where operational refers to risks that occur within the internal operations of the company and supply and demand risks are those located in the supply side and demand side of the company's supply chain as shown in Figure 4.1.

While this is a useful approach, what's key to understanding, and ultimately mitigating risk, is the risk factors that can impact anywhere along the supply chain, such as risk of company insolvency or natural disaster. While there are a number of supply chain risk frameworks (for example Tummala and Schoenherr, 2011, Blackhurst et al., 2008) none of them cover the full range of risk types that can be encountered across a supply chain. To fill this gap in our knowledge Hasan Khan, through a Doctoral Systematic Literature Review, has developed a supply chain risk framework shown in Figure 4.2, building on all existing frameworks, where risks are categorised into eight groups as follows:

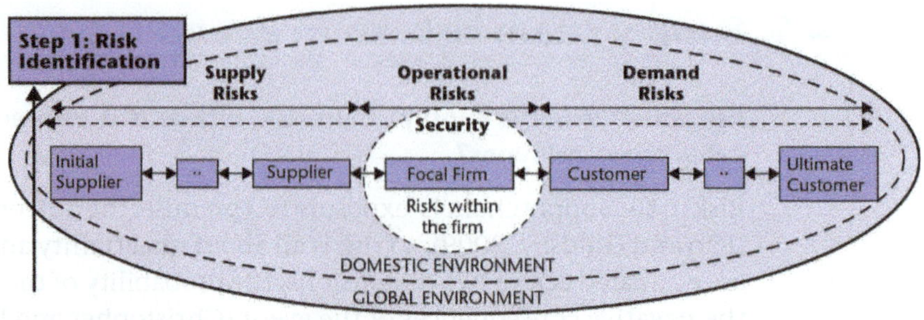

Figure 4.1 Supply chain risk by location.
(Source: Adapted from Manuj & Mentzer, 2008.)

1. Geopolitical
2. Operational
3. Financial
4. Logistics and transportation
5. Technological
6. Sustainability
7. Supplier specific
8. Demand specific

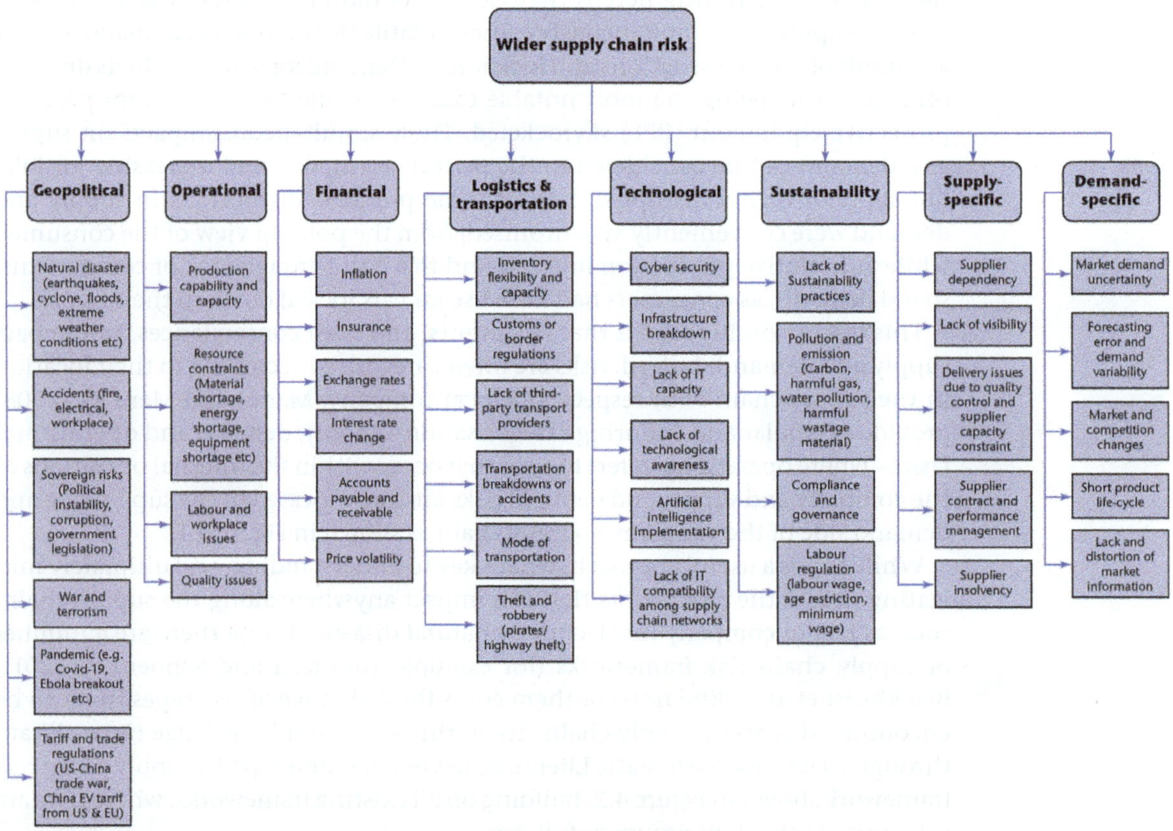

Figure 4.2 Supply chain risk categories and types.
(Source: Hasan Khan, 2024.)

The first six risk categories can act anywhere along the supply chain, whereas the supply-specific risks only apply to the supply side of a company's supply chain and the demand-specific risks only apply to the outbound flows from a company.

4.1.1 Geopolitical risks

Geopolitical events can profoundly disrupt supply chains, as evidenced by recent occurrences such as the COVID-19 pandemic, Russia–Ukraine war and the trade disputes between the Chinese and United States governments (Roscoe et al., 2020; Sheth and Uslay, 2023). Unpredictable natural disaster events, such as floods and earthquakes, and manmade events, for example war and terrorism, have all disrupted the globally extended and heavily outsourced manufacturing supply chains we see today. Geopolitical risk encapsulates all of these risks:

- Natural disaster
- Accidents
- Sovereign
- War and terrorism
- Pandemic
- Tariff and trade regulations

Natural disaster

Catastrophic events such as earthquakes, floods, tsunamis and extreme weather conditions can disrupt the entire supply chain (Chopra and Sodhi, 2014; Huma et al., 2020). Given the devastation caused by natural disaster various researchers, as well as governmental organisations, have proposed different classifications. A widely used system developed by the Centre for Research on the Epidemiology of Disasters (CRED) categorises different natural disasters into the following four primary groups and is used in the EM-DAT (Emergency Events Database) maintained by CRED (Guha-Sapir et al., 2017):

- Climatological events: This category includes occurrences like heatwaves, freezes, wildfires and droughts.
- Hydrological events: Encompassing flash floods, river floods, storm surges and mass movements (landslides).
- Meteorological events: The most diverse category, including tropical storms, winter storms, severe weather, hailstorms, tornadoes, local storms, hurricanes and blizzards.
- Geophysical events: These events, such as earthquakes and volcanic eruptions, are driven by tectonic movements.

An example of a hydrological event was the flood in Thailand, which resulted in major disruption for Ford Motors and stopped production of one of its major vehicle lines (Simchi-Levi et al., 2015). The Tohoku earthquake in Japan in 2011 was a geophysical event that severely damaged a significant geographical area resulting in major disruption in the semiconductor supply chain (Matsuo, 2015). In coastal areas, petrochemical complexes suffered severe damage, leading to a shortage of speciality chemicals such as hydrogen peroxide, which is essential for semiconductor manufacturing. The disruption in the semiconductor supply chain resulted in severe disruption in Toyota Motor Corporation's supply chain operations and financial repercussions.

Later in this chapter in Section 4.3.4 reactive risk mitigation strategies are presented to reduce the negative share price reactions to natural disaster induced supply chain disruptions.

Accidents

Accidents such as fire, electrical and poorly maintained workplace are commonplace and cause supply chain disruption. For instance, a fire accident in an Ericsson plant caused a revenue loss of €400 million (Huma et al., 2020).

Sovereign risks

These include political instability, government legislation and regulations (Schoenherr et al., 2008). Political uncertainty and instability are typically caused by changes in government and political regimes, but not always. For instance, a weak government might affect domestic firms and, subsequently, their trading partners in other countries (Rao and Goldsby, 2009). For example, the 2019 political protests in Hong Kong, which shut down the city centre and disrupted transportation networks, caused major supply chain disruptions (Roscoe et al., 2020). Political unrest in Bangladesh was a key factor that led large firms, such as Wal-Mart and Hanesbrands, to cease business in the country (Rao and Goldsby, 2009). Changes in government often cause disruptions in the supply chain as firms might be apprehensive about the subsequent new regulations and policies.

War and terrorism

These have become widely recognised in recent years due to the 9-11 Al Qaeda US terrorist attack, Russia–Ukraine war and the Israel–Palestine war. The Russia–Ukraine war has caused significant global supply chain disruption for certain materials supplied by Ukraine, for example coal, steel and grain, leading to shortages and higher prices. Previously, 9/11 was a significant reminder of the gravity of terrorism-related risks in the supply chain.

Pandemic

Pandemics have been one of the major concerns in recent years after COVID-19 caused severe disruption in global supply chains for most products (Chervenkova and Ivanov, 2023; Hoek, 2020). COVID-19 not only disrupted the supply chain during the pandemic, but has continued to have long-term effects known as post-COVID-19 impacts (Hoek, 2020). COVID-19 emerged and rapidly spread to nearly all countries worldwide. In addition to causing social and humanitarian crises, the pandemic has disrupted trade and supply chains, leading to significant economic losses (Choudhury et al., 2023). Global supply chains typically found that their existing risk approaches were woefully inadequate and have since attempted to review and improve their risk response strategies, hence supply chain risk management has received more attention since 2020. Prior to COVID-19, the world had already witnessed the emergence of rare infectious diseases, beginning with SARS in 2002, followed by bird flu in 2003, swine flu in 2009, MERS in 2012, Ebola in 2014 and Zika virus in 2015. Even the plague, traditionally considered a historical phenomenon, experienced a significant outbreak in Madagascar in 2017 (Choudhury et al., 2023). So, it can be said that pandemics are more probable than perhaps previously recognised.

Tariff and trade regulations

The US–China trade war was a highly disruptive and recent example where the US imposed 25 per cent tariffs on Chinese imports, followed by similar retaliatory actions by the Chinese on US imports. More recently, the US imposed 100 per cent tariffs on electric vehicles made in China, and the European Commission imposed 17.4 per cent to 37.6 per cent tariffs, both aiming to protect their domestic motor industry from a value for money import that they claim is heavily subsidised by the Chinese government (Silva, 2024). The recent shift towards tariffs and trade wars has significantly impacted supply chain operations and is a prominent risk for international supply chains. Common consequences include diminished foreign investment, trade restrictions, damage to global reputation, increased security risks, withdrawal of foreign businesses and disrupted supply chains – all of which have been evident in the context of the Russian–Ukrainian war (Sheth and Uslay, 2023).

In Section 4.3.4 a study (Roscoe et al., 2020 and 2022) is presented on how supply chain uncertainty, and thus disruptions, arising from geopolitical risk events (excluding accidents and natural disasters) may be managed.

4.1.2 Operational risks

Operational risks are mainly concerned with risks located within the company concerned. Production capability and capacity along with resource constraints and quality issues can all be categorised as operational risk types:

- Production capability and capacity
- Resource constraints
- Labour and workplace issues
- Quality issues

Production capability and capacity

Lack of production capacity caused by lack of equipment or indeed labour can cause delays in product and thus deliveries to customers. Equally, lack of production capability can lead to poor efficiencies, or poor flexibility in terms of the speed with which production can be switched to other demand products. Again delays or perhaps poor quality products are likely to result.

Resource constraints

Lack of resources such as material, equipment, energy or manpower is a risk factor that negatively affects supply chain operations (Hajmohammad et al., 2024). Considering the electrification trend in the automotive industry, as well as a rapid increase in technology industries, the required energy for production is a key global risk. Further, energy crises are not new and have been observed from the seventies to earlier 2003 to 2008 when the oil industry struggled to cope with rising demand (Sheth and Uslay, 2023) and are likely to continue given disruptions in oil supplies caused by war and conflict such as the Russian–Ukrainian.

Labour and workplace issues

Labour disputes or strikes can happen with little warning due to poor management (Ho et al., 2015) and can halt a production line and cause severe delays in production flow. An example is the labour strikes at the Maruti Suzuki plant in India, which halted car production for nearly a month (Samvedi et al., 2013). Lack of training also falls under this risk type, caused mostly by disorganised management, and disrupts the flow of production.

Quality issues

In an extreme case poor quality in a product can result in enterprises' exit from the market, for example Nokia initially possessed the potential to be the quality leader in the mobile phone market, but due to poor quality they exited the market leaving other companies such as Apple and Samsung to take leadership (Lamberg et al., 2021). Poor quality can also lead to highly disruptive and costly product recalls. In 2016 Samsung were forced to discontinue and recall 2.5 million Galaxy Note 7 after some of them started bursting into flames (Burrows, 2018). The total cost of the recall was $5.3 billion, but the diversified electronics giant was more than able to withstand the blow launching its Samsung Galaxy Note 8 the following year to strong reviews and sales.

4.1.3 Financial risks

Financial risks, including currency fluctuation, inflation, insurance issues, exchange rates and credits payable, naturally increase costs and reduce profits. Currency fluctuation is known to be one of the major economic risks followed by inflation in recent years and can cause significant harm to an organisation's financial status (Kırılmaz and Erol, 2017). Financial risk types are:

- Inflation
- Insurance
- Exchange rates
- Interest rate change
- Accounts payable and receivable
- Price volatility

Inflation

Unmanageable inflation constitutes a significant financial risk in current global supply chains. Inflation might occur due to several reasons such as pandemics and wars. Sheth and Uslay (2023) argue that while pandemics reduce aggregate demand and do not inherently lead to inflation, extended conflicts (as we see in the Russian–Ukrainian and Israel–Palestine wars) elevate aggregate demand and are generally accompanied by increased interest rates, higher levels of investment and inflation. While countries like the UK and US will argue that they have inflation under control, considering the current global scenario, inflation remains one of the prominent financial risks in supply chains.

Insurance

Not having proper insurance policies for different parts of the supply chain, such as business interruption insurance, and engaging in the buying and selling of financial instruments, such as forward and futures contracts are likely to result in financial risks (Simangunsong et al., 2012). Should a risk event occur, for example a factory fire, for which a company has no insurance not only will the business be immediately disrupted, but it is likely it won't be recoverable without an insurance pay out to rebuild the facility.

Currency exchange rates

Bank exchange rates play a critical role for enterprises trading with suppliers and customers internationally (Tummala and Schoenherr, 2011). Fluctuations in currency exchange rates are of course themselves often caused by risk events, such as natural disaster and terrorism.

Interest rate change

This particularly impacts company's borrowing, which may be an overdraft to support working capital (for example inventory holding and salaries) or it could be some type of longer-term loan, to support fixed capital investment in equipment or buildings. Increases in a national banks interest rates will have an almost immediate effect on the interest rates charged by banks and increase costs, potentially a long way beyond the businesses budget.

Accounts payable and receivable

Accounts receivable from customers represent a financial risk as customers may default on payment and this may affect the company's ability to pay its own supplier, potentially causing defaults up the supply chain.

Price volatility

Price volatility and increases in cost for certain commodities contribute to financial risks (Hallikas et al., 2020). Sudden and/or significant price increases can negatively affect enterprises' financial status. For instance, sudden increases in semiconductor prices are affecting a wide range of sectors across the globe (Sheth and Uslay, 2023).

4.1.4 Logistics and transportation risks

Logistics and transportation are critical elements of any supply chain and therefore pose significant risks including inventory, warehouse and delivery-related risks. Leading manufacturers maintain supply chain reserves, which encompass warehouse capacity and buffer inventory. The challenge for managers is to mitigate risk by strategically positioning and sizing supply chain reserves without diminishing profits. While accumulating inventory can protect a company against supplier delivery delays, indiscriminately building reserves can increase costs and negatively impact the bottom line (Chopra and Sodhi, 2004). Logistics and transportation-related risks are:

- Inventory flexibility and capacity
- Customs or border regulations
- Lack of third-party transport providers
- Transportation breakdowns or accidents
- Mode of transportation
- Theft and robbery

Inventory flexibility and capacity

One of the biggest challenges for top enterprises is to determine and build the right level of inventory reserves to protect against supply disruptions, while not increasing costs too high. Lack of inventory flexibility is another risk where material inventories can only be used on a very small range of products. Flexibility serves as a form of resource pooling, enabling the utilisation of the same inventory (and perhaps production capacity) across a diverse range of products.

Customs or border regulations

Global supply chains require goods and materials to cross many borders and therefore they're subject to customs and border regulations, which represent a risk. Brexit, when the United Kingdom left the European Union, is a good example of such risks, and all supply chains exporting from the UK to the EU or vice versa were exposed to this risk. When the UK did leave the EU on 31 December 2020, fortunately a deal had been negotiated and the worst-case scenario of World Trade Organization (WTO) trade tariffs were avoided. However, the UK and the EU are now in separate customs and regulatory regimes, so the EU applies its usual third-country customs and regulatory regime to goods imported from UK to the EU, to ensure such aspects as safety and security obligations are fulfilled. This means that goods exported from the UK to the EU face border checks, which are particularly intrusive in the case of food, and are in any case time consuming and incur extra costs (Reland and Jurkovic, 2024).

Third-party transport providers

Delays due to third-party transport providers are quite common incidents. The involvement of third-party transport providers creates risk in the global supply chain operations. Although most of the time transport providers are reliable, it is evident that they can sometimes cause damage to products and also delays (Gaudenzi and Borghesi, 2006).

Transportation breakdowns or accidents

Accidents in transportation are another risk factor that can disrupt the global supply chain. Further, vehicle breakdowns and malfunctioning contribute to transportation-related risks and result in delayed deliveries (Tummala and Schoenherr, 2011).

Mode of transportation

The mode of transportation also contributes to transportation-related risks, for example air, sea and road transportation can bring different types of delays due to extreme weather conditions, vehicle breakdowns and port clearance (Tummala and Schoenherr, 2011).

Theft and robbery

This includes highway theft, maritime pirate attacks, aeroplane hijacks and robberies, which can clearly disrupt supply chain operations. Cargo theft is on the increase and a particular global risk. Through 2019 and 2020, TAPA (Transported Asset Protection Association) EMEA (Europe, the Middle East and Africa) recorded over 15,000 cargo losses from supply chains, with a total loss value of over €310m, which is the equivalent of €424,000 of goods being stolen every single day (TAPA EMEA, 2021). The consequences of cargo theft are more extensive than is immediately obvious. When a single cargo theft accident occurs, the involved supply chain costs six times the cargo value because the accident affects the costs of product replacement, accident handling, increased insurance premium, loss of sales and negative impact on the business reputation (Burges, 2013).

4.1.5 Technological risks

In the age of digital transformation, **technological risks** can severely disrupt supply chain operations. Cyber security and AI integration are some of the most crucial factors in technological risk in recent years (Sheth and Uslay, 2023), but it is wider than this and includes:

- Cyber security
- Infrastructure breakdown
- Lack of IT capacity
- Lack of technological awareness
- Artificial intelligence implementation
- Lack of IT compatibility among supply chain networks

Cyber security

System security is being jeopardised by cyber threats, massive data fraud and theft incidents, intellectual property breaches and data management risks. Current common cyber threats impacting digital assets include ransomware, data leakage, phishing, hacking and insider threats. This is due to the proliferation of information, globalisation and the adoption of cloud-based systems (Deiva Ganesh and Kalpana, 2022) and is a particular problem for supply chains, because, to ensure their smooth running, it is necessary for organisations to share high levels of supply and demand data, which leaves them exposed to cyber security risks.

Infrastructure breakdown

The more a company integrates its information systems, the greater the risk that a failure in one area can lead to widespread systemic failures. The breakdown of information infrastructure can devastate highly networked supply chain environments (Chopra and Sodhi, 2004). A pertinent example played out on 19th July 2024, when a software bug in CrowdStrike's system caused 8.5 million Windows-based computers to crash. The largest IT outage in history, disrupted airports, ports and railways worldwide, with planes and cargo stranded at major hubs in Europe, Asia and North America (Kelly, 2024).

Lack of IT capacity

Technological advancement and digitalisation are common trends in the global supply chain (Wang et al., 2024). Therefore, lack of IT capacity or compatibility among supply chain partners in a global supply chain can result in disruption.

Lack of technological awareness

Lack of IT-related training and awareness can result in internal conflict and disrupt the supply chain in this era of digitalisation (Deiva Ganesh and Kalpana, 2022).

Artificial intelligence implementation

In the rapidly advancing digital era, artificial intelligence (AI) plays a crucial role as one of the most prominent technologies (Deiva Ganesh and Kalpana, 2022). In recent years, research in supply chain risk management (SCRM) has begun to benefit from AI-driven applications. Misuse of AI, or errors induced by generative AI, in the supply chain can also be considered an important technological risk.

Lack of IT compatibility among supply chain networks

Lack of IT compatibility among supply chain networks and poor IT security are also technological risk factors (Tummala and Schoenherr, 2011).

4.1.6 Sustainability risks

Sustainability risks have gained significant attention in recent years and as described in section 1.3, this covers the triple bottom line: environmental, social and economic values. Further, the term environmental, social and governance (ESG) has grown in importance as a way of capturing sustainability performance adding the governance dimension. Sustainability risk thus includes the following types:

- Lack of sustainability practices
- Pollution and emission
- Compliance and governance
- Labour regulation

Lack of sustainability practices

Supplier sustainability risk is broadly defined as a sustainability-related condition, or potential event, occurring among a buying firm's suppliers that may elicit adverse reactions from stakeholders (Hajmohammad et al., 2024). Lack of sustainability practices in enterprises can be a major risk in the current global supply chain, since most big enterprises are under pressure to comply with sustainability regulations (Lintukangas et al., 2016).

Pollution and emission

This is environmental risk exposure related to climate change issues (such as greenhouse gas emissions) and resource utilisation (including water, land, energy, materials use, recycling and disposal) (Tummala and Schoenherr, 2011). Green House Gas (GHG) emissions are normally measured in terms of kilograms of CO_2 equivalent (or carbon footprint) as described in Section 1.3.3. A particular risk associated with this is the cost of carbon, in terms of taxes and emissions trading schemes (ETS) as detailed in Section 3.5.

Compliance and governance

Supply chain sustainability risks are often related to direct and indirect governance (Kähkönen et al., 2023). Governance provides a framework for managing organisations and identifies who can make decisions, who has the authority to act on behalf of the organisation and who is accountable for how an organisation and its people behave and perform (Chartered Governance Institute). In the context of ESG it is concerned with environmental and societal performance. Risk emerges when the governance is not in place to achieve this performance and/or assure compliance with ESG regulations.

Labour regulation

Complying with labour regulations (for example working conditions, age restriction, minimum wage) falls under the social aspect of the sustainability risks

(Kähkönen et al., 2023), as discussed in Section 1.3.3. child labour, forced labour and minimum hourly wage are examples of labour regulation risks that can lead to reputational damage and losses in revenue (Zimmer et al., 2017).

4.1.7 Supply-specific risks

Supply-specific risks can be defined as the risks that originate from suppliers, or can affect the purchasing organisation, to meet customer demand and they include:

- Supplier dependency
- Lack of visibility
- Delivery issues
- Supplier contract and performance management
- Supplier insolvency

Supplier dependency

Supplier dependency is one of the major aspects of supply-specific risks. Firms often rely on one supplier, which can cause harm if the major supplier confronts any disruption. For example, in 2007 the earthquake that damaged Rikon Corporation, a major supplier of piston and seal rings, caused production delays for Toyota, Mitsubishi, Honda and Suzuki Motor Corporation as they were all dependent on Rikon Corporation (Blackhurst et al., 2008). Supplier dependency can result in major harm to enterprises and companies try to avoid relying on a single supplier (Simchi-Levi et al., 2015).

Lack of supply visibility

Supply visibility is another crucial aspect of supply-specific risk as it provides companies with knowledge of their supply network, and potentially control, over it (Christopher and Peck, 2004). Attaining this visibility is challenging due to the interconnected nature of supply networks. The importance of supply chain transparency and visibility is highlighted by a 2013 survey of 149 companies conducted by the Aberdeen Group, where 63 per cent of the respondents identified supply chain visibility as their foremost priority (Sarker et al., 2016). However, suppliers are often reluctant to share information and unwilling to provide access to data, which results in a lack of transparency and visibility that can lead to major disruptions.

Delivery issues

Delivery and quality issues often delayed deliveries, and poor product quality can cause harm to the focal organisation (Tummala and Schoenherr, 2011). Supplier capacity constraints, sometimes exposed by increasing demand, can also arise as a significant risk factor for delaying product delivery. Controlling an intricate and widely diversified supply chain often results in delivery issues due to poor monitoring of the suppliers, which can be linked to the supplier's quality and capacity.

Supplier contract and performance management

Deteriorating supplier performance can result in immediate production disruption and long-term negative effects on supply chain (Huma et al., 2020). Offering long-term contracts to reliable suppliers and short-term contracts to less reliable suppliers increases the loyalty of supplier base to an enterprise. Monitoring supplier performance and keeping contracts up to date is essential to avoid disruption in supply chain (Huma et al., 2020).

Supplier insolvency

Supplier bankruptcy, or insolvency, can cause disruption in the supply chain simply because the supplier is likely to cease operations, and therefore supply to the company. Delayed reports of insolvency can increase the disruption to the focal company, as there may be insufficient time to arrange alternative supply. For example, in 2001 bankruptcy of UPF-Thompson, the sole chassis supplier for Ford Motor Company's Land Rover division, created significant challenges for the automaker (Chopra and Sodhi, 2004).

4.1.8 Demand-specific risks

Demand-specific risk refers to the potential occurrence of events related to outbound product flows that could impact the probability of customers placing orders with the focal firm, as well as variability in the volume and variety of products desired by customers. Demand-specific risks are:

- Market demand uncertainty
- Forecasting error and demand variability
- Market and competition changes
- Short product life cycle
- Lack of or distortion of market information

Market demand uncertainty

Sudden, unexpected increases, or reductions, in demand cause market demand uncertainty. For example, due to COVID-19 the culture of working from home increased rapidly, which caused skyrocketing demand for electronic products (Zhang et al., 2024). Apple faced major disruption due to the spike in demand for electronic products on the one hand, and the global semiconductor shortage on the other. A similar example can be observed in the Automotive industry where the rapid increase in demand for electronic vehicles drove high demand for Tesla cars at the same time as the semiconductor shortage caused production delays resulting in disruptions to customer deliveries (Biney et al., 2024).

Forecasting error and demand variability

Forecast risk arises from discrepancies between a company's forecasts and actual demand otherwise known as forecast error. When demand is under forecasted then insufficient products may be made leading to low product availability and possibly stockouts and lost sales. Conversely, overly optimistic forecasts can lead to excess inventory and, consequently, necessitate price markdowns. For instance, in late 2003, product shortages in Western Europe led Nokia's customers to place larger orders than necessary to safeguard against potential rationing or allocations by Nokia (Chopra and Sodhi, 2004). This overordering distorted Nokia's market perceptions, resulting in inaccurate sales forecasts for the company.

Market and competition changes

Any changes in market or rise of new competitors are examples of demand side risk. For instance, a rumour about the depletion of an essential commodity can trigger panic, causing a dramatic surge in demand for that product (Samvedi et al., 2013). The case of Nokia can again be mentioned to relate to market changes and the rise of new competitors resulting in the exit of Nokia from being one of the top electronics manufacturers (Lamberg et al., 2021).

Short product life cycle

Shorter product life cycles can result from rapidly evolving customer preferences, as well as expansion into international markets and production (Wagner and Neshat, 2010). Product and technology life cycles have significantly shortened, and frequent competitive product introductions make it challenging to predict changes in demand over the product life cycle.

Lack of or distortion of market information

Along with forecasting errors sometimes information distortion and lack of market information such as market changes and competitors' movement can also contribute to demand-specific risks (Tummala and Schoenherr, 2011).

4.1.9 High risk exposure in automotive supply chains

Automotive supply chains consist of a complex, interconnected and vast network of suppliers across the globe, which have relatively fixed geographic locations due to the clustering of suppliers and high levels of capital investment required in production (Roscoe et al., 2022). Consequently, automotive supply chains are particularly exposed to risk. They have faced heightened risks in recent years due to a series of global events that have disrupted their production and distribution networks, including Israel–Palestine war, Russia–Ukraine war, and the COVID-19 pandemic (Hoek, 2020; Lin et al., 2024; Sheth & Uslay, 2023). The transition to electric vehicles (EVs), has further exacerbated automotive supply chains' challenges. Both the Israel–Palestine and Russia–Ukraine wars disrupted raw material supplies, some of which are critical and required in semiconductor production. Case Study 4.1 describes how a European automotive assembler, AutoCo, classifies and prioritises supply chain risks, based on their experience of supply chain disruptions in recent years.

CASE STUDY 4.1

Supply chain risk categorisation and prioritisation at AutoCo: evidence from the automotive industry

AutoCo has been operating as a major automotive assembler for over 70 years and like other automotive companies, AutoCo has faced significant disruption due to recent events such as Israel–Palestine war, Russia–Ukraine war and COVID-19 pandemic. The semiconductor shortage has been another major disruption (Biney et al., 2024) that has impacted AutoCo's production line. The company identified the risk factors shown in Figure 4.3 (and explained next), based on the disruptions they have faced including the 9/11 attack, the Tohoku earthquake, semiconductor shortage and recent wars and COVID-19.

Operational risks are high priority for automotive manufacturers such as AutoCo, as the company is required to ensure production stability without disruption in order to meet customer delivery dates. COVID-19 pandemic resulted in social distancing and workplace regulation changes, which impacted directly the manpower for AutoCo (Sarker et al., 2022). The Israel–Palestine war resulted in a lack of raw commodity materials and the Russia–Ukraine war disrupted critical raw material supply required to produce semiconductors (Lin et al., 2024; Sheth and Uslay, 2023). Considering the electrification trend in the automotive industry this significantly impacted AutoCo.

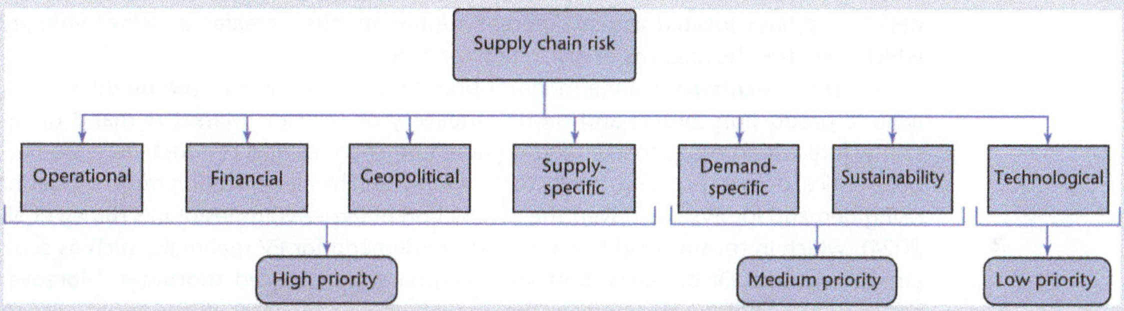

Figure 4.3 **Supply chain risks categories and prioritisation at AutoCo.**

Financial risks are important to most companies as they directly impact their revenue and profit, and this is the case for AutoCo, who view them as being high priority. AutoCo considers inflation, currency fluctuation, exchange rates, material cost increase, reduced revenue and tariff prices as their financial risks. Recent wars between Russia–Ukraine and Israel–Palestine have increased aggregate demand resulting in high interest rates, investment uncertainty and inflation (Sheth and Uslay, 2023). US–China trade war has caused an increase in tariff prices as sales tax (Chen, 2024) and increased cross-border customs costs (Moradlou et al., 2021) both of which have affected AutoCo. Moreover, production line disruption from operational risks directly impacts the financial aspects of AutoCo as an automotive manufacturer. For instance, material shortages inevitably drive up material prices and may lead to late deliveries.

Geopolitical risks such as pandemics and natural disasters, in the past, occurred once every few years such as the 9/11 incident in 2001, swine flu in 2009, the flood in Thailand and Tohoku earthquake in 2011 and Ebola in 2014, (Choudhury et al., 2023; Matsuo, 2015; Simchi-Levi et al., 2015). Due to the lower frequency, therefore probability, of these geopolitical risks occurring once every few years, and their risk impact being comparatively low, AutoCo regarded them as medium priority. But in recent years, due to the electrification trend, as well as frequent breakout of war (Israel–Palestine, Russia–Ukraine) along with the COVID-19 pandemic creating major havoc across the global supply chain, AutoCo has increased the priority level of geopolitical risks from medium to high. Moreover, sovereign risks including political instability and shifts in government policies driven by geopolitical factors – exemplified by Brexit – have heightened the emphasis on managing geopolitical risks.

Supply-specific risks are driven by automotive companies' interconnected and complex network of suppliers across the globe (Simchi-Levi et al., 2015) and AutoCo is no different. AutoCo has a diverse supplier base spanning Asia, Europe, America and Africa, including almost 1000 active tier-1 suppliers, which are spread over 800 manufacturing sites across different countries, making supply-specific risks a major concern for the company. Considering multiple tiers of suppliers, which can often exceed 10-tiers, creates extreme complexity in AutoCo's supply-specific risks, which include supplier dependency, lack of visibility, supplier performance management, supplier delivery issues, supplier capacity constraint and supplier insolvency. The electrification trend introduced a new set of potential suppliers for EVs further increasing supplier-specific risk. Moreover, since many EV battery suppliers are in China (Ren et al., 2024) this increased supplier dependency towards a specific country, which is not considered a 'friendly' nation by many European countries. Finally, the high number of interconnected suppliers located across different continents often creates a lack of visibility, which increases the chances of disruption for AutoCo.

Demand-specific risks are a medium priority risk at AutoCo driven by the need to achieve production targets and on-time delivery of vehicles. Market demand uncertainty, forecasting error, market and competition changes and product life cycle have been critical demand-specific risk factors for AutoCo. The electrification trend triggering rising demand for EVs has driven the production of larger volumes of EVs (Biney et al., 2024), which in turn has led to an increase in demand for EV materials, such as semiconductors, and EV batteries, both of which have experienced shortages. Moreover, the transition to EV's is a change in the market where new competitors might arise for AutoCo, and EV batteries have a limited life span (Botelho Junior et al., 2021), which introduces product life cycle-related challenges for AutoCo.

Sustainability risks have been a major concern in recent years for the global supply chain, particularly in terms of the environment due to global warming and net-zero carbon emission targets, at both national and company levels. Lack of sustainability practices, pollution and emission, compliance, governance and labour regulations have been sustainability risks at AutoCo. Reducing environmental pollution and emissions is one of the major sustainability goals for AutoCo, and they are working towards achieving their carbon net zero target within the next decade. Due to the increase in sustainability issues, governments are employing environmental regulations that reduce risk (Torres-Ruiz and Ravindran, 2018) to which AutoCo is aiming to adhere strictly. Even though sustainability risks might not be as critical as operational, financial or geopolitical for AutoCo, it certainly has had a major impact in recent years and is considered to have a similar importance to demand-specific risks, medium priority.

Technological risks at AutoCo include cyber security, AI implementation, lack of technological awareness and lack of IT compatibility among supply networks. AutoCo, aiming towards a digitalised supply chain system, is very much aware of these risk factors and considers information infrastructure breakdown a critical technological risk. For example on 19th July 2024 Windows-based computers crashed due to a software bug in CrowdStrike's system causing unforeseen disruption for AutoCo. Due to well-maintained technological infrastructure, the damage was minimal, but it brought previously unforeseen technological risks to their attention. AutoCo is proactive in increasing technological awareness among employees and wants to achieve a digitalised supply chain system with high levels of IT literacy among their employees. Further, they are aiming to achieve IT visibility by increasing IT compatibility among supply network partners. Technological risks are a recent aspect of risk for AutoCo emerging due to recent supply chain digitalisation; therefore they are labelled as low priority, but the company expects that due to the rapid globalisation and AI integration in supply chains (Deiva Ganesh and Kalpana, 2022) the priority might increase to medium.

The case study describes the scenario of a major automotive assembler to provide current insights into supply chain risks in the automotive industry. It can be observed how risks in recent years have affected the automotive industry severely through the case study. AutoCo aims to achieve a digitalised supply chain system with proactive risk management to stay at the top in managing their global supply network.

(Source: Courtesy of Hasan Khan.)

Study questions:

1. Considering risk probabilities, and likely consequences, review AutoCo's risk category prioritisation – do you agree with it?
2. Compare AutoCo's risk categorisation and prioritisation with a company from another sector you are familiar with. Is it very different?

4.2 Redesigning international supply chains to mitigate risk

***Key issues:* How can international supply chains be redesigned in response to risk events and the disruptions they cause? What aspects can be changed and how will they mitigate risk?**

International supply chains extend across multiple countries, and this leads to many inherent risks. For example:

- extended lead time of supply;
- extended and unreliable transit times;
- multiple consolidation and break points;
- multiple freight modes and cost options;
- price and currency fluctuations.

Further, international supply chains are exposed to the many different types of risk described in Section 4.1. In response to these risks, and in particular, the recent geopolitical risks (e.g. Brexit, COVID-19, US–China trade war and Ukraine War), companies are reviewing and changing the strategic design of their global supply chains to mitigate the supply chain risks. In this section we will cover the following three design dimensions:

- Geographical location of operations
- Focused factories or focused markets
- Centralised or decentralised inventories

4.2.1 Geographical location of operations

A major design choice that affects risk exposure is the geographical location of operations, such as manufacturing facilities and distribution centres, both within the company's in-house operations and outsourced to suppliers. Arguably the most critical operation in a supply chain is manufacturing, where materials or components are transformed to produce products of greater value than the sum of the materials' value. Since the 1970s, companies have deliberately established manufacturing facilities in low-wage economies to minimise costs and gain access to emerging markets (de Sa et al., 2019). The most notable low-cost manufacturing destination is China, which, it can be argued, has become the manufacturing superpower of the world, accounting for 28.7 per cent of global manufacturing output compared to the United States, which is second at 16.8 per cent, according to the United Nations Statistics Division 2019 output figures (Richter, 2021). However, this globalisation has left companies, and their supply chains, exposed to many different types of risk (see those described in Section 4.1) and the subsequent disruptions that can occur at any point along internationally dispersed supply chains. Managers are often obliged to re-evaluate the manufacturing location decision to mitigate these supply chain disruption risks.

The manufacturing location decision refers to whether a company operates in its own country (i.e. the country in which the company is registered) or across national borders, and it takes a range of forms including offshoring, nearshoring, reshoring and more recently friend shoring:

- **Offshoring** refers to when production is sent to another country, typically overseas; it is often driven by cost minimisation objectives including access to low-cost labour and raw materials (Ellram et al., 2013; Tate and Bals, 2017). However, the cost advantages of offshoring production to other countries are gradually eroding, resulting in companies repatriating their production to home countries (Moradlou and Backhouse, 2016). Further, offshoring production increases exposure to many types of risks including logistical, geopolitical, operational and financial. For instance quality issues are not discovered until delivery to the home country, which may be months after production and leave the company with product shortages. Also, using offshore suppliers in low-cost countries creates financial risk through currency exchange rates and lack of credit provided by suppliers leading to cash flow issues.
- **Reshoring (or backshoring)** refers to repatriating production from a previously offshored location to the home country (Tate and Bals, 2017). Moradlou et al. (2017) studied the automotive sector in the UK and identified a lack of

responsiveness in the supply chain and long lead times to be the primary motivation behind reshoring manufacturing activities from India to the UK. Another study by Theyel et al. (2018) identified the overestimation of cost saving in offshoring, quality problems, product development and intellectual property as the reasons behind reshoring to the UK. Reshoring is widely understood to reduce supply chain risk exposure.

- **Nearshoring** refers to the repatriation of production activities from a lower-cost country, such as China, to another lower-cost country, such as Poland, that is nearby a major market such as Europe (Hartman et al., 2017). This is an approach which can mitigate many of the risks associated with offshoring while still benefiting from lower manufacturing costs.
- **Friend shoring** refers to when production is sent only to countries deemed to be trusted political allies by the government of the home country (Gordon, 2023). This is designed to reduce exposure to political risk and improve security, particularly for critical products like defence and health. However, there are lots of concerns with this strategy, for instance how does the government determine which countries are 'friendly'. For instance, the US government deems China to be an unfriendly nation, but in addition to its traditional allies, the Biden Administration has identified Brazil, India, South Korea, Japan, Indonesia, Vietnam and Malaysia as trustworthy nations. However, can these emerging industrial powerhouses prove to be a viable substitute for Chinese manufacturing bases?

The general consensus is that cost and company strategy are the key criteria for the location decision (Ellram et al., 2013; Tate and Bals, 2017). For example, factors such as transportation and fuel costs, labour costs and productivity, supply chain responsiveness, end customer proximity and currency valuation volatility have been identified as drivers of global manufacturing location decisions (Ellram et al., 2013). However, pursuing an offshoring decision is not necessarily easy as Case study 4.2 illustrates.

CASE STUDY 4.2

Moving offshore – not so easy or straightforward: the experience of Smiths

Aerospace

Smiths Aerospace is a largely UK-based supplier to both military and civilian aircraft and engine manufacturers, and it is owned by General Electric of the USA. Several years ago, Smiths launched an initiative to outsource production of parts from UK suppliers to Chinese suppliers in a drive to benefit from lower costs. Amongst the beneficiaries of the new initiative was the Mechanical Systems Division, which intended to source high-volume, low-cost products from lean, low-cost suppliers in China. The remaining volume was to be sourced from domestic suppliers that could operate more flexibly. The scope of the restructuring included machined civilian aircraft parts from four UK sites under the Mechanical Systems Division, based in four locations in the UK: Wolverhampton, Cheltenham, Hamble and Dowty Propellers (Gloucester).

Global supply chain teams based in the UK and the USA, in conjunction with each of the Smiths Aerospace divisions, were given responsibility for the deployment of the outsourcing programme. The reconfigured supply chain was to result in the transition of approximately 5,000 to 15,000 parts from traditional suppliers to low-cost economy suppliers over a five-year period. Plans stated that, on average, 40 per cent of the spend would remain within the UK because of high switching costs. As the long-term contracts expired, the parts would either be manufactured internally or outsourced, depending on intellectual property rights and technology protection. However, several years into the initiative, only parts of the original plans have been accomplished. Much of the delay was attributable to the change process, which was not so simple as originally envisioned. There were also challenges with how that change was being managed. For example, in the words of one company executive:

> **Failure to manage exit from the existing supplier, and failure to coordinate the transition, led to catastrophic failure of supply.**

In this restructuring initiative, several keys to a successful supply chain initiative have been met:

- The initiative directly relates to corporate strategic priorities and there is top executive recognition of its importance.
- There are clear considerations for switching production to China.
- There is a clear business (four units, two of which serve as pilots) and operating scope defined (those that require less flexibility).
- There is a launch point for 'quick wins' (high-volume, labour-intensive parts).
- Teams around the world have been allocated to the initiative.

However, as is also clear from the above quote from the executive, there are real risks involved. As much as there have been many companies moving supply chain operations to China, there are also clear negative impacts on supply chain performance that need to be considered and incorporated into the change plan.

Study questions

1. What are the risks in relocating parts of the supply chain and how can they be mitigated?
2. Despite the recognised need to coordinate the transition process, the sites lacked a documented method to specify how this would take place. There were also challenges with the change process itself. Propose what steps might have been included to address these shortcomings.

Geopolitical risk

Geopolitical risk, and its subsequent disruptions, are certainly a driver for relocating manufacturing and distribution facilities. Recent events such as the dissolution of NAFTA and the US–China Trade war have seen companies move production and distribution facilities either from or to affected countries (Forbes, 2020; New York Times, 2020a, b). A study by Moradlou et al. (2021) investigated the impact of Brexit on the operations location decision of managers in UK multinational firms. The findings indicate that the majority of companies planned, or have already relocated, production facilities from the UK to the EU, and distribution centres from the EU to the UK. This was because of:

- **market-seeking advantages**: being close to major centres of demand, ease of access to local and international markets, and
- **efficiency-seeking advantages**: costs related to expected delays at ports, tariff and non-tariff barriers.

Another study by Roscoe et al. (2022) examined:

How can companies redesign their global supply chains in the face of compounding geopolitical disruptions?

It investigated how managers redesigned their global supply chains, across nine different industries, when faced with the high levels of uncertainty created by compounding geopolitical disruptions - Brexit, US–China trade war and COVID-19 - which unfolded over a similar period. The study found that managers made their decisions by considering three dimensions:

1. **the perceived intensity of institutional pressures**, such as those from governments, including trade tariffs;
2. **the relative geographic mobility of suppliers** and supply chain assets; and
3. **the perceived severity of the potential disruption risk.**

There was some support for companies in the same industry selecting the same supply chain design, such as technology companies who nearshored production to Mexico and Vietnam during the US–China trade war, or pharmaceutical companies who moved production facilities from overseas and localised production in the UK and USA. However, intense government pressure and persistent geopolitical risk do not necessarily impact companies in the same industry in the same way. For example, managers in the oil and gas, manufacturing, and clothing industries adopted a near-shore or on-shore supply chain design. In contrast, companies in the automotive industry had to 'Grin and Bear It' due to entrenched suppliers, leading to the maintenance of an offshore design. Where suppliers are relatively immobile and supply chain assets are relatively fixed, this produces a dominant logic that can override both institutional pressure and perceived risk. For example an interviewee from the automotive industry revealed that:

tariffs on steel and aluminium would need to be significantly higher than 25% to justify switching from a brake motor supplier in northern China to a domestic U.S. supplier

This suggests that in the automotive sector an entrenched supply base, coupled with high sunk costs in existing facilities, informs a rationale for continuing an offshoring strategy, despite persistent institutional pressures and disruption risks.

Roscoe et al. (2022) identified eight predominant supply chain logics, depending on the aforementioned three dimensions and these are shown in Figure 4.4:

1. Navigate the Policy Environment;
2. Maintain Market Access and Supply Continuity;
3. Close to the Customer;
4. Almost Home;

5. Tactical Warfare;
6. Keep it Simple;
7. Grin and Bear it; and
8. Ready for Every Scenario.

This shows that where suppliers and facilities are entrenched and not mobile the supply chain logics, and therefore designs, are quite different in response to geopolitical risk.

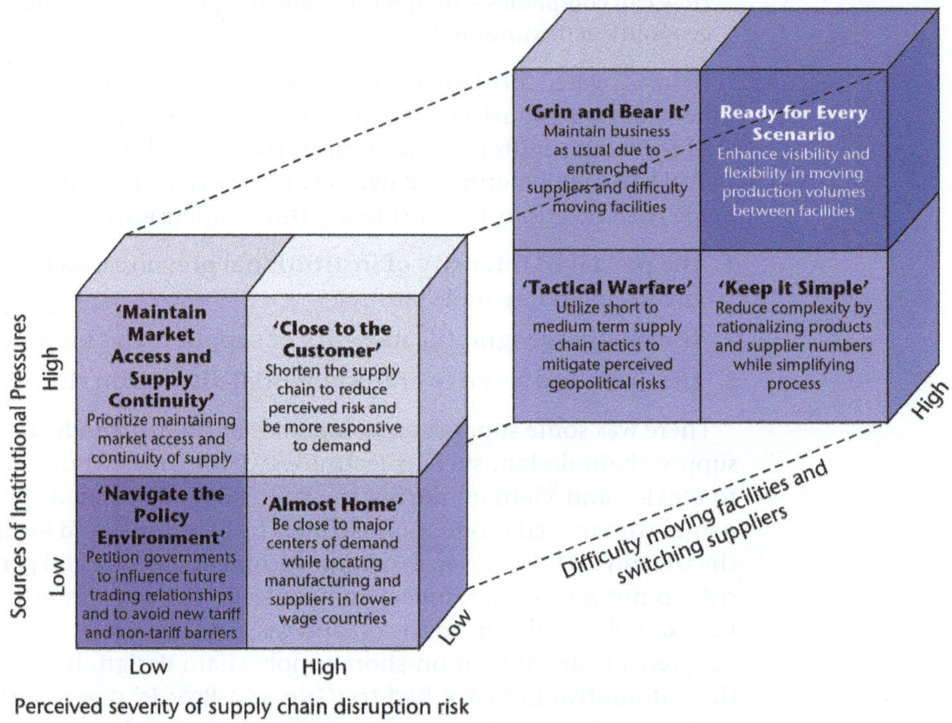

Figure 4.4 Supply chain logics in response to compounded geopolitical risks.
(Source: Roscoe et al., 2022.)

4.2.2 Focused factories or focused markets

Many international companies, particularly in Europe, originally would have organised their production nationally. In this situation, factories in each country would have produced the full product range for supply to that country. Over time, factories in each country might have been consolidated at a single site, which was able to make all the products for the whole country. This situation, in which there is a focus on a limited segment of the geographical market, is shown in Figure 4.5(a).

The focused factory strategy involves a company's consolidating production of products in specific factories. Each 'focused factory' supplies its products internationally to a wide market and focuses on a limited segment of the product assortment. This situation is shown in Figure 4.5(b). Traditional thinking is that this organisational strategy will deliver cost advantages to a global company. Whilst this is true for production costs, through economies of scale, the same is not necessarily true for inventory-holding costs and transport costs. Further, it can be argued that the focused factories are more exposed to risk, not just through the higher levels of transportation, but also through limiting the production of each product to one site globally. If this site is disrupted by some risk event, for instance natural disaster, then the supply of that product is disrupted globally with no back up supply.

While using the focused factory strategy companies need to be mindful of the risks that this brings and perhaps sacrifice production economies of scale, to assure supply of their products globally.

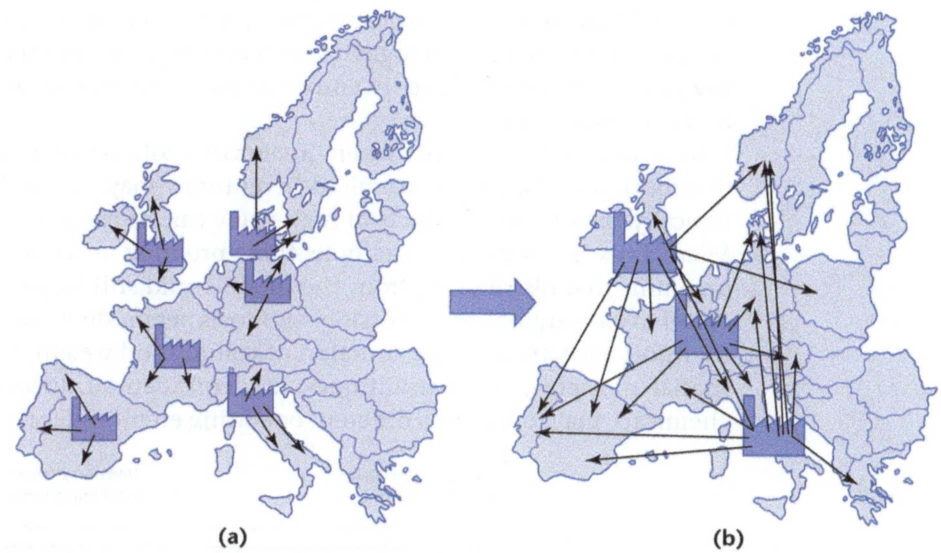

Figure 4.5 (a) Focused markets: full range manufacture for local markets (b) focused factories: limited range manufacturing for all markets.

Activity 4.1

Focused factories have an impact on performance, in particular cost and delivery lead time. Make a list of the advantages and risks of focused factories. Some examples have been entered in this table to start you off.

	Cost	Leadtime
Advantages	Lower production costs through economies of scale	Specialised equipment may be able to manufacture more quickly
Risks	Higher transport costs	Longer distance from market will increase lead time and reduce responsiveness

4.2.3 Centralised or decentralised inventories

In the same way that the consolidation of production can deliver cost benefits, so can the consolidation of inventory. Rather than having a large number of local distribution centres, bringing these together at a small number of locations can save costs. Savings can be achieved in this way by coordinating inventory management across the supply pipeline. This allows duplication to be eliminated and safety stocks to be minimised, thereby lowering logistics costs and overall distribution cycle times. Both may sound contrary to the fact that the transport pipeline will extend, owing to the longer distribution legs to customers from the central warehouse in comparison with a local warehouse. Nevertheless, through centralising inventory, major savings can be achieved by lowering overall speculative inventories, very often coupled with the ability to balance peaks in demand across regional markets from one central inventory. Figure 4.6 characterises the different operating environments (in terms of logistics costs on the x axis and service dimensions on the y axis) where centralised inventory (continental level of centralisation) may be more or less relevant.

In product environments where inventory costs are more important than the distribution costs, then centralised inventories may be the best option. This is typically the case for products of high value (measured in costs per volume unit). Microchips are an extreme example: these products are of such high cost per volume unit that distributing from the moon could still be profitable! Distribution costs have a marginal impact on logistics costs per product, assuming of course that transport costs are mainly a function of volume and weight. Products that require special transport, such as antiques, art, confidential documents or dangerous chemicals, may represent a different operating environment.

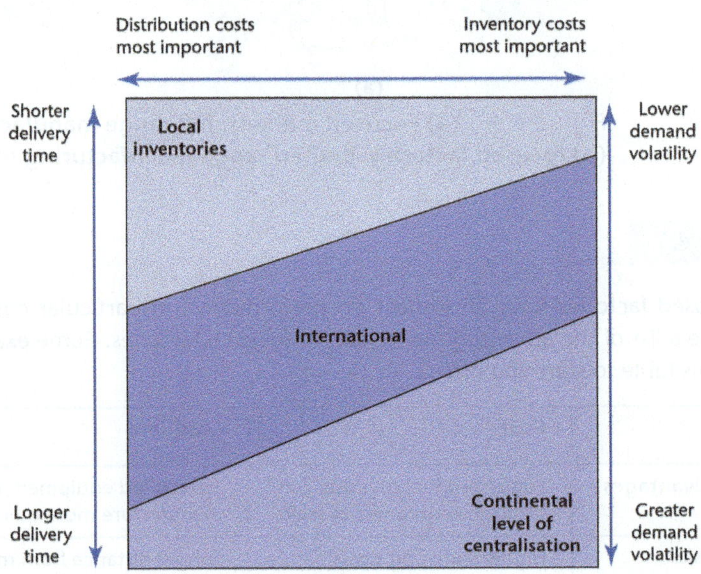

Figure 4.6 Inventory centralisation versus local inventories against logistics costs and service dimensions.

A second dimension that needs to be taken into consideration is that of distribution lead times. Here, we focus on physical distribution from warehouse to customer, and not on the inbound pipeline. Centralising inventory may lead to lower factory-to-warehouse distribution costs because shipments can be consolidated into full container loads. Where customers require short delivery lead times, there may not be sufficient time to ship products from a central warehouse. This is why, for example, hospitals and pharmacies retain inhouse stocks of products, almost irrespective of their inventory costs. Critical medicines and surgical appliances need to be available instantly and locally, regardless of inventory costs.

In general, transport costs have continued to decline over time as a relative cost item be-cause of innovations in transport technology, the commoditisation of transport (such as container ships) and the oversupply of transport capacity for basic transport. These factors in themselves contribute to the increasing internationalisation of logistics: physical distance be-comes less important, even for bulky products. However, customer demand can be very volatile and unpredictable. Accuracy of delivery (the right quantity) therefore can be a more demanding challenge than speed (the right time). Speed is available through different transport modes (container ship, air cargo, express, courier, for example) at reasonable prices. In very volatile markets, control over international inventories by means of centralised inventories can be crucial. Overall delivery reliability ('on time in full') tends to increase significantly, to the benefit of an organisation's performance in terms of service requirements. The ability to balance peaks across market regions from a central inventory is amongst the additional advantages. Different levels of inventory centralisation can be applied according to different dimensions. Taking the European market as an example, the range is from local inventories (by country or even by location) through international (a selection of countries) to the complete continent. Many companies now include the Middle East and Africa as a trading bloc (Europe, Middle East and Africa – EMEA).

Centralisation or localisation of inventory enables different delivery strategies with different advantages and risks. Figure 4.7 depicts a simple distribution network that enables three different delivery strategies to be applied, depending on the demand profile, as described in Table 4.1. For example, an opportunity to think globally with centralised inventory arises where the key product relies more on the designer label and its promotion and marketing and less on its manufacturing origins. The key to success in clothing is often about fashionable design and labelling. Low labour costs (rather than material costs) of production can then be achieved by outsourcing to low-wage economies, often in the Far East.

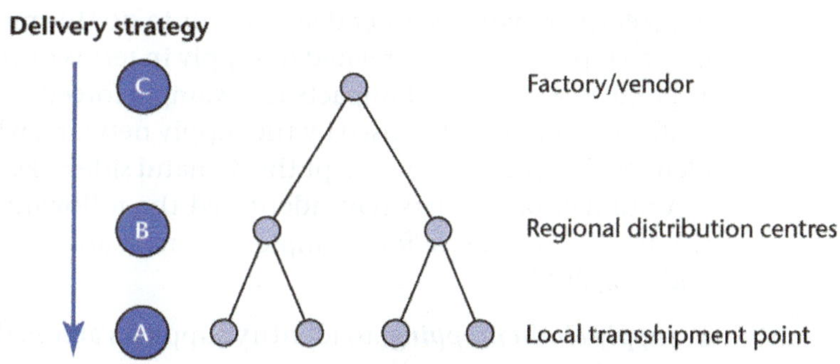

Figure 4.7 **Delivery strategies in a global network.**

Table 4.1 Three different delivery strategies and their risks, depending on demand profile.

Delivery strategy	Demand profile	Description	Advantages	Risks
A: Local inventory	High volume, stable demand	Direct shipment of fast-moving, predictable lines. Held locally, probably pre-configured (finished)	Short lead time to customer	Multiple inventory points leading to duplication of stocks, high inventory costs and higher risk of obsolescence
B: Regional inventory	Medium volume, variable demand	Inventory of medium velocity, less predictable demand lines held at generic level awaiting final configuration (postponement, Section 7.2.2)	Lower overall levels of inventory, consolidated shipments to distribution centres and concentrated handling	Longer lead times and transport distances to customers incurring higher risk of transport disruption and late deliveries
C: Centralised inventory	Low volume, volatile demand	Slowest-moving lines, least predictable. Perhaps one shared continental/global inventory or make to order	Low overall inventory levels	Longest lead times and transport distances to customers incurring highest transport and possibly customs risk

4.3 Supply risk management process

***Key issues:* What are the key steps to be followed to identify, evaluate and mitigate risk in the supply chain? How can supply chains be mapped and risk be measured and evaluated against a company's risk appetite?**

Supply chain risk management is the mitigation of supply chain risks through strategic coordination and collaboration among supply chain partners to ensure both profitability and operational continuity (Tang, 2006). It requires the identification, evaluation and mitigation of risks across the whole supply chain. Typically, companies are most concerned about the risk posed by their supplier network, because disruptions are likely to occur that will jeopardise the company's ability to meet their own customer demands, or to do this profitably. Alternatively, there may be reputational risk related to supply in terms of environmental impacts, such as pollution, or societal impacts for example forced or child labour. Therefore, we shall focus on the risks posed by the supply network, which covers all the risk types identified in Section 4.1, except the demand side risks.

A number of scholars have identified the following four major steps to supply risk management (see for example Tummala and Schoenherr, 2011 and Kırılmaz and Erol, 2017):

- ***supply chain mapping***, to identify suppliers across the different tiers to identify the critical nodes;
- ***risk identification*** through gathering supply risk data from various channels both internal to the company and external;

- ***risk evaluation*** through measurement and assessment against a company's risk appetite; and
- ***risk mitigation*** by developing plans to reduce the potential disruption.

In the following sub sections we will discuss how these processes work and some of the challenges involved.

4.3.1 Supply chain mapping

To manage risk across a supply network it is first necessary to improve visibility of the flow of goods and services, ideally from the origin, by identifying suppliers across the tiers up to the company in question, who we shall call the 'focal company'. This is known as **supply chain mapping**. It's important to be able to identify risks, even in the lowest tiers near the origin of the materials (Ho et al., 2015), as quite often some of the most serious risks occur there. For example, the reputational risk of child labour and modern slavery is often found in mines for precious metals and minerals, as was the case for cobalt mining in the Democratic Republic of the Congo (Boyle, 2023). Cobalt is used for components in various electronic products - smartphones, tablets, laptops, e-scooters, electric vehicles - and therefore is at the beginning of the supply chain for some of the world's largest and most successful companies. Around 75 per cent of the world's cobalt is mined in the DRC and it is in high demand (Boyle, 2023). The rare silvery metal is an essential component in every lithium-ion rechargeable battery, a necessary part of the booming electric vehicle (EV) industry.

A map of the supply network enables companies to address a risk pre-emptively, to avoid disruption to supply. For instance, if the risk of a hurricane is identified near a supplier location, and is likely to disrupt production, the supply may be temporarily switched to an alternative supplier, preventing supply disruption.

A supply chain map consists of two key elements (Maccarthy, 2022):

1. ***Nodes:*** these may be primary participants, which are entities that contribute directly to value-adding activities in the processing stages of a supply chain. Secondary participants may include third-party logistics providers, customs agencies, auditors, regulators, financing and insurance companies, etc.
2. ***Links:*** how the participants in the supply chain are connected via flows of material, information and financial. Other types of links between entities can also be captured in the map, such as competition, contractual relationships and cooperation and technology transfer.

Figure 4.8 shows a high-level example of a supply chain map provided by Resilinc (2023). It demonstrates a typical scenario where tier 2, and beyond, are not visible to the Original Equipment Manufacturer (OEM), which in this case is the focal company. Consequently, when a factory fire renders a tier 2 supplier inoperative the first the OEM hears about it is when the first-tier supplier pushes out the delivery date, which is too late to prevent disruption and ultimately late delivery, potentially to the OEM's customers. This map also demonstrates that this supplier is critical to the supply network, as it supplies a number of first-tier suppliers. As indicated by the red lines it supplies both the Original Design Manufacturer (ODM) and the sub-assembly manufacturer, who in turn supplies a further three

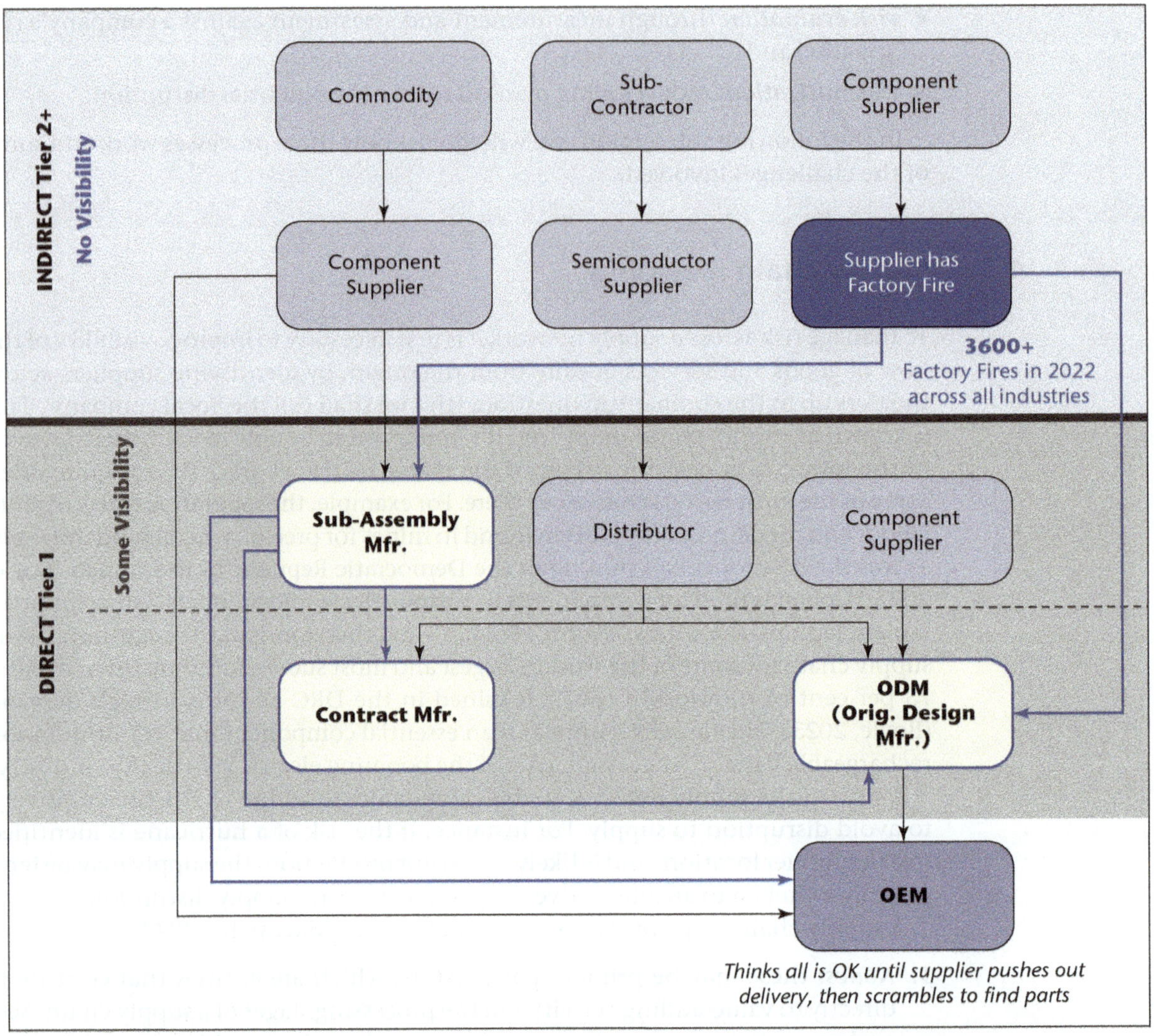

Figure 4.8 **Supply chain map for an OEM demonstrating the lack of visibility in the second tier.**
(Source: Adapted from Resilinc, 2023.)

companies: the OEM direct, the contract manufacturer and the ODM. All these flows are disrupted by the factory fire at this supplier, indicating that this supplier is a ***critical node*** in the supply network and risks affecting this supplier should be closely monitored to prevent disruption. A supply chain map helps understand the different relationships between suppliers, such as competitor, dual supplier and buyer–supplier, and exactly which suppliers (or nodes) would cause most disruption to the network if inoperative, and therefore could be deemed critical nodes!

However, while the benefits of supply chain maps are clear, developing them is far from easy. Most companies have many first-tier suppliers, which then multiply into many more at second tier and beyond. The automotive industry is an extreme example, where the supply base is broad, often extends to tier-10 or further, and is dependent on a worldwide supplier network, thus increasing the likelihood of risk events and rendering it particularly difficult to map.

So, what are the approaches to mapping the supply chain? Broadly they fall into two categories:

- ***automated analysis*** of large publicly available data sets on company, shipping and cross border transactions
- ***manual identification*** of suppliers through direct communication.

The ***automated approach*** requires the first-tier suppliers to be identified by the focal company. From there a variety of publicly available data can be analysed to identify the second-tier suppliers and beyond, sometimes to original source. The type of data used includes transactional data between companies, shipping data and customs or transborder data. This approach is quick and avoids the time-consuming communications normally required with suppliers. However, this requires capabilities to analyse very large data sets and ultimately the supply map generated is only an approximation, as it incorporates ***all*** suppliers regardless of whether they are supplying the precise components and products the focal company is buying. There are ways of limiting the network more closely to that actually supplying the focal company, by using different types of product codes, which can be found in customs data. For example, the European Commission (2024) has established a Harmonised Commodity Description and Coding System (HS), commonly referred to as the Harmonised System, which is an international system to classify goods developed by the World Customs Organization (WCO). It is a classification system of around 5,000 six-digit product categories. Nevertheless, these codes are broad and don't identify the precise products supplied to the company. There are various companies who offer supply chain mapping and risk management services, such as Resilinc, Everstream Analytics and Altana. Case study 4.3 describes Altana's approach, which provides a unified map of the global supply chain using AI.

CASE STUDY 4.3

Altana's unified global supply chain map generated using AI

Altana is a New York company founded in 2018, which uses Artificial Intelligence (AI) to generate a ***unified map of the global supply chain*** to enable the private and public sectors to manage global value chains. AI makes it possible to process billions of messy logistics and commercial data points, across different languages and data types, rendering a clean, unified and dynamic view of the global supply chain network. It can further reveal the precise supply chains of individual products and automatically track the changes to each supply chain as the network evolves over time, thus providing a current up-to-date global supply chain map.

It was thought that AI requires pooling everyone's sensitive data for learning, but not anymore. Through federated architecture and machine learning, it is possible to overcome the limitations on sharing data, making learning across data silos a possibility. Altana has pioneered a unique federated learning architecture that connects and organises the largest body of supply chain data ever assembled – across public and private data – providing a dynamic, intelligent, universal map of the global supply chain, all while ensuring data privacy, security and sovereignty for each of the network participants. The result is a shared source of truth on the global supply chain incorporating:

- 567 million companies
- 3+ billion shipments
- 137 million buyer–supplier relationships

Businesses are now increasingly required to gather and share insights across multi-tier value chains from raw materials, intermediate goods, final assembly and consumption. From the perspective of companies in both the private and public sectors around the world, they can access Altana's unified global supply chain map to:

1. gain visibility of their own supply network structure (see Figure 4.9 for example),
2. generate and manage product-level value chains (see Figure 4.10 for example) and
3. collaborate with both their suppliers and regulators on this common operating picture in order to generate growth and resilience through value chain design and industrial policy.

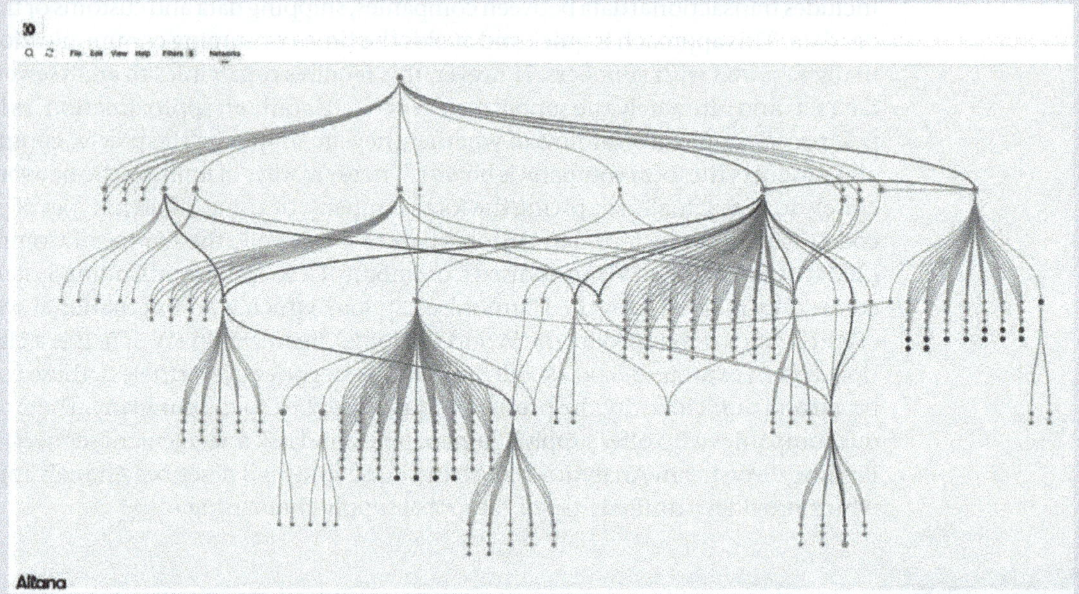

Figure 4.9 Expanding supplier network structure.

(Source: Ryan Heath, Customs and Border Protection is using AI to crack down on fentanyl trafficking. Retrieved from https://www.axios.com/2023/12/07/fentanyl-trafficking-ai-border-patrol.)

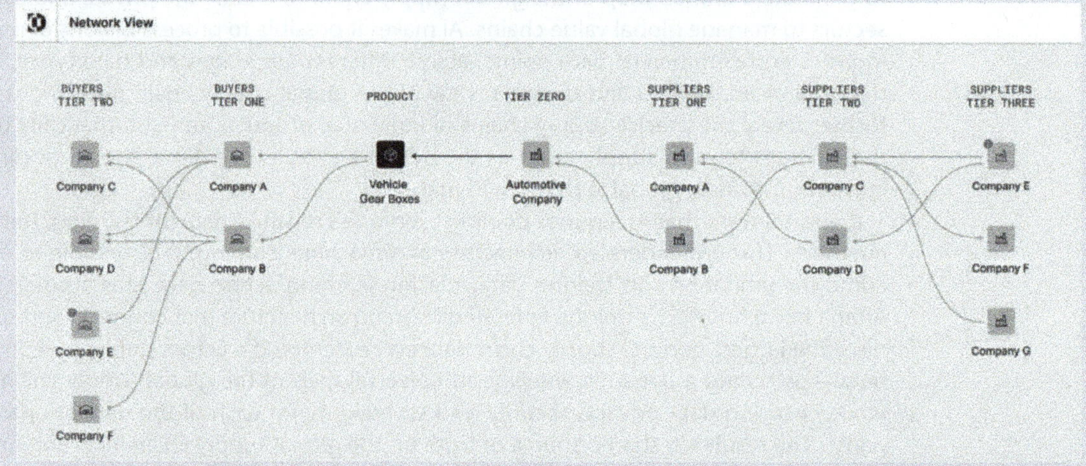

Figure 4.10 Product value chain view – the specific component development into a finished product.

(Source: Team Altana June 2024, Compliance: Move Beyond Flagging Risk to Orchestrate a Compliant Network. Retrieved from https://altana.ai/resources/compliance-value-chain-management-system.)

Access to Altana's unified global supply chain map provides a company with business intelligence on cross-border trade and compliance, sourcing, procurement, sustainability, financing, insurance, market intelligence and more. For instance, compliance covers everything from sanctions to forced labour, deforestation, carbon and more. Some examples:

- Workers' rights: the Uyghur Forced Labor Prevention Act (UFLPA) in the US
- Climate and sustainability: the EU's Corporate Sustainability Due Diligence Directive (CSDDD) and the EU's Carbon Border Adjustment Mechanism (CBAM)
- Geopolitically related sanctions (the UK and EU's multi-tier Russian Steel Sanctions)
- Critical minerals (Foreign Entities of Control Requirements in the Section 30D Clean Vehicle Credit)

A screenshot of compliance reporting is provided in Figure 4.11.

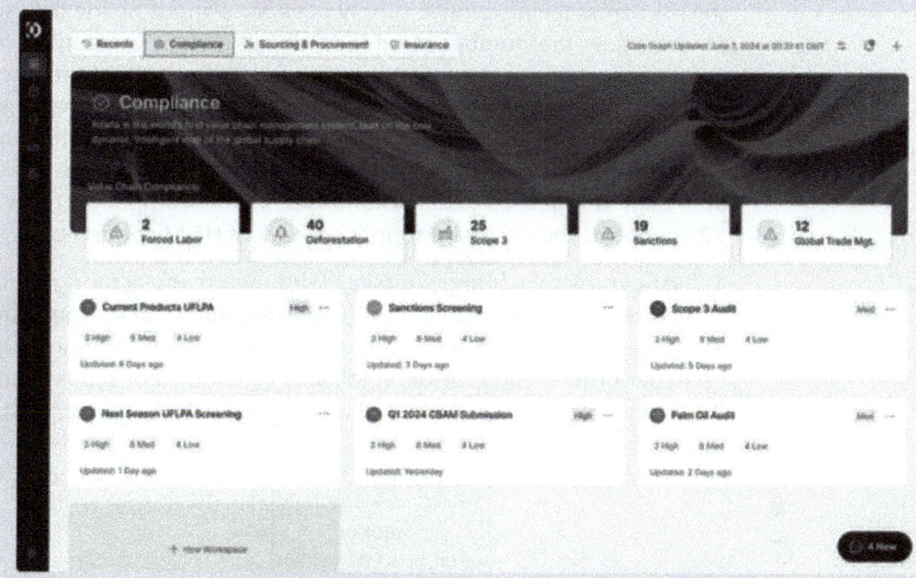

Figure 4.11 Screenshot of Altana's compliance reporting.

(Source: Team Altana June 2024, Compliance: Move Beyond Flagging Risk to Orchestrate a Compliant Network. Retrieved from https://altana.ai/resources/compliance-value-chain-management-system.)

Written with Tom Morrison of Altana.

(Sources: Beyond Supply Chain Management — Master Your Value Chains and Transform Your Business (Evan Smith CEO, Altana), Altana: comparing supply chain risk management applications to Altana's Value Chain Management System, Altana website, accessed on 22/08/2024 at https://altana.ai/resources/compliance-value-chain-management-system.)

The ***manual identification*** of suppliers through direct communication is far more time and resource consuming, often entailing questionnaires, email correspondence, telephone calls and even site visits to verify that these are the suppliers of the materials and components used by the focal company. Further, suppliers are not always cooperative in revealing their own suppliers fearing that this information will be shared with competitors or used against them in price negotiations. However, on the positive side the manual approach generates the precise map of the supply network for the specific products and components supplied to the focal company.

Naturally, the automated and manual mapping approaches can be combined, where the supply chains for critical suppliers or nodes can be mapped more precisely through a more manual method. Some companies specialise in the more precise mapping of supply chains for specific products combining data analytics with the manual method. For instance, Circulor specialises in supply chain traceability for environmental and societal sustainability. Case study 4.4 shows how Hennes & Mauritz's (H&M) mapped its supply chain using a mix of manual and automatic methods.

CASE STUDY 4.4

Hennes & Mauritz's (H&M) supply chain mapping

Like many companies, Hennes & Mauritz's (H&M), a leading Swedish global apparel retailer, has completed a supply chain mapping exercise to enable them to manage the risk across their extensive supply network. Various online data sources (e.g. annual reports show the number of opened/closed stores per country, revenue per market and the number of employees) were researched to find information about H&M's distribution centres and markets to map the company's downstream network (MacCarthy, 2022) as shown in Figure 4.12, where the solid line arrows show material flow. H&M products are transported to a centralised distribution centre in Hamburg, Germany and then shipped to local warehouses in the company's main markets spanning 72 countries. The upstream supply network of H&M consists of:

1. first-tier manufacturing suppliers who own manufacturing facilities known as 'cut and sew' factories located in 40 countries, mainly in Asia and Europe;
2. garment processing factories that the first-tier manufacturing suppliers subcontract to perform certain activities (indicated by bi-directional links); and
3. second-tier suppliers (yarn and fabric mills) (H&M Suppliers List, 2019).

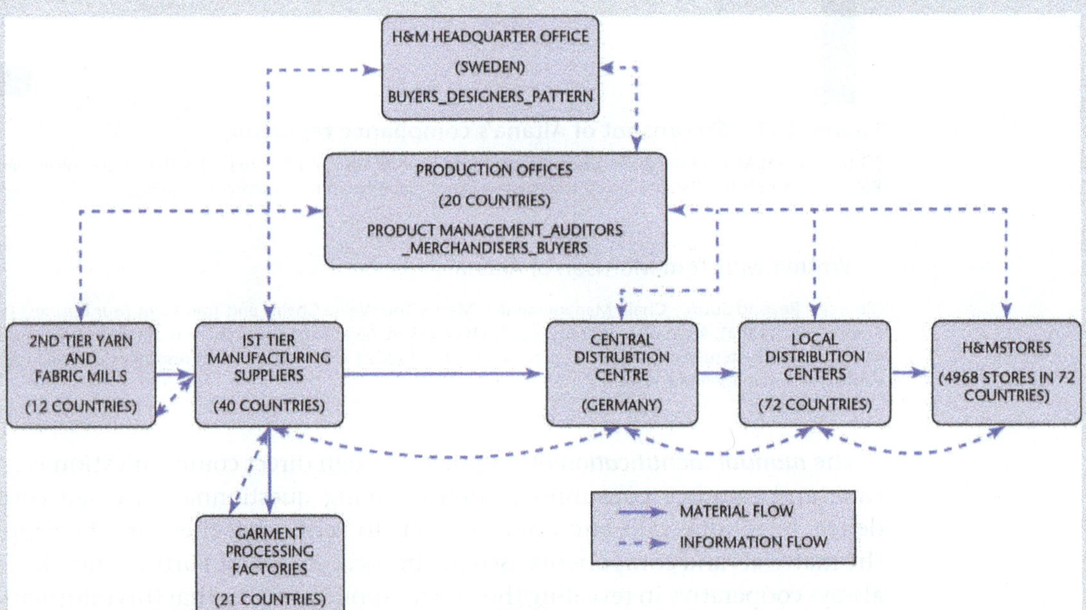

Figure 4.12 H&M high-level supply network map.
(Source: MacCarthy et al., 2022.)

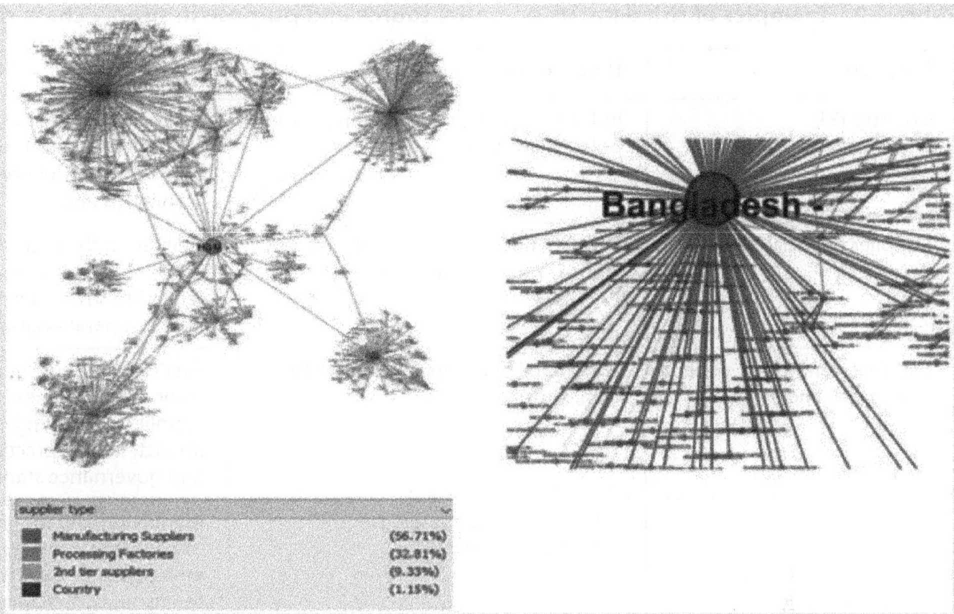

Figure 4.13 H&M supply network map at firm and country level.
(Source: MacCarthy, 2022.)

This provides a macro-view, but we can also visualise the specific supply network at the firm level, which is shown in Figure 4.13, also zooming into the sub-network in a specific country (Bangladesh).

This shows how their first-tier manufacturing suppliers, the processing factories they subcontract and the second-tier suppliers are clustered in just a few low labour cost countries. However, it also demonstrates that there are a high number of suppliers, suggesting a high overall manufacturing capacity and the opportunity to switch supply away from risk events when they occur.

(Source: MacCarthy (2022) and H&M Suppliers List (2019).)

4.3.2 Risk identification

Once a company's supply network has been mapped, the next stage is to gather supply risk data from various channels, both internal to the company and external, to identify risks (described and categorised in Section 4.1) that may affect either a node or a link in the network. Various types of data like country risk data, supplier financial stability data, ESG data and sanctions data can be collected from diverse sources like shipping data, social media, industry reports and meteorological reports. Examples of such data, its sources and purpose are shown in Table 4.2.

Data on supply chain risk can be gathered and assessed using methods such as data mining, predictive analytics and supplier surveys (Cylynx, 2021). Data warehousing, Application Programming Interface (API) integration, and Extract, Transform, Load (ETL) processes are used to integrate this data from diverse sources while utilising big data analytics to identify potential threats. Dashboards, Geographic Information Systems (GIS) and heat maps are examples of visualisation approaches that can be used to communicate risk insights clearly and quickly. Case study 4.5 provides an outstanding example of real-time supply chain risk management dashboards at Flex.

Table 4.2 Examples of risk data, its potential source and purpose in supply chain risk management.

Data type	Data source	Purpose/Usage in SCRM
Country risk	Industry reports, economic indicators, political analysis	Assessing the potential risks associated with specific countries, including political instability, regulatory changes, economic conditions and trade relationships
Supplier financial/stability	Supplier financial statements, credit ratings, supplier audits	Evaluating the financial health and stability of suppliers to identify potential risks related to their solvency, creditworthiness or operational capabilities
ESG (environmental, social and governance)	Sustainability reports, social media data, supplier audits	Assessing the sustainability and responsible business practices of suppliers, including environmental impact, labour practices, ethical sourcing and governance standards
Sanctions	Government databases, Trade compliance reports	Identifying and monitoring suppliers or countries subject to trade sanctions, embargoes or export control regulations to ensure compliance and mitigate legal and reputational risks

CASE STUDY 4.5

Flex Pulse supply chain risk data visualisation

Flex, formerly Flextronics, manufacture over 1,000,000 SKUs for markets, such as automotive, consumer electronics and healthcare, using their global manufacturing network of approximately 100 production sites across 30 countries. They have built one of the world's largest and most diversified supply chains operating at scale across multiple industries. Powering this massive, nimble network are 7,000+ supply chain professionals across their sites in approximately 30 countries who utilise strong relationships with a diverse base of 16,000 suppliers to source more than 1 million parts.

Figure 4.14 Flex Pulse dashboards at a Pulse centre.
(Source: Courtesy of Flextronics International Limited.)

Flex's digital supply chain visualisation tool, Flex Pulse, gives real-time visibility across multiple data streams, including transportation, manufacturing and inventory, resulting in greater resilience and faster time-to-market. Flex Pulse was released in 2015 providing real-time actionable data and global intelligence, drawing from over

9,000 supply chain experts. It was designed to pull from over 200 unique data streams, programs and processes, making it possible to understand the big picture without losing details. Flex Pulse serves as a single source of truth, providing supply chain teams with the real-time, high-integrity data they need, while providing secure access to data from anywhere, whether it's a Pulse centre (as shown in Figure 4.14), factory site, desktop or mobile device.

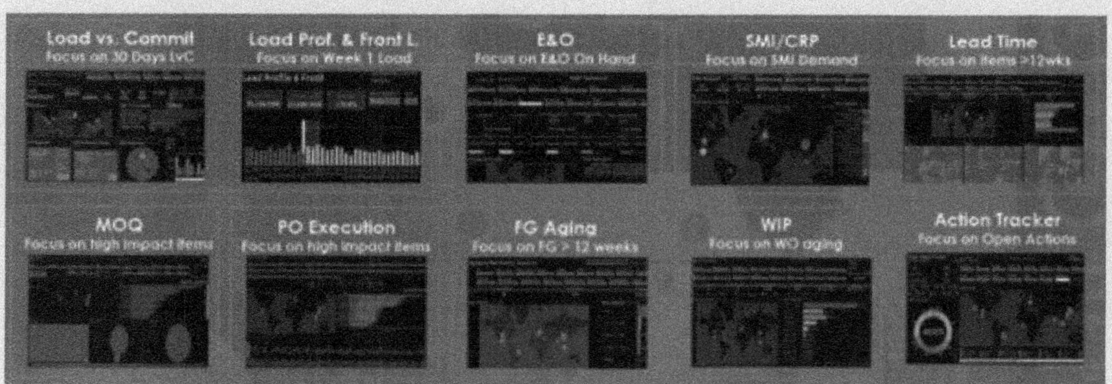

Figure 4.15 Flex Pulse real time dashboards focusing on actionable inventory insights.
(Source: Courtesy of Flextronics International, Limited.)

Dashboards, like those shown in Figure 4.15, provide inventory insight to mitigate risk before they turn into major disruptions, and an action tracker drives progress from action open to action close. Continuous improvement is prioritised, and Key Operational Indicator dashboards track outcomes and optimise processes over time. The intelligent platform identifies issues early and distributes consolidated data so that all employees have access to the information they need, at the moment they need it, to enable real-time action, active collaboration and avoid constant delays. Bringing all this together allows Flex to navigate the shifting business landscape, reduce risk, make data-driven decisions, harness real-time data, visibility and analytics, and sustain a more responsive, resilient supply chain.

(Source: Based on the datas from Flex website (http//flex.com).)

Activity 4.2

Select a food supply chain and use the template provided to answer these questions:

1. What are the risk factors across the supply network? (See Section 4.1 for a description of the possible risk categories.)
2. Consider how these risks might be identified and monitored – what is the data source and type?
3. Develop possible response actions to manage/mitigate the risk.

Risk factor	Risk identification (data source and type)	Risk mitigation actions

4.3.3 Risk evaluation

Risks are measured, assessed and evaluated against the risk appetite of a company in this stage of supply risk management. The key to measuring supply chain risk is to remember that it is evaluated across two dimensions: the probability of the risk event occurring and the negative consequences of the event (Christopher and Peck, 2004). This could be expressed as:

Risk = Probability (of the event) × Business Impact (or severity of the event)

The ISO 31000 standard for risk management provides principles, a framework and a process for managing risk in organisations of any size, activity or sector. One of the tools provided is the risk assessment matrix, an example of which is shown in Figure 4.16.

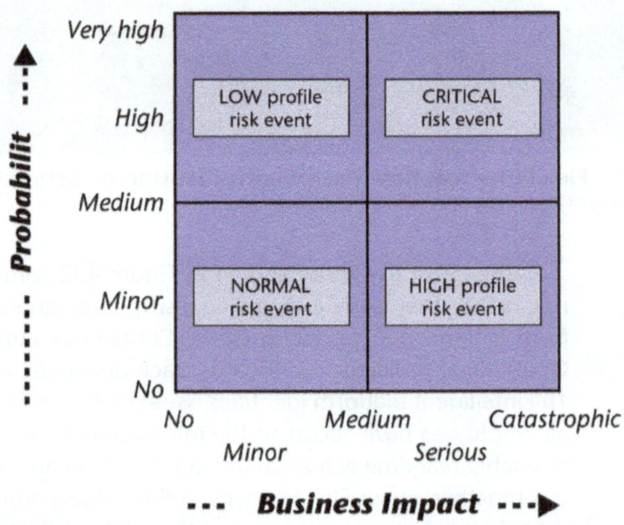

Figure 4.16 **Risk Assessment Matrix.**

(Source: Adapted from Norrman & Jansson, 2004.)

Risk events can be plotted on a risk matrix as a way of illustrating the measurement of the risk. Risks that fall in the high-probability and high-impact quadrant of the matrix are considered the most critical and would normally demand immediate attention. The risk appetite of a business determines how risks are assessed or evaluated. A business with a low appetite for risk, for instance, may not tolerate even low-profile risks (high probability of occurrence but low impact), whereas a company with a high appetite for risk might tolerate even high-profile risks (low probability of occurrence but a high impact), such as natural disaster risk events.

Thun and Hoenig (2011) provide a risk assessment matrix (in Figure 4.17), which illustrates the risk appetite of a particular company showing when immediate action is required, observation/analysis only and when no action is required. The shading shown on this matrix is a graphic representation of a particular risk appetite.

Thun and Hoenig (2011) conducted a survey of supply chain risk faced by 67 German automotive manufacturing plants, and the risk assessment matrix in Figure 4.18 is for one of these companies, illustrating how differently risks are assessed. Supplier quality problems are regarded as a critical risk since they have both a high probability and

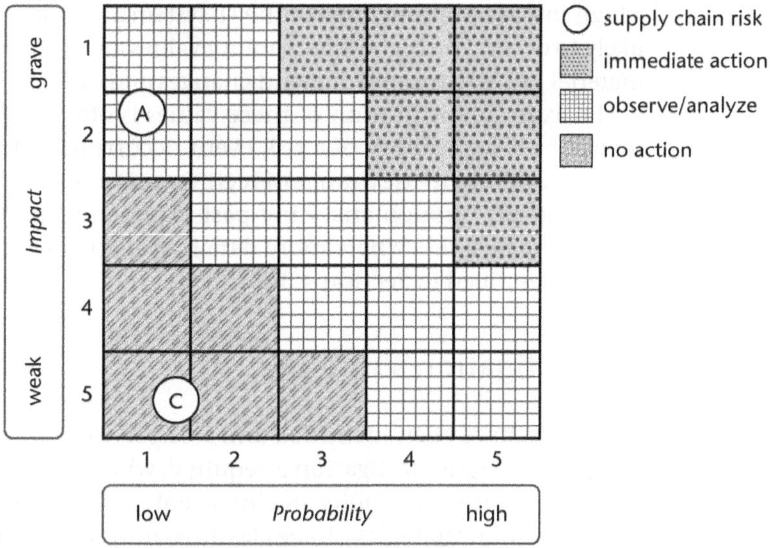

Figure 4.17 Risk Assessment and Appetite Matrix.
(Source: Adapted from Thun and Hoenig, 2011.)

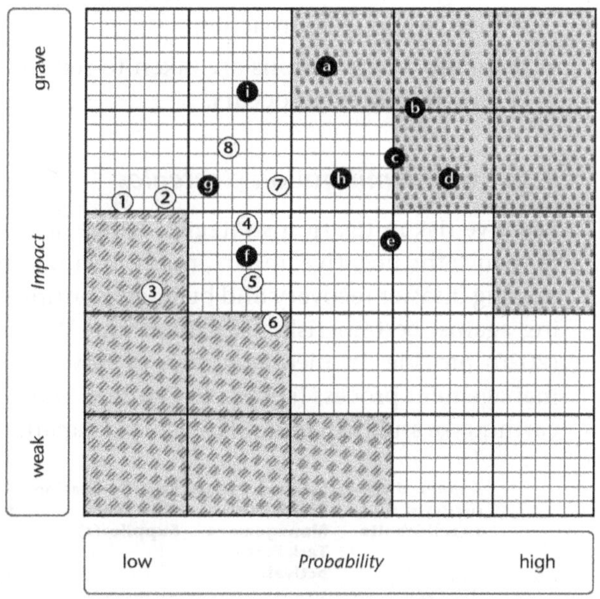

○ external supply chain risks	● internal supply chain risks
1. war	a. supplier failure
2. natural disaster	b. supplier quality problems
3. terriorist attack	c. change in customer demand
4. import restriction	d. increasing raw material prices
5. oil crisis	e. delivery chain disrupts
6. increasing customs duty	f. technological change
7. strike	g. transportation failure
8. accident (e.g. fire)	h. machine breakdowns
	i. malfunction of IT system

Figure 4.18 Risk Assessment and Appetite Matrix evaluating risk events.
(Source: Adapted from Thun and Hoenig, 2011.)

a high impact. Malfunctions of the IT system are seen as severe problems but are less likely to occur. The highest probability values are observed in terms of increasing raw material prices, customer demand changes and delivery chain disruptions.

The exact quantification of these values is often difficult, since a precise assessment of the probability of a risk event occurring and its effect is itself uncertain. Companies tend to use a range of techniques from expert group opinion within the organisation, through analysing past experience (particularly applicable to risks within the business where more data is available) to sourcing external data about risks as described in Section 4.3.2.

4.3.4 Risk mitigation strategies

Once risks have been identified and assessed to be beyond the risk appetite of the company, then risk mitigation is required, which involves the development of plans that decrease the probability and impact of risks in the supply chain (Mamun, 2023). Risk mitigation strategies can be classified into two groups (Kırılmaz and Erol, 2017):

- ***reactive*** where no action is taken in advance of a risk event, but action is taken to mitigate its impact once it has already happened. The risk probability is not reduced in these approaches.
- ***proactive*** where actions are taken to reduce the risk probability and/or impact before the risk event occurs.

Reactive risk mitigation strategies

Reactive risk mitigation strategies, where action is only taken after the risk event to reduce the negative impact, might include creating emergency response teams, putting disaster recovery and business continuity strategies into action, and insuring against certain risks (Norrman and Wieland, 2020). Norrman and Wieland (2020) provide detailed examples of how Ericsson's reactive supply chain crisis management process (shown in Figure 4.19) was used in crises, including the 2011 earthquake and tsunami in Fukushima, Japan.

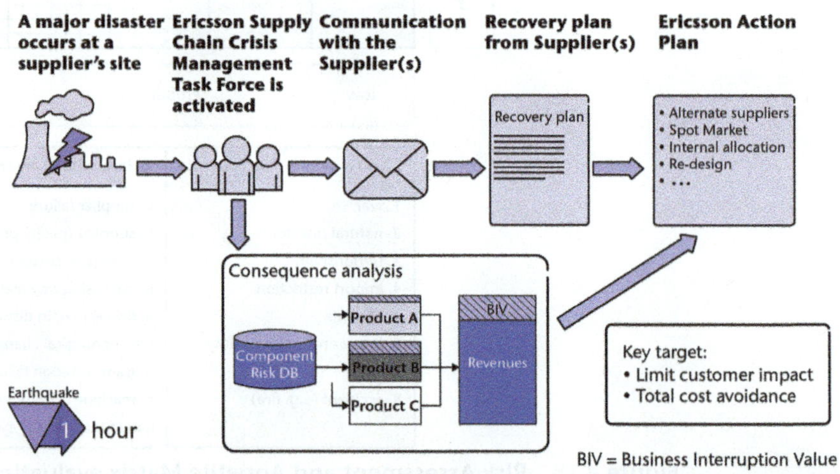

Figure 4.19 Ericsson's overall Supply Chain Crisis Management process.
(Source: Norrman & Wieland, 2020.)

Reactive risk strategies are often used in the event of ***natural disasters*** (described in Section 4.1.1), which are difficult to predict but have catastrophic effects on supply chains, disrupting entire regions, resulting in damage to infrastructure, transportation and communication systems. The consequences of such disruptions can be felt far beyond the immediate disaster area, affecting supply chains on a global scale.

Hurricanes are particularly destructive, and the annual average damage in the US due to hurricanes is $54bn, of which $9bn is to commercial businesses (Congressional Budget Committee, 2019). Dr Priscilla Schelp (Schelp et al., 2024) conducted research at Cranfield University on reactive risk mitigation strategies to reduce the negative share price reactions to hurricane-induced supply chain disruption, which account for 82 per cent of disaster incidents involving firms listed on the New York Stock Exchange (NYSE) (Schelp et al., 2024). This research provides guidelines to managers who need to make decisions on how to communicate supply chain disruptions to their customers and shareholders. The findings show that:

> **firms should communicate hurricane-induced disruptions in a transparent way, as this reduces shareholders' uncertainty, so the stock price reactions are less negative. For instance, providing details on actual damage leads to a less negative, and mostly positive, stock price reaction and providing information on preventative closures mainly prevents negative stock reaction.**

Proactive risk mitigation approaches could include establishing strong control systems, designing robust processes, providing redundancy to the supply chain and diversifying the suppliers (Norrman and Wieland, 2020). Jüttner et al. (2003) define proactive supply risk management strategies in terms of: avoidance, control, co-operation and flexibility and they provide specific practices for each strategy as displayed in Table 4.3. These approaches have stood the test of time and are as relevant today as they were when first published.

Table 4.3 Proactive risk mitigation strategies in supply chains.

Avoidance	Dropping specific products/geographical markets/supplier and/or customer organisations
Control	Vertical integration
	Increased stockpiling and the use of buffer inventory
	Maintaining excess capacity in productions, storage, handling and/or transport
	Imposing contractual obligations on suppliers
Cooperation	Joint efforts to improve SC visibility and understanding
	Joint efforts to share risk-related information
	Joint efforts to prepare SC continuity plans
Flexibility	Postponement
	Multiple sourcing
	Localised sourcing

(Source: Kırılmaz and Erol, 2017), after Juttner et al., (2003).)

Aside from natural disasters and accidents, geopolitically induced supply chain disruption (described in Section 4.1.1), such as trade wars, can be to some extent anticipated, and consequently planned for. But not with total certainty. For, while it might be possible to predict the probable broad shape of events, the precise nature of specific supply chain outcomes and their consequences can only be guessed at. For example, by June 2022 the post-Brexit border checks had still not been introduced at UK ports, having been delayed four times since the end of the Brexit transition period in December 2020 – a full six years after the referendum of June 2016. Roscoe et al. (2020 and 2022) conducted research on how supply chain uncertainty, arising from geopolitical disruptions (excluding accidents and natural disasters), may be managed by studying the pharmaceutical industry during Brexit from June 2016 (vote taken) to end of January 2020. Twenty-seven interviews were conducted with senior-level managers from eight real-life businesses and four expert organisations, all drawn from the pharmaceutical industry chosen because of its significant two-way cross-border trade flows, life-critical products and the existence of government mandates requiring assurances of continued supply. The research addressed the questions:

- ***Q1: How do businesses formulate and implement strategies to manage potential supply chain disruption in the face of such uncertainty?***
- ***Q2: Do firms of different sizes approach the challenge differently?***

Building on proactive strategy ideas in Jüttner et al. (2003) (shown in Table 4.3) and later academic literature, four distinct risk mitigation strategies were defined, of which the latter three are proactive:

- ***A passive strategy*** (same as reactive strategy described earlier), characterised by a *'do nothing'* approach in which businesses carry on as usual until after the event has materialised, and only then taking any actions required in order to minimise disruption to the supply chain.
- ***A 'wait-and-see' strategy***, in which businesses attempt to reduce uncertainty by *acquiring knowledge*, investing in intangible resources, such as relationships with suppliers, government bodies, trade associations, or policymakers, or initiate internal data-gathering programmes.
- ***A reactive strategy*** (which in this study is proactive compared to the reactive strategy described earlier), aimed at *reducing the severity of adverse outcomes* through *operational and tactical decision* making and investment in variable assets, building *redundancies* in the supply chain, for example:
  - Building inventory, accumulating safety stock
  - Shifting inventory to different distribution and warehousing facilities
  - Moving production quantities to different manufacturing facilities
  - Increasing capacity in transportation network through additional modes of transportation or transportation providers.
- ***A proactive strategy***, aimed at *reducing or eliminating the possibility of an adverse outcome* through *strategic decision making* and investments in tangible fixed assets, reconfiguring the supply chain, for example:

- Establishing new supplier contracts: multi-sourcing/dual sourcing
- Building new storage and distribution facilities
- Moving supply chain facilities away from high-risk locations
- Investing in enterprise risk management and systems
- Using tools and software to identify risk.

The study (Roscoe et al., 2020 and 2022) included companies of different sizes, and every company was interviewed at least twice, in order to see how their strategies evolved over time. The study findings showed that:

- ***Small- and medium-sized enterprises (SME) (1–500 employees)*** at first responded passively and then adopted a 'wait-and-see' strategy. Constrained by a lack of resources, they delayed acquiring knowledge until the shape of the questions become clearer. 'As far as I see it, we don't have any strategy [for Brexit],' one managing director stated. 'We've sent questionnaires [to our suppliers],' an operations director said. 'Some have said they're looking into it, others haven't come back at all, so we're chasing them up.'
- ***Large companies' (500+ employees)*** initial response was to adopt the information-gathering 'wait-and-see' approach, followed by both reactive and proactive responses, conducted in parallel, based on the conclusions that they drew. 'We're meeting very frequently with trade associations', a director of supply chain operations said. 'We have positioned buffer stocks, and [invested in the] capacity to make products. It's not just a wait-and-see approach anymore.'
- ***Multinational enterprises (MNE) (50,000+ employees)*** were the most aggressive in reducing uncertainty. Without exception, they assumed *worst-case scenarios* – in this case, a 'hard' Brexit under World Trade Organization (WTO) rules – and moved quickly through the information-gathering wait-and-see phase into both reactive and proactive strategies, again conducted in parallel. 'We don't have [any] uncertainty because of the worst-case assumptions that we've made,' a head of global logistics and warehousing told us. 'From Day One we've assumed full WTO conditions, and full customs and regulatory frictions on the way in, on the way through, and on the way out of the European Union,' added a global operations director.

How these differing strategic responses depend on company size is illustrated in Figure 4.20, demonstrating how the chosen strategies evolve over time as the disruptive event approaches and the extent of the uncertainty reduces.

Considering these study findings, first it appears that resource-poor small- and medium-sized enterprises (SMEs) are doomed by their lack of resource to live in a state of perpetual unpreparedness. But this is not necessarily the case. SMEs could instead be cannily banking on their greater agility and streamlined decision-making processes, and waiting until the shape of what may emerge is more certain before investing time and resources on what may be wasted information-gathering.

Second, it is difficult not to be impressed by multinational enterprises' (MNEs) ability to define, envisage and agree a worst-case scenario. There are costs to doing so, but multinational enterprises clearly judge that they can afford them.

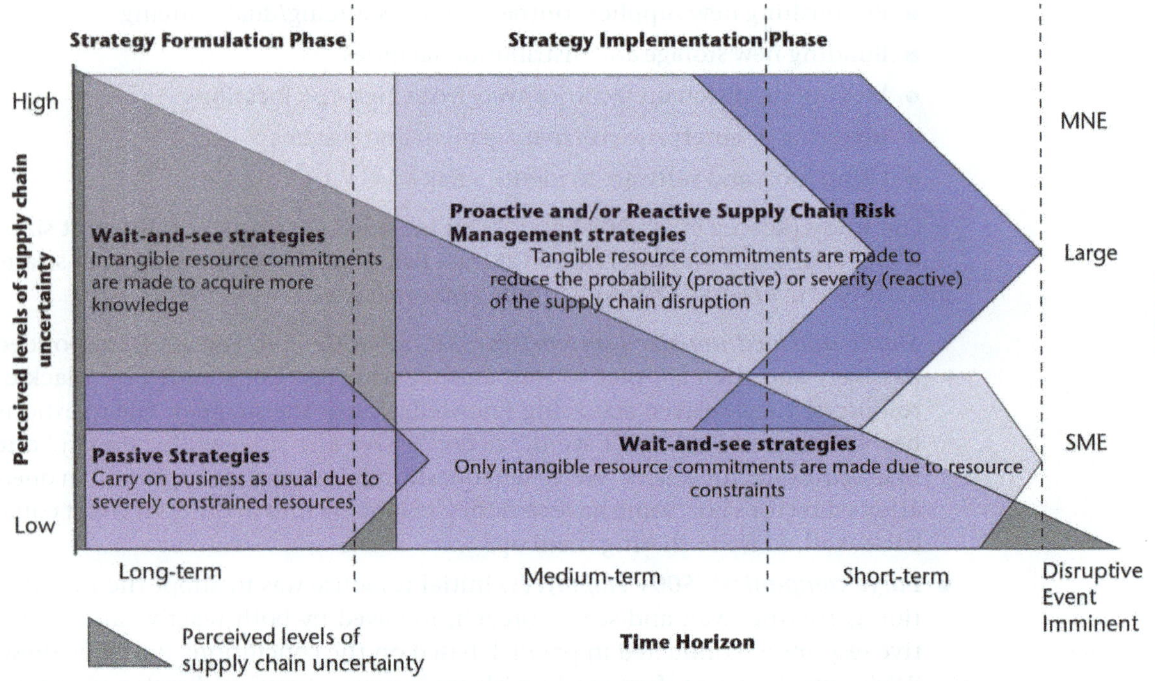

Figure 4.20 Risk mitigation strategies for different sized pharmaceutical companies managing supply chain uncertainty created by Brexit.

(Source: Roscoe et al., 2020 and 2022.)

Finally, large companies seem to take a more balanced middle-of-the-road approach – first gauging the risk and reducing the uncertainty by information-gathering, and then making decisions in which tangible resources to invest so as to reduce the impact of any disruption.

Proactive risk mitigation

Proactive risk mitigation is particularly challenging to apply across a broad and deep (10 echelons) supply network incorporating thousands of suppliers, as is typical for automotive assemblers. Supplier segmentation is an emerging purchasing approach to risk management, which enables supply risk to be mitigated across a vast supplier network, while minimising the resource required to do it. Suppliers are grouped (or segmented) using measures that determine the nature of the risk and therefore the risk mitigation approach. For example, a supplier risk assessment matrix, like that shown in Figure 4.17, could be used where suppliers are plotted according to the probability of a risk event occurring at the supplier's site and the impact on the company of such a risk event. Subsequently, the suppliers are segmented into each quadrant and different risk mitigation strategies developed for each. The axes of such a supplier segmenting matrix could include other parameters, such as supply risk (indicated by the number of alternative qualified suppliers available) as used by Kraljic (1983) in his enduring purchase portfolio matrix (covered in Section 9.3.2). As detailed in Case study 4.6, Ford Motor Company segment suppliers against total spend at supplier site and impact on business performance to determine proactive supplier risk mitigation strategies (Simchi-Levi et al., 2015).

CASE STUDY 4.6

Supplier segmentation at Ford Motor Company driving proactive risk mitigation strategies

Ford Motors used a supplier segmentation approach to enable more effective proactive supplier risk mitigation, using the same resource now focused on the more risky suppliers. Ford included more than 4,400 tier-1 suppliers, hundreds of thousands of lower-tier suppliers, 50 Ford-owned facilities, 35 billion total parts and more than $80 billion spend annually. Figure 4.21 shows the geographical location of the critical suppliers to Ford across tiers 1 to 10, which were included in the segmentation approach.

Figure 4.21 Geographical location of Ford critical suppliers where the size of a circle indicates the magnitude of the impact on Ford's performance if a supplier is disrupted.

(Source: Simchi-Levi et al., 2015.)

Rather than focusing this analysis on supplier companies, Ford focused on supplier sites, because risk events are often at specific locations, for example factory fires and natural disaster. For each supplier site Ford measured the total spend and the performance impact, in terms of lost profits for Ford, of a disruption at the supplier site in question. They were not concerned with the type of risk at the supplier, but more interested in how a disruption in supply would affect their profits. They then plotted the supplier sites on the matrix as shown in Figure 4.22. Interestingly, it can be seen that Ford's spend at a supplier site does not correlate with the profit performance impact on Ford. Indeed the red oval highlights that the supplier sites where a disruption causes the highest negative profit impact on Ford account for the lowest Ford spend.

Ford segmented the supplier sites into three segments, as shown in Figure 4.22:

- *Low-exposure suppliers (left side of matrix):* these supplier sites cause low negative profit performance impact and typically have low total spend, as shown by the spread on the chart. Ford's risk mitigation strategies for these suppliers include long-term supply contracts and tracking inventory.

- ***High-exposure strategic suppliers*** (top right of matrix): there are only a few supplier sites in this segment, but they provide critical components that strongly affect customer experience and account for a high Ford spend on material. Ford typically refers to these suppliers as 'strategic suppliers' and focuses on long-term partnerships, risk-sharing strategies and close performance tracking of them. Additionally, Ford requires these strategic suppliers to supply out of multiple sites to enable possible switching of supply to another location.
- ***Challenging suppliers*** (bottom right of matrix): this category includes suppliers that account for low total spend but have a high negative profit performance impact on Ford. These suppliers pose challenges in terms of ensuring a stable supply. Mitigation strategies include inventory investment, dual sourcing or requiring suppliers to have backup supply sites in different regions. In the longer-term efforts may be made to change the product design to avoid these suppliers.

Ford also categorised each supplier in terms of the specific vehicle model – 'vehicle impacted' – such that they could identify the specific vehicle that would be affected by disruptions.

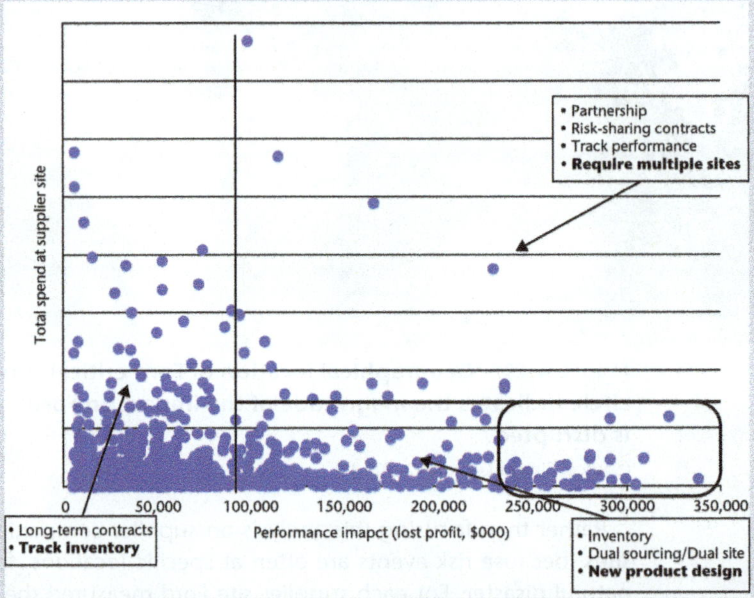

Figure 4.22 Supplier segmentation and associated risk mitigation strategies at Ford.
(Source: Simchi-Levi et al., 2015.)

Based on the supplier segmentation, and associated risk mitigation strategies, Ford reallocated its resources to protect itself from the highest-impact risk exposures in its operations and supply chain. This reallocation involved shifting resources away from low-exposure suppliers, that were receiving excessive attention, towards high-exposure strategic suppliers that required more focused risk management efforts.

Following the supplier segmentation approach, Ford identified over 400 supplier sites, which were currently receiving excessive allocation of Ford's risk management resource, that posed a very low performance risk to the company, if disrupted. By recognising these low-exposure sites, Ford could reallocate its risk management resources to the high-exposure strategic suppliers, ensuring that precious resources were directed towards suppliers with the highest impact on Ford's profit.

(Source: Based on Simchi-Levi et al., 2015.)

Questions

1. What are the two parameters you would use to segment suppliers of a company, you are familiar with, to drive proactive supplier risk mitigation strategies? How would you then segment?
2. What are the risk mitigation strategies you would suggest for each segment?

4.4 Supply chain resilience

***Key issues:* What is a resilient supply chain? What are the chronological phases in response to a risk event and the resilient supply chain capabilities required?**

While supply chain risk management is about mapping the supply network and monitoring risks affecting it to enable risk-induced disruption to be prevented or reduced, supply chain resilience accepts that disruptions will happen and it focuses on how to prepare for, respond to, recover from and ultimately adapt to these disruptions. A seminal work by Emeritus Prof Martin Christopher (Christopher and Peck, 2004, page 2) defines a resilient supply chain as one that can 'return to its original state, or move to a new more desirable state, after being disturbed'. This has been an enduring definition that still applies today.

It's widely accepted that supply chain resilience is enacted across chronological phases, as suggested by Hohenstein et al.'s (2015, page 1) definition developed from a systematic review of previous research:

> **The supply chain's ability to be prepared for unexpected risk events, responding and recovering quickly to potential disruptions to return to its original situation or grow by moving to a new, more desirable state.**

4.4.1 Chronological phases and capabilities

According to most definitions of supply chain resilience, the key chronological phases in relation to a risk event are as follows where the readiness phase prior to the disruption is proactive and the remaining phases following disruption are proactive:

- ***Preparedness or readiness*** for the disruption, which allows the disruption to be absorbed or even avoided
- ***Response*** to the disruption which tends to be immediate and quick
- ***Recovery*** from the disruption that may take more time and aims to return to the original pre-disrupted state
- ***Growth or adaptability,*** which aims to exploit the disturbance by not only returning to the original state through adaptation, but surpassing it by expanding and developing specific elements to boost performance.

Table 4.4 Resilience capabilities required during the resilience phases I.

Capabilities for ALL resilience phases	Proactive readiness phase	Reactive phases – response, recovery and growth
Collaboration	Inventory management	Agility
Human resource Management	Predefined contingency plans	Flexibility
Redundancy	Visibility	

(Source: Adapted from Hohenstein et al., 2015.)

Now let's consider the ***capabilities required for resilience***. According to most research the core capabilities are flexibility; redundancy; collaboration and visibility; and agility and multiple sourcing. But what matters is how these capabilities contribute to resilience through the four chronological phases as shown in Table 4.4. Hohenstein et al. (2015) identified three main capabilities that contribute to ***all four phases***:

1. **Collaboration** to share crucial information and valuable knowledge and establish joint efforts. Consists of coordination, cooperation, joint decision making, knowledge sharing, supplier certification and supplier development.
2. **Human resource management** to train and educate employees in dealing with risk events and to establish cross-functional teams. Consists of employee training and education, risk-sensitive culture and mindset, and experienced employees for crisis management.
3. **Redundancy** such as multiple suppliers and production locations, and excess capacity in production or transport that can be used as 'shock absorbers' for short-term disruptions.

Hohenstein et al. (2015) identified three further capabilities that contribute to the ***proactive readiness*** phase by anticipating and mitigating the impact of disruptions:

1. **Inventory management** by using safety stocks to buffer unexpected events and reduce the probability of stockouts and lost sales.
2. **Predefined contingency plans** as well as communication protocols to decrease response time and reduce mistakes during execution.
3. **Visibility** such as early warning indicators and real-time financial monitoring to prevent disruptions.

Finally, a further two capabilities that contribute to the ***reactive post disruption phases – response, recovery and growth*** – by providing the ability to cope with, and adapt to, unexpected disturbances:

1. **Agility** consisting of communication, information sharing, velocity to accelerate speed, responsiveness to changes in demand/supply and quick supply chain redesign to reduce the impact of disruptions and facilitate recovery.
2. **Flexibility** (which is a subset of agility) through backup suppliers, easy supply switching, flexible production systems (enabling volume flexibility), flexible distribution channels and multi-skilled workforce.

COVID-19 tested the resilience of all supply chains, and one could argue none more so than healthcare. Sawyerr and Harrison (2023) investigated the supply chain resilience of the ***UK's National Health Service (NHS)*** in response to COVID-19. They found that supply chains were largely unprepared, which was not particularly surprising even though the availability of gloves was significantly better compared to the other personal protective equipment (PPE). Techniques adopted to ensure response and recovery included unsanctioned methods such as extended use of PPE beyond recommended use, redefinition of guidelines, protocols and procedures by infection control and the use of expired PPE – all of which compromised healthcare worker and patient well-being. They make recommendations to improve the capabilities to sense and shape during the preparedness phase and to seize and maintain during response and recovery.

Supply chains in the private sector are typically more resilient and one particularly strong example can be found at Flex, as described in Case study 4.7.

CASE STUDY 4.7

Flex's supply chain resilience levers

Flex, formerly Flextronics, manufacture over 1,000,000 SKUs for markets, such as automotive, consumer electronics and healthcare, using their global manufacturing network of approximately 100 production sites across 30 countries. They have built one of the world's largest and most diversified supply chains operating at scale across multiple industries. Powering this massive, nimble network are 7,000+ supply chain professionals across their sites in approximately 30 countries who utilise strong relationships with a diverse base of 16,000 suppliers to source more than 1 million parts.

In keeping with the research ***flexibility, visibility and collaboration*** are Flex's key pillars of resilience to reinforce production and distribution systems. Flexible organisations can adapt to disruptions with minimal impact. For example, one way to build flexibility is to develop multiple suppliers in the event of service interruptions by your primary suppliers. When it comes to gaining visibility, this is critical to help you anticipate risks in real time, whether it's understanding a weather event such as the path of a monsoon or the ESG reputation of a second-tier supplier. Finally, collaboration entails bringing together stakeholders to work towards a common goal, and this includes information-sharing both inside and outside of the organisation. The stronger the collaboration between companies in a supply chain, the faster and more effectively they respond to disruptions.

Flex identify, evaluate and mitigate risks through three lenses: customer, suppliers and partners and market, as shown in Figure 4.23.

1. **Serving customers**: understanding obligations to customers requires an understanding of the risks in the chain. This begins with identifying the most critical components and mapping out their associated risks. For example, are there seasonal shortages of critical parts or potential price fluctuations that need to be planned for?
2. **Taking the pulse of suppliers and partners continuously**: how financially stable are our partners? Are there emerging risks to quality and timely shipment?
3. **Keeping tabs on potential marketplace disruptions**: these include political, environmental and other external threats.

▶

Figure 4.23 Three lenses through which Flex identify evaluate and mitigate risk.
(Source: Applying supply chain resilience levers nov 16, 2020, Flex. Retrieved from https://flex.com/resources/applying-supply-chain-resilience-levers.)

Table 4.5 shows the various risk mitigation strategies, tools and techniques Flex apply across the three pillars of resilience: flexibility, visibility, and collaboration.

Table 4.5 Risk mitigation strategies, tools and techniques Flex apply across the three pillars of resilience.

	Visibility and velocity	Flexibility and agility	Collaboration and relationships
Customers	Understand the shifts that can disrupt your processes and production such as changes to your customer's product demand forecast and launch plans	Build supply buffers of mission-critical parts by stocking extra inventory	Be a genuine partner to your customer and stay current on the developments in their business and markets. This extra effort will allow you to have meaningful conversations and information sharing
	Identify critical components, their lead times and any specialised tooling required for custom parts	Configure facilities for nimble production, which can be designed in a way to shift product mix quickly	
Suppliers and partners	Audit preferred first-tier suppliers for financial health, ESG standards and other relevant attributes	Develop dual- or multi-source supply base	Build on your customers' existing relationships with customers
		Understand suppliers' product lifecycle plans to get ahead of discontinued parts	Strengthen supplier relationships through ongoing engagement such as site visits and regular check-ins
Market	Analyse data from many sources to build a wide-ranging view of real-time market risks	The growing complexities in our world require risk mitigation models on multiple fronts	Build relationships with organisations having visibility and expertise in domains that matter to your business.

	Visibility and velocity	Flexibility and agility	Collaboration and relationships
	At Flex, we use Flex Pulse, a real-time dashboard that ingests data from hundreds of external and internal sources to give us a real-time view. We draw on wide-ranging data sources that include our purchase order systems to third-party weather forecasts	Line up alternative suppliers in different geographies to mitigate the effects of tariff wars and other trade disruptions	This includes research firms and government agencies. During COVID, the information we got from government officials helped us make decisions in a highly dynamic environment

(Source: Applying supply chain resilience levers nov 16, 2020, Flex. Retrieved from https://flex.com/resources/applying-supply-chain-resilience-levers.)

Building a resilient supply chain is a proactive de-risking process that never ends. Like any insurance policy, it comes with a cost.

(Source: Based on Applying supply chain resilience levers nov 16, 2020, Flex. Retrieved from https://flex.com/resources/applying-supply-chain-resilience-levers.)

Questions

1. Apply Flex's three pillars of resilience through the three lenses they propose, to a sector/company you are familiar with. What risk mitigation strategies, tools and techniques can you identify across a grid like that shown in Table 4.5?

Summary

What is supply chain risk and what are its sources, risk categories and factors?

- Supply chain risk is evaluated across two dimensions: the probability of the risk event occurring and the negative consequences of the event (Christopher and Peck, 2004), which leads to disruptions and reductions in operational performance across quality, cost and speed. Risks are categorised according to their location in the supply chain with respect to a focal company – supply, demand and operational. But also, according to the different risk factor groups: geopolitical, operational, financial, logistics and transportation, technological, sustainability, supplier specific and demand specific.

How can a company's supply chains mitigate the effects of these risks and prevent the disruption and reputational damage that may follow? There are three schools of thought in this chapter:

- International supply chains can be redesigned to mitigate the risk-induced disruption through changing the geographical location of operations (e.g. reshoring, offshoring, nearshoring and friend shoring), establishing focused factories (or not) and centralising or decentralising inventories.
- Supply chain risk management seeks to identify, evaluate and mitigate risks across the supply network with the aim of preventing (or at least reducing) the disruption.

It starts with mapping the supply network to the nth tier, which can be conducted automatically using AI or manually, although this is not possible at scale.

- Supply chain resilience accepts that disruptions will happen and focuses on preparedness, response, recovery and ultimately adaptation to the disruption to improve the resilience of the supply chain. It requires certain core capabilities which are: flexibility; redundancy; collaboration and visibility; and agility and multiple sourcing.

Discussion questions

1. How do the risk categories and factors described in Section 4.1 vary across sectors? Select two very different sectors and compare and contrast the risks.
2. Considering the three dimensions across which supply chain might be redesigned (geographical location of operations, establishing focused factories (or not) and centralising inventories) to mitigate risk-induced disruption, discuss the trade-offs against risk for each one.
3. Supply chain mapping and risk monitoring and evaluation require resource even if enabled by AI. How would you identify the most critical supply chains in your supply network to focus on? What criteria would you use?
4. Considering resilience capabilities across the chronological phases of resilience, how would you prioritise them and what types of risks (e.g. sources, categories and factors) do you think would prove the greatest challenge to resilience?

References

Blackhurst, J.V., Scheibe, K.P. and Johnson, D.J. (2008) 'Supplier risk assessment and monitoring for the automotive industry', *International Journal of Physical Distribution & Logistics Management'*, vol. 38, no. 2, 143–65. https://doi.org/10.1108/09600030810861215

Biney, J., Jones, E.C.J. and Jones, E.C. (2024) 'Understanding the EV semiconductor chip sustainable supply chain chip shortage', *International Supply Chain Technology Journal*, vol. 10, no. 2. https://doi.org/10.20545/isctj.v10i2.336

Boyle, L. (2023) '"Here it is better not to be born": cobalt mining for Big Tech is driving child labor, deaths in the Congo', *Independent*, Thursday 23 February, 2023.

Burges, D. (2013) *Cargo Theft, Loss Prevention, and Supply Chain Security*, Elsevier, ISBN 978-0-12-416007-1

Burrows, D. (2018) '10 Biggest product recalls of all time', Kiplinger, 26th March 2018, accessed on 05/08/2024 at https://www.kiplinger.com/slideshow/investing/t052-s000-10-biggest-product-recalls-of-all-time/index.html

Chervenkova, T. and Ivanov, D. (2023) 'Adaptation strategies for building supply chain viability: a case study analysis of the global automotive industry re-purposing during the COVID-19 pandemic', *Transportation Research Part E: Logistics and Transportation Review*, 177, 103249. https://doi.org/10.1016/j.tre.2023.103249

Chopra, S. and Sodhi, M.S. (2004) 'Managing risk to avoid supply-chain breakdown', *MIT Sloan Management Review*, vol. 46, no. 1, 53–61+87.

Chopra, S. and Sodhi, M.S. (2014) 'Reducing the risk of supply chain disruptions', *MIT Sloan Management Review*, vol. 55, no. 3, 73–80.

Choudhury, N.A., Ramkumar, M., Schoenherr, T. and Singh, S. (2023) 'The role of operations and supply chain management during epidemics and pandemics: potential and future research opportunities', *Transportation Research Part E: Logistics and Transportation Review*, 175, 103139. https://doi.org/10.1016/j.tre.2023.103139

Christopher, M. and Lee, H. (2004) 'Mitigating supply chain risk through improved confidence', *International Journal of Physical Distribution & Logistics Management*, vol. 34, no. 5, 388–96. https://doi.org/10.1108/09600030410545436

Christopher, M. and Peck, H. (2004) 'Building the resilient supply chain', *The International Journal of Logistics Management*, vol. 15, no. 2, 1–14. https://doi.org/10.1108/09574090410700275

Congressional Budget Committee (2019) 'Expected Costs of Damage From Hurricane Winds and Storm-Related Flooding', Congressional Budget Office (cbo.gov)

Cylynx (2021) 'Visualizing supply chain networks with Motif', 14th July 2021, accessed 31/07/2024 at https://www.cylynx.io/blog/visualizing-supply-chain-networks-with-motif/

Deiva Ganesh, A. and Kalpana, P. (2022) 'Future of artificial intelligence and its influence on supply chain risk management – A systematic review', *Computers & Industrial Engineering*, 169, 108206. https://doi.org/10.1016/j.cie.2022.108206

de Sa, M.M., Miguel, P., Brito, R. and Pereira, S. (2019) '"Supply chain resilience: the whole is not the sum of the parts', *International Journal of Operations and Production Management*, vol. 40, no. 1, pp. 92–115.

Ellram, L.M., Tate, W.L. and Petersen, K.J. (2013) 'Offshoring and reshoring: an update on the manufacturing location decision', *Journal of Supply Chain Management*, vol. 49, no. 2, pp. 14–22, John Wiley & Sons.

European Commission (2024) Harmonised System, accessed on 29th July at https://trade.ec.europa.eu/access-to-markets/en/content/harmonised-system-0#:~:text=The%20Harmonised%20System%2C%20HS%2C%20nomenclature,customs%20authorities%20around%20the%20world

Gordon, J. (2023) 'What friendshoring means for global supply chains', *Supply Chain and Procurement, Raconteur*, 19th March 2023.

Guha-Sapir, D., Below, R. and Hoyois, P. (2017) 'EM-DAT: The CRED/OFDA International Disaster Database', Université catholique de Louvain.

H&M Suppliers List, 2019 H&M Group Supply Chain, H&M Group. https://hmgroup-prd-app.azurewebsites.net/sustainability/leading-the-change/transparency/supply-chain/. accessed 04/01/2019.

Hajmohammad, S., Klassen, R.D. and Vachon, S. (2024) 'Managing supplier sustainability risk: an experimental study', *Supply Chain Management: An International Journal*, vol. 29, no. 1, 50–67. https://doi.org/10.1108/SCM-02-2023-0106

Hallikas, J., Lintukangas, K. and Kähkönen, A.-K. (2020) 'The effects of sustainability practices on the performance of risk management and purchasing', *Journal of Cleaner Production*, 263, 121579. https://doi.org/10.1016/j.jclepro.2020.121579

Hartman, P.L., Ogden, J.A., Wirthlin, J.R. and Hazen, B.T. (2017) 'Nearshoring, reshoring, and insourcing: moving beyond the total cost of ownership conversation', *Business Horizons*, vol. 60, no. 3, pp. 363–73.

Ho, W., Zheng, T., Yildiz, H. and Talluri, S. (2015) 'Supply chain risk management: a literature review', *International Journal of Production Research*, vol. 53, no. 16, 5031–69. https://doi.org/10.1080/00207543.2015.1030467

Hoek, R.V. (2020) 'Responding to COVID-19 supply chain risks—insights from supply chain change management, total cost of ownership and supplier segmentation theory', *Logistics*, vol. 4, no. 4, 23. https://doi.org/10.3390/logistics4040023

Hohenstein, N.-O., Feisel, E., Hartmann, E. and Giunipero, L. (2015) 'Research on the phenomenon of supply chain resilience: a systematic review and paths for further investigation', *International Journal of Physical Distribution & Logistics Management*, vol. 45, no. 1/2, pp. 90–117. https://doi.org/10.1108/IJPDLM-05-2013-0128

Huma, S., Ahmed, W. and Najmi, A. (2020) 'Understanding the impact of supply-side decisions and practices on supply risk management', *Benchmarking: An International Journal*, vol. 27, no. 5, 1769–92. https://doi.org/10.1108/BIJ-06-2019-0272

Jüttner, U., Peck, H. and Christopher, M. (2003) 'Supply chain risk management: outlining an agenda for future research', *International Journal of Logistics Research and Applications*, vol. 6, no. 4, 197–210. https://doi.org/10.1080/13675560310001627016

Kähkönen, A.-K., Marttinen, K., Kontio, A. and Lintukangas, K. (2023) 'Practices and strategies for sustainability-related risk management in multi-tier supply chains', *Journal of Purchasing and Supply Management*, vol. 29, no. 3, 100848. https://doi.org/10.1016/j.pursup.2023.100848

Kelly, P. (2024) 'Microsoft IT outage disrupts global supply chains', *Logicall*, 29th July, 2024, accessed on 06/08/2024.

Kırılmaz, O. and Erol, S. (2017) 'A proactive approach to supply chain risk management: shifting orders among suppliers to mitigate the supply side risks', *Journal of Purchasing and Supply Management*, vol. 23, no. 1, 54–65. https://doi.org/10.1016/j.pursup.2016.04.002

Kraljic, P. (1983) 'Purchasing must become supply management', *Harvard Business Review*, vol. 61, no. 5, 109–17.

Lamberg, J.-A., Lubinaitė, S., Ojala, J. and Tikkanen, H. (2021) 'The curse of agility: the Nokia Corporation and the loss of market dominance in mobile phones, 2003–2013', *Business History*, vol. 63, vol. 4, 574–605. https://doi.org/10.1080/00076791.2019.1593964

Lintukangas, K., Kähkönen, A.-K. and Ritala, P. (2016) 'Supply risks as drivers of green supply management adoption', *Journal of Cleaner Production*, 112, 1901–09. https://doi.org/10.1016/j.jclepro.2014.10.089

MacCarthy, B.L., Ahmed, W.A.H. and Demirel, G. (2022) 'Mapping the supply chain: why, what and how?', *International Journal of Production Economics*, 250. https://doi.org/10.1016/j.ijpe.2022.108688

Mamun, M. (2023) 'Supply chain risk management in a digital era: evidence from SMEs of clothing retailers in Australia', *Journal of Risk and Financial Management*, vol. 16, no. 4. https://doi.org/10.3390/jrfm16040242

Manuj, I. and Mentzer, J.T. (2008) 'Global supply chain risk management', *Journal of Business Logistics*, vol. 29, no. 1, 133–55. https://doi.org/10.1002/j.2158-1592.2008.tb00072.x

Matsuo, H. (2015) 'Implications of the Tohoku earthquake for Toyota's coordination mechanism: supply chain disruption of automotive semiconductors', *International Journal of Production Economics*, 161, pp. 217–27. https://doi.org/10.1016/j.ijpe.2014.07.010

Moradlou, H. and Backhouse, C.J. (2016) 'A review of manufacturing re-shoring in the context of customer-focused postponement strategies', Proceedings of the Institution of Mechanical Engineers – *Part B: Journal of Engineering Manufacture*, vol. 230, no. 9, pp. 1561–71.

Moradlou, H., Backhouse, C. and Ranganathan, R. (2017) 'Responsiveness, the primary reason behind re-shoring manufacturing activities to the UK: an Indian industry perspective', *International Journal of Physical Distribution and Logistics Management*, vol. 47, nos 2–3, pp. 222–36.

Moradlou, H., Reefke, H., Skipworth, H. and Roscoe, S. (2021) 'Geopolitical disruptions and the manufacturing location decision in multinational company supply chains: a Delphi study on Brexit', *International Journal of Operations and Production Management*, vol. 41, no. 2, pp. 102–30.

Norrman, A. and Jansson, U. (2004) 'Ericsson's proactive supply chain risk management approach after a serious sub-supplier accident', *International Journal of Physical Distribution and Logistics Management*, vol. 34, no. 5, 434– 56. https://doi.org/10.1108/09600030410545463

Norrman, A. and Wieland, A. (2020) 'The development of supply chain risk management over time: revisiting Ericsson', *International Journal of Physical Distribution and Logistics Management*, vol. 50, no. 6, 641–66.

Rao, S. and Goldsby, T.J. (2009) 'Supply chain risks: a review and typology', *The International Journal of Logistics Management*, vol. 20, no. 1, 97–123. https://doi.org/10.1108/09574090910954864

Reland, J. and Jurkovic, P. (2024) 'The UK's border with the EU', UK in a Changing Europe, 30th January 2024, accessed on 06/08/2024 at https://ukandeu.ac.uk/explainers/the-uks-border-with-the-eu/

Richter, F (2021) 'China is the world's manufacturing superpower', *Statista*, 4th May 2021, accessed at https://www.statista.com/chart/20858/top-10-countries-by-share-of-global-manufacturing-output/

Roscoe, S., Skipworth, H., Aktas, E. and Habib, F. (2020) 'Managing supply chain uncertainty arising from geopolitical disruptions: evidence from the pharmaceutical industry and Brexit', *International Journal of Operations & Production Management*, vol. 40, no. 9, 1499–1529. https://doi.org/10.1108/IJOPM-10-2019-0668

Roscoe, S., Skipworth H., Aktas, E. and Habib, F. (2022) 'Decision making in the dark', *Focus*, Chartered Institute of Logistics and Transport (CILT), July edition. pp. 56–8.

Roscoe, S., Aktas, E., Petersen, K., Skipworth, H., Handfield, R. and Habib, F. (2022) 'Redesigning global supply chains during compounding geopolitical disruptions: the role of supply chain logics, *International Journal of Operations and Production Management*, vol. 42, no.9, pp. 1407–34.

Samvedi, A., Jain, V. and Chan, F.T.S. (2013) 'Quantifying risks in a supply chain through integration of fuzzy AHP and fuzzy TOPSIS', *International Journal of Production Research*, vol. 51, no. 8, 2433–42. https://doi.org/10.1080/00207543.2012.741330

Sarker, S., Engwall, M., Trucco, P. and Feldmann, A. (2016) 'Internal visibility of external supplier risks and the dynamics of risk management silos', *IEEE Transactions on Engineering Management*, vol. 63, no. 4, 451–61. https://doi.org/10.1109/TEM.2016.2596144

Sawyerr, E. and Harrison, C. (2023) 'Resilience in healthcare supply chains: a review of the UK's response to the COVID19 pandemic', *International Journal of Physical Distribution & Logistics Management*, vol. 53, no. 3, pp. 297–329. https://doi.org/10.1108/IJPDLM-09-2021-0403

Schelp, P., Skipworth, H., Aktas, E. and Vieth, B. (2024) 'Supply chain disruptions and stock prices: the effects of hurricane-induced disruptions on company stock prices', *Springer Nature*, 31st May, 2024.

Schoenherr, T., Rao Tummala, V.M. and Harrison, T.P. (2008) 'Assessing supply chain risks with the analytic hierarchy process: providing decision support for the offshoring decision by a US manufacturing company', *Journal of Purchasing and Supply Management*, vol. 14, no. 2, 100–11. https://doi.org/10.1016/j.pursup.2008.01.008

Sheth, J.N. and Uslay, C. (2023) 'The geopolitics of supply chains: assessing the consequences of the Russo-Ukrainian war for B2B relationships', *Journal of Business Research*, 166, 114120. https://doi.org/10.1016/j.jbusres.2023.114120

Silva, J. (2024) EU hits Chinese electric cars with new tariffs, BBC Business News, 4th July 2024, accessed 05/08/2024 at https://www.bbc.co.uk/news/articles/cy99z53qypko#:~:text=The%20European%20Union%20has%20raised,electric%20cars%20imported%20from%20China

Simangunsong, E., Hendry, L.C. and Stevenson, M. (2012) 'Supply-chain uncertainty: a review and theoretical foundation for future research', *International Journal of Production Research*, vol. 50, no. 16, 4493–523. https://doi.org/10.1080/00207543.2011.613864

Simchi-Levi, D., Schmidt, W., Wei, Y., Zhang, P.Y., Combs, K., Ge, Y., Gusikhin, O., Sanders, M. and Zhang, D. (2015) 'Identifying risks and mitigating disruptions in the automotive supply chain', *Interfaces*, vol. 45, no. 5, 375–90. https://doi.org/10.1287/inte.2015.0804

Tang, C.S. (2006) 'Perspectives in supply chain risk management', *International Journal of Production Economics*, vol. 103, no. 2, 451–88. https://doi.org/10.1016/j.ijpe.2005.12.006

Tate, W.L. and Bals, L. (2017) 'Outsourcing/offshoring insights: going beyond reshoring to rightshoring', *International Journal of Physical Distribution and Logistics Management*, vol. 47, nos. 2–3, pp. 106–13.

Theyel, G., Hofmann, K. and Gregory, M. (2018) 'Understanding manufacturing location decision making: rationales for retaining, offshoring, reshoring, and hybrid approaches', *Economic Development Quarterly*, vol. 32, no. 4, pp. 300–12.

Thun, J.-H. and Hoenig, D. (2011) 'An empirical analysis of supply chain risk management in the German automotive industry', *International Journal of Production Economics*, vol. 131, no. 1, 242–9. https://doi.org/10.1016/j.ijpe.2009.10.010

Torres-Ruiz, A. and Ravindran, A.R. (2018) 'Multiple criteria framework for the sustainability risk assessment of a supplier portfolio', *Journal of Cleaner Production*, 172, 4478–93. https://doi.org/10.1016/j.jclepro.2017.10.304

Tummala, R. and Schoenherr, T. (2011) 'Assessing and managing risks using the Supply Chain Risk Management Process (SCRMP)', *Supply Chain Management: An International Journal*, vol. 16, no. 6, 474–83. https://doi.org/10.1108/13598541111171165

Wagner, S. M. and Neshat, N. (2010) 'Assessing the vulnerability of supply chains using graph theory', *International Journal of Production Economics*, vol. 126, no. 1, 121–9. https://doi.org/10.1016/j.ijpe.2009.10.007

Wang, S., Ghadge, A. and Aktas, E. (2024) 'Digital transformation in food supply chains: an implementation framework', *Supply Chain Management: An International Journal*, vol. 29, no. 2, 328–50. https://doi.org/10.1108/SCM-09-2023-0463

World Economic Forum Insight Report 7th Ed., 2012. Global Risks 2012.

Zhang, X., Zhang, Y. and Li, G. (2024) 'Strategic inventory in semi-conductor supply chains under industrial disruption', *International Journal of Production Economics*, 272. https://doi.org/10.1016/j.ijpe.2024.109254

Zimmer, K., Fröhling, M., Breun, P. and Schultmann, F. (2017) 'Assessing social risks of global supply chains: a quantitative analytical approach and its application to supplier selection in the German automotive industry', *Journal of Cleaner Production*, 149, pp. 96–109. https://doi.org/10.1016/j.jclepro.2017.02.041

CHAPTER 5

Managing the lead-time frontier

Objectives

The intended objectives of this chapter are to:

- **introduce time-based competition and the virtuous circle of speed;**
- **show how the lead time needs to be managed to serve customer expectations;**
- **explain how organisations compete through responsiveness.**

By the end of this chapter you should be able to understand:

- **how organisations compete through managing lead time;**
- **how time can be used as a performance measure;**
- **P-times and D-times and the consequences when they do not match;**
- **different solutions to reduce P-times.**

Introduction

This chapter takes a strategic and a managerial view of time, and of the impact of time on logistics performance. It provides an introduction to the nature of time-based competition and how time can provide competitive advantage in logistics. As we saw in Section 1.3, logistics supports the competitiveness of the supply chain as a whole by meeting end-customer demand through supplying what is needed, when it is needed and at low cost. Because logistics supports time and place commitments in the supply chain, it can be argued that the lead-time frontier accounts for at least half of logistics success.

Competing on time is the principle of taking timely completion of supply chain tasks to a higher level: that of compressing **cycle times** for supply chain operations for internal and external benefits. External benefits include:

- lowering overall cycle time and providing products and services on a shorter **lead time**, which is increasingly important in many different markets today;
- out-performing the competition.

These benefits are especially important in the context of improving responsiveness to customers and volatile markets. Chapter 7 will return to these points by addressing agile supply chains.

Internal benefits include:

- removal of non-value adding processes that could be termed as waste;
- lowering inventories in the supply chain by speeding up processes, such that sales forecasts are more accurate and safety stock can be reduced;
- shorter cash-to-cash cycles, thereby releasing working capital, improving liquidity and reducing asset intensity of the supply chain (as discussed in detail in Chapter 3).

These benefits are especially important within lean or waste elimination approaches, as will be developed in Chapter 7. This chapter focuses on how time-based solutions link with competitive strategy and details the time-based process mapping approach, which can be used when implementing lean thinking.

Key issues

This chapter addresses four key issues:

1. **The role of time in competitive advantage:** using time in logistics management and strategy.
2. **Time-based process mapping:** how to create visibility of time across the network.
3. **P:D ratios and differences:** the gap between the time it takes to produce and distribute the product (P-time) and the time the customer is prepared to wait (D-time).
4. **Managing timeliness in the logistics pipeline:** strategies and practices for coping when P-time is greater than D-time.

5.1 The role of time in competitive advantage

***Key issues:* What is time-based competition, how does it link to other initiatives, and what is the purpose of it?**

5.1.1 Time-based competition: the virtuous circle of speed

Many attempts at business improvement focus on cost reduction and quality improvement. Whilst a great deal of benefit has been achieved by many organisations through these efforts, most of the obvious opportunities for improvement have now been taken. This has led to time emerging as a fresh battleground in the search for competitive advantage. A working definition of competing on time is:

The timely response to customer needs

The emphasis in this definition is on 'timely'. This means responding to customers' needs on time – neither early nor late. The implication of this definition is that the organisation must focus its capabilities on being responsive to the customer.

However, achieving this is not straightforward as, traditionally, people have had the opinion that you cannot have low cost *and* fast delivery or high quality.

The belief is that some kind of trade-off is necessary, meaning that more of one advantage means less of another. For example, better quality means putting in more inspectors, which increases costs. Such thinking was shown to be flawed when the quality movement of the 1980s demonstrated that good quality actually *reduces* costs (Crosby, 1979). The trade-off between cost and quality can be altered by *preventing* defects from happening in the first place through such measures as designing the process so that defects cannot occur (error proofing) and statistical process control as in Six Sigma. This leads to savings in *detecting* defects, by removing the need for inspection, and in avoiding the *failures* that lead to scrap and the cost of resolving customer complaints. The result is that overall quality costs (prevention + detection + failure) can be reduced by spending more on prevention. Thus reduced costs and improved quality can be achieved simultaneously and the cost versus quality trade-off overcome.

Similarly, there is a belief that fast delivery incurs higher cost. Certainly, on the face of it, if you employ air freight rather than road freight, it will be faster, but will incur a higher cost per unit. However, this analysis does not take into account the wider implications of speed for the supply chain. These are best expressed in terms of the virtuous circle of speed, shown in Figure 5.1.

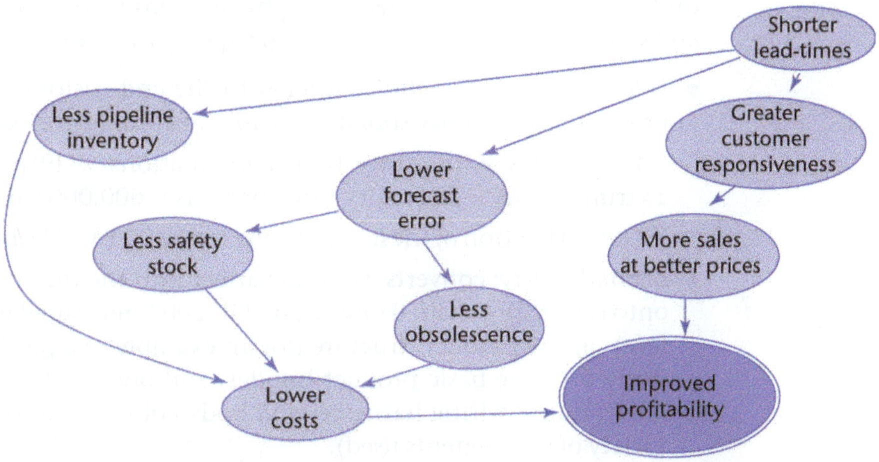

Figure 5.1 The virtuous circle of speed.
(Source: Adapted from Christopher, 1998.)

Naturally if processes such as delivery have shorter lead times then customers do not have to wait as long for products ordered and a greater customer responsiveness is achieved. Additionally, through this improved speed you may gain competitive advantage and increase sales, revenue and thereby profitability. However, this is only part of the impact; the left side of the virtuous circle shows how reduced lead times, such as production and distribution, can also reduce costs by:

- reducing pipeline inventory to buffer against long and unreliable supply lead times;
- reducing the time horizon upon which sales forecasts are made. As with all forecasts – consider weather forecasts – this has the impact of improving **forecast accuracy**, which in turn reduces the safety stocks to buffer against inaccuracies. Further, the match between supply and demand is better, leading to reduced

obsolescence or mark-downs where forecasts were overestimated, or reduced stock-outs and lost sales where forecasts were underestimated.

The agility strategy is predicated on this virtuous circle of speed to respond to unpredictable and volatile demand, and approaches required to enable this are described in Chapter 7. Equally, shorter process lead times can be achieved through time-based process mapping (as described in Section 5.2 in this chapter) and identifying the non-value-adding, wasteful processes such that they can be eliminated or reduced by applying lean thinking approaches, as also described in Chapter 7.

5.1.2 Variety and speed

Product variety has been increasing since the 1990s, with most products now available in more variants. For example, when we enter a supermarket we are faced with a seemingly endless choice of products as simple as toothpaste. Different brands, flavours, functionalities, pack types and pack sizes lead to multiple shelves packed with just this one type of product and hundreds of SKUs, driving up inventories and therefore logistics lead time (P-time, as discussed later in this chapter). More understandable is the variety of high-value products such as cars that is offered, and so it is useful to distinguish two perspectives on variety:

- *External variety*: the choice offered to the end-customer, or potential finished product SKUs. Choice soon builds up - an automotive example would be:

  2 body styles $\times$ 15 power train combinations $\times$ 19 painted body colours $\times$ 15 trim colours $\times$ 70 factory fitted options $=$ 600,000 variations.

  Yet only a fraction of these variations, say 20,000, will be bought by the customer.
- *Internal variety*: converts external variety into the internal requirements placed onto the supply chain. Holweg and Pil (2004) measured internal variety at three levels in the product structure (for an example of a product structure, see Case study 6.1): the basic product (models and body styles), intermediate (such as power trains, wiring harnesses and body colours) and peripheral (number and variety of components used).

But while customers drive up product variety, this doesn't come for free. There are a number of important implications of product variety for both speed and cost in the supply chain:

- More components and materials are required, which increases the number of inbound inventories and the number of suppliers to manage increasing both processing time and costs.
- In production, product variety may require more changeovers from one type of product to another, which increases processing time and costs. Further, particularly where there is a high level of customisation (for example bespoke cars) the level of variety in the production processes increases drastically, and scheduling and meeting deadlines, through allocation of standard times, becomes ever more difficult, as discussed in more depth later in this chapter in Section 5.3.2.

- For finished product inventories the demand variability, and thus uncertainty, at finished item level is much higher where variety is high. This leads to inaccurate sales forecasts and increased safety stocks, thus increasing both lead time and costs.

It can be concluded that product variety costs more and increases the lead time, so how can this be addressed?

- Variety should be increased only when it contributes to added value. Heineken, the Dutch beer manufacturer, reduced SKUs from 2,500 across Europe to a few dozen. The 'right' level of product variety starts with consumer research (Mahler and Bahulkar, 2009) rather than 'tail cutting' (Activity 2.2).
- External product variety offered to customers can be somewhat superficial and does not have to increase component and process variety to the same extent internally. For example the Smart Car offers lots of choice to the customer but the manufacturing processes are standardised, as described in Case study 7.3.
- System redesign can reduce the cost impact of an increase in variety. The antidote to complexity caused by variety is *simplicity*, so auto manufacturers have implemented modular design and manufacture to offer external variety without making internal operations too complex (see Case study 8.5).

For more strategies to deliver high product variety while reducing impact on speed and cost see Chapter 7.

5.1.3 Time-based opportunities to add value

There are several ways in which a company can use time to help meet customer needs better and therefore add more value. The most common examples are:

- increased responsiveness to customer needs;
- managing increased variety;
- increased product innovation;
- improved return on investment for new products;
- reducing risk by relying less on sales forecasts.

We deal with each of these opportunities in turn.

Increased responsiveness to customer needs

Increased responsiveness to customer needs (as discussed in Section 5.1.1 for the virtuous circle of speed) is the most common reason for organisations to invest in time-based approaches to performance enhancement. Many elements of customer service are dependent upon time. These include how long it takes to deliver a product or service, achieving on-time delivery and how long it takes to deal with customer queries, estimates and complaints.

High levels of responsiveness to customers tend to correlate to greater loyalty from them and therefore more business over time. Such responsiveness is also addictive to the customer, creating customer lock-in. Once they get used to short lead times, industrial customers often reorganise their own products and services to customers to make use of responsiveness from their suppliers, such as by holding less inventory and promising their own customers shorter lead times. Once they start to do this they find it hard to accept longer times again.

Industrial customers of time-based organisations do not have to carry as much raw material or component stock and therefore benefit from a cost saving. In order to profit from the service they provide, a time-based organisation needs to demonstrate to customers that the total cost of doing business is lower, and then recover some of this value. This can be achieved by winning more business and/or by charging more.

Managing increased variety

We discussed the impact of variety on lead times in Section 5.1.2. Shortened lead times in product development, the supply chain and manufacturing help factories deliver a variety of products without the traditional cost penalty (as discussed in detail under agility in Chapter 7). By reducing overall lead time, product complexity and process set-up times, the production of a particular product can be scheduled more frequently with smaller production batches. This improves the variety of products available to a customer at any given time.

Increased product innovation

Time-based organisations are more likely to meet customer needs accurately by using short product development times to produce new products that meet customer needs. The shortening of product development lead time means that innovations can be capitalised to maximum effect. If a company innovates through product design faster than its competitors it will become increasingly competitive. Conversely, if your competitors are innovative, then reducing the time to develop imitations will underpin a 'fast follower' strategy to keep up.

Improved return on investment for new products

Reducing product development lead time means that a product can get to market earlier. This has a number of important advantages:

- the sales life of the product is extended;
- a higher price can be charged;
- new customers can be won;
- a high market share can be won through building upon the initial lead.

Each of these benefits can add to the other. Therefore, being first to the market allows a higher initial price to be charged, helping to recoup development costs more quickly. This revenue will support investment into further developments necessary to retain these initial customers. Meanwhile, the initial product can continue to be sold, generating cash through its high market share. Being first in the market maximises the product life until the time when it becomes obsolete.

The related argument here is that of *break-even time* rather than the break-even volumes discussed in Chapter 3. Traditional break-even analysis focuses on the volume of product needed to be moved before the investment pays off. Given compressed product life cycles – the curves of modern product life cycles have changed from flat and shallow to peaked and short lived (e.g. from 6 months to 45 days of shelf life for Nike footwear) the analysis shifts towards the question 'how long before break-even is reached?' Figure 5.2 illustrates the point.

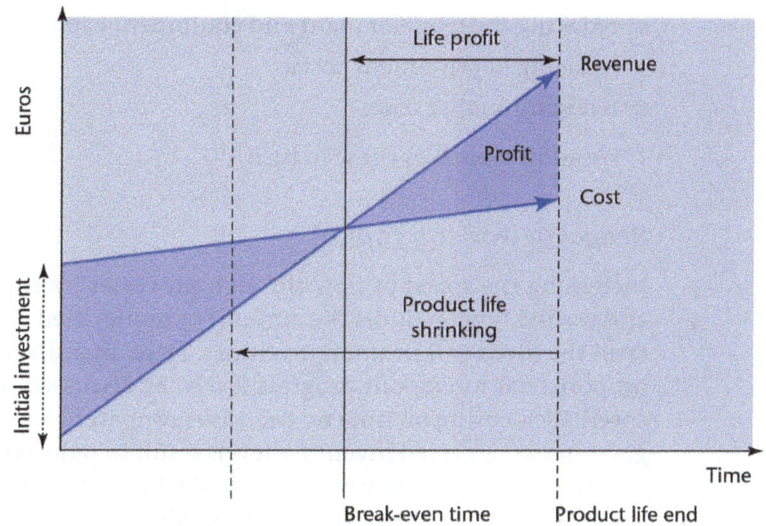

Figure 5.2 Break-even time.

As product life cycles shrink, so the time window of opportunity for making profits also shrinks. This consideration means that a new product must achieve its break-even time more quickly.

Reducing risk by relying less on sales forecasts

There is a saying in industry that there are only two types of forecast: wrong ones and lucky ones, and there are precious few of the latter! It is certainly true that the further ahead a company tries to forecast, the less likely the forecast is to be correct, as described in Section 5.1.1 for the virtuous circle of speed. When the production lead time is reduced, the period when demand is uncertain becomes shorter and the forecasts more accurate, decreasing the risk of stock-outs or obsolete stock. It also reduces the amount of finished goods stock needed, which frees up working capital.

The ultimate goal is to reduce production time so it lies within the lead time it has been given by the customer to deliver. In this situation, no forecasting is needed and all production is done to firm demand – customer orders – rather than uncertain demand – forecasts. The implications of reducing production time in relation to the demand time of customers are very significant and we have devoted Sections 5.3 and 5.4 to addressing them.

5.1.4 Time-based opportunities to reduce cost

The second key element of time-based competition is to reduce cost by the elimination of non-value-added time in processes. This means that wasted lead time and unnecessary tasks that are not actually adding any value in the customers' eyes should be identified and eliminated. Stopping unnecessary tasks and removing wasted time from those that remain lowers cost by:

- reducing the need for working capital;
- reducing the need for plant and equipment capital;
- reducing development costs;
- reducing quality costs.

We address each of these in turn.

Reducing working capital

Increasing the speed of flow through processes by eliminating unnecessary steps and wasted time, reduces the amount of money tied up in the system. In the short term the focus will be upon inventory. Here, manufacturing lead time is inversely proportional to work-in-progress levels, as discussed under the virtuous circle of speed. By focusing on time we decrease raw material, work-in-progress and finished good stocks. Lowered inventory levels result in reduced working capital. As already mentioned, returns on working capital will be improved by reducing obsolescence caused by making to stock and not to order.

Reducing plant and equipment capital

Over the longer term, processes become more visible, inventory levels reduce and opportunities to minimise capital expenses become more visible. These opportunities include the removal of equipment not employed in activities that add value. Initial items to remove will include the racking and pallets formerly used to store inventory. Next will be a purge of unnecessary equipment in offices, stores and production, including the jigging for unnecessary operations of obsolete parts.

As a company embraces time-based competition, success in the marketplace will increase demand for products and services that the customer really values. To make way for these means that space will be at a premium in the company. This is just the driver needed to replace the old with the new.

Reducing development costs

Shortened lead times in product development are achieved in part by more effective use of development resources through elimination of rework and reduction of distracting superfluous projects. This leads to cost reductions as the time spent on a given project is less.

Reducing quality costs

One of the main elements in improving quality is to reduce the time between an error being made and the problem being detected. The sooner the error is detected the smaller the amount of the product affected by it. Reducing lead times has a positive effect on the speed of feedback and hence quality costs are reduced.

In keeping with the total quality movement, time-sensitive organisations will become consistently responsive only if they strive to maintain quality processes. This means that, as defects and errors arise, they are detected quickly, root causes are identified and effective solutions installed to ensure they cannot recur.

Activity 5.1

List six applications of responsiveness in an organisation; for example, 'external phone calls answered within five rings'. How many organisations can you think of that compete overtly on time, such as the Vision Express example given in Chapter 1?

5.1.5 Limitations to time-based approaches

Despite the clear benefits of time-based approaches to logistics management described above, there are often barriers to its application, as well as limitations to its relevance.

Two basic limitations to the need for time-based logistics management are the need for speed and the degree of speed required. Not all operating environments require speed. Product demand that is very predictable, such as high-volume, low-value commodity products, can be planned well in advance and processed without particular speed. Not all customers value speed as they may be able to order well in advance of delivery. Delivery before the parts are needed creates unnecessary inventories. In particular, when there are costs involved in creating speedy delivery, customers may trade that off against ordering in advance. Only selected parcels need to be shipped with express carriers, for example.

A particular issue with the costs involved in speeding up logistics processes in the supply chain is the distribution of those costs between companies in the supply chain. It is well known that just-in-time (JIT) deliveries, for example, may generate significant costs for suppliers, whereas the customer may experience most of its benefits (such as low process inventories and rapid delivery). Toyota is capable of manufacturing a car in five days, but has decided not to do so because of the pressure it would place on its suppliers and its distribution processes, creating costs that are not expected to be outweighed by revenue opportunities in current market circumstances.

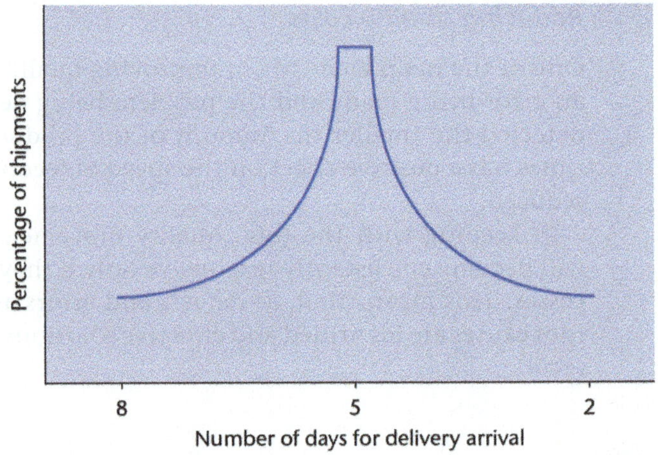

Figure 5.3 Distribution of shipment cycle times in days.

An additional issue is that time-based approaches might lead to superior performance only being achieved on a limited number of occasions. An illustration of this situation is shown in Figure 5.3. In this example, a supplier demonstrates that it is able to deliver in only one day. However, it is clear that this was achieved for only a minor portion of shipments, which does not mean that customers can depend on shipments being consistently completed within a day. Rather customers will order seven days in advance, where the required 99 per cent service level for deliveries is achieved. Time-based approaches are not about managing exceptions but managing for speed reliably.

5.2 Time-based process mapping

***Key issue:* How do you go about measuring time in a supply network?**

The purpose of supply chain mapping is to generate visibility of the processes within the supply chain. Once this visibility has been achieved it is possible to benchmark similar processes. The processes we need to map are the actual processes that are taking place, not what is supposed to happen. Quality standards based on ISO 9000 require processes to be documented, but within the organisation the actual process undertaken may often differ considerably. When undertaking a supply chain mapping exercise it is the *actual* process that we need to focus on. The key is to track one order, one product or one person through the process with respect to time. A map is a snapshot taken during a given time period. Workloads may vary during the course of a month, and so may the individual process times. Record the actual times that you observe. Most processes take place in batches, so if you are mapping a trailer being filled with tyres, record the time that the median (middle) tyre waits before being moved. The method of documentation of the process and the symbols to use are illustrated in Table 5.1. Key operations and the subprocesses that can consume the most time

Table 5.1 Example of process document.

Step	Description	Symbol	Time	Notes
1	Machine complete	❍	1:37	
2	Inspect	❒	0:45	
3	Wait transport	D	5:53	
4	Transport to heat treat	➪	0:08	
5	Wait heat treat	D	3:34	
6	Heat treat	❍	4:15	

Symbol	Description
➪	Transport
▼	Store
❍	Operation
❒	Inspect
D	Delay

and generate the greatest inefficiencies (e.g. waiting for transport) are revealed, enabling problem solving and improvement of the supply chain.

The following sections give an overview of the key stages involved in the time-based mapping process.

5.2.1 Stage 1: Create a task force

Before the mapping process can be undertaken, it needs to be recognised that supply chain processes cross all functions of the organisation. It is therefore important to have all key functions represented. The task force must be assured of top management support. A project champion may also need to be appointed.

5.2.2 Stage 2: Select the process to map

It may not be feasible to map the total supply chain initially. Take an overview of the core processes within the organisation and the time they take before deciding on the priorities for detailed mapping. To get the organisation to 'buy in' to the project, a subprocess may be identified that has been a particular problem. This can act as a pilot for the task force, enabling them to prove that their methods really work. When selecting the process, ensure that there is a generic customer or group of customers that the process serves. A clear start (or trigger) and finish to the process should also be present.

5.2.3 Stage 3: Collect data

The most effective way to collect the data is to follow an item through the process. This is referred to often as *walking the process*. An actual component or order will be followed through all the stages of the process. Identify someone who is actively involved in each part of the process and knows what is really happening within the process: interview these key individuals. Get the interviewee to describe each movement of the item with respect to time. It can be useful to ask the interviewee to describe 'a day in the life of' that product or order. Remember, the steps an item goes through are not just those where something is done: for example, items could be waiting or being moved, or may be sitting waiting for a decision to be made. Identify an appropriate level of detail at which to map the process. Initially it might be better to map at a high level to gain an overview of the process; one can always map in more detail if needed later.

5.2.4 Stage 4: Flow chart the process

Use the data collected by walking the process and the interviews with operators to sketch a flow chart so linkages and dependencies between steps can be clarified before constructing the time-based process map. This flow chart is used by the task force to ensure they have not missed any steps in the process.

5.2.5 Stage 5: Distinguish between value-adding and non-value-adding time

A rough definition of value-adding time is time when something takes place on the item that the end-customer is willing to pay for. The definition of value-adding time requires due consultation and should be aligned with the overall business strategy. The business strategy should define the markets and segments, and the accompanying order qualifiers and order winners (see Chapters 1 and 2). Once the value-adding criteria at the strategic level have been defined, these can be translated into value-adding criteria at an operational level. The time data collected in stage 3 can then be analysed to identify the value-adding time. Value-adding time is characterised using three criteria:

- whether the process (or elements of the process) physically transforms the material that forms the input to that process;
- whether the change to the item is something that the customer values or cares about and is willing to pay for;
- whether the process is right the first time and will not have to be repeated in order to produce the desired result that is valued by the customer.

Non-value-adding activity can be split into four categories: delay, transport, storage and inspection, using the categories from Table 5.1.

5.2.6 Stage 6: Construct the time-based process map

The purpose of the time-based process map is to represent the data collected clearly and concisely so that the critical aspects of the supply network can be communicated in an easily accessible way. The ultimate goal is to represent the process on a single piece of paper so that the task force and others involved in the project can easily see the issues. A simple Gantt chart technique can be used to show the process, and different categories of non-value-adding time can be represented on this. These categories will be dependent on the nature of each process. Figure 5.4 shows three operations processes (delivery, production and goods in), with the last one magnified to show four types of waste.

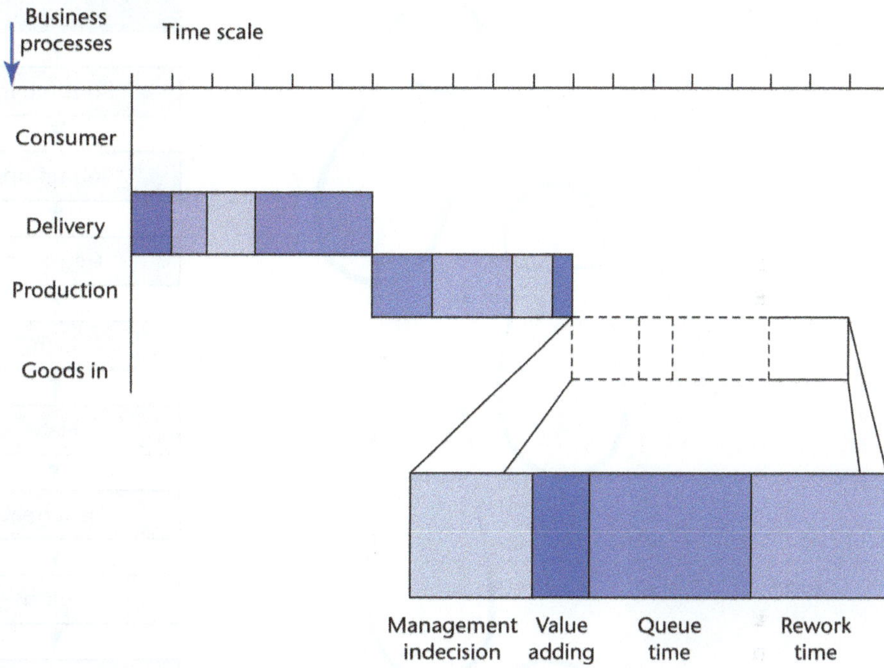

Figure 5.4 Process activity mapping and sources of waste.

From the interviews and data from walking the process, extract the relevant data. It is sometimes useful to sketch a flow diagram so that linkages and dependences between steps can be clarified before constructing the map. This flow diagram can be used to approximate the total time that the business process consumes.

5.2.7 Stage 7: Solution generation

Once the time-based process map has been produced, the opportunities for improvement are generally all too obvious. The task force can collect ideas and categorise causes of non-value-adding activity using problem-solving approaches such as cause-and-effect diagrams. (A helpful condensed guide to problem-solving tools and techniques will be found in Bicheno and Holweg, 2008.)

The Auto Parts Ltd case study (Case study 5.1) describes how the above principles were applied to a focal firm that produces electroplated parts for the automotive industry.

CASE STUDY 5.1

Auto Parts Ltd

Auto Parts Ltd electroplates parts for the automotive industry. A typical example of its work is emblem badges which are mounted on cars. Auto Parts Ltd are finding that customers want increasingly high value for money and therefore there is a need to review its internal supply chain. The first part of the analysis identified 12 key processes, as shown in Figure 5.5.

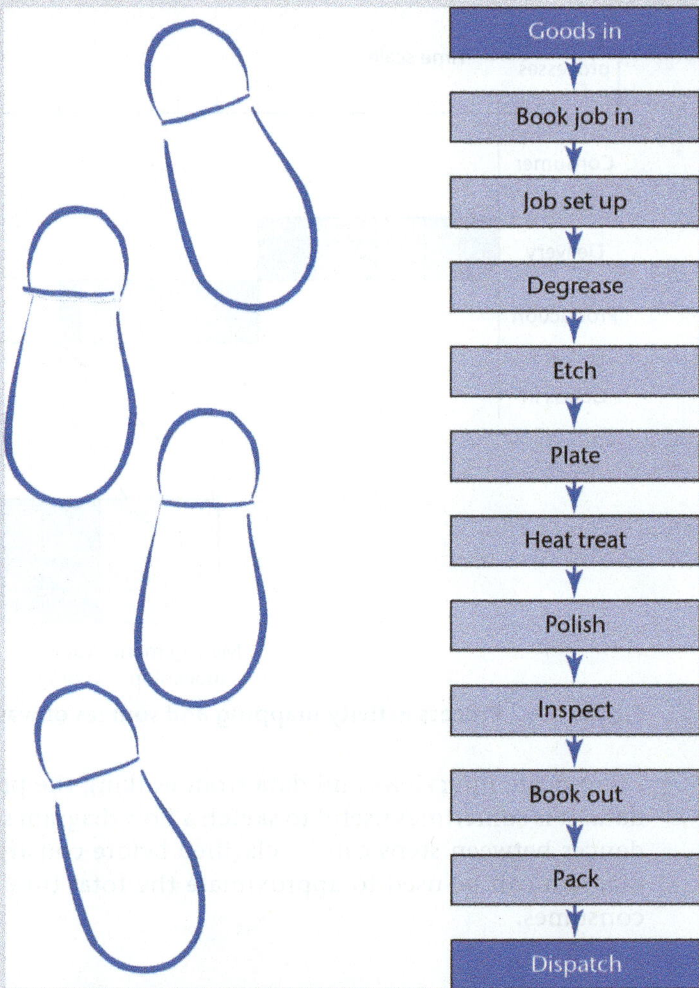

Figure 5.5 Walk the process (12 steps).

Following the establishment of this first process map, each process was mapped in detail identifying around 60 steps, which are summarised as a flow diagram in Figure 5.6.

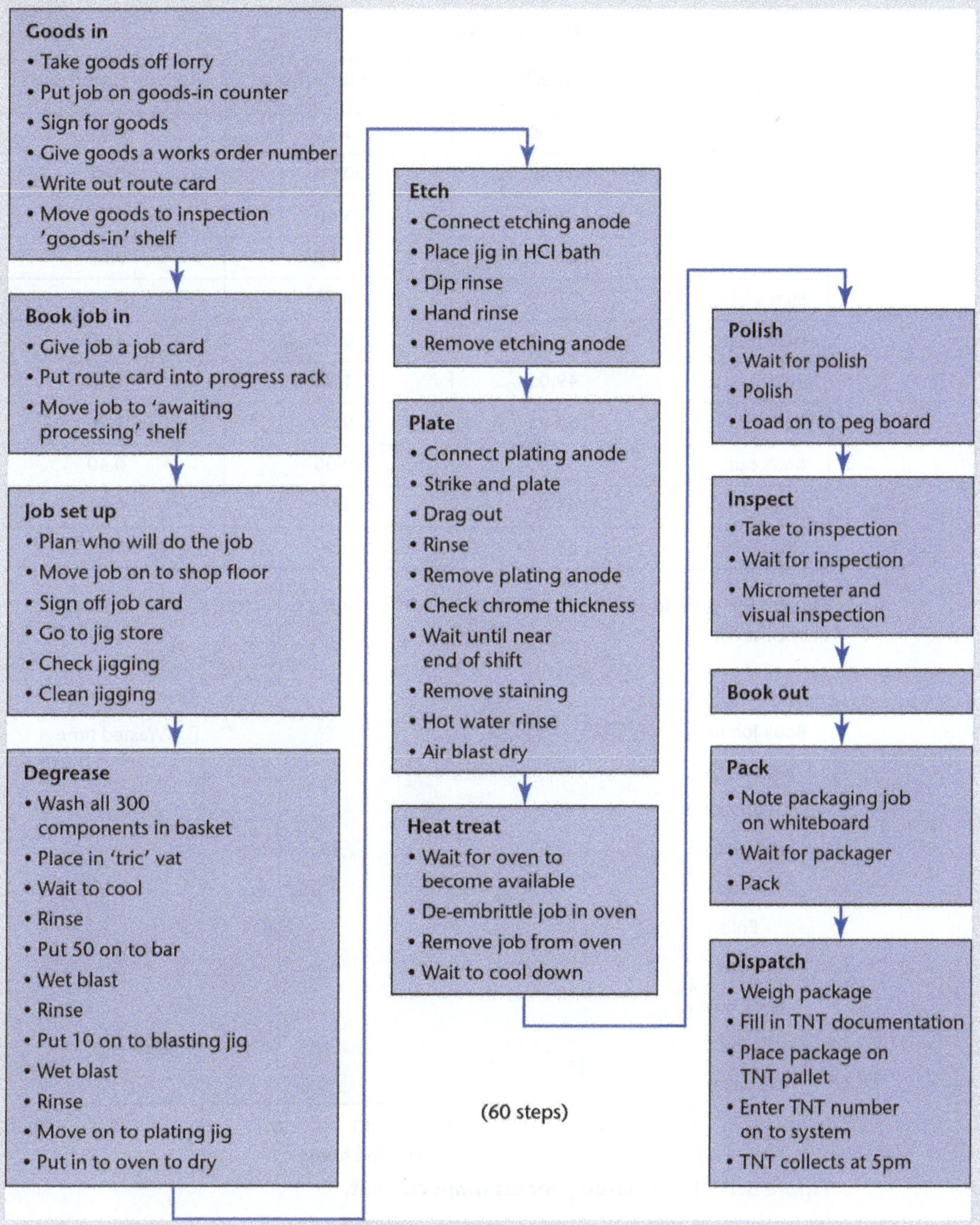

Figure 5.6 Identify every process step.

Process steps were then analysed to identify value-adding and non-value-adding time and this is shown in Table 5.2, which summarises the total elapsed time, non-value-adding (wasted) time and value-adding time for each of the 12 key processes.

Table 5.2 Time-based analysis data.

	Total time/hours	Wasted time/hours	Activity time/hours
Goods in	0.00	3.91	0.41
Book job in	4.32	20.00	0.41
Job set up	24.73	5.50	1.77
Degrease	32.00	1.00	0.60
Etch and plate	33.60	8.75	2.20
Heat treat	44.55	0.00	4.50
Polish	49.05	1.95	1.95
Inspect	52.95	9.50	1.00
Book out	63.45	0.00	0.40
Pack	63.85	4.00	0.85
Dispatch	68.70	0.00	0.40

Figure 5.7 provides a map with these times across 11 steps (etch and plate were combined).

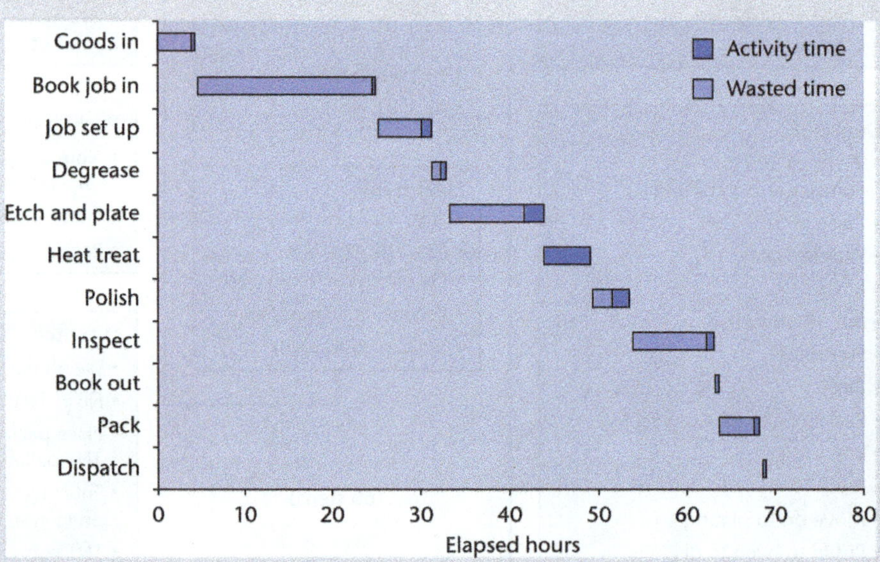

Figure 5.7 Time-based process map: current.

This initial analysis showed the total elapsed process time to be approximately 70 hours. To identify the causes of the non-valued added time, all the employees involved in the process held a meeting and conducted a brainstorming session producing the cause-and-effect diagram illustrated in Figure 5.8. From this actions were identified to reduce the wasted time and improve the efficiency of the process. For instance, jobs arriving at 9.00 am, or anytime during the day, would not be logged in the system until 5.00 pm, since the operator only inputted data once each day at 5:00 pm. inconsequently, manufacturing did not see the new orders until 9.00 am the next morning. The action to

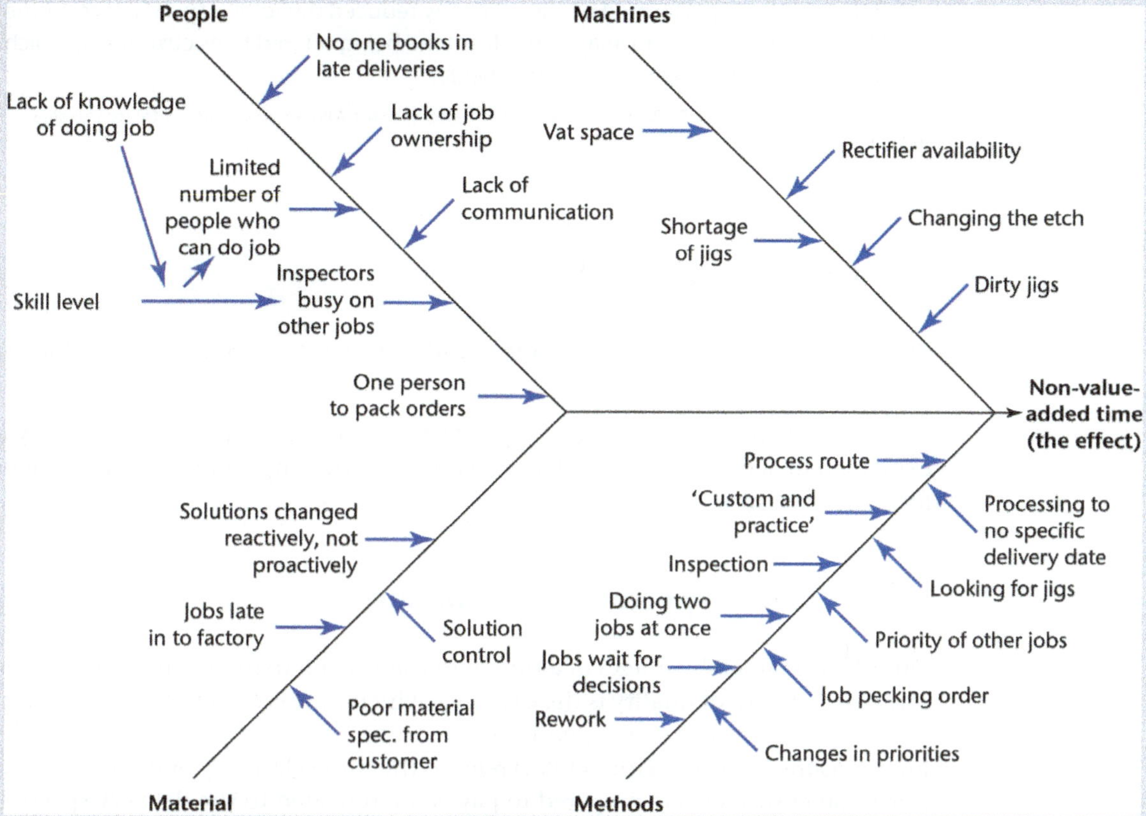

Figure 5.8 Cause-and-effect diagram.

reduce this wasted time was to conduct the booking-in process at the same time as the goods inwards process. Figure 5.9 shows the re-engineered process.

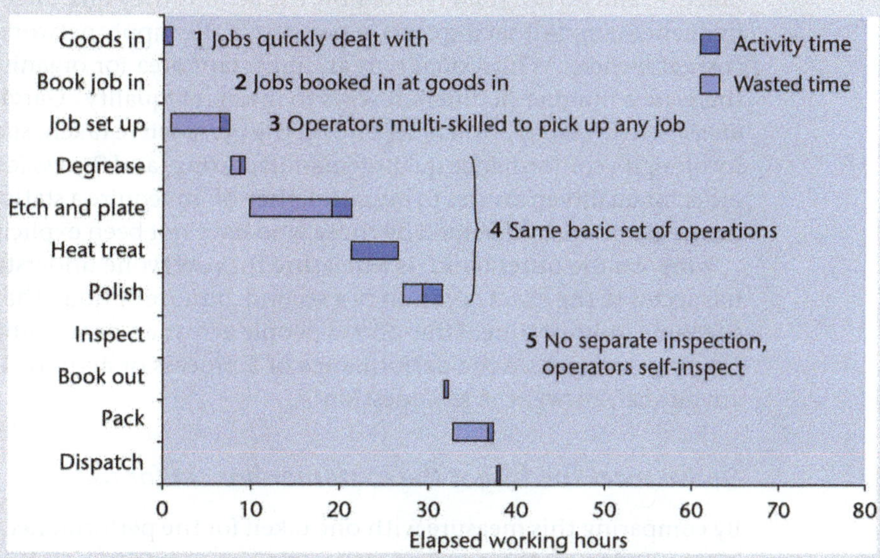

Figure 5.9 Time-based process map: re-engineered.

A series of actions performed by the company reduced the total elapsed process time to 37 hours. This culminated in a shorter leadtime being offered to its customers, which in turn resulted in increased sales and revenue.

(Source: Based on a study by Dr Paul Chapman and Professor Richard Wilding, Cranfield Centre for Logistics and Supply Chain Management.)

5.3 P:D ratios and differences

***Key issues:* What are P- and D-times, and why are they important to logistics strategy?**

P-time and D-time are measures of performance of the supply pipeline. They are explained in Section 5.3.3, but let us first look at the importance of time as a performance measure.

5.3.1 Using time as a performance measure

One of the major advantages of a time-based approach to managing processes over one based on cost or quality is the ease with which time is understood as a measure. Whilst cost and quality are open to differences in interpretation, time is an absolute measure. Stalk and Hout (1990) refer to the 'time elasticity of price', where the price that customers are prepared to pay is often related to the delivery speed. For example, Talleres Auto, in Case study 1.6, was able to charge premium prices for spare parts in breakdown situations because these were 'distress purchases'.

Cost is a more subjective measure that is open to interpretation, three examples of which we saw in Section 3.4. Many people have a poor grasp of how costs work in practice, and do not understand how the actions they take affect others. An all too frequent example is saving costs in one part of the supply network only to cause extra costs elsewhere. Whilst quality is an important area for organisations to improve, there are a number of different ways to interpret 'quality'. Garvin (1988) lists eight *dimensions of quality*, which depend on the perspective taken, such as product quality (design), conformance quality (manufacturing) and fitness for use (customer). In order for quality measures to be useful, they often require a statistical approach that can easily be misunderstood by those who have not been explicitly trained.

Time, on the other hand, is a measure that everyone understands. Every person has access to the exact duration of a second, minute or hour, thanks to clocks using the same units of time. Time allows people across an organisation, with very little training, to measure the performance of a process or activity. Using this measure anyone can answer the key question:

Do we meet the target the customer has set for us?

By comparing this measure with one taken for the performance of competitors, we can easily answer the next key question:

How good are we compared with the competition?

If we take a reason for measuring performance as being to understand the effect of making changes to a process, we can more easily answer the question:

Is our performance getting better or worse?

By using measures that are simple to understand, people can see the big issues more easily. They can measure and quantify the flow of activities directly, and ask themselves whether each of the steps in a process is adding real value or just adding cost. By following the flow through a process we can see where time is lost. This allows us to translate the data into time-reduction and cost-reduction opportunities. Looking at cost analyses alone does not tell anyone where to save time.

5.3.2 High variety poses a challenge to conventional clock-time

Before we go any further in examining the use of time as a measure of performance, it is worth considering two different perspectives on time and the challenge that high variety poses to the widely accepted notion of time, that is, 'clock time', the predominant perspective of time in operations management. In Western societies, time is mainly viewed objectively and is assumed to be homogeneous, linear, discrete and subject to precise measurement. The commoditisation of time that developed from this perspective is encapsulated in phrases such as 'time is money', 'time is our most valuable commodity' and 'time is of the essence'.

However, there is another perspective of time, that of 'lived time' (Chen and Miller, 2011). The 'lived-time' perspective is derived from human experience based on temporal continuity of flow from the past, to the present, and on to the future. From a 'lived-time' perspective, people view and value time differently. Powel and Schultz (2004) examined behaviour in serial lines, expecting operators to work at the pace of the production line; however they found that time was used as a malleable buffer by operators to avoid idle time in the group.

The trade-off between routinisation and variety of processes influences the normative regulation – clock time or lived time. Routinisation implies repetition of an activity and standard operating procedures. This aligns with a clock-time normative regulation based on how time is managed – the perspective we tend to use. However, variety in the range of activities in a process may challenge routinisation and thus the way time is managed. Within customised or high variety production environments – for example customised cars made to individuals' specifications – it is not always economically viable to prescribe each step within the production process. This requires individuals and the organisation to develop a normative regulation based on people being 'mindful of time use' when executing processes which contain discretionary activities, as we suggest (Aitken et al., 2018). Being mindful of time reflects the need for people to be conscious of the time they take to complete activities, which is determined by an individual worker's subjective standards and therefore is more difficult to manage.

5.3.3 Using time to measure supply pipeline performance

In the same way that time can be used to measure the performance of a process within a company, so it can be used to measure the supply pipeline. The next two measures presented (and illustrated in Figure 5.10) are key to understanding supply pipeline performance: P-time and D-time.

P-time

The first measure of performance for the total supply process is to determine how long it takes for a product or service to pass through it. This measure is used to identify the total logistics lead time, also known as the *P-time* or production time.

Just to be clear, the P-time is a measure of the total time it takes for a product to go through a pipeline. Thus, it includes source, make and deliver lead times: it is not just the time it takes to supply from stock.

The measure starts the moment a new order is raised. It includes all the time needed to take a product through all the processes necessary to make and deliver that product including time in storage (work-in-progress or finished inventory). It is important to be clear about when these activities start and end in order for the measure to be consistent, should you want to measure performance for a number of processes, including those of competitors. For a first attempt at this measure, take the starting time as the point when the first order for materials is raised. Consider the total time needed to make and deliver a new product or batch of products. This includes the time needed to procure the longest lead parts and the total manufacturing time. The end of the process is the time when you fulfil an order and the product is received by the customer, rather than the time when you dispatch it.

This measure incorporates the steps the customer takes to receive your delivery and get it to where it is needed. Exploring this process will reveal useful opportunities where you can help the customer to help themselves, thus strengthening your competitive position.

D-time

The time for which customers are willing to wait to have their demand fulfilled is the *D-time* or demand time. It is measured from when the person in the customer company realises they have a need, and the end point is when the product is received by that person.

D-time varies considerably. For example, the time a customer is willing to wait for 'fast food' is comparatively short. Assuming you are in a city with plenty of options, once you realise you are hungry, you probably will want to be eating within 10 minutes. This D-time will include the time it takes to walk to the cafeteria/restaurant, wait in a queue, sit at a table and be served. By contrast, as a customer of an upmarket restaurant, you may have travelled for an hour, spent 20 minutes in a reception area over an aperitif and studied the menu for 15 minutes, before happily waiting for a further half an hour for the meal to be cooked and served.

In addition to the obvious differences in grade and choice of food, the implication from a supply chain point of view is that the two restaurants must be organised in totally different ways to deliver the food within their customers' D-time. Interestingly, the same customer may visit both restaurants on the same day and accept the two different delivery systems. You do not *expect* to wait at a fast-food counter, but you *do* expect to linger over a meal in a high-quality restaurant.

Similar examples can be found in other industries. Buyers of new premium cars expect to wait a few months or even a year for delivery when they place an order. Indeed, when Tesla launched the Model 3, customers put down deposits of $1,000 in April 2016 on the basis that production would begin at the end of 2017 – a wait of a year and nine months! However, nearly two years later, in February 2018, Tesla informed many of its nearly half a million reservation holders that Model 3 production challenges meant deliveries were taking longer than planned and the standard model wouldn't go into production until late 2018 (Ohnsman, 2018). At that point some customers were asking for their deposit back. Many people are not prepared to wait so long, but may, for example, be prepared to accept a second choice of colour instead of their first, especially if the dealer gives a discount! Manufacturers of vehicles for customers with short D-times face increased supply chain challenges compared with those who have long ones. If it is not possible to make a car to order within the expected D-time, then the manufacturer is forced to carry out some or all of the logistics processes speculatively. The most risky scenario is to make the whole car for stock, hoping that the forecast mix of diesel and petrol, of left- and right-hand drive and so on is correct. But taking such a risk is necessary to cope with the customer who wants to drive away a vehicle the same day he or she enters the dealer's showroom.

5.3.4 Mapping P-time and D-time

P-time should be measured for each separate product group, because each will have different internal processes. D-time should be measured for each different market segment that is served, because customers may have different needs (e.g. prepared to wait/not prepared to wait).

Armed with this data, P-times and D-times should be contrasted for each product/customer group to see if P-time is more than D-time. A simple way to do this is by drawing them on a graph as time lines, as shown in Figure 5.10. The length of the arrows shown in Figure 5.10 represents *time*. The arrow for the P-time represents

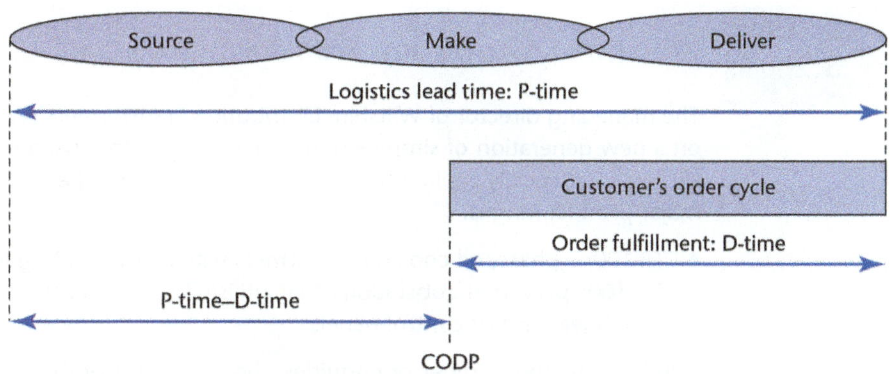

Figure 5.10 When P-time is > D-time.

the time taken for source, make and deliver processes. The D-time arrow represents the time the customer is prepared to wait for an order to be fulfilled.

Comparing the length of the two arrows, it can be seen that the time it takes to respond to an order is longer than the customer is prepared to wait, thus the P-time is greater than D-time. The consequence is that this focal firm is not able fully to make to order. On the other hand, it may be possible to complete the final 'make' processes such as assembly and test within the customer-required D-time. Such a strategy is called *assemble to order* (ATO). This is basically how Dell manages to supply the computer you want so quickly.

Activity 5.2

Assess the benefits and concerns that may arise as a result of the relative sizes of P-time and D-time. Compile your views in the template provided:

	P-time greater than D-time	P-time = D-time	P-time less than D-time
Benefits	•	•	•
	•	•	•
	•	•	•
Concerns	•	•	•
	•	•	•
	•	•	•

The vertical broken line that separates D-time from P–D time in Figure 5.10 is *the customer order decoupling point* (CODP): downstream from this point the focal firm carries out processes to known customer orders, whereas upstream from this point the processes are carried out speculatively. We return to the importance of the CODP in terms of planning and controlling materials in Chapter 6 and later in Chapter 7 in relation to form postponement.

We now consider a case study where time-based approaches are used to reduce the time the customer waits for delivery of an industrial product, such that order fulfilment lead time is closer to D-time.

CASE STUDY 5.2

Wiltshire Distribution Transformers

The managing director of Wiltshire Distribution Transformers (WDT) had concentrated on a new generation of simplified, modular designs that used proven US technology. He had energetically exploited the market advantages this had given. WDT now has two major product ranges:

- TR 100: 3-phase, oil-cooled transformers with a power rating from 200 to 2000 kVA;
- PS 300: packaged substations that utilise TR 100 transformers with appropriate switchgear and LV control panels.

Judging by the number of enquiries, the market for both product ranges was now increasing.

The new JIT system

Each product must be individually engineered to order (ETO). Previously, this process had taken two weeks, because an engineer had to develop an entirely new design from scratch based on the customer order. Designs have now been modularised (refer to Section 7.2.2) as a result of the new system: that is, a new design is produced from a few hundred standard 'modules' that are held on file. This can be done by a sales engineer in a matter of hours. If a tender was accepted by a customer, it had formerly taken another two weeks to convert the tender information into specifications and drawings for manufacture. Today, it is possible simply to send the accepted tender information to the shop floor, and to use the set of standard engineering information already held on file to act as manufacturing instructions. The following is a list of the main features of the new JIT system.

Enquiry processing

The engineer enters major design details (kVA rating, voltage ratio, product classification and quantity) into a computerised estimating program. From a list of 700 possible options, the selected ones to suit the tender requirements are added. From a library of material, labour and overhead costs, a tender price is calculated.

Should the customer accept this price, then a customer delivery date is agreed and the tender becomes the works (factory) order.

Engineering instructions

WDT's efforts had resulted in the completion of a comprehensive library of standard drawings and instructions that covered all major options. The works order simply calls these up by reference number and description. The one exception is the fabricated cubicle that houses the packaged substations. This has to be individually designed. A simple CAD/CAM system enables the design and associated manufacturing instructions to be completed quickly. Presentations of the panels can be separately worked on and designed. The output is a set of computer numerical control (CNC) tapes for the relevant machines in the fabrication shop, and a set-up schedule indicating sheet size, clamp positions, list of tools, etc.

Master production scheduling (MPS)

Activity durations for each manufacturing process vary according to specific designs and are picked up from the works order. Only bottleneck operations are scheduled and can be loaded only up to 100 per cent of their capacity. Given the customer requirement date, the scheduling programme works backwards and loads activities to key resources so that the final assembly date will be met. The MPS is executed by allowing demand to be pulled through the manufacturing system (a process called *pull scheduling*).

Material requirements for each work centre for each order are calculated by means of a modular bill of material, which has been simplified as a result of the modular designs.

Shop scheduling

The MPS generates operation release tickets (ORTs) for each scheduled process. The type and quantity of units required by the next process are withdrawn from the previous one as they are needed. When a work square becomes empty, an ORT is passed back to the preceding work centre to trigger a manufacturing operation. This serves as a signal *(kanban)* to the previous process to produce just enough units to replace those withdrawn.

Work is performed in sequence of ORTs and is carried out only when an output square is available. Completed operations are marked up on the hard copy of the MPS, which is pinned to the wall of the works manager's office by the supervisors at the end of each shift. The MPS is updated for completed operations and new orders each week.

A combination of four weeks' reduction in the time taken to tender and the time taken to produce a manufacturing design, and a further two weeks' reduction in manufacturing times, has placed WDT in a pre-eminent position in the marketplace. Customers want to place orders for this type of equipment later and later in their own projects, so short lead times are a major benefit to WDT in the marketplace.

Questions

1. Sketch out the main processes between a customer placing an enquiry and receiving delivery of a WDT transformer. Where has WDT really scored in terms of reducing this time?
2. What are the potential negatives of WDT's new JIT system in terms of limiting customer choice and short-circuiting the design process?

5.4 Managing timeliness in the logistics pipeline

***Key issue:* When P-time is greater than D-time, what time-based strategies and practices can help to improve competitiveness?**

Two basic strategies for managing timeliness in the logistics pipeline are make to stock (MTS) and make to order (MTO). In between, we have assemble to order (ATO). We begin with a brief description of each:

- *Make to stock (MTS).* Here, the key task is to offer products for customers to buy from available inventory. Customer service is determined by this availability, so a key performance measure in supermarkets is *on-shelf availability* (OSA). Achieving 100 per cent OSA would mean holding infinite inventories so, in practice, a compromise of say 98.5 per cent OSA across most products at most times is targeted. MTS firms have to plan the availability of their inventory by means of a distribution network, which may involve several levels (regional, national and local). In turn, this requires that models are determined for *stock replenishment* – how much, when and where.
- *Assemble to order (ATO).* By shifting the decoupling point (CODP, Figure 5.3) upstream, it is possible to greatly reduce risk – of holding inventories of finished products that do not sell, and of missing out on sales opportunities because the

desired product was unavailable at the time. Thus Dell computers and BMW cars use ATO as their basic strategies. A BMW 3-series is available in around a million finished vehicle specifications, and it would be risky and impractical to have all of these available in the distribution pipeline. This means that the vehicle must be designed flexibly in terms of *components, options and modules*.

- *Make to order (MTO)*. Here, the CODP is moved to just after product design, and just before manufacturing begins, thus reducing the need for speculative processes even further. In the Wiltshire Distribution Transformers case (Case study 5.1), we saw how a focal firm had moved from an engineered (design) to order (ETO) to an MTO strategy. It had achieved this by developing standard modular designs, which meant that customer orders could be configured by the sales engineer, rather than having to be designed from scratch for every customer order.

Let us now consider the strategies and practices that can be used to cope when P-time is greater than D-time.

5.4.1 Strategies to cope when P-time is greater than D-time

When faced with a D-time shorter than the corresponding P-time, a company has a number of options. In the short term it can attempt to make to order, or it can forecast demand and supply from stock (MTS). Making to order in these circumstances is likely to dissatisfy customers. If competitors exist that can deliver within the customer's D-time, or there are substitute products available that will, then the customer is likely to select them. If there are no alternatives, then it may be possible to continue supplying to order for the short term. In the longer term it is likely that the customer will seek to develop alternative suppliers, or re-engineer its products to remove the need for yours.

The more common solution is to forecast customer demand, make products to stock and supply from there. This stock may be held as finished goods if the D-time is very short, or it could be work-in-progress held in the manufacturing process that can be finished in time. This option incurs a number of penalties. The stocks of goods will need to be financed, as will the space needed to store them. There is also the risk that the customer may not order those goods already made within their shelf-life, causing them to become obsolete.

There are a number of strategies for reducing the risks of speculative manufacturing and distribution where P-time is greater than D-time:

- seek the customer's help;
- product development;
- process improvement to reduce P-time.

Each of these areas is analysed next.

Seek the customer's help

There are various ways in which you can reduce risk with help from the customer. For example, ask the customer to cooperate by supplying more detailed demand information at an earlier stage in the planning process, such as promotion or new product launch plans. Speed up the access to demand data, perhaps by establishing internet-based frequent sharing of sales figures. The customer may be prepared to wait longer than stated if you can guarantee delivery on time.

Product development

Different approaches can be used in product development which subsequently reduce production time. These are described in detail in Section 7.2.2, and may include using design for manufacture techniques, where the number of materials and components are reduced such that there is a corresponding reduction in the number of production and assembly steps. Another approach is design for supply chain such that the product can be stocked in a generic form and then completed to a customer order using an approach called form postponement (see Section 7.2.3).

Process improvement to reduce P-time

Time-based organisations come into their own by changing the way they go about their business. They engineer their processes to eliminate unnecessary steps, and take wasted time out of those that remain. Engineering your key processes means focusing on those things the customer cares about and getting rid of all the rest. Having done this once, the best organisations go on to do it again and again as they learn more about their customers and grow in confidence in what they can change. Typically this is done under the umbrella of lean thinking, as described in Section 7.1.

5.4.2 Practices to cope when P-time is greater than D-time

There are a number of practices to reduce P-time. These can be summarised as follows:

- *Control* by improving balance between demand and capacity.
- *Simplify* by untangling process flows and reducing product complexity.
- *Compress* by reducing waste and batch sizes.
- *Integrate* by improving communications and implementing teams.
- *Coordinate* by conducting process in parallel rather than series.

Control

In any process, lead time depends on the balance between load and capacity. If demand rises above available capacity, lead times will increase unless resource is also increased, for example through overtime or subcontracting work. Therefore, in order to maintain or reduce lead time, it is necessary to balance this equation effectively by optimising throughput.

Simplify

Simplification is concerned with cutting out sources of process complexity and of product complexity. Process complexity is often caused by many different products *sharing the same process*. This process becomes a bottleneck, and process flows become tangled because they all have to go through this single, central process. In manufacturing, the solutions are based on cellular manufacturing: in distribution, the solutions are based on different distribution channels. Product complexity is often related to the *number of parts*. The more parts there are in a product the more difficult it is to plan, to make and to sell. One way to reduce product complexity is to reduce the number of parts, by integrating several components into one. The other is to reduce the number of parts by standardising them between products.

Compress

Compressing P-time is concerned with squeezing out waste in each process step. There are two main ways to achieve this. First, straighten the process flow by making a linear flow for each product. Second, reduce the batch size so that flow is improved and queuing time is minimised.

Integrate

Integrating different value-adding activities so that they work more closely together helps to reduce P-time. Integration is, in turn, helped by improving the speed and accuracy of information to the process owner. Important issues are demand information (what to do next?), product information (what is it?) and process information (how is it done?). Ways of speeding up information range from simple, paperless systems such as *kanban*, through simple IT systems such as electronic data interchange (EDI) (see Chapter 8 for further explanation of this), to more complex systems such as making EPOS data available in real time through the internet. Integration is also helped by forging relationships between departments or organisations that need to communicate. Teams and partnerships help to integrate activities that are otherwise disconnected. Further approaches to supply chain integration are covered in Chapter 8.

Coordinate

Other approaches to reducing P-time aim to reorganise value-adding activities so that they are done in parallel and/or in the best order. Thus running activities at the same time (in parallel) instead of one after another (in series) will reduce lead times. Sometimes it is possible to reduce lead times by doing the same activities in a different order. This may make it possible to combine activities or allow them to be done in parallel. It may also make better use of resources by fitting an extra job into a shift, or by running long tasks that need no supervision overnight.

5.4.3 Technologies to cope when P-time is greater than D-time

Technologies should be used last, once all the practices in Section 5.4.2 have delivered their improvements (do not automate waste!). The aim is to reduce lead time through the use of appropriate technologies. One approach for particularly high variety, customised, prototype or spare part products is 3-D printing, covered in Section 7.2.2 on manufacturing for agility. Four other approaches are covered here: traditional automation, industrial robots, augmented reality and the use of Artificial Intelligence. Automation approaches were traditionally best focused on bottleneck steps in the overall process, but today these technological investments are more widely applied with a focus on more repetitive tasks. The aim is to improve process capability and reliability as well as speed.

Traditional automation

Automation is not a new concept and has been used since the nineteenth century when, during the industrial revolution, machines such as textile looms were invented and powered by water mills and steam, dramatically speeding up labour-intensive processing. The aim is to automate highly repetitive tasks such that the process requires far less time (reducing P-time) and the labour required and associated costs are drastically reduced. Inherent in the traditional automation concept is the efficiency versus flexibility trade-off where efficiency (in terms of much shorter throughput times) is the priority and the process is typically more reliable and accurate, providing higher quality levels. However, the downside is that an automated process is less flexible, for example less able to accommodate new products, which necessitates the introduction of different processes. Therefore investment in traditional automation should be based on credible forecasts of future business, or should be used where the processes are not subject to particular change.

Industrial robots

Industrial robots – machines that can be automatically controlled and reprogrammed and that can manipulate objects and move along three or more axes – were first introduced in Europe, Japan and the US in the 1960s, with particular prominence in the automotive industry. Their reprogramming capability mitigates the efficiency versus flexibility trade-off inherent in traditional automation, which is particularly important as product life cycles reduce and product variety increases.

In recent years robots have become more accessible and affordable, providing the short payback periods demanded by business. For example, the Boston Consulting Group (Sirkin et al., 2015) has estimated that while 'a human welder earns around $25 per hour, including benefits, the equivalent operating cost per hour for a robot is around $8' and this gap is expected to widen further and drive a much faster robot adoption rate in industry. The new World Robotics 2023 Industrial Robots and Service Robots report said that 553,052 industrial robots were installed in factories around the world in 2022 – a year-over-year growth rate of 5 per cent. By region, 73 per cent of all newly deployed robots were installed in Asia, 15 per cent in Europe and 10 per cent in the Americas, according to the International Federation of Robotics (IFR). 'The world record of 500,000 units was exceeded for the second year in succession,' stated Marina Bill, president of the IFR, in a release.

Unlike traditional automation, robots are more flexible and can be reprogrammed to complete a much broader range of processes, although still they are best considered for more repetitive operations. Further, they achieve higher quality levels and can work almost continuously with no breaks (other than for servicing and repair), in sharp contrast to humans who require sleep, rest breaks and holidays, and fall sick. Thus over days and weeks robots are far more productive than humans and can achieve much shorter P-times. However, robots may not be quicker than humans in terms of the speed with which they perform individual tasks, especially when they are first programmed and there has been no opportunity to optimise the movements, as described in Case study 5.3 about GKN Driveline.

The positive impact on P-time is further amplified by the opportunity afforded by robotics to reshore manufacturing from low-cost economies closer to markets where labour is typically at a premium, thereby eliminating the time-consuming shipping process. This is illustrated by Zara who – faced with the prospect of sub-contracting manufacturing to Asia to reduce costs – built 14 highly automated Spanish factories, where robots work 24 hours a day cutting and dyeing fabrics and creating unfinished 'grey goods' – the basis of the final products. This enabled Zara to reduce operating costs and P-time simultaneously.

More flexible and cheaper robots are now being produced which challenge the efficiency versus flexibility trade-off further using clever yet simple reprogramming approaches. Advanced robotics companies such as Rethink Robotics (www.rethinkrobotics.com) and their flagship robots 'Baxter' and 'Sawyer' have created new possibilities for companies who previously assumed that robots were outside their budget, according to Sean Culey, a business transformation expert (Culey, 2017). Baxter can handle a wide range of tasks – from line loading and machine tending to packaging and material handling. Sawyer features a 7 degree of freedom robot arm with a 1,260 mm reach that manoeuvres into tight spaces and operates in work cells designed for humans. Built-in force-sensing capabilities allow Sawyer to make adaptive decisions as tasks run, enabling it to work precisely (+ / − 0.1 mm) while operating safely next to people. Arguably just as important is the ease with which these robots can be reprogrammed, promoting enhanced flexibility. These collaborative robots, or 'cobots', can be reprogrammed by non-engineering personnel simply by moving the arm through the motions to train it how to do a task. The cobots enable smaller companies to produce items with lower operating costs than if they offshored their activities, and without the increased lead times incurred by shipping and large batch sizes.

But these types of new industrial robots are not restricted to small companies in developed countries, as the GKN Driveline case study that follows demonstrates.

CASE STUDY 5.3

Cobot pilots at GKN Driveline

As a global business serving the world's leading vehicle manufacturers, GKN Driveline develops, builds and supplies an extensive range of automotive driveline products and systems, for use in everything from the most sophisticated premium vehicles that demand complex driving dynamics, to the smallest ultra-low-cost cars. In 2017 GKN Driveline sales were £3.5 billion, it employed around 20,000 people and operated 38 manufacturing locations in 18 countries.

A complete GKN Driveline solution

As part of their Industry 4.0 roadmap in 2016 GKN Driveline decided to implement collaborative robots (cobots) and a central fund was allocated for applications giving a 1-year payback (Figure 5.11). It was decided to apply cobots in assembly and material handling applications, as before the implementation:

- in machining most of the component production was automated using classic automation involving mainly gantries, pick and place units and 6 axis robots. Automation levels differed between low and high labour cost countries with the latter tending to use higher levels of automation. Loading and unloading stations were mainly manual.
- in assembly automation was around sub-assemblies with final assembly predominantly manual.

Figure 5.11 An example of the type of cobot implemented.
(Source: MikeDotta/Shutterstock.)

As a pilot project, within one year 14 cobots were launched for a range of activities from simple pick and place to complex assembly. There were no safety incidents showing that, despite the close working proximity with people, the cobots were still safe. However, there were many lessons learned which fell into four categories as explained next.

Health and safety

- *Regulations – need thorough risk assessment.* Deployment of Cobots working alongside Humans is a relatively new concept and current health and safety regulations may need to be upgraded to reflect this.

- *Programs were very easy to change on some units, which itself presented a risk.* There needs to be a limit on who can change the program for a cobot to avoid instability in processes and to reduce the risks around safety.
- *Sensors and vision systems need to be tested thoroughly testing.* Off the shelf systems work well in most cases but some applications require additional safeguards.
- *Drops and slippages could be a problem, especially at high speed.* Typical cycle times obtained with robots or operators are not always feasible with use of cobots. Generally cobots operate slower than robots. When trying to achieve certain cycle times, dropping of parts or slippages within the grippers were a concern.
- *Safety issues around grippers, which were not part of cobot equipment supplied* Whilst the cobots came equipped with sensors or vision systems, the grippers needed special attention for sensors (i.e. a sensor detecting an obstruction of a metallic part did not necessarily detect a human finger).

Limitations

- *Speed.* This was the biggest issue as the speed with which the cobots performed individual tasks was generally not quicker than humans.
- *Variations in pallets or fixtures and components caused issues.* Any variations in component geometry, fixture positions or component tolerances need to be built into the algorithm for vision system. Similarly pallet and component trays with wider tolerances require additional safeguards and fine-tuning of vision systems.
- *Not suitable everywhere so robots and gantries were still required.* Cobots were not the solution for all applications; classic automation (robots and gantries) was better for some applications.
- *Technical support required from suppliers who themselves were still learning.* Applications differ greatly at each customer; therefore, the suppliers are in their early days of learning and development. Close collaboration with suppliers was essential for the success of each project.

Applications

- Simplest applications work the best – simple applications for moving parts from A to B which required little development worked well. Where there was integration involved with other systems, it took a lot longer to achieve and the cost of system increased.
- Need design of grippers to finalise sensors. The main considerations were for safety of operators (to detect hands/fingers) and security of part once in the gripper to avoid dropping parts on moving parts, equipment or floor.
- Test assumptions for each application using simulation. Although time consuming at the start, simulating the application saves time later. This is assuming the site has the necessary software for such simulations.
- Complex applications require significant development time. If a cobot is required to pick and place parts, receive inputs from other equipment, make decisions, slow down if an operator appears close, or change grippers for different operations, then the development time for such applications becomes significant.

Benefits

- The cobots are low cost.
- Short lead time for supply of cobots.
- Flexible and easy to redeploy on other tasks.
- No safety barriers required.
- Productivity improvements. In most cases we could replace a person with a cobot. This was ideal, especially for the repetitive tasks with ergonomic issues (i.e. lifting heavy parts from bins to conveyors).
- Generally well accepted. There was generally no resentment to the deployment of cobots.

The results of these pilots were incorporated into new equipment standards and GKN plan further use of them in new automation projects.

(Source: Based on Mohammed Zameer, GKN Driveline, 2018.)

Question

1. Considering the lessons learned by GKN, discuss the context in which cobots are most beneficial in terms of the type of company and the specific operations.

Other examples of cobot applications include Foxconn, the Taiwanese manufacturing giant behind Apple's iPhone and numerous other major electronics, which has embarked on an extensive automation programme despite being located in a relatively low-cost labour region. In March 2016, Foxconn declared that it had automated away 60,000 repetitive or dangerous jobs at one factory alone (Statt, 2016). The second phase involves improving efficiency by streamlining production lines to reduce the number of excess robots in use, which indicates that the P-time reduction practices outlined in Section 5.4.2 may not have been followed in Foxconn, leading to automating waste! The third and final phase involves automating their entire factories. Cobots are quicker, cheaper, union free and prepared to work 24/7, 365 days a year (Culey, 2017).

Augmented reality (AR)

Augmented reality (AR) is defined as the expansion of physical reality through adding layers of computer-generated information to the real environment through a wearable device (Carmigniami et al., 2011). Like cobots, it challenges the efficiency versus flexibility trade-off, but in a quite different way. AR combines the flexibility of humans with the efficiency and speed improvements offered by computer-generated real-time information.

AR can be supported by different technologies (such as computers, TVs, smartphones and tablets, glasses and wearables) and although it can include audio and other senses such as smell, it is mainly associated with the visual aspect. An AR system should:

- operate in real time;
- mix virtual computer-generated information with reality;
- be integrated in a 3D environment.

Stoltz et al. (2017) identified four main warehouse operations where AR is used:

- receiving
- storing
- order picking
- shipping.

They also provide a helpful list of the potential uses of AR in warehouse operations, examples of which are shown in Table 5.3

Table 5.3 Potential uses of AR in warehouse operations.

Operation	Potential uses
Receiving	Show where to put the items/how to arrange them in the waiting zone
Storing	Indicate route to storage location
	Indicate picker's current status as well as the next step of the process
	Check locations requiring replenishment while storing
Picking	Inform about errors and disruptions
	Scan the item's barcode to assign to picking cart or to see more information
	Highlight where to put each item on the picking cart for sorting while picking
	Give information to prevent congestion in aisles
	Monitor picker's condition and performance
Shipping	Show where to place each order on a pallet/in a truck according to type of orders, destination, fragility
	Indicate appropriate loading area
	Check/Count products/orders to be loaded on a truck

(Source: Adapted from Stoltz et al., 2017.)

Order picking has received the most attention, perhaps due to the fact that it accounts for more than 50 per cent of warehousing costs (Giannikas et al., 2016). The goal is to enable picking which is fast, error free and user friendly while guiding a human operator. Head mounted displays and smart glasses are most popular as they offer a hands-free solution and the user can communicate effectively with the physical world while wearing them, which is crucial in industrial applications.

In their study of AR in picking operations Stoltz et al. (2017) identified a number of benefits with example justifications given by the operators:

- *Reliability improvement:* picking instructions are easy to understand, which enables temporary workers to quickly become effective. Also, it is possible to share photos of an issue with the supervisor enabling quicker and more effective resolution.

- *Error reduction:* the visual display helps prevent the wrong product being selected and the provision of instructions reduces the need for the operator to remember and make decisions.
- *Flexibility improvement:* the hands-free capability ensures the operator is unhindered by the device and, if the operator is disrupted, the visual instructions are a reminder. Plus the visual display is provided anywhere in the warehouse.
- *Speed improvement:* Re-work is reduced by the reduction in errors and it's not necessary to walk to and from fixed computers. Also, optimised routing information results in less movement.
- *Safety:* hands-free capability helps prevent accidents and allows operators to immediately warn of danger.

Interestingly, it was found that AR did not necessarily increase the speed of the operation directly but, rather, through the above indirect effects. The main challenges of AR were found to be:

- Hardware limitations such as batteries not being designed to last long, processors overheating, problems with wearability such as eye strain.
- Software challenges including user-friendliness of interface.
- Acceptance such as users not being willing to wear a device with a camera due to privacy issues.
- Cost, since the total cost of ownership is still quite high especially if the wearable devices are considered to be personal equipment (i.e. due to hygiene issues).

Though AR is not considered to be a new technological development, its usage in manufacturing and logistics operations is still significantly behind other industries such as retail and gaming. Stoltz et al. (2017) concluded that some of the challenges identified here, together with the sometimes limited benefits it can provide compared to existing well-adopted solutions, are probably the reason for this. In other words, it could be that AR technology applied to logistics may not yet be a mature technology. However, companies such as Knapp, Picavi, SAP and DHL have started developing AR solutions that focus on different hardware and software elements. Case study 5.4 describes DHL's vision picking system that the company has developed and applied for multiple customers.

CASE STUDY 5.4

Vision picking by DHL

The vast majority of warehouses in the developed world still use the pick-by-paper approach. But any paper-based approach is slow and error prone. Furthermore, picking work is often undertaken by temporary workers who usually require cost-intensive training to ensure they pick efficiently and without making errors. DHL has developed a vision picking system using AR which has been integrated into a number of operations around the world.

By wearing advanced Smart glasses pickers use a hands-free visual guide throughout the picking process. The Smart glasses:

- identify the location number;
- provide the best route using indoor navigation;

- scan the product barcode and, using image recognition technology, check that it is correct;
- identify the number of items to be picked;
- show where each item should be placed in the trolley;
- offer seamless integration of information with the Warehouse Management System (WMS).

Good for both single and multi-order picking, vision picking allows picking at a faster pace and reduces the error rate. Although today's picking error rate is very low, even using a pick-by-paper approach, every error must be prevented, because it typically results in high follow-up costs. DHL's customer applications have reported various benefits, including:

> **About 50% of the man hours we spend in a typical warehouse are spent on picking. At the moment we have about a 15% productivity improvement as a result of implementing the vision picking technology. We have also seen that training is much quicker, as it's learning by doing.**

Director, Technology & Automotive Benelux, DHL Supply Chain

> **We are in an extremely aggressive market so its vital that we remain in front with . . . Vision picking has distinctive advantages when it comes to quality and productivity. Effectiveness originates from the way that the administrators can do the picking hands free and the quality originates from the visual guides they need to sort the items into the correct bits.**

Director of Operations, Europe Supply Chain Management

(Source: sunchai/Adobe Stock Photo.)

Question

1. What challenges might you envisage and how might these restrict the possible applications?

(Source: DHL Supply Chain, 2017.)

Activity 5.3

Consider an operation in a warehouse setting, or another aspect of logistics you are familiar with, and determine how AR could speed up the operation. Identify all the possible benefits and challenges of its implementation, paying particular attention to its likely impact on speed. Would you recommend its implementation. If so, why?

Demand forecasting using Artificial Intelligence (AI)

Predicting, or forecasting, demand across the products and markets served by a company is critical where P-time is greater than D-time, and therefore operations such as procurement and manufacturing, are driven by forecasts, rather than firm customer orders. Demand forecasting is also the first step in the Sales and Operations Planning process (as described in Section 6.1.2), and it is required for inventory management (as detailed in Section 6.1.3). The more accurate the forecast the higher the availability of product and lower the safety stock required leading to a shorter P-time.

However, classical statistical methods are not always appropriate for accurate and reliable forecasting, especially when demand is highly variable and unpredictable as is often the case for high-variety (or customised) products or those subject to promotions. Many companies, particularly retailers like Amazon, are using AI to monitor competitors' prices, market trends and customer behaviour to forecast demand. According to McKinsey (Amar, et al., 2022) AI-driven forecasting can reduce supply chain errors by between 20 and 50 per cent, leading to a 65 per cent boost in efficiency through fewer lost sales and unavailable products.

AI demand forecasting methods combine traditional time series forecasting with machine learning methods or use artificial neural networks to refine and improve the demand forecasting process (Shen and Chan (2017). Machine learning (ML) is a subarea of AI which works with self-learning algorithms. ML methods aim to improve their results based on experience gained from available historical data (Moroff and Sardesai, 2019). Furthermore, ML methods have been shown to perform well with large amounts of noisy data, such as those typically found in historical demand data; however, there are many different approaches.

Mediavilla et al. (2022) review all the AI methods published between 2017 and 2021 and provide a useful classification system of those approaches that provide the best results. It is based on the Liu et al. (2019) taxonomy, where AI methods are classified into traditional ML methods and deep learning methods that can achieve outstanding performances and are better at dealing with big data. Subsequently, each category can be divided into supervised and unsupervised learning. *Supervised learning* relies on the data being labelled; consequently manual data labelling is required, which is expensive and time consuming. The lack of sufficient labelled demand data forms the main bottleneck to supervised learning. In contrast, *unsupervised learning* extracts valuable feature information from unlabelled data, making it much easier to obtain training data; however, the performance of unsupervised learning methods is usually inferior.

To support companies in selecting suitable AI forecasting methods, Mediavilla et al. (2022) propose a classification system based on the following demand data characteristics:

- dimensionality of the data: univariate versus multivariate;
- the volume of data; and
- the time horizon over which the methods offer the best results.

Summary

What is time-based competition?

- Competing on time demands a fast response to customer needs. Time-based approaches focus on the competitive advantage of speed, which reduces the time horizon upon which forecasts are required and thus improves forecast accuracy, leading to a reduction in expensive safety stock. Speed also helps a network to cope with variety and product innovation, whilst also improving returns on new products.
- Speed of response helps to lower costs by reducing the need for working capital, and plant and equipment. It also helps to reduce development costs and the cost of quality.

How do we measure and implement time-based strategies?

- Time-based mapping aims to generate visibility of time in the supply network. A seven-step approach to mapping involves creating a task force, selecting the process, collecting data, distinguishing between value-adding and non-value-adding activities, constructing the time-based process map and generating a solution.

What is the lead-time frontier and how can it be managed?

- The lead-time frontier is concerned with reducing P-time (time needed to produce a product or service) to less than D-time (the time the customer is prepared to wait).
- The difference between P-time and D-time is referred to as the lead-time gap. This gap has strategic implications for marketing, product development and process development. P-time can be reduced by a six-stage process: control, simplify, compress, integrate, coordinate and apply technology.

Discussion questions

1. Why is time important to competitive advantage? Identify and explain six key contributions that speed can make to logistics strategy.
2. 'Variety yes, complexity no'. Discuss the implications of this statement to logistics strategy.
3. Explain the significance of P:D ratios. How can the production lead time be reduced?

References

Aitken, J., Deakins, E., Skipworth, H. and Cole, R. (2018) *The Role of Temporal Norms and Orientations in Operations Management.* 25th EurOMA Conference, Budapest, 24–6 June 2018.

Amar, J., Rahimi, S., Surak, Z. and von Bismark, N. (2022) 'Too many companies still rely on manual forecasting because they think AI requires better-quality data than they have available. Nowadays, that's a costly mistake.', McKinsey & Company, 15th February 2022. Accessed at https://www.mckinsey.com/capabilities/operations/our-insights/ai-driven-operations-forecasting-in-data-light-environments

Bicheno, J. and Holweg, M. (2008) *The Lean Toolbox – The Essential Guide to Lean Transformation*, 4th edn. Buckingham: Picsie Books.

Carmigniami, J. and Furht, B. (2011) 'Augmented Reality: An Overview', in Furht, B. (ed.) *Handbook of Augmented Reality*, pp. 3–46. New York, Springer.

Chen, M.J. and Miller, D. (2011) 'The relational perspective as a business mindset: managerial implications for east and west', *Academy of Management Perspectives*, vol. 25, no. 3, pp. 6–18.

Christopher, M. (1998) *Logistics and Supply Chain Management.* London: Financial Times Pitman Publishing.

Cooper, J. and Griffiths, J. (1994) 'Managing variety in automotive logistics with the rule of three', *The International Journal of Logistics Management*, vol. 5, no. 2, pp. 29–40.

Crosby, P.B. (1979) *Quality is Free: The Art of Making Quality Certain.* New York: McGraw-Hill.

Culey, S. (2017) 'Revitalizing the rust belt', *Forbes*, 8 September, at https://www.forbes.com/sites/realspin/2017/09/08/revitalizing-the-rust-belt/#5eceeaa946f2

Garvin, D.A. (1988) 'The multiple dimensions of quality', *Managing Quality*. New York: Free Press.

Holweg, M. and Pil, F. (2004) *The Second Century: Reconnecting the Customer and Value Chain Through Build-to-Order*, Cambridge, MA: MIT.

Liu, H. and Lang, B. (2019) 'Machine learning and deep learning methods for intrusion detection systems: a survey', *Applied Sciences*, vol. 9, no. 20, 4396. https://doi.org/10.3390/app9204396

Mahler, D. and Bahulkar, A. (2009) 'Smart complexity', *Strategy and Leadership*, vol. 37, no. 5, pp. 5–11.

Mediavilla, M.A., Fabian, D. and Palma, D. (2022) 'Review and analysis of artificial intelligence methods for demand forecasting in supply chain management', 55th CIRP Conference on Manufacturing Systems, pp. 1126–31. https://creativecommons.org/licenses/by-nc-nd/4.0

Moroff, N.U. and Sardesai, S. (2019) 'Machine learning in demand planning cross-industry overview'. epubli GmbH.

Ohnsman, A. (2018) 'The elusive $35,000 model 3: a Godot-like wait for the "Mass-Market" Tesla', *Forbes*, 20 February, at https://www.forbes.com/sites/alanohnsman/2018/02/20/the-elusive-35000-model-3-a-godot-like-wait-for-the-mass-market-tesla/#64d9a56b4251

Shen, B. and Chan, H.-L. (2017) 'Forecast information sharing for managing supply chains in the Big Data Era: recent development and future research', *Asia Pacific Journal in Operations Research*, vol. 34, no. 01,1740001. https://doi.org/10.1142/S0217595917400012

Sirkin, H., Zinser, M. and Rose, J. (2015) 'How robots will redefine competitiveness', Boston Consulting Group, at https://www.bcg.com/en-gb/publications/2015/lean-manufacturing-innovation-robots-redefine-competitiveness.aspx

Stalk, G. and Hout, T. (1990) *Competing Against Time*. New York: Free Press.

Statt, N. (2016) 'Foxconn cuts 60,000 factory jobs and replaces them with robots', The Verge, at https://www.theverge.com/2016/5/25/11772222/foxconn-automation-robots-apple-samsung-smartphones

Stoltz M.H., Giannikas V., McFarlane D., Strachan J., Um J. and Srinivasan R. (2017) 'Augmented reality in warehouse operations: opportunities and barriers', Institute for Manufacturing, Department of Engineering, University of Cambridge, Cambridge, UK.

Suggested further reading

Galloway, D. (1994) *Mapping Work Processes*. Milwaukee, WI: ASQC Quality Press.

Hammer, M. (2007) 'The process audit', *Harvard Business Review*, April, pp. 111–23.

Rother, M. and Shook, J. (1999) *Learning to See*, version 1.3. Brookline, MA: The Lean Enterprise Institute Inc.

CHAPTER 6

Supply chain planning and control

Objectives

The intended objectives of this chapter are to:

- **explain the processes by which material flow is planned and executed within a focal firm and between partners in a supply chain;**
- **explain the initiatives that have been developed to overcome poor coordination in retail supply chains.**

By the end of this chapter you should be able to:

- **appreciate the sophistication that lies behind an integrated model of material flow in a supply chain, and why this model is so easily corrupted;**
- **understand how creating a sales and operations planning platform can improve coordination and information flow;**
- **understand how corruption of flow causes loss of focus on ability to meet end-customer demand;**
- **recognise enemies of flow in the supply chain;**
- **appreciate initiatives that have been developed to restore flow.**

Introduction

In Chapter 3, we introduced the simple framework for coordinated processes across the supply chain that has become known as the 'SCOR model' (Figure 3.19). This model creates a vision of integration of supply chain processes both upstream and downstream. A shared planning process – that coordinates movements seamlessly from one process to the next – orchestrates material flow.

The reality of supply chain management today reveals a very different picture as coordination shifts from organising a linear, unidirectional entity and becomes: 'adaptive to both supply and demand as well as being reactive and pro-active to wider geo-political, business, economic, environmental, and social factors' (Stevens and Johnson, 2016). The factors behind the gap between vision and reality are many, reflecting the sophisticated web of processes and coordination that lie behind the vision and the almost endless ways of corrupting it. Decisions based on advantages internal to a focal firm and on the search for cheaper prices are but two common factors in corrupting the flow of materials and information, and the focus on the end-customer. Corruption is displayed by poor customer service, stock write-offs or mark-downs, and a lot of resource is devoted to 'fire fighting'.

This chapter aims to summarise the detail of an integrated planning and control system. The most comprehensive models originate from manufacturing, and link key activities such as resource planning, **demand management** and **capacity planning** into a holistic framework. Individual firms have been quite successful not only in developing effective **manufacturing planning and control (MPC)** systems, but also in integrating them with other business functions such as finance and human resources through **enterprise resource planning (ERP)**. However, linkages *between* the MPC systems of supply chain partners are relatively weak (Vollman et al., 2005: 578), and those between MPC systems at manufacturers and 'service' processes such as distribution and back of store are even weaker. Skim the detail at your peril! Far too many logistics 'decisions' are made on the basis of lack of understanding of the sheer scale and scope of the intricacies of balancing load and capacity, of coordinating marketing wants and supply chain realities.

One of the principal techniques used by manufacturers to overcome some of the potential pitfalls of poor coordination is **sales and operations planning (S&OP)**. Developed in the 1980s by Oliver Wight, S&OP is an integrated business management process which encourages medium-term forecasting from both a demand and a supply perspective. The purpose of the S&OP module is to set demand (in terms of orders and sales forecasts for existing and new products) and to translate them into operations plans for sourcing, making, storing and delivering to demand.

Next, we examine the planning and control processes in retail, and explain the implications for integrating material flow across the supply chain. Retail supply chains are of particular interest because end-customer demand is tracked continuously through POS data. There should, accordingly, be every opportunity to develop a seamless coordination between demand and supply, as envisaged in Figure 1.7. There are challenges enough to cope with, notably the integration of manufacturing, distribution and service processes. However – historically at least – retailers have given priority to the market and have expected manufacturers to keep pace without investing much in terms of coordinating demand and supply. This has resulted in such problems as amplification of demand upstream – the so-called '**bullwhip effect**' – high inventories and lengthy P-times. The second part of this chapter therefore continues by reviewing some of the key initiatives that have been developed in recent years to improve planning and control of materials in retail supply chains.

Key issues

This chapter addresses three key issues as follows:

1. **The supply chain 'game plan'**: planning and control in manufacturing. Managing independent demand items. Retail supply chains – driven by the market rather than by the supply chain. Implications for supply chain planning and control and the alignment role of sales and operation planning (S&OP).
2. **Overcoming poor coordination in retail supply chains**: initiatives to improve coordination in retail supply chains. Efficient consumer response (ECR) and Quick response (QR).

6.1 The supply chain 'game plan'

***Key issues*: What are the key steps in planning and executing material flow and information flow within the focal firm? What are the key steps in planning and executing material flow and information flow between partners in a supply network? What are the implications for planning and controlling the supply chain as a whole?**

In this section, we consider planning and control processes across a simple supply chain, such as that shown in Figure 1.1. We start with planning and control processes at the manufacturer, and the demands this generates on the supplier (well documented in such publications as Silver, Pyke, and Thomas, 2016). Once it has been made, a fresh batch of product turns into *finished product inventory* – initially stored in the manufacturer's national distribution centre (NDC). So, next we turn to the management of inventory in the supply chain, showing that *different* models are likely to be used by manufacturers and retailers to determine how much and when to order. We then explain planning and control from the retailer's perspective, and conclude with the implications for planning and controlling the supply chain as a whole.

6.1.1 Planning and control within manufacturing

The purpose of a manufacturing planning and control (MPC) system is to meet customer requirements by enabling managers to make the right decisions. The system coordinates information on key 'source–make–deliver' processes to enable material to flow efficiently and effectively. Three time horizons are involved for all of these processes:

1. *Long term:* to support decisions about capacity provision. These decisions are essentially strategic, and answer the questions how much capacity is needed, when and of what type? Thus Mercedes-Benz may plan new model ranges for 20 years ahead – including outline volumes, internal and supplier capacities and distribution strategies.
2. *Medium term:* to match supply and demand. Here, Mercedes may plan in more detail over the next 12 months to ensure that forecast demand can be met by correct material provision, together with capacity and resource (such as manpower) availability. The plan would be refreshed monthly.
3. *Short term:* to meet day-to-day demand as it unfolds. Here, Mercedes makes weekly production plans to meet specific customer orders. There may be numerous changes that affect achievement of the medium-term plan. These include changes in customer demand, facility problems and supplier shortages. The short-term plan helps managers to decide what corrective actions are needed to resolve such problems, and would be refreshed daily or weekly.

Figure 6.1 shows the main modules in an MPC system. The top section is called the 'front end', and provides an overall match of demand and resource. We summarise here the main front-end modules, followed by a summary of engine and back end:

1. *Demand management:* collates demand from all sources – external (forecasts and orders), internal (other firms within the organisation) and spares. Such demand is called *independent* – that is, it is independent of the actions of the focal firm. Referring to Figure 5.10, demand is independent up to the **customer order decoupling point (CODP)**. At this point, demand changes from independent to *dependent*. Upstream from the CODP, in the area referred to as 'P-time–D-time', the focal firm assumes responsibility for sourcing and making speculatively – on the assumption that orders eventually will transpire. Thus *make to order* (MTO, Section 5.4) incurs less speculation than *assemble to order* (ATO) and much less than *make to stock* (MTS). Speculation implies that it is necessary to *forecast* demand for the relevant module. Thus, forecasting for sales and operations planning is carried out monthly or quarterly and is at the level of the overall product line. Forecasts for master production scheduling purposes are refreshed frequently for the next few days or weeks, and are made at the level of the individual SKU (stock keeping unit). Forecast accuracy (comparing forecast and actual values) is measured by such techniques as Mean Absolute Percentage Error (MAPE, Section 2.2). It is necessary to forecast only for independent demand items: demand for dependent items can be calculated using material requirements planning – described next.
2. *Resource planning:* pooling demand and passing it on to manufacturing *must* be moderated by capacity to deliver. Otherwise, a focal firm is at risk of being unable to fulfil marketing plans that do not take into account the realities of what

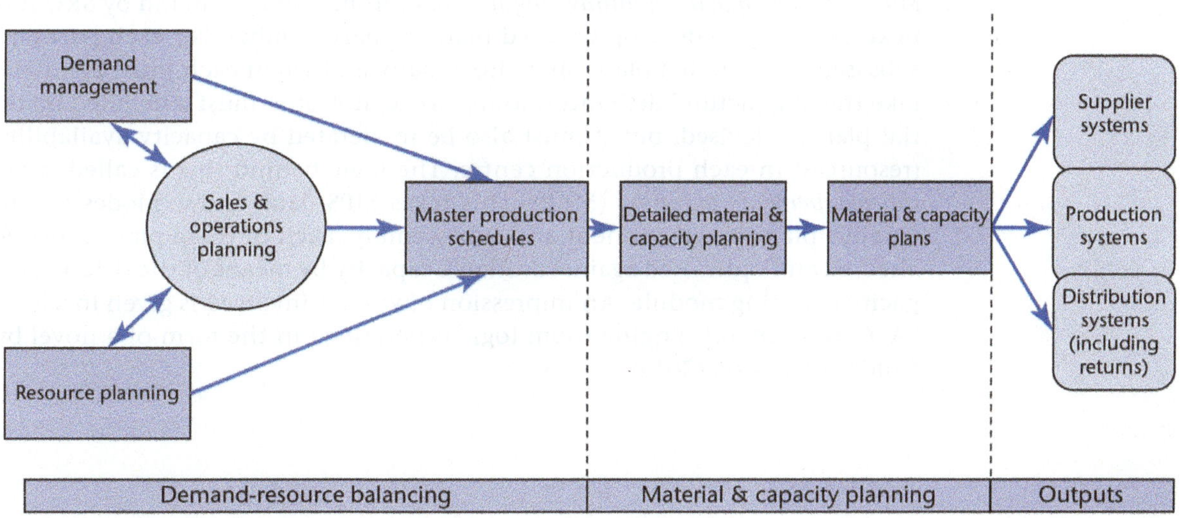

Figure 6.1 Manufacturing planning and control systems.

can be done. Again, this would mean that marketing plans are not actionable (Section 2.1). Resource planning is concerned with manufacturing capacity in the longer term (output measure), and with machine and manpower loading (input measure) in the shorter term.

3. *Sales and operations planning (S&OP):* is the module concerned with matching of demand management and resource planning. Therefore, it is crucial that compatible measures of demand and capacity are used - for example, tonnes/week or '000 units produced/week. Sales and marketing must check with manufacturing that new enquiries can be made and delivered within requested lead times. This may well require coordination across several manufacturing units in different countries. The aim of S&OP is to maintain *balance* between demand and supply. Create too much demand in terms of capacity, and manufacturing will be under pressure to work overtime and to rush work through. If there is too little demand, margins will be under pressure from under-utilised resources, layoffs and price cuts. S&OP is discussed in more detail in Section 6.2.
4. *Master production scheduling (MPS):* is the disaggregated form of the S&OP. This means that the S&OP is broken down from high level measures like product families into the detail of SKUs by major production facility. The MPS is the link between demand-resource section and manufacturing and capacity planning of the MPC system. On the one hand, it receives S&OP data about sales and forecasts. On the other hand, it feeds data back to S&OP on orders and stock replenishment status so that customers and distribution can be kept up to date. The MPS handles the detail of what is planned and what is happening. For MTS environments, the priority is inventory management: for MTO environments, the priority is timely execution of all of the processes from design through to delivery.
5. *Material and capacity planning (engine room):* from overall demand by SKU it is next necessary to develop detailed plans by part number. For each part and subassembly, detailed plans show how many and when each must be made. Like the 'big picture' demand-resource logic, not only must a detailed material plan be devised, but it must also be moderated by capacity availability (resources) in each production centre. The logic behind this is called *material requirements planning* (MRP). This takes MPS data, and explodes it into detailed plans by component and subassembly. Each of these plans must be checked and optimised against available capacity by means of the detailed capacity planning module. An impression of what is involved is given in Victor SA, Case study 6.1. Engine room logic is described in the form of a novel by Goldratt and Cox (2016).

CASE STUDY 6.1

Victor SA

Victor SA makes 'fantastically good cakes' from basic ingredients such as flour, eggs and butter. Demand for Victor sponge cakes comes from two sources. Some big retailers place their order with the firm two days in advance, whilst other customers arrive at Victor's own shops without prior warning and select from cakes that are on display. This means that some cakes are made in line with orders, whilst a forecast is also required to predict day-to-day demand.

Whilst there are many varieties of cake, the bill of material for the famous Victor sponge cake is shown in Figure 6.2.

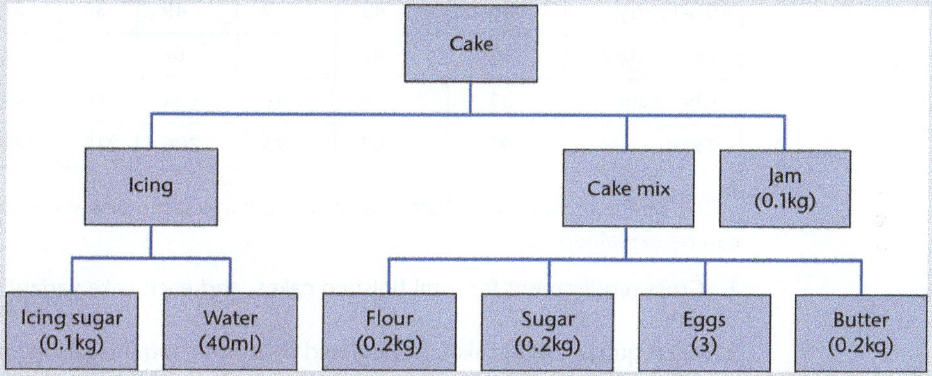

Figure 6.2 Structured bill of materials for sponge cake.

When overall demand across the range has been collated, Victor SA is able to determine how much of each ingredient will be needed to make the right number of cakes. Too many and cakes will have to be thrown away, because the shelf life is five to eight days (Victor does not use stabilisers such as potassium sorbate). Too few and sales will be lost. Accurate planning is thus crucial to the efficiency of the whole operation. The ideal situation is that cakes are made and delivered *just-in-time* to meet customer demand because inventories will be low and freshness at its best.

In an effort to increase sales, Victor SA decided to increase the product range. Strawberry jam is the traditional filling, but marketing considers that customers would also like other types of filling and decides to try blackberry jam, apricot jam, lemon curd and chocolate. Over the course of the next few months, the experiment appears to be working. Overall sales are up by 10 per cent, with each of the new varieties contributing well. The problem, however, is that no stable pattern exists in the mix of sales. For example, some days the chocolate-filled cakes sell out, whilst on other days hardly a single chocolate-filled cake is sold. Major retail customers are complaining about wastage and lost sales opportunities.

The issue appears to be that offering increased variety has led to less stability in the demand pattern, as illustrated by the master production schedule (MPS) in Table 6.1. Whilst total daily cake demand is reasonably stable, at around 200 cakes, the demand for each variant is highly uncertain. This leads to high inventory levels, due to inaccurate sales forecasts, and increased complexity in the production operation, as shown by the MRP calculation for gross and net requirements in Table 6.2.

Table 6.1 Master production schedule (MPS) for sponge cakes (before postponement).

	Sales							
Cake variant	Orders & forecast		Forecast only					
	Mon.	Tue.	Wed.	Thur.	Fri.	Sat.	Sun.	Total
Strawberry	34	52	56	13	64	62	57	338
Apricot	58	39	33	43	7	57	28	265
Blackberry	36	43	9	49	39	37	17	230
Lemon curd	40	47	51	67	59	18	61	343
Chocolate	23	6	46	34	49	49	23	230
Total	**191**	**187**	**195**	**206**	**218**	**223**	**186**	**1,406**

The MRP calculations, which are shown for the same one-week period as the MPS, can be explained as follows:

1. Gross requirement for total finished cakes, and each cake variant, is taken from the MPS.
2. Net requirement of cakes is calculated by subtracting the existing inventory from the gross requirement.
3. Inventory of finished cakes is high (equivalent to almost four days' demand) because demand for each variant is highly uncertain and therefore sales forecasts are inaccurate.
4. The net requirement for total finished cakes is exploded (by multiplying it by the BOM quantity for each cake mix ingredient plus icing) to give the gross requirement for each of the cake mix ingredients and the icing.
5. The net requirement for each of the cake ingredients is calculated by subtracting the existing inventory and any scheduled receipts.
6. The inventory of cake mix ingredients is low (equivalent to about one day's demand with another day's demand scheduled for receipt). This is a result of the relatively stable demand for the total number of cakes leading to accurate sales forecasts.
7. The net requirement for each of the finished cake variants is exploded (by multiplying it by the BOM quantity for jam) to give the gross requirement for each jam flavour. The net requirement of jam is calculated in the same way as for cake mix ingredients (point 5 above).
8. Inventories of the various jams are high (they cover requirements for the coming weeks without need for scheduled receipts), and therefore the net requirement is zero. This is due to inaccurate sales forecasts caused by the uncertain demand for each cake variant.

To fix the unexpected problems, Victor SA decided on a new way of working. It is recognised that demand is not going to stabilise, given the increased product range. The firm decided to adopt a *postponement* strategy by making standard cakes and then

Table 6.2 Gross and net requirement calculations for one week demand for sponge cake (before postponement). 'Exploding' is indicated by arrows.

Component	BOM* quantity	units	Inventory	Scheduled receipts	Gross requirement	Net requirement
Total finished cake	n/a	cakes	723		1,406	683
Strawberry cake	n/a	cakes	188		338	150
Apricot cake	n/a	cakes	103		265	162
Blackberry cake	n/a	cakes	145		230	85
Lemon curd cake	n/a	cakes	212		343	131
Chocolate cake	n/a	cakes	75		230	155
Flour	0.2	kg	40	40	137	57
Sugar	0.2	kg	40	40	137	57
Eggs	3	eggs	600	600	2,049	849
Butter	0.2	kg	40	40	137	57
Icing sugar	0.1	kg	20	20	68	28
Strawberry jam	0.1	kg	21	10	15	0
Apricot jam	0.1	kg	18		16	0
Blackberry jam	0.1	kg	14		9	0
Lemon curd	0.1	kg	14	10	13	0
Chocolate	0.1	kg	16	10	16	0

*BOM = bill of material (quantity required for each cake)

postponing final assembly until known demand is available. The basic cake is a *standard component*, whilst the filling is non-standard and represents the source of complexity and variable customer demand. Cakes are therefore kept in the standard form and turned into the final form only by adding the filling once customer orders have been received. Victor SA applied postponement to the supply chain and introduced a *decoupling point* (Section 5.3) at the end of the cake making process. Upstream of the decoupling point, overall demand is forecasted to inform sourcing decisions. Standard components are baked each morning. Downstream of the decoupling point, cakes are assembled to order in line with customer orders. The time this activity takes has been minimised by setting up a workstation with cakes, filling and spreading tools arranged in a mini flow-line. This brings the production time (P-time: see Section 5.3) within the time the customer is prepared to wait (D-time). Carrying out the operation in view of the customer also helps engage them and extends their D-time to a minute or so, long enough to complete the final assembly task.

The flexibility of the new operation means that customers no longer need to place an order two days in advance. Victor SA can now supply from the new process if orders are received by major customers the day before. An unexpected benefit of the new approach is the ease with which innovations can be test marketed and adopted.

(Source: Based on Chapman, P. (2010) 'Reducing product losses in the food supply chain', in Mena, C. and Stevens, G. (eds) Delivering Performance in Food Supply Chains. New York: McGraw Hill.)

Question

1. How do you think the MPS, the MRP gross/net requirements calculations and the inventories (finished cake and ingredients) might be different after the implementation of postponement?

MPC execution systems (back end): the outputs from material and capacity plans in the engine are sets of instructions to suppliers, manufacturing and distribution. These schedules are in the form of purchase orders, works orders (or schedules for MTS) and shipping orders – hence the familiar 'source–make–deliver' processes at the bottom of Figure 6.1. The basic format is 'how many' and 'when' for each part number for each planning process for the relevant planning period (for example the next two weeks, or the next four weeks). Achievement against schedule has to be monitored by minute, by hour or by day. Failures to meet schedule – as a result of, for example, breakdowns or quality problems – require that remedial action is taken, such as overtime working or outsourcing. An example here is the Procter & Gamble supply problem described in Case study 1.4.

Front end, engine and back end MPC modules are all connected to the *enterprise resource planning* (ERP) database. This enables MPC modules to be connected seamlessly to human resource management, finance and sales and marketing modules. SAP includes MPC systems as part of its supply chain software – supply chain planning, execution, collaboration and coordination. One of the key modules for ensuring that the front end of MPC supports the organisation in delivering value is sales and operations planning where demand management and resource planning are aligned.

6.1.2 Sales and operations planning (S&OP)

Sales and operations planning (S&OP) is an integrated business management process developed in the 1980s by Oliver Wight, which encourages medium-term forecasting from both a demand and a supply perspective. The purpose of the S&OP module (as introduced in Section 6.1.1) is to set demand (in terms of orders and sales forecasts for existing and new products) and to translate them into operations plans for sourcing, making, storing and delivering to demand, in other words to balance supply and demand. The American Production and Inventory Control Society (APICS) provides a formal, albeit production-centric, definition of S&OP:

> **Johnsson et al., (2021) define S&OP as "the matching of supply and demand in the medium term by providing a process for the vertical alignment of business strategy and operational planning and execution, and for the horizontal alignment of demand and supply plans".**

S&OP requires internal integration (which is further discussed in Section 8.1.1) to make the process work, at least between sales, marketing and operations and ideally with other functions such as product development and finance. However, these functional areas traditionally specialise in portions of the planning activities, which results in conflicts of priorities. Oliva and Watson (2011) show that the S&OP *process* can achieve integration, rather than requiring it in the first place, and this is despite formal functional incentives (such as performance-related pay). Further, it is widely acknowledged that companies that implement S&OP successfully can meet customer demands at the highest levels with reduced lead times for orders and time-to-launch for new products, whilst maintaining reduced inventories and minimising supply chain operating costs (for example, Ambrose et al., 2018). However, many companies do not realise these benefits because S&OP is not measured or implemented properly (Hulthén et al., 2017; Wallace 2013)).

In her lectures, Godsell (2006) provides a good example of an S&OP process at Corus Group plc, a multinational steel-making company, now wholly owned by Tata Steel. The schematic in Figure 6.3 shows how the S&OP is positioned at a tactical level. So it is not concerned with the day-to-day, week-to-week operations, but instead provides governance in line with the corporate strategy (across products, marketing and operations) with a horizon of up to 24 months.

The four fundamentals of S&OP

There are four fundamentals of S&OP, as indicated by Dougherty and Gray (2006) and shown in Figure 6.4.

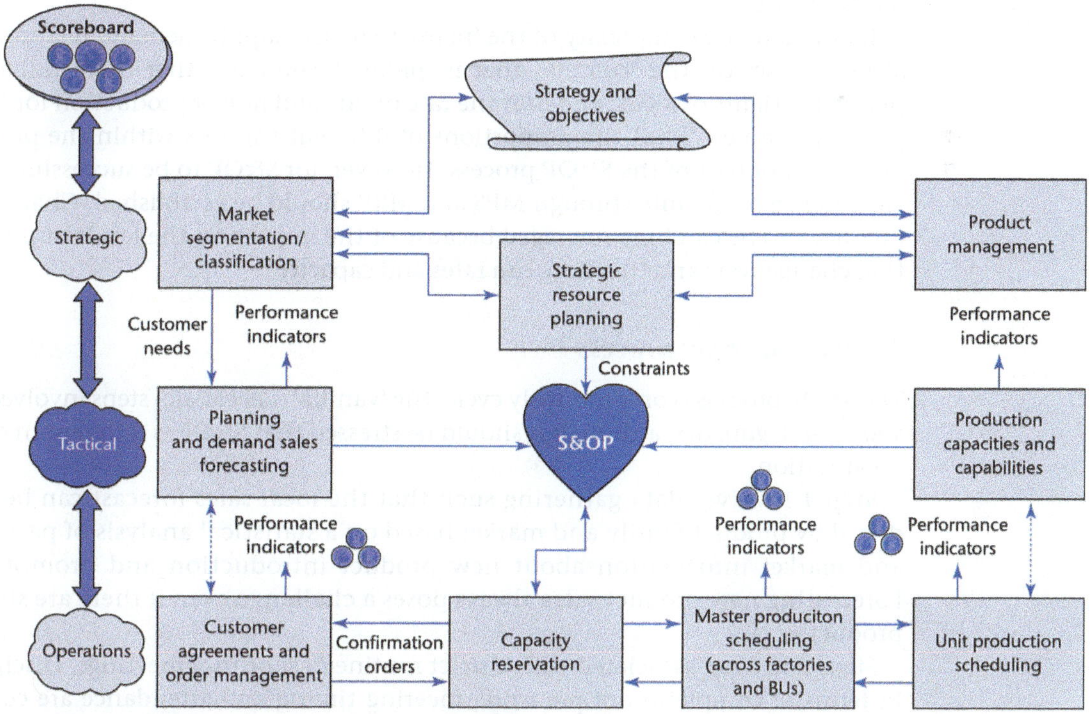

Figure 6.3 Overview of the Corus S&OP process.
(Source: Adapted from Godsell, 2006.)

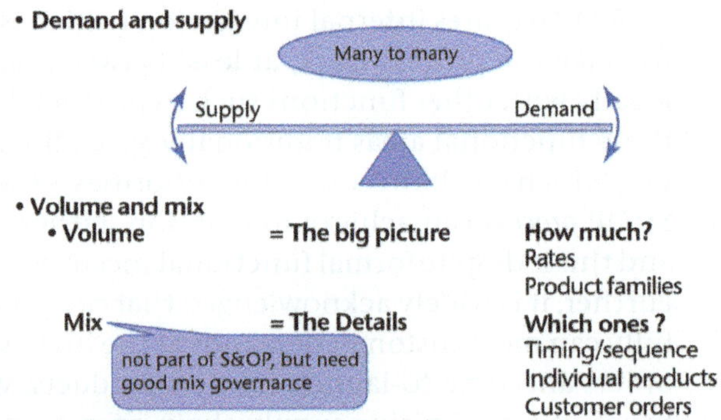

Figure 6.4 The four fundamentals of S&OP.
(Source: Dougherty and Gray, 2006.)

The aim of S&OP is to balance supply and demand across the projected planning period. Typically, this involves many sources of supply – whether 'in-house factories or external suppliers or both – and many sources of demand across a range of products and markets in a variety of geographical regions. If supply exceeds demand the result is high inventories of raw materials and finished product, leading to high inventory holding cost, obsolescence, long cash-to-cash cycle times and high levels of working capital. On the other hand, if demand exceeds supply then it will lead to poor customer service levels in terms of availability and on time in full which will probably lead to lost sales and/or market share.

To mitigate the complexity of the 'many to many' supply–demand relationship S&OP focuses on the 'volume', that is, product families rather than individual product variants or SKUs, and uses the rate of sale and rate of production for these product families. 'Mix', the proportions of different variants within the product family, is not part of the S&OP process. However, for S&OP to be successful, good governance of the mix through MPS and MRP should be established. Changes in mix need to be carefully managed because of the impact on the levels of production changeovers and therefore run rates and capacity.

The vanilla S&OP process

The S&OP process is on a monthly cycle; the 'vanilla' (i.e. classic) steps involved are shown in Figure 6.5, although it should be stressed that S&OP is different in every organisation.

Step 1 involves data gathering such that the local sales forecast can be produced by product family and market based on a statistical analysis of past sales and market information about new product introduction and promotions. Forecasting new product sales always poses a challenge even if there are similar products.

Steps 2 to 5 are associated with a strict routine of monthly meetings. Discipline in terms of completion of pre-work, meeting timing and attendance are cornerstones of this process.

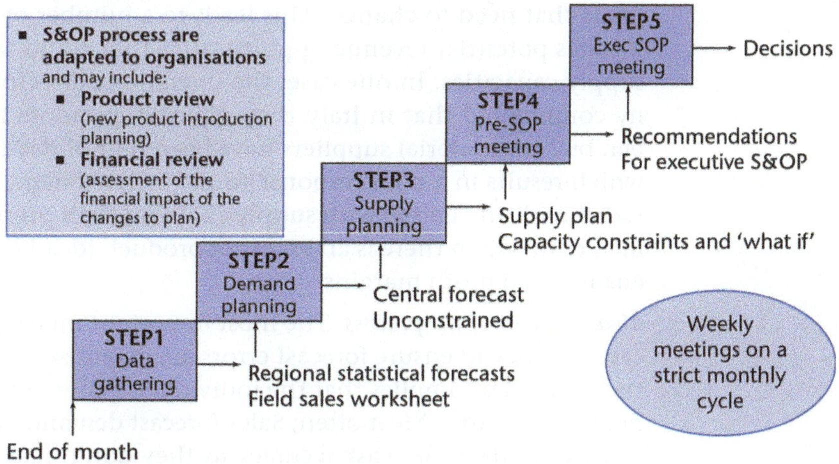

Figure 6.5 The S&OP 'vanilla' process.
(Source: Wallace and Stahl, 2006.)

Step 2 is demand planning, which aggregates the local forecasts into one central sales forecast across product families, assuming unconstrained demand. It is important that an unbiased baseline forecast is used to start the process, because it forms the working draft from which S&OP participants develop final supply and demand plans.

Step 3 is rough-cut supply planning where supply plans across purchasing, manufacturing and distribution are created to satisfy the central forecast. This takes into account production rates for the different product families and various capacity constraints, such as planned shut-downs for maintenance or even short-falls of raw materials. Typically, various what-if scenario simulations are performed to understand the impact on inventory and customer service of possible resource constraints.

Step 4 is the pre-S&OP meeting where the proposed supply plan is reviewed to determine the impact of the plan on the various financial targets/budget, such as revenue growth, profit and potentially cash generation. This meeting is attended by all the different functions involved and more than one supply plan may be developed.

Step 5 is the executive meeting where the executives representing the different functions, such as sales and marketing, production, procurement, product development and finance, will make the final decision on which plan is adopted.

So what makes the S&OP process successful? Lapide (2004) identifies 12 success factors, 4 of which are particularly pertinent:

1. *Cross-functional participation*. S&OP process is cross-functional, involving demand-side managers from sales, marketing and customer service and supply-side managers from procurement, manufacturing and logistics. In addition, finance and product development/engineering are highly relevant. The meetings, and associated communications, are important forums through which to resolve conflicts.
2. *Joint supply and demand planning to ensure balance*. Most S&OP processes tend to presume that the sales and marketing plans are fixed and that it is the supply

plans that need to change. This leads to a number of problems; for example, it hides potential revenue opportunities that could take advantage of excess supply capacities. In one case, the operations director of a global oil company commented that in Italy they typically promote lubricant oil in September, but raw material suppliers have been on holiday for the last two months, which results in a poor response to the inflated demand. It would be better if merchandising liaised with supply chain on their promotion plans and scheduled them when there is an excess of product, ideally available at lower cost to ensure good profit margins.

3. *Measurement of the process*. The most important metric to track is demand forecast accuracy to ensure forecast errors are diagnosed and accuracy improved in the future. This implies that the individuals generating the forecasts should be held accountable. Most often, Sales forecast demand, but they have limited incentives to drive forecast accuracy as they don't 'have to live with the consequences – indeed under-forecasting could make it easier to hit sales targets. To help improve the S&OP process, other metrics should be monitored, such as adherence to sales, marketing and operations plans.
4. *Supported by integrated supply – demand planning technology*. Many S&OP processes are supported by a myriad of spreadsheets or by separate demand forecasting and resource planning applications. What is important is that the software allows the demand- and supply-side views to be brought together.

Whilst the above vanilla S&OP process and success factors may seem clear and sensible, many companies have found that it is still not easy to derive value, in terms of increased profit, from S&OP.

A global oil company implemented S&OP but found that it became a 'tick box' process and did not deliver increased value. They have now introduced a series of value levers, which ultimately focus on increasing the average profit margin across their product range. During the S&OP process they review each product family against contribution to profit and supply chain ratio: margin over working capital. They attempt to move as many products into the upper quadrant by product rationalisation, cost reduction and inventory reduction. This provides visibility of a product's profitability, giving prominence to those that are more profitable and triggering a supply review of those that fall below a profit-margin threshold.

Tom Wallace is a Distinguished Fellow at Ohio State University and for the last 35 years has specialised in S&OP. He considers what the future holds for S&OP (Wallace, 2013) and concludes that:

> **S&OP is here to stay; it'll get better and better; and will at some point in the future be widely accepted as the standard set of processes with which to run a business. Neglect it at your peril!**

Case study 6.2 illustrates 'the important supply planning step of the S&OP process for a company with a many-to-many, supply-to-demand scenario, to understand better the dilemma's faced.

CASE STUDY 6.2

Cranfield Currency Company

This case study, although simplified, has been derived from a real world industrial situation. The Cranfield Currency Company (CCC) manufactures various types of cash machines under three product families, which are each produced in three variants:

- The standard dispenser (made in the USA), which needs to be filled with currency to be dispensed.
- The recycling dispenser (made in the UK), which is able to take in currency through ongoing deposit transactions and uses the same notes to dispense. It is thought that the market is shifting towards recycling dispensers, which have the biggest profit margin (32 per cent), and marketing plan to launch sales promotions for this product range.
- The counting machine (made in France), which is sold to businesses that need to be able to count cash in large quantities quickly, e.g. retailers, and therefore targets a different market from the dispensers, which are sold to banks.

CCC has five main markets for its cash handling technology, as shown in Figure 6.6. The markets vary in size, with the UK and US being the largest. China is a relatively small market but has been growing recently. CCC has had a challenging time coordinating supply and demand between its five markets and its three plants, each of which supplies all five markets. This case study has been simplified so that each machine is only made in one factory and is sold for the same price irrespective of the market.

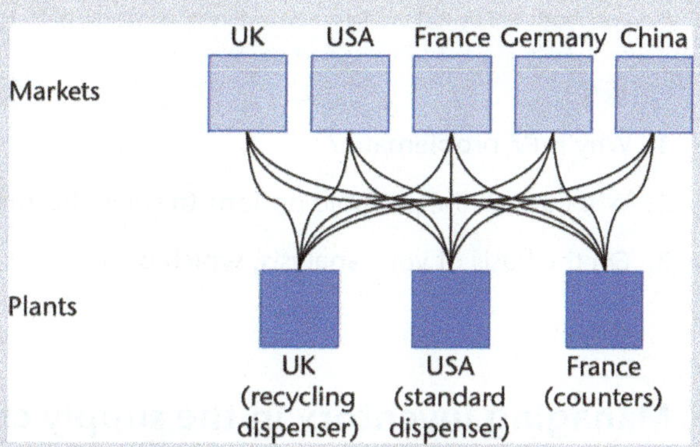

Figure 6.6 Production plants and markets supplied by CCC.

The demand planning stage has been completed and each of the three plants has received its sales forecast and produced a master production schedule to enable it to consider capacity. Let's consider the UK plant, producing recycling dispensers, in supply planning period 1 (P1). The plans are shown in Figure 6.7.

Sales of recycling dispensers are forecast to peak in period 7 (P7) owing to marketing's plan to run promotions in Germany, the US and France, where sales are forecast to be stagnant. The UK plant produces a capacity plan by determining the number of production days per month and the capacity per day, giving the available capacity per month. The available capacity drops in P7 and slightly in P8 due to a scheduled two-week factory shut-down.

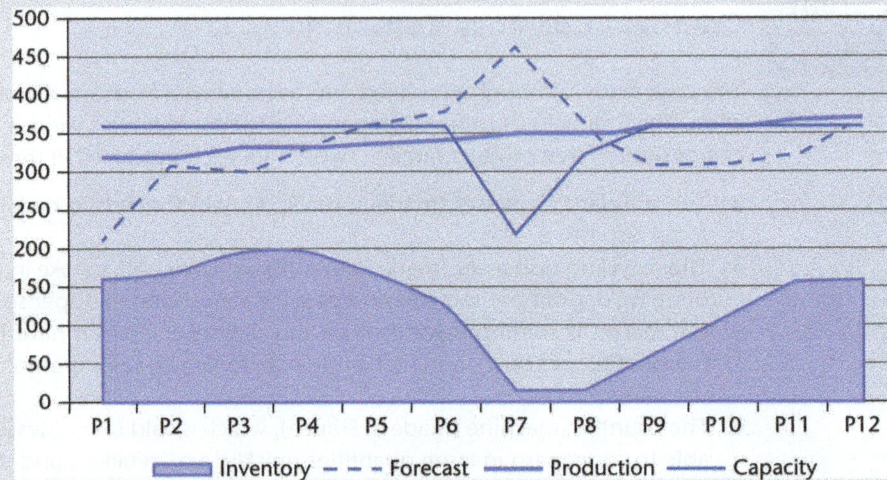

Figure 6.7 UK plant P1 sales forecast and production plan for recycling dispensers across all five markets.

Note: Inventory is calculated on the basis of the product plan. Starting with the opening balance of inventory, the planned production for P1 is added and the forecast sales subtracted, giving the inventory for P1.

Production plan to produce 320 machines per month (increasing to 370 per month by year end to satisfy the forecast increasing demand) and have determined the rate per day which will be needed to achieve this. However, it has been observed that P7 seems to be particularly problematic.

(Source: Produced by Richard Renshaw with the assistance of Dr Heather Skipworth, 2015.)

Questions

1. Why is P7 problematic?
2. What are all the possible options to solve this problem? Are they feasible?
3. On the basis of your analysis, which is the best solution?

6.1.3 Managing inventory in the supply chain

Planning and controlling factory output is but part of the challenge of managing material flow in the supply chain. A focal firm positioned in a network, such as that shown in Figure 1.2, is at the centre of many possible connections with other supplier and customer companies. Upstream processes, such as distribution and retail for both finished products and spare parts, are subject to independent, random demand. Such demand is independent in that it is not affected by the actions of the focal firm (although demand may of course be stimulated through promotions). Dependent demand, on the other hand, is fixed by the actions of the firm – such as order acceptance and determining forecasts. This section is concerned with the management of inventories of **independent demand** items using *order point* methods. These are aimed at optimising the trade-off between inventory holding costs and the preparation costs of changeover (manufacturing) or of placing an order (retailing and manufacturing). Whilst the concept of 'economic' batch sizes and order sizes has been superseded widely by other considerations, as we shall see, its principles help us to grasp the nature of some of the hidden costs of inventory decisions.

'Economic' batch sizes and order sizes

The question of how many parts to make at a time traditionally has been answered by reference to a longstanding concept called the 'economic' batch quantity (EBQ) formula. Similar principles are used to determine how many parts at a time to order from suppliers in 'economic' order quantities (EOQs). Both EBQ and EOQ assume that parts are used at a uniform rate (i.e. that demand is stable), and that another batch of parts should be made or ordered when stock falls below the *reorder point*. The principle behind reorder point, which sets out to answer the question when to order, is shown in Figure 6.8.

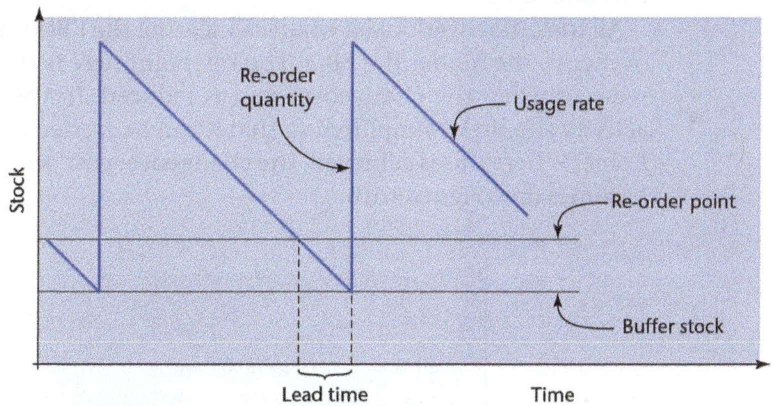

Notes:
1 Re-order point = Demand during lead time + safety stock
2 Re-order quantity = Economic order quantity
3 Buffer stock = *f*(service level.lead time variability.demand variability)

Figure 6.8 When: the reorder point.

A buffer (or safety) stock line is shown below the reorder level. Buffer stock acts as a 'safety net' in order to cushion the effects of variability in demand and lead times. Buffer stock is a function of the service level (risk of stock-outs), lead time variability and demand variability. The reorder point is therefore the sum of the forecast demand during the lead time plus the buffer stock requirement. There are various ways of calculating buffer stock (for a detailed coverage, and for details of EBQ and EOQ calculations, see Waters, 2008).

In the case of manufacturing batch sizes, the EBQ is determined by optimising the trade-off between changeover cost between one batch and the next (for example, cleaning out the process plant between one type of cheese and the next, or resetting the packing line from 250 g to 500 g carton sizes) and inventory carrying cost:

1. *Changeover cost per unit*, C_S. The cost associated with changing over a given machine from the last good part from a batch to the first good part from the succeeding batch.

2. *Inventory carrying cost, C.* The cost of holding stock, calculated from the total inventory cost and the annual rate charged for holding inventory.

To these assumptions we need to add that the usage rate, z, is known and constant and that the manufactured cost of the SKU, c, is also known and constant. A little algebra applied to these assumptions leads to the so-called Wilson formula:

$$\text{EBQ} = \frac{\sqrt{2zC_s}}{cC}$$

Thus EBQ increases with usage rate and changeover cost, and reduces with manufactured cost per unit and inventory carrying cost. Figure 6.9 shows how changeover costs reduce as the batch size increases: the bigger the batch size, the lower the changeover costs per unit. On the other hand, inventory carrying costs increase linearly with batch size: the bigger the batch size, the bigger the carrying costs. A total cost line can be added, which is at a minimum when the two lines cross.

All too often overlooked when calculating the EBQ is that the higher the changeover cost, the higher the EBQ. The key point here is that the EBQ can therefore be reduced when the changeover cost is reduced. In the ideal case, the changeover activity should be simplified so that it can be carried out in seconds rather than in hours. Where this is achieved, the changeover cost becomes negligible and the EBQ becomes one (Figure 6.10).

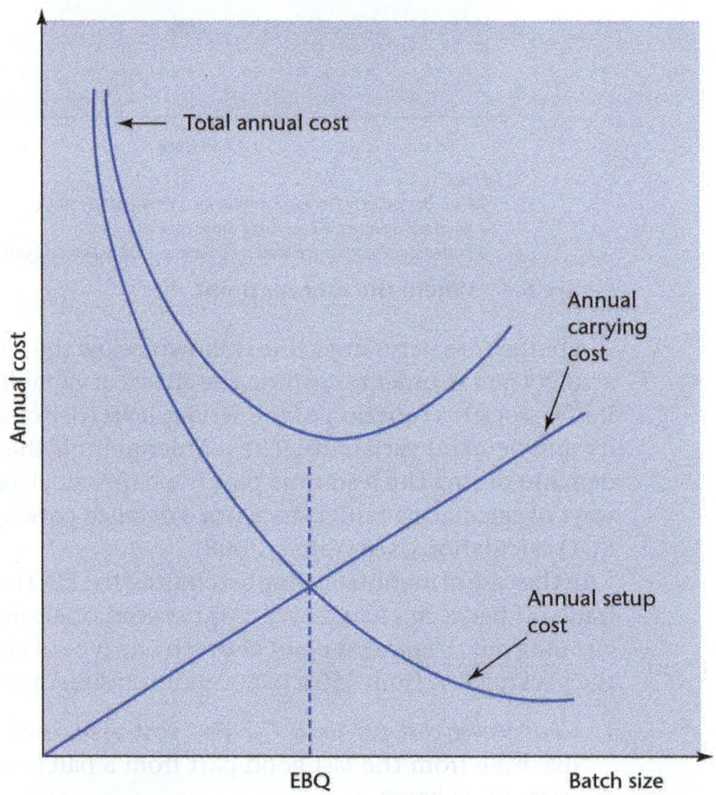

Figure 6.9 Economic batch quantity (EBQ).

Given zero changeover costs, the EBQ formula obeys the JIT ideal of pull scheduling – only make in response to *actual* demand. Actual demand, of course, is likely to vary from one day to the next, unlike the assumption for demand rate shown in Figures 6.8 and 6.9. Pull scheduling is more sensitive to demand changes, because only what is needed is made. Note that *annual* costs and demand have been quoted in Figures 6.9 and 6.10, but under current market turbulence, this is unrealistic and much shorter history periods (perhaps two or three months) should be used. A further major problem with use of EBQs in manufacturing is that it leads to different stockholdings for different part numbers. Synchronisation of parts movements becomes impossible.

The concept of the economic order quantity (EOQ) is based on similar assumptions to the EBQ. Here, the calculation addresses the question 'how many parts will we order?' The trade-off this time is between the cost of placing an order and inventory carrying cost, where:

1. *Cost of placing an order:* All order-related costs, including purchase department costs, transportation costs from the supplier, and goods-in inspection and receiving.

EOQ again increases in line with the cost of placing an order and reduces in line with the inventory carrying cost. Again the trade-off can be changed. If the cost of placing an order can be simplified to a routine basis whereby parts are ordered by paperless systems such as cards and collected on regular pick-up routes called 'milk rounds', the EOQ again can be reduced towards the JIT ideal.

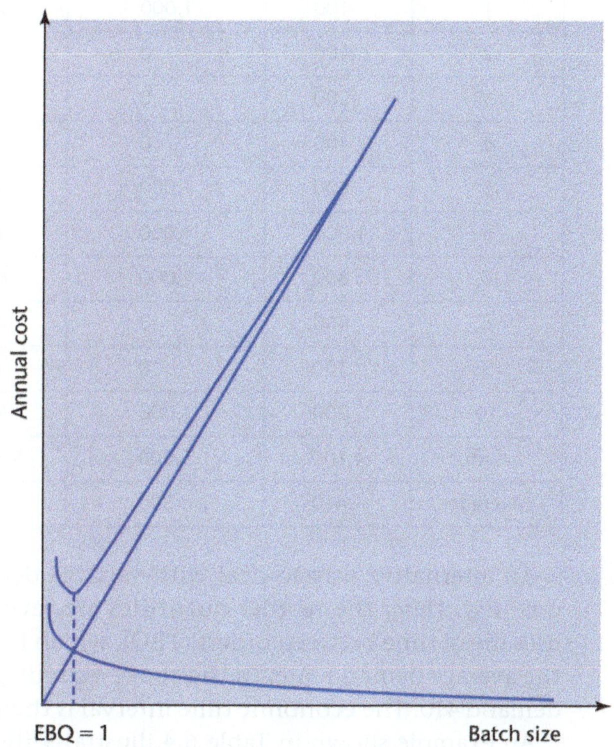

Figure 6.10 As EBQ becomes one.

In retailing, similar economies can be made by using POS systems and centralised (as opposed to stores-based) ordering. EOQ principles are still widely used for ordering 'independent demand' items that are not directly used to manufacture products, such as automotive spare parts, class 'C' parts in retail and office supplies.

Periodic order quantity and target stock levels

Various methods have been adopted to overcome some of the deficiencies of EOQ models, which mean that a set order size is placed on a supplier whenever the inventory level falls below the reorder level. The effect upon suppliers is that, although a regular amount is ordered, the time the order is placed can vary enormously. An EOQ system finds it very difficult to cope if demand goes up or down rapidly. If demand goes up rapidly, then an EOQ system would tend to make replenishments that lag the demand trend.

To illustrate, let us assume a sequence of 10 weeks where demand fluctuates between 100 and 1,000 units. The economic order quantity (EOQ) has been established as 1,000 units, and the safety stock at 100 units. Inventories at the start and end of each week can then be calculated as shown in Table 6.3.

Table 6.3 **Economic order quantity example.**

Week no.	Demand	Ord. quantity	Inv. end	Inv. start	Inv. holding
1	100	1,000	900	1,000	950
2	100	0	800	900	850
3	200	0	600	800	700
4	400	0	200	600	400
5	800	1,000	400	200	300
6	1,000	1,000	400	400	400
7	800	1,000	600	400	500
8	400	0	200	600	400
9	100	0	100	200	150
10	200	1,000	900	100	500
Sum	4,100	5,000	5,100	5,200	5,150
Average	410	500	510	520	515

An alternative way to deal with variable demand is to use the periodic order quantity. Here, the reorder quantities are revised more frequently. The method uses mean time between orders (TBO), which is calculated by dividing the EOQ by the average demand rate. In the above example, the EOQ is 1,000 and the average demand 410. The economic time interval is therefore approximately 2.

An example shown in Table 6.4 illustrates the same situation as in Table 6.3 in terms of demand changes and safety stock level. However, the reorder quantity

Table 6.4 Periodic order quantity example.

Week no.	Demand	Ord. quantity	Inv. end	Inv. start	Inv. holding
1	100	200	100	200	150
2	100	0	0	100	50
3	200	600	400	600	500
4	400	0	0	400	200
5	800	1,800	1,000	1,800	1,400
6	1,000	0	0	1,000	500
7	800	1,200	400	1,200	800
8	400	0	0	400	200
9	100	300	200	300	250
10	200	0	0	200	100
Sum	4,100	4,100	2,100	6,200	4,150
Average	410	410	210	620	415

is based on total demand for the immediate two weeks of history. This reorder method is called *periodic order quantity* (POQ).

POQ normally gives a lower mean inventory level than EOQ in variable demand situations. In this example, the average inventory holding has fallen from 5,150 to 4,150. The same number of orders (Chase et al., 2005) have been used, but the order quantity varies from 200 to 1,800.

Periodic review

A widely used model for inventory control in retailing is *periodic review*. This works by placing orders of variable size at regular intervals – the *review period*. The quantity ordered is enough to raise stock on hand plus stock on order to a target level called the *target stock level* (TSL):

$$\text{Order quantity} = \text{Target stock level} - \text{Stock on hand} - \text{Stock on order}$$

The TSL is the sum of cycle stock (average daily demand over the review period and replenishment lead time) and the safety stock. An example of the way the TSL is calculated is:

$$\begin{aligned} \text{TSL} &= \text{cycle stock} - \text{safety stock} \\ &= D \times (T + LT) + Z \times \sigma \times U(T + LT) \end{aligned}$$

where D = daily demand per SKU, T = review period in days and LT = lead time in days. Z = number of standard deviations from the mean corresponding to the selected service level, and σ = standard deviation of demand over $T + LT$. D may be raised to weekly intervals for slow moving items and lowered to hours for fast movers.

6.1.4 Planning and control in retailing

Retailing is faced with planning and control challenges that are quite distinct from manufacturing:

1. A retailer cannot generate sales without stock, and stock that is bought for sales that do not happen 'constitutes a retailer's nightmare' (Varley, 2014). Retailers are constantly walking the tightrope between too much stock and not enough.
2. The product range that has to be supported on the shelf is comparatively wide – 20,000 different products in the Tesco example in Case study 1.1, and perhaps four times that number of individual SKUs. *On-shelf availability* (OSA) is a key performance indicator. The aim is that OSA targets are maintained across all SKUs at all times of the day and night so that every product is available at any time that a customer visits a store. In practice, categories such as fresh fish and bread are withdrawn from sale by 18:00 hours to avoid excessive stock write-offs when demand is comparatively low.
3. Several stages of the internal supply chain must be coordinated – depots, back of store and front of store. Again, it matters less if a product is in stock at the depot – it *does* matter that it is on the shelf, without which sales cannot be generated.
4. Retail profit margins in grocery are tighter (2–4 per cent) than for large, branded manufacturers (8–10 per cent). Retail margins are prone to erosion by *shrinkage*, which is caused by losses resulting from internal and external theft and process failures such as damage and stocktaking errors. Average shrinkage in grocery is 1.52 per cent (Chapman, 2010) and is much higher for categories such as health and beauty, pharmaceutical and floral. Demand can be affected by changes that are difficult to forecast, such as seasonality (Section 2.3), fashion, endorsements (such as the impact of a famous TV chef on the sale of brown eggs) and promotions (Case study 2.2).
5. 'Best before' and 'use by' dates for fresh produce increase obsolescence pressures and inventory turns. Reverse logistics (Section 4.6) is more complicated because product is being reversed from one point (the store) to a multitude of supply chains (suppliers).

As we have seen in Chapter 2, customers' choices in retailing 'drive everything'. Retailers become more connected to the market than to the supply chain. The core capability in retailing is *trading* – buying and selling goods at a profit. To a degree, manufacturing suppliers become the means to an end, and the constraints of manufacturing are poorly understood by retailers. We expect the manufacturers to supply what we want when we say we want it. This ignores the S&OP discipline.

Consider the demand series shown in Figure 6.11. This is for a high-volume ambient product – in this case a washing powder for which demand is comparatively stable.

Examination of this very typical retail demand series shows that the overall demand pattern for each week is similar, but is by no means identical. Peak demand is usually (but not always) on a Saturday, whilst lowest demand is on Sundays when trading hours are restricted. There is a degree of *uncertainty* (Section 2.3) about the

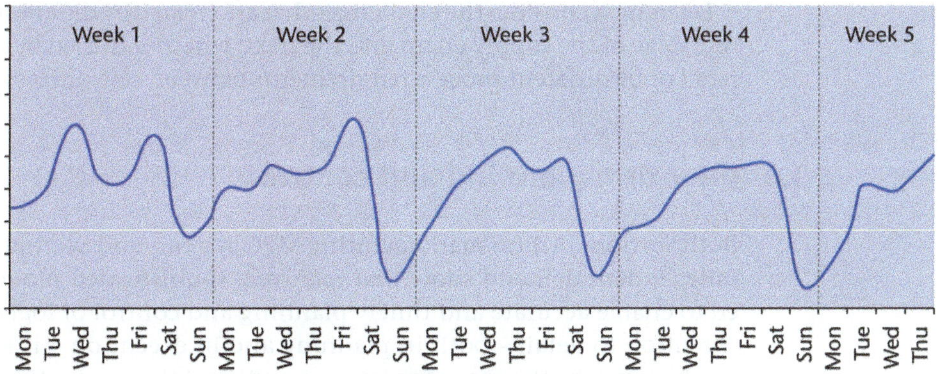

Figure 6.11 EPOS data for the last five weeks.

actual demand for each day. Retailers expect suppliers to cope with this demand uncertainty – and other uncertainties in the supply chain caused by problems such as shrinkage and variable transport times – by holding *buffer stocks*. Case study 8.7 shows that these buffer stocks – often duplicated in the retailer's depots – can be equivalent to several days of demand.

How does the manufacturer cope with such retailer expectations? Washing powders are manufactured in Europe at Procter & Gamble's (P&G's) factory near London. The process involves mixing the ingredients of individual products (such as Ariel and Bold) in *batches* and then drying and granulating each batch into powder in a 'blowing tower'. Whilst the tower is blowing Bold, it cannot blow Ariel. Each brand has several different formulations, such as Bold Automatic and Bold Low Temperature. This further constrains manufacturing capability (although some products can be formulated finally by clever use of additives at the filling and packing stage). Blowing towers are expensive pieces of capital investment, so the site has only two. It is, therefore, *impossible* for P&G to produce each product formulation in line with demand.

Therefore, P&G has to manufacture its products in advance of retail orders, using the principles of the reorder point shown on Figure 6.8, and must use forecasts to calculate the batch sizes. Further allowance must be made for the time it takes to ship the product from the National Distribution Centre (NDC, which is positioned close to P&G's packing lines on the London factory site), the retailer's depots and its stores. Fortunately, in the case of demand as shown in Figure 6.11, forecast accuracy should be high and it is then possible to plan production batch sizes and buffer stocks accurately as well. But promotions can distort even this high forecast accuracy demand.

In practice, retailers use projective forecasting for planning replenishment quantities of stable demand items, such as that shown in Figure 6.11, from suppliers such as P&G. Using sales-based ordering (SBO), retailers attempt to match supply with POS demand as closely as possible. POS data from each of the stores that it serves are sent to the depot, which collates sales data and so provides a smoothing effect on demand forecasting. Even when a close logistics relationship has been established with suppliers, coordination comes under strain because of pressures brought by the trading function of the retailer to squeeze suppliers' prices.

Let us next consider the challenges that are created by different processes between one stage of the supply chain and the next, whether caused by manufacturing and retail or by different process requirements between one process and another.

6.1.5 Inter-firm planning and control

Both Section 6.1.1 on manufacturing MPC systems and Section 6.1.3 on managing independent demand show that relatively sophisticated modelling data is needed to enable accurate and timely planning and control of logistics in a focal firm. Attention to detail - both in planning and in execution - is key. The greater the product variety, the more component parts and the greater the number of levels in the BOM, the more challenging the task. When it comes to coordinating logistics between supply partners, the challenges multiply because the number of processes at stake is so much greater. There are many other factors that make life even more challenging, resulting from differences between the partners:

1. *Differences in process technology:* a supplier of aluminium cans to a soft drinks manufacturer is positioned between producers of aluminium rolled sheet, and high-speed canning lines. At the can supplier, the sheet has to be deep drawn and printed with increasingly sophisticated designs. High-speed filling machines (1,500 cans/minute) at the soft drinks manufacturer mean that the lengthy changeovers are carried out as infrequently as possible. During the peak summer sales period - when sales can double during a hot spell of weather - the whole logistics pipeline is under pressure. The can supplier - situated next to the factory of the drinks manufacturer - supplies cans through a 'hole in the wall' conveyor, which enables just-in-time delivery. Coordinating these three quite different manufacturing processes is a major challenge. The default solution is to hold huge stocks at the can supplier - but, even then, you have to hope that the forecasts were correct! If we move to the NDC for the drinks manufacturer, the even tougher challenge is to interface manufacturing with service processes - distribution and retail. Retail demand is not based on manufacturing batch sizes, but on end-customer demand through the till - moderated by weather forecasts and promotions.
2. *Differences in working routines:* shift patterns, conditions of employment, holidays and shut-downs are but a few of the possible differences in working routines between partners in a supply chain. Retailers complain that they work 24/7, whilst manufacturers may work only five days/week. In turn, this means that replenishments for weekend sales (the highest of the week) have to be made up by extra quantities delivered on Monday and Tuesday. *Priority planning*: whilst an order for a major customer may be priority number 1 for the focal firm in Figure 1.3, the existence of the order may not be visible to upstream partners. Each has different priorities to manage - and each has a different perspective about which order should be processed next.
3. *Inadequacies in MPC systems design:* we documented the case of a manufacturer of electrical cables ('ElectriCo') to specific customer orders against very short lead times (Skipworth and Harrison, 2004). Orders from the customer - a distributor

of power leads – were placed daily against generic stocks held at ElectriCo (MTS). Attempts to cut out these stocks at ElectriCo by changing to MTO were frustrated by weekly MRP planning intervals, and by the fact that each planning run took 36 hours to complete. We have surveyed a number of firms to identify best practice in demand planning and forecasting (Harrison et al., 2004). This survey provided dozens of examples of good practice and bad practice in these areas. Partners in a network who have weak MPC systems potentially create problems for everyone else.

Implications of poor coordination

One consequence of poor coordination within a supply network is amplification of changes in demand upstream. Amplification of demand changes has been called the *bullwhip effect*. For example, a retailer may order only full truck loads from its suppliers. Instead of understanding the actual end-customer demand, the suppliers see huge swings in orders that are due essentially to the retailer's desire to minimise transport costs. This has the unfortunate impact of increasing manufacturing costs at the suppliers, because they are asked to make large quantities at irregular time intervals. What originally may have been stable demand through the till becomes heavily distorted.

Figure 6.12 shows an example of the bullwhip effect. Demand through the till (the EPOS series) is relatively stable, but suppliers' shipments are anything but stable! The original range of variation has been amplified into something much worse. The only way in which the manufacturer can respond is to hold stocks – and even those vary enormously from one week to the next. Uncertainty about customer demand leads to large up-and-down swings in the need for capacity and

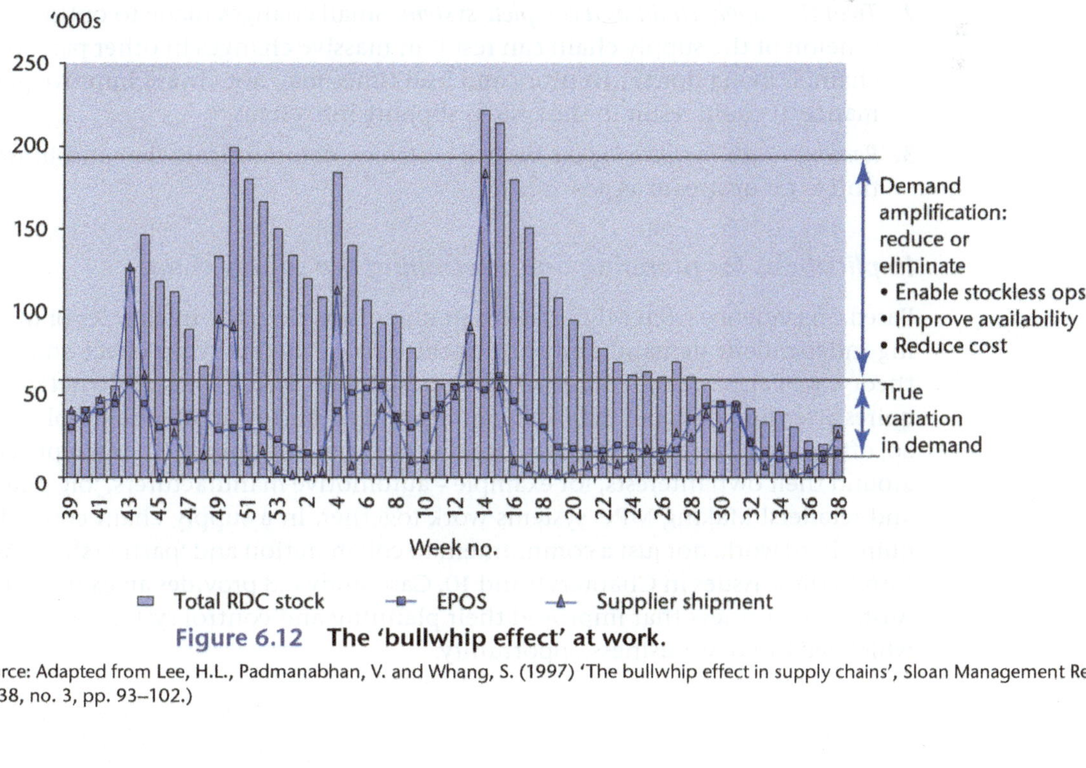

Figure 6.12 The 'bullwhip effect' at work.

(Source: Adapted from Lee, H.L., Padmanabhan, V. and Whang, S. (1997) 'The bullwhip effect in supply chains', Sloan Management Review, vol. 38, no. 3, pp. 93–102.)

in inventory levels. This effect ripples through the supply chain. Batching rules at the manufacturer make things even worse for its own suppliers upstream. Lee et al., (1997) identify four major causes of the bullwhip effect:

1. *updating of demand forecasts:* resulting in changes to safety stock and stock in the pipeline;
2. *order batching:* whilst retail customers may buy mostly on Saturdays, MPC systems may batch orders according to different timing rules;
3. *price fluctuations:* promotions most often result in lumping of demand into peaks and troughs, when the ongoing pattern is stable;
4. *rationing and shortage gaming:* when the latest games console is in short supply, retailers are rationed by manufacturers. Customers place multiple orders on different retailers and thus create apparent demand amplification.

To make matters even worse, it is quite possible for material movements in supply chains to descend into *chaos* (Wilding, 1998). Chaos is characterised by the following:

1. The same state is never repeated ('aperiodic').
2. On successive iterations, the state stays within a finite range and does not approach infinity ('bounded').
3. There is a definite rule with no random terms governing the dynamics ('deterministic').
4. Two points that initially are close will drift apart over time.

Wilding lists several implications for management, three of which are:

1. *Supply chains do not reach stable equilibrium:* small perturbations will always prevent equilibrium being achieved.
2. *Treat the supply chain as a complete system.* Small changes made to optimise one echelon of the supply chain can result in massive changes in other parts of the chain. Driving down inventory and lead times may not always improve performance. It could result in the system slipping into chaos.
3. *Remove chaos by focusing on the end-customer:* communicate demand information as far upstream as possible.

Implications for planning and controlling the supply chain

Based on evidence from MPC systems in manufacturing, the intricacies of managing independent demand and the conclusions of the bullwhip effect and chaos theory, we can say that coordinating material flow across the supply network requires attention to detail in both planning and execution across the supply chain. So, often, firms have 'orchestrated' (or did we mean 'optimised'?) the supply chain around their own interests, for example – automotive manufacturers, 'big pharma' and retailers! Making MPC systems work together, in a supply chain context, requires hard work, not just a commitment to collaboration and 'partnership'. We return to these issues in Chapters 9 and 10. Case study 6.3 provides an example of an Australian business that improved their planning and control systems for oysters, which led to a new business opportunity.

CASE STUDY 6.3

Oceanfarmr

The aquaculture case study company, Oceanfarmr, was officially launched in 2017 in New South Wales, Australia. The founder of the business was an oyster farmer who sensed an opportunity to improve his operation through automating his planning and control approach. Historically, the traditional cottage industry relied on the mental capacity of owners memorising the locations of thousands of pots and taking timely action to rotate the oysters. This methodology was both inefficient and stressful.

Through the development of an app that GPS maps the location of pots and recommends when to rotate the oysters (necessary to keep fresh water flowing across them as they grow) farmers time was liberated from manually assessing and monitoring activities (see Figure 6.13).

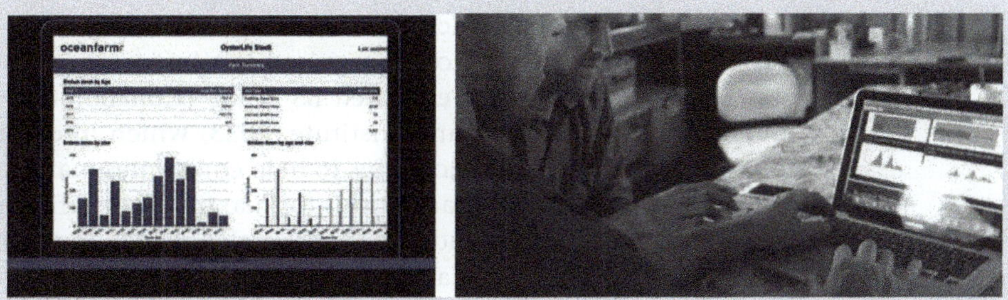

Figure 6.13 Location data.
(Source: Oceanfarmr App & Dashboard, Oceanfarmr PTY LTD.)

The app migrated farmer knowledge from a tacit to codified format providing the platform for demand management and resource planning to occur. The software provides them with yield forecasts enabling, with increased confidence, the coordination of deliveries to customers locally and internationally, overcoming potential challenges of customer rationing and shortage gaming. Simultaneously, the farmer through visualising workload, via the app, can coordinate resources to improve yields and increase capacity. The planning and control systems that were once manual are now digitised to facilitate sharing of information within and across organisational boundaries.

Oceanfarmr was founded, with the goal of 'getting the farm out of the farmer's head' and ensuring that farm management was digital-ready: however, delivering this objective was not viewed as a singular achievement. Environmental and social benefits were also expected in addition to economic gains. Oysters are a natural purifier of water systems, which supports the health of the ecosystem. Through digitising the planning and control processes farmers are no longer tied to the site, facilitating an improved work-life balance. This synergetic benefit proffers an attractive package to markets across the globe for Oceanfarmr.

Questions

1. Discuss the supply chain benefits of digitising the planning and control systems.
2. Explain how the synergetic benefits derived from the app could be used in market segmentation and become incorporated into the Sales & Operations Planning (S&OP) process of oyster farmers.

6.2 Overcoming poor coordination in retail supply chains

***Key issue:* How can collaboration be extended across the supply chain to focus on meeting consumer demand?**

As a result of the challenges listed in Section 6.1.4, a number of initiatives have been launched to promote better coordination between supply chain processes in retailing (Hill et al., 2018). The principle being aimed for is that stock in a retailer's stores is replenished in response to POS data. Whilst retailers initially wanted manufacturers to do this by imposition, more recent initiatives recognise that collaboration is needed - at least between logistics processes at each stage of the supply chain. There are potential benefits all round - more accurate replenishment quantities mean lower inventories, faster response to demand fluctuations and improved on-shelf availability (OSA), which all lead to improved sales.

British Standards have now recognised the importance of collaborative business relationships and have created BS 11000 (Collaborative Business Relationship System; British Standards Institute, 2023) which 'provides a framework for collaborative business relationships to help companies manage and develop their interactions with other organisations for maximum benefit for all'. We cover two collaborative approaches and provide examples of enabling technologies deployed to improved supply coordination:

1. *Efficient consumer response (ECR)*, which has been targeted primarily in food and fast-moving categories in the grocery sector.
2. *Quick response (QR)*, which has been targeted primarily at non-food categories.

6.2.1 Efficient consumer response (ECR)

Established as a grocery industry initiative, **efficient consumer response (ECR)** is designed to integrate and rationalise product assortment (range), promotion, new product development and replenishment across the supply chain. It aims to fulfil the changing demands and requirements of the end-customer (consumer) through effective collaboration across all supply chain members, in order to enhance the effectiveness of merchandising efforts, inventory flow and supply chain administration (PE International, 1997).

The origins of ECR can be traced back to work carried out by Kurt Salmon Associates (in the USA) for the apparel sector (Salmon, 1993) and, subsequently, in the grocery sector (Fernie, 2009). Since then, ECR has increased industrial awareness of the growing problem of non-value-added supply chain costs (Section 5.2.5).

The focus of ECR is to integrate supply chain management with demand management. This requires collaboration between suppliers (manufacturers) and retailers, and emphasises the end-consumer. However, the current ECR initiatives and tools tend to focus on the supply side, rather than managing demand in terms of product assortment or promotions.

The main areas addressed under ECR initiatives are category management, product replenishment and enabling technologies. These can be broken down into 14 smaller areas where individual as well as well-integrated improvements can be made to enhance efficiency (see Figure 6.14).

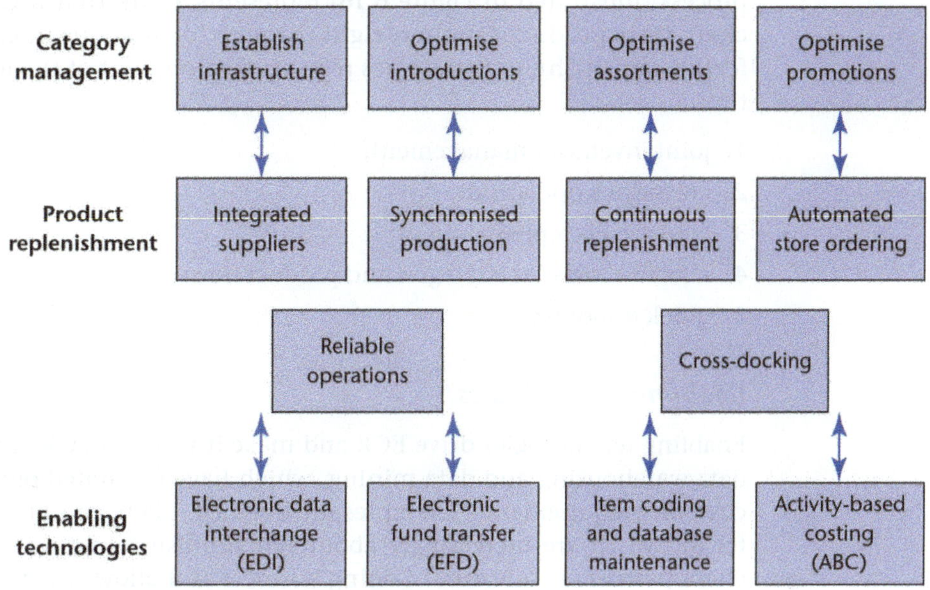

Figure 6.14 ECR improvement categories.
(Source: Fernie, 2009: 30.)

Category management

As demand management principles have become more important to supply chain initiatives, the category management process has increased in popularity. With an objective of preventing stockout situations and improving supplier-retailer relationships, category management aims to balance retailers' product volume and variety objectives. Among activities included in the category management process are the capture and utilisation of knowledge of the drivers behind consumer attitudes and choices.

By focusing on category management and measuring promotional efficiency, ECR enables organisations to utilise their joint resources to reduce supply chain inventory levels, streamline product flows and use cross-docking options where appropriate. This category management represents a focus on the development of at least some of the following capabilities:

1. account management;
2. demand management;
3. multifunctional selling teams;
4. price list restructuring;
5. effective and customised promotions.

Continuous replenishment

Continuous replenishment offers both retailers and their suppliers the opportunity to manage their inventory in a more efficient manner (Mitchell, 1997; PE International, 1997). Each of the six stages making up the product replenishment process (illustrated in Figure 6.16) represents a link that integrates the supply chain from product suppliers right through to end-consumers. In addition, effective replenishment strategies require development of the following capabilities:

1. joint inventory management;
2. cross-dock operations;
3. continuous replenishment;
4. effective logistics strategies and product flows;
5. quick response.

Enabling technologies

Enabling technologies drive ECR and make it work. They include scanning data, data warehousing and data mining, which have facilitated our understanding of customer requirements. Examples include EDI, EPOS and Blockchain (see Chapter 8), which are increasingly about synchronising trading data among supply chain partners in advance of doing business as it allows the transmission of forecasting data back up through the supply chain. Other capabilities required by organisations in order to implement an effective ECR initiative include:

1. effective information sharing;
2. automated order generation;
3. barcoding and the use of other scanning technologies.

In addition, the data to be shared and communicated at various stages in the supply chain depends on what will provide the most overall benefit. This data should include:

1. demand/consumption/sales information;
2. cash flow;
3. stocks of finished goods/work in progress;
4. delivery and output status.

However, many of the problems with sharing and using this data and implementing EDI networks are related to difficulties in achieving a critical mass of companies sufficient to generate substantial benefits.

ECR programmes in operation

In Europe, ECR programmes commenced in 1993 with the commissioning of a series of projects, for example the Coopers & Lybrand survey of the grocery supply chain (Coopers & Lybrand, 1996). Other examples of studies sponsored by ECR Europe initiatives include the *Optimal Shelf Availability* report (Roland Berger Strategy Consultants, 2003) and the *Shrinkage in Europe* report (Beck, 2004).

ECR UK is run by the Institute of Grocery Distribution (IGD) and is organised around 'various workgroups involved in supply improvements, focusing on using collaboration to fulfil shopper wishes better, faster and at less cost'. It also offers a range of tools and resources, which companies can access freely. Initiatives and tools available during 2018 on the ECR UK website include:

Supply chain waste prevention

A top-level estimate of the annual volume and value of food and drink waste along the UK grocery supply chain is shown in Figure 6.15, illustrating the extent of the problem. This enables companies to link up with companies they trade with, specifically to address total supply chain waste from factory in-gate to retailer check-out till. ECR UK also provides a supply chain waste prevention guide (2013) identifying how to prevent product and packaging waste and providing best practice examples from retailers and manufacturers.

ECR UK proposes a hierarchy of preferred options for reducing waste (as shown in) and emphasises that a company should start at the top:

1. *Prevent* or eliminate waste by reducing the price of short-dated or damaged stock to sell through before the food becomes waste. A five-to-drive plan for prevention – measure, engage, forecast, design and range – is also proposed.
2. *Redistribute* to alternative markets. For example, surplus to charities or animal feed. Up to 10 times more commercial and environmental value can be gained through prevention than can be salvaged through waste recovery.
3. *Recycle* or process into a fresh supply of the same or similar material and reduce consumption of virgin material.
4. *Recover* via anaerobic digestion composting, used cooking oil, rendering, energy recovery and mechanical heat treatment.
5. *Dispose* of via landfill, thermal treatment without energy recovery or via sewer/controlled water course.

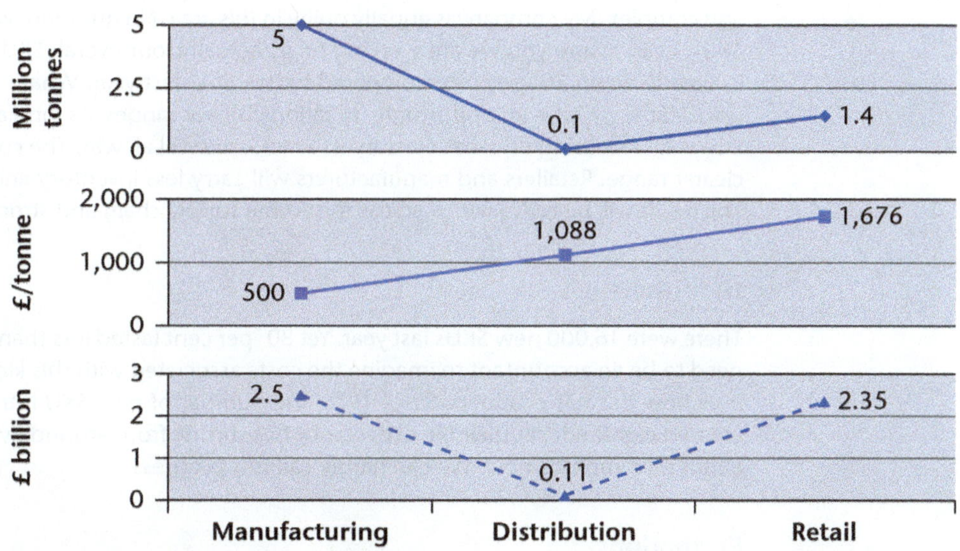

Figure 6.15 Top-level estimates of food and drink waste along the UK grocery supply chain.

(Source: Adapted from Lee, P. and Willis, P. (2010) Waste arising in the supply of food and drink to households in the UK, WRAP.)

Reducing wasted miles

ECR UK have set up a workgroup focusing on how to reduce costs and waste of vehicles running empty or part-loaded. Currently 29 per cent of trucks on the roads are running empty, creating a major economic and environmental cost. With changes in the retail landscape due to a growth in the convenience, discount and online sectors the waste in miles could accelerate rapidly without intervention. Smaller and more frequent deliveries are challenging transport operations in terms of economies of scale and efficient loads. The workgroup is investigating how data, flexible flow, streamlined stock holding, shared services and tailored transport could alleviate these increasing wastes.

CASE STUDY 6.4

ECR in the UK

The Institute of Grocery Distribution (IGD) supports the development and progress of ECR initiatives in the UK and across Europe. IGD aims to fulfil consumer wishes better, faster and at less cost with forums such as reducing wasted miles (2018). The work of the ECR forums is based on the foundational principles of ECR, exemplified through the speech of Paul Polman, a former general manager of Procter & Gamble UK. Whilst admiring the UK's advanced retailing systems, he saw opportunities for all four 'pillars of ECR': range, new items, promotions and replenishment. The following is extracted from the text of a speech he made to the IGD.

Range

The average store now holds 35 per cent more than five years ago, yet a typical consumer buys just 18 items on a trip. A quarter of these SKUs sell fewer than six units a week! The number of SKUs offered by manufacturers and stores has become too large and complex. My company is equally guilty in this area. No question, we make too many SKUs. I can assure you we are working on it. Actually, our overall SKU count in laundry is already down 20 per cent compared to this time last year. What's more, business is up. Clearly, we have an opportunity to rationalise our ranges. As long as we do this in an ECR way – focusing on what consumers want – we will all win. The consumer will see a clearer range. Retailers and manufacturers will carry less inventory and less complexity. The result will be cost savings across the whole supply chain and stronger margins.

New items

There were 16,000 new SKUs last year. Yet 80 per cent lasted less than a year. You don't need to be an accountant to imagine the costs associated with this kind of activity. And look how this has changed. Since 1975, the number of new SKU introductions has increased eightfold. Yet their life expectancy has shrunk from around five years in 1975 to about nine months now. We can hardly call this progress.

Promotions

In promotions it's the same story. Take laundry detergents. This is a fairly stable market. Yet we're spending 50 per cent more on promotions than two years ago, with consumers buying nearly 30 per cent more of their volume on promotions. This not only creates an inefficient supply chain, or in some cases poor in-store availability, but, more importantly, has reduced the value of the category and likely the retailers' profit. We're all aware of the inefficiencies promotions cause in the system, such as problems in production, inventory and in-store availability. They all create extra costs, which ultimately have to be recouped in price. But there's a higher cost. As promotions are increasing, they are decreasing customer loyalty to both stores and brands by 16 per cent during the period of the promotion.

We commissioned a report by Professor Barwise of the London Business School. He called it 'Taming the Multi-buy Dragon'. The report shows us that over 70 per cent of laundry promotional investment goes on multi-buys. The level of investment on multi-buys has increased by 60 per cent over the last three years. There's been a 50 per cent increase behind brands and a doubling of investment behind own labels. Contrary to what we thought, most of this volume is not going to a broad base of households. It is going to a small minority. Seventy-one per cent of all multi-buy volume is bought by just 14 per cent of households. Just 2 per cent of multi-buy volume goes to 55 per cent of households. We really are focusing our spending on influencing and rewarding a very small minority of people indeed.

Replenishment

Based on the escalating activity I've just [referred to], costs are unnecessarily high. There are huge cost savings also here, up to 6 per cent, by removing the non-value-added SKUs and inefficient new brand and promotional activity.

Questions

1. Cutting down on range, new items and promotions is presumably going to lead to 'everyday low prices'. Discuss the implications for the trade-off between choice and price.
2. Procter & Gamble's major laundry brand in the USA is Tide. This is marketed in some 60 pack presentations, some of which have less than 0.1 per cent share. The proliferation of these pack presentations is considered to have been instrumental in increasing Tide's market share from 20 to 40 per cent of the US market in recent years. Clearly, this is a major issue within P&G. What are the logistics pros and cons of SKU proliferation?

6.2.2 Quick response (QR)

Quick response (QR) is an approach to meeting customer demand by supplying the right quantity, variety and quality at the right time to the right place at the right price. This concept originated in the US textile and apparel industry in response to the threat posed by overseas competitors. The concepts behind QR are based on taking a total supply chain view of an industry. From this perspective it is possible to understand overall performance and the causes of poor performance, and to identify opportunities for improvement.

Understanding overall performance involves mapping the processes needed to convert raw material into the final product (see Chapter 5). The performance of the process is also assessed to determine its effectiveness. In the case of the apparel industry, mapping followed the process of converting raw material into fibre, then into fabric, then into apparel and, finally, delivery to the retailer. Key measures of the process were lead times, inventory levels and work in progress.

This investigation found that the total process of converting raw material into clothing took 66 weeks. A basic analysis of the process identified that 55 weeks were taken up with products sitting in various stores as inventory. The principal cause of this inventory was identified as being lack of communication between the organisations in the supply network.

Such analysis is similar to that described in Chapter 5, with the process considered, in this case, being the whole supply chain from end to end. There are two main differences between QR and a time-based approach to improvement. First, there is an emphasis on using actual customer demand to pull products through the distribution and manufacturing system. Second, there is extensive use of information technology as the preferred way to achieve pull. These two issues are explored in more detail next.

Role of enabling technologies

High variety in clothing markets – due to different sizes, styles and colours – and in grocery markets has led these industries to use information technologies as a means of enabling QR. These technologies are based around the use of uniform product codes, electronic data interchange (EDI) and electronic point of sale (EPOS). EPOS, through the application of bar code scanners in stores, facilitates the collection of real-time data on inventory levels and sales. This enables high levels of shelf availability and the automatic reordering of inventory. The process involves collecting merchandise information at the point of sale from the product barcode. EPOS data is sent to the supplier via EDI, where it is compared with an inventory model for the store concerned. When appropriate, production is ordered for the specific items needed to restock the store to the requirements of the model. Once these items have been made, the cycle is completed when they are packed, shipped to the store and delivered to the shelf.

This process has enormous implications for links across the supply chain. With each retailer having a range of suppliers, and each supplier servicing a number of retailers, there is the need for common barcode standards across the industry. The retailer needs to have a scanning and data capture system to identify the item being sold. It will need to have a reordering system that links the item to its manufacturer, and that places an order. Information needs to be exchanged between the parties in a common data format that can be read by different IT systems. The high volume of transactions means that the systems handling the data exchange need to be robust and reliable. Having been informed of the sale, the supplier inputs this information to its manufacturing planning system in order to schedule production and the ordering of supplies.

It is hardly surprising that it is extremely difficult to achieve this integration across the whole of a supply network. There are significant implications for small businesses, which have difficulty justifying the cost of the IT system and the associated training. These set-up costs can deter new companies with innovative products from being able to supply. However, recent developments in internet-based applications are helping to resolve this situation because the implementation and data transfer costs are much lower. Case 6.5 illustrates how technology is providing a competitive edge for craft beer producers and their customers through the application of IoT (Internet of Things). Improved visibility and real-time availability of data across the supply chain are shown to improve product quality, information flow and the S&OP process.

CASE STUDY 6.5

Improving information flow and S&OP through massive IoT sensor technology

BinaryBeer is an Australian organisation that is a global leader in smart keg technology, boasting numerous patents and a long list of 'world first' accomplishments. Their mission is to connect the world's beer kegs to the cloud to reduce waste, uncertainty and improve customer experience of macro and craft brewers. BinaryBeer has been deploying smart keg technology (see Figure 6.16) since 2018 to improve the quality and profitability of macro and craft brewers, allowing the industry to track assets and monitor quality.

Figure 6.16 Smart keg technology.

(Source: BinaryTech subsidiary, BinaryBeer is selected by Asahi Europe & International for smart keg deployment, 12th September 2023, Binary Tech.)

Tracking assets is particularly important for craft brewers as their beers are preservative free and hence, are more vulnerable to loss of quality through inappropriate handling of kegs in the beer distribution network. Craft beers are also predominantly consumed within the same geographical area where it is brewed. Handling of the kegs itself, exposure to high temperature and low volume while being on tap are all potential quality impact factors. Traditionally, craft brewers lose control over their kegs once dispatched to a venue leaving brewers with a high reputational risk.

BinaryBeer's smart keg sensors are equipped with 5G wireless connectivity and bespoke IoT (Internet of Things) sensors able to monitor key data points including location, temperature, tilt and volume while identifying the exact moment when the beer is put on tap, providing brewers with information to monitor quality and reduce uncertainty around the management of their product. Therefore, protecting their unique brands and reputations.

IoT sensor deployment uncovers live, actionable insights from the distribution network that have historically been unavailable to brewers. Data-driven insights improve logistical routing support and enhance the sales and operational planning process (S&OP). Table 6.5 provides an overview of the brewer's system ability to improve supply chain visibility, quality and S&OP through massive IoT deployment. Improvements through information flow (see Section 1.2.2) were found across four key areas – demand, control, process and supply.

Table 6.5 Information flow improvement due to massive IoT deployment.

Information flow	Areas of improvement through massive IoT deployment
Demand	Volume tracking using infrared laser sensors at the top of the keg
	Time stamp when keg goes on tap using an infrared laser sensor
Control	Asset tracking of beer kegs using a geo-location sensor
	Quality control using temperature and tilt sensors
Process	Information on volume per type of beer, in-house stock levels, location of venue and kegs per venue allows for S&OP processes regarding batch prioritisation
	Lead-time compression (production to distribution time)
	Digital integration
Supply	Sharing of S&OP planning data with upstream suppliers and 3PL companies for scheduling purposes

Through the application of IoT brewers have compressed production-to-distribution time, from an average of 15 days to 4. This 74 per cent reduction has been achieved through comprehensive location mapping of breweries and distributors, enabling analytics to compare and optimise travel times across various transportation routes. Through tracking keg activity, BinaryBeer were able to measure the following for brewers:

- Time to tap: Measuring the duration between keg filling and consumption (tracking freshness and outlet performance);
- Time on tap: Enabling comparison of keg consumption rates across different venues;
- Time off tap: Enabling one-time keg collection routes to enhance logistics efficiency.

Through a 'freshness score' for each keg based on its specific contents (e.g. beer type, alcohol content) and current environmental conditions (heat, tilt), BinaryBeer provides real-time information to brewers and their customers of potential freshness issues. This score, ranging from 100 per cent (optimal) to 0 per cent (significantly degraded), offers a holistic view of how each product fares throughout the supply chain.

Through massive IoT implementation, BinaryBeer has improved the flow of information across the supply chain from downstream customers to upstream suppliers, enabling brewers, large and small, to enhance their S&OP through gathering real-time demand data to plan beer production, 3PL scheduling and acquisition of raw materials. As a result, BinaryBeer's 'intelligent' kegs have improved the balancing of demand and supply for brewers, enabling producers to enhance their customer value proposition.

Questions

1. Through depying IoT brewers are gathering real-time data on keg usage. Improved information flow has the potential to address some of inter-firm planning and control issues identified in Section 6.1.5. If you were the supply chain director of a brewery, what steps would you take to implement the technology with customers to improve S&OP?
2. BinaryBeer offer scalable technology solutions that enable seamless connectivity and real-time data exchange, empowering businesses to drive efficiency on a global scale. Brewers are one example of an industry that is benefitting. What other sectors could gainfully deploy the technology? How could the technology improve S&OP in those sectors?
3. What alternative data points/information could be gathered using IoT technology to further reduce uncertainty from the supply chain and enhance material, information and cash flow?

Summary

How is material flow planned and controlled in the supply chain?

Material planning and control in manufacturing is based on three time periods – long term, medium term and short term.

The focal firm 'game plan' comprises a set of inter-linked modules ranging from 'front end' (demand management, resource planning, sales and operations planning and master production scheduling) to 'engine' (materials and capacity planning) to 'back end' (detailed planning and control of source–make–deliver processes). All are linked to the enterprise resource planning (ERP) database.

Sales and operations planning (S&OP) is an integrated business management process, developed in the 1980s by Oliver Wight, which encourages medium-term forecasting from both a demand and a supply perspective. Ultimately it enables supply to be aligned with demand and is particularly important where demand is variable and unpredictable.

After manufacture, replenishment of independent demand items in the supply chain is usually managed by order-point methods like EOQ and POQ. Periodic review places orders of variable size at fixed intervals.

Retail processes have other, distinct challenges when it comes to material planning and control. Stock must be available to generate sales, so OSA is a key performance measure. Sales must be supported across a much wider range of SKUs. The top priority of retailers has been to serve the market, and manufacturers traditionally have been expected to serve retail processes. Shrinkage (stock losses) and the impact of promotions are further challenges.

Coordinating material planning and control between firms greatly increases the need for management of detail. There are many more ways to inhibit the accurate exchange of data than within a focal firm. This results in undesirable symptoms like the bullwhip effect and even chaotic behaviour of material movements.

How is it possible to improve coordination between retail and manufacturing processes?

Efficient consumer response (ECR) is aimed at integrating SCM with demand management by means of category management, product replenishment and enabling technologies.

Quick response (QR) is based on taking a total supply chain view, starting with supply chain mapping.

Discussion questions

1. Apply the MPC framework in Figure 6.1 to a restaurant. Pay special attention to identifying the front end, engine and back-end components.
2. Evaluate the impact of international supply chains on the challenges to MPC systems in practice. Does increasing the physical distance between processes mean that they are more difficult to plan and control?
3. Demand changes from independent to dependent at the customer order decoupling point (CODP). What actually happens to end-customer demand, and why is this change so important in managing material flow?
4. Explain the difference between pull scheduling and push scheduling. In what circumstances might push scheduling be appropriate?
5. What actions are needed to address the problems of inter-firm planning and control listed in Section 6.1.4? How would you go about orchestrating material movements (for example the cheese supply chain, shown in Figure 1.1) across a grocery supply chain?
6. Paul Polman, chief executive of Unilever, said, 'I do not work for the shareholder, to be honest, I work for the customer. I don't drive this business by driving shareholder value.' What matters more: value to the customer or value to the shareholder? Refer to Section 3.8 when formulating your response. How would you expect this question to impact on Unilever's long-term MPC strategy?

References

Ambrose, S.C., Matthews, L.M. and Rutherford, B.N., (2018) Cross-functional teams and social identity theory: A study of sales and operations planning (S&OP), *Journal of Business Research*, vol. 92, pp. 270–78.

Barratt, M. and Oliveira, A. (2002) 'Supply chain collaboration: exploring the early initiatives', *Supply Chain Planning*, vol. 4, no. 1, pp. 16–28.

Beck, A. (2004) *Shrinkage in Europe 2004: A Survey of Stock Loss in the FMCG Sector*. Brussels: ECR-Europe, at www.ecrnet.org

British Standards Institute (2023) *Collaborative Business Relationships Systems*.

Chapman, P. (2010) 'Reducing product losses in the food supply chain', in Mena, C. and Stevens, G. (eds) *Delivering Performance in Food Supply Chains*. New York: McGraw Hill.

Chase, R., Jacobs, R. and Aquilano, N. (2005) *Operations Management for Competitive Advantage*, 10th edn. New York: McGraw Hill.

Coopers and Lybrand (1996) *European Value Chain Analysis: Final Study*. Utrecht: ECR Europe.

Dougherty, J. and Gray, C. (2006) *Sales & Operations Planning – Best Practices*. Trafford Publishing.

Fernie, J. (2009) 'Relationships in the Supply Chain', in Fernie, J. and Sparks, L. (eds) *Logistics and Retail Management: Emerging Issues and New Challenges in the Retail Supply Chain*, pp. 38-62. London: Kogan Page.

Goldratt, E.M. and Cox, J. (2016) *The Goal: a process of ongoing improvement*. Routledge.

Harrison, A., Chapman, P., Rutherford, C. and Stimson, J. (2004) *Demand Planning and Forecasting: Survey of Best Practice*. Cranfield: Cranfield University.

Hill, C.A., Zhang, G.P. and Miller, K.E. (2018) 'Collaborative planning, forecasting, and replenishment & firm performance: An empirical evaluation', *International Journal of Production Economics*, vol. 196, pp.12–23.

Lapide, L. (2004) 'Sales and operations planning. Part1: The process', *The Journal of Business Forecasting*, vol. 23, no. 3, pp. 17–9.

Hulthén, H., Näslund, D. and Norrman, A. (2017) 'Challenges of measuring performance of the sales and operations planning process'. *Operations and Supply Chain Management: An International Journal*, vol. 10 no. 1, pp. 4–16.

Lee, H.L., Padmanabhan, V. and Whang, S. (1997) 'The bullwhip effect in supply chains', *Sloan Management Review*, vol. 38, no. 3, pp. 93–102.

Lee, P. and Willis, P. (2010) *Waste arising in the supply of food and drink to households in the UK*, WRAP.

Mitchell, A. (1997) *Efficient Consumer Response: A New Paradigm for the European FMCG Sector*. London: FT Pearson Professional.

Oliva, R. and Watson, N. (2011) 'Cross-functional alignment in supply chain planning: A case study of sales and operations planning', *Journal of Operations Management*, vol. 29, no. 5, pp. 434–48.

PE International (1997) *Efficient Consumer Response – Supply Chain Management of the New Millennium*. Corby: Institute of Logistics.

Roland Berger Strategy Consultants (2003) *Optimal Shelf Availability*. Brussels: ECR-Europe, at www.ecrnet.org

Salmon, K. (1993) *Efficient Consumer Response: Enhancing Consumer Value in the Supply Chain*. Washington, DC: Kurt Salmon.

Silver, E.A., Pyke, D.F. and Thomas, D.J. (2016) *Inventory and Production Management in Supply Chains*. CRC Press.

Skipworth, H. and Harrison, A. (2004) 'Implications of form postponement to manufacturing: A case study', *International Journal of Production Research*, vol. 42, no. 10, pp. 2063–81.

Stevens, G.C. and Johnson, M. (2016) 'Integrating the supply chain . . . 25 years on'. *International Journal of Physical Distribution & Logistics Management*, vol. 46, no. 1, pp.19–42.

Stefan Stern. Outsider in a hurry to shake up Unilever, Financial Times, April 4, 2010.

Varley, R. (2014) *Retail Product Management: Buying and Merchandising*. Routledge.

Vollman, T.E., Berry, W.L., Whybark, D.C. and Jacobs, F.R. (2005) *Manufacturing Planning and Control for Supply Chain Management*, 5th edn. New York: McGraw Hill Higher Education.

Wallace, F. and Stahl, R.A. (2006) *Sales & Operations Planning: The Executive Guide*, T.F. Wallace and Co.

Wallace, T. (2013) 'Sales & operations planning: where is it going?', *The Journal of Business Forecasting*, Summer.

Waters, D. (2008) *Inventory Planning and Control*. New York: John Wiley and Sons Ltd.

Wilding, R. (1998) 'The supply chain complexity triangle: uncertainty generation in the supply chain', *International Journal of Physical Distribution and Logistics Management*, vol. 28, no. 8, pp. 599–616.

Jonsson, P., Kaipia, R. and Barratt, M., 2021. Guest editorial: the future of S&OP: dynamic complexity, ecosystems and resilience. International Journal of Physical Distribution & Logistics Management, 51(6), pp.553-565.

Suggested further reading

Crum, C. and Palmatier, G. (2003) *Demand Management Best Practices: Process, Principles and Collaboration*. Fort Lauderdale, FL: J. Ross Publishing.

Fernie, J. and Sparks, L. (eds) (2004) *Logistics and Retail Management*, 2nd edn. London: Kogan Page.

Randall, G. and Seth, A. (2005) *Supermarket Wars: Global Strategies for Food Retailers*. Basingstoke: Palgrave Macmillan.

Storey, J., Emberson, C., Godsell, J. and Harrison, A. (2006) 'Supply chain management: theory, practice & future challenges', *International Journal of Operations and Production Management*, vol. 26, no. 7, pp. 754–74.

Wild, A. (2002) *Best Practice in Inventory Management*. Oxford: Elsevier Butterworth Heinemann.

CHAPTER 7

Lean thinking and agile supply chains

Objectives

The intended objectives of this chapter are to:

- explain how lean thinking can be used to avoid the build-up of waste within and between supply chain processes;
- introduce the concept of the agile supply chain as a broad-based approach to developing responsiveness advantages;
- explore the challenges of coping with volatile demand situations;
- explain how capabilities can be developed and specifically targeted at thriving in conditions of market turbulence;
- describe how lean and agile approaches can be combined to meet market needs.

By the end of this chapter you should be able to:

- understand how lean thinking can be used to improve performance of the supply chain in meeting end-customer demand by cutting out waste;
- identify the type of market conditions under which agile strategies are appropriate, and how they can be operationalised;
- understand the distinctions between lean and agile strategies, and how the two can work together.

Introduction

In Chapter 6 we considered the way in which organisations approach their planning and control of supply chains. One important way of increasing the control of processes and improving reliability of plans is through the reduction of non-value-added activities – waste. The elimination of waste has been promoted under the banner of '**lean thinking**' (Womack and Jones, 2003), who advise:

> **To hell with your competitors; compete against *perfection* by identifying all activities that are *muda* and eliminating them. This is an absolute rather than a relative standard which can provide the essential North Star for any organisation.**

Lean thinking and the **just-in-time (JIT)** pull approach to coordinating material flow across the supply chain share the same roots and originate from competitive strategies developed by the Japanese. Toyota Motor Company is held up as the role model and, although the Toyota brand has been damaged in recent years by widespread quality problems (Section 1.3.1), this focal firm's operational excellence has had a major influence on logistics thinking today.

A common view is that lean thinking works best where demand is relatively stable - and hence predictable - and where variety is low. But in situations where demand is volatile and customer requirement for variety is high, the elimination of waste in itself becomes a lower priority than the need to respond rapidly to a turbulent marketplace. So the second part of this chapter reviews developments under the banner of the '**agile supply chain**'.

Marketplaces of the twenty-first century are often characterised by a proliferation of products and services, shorter product life cycles and increased rates of product innovation. Simply responding quickly and at the right time is not enough to meet the needs of such marketplaces. The mission of modern logistics is to ensure that it is the right product - to meet exact end-customer needs - that gets delivered in the right place at the right time. Such a mission means that the *end-customer comes first*. Section 7.2 proposes the agile supply chain as an approach that elevates speed capabilities in a given supply chain to much higher levels than would be possible using the tools and techniques discussed in Section 7.1.

We review the important capabilities required for an agile supply chain - market sensitive, process integration, network based and **virtual integration** - and how these are necessary to meet both predictable and unpredictable demand variability. Practices to enable agility are many, so we present those that are key, spanning: planning, product design, manufacturing and supply partnerships. Agility can increase costs in terms of the necessary capacities required to respond to volatile demand, so it is necessary to consider the preconditions to applying agility.

Finally, we consider the different ways in which lean and agile approaches can be combined to meet the changing market needs, building on the ideas of segmented supply chain strategy presented in Chapter 2. Lean and agile strategies must be combined and led in order to meet changing customer needs in the most efficient manner.

Key issues

This chapter addresses three key issues:

1. **Lean thinking:** the principles of lean thinking to improve material flow and minimise waste whilst ensuring customer value is delivered. Cutting out waste in all business processes. Simple, paperless systems versus central control.
2. **The concept of agility:** the dimensions of the agile supply chain, and the environments that favour agility. Agile practices: addressing the challenges of market turbulence, rapid response logistics and managing low-volume products.
3. **Combining lean and agile:** careful consideration of the how to minimise waste while delivering the flexibility and responsiveness demanded by the market is a conundrum facing for many organisations. The options available to balance the apparently competing demands need to take into account the skills and leadership challenges that may arise.

We acknowledge and are grateful for Corrado Cerruti's assistance with expanding and improving the section on agility, in particular his research on agile partnerships.

7.1 Lean thinking

***Key issues:* What are the implications of lean thinking principles for logistics? How can lean thinking be applied to other business processes and what are the practices associated with it?**

Lean thinking (Krafcik and MacDuffie, 1989) was the term used in the West to refer to the just-in-time production methods used by Japanese automotive manufacturers, such as the Toyota Production System. Suffering shortages and lack of resources in the 1950s and 1960s, Japanese car manufacturers responded by developing production processes that operated with minimum waste. The term 'lean' was used in the West because production required less space, resource and inventory due to the emphasis on minimising waste. However, waste comes in many forms, as we shall see in the next section.

7.1.1 Types of waste

In Chapter 5 we saw how any activity that does not add value but consumes resource, is a form of waste. By mapping processes through the supply chain, it is possible to sort value-adding and non-value-adding activities (transport, store, inspect and delay). Lean thinking goes further by adding three more types of 'waste' to make seven in all. They are as follows:

- *The waste of overproduction:* making or delivering too much, too early or 'just in case'. Instead, the aim should be to make 'just-in-time' – neither too early nor too late. Overproduction creates unevenness or lumpiness of material flow, which is bad for quality and productivity. It is often the biggest source of waste.
- *The waste of waiting:* takes place whenever time is not being used effectively. It shows up as waiting by operators, by parts or by customers.
- *The waste of transporting:* moving parts around from one process to the next adds no value. Double handling, conveyors and movements by fork-lift truck are all examples of this waste. Placing processes as close as possible to each other not only minimises the waste of transport but also improves communications between them.
- *The waste of inappropriate processing:* using a large, central process that is shared between several lines (e.g. a heat treatment plant) is an example of this type of waste. Another example is a process that is incapable of meeting quality standards demanded by the customer – so it cannot help making defects.
- *The waste of unnecessary inventory:* inventory is a sign that flow has been disrupted, and that there are inherent problems in the process. Inventory not only hides problems, it also increases lead times and increases space requirements.
- *The waste of unnecessary motions:* if operators have to bend, stretch or extend themselves unduly, then these are unnecessary motions. Other examples are walking between processes, taking a stores requisition for signature, and decanting parts from one container into another.

- *The waste of defects:* producing defects costs time and money. The longer a defect remains undetected (e.g. if it gets into the hands of the end-customer), the more cost is added. Defects are counteracted by the concepts of 'quality at source' and 'prevention, not detection'.

Lean thinking invites us to analyse business processes systematically to establish the baseline of value-adding processes and identify the incidence of these seven wastes. The aim is to get parts and data to flow through business processes evenly and synchronously. The more detailed approach, prompted by the concept of seven wastes, encourages a greater analysis and understanding of processes and their relationships than is made by supply chain mapping.

Gradually, the principle of minimising waste spreads from the shop floor to all manufacturing areas, and from manufacturing to new product development and supply chain management. Thus, the term *lean thinking* refers to the elimination of waste in all aspects of a business and its supply chain.

7.1.2 The principles of lean thinking

Lean thinking is a cyclical route to seeking perfection by eliminating waste (the Japanese word is *muda*) and thereby enriching value from the customer perspective. The end-customer should not pay for the cost, time and quality penalties of wasteful processes in the supply network. Four principles are involved in achieving the fifth, seeking perfection (see Figure 7.1):

- specifying value;
- identifying the value stream;
- making value flow;
- pull scheduling.

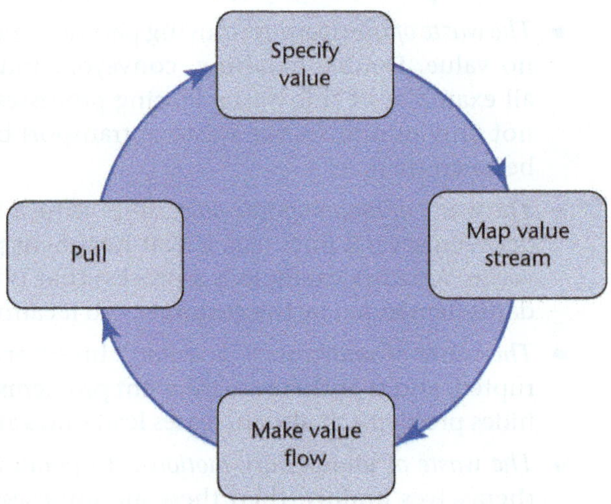

Figure 7.1 Lean virtuous improvement cycle: striving for perfection.

Principle 1: Specify value

Value is specified from the customer perspective. In Chapter 2 we discussed value from the customer perspective. Value is added along the supply network as raw materials from primary manufacture are converted progressively into finished product bought by the end-customer, such as the aluminium ore being converted into one of the constituents of a can of cola (see Chapter 1, Section 1.1). From a marketing and sales perspective, the can of cola should be 'always within reach of your thirst'. That is an attempt to define value from the end-customer perspective. Another is Porter's concept of the *value chain* (Porter, 1985), which sees two types of activity that are of value to the customer. The first is the primary value activities of transforming raw materials into finished products, then distributing, marketing and servicing them. The second is support activities, such as designing the products, and the manufacturing and distribution processes needed to underpin primary activities.

Principle 2: Identify the value stream

Following on from the concept of value, the next principle is to identify the value stream – the whole sequence of processes along the supply network. The principles of time-based mapping are discussed in Section 5.2 and can be used to map the current state and the future state of the value stream.

Principle 3: Make value flow

In essence, this means eliminating the seven wastes, as identified earlier in Section 7.1. Minimising delays, inventories, defects and downtime supports the flow of value in the supply network. Simplicity and visibility are the foundations to achieving these key factors.

Principle 4: Pull scheduling

Make only in response to a signal that more is needed from the customer (the next process downstream). This implies that demand information is made available across the supply chain. Where possible, supply from manufacturing, not from stock. Where possible, use customer orders not forecasts.

Principle 5: Seek perfection

The fifth principle is achieved by getting better gradually at everything we do, squeezing waste out at every step.

Many supply chains attempt to apply the principles of lean thinking, and Case study 7.1 provides a good example of a food supply chain applying these principles in order to reduce waste and improve flow.

We continue this section by considering the way in which lean thinking can be applied to enriching value in business processes other than manufacturing, where it originated.

CASE STUDY 7.1

Improving value flow in Bernard Matthews' poultry supply chain

Almost a fifth of the UK's wheat crop goes into poultry feed and, although feed supply chains are often short and integrated, there are opportunities to improve the performance, even in these commodity chains. This was found to be the case during a project examining value flow in the feed supply chain for Bernard Matthew's' poultry farms, shown in Figure 7.2.

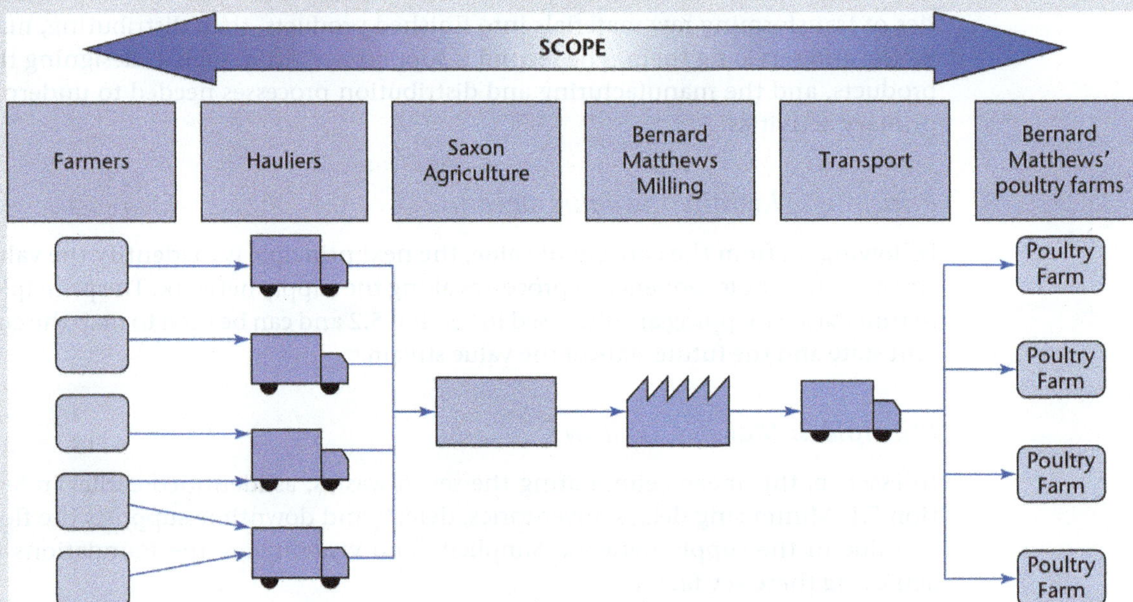

Figure 7.2 Project scope from grain trading to point of delivery into poultry farms.

Principle 1: Specify value

In a supply chain it is complex to understand value, since all participants in the chain will have their own needs and expectations about what their internal or external suppliers should deliver. However, by understanding value it is possible to identify activity that does not add value and seek to reduce or eliminate it. A team of four people from Bernard Matthews and Saxon constructed a map of value in the supply chain (as shown in Figure 7.3) by analysing the value at each stage of the process.

The value map was used to understand the impact of various activities on customer value and to define non-value-adding activities. It is interesting to note that the value proposition changes substantially as we go through the chain. Earlier stages focus mainly on price and, to some degree, on quality and delivery, indicating the product's commodity status. However, at the retailer and consumer end, the value proposition appears to be considerably more complex, with the emergence of issues such as choice, brand, packaging, innovation and promotions.

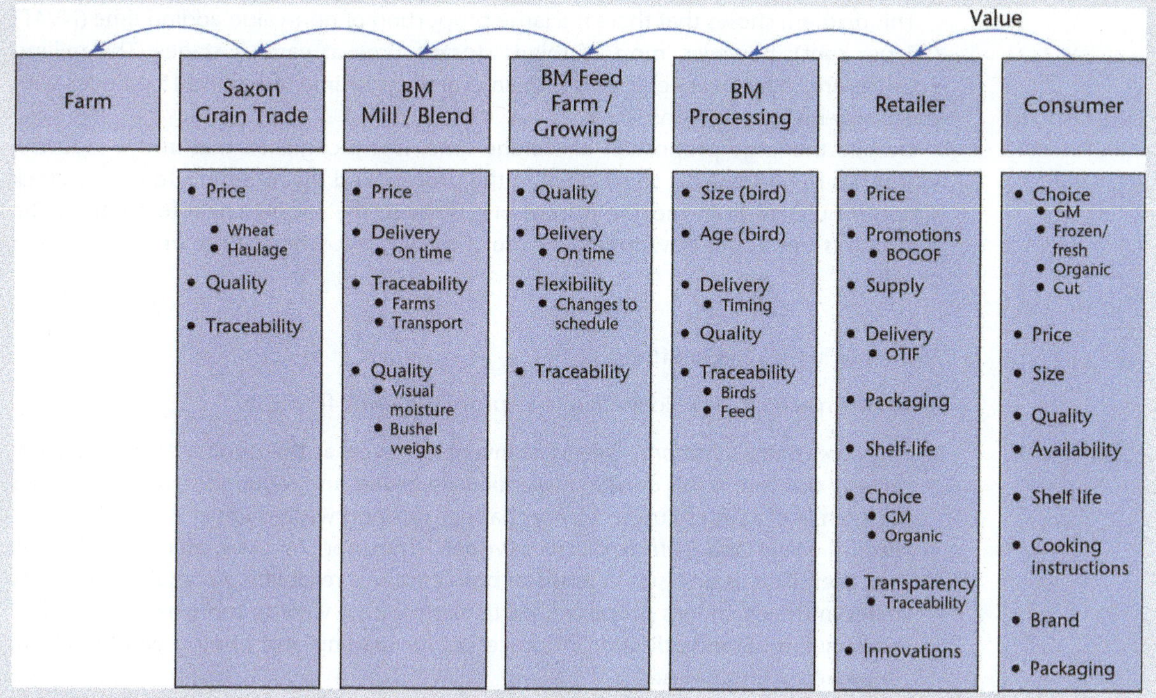

Figure 7.3 Value across the supply chain.

Principle 2: Identify the value stream

Both the information and product flows along the supply chain were analysed and the time-based process map, shown in Figure 7.4, was produced.

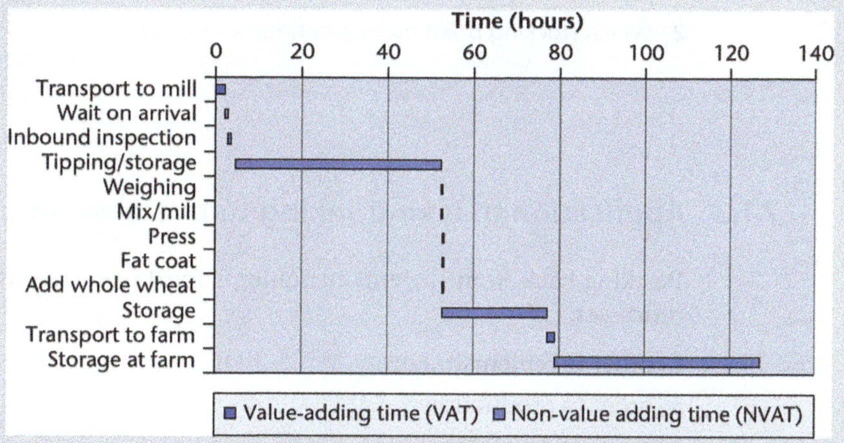

Figure 7.4 Time-based process map from Saxon agricultural transport to Bernard Matthews' poultry farm.

This diagram shows that there is a large proportion of non-value-adding time (NVAT) (97 per cent); however, most of this is storage time at various stages. The milling activities are, in fact, very efficient, with an overall cycle time of around 15 minutes with practically no interruptions.

Despite the large proportion of storage time, it is recognised that in this industry, wheat has to be stored at some point in the process and that attempts to reduce stock simply would result in moving it from one stage in the supply chain to another. The question is not about how much inventory is held, but where is the optimal holding point.

Principle 3: Make value flow

Three main actions were identified to improve the value flow:

- *Improve communications*. Details of inventory levels at the poultry farms were not always visible and this created disruptions in orders and required schedule changes at the mill, leading to unnecessary changeovers and wasted time.
- *Reduce delays and inefficiencies in transport*. Transport of raw materials to the mill was identified as an issue in terms of both cost and reliability. An analysis of empty miles in the chain was proposed, particularly with a view to more extensive use of backhauling. Standardisation of processes for loading and tipping would help to improve waiting times.
- *Reduce the frequency of grain sampling*. Grain was being sampled by a number of participants and on several occasions. The use of an independent sampling service would help reduce the wasted time and effort associated with multiple sampling.

(Source: Dr Carlos Mena, Cranfield School of Management.)

Questions

1. How might each of the improvement actions identified allow the reduction of inventory at each of the three storage points identified (see Figure 7.4)?
2. Which stocking point may be optimal and why?

7.1.3 Application of lean thinking to business processes

Working back from the end-customer, a focal firm should consider the following processes:

- order to replenishment;
- order to production;
- product development.

In each of these processes, the application of lean thinking involves examining the process, quantifying waste within it, identifying root causes of the waste, and developing and implementing solutions. Examining the process involves mapping it using a variety of techniques, such as flow charting, depending on the nature of the process. Performance is quantified by taking measures of the different kinds of waste. For a first attempt, using the time-based measures of lead time and value-adding time often reveal the main incidences of waste. Having identified waste, lean thinking applies the problem-solving tools associated with total quality control (TQC) to identify root causes and develop solutions.

The application of lean thinking is the means by which many companies bring their processes under control. Following a systematic approach to tackling waste, they seek to minimise defects, to minimise inventory and to maximise simplicity and visibility.

Order to replenishment

The order replenishment cycle concerns the time taken to replenish what has been sold and assumes that a 'make to stock' approach is being used. Lean thinking seeks to manage the order replenishment cycle by replacing only what has been sold within rapid replenishment lead times. Typically, a *kanban* approach to material flow is used where a *kanban* quantity is defined – this is a fixed replenishment quantity where the replenishment is initiated by the 'customer' of the process sending back a *kanban* ticket.

Order to production

The order to production cycle assumes a 'make to order' approach and is the series of steps that are followed to respond to an order, organise and undertake production, and deliver the product to the customer. This 'make to order' process may be contained within a company or can extend up the supply chain.

Product development

Product development delivers new products or services that can be sold. This process is essential if an organisation is to have future success. Lean thinking can be applied to this process to make it more effective by supporting the development of products with desirable attributes and features, whilst minimising time to market. It can also make the process more efficient and ensure that products are developed to cost. Beyond lean thinking, product development for agility, covered in Section 7.2.2, can reduce further time to market, product development costs and, ultimately, the costs inherent in the supply chain that delivers the product.

7.1.4 Lean manufacturing practices

Lean thinking is associated with a number of operational practices that help to deliver the aim of waste minimisation. Two of the most significant are:

- small-batch production;
- rapid changeover.

These two practices are associated closely with each other, but are considered separately here to aid clarity.

The target in small-batch production is a batch size of 1. The traditional logic behind large batches is to take advantage of reduced costs through economies of scale. The established approach to determining the appropriate batch size in manufacturing is the economic batch quantity (EBQ) (see Section 6.1.3), which is the optimum batch size that mitigates the trade-off between changeover costs and inventory holding costs, given an average demand rate. This is a fair approach, as it considers both production costs and inventory costs. However, since changeovers are typically lengthy and therefore costly, this pushes the EBQ up, leading to large batch sizes, which result in a lack of flexibility. The rationale behind small batches is that they can reduce total cost across a supply chain, such as removing the waste of overproduction and excessive inventory. They help to deliver products that the end-customer wants within the expected lead time (D-time – Section 5.3).

The discussion above links changeover time to batch size – shorter changeovers are lower cost and enable reduced batch sizes (i.e. EBQs). The contribution of rapid changeover was shown graphically by the changeover of press tools used to make car body panels. These cumbersome pieces of equipment can weigh up to 10 tonnes, and historically took up to 8 hours to change within the large presses. The consequence of these long changeover times was that component production runs (batch sizes) were long, often going on for days before the press tools were changed so that another component could be made. Extensive work, again pioneered by Toyota, was undertaken on press design, tooling design and component design over a number of years to help reduce changeover times. The effect has been to reduce changeover times for tools for large pressed parts to around five minutes. Consequently, practices that reduce changeover times are often known as *single minute exchange of dies* (SMED; Shingo, 1988). The ability to undertake rapid changeovers allows a batch of each different body panel to be produced each day in line with current demand, instead of having to produce to forecast.

The lesson from the automotive industry is that even very large pieces of equipment can be developed to allow rapid changeovers. This effort may take a number of years, and is reliant upon developments in machinery and product design. The effect is to provide the flexibility to make possible small-batch production that responds to customer needs.

7.1.5 Lean and resilience

Lean approaches to managing inventory, through techniques such as Just-In-Time (JIT), have come under criticism as global supply chains experience disruption. Events such as the 'Ever Given' container ship blockage of the Suez Canal and the COVID-19 pandemic created disturbances in the global flow of goods leading to temporary shortages of raw materials, component and finished goods. Lean thinking was criticised for reducing inventory to levels which endangered the resilience of supply chains. However, JIT was developed as a concept to synchronise production with (stable) demand, through the supply of parts and material, and encourage the co-location of suppliers. The concept was designed, in part, as a tool to minimise excess inventory not as a method for removing it entirely. Globalisation and the associated lengthy lead-times are not suitable for the operation of a JIT approach.

Long transit times require businesses to build in inventory as buffers to compensate for potential disruptions. Misconceptions of how to apply JIT is the problem, not the actual concept (see Choi et al., 2023 for a more detailed discussion).

7.2 The concept of agility

The 'agile supply chain' is essentially a practical approach to organising logistics capabilities around changing end-customer demands. It is about moving from supply chains that are structured around a focal company and its operations (for example, Ford Production System) towards supply chains that are focused on end-customers. Enabling the agile supply chain requires many significant changes: as an example, consider the position of Li & Fung, the largest exporter of textiles into the USA. The organisation coordinates manufacturers mainly across Asia to supply major customers, such as Levi's, mostly in the USA (as described in Case study 7.4). One of the key features of the Li & Fung approach is to establish an organisation that is customer centric, rather than being split into geographic divisions that end up competing against each other for global customers. The customer-focused divisions were separate profit-making units often dedicated to serving one customer and lead by an entrepreneurial manager.

Mason-Jones et al., (1999) developed a helpful comparison between agile and lean supply, shown in Table 7.1. We have extended this table into our comparison of further characteristics of lean and agile supply, shown in Table 7.2.

There is no reason why there should be an 'either-or' approach to logistics strategy. Thus, many supply chains can adopt a 'lean' capability up to a given downstream process, and then adopt an 'agile' capability thereafter. This enables high productivity, low cost processes to start with, followed by responsive processes to allow high levels of customisation thereafter. Such a strategic choice has been referred to as 'leagility' because it combines the benefits of both supply capabilities. The concept of leagility is close to that of postponement, which we discuss later in this chapter.

The comparisons in Tables 7.1 and 7.2 help us to place 'agile' in relation to 'lean', and thus to complement our earlier concept of logistics performance objectives. In Table 1.1 (in Chapter 1), we considered the issue of competing through logistics. The relative importance of the three logistics objectives (quality, time and cost) can be assessed with the help of order winners and order qualifiers (see Section 1.3.4). To actually win orders demands that performance of the focal firm must be superior to that of its competitors, so that products win orders in the marketplace. The order winner provided by a lean supply chain is *price* as the focus is on waste, and therefore cost minimisation, whereas the order winner enabled by an agile supply chain is *availability* of the product, despite it being subject to volatile demand. In fact, agility is typically appropriate either in the early stages of the product life cycle – during the introduction and growth phase – or for products that simply are not allowed to mature, for example fashion products or consumer electronic goods (e.g. mobile phones) where the product life cycles are short.

Table 7.1 Comparison of lean supply with agile supply: the distinguishing attributes.

Distinguishing attributes	Lean supply	Agile supply
Typical products	Commodities	Fashion goods
Marketplace demand	Predictable and stable	Volatile
Product variety	Low	High
Product life cycle	Long	Short
Order winner	Price	Availability
Profit margin	Low	High
Dominant costs	Physical costs	Marketability costs
Stockout penalties	Long-term contractual	Immediate and volatile
Purchasing policy	Buy materials	Assign capacity
Information enrichment	Highly desirable	Obligatory
Forecasting mechanism	Algorithmic	Consultative

(Source: Adapted from Mason-Jones et al., 1999.)

Table 7.2 Further characteristics of lean and agile supply.

Characteristic	Lean	Agile
Logistics focus	Eliminate waste	Responsiveness to customers and markets
Partnerships	Long term, stable	Fluid clusters, frequently reconfigure
Performance measures	'World class' output measures, like productivity and cost	Measure capabilities, like responsiveness and flexibility, and focus on customer satisfaction
Employee process focus	Work standardisation, conformance to quality and productivity standards	Focus on operator self-management to maximise autonomy

So far we have focused on the differences between lean and agile. However, there are similarities. Both lean and agile supply chains aspire to establishing product flow synchronised with demand, but of course for lean supply chains this is far simpler as demand is stable and predictable. As discussed under lean practices, in Section 7.1.4, large batches lead to lack of flexibility in responding to changes in demand volume or demand mix (the range of different product variants). It therefore follows that small batch sizes are desirable for both lean and agile supply chains to ensure product flow is synchronised with demand. However, the main drivers for small batches are different – lean requires reduced waste (inventory, changeover time, etc.), whilst agility requires flexibility to changes in demand.

Case study 7.2 compares and contrasts two supply chains for the same cured fish product (bacalao) but that supply two different markets and employ different strategies akin to lean and agile.

CASE STUDY 7.2

Bacalao – two supply chains for two markets

Bacalao is fish that has been salted and dried, traditionally in the open air on rocks; today it is done in a drier. It has been produced in Norway since about 1640, can be kept refrigerated for several years, and is said to improve over time. It has developed a strong position in the food cultures of many Latin countries – such as Brazil, the Dominican Republic and Portugal – where consumers often follow the Catholic tradition of eating more fish on Fridays and in the run-up to Easter. Marketing over many years has created the association with Norway as 'the land of bacalao', or *'bacalhau da Noruega'*, as it is called. It is a matter of great pride amongst consumers to master a variety of recipes for serving bacalao.

The overall supply chain is illustrated in Figure 7.5. It takes at least four weeks to make the end-product. The best fish is wild and taken by line, but trawled fish is also good, whilst nets give the lowest quality because the fish can be dead for a while before being hauled up. Today, the fish is increasingly farmed as well. The raw material is the major cost item: prices are set by the Råfiskelaget (the Norwegian raw fish association). Prices can vary a lot – for example from NOK26/kg to NOK15/kg within a year. Electricity and insurance are the other two major cost items. The fish is slaughtered (and bled on the boat for the best quality), then matured in salt for two to three weeks. After salting, it is dried, sorted, packed and distributed. There are no reliable ways of measuring salt and water content, so manual methods of touching and feeling the fish during each stage are used to ensure consistent quality and weight.

Bacalao is produced mainly from cod, which is preferred by Portuguese customers. But consumers in the Dominican Republic prefer pollock, which is a darker-fleshed fish that is more abundant in the North Atlantic. Cod is up to three times more expensive than pollock. The Norwegian fish industry is highly fragmented, with many small-scale fish farmers, fishermen and producers. Marketing activities are coordinated by the Norwegian Seafood Export Council.

Consumers are very quality conscious when buying bacalao. Quality is determined by colour, texture and firmness, as well as water content and size. Portuguese consumers prefer smaller cod, around 2.5 kilos, whilst consumers in the Dominican Republic are less concerned with size. Note that quality here refers to *grade* of fish rather than to conformance quality: both grades are fit for purpose in the markets they serve.

Bacalhau da Noruega

Company Noruega (CN) has 150 employees and built its bacalao production facility in 1997 in the Port of Ålesund – which has one of the largest harbours in Norway and one of the most modern fishing fleets in Europe. The company focuses on volume in order to benefit from the economies of scale. Production is stabilised through the year by ensuring a stable supply of fish through sourcing a combination of frozen and fresh fish, creating a buffer of some three to four months' supply. The company trades only in full truckloads, which are distributed via Hamburg or Rotterdam. Product is sold under the generic brand name of *Bacalao da Noruega* in standard transport packaging. Whilst CN serves most Latin markets, 80 per cent of its sales go to the Dominican Republic as pollock bacalao. This market is relatively stable throughout the year, which matches CN's stable production policy. CN is experimenting with pollock farming further to improve supply reliability.

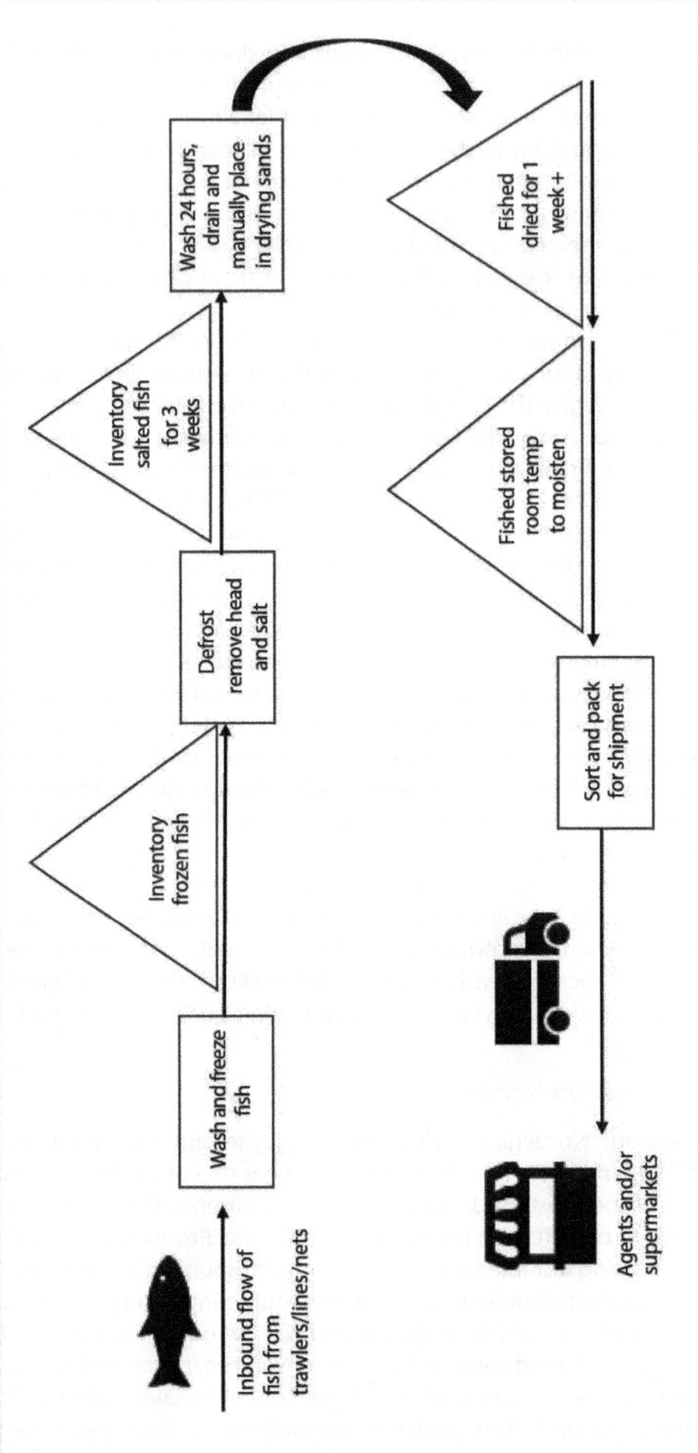

Figure 7.5 The overall supply chain for bacalao.
(Source: Adapted from Jahre and Refsland-Fougner, 2005.)

Bacalao Superior

Company Superior (CS) is also based in the Ålesund area, and accounts for 15–20 per cent of Norwegian bacalao exports to Portugal. Only cod bacalao is exported to this market, which commands a 10–15 per cent price premium over other Norwegian bacalao. The product is popular with consumers, which creates a strong relationship with the single supermarket chain that sells it. Fish are sold whole, with a CS tag showing guarantee of origin from fresh Norwegian cod, which was an idea that came from the supermarket customer. This ensures that CS bacalao stands out from other offerings. Joint marketing campaigns are funded by both CS and its supermarket customer, and include TV promotions. Only fresh cod is used in *bacalao superior*, caught by the coastal fleet in small boats. During the winter, supply is heavily dependent on quotas that are permitted in the famous Lofoten fishing field in the far north. CS buys from three fresh cod suppliers, and from 15–20 suppliers of salt fish. Processing follows traditional routes, but some technology has been introduced into cutting and drying. Finished product is transported to Portugal in 22-tonne truckloads three times per week. Storage of finished product is in Lisbon at the customer's warehouse.

Comparing da Noruega and Superior

Table 7.3 summarises some of the major differences between these two products.

CN accepts more variation in its raw material source to enable continuous supply. This applies to type of fish as well as where and how it is caught. Farming and a healthy stock of frozen fish help to reduce further supply variations. On the other hand, CS seeks the best quality with minimum variation. The only inbound stock that is permitted is small quantities of salted cod.

Table 7.3 Comparing da Noruega and Superior.

Characteristic	da Noruega (Dominican Rep.)	Superior (Portugal)
Raw material	• Fresh/frozen pollock • Different sizes • Line/trawl/net/farm • Continuous supply • 3–4 months' inbound stocks	• Fresh cod, some salted • Size specific (around 2.5 kg) • Mostly line • Seasonal supply • Small inbound stock
Production process	• High volume • All types of fish processed in a single factory • Undifferentiated packaging	• Low volume • Cod only in single, focused factory • Whole fish individually tagged
Marketing	• Continuous consumption • Generic marketing through Seafood Export Council • Low price • Generic packaging • Little differentiation	• Special occasions • Joint promotion with supermarket customer • Premium price • Tagged to show origin • Differentiated by market

▶

Whilst the raw materials and end-product have many similarities, there are substantial differences in inbound and outbound logistics as well as processing and distribution strategies. These differences are fundamental to the need to support the brand (raising consumer expectations) by means of logistics strategy (meeting consumer expectations). We can conclude as follows:

- *Two fundamentally different inbound strategies:* CN focuses on secure, continuous supply and accepts greater variation in terms of type of fish, where and how caught – so farming is encouraged. They buffer and store extensively. CS goes for consistently high quality by not accepting much by way of variation: size, line catching and location are all important requirements. They do not store fresh fish or use frozen.
- *Internally consistent marketing and logistics:* CN matches the low price, continuous availability marketing mix by means of efficient sourcing and continuous availability, and of 'lean' production and distribution methods. This enables high and consistent production volumes supported by a flexible product mix. There is less to go wrong in terms of supply, but the generic nature of the product works against better margins or customer loyalty. CS matches the high price, seasonal availability marketing mix by means of highly selective sourcing and by focused factory production that is seasonal and relatively inefficient. Production is possible only when high-quality, line-caught fresh fish are available. Limited and sporadic availability mean that the product has to reassert itself following supply interruptions, so the marketing pull must be consistent and strong. Traceability through tagging reinforces the superior quality image in consumers' minds, supported by joint marketing with the major retail customer.

The way that the two supply chains have evolved illustrates the trade-offs at stake: more of one thing means less of another. The CS supply chain has become focused on top quality (grade) product, but at relatively high cost and sporadic availability. The CN supply chain has become focused on the opposite: low cost and continuous availability, but at average quality (grade).

(Sources: Jahre and Refsland Fougner, 2005; Alan Harrison, 2010.)

Question

1. Discuss and evaluate to what extent Company Noruega (CN) has a lean supply chain and Company Superior (CS) has an agile supply chain.

There is no reason why there should be an 'either-or' approach to logistics strategy. Lean and agile can be combined in different ways (as described in Section 7.3). Further, as discussed in Section 2.3.2, agility costs more. Wherever possible, the supply chain should be lean and waste minimised. However, to respond to volatile demand, capacity and inventory buffers are required.

> **Agility is defined in many ways but it is understood that it centres on being able to compete and prosper within a state of dynamic change, which involves two aspects: responding to changes (anticipated or unanticipated) in proper ways and due time; exploiting changes and taking advantage of changes as opportunities.**
>
> **(Source: Zhang and Sharifi, 2007.)**

Zhang and Sharifi (2007) go on to define a taxonomy based on three types of agility:

1. capability to satisfy and be close to customers;
2. capability to thrive in changes that may be anticipated, e.g. seasonality, promotions;
3. capability to cope with unanticipated changes, e.g. disruption in supply, competitor product introductions.

Whether changes are anticipated or not depends on the organisation's predictive capabilities in terms of sales forecasting (as covered in 'Demand Profiling', Section 2.2), risk management (see Section 4.3) and market research.

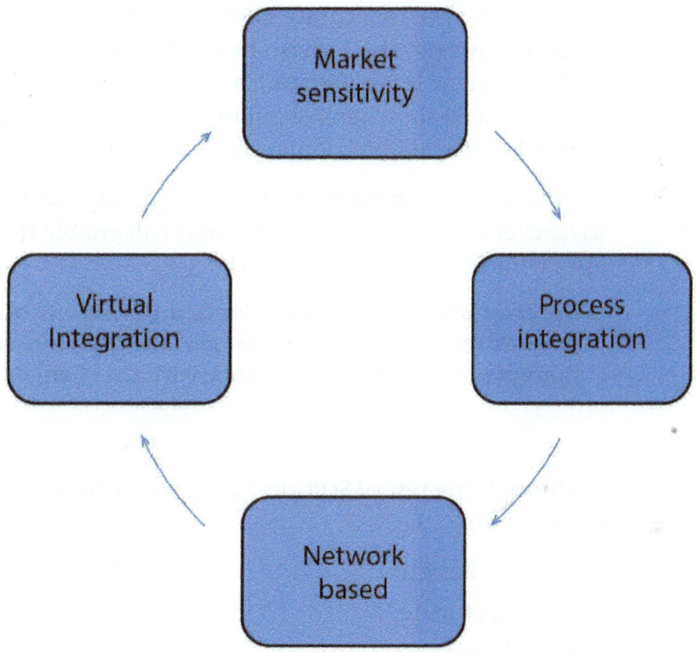

Figure 7.6 Model of agile capabilities.
(Source: Adapted from van Hoek, et. al., 2001.)

Compatible with this view is an earlier understanding of agile capabilities (van Hoek et al., 2001), which defines agility as the capability to read and respond to changing end-customer demand and identifies four distinct capabilities that are required, as shown in Figure 7.6:

- *Market sensitive*. Organisation requires a strong ability to 'read' the market, both in terms of demand for existing products and services and new, hitherto undefined, products and services. This requires strength in terms of market research and being close to the customer.
- *Process integration*. The supply chain can be viewed as a system of business processes, which, if integrated and synchronised (as described in Section 8.1), can avoid the time, cost and quality penalties associated with 'stand-alone' processes.

For example, where the component delivery process is not synchronised with the manufacturing process, the penalty will be a high inbound component inventory.

- *Network based*. A network of supply chain partners collaborate to meet the end-customer needs and demand by collaboratively planning across the supply chain. In the case of Li & Fung they configured and orchestrated the whole supply network, as described in Case study 7.4. The competitive strength is gained through focusing the distinct capabilities provided by each company on the end-customer needs.
- *Virtual integration*. This depends on capturing electronic point of sale (EPOS) demand data and sharing it across the supply chain, such that member companies see the 'real time' demand, rather than the distorted picture of demand provided by sales forecasts. This reduces the level of inventory required to buffer against the inaccurate sales forecasts, thus replacing inventory with demand data. However, the proviso here is that even the EPOS data is past demand from the moment it is generated, as opposed to future demand (such as customer future orders) so, when we refer to sharing 'real time' demand data, it is more like the 'latest available' demand data, which can improve forecast accuracy.

Now we have an understanding of the capabilities required for agility, it is time to further consider the practices that will enable these capabilities. However, there are a wide range of practices and:

> **Different organisations experience different sets of changes, and different levels of pressure resulting from the changes, and therefore would require different combinations of practices and tolls to cope with the changes.**
>
> **(Source: Zhang and Sharifi, 2000.)**

Through the rest of Section 7.2 we will consider a selection of agile practices concerned with:

- product design;
- manufacturing;
- logistics; and
- supply partnerships.

This will culminate in a consideration of three preconditions for agility.

7.2.1 Product design for agility

Agile supply chains are a response to shortening product life cycles, typical of fashion products, and proliferating product variants. Equally, agile supply chains must respond to unanticipated changes in demand due to technological or environmental changes, as illustrated by a leading global oil company supplying marine oil for large freight ships. The engines powering these enormous vessels burn considerable oil on every long trip and therefore top-ups are required in each port. Following the financial crisis of 2008, and subsequent global recession, freight ships reduced their speeds to improve fuel consumption. However, an unexpected consequence of this behaviour was an increase in oil consumption. Effectively, the oil was not designed for the new slow speeds. A new marine oil was developed quickly that was appropriate for the slower speeds and, ironically, drew on an old technology from days when ships were slower.

Crucial to achieving market sensitivity necessary for agility is the capability to develop products quickly and efficiently – time to market must be short or the product will have been superseded before it is available, or the competition will have cornered the market! But, just as important as the time to market are production cost and speed. Both these goals can be achieved through product development being coordinated with supply chain design (manufacturing, sourcing and logistics).

Unfortunately, far from being a coordinated process of product and supply chain design, supply chain considerations, such as component sourcing and manufacturing location, are often afterthoughts. As Ellram et al., (2008) observed, there is a lack of inclusion of supply chain decisions in product design, despite the fact that 75 per cent of life cycle costs are determined by product specification (Balasubramanian, 2001). This can lead to higher purchasing costs, excessive transportation and unresponsive supply chains that fail to meet end-customer needs. Here we will discuss a number of approaches to product design for agility.

Design for manufacture and assembly

Recognition of the criticality of coordinating product design and manufacturing process design decisions has led to 'design for manufacture and assembly' (Boothroyd et al., 1994), which is 'both a philosophy and a methodology whereby products are designed in a way that is as amenable as possible for downstream manufacturing and assembly' (Gao et al., 2020). This involves the careful consideration of component manufacture and assembly early in the product design cycle, reducing the number of components, materials and assembly steps where possible. It thereby reduces the time to market and the production costs through simplification of design.

Concurrent engineering (CE)

Concurrent engineering (CE) requires that the related functions, such as product design, manufacturing and logistics, work concurrently on the product design rather than the 'over the wall' approach. It is renowned for reducing time to market.

Design for supply chain (or design for logistics)

The aim is to keep the product in a 'vanilla' (or generic) form for as long as possible in the manufacturing process by delaying product differentiation. Indeed it is sometimes referred to as *delayed product differentiation* and, as we shall see in Section 7.2.2, it is important to enable the application of form postponement.

Lee (1993 and 1995) develops ideas in this area and identifies three main approaches to design for supply chain or logistics:

- *Product and process modularisation* (Ulrich, 1994; Pine, 1993). Ulrich (1994) claims that 'a completely modular design embodies a one-to-one correspondence between each functional element and physical component, in which every interaction between components is critical to the function of the system'.

The idea is that many product variants can be assembled from a relatively narrow range of modules. Pine (1993) identifies six different types of modularity (as shown in Figure 7.7). 'Component swapping' is the complement of 'component sharing' and is where different components are paired with the same basic product, creating as many products as there are components to swap. In many cases the distinction between component sharing and component swapping is a matter of degree. Consider Swatch watches: are the basic watch elements a component shared across all the range of watches (component sharing) or are the watch parts the basic product and the incredible variety of face styles the components (component swapping)? Component swapping is associated often with the creation of product variety as perceived by the customer, as we will see later in the Smart Car Case study 7.3.

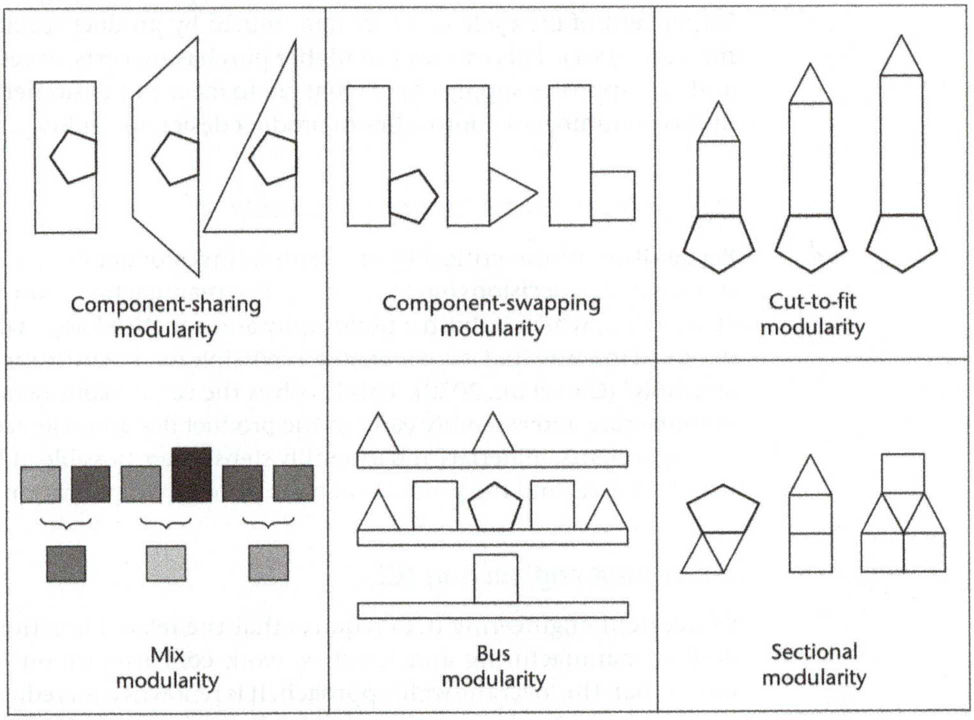

Figure 7.7 Illustration of the six types of modularity.
(Source: Adapted from Abernathy and Utterback, 1978.)

- *Product and process standardisation* (Erixon, 1996). This involves standardising and rationalising components across the product range. Ultimately this leads to a standardised product.
- *Process re-sequencing* (Lee and Tang, 1998), such that the differentiating products are postponed. Benetton provides the classic example when the dyeing and knitting processes were swapped, such that the jumpers were knitted out of natural yarn and then dyed when more accurate sales forecasts were available. Dyeing is the main differentiating process – think of the colours of Benetton – so, by delaying it until after the lengthy knitting process, it radically reduced forecast horizon for jumpers by colour.

Three-dimensional concurrent engineering (3DCE)

Fine (1998) effectively brings together concurrent engineering (CE) and design for supply chain by proposing the extension of CE to supply chain design in an approach termed *three-dimensional concurrent engineering* (3DCE). Fine's framework for 3DCE proposes that only those activities that fall into the overlaps between product, manufacturing process and supply chain design need to be undertaken concurrently by the integrated product team. Many authors cite coordinated product and supply chain design as an area requiring further research. Rungtusanatham and Forza (2005) claim that:

> **Despite the undeniable appeal and importance of coordinating decisions across product, manufacturing process and supply chain design to both science and practice, we know very little about how to do so to maximise operational, supply chain and firm performance.**

They find that coordinating product and supply chain design decisions improves performance in terms of reducing supply chain costs and improving customer service.

7.2.2 Manufacturing for agility

Agility – responding to changes and exploiting changes – requires responsive and flexible manufacturing, which can be adapted quickly to new products and accommodate changes in mix (range of variants) and volume of production with minimum cost or time penalties. Allocation of finished goods to given customer orders is a familiar way of responding quickly to demand – for example, selling cars from a dealer forecourt. But this approach to supply means that inventories of finished goods must be built up first – made-to-stock (MTS). The problem is that they must be built up in anticipation of *unknown* demand, which depends on accurate forecasts. If stocks pushed by a manufacturer onto its dealer network are too high, they will have to be discounted. If they are too low, sales are lost to competitors. Reducing the risks of speculative manufacture by delaying the exact specification of the car until the customer order is known, and then delivering it within an acceptable D-time, is called *form postponement*. The concept of 'postponement' now is increasingly widely employed by organisations in a range of industries (van Hoek, 2001). Form postponement is widely used to improve responsiveness and is defined (Skipworth and Harrison, 2004) as:

> **The delay, until customer orders are received, of the final part of the transformation processes, through which the number of SKUs proliferates, and for which only a short time period is available. The postponed transformation processes may be manufacturing processes, assembly processes, configuration processes, packaging or labelling processes.**

For example, the aim of the 'three-day car' project is to complete paint, trim, final assembly and delivery of a car to dealer within three days (Holweg and Miemczyck, 2003). However, many less ambitious form postponement applications delay packaging, labelling, adding documentation or product peripherals, all of which are frequently conducted in distribution centres. Further, the postponed process may take place even further downstream, such as paint mixing in DIY retailers, where the customer can choose almost any shade of any colour and the 'vanilla' paint is mixed with a customised combination of pigments to give the precise colour required.

The customer order decoupling point and form postponement

There are two main types of postponement, as illustrated in Figure 7.8, which are distinguished by the location of the customer order decoupling point (CODP), the point in the value-adding process where a product is linked to a specific customer order. Therefore, downstream from this point production is order-driven and upstream it is forecast-driven. As we discussed in Section 5.3 on P:D ratios, for MTO the production process is entirely order-driven and the CODP is positioned before the beginning of the first transformation process. In contrast, for MTS the entire production process is forecast-driven, because the CODP is located after the end of the last transformation process. In the case of form postponement (FPp), the CODP is at the semi-finished product stage, where the product, or component modules, are in a generic form, as shown in Figure 7.8, thus mitigating the weaknesses of MTO and MTS by enabling a high variety or customised product to be provided on a short lead time with minimum (and generic) inventory. The other type of postponement – logistical postponement – is in essence MTS, where only the distribution is postponed until the receipt of an order. Thus it is akin to centralisation of inventory in, say, a Central European distribution centre.

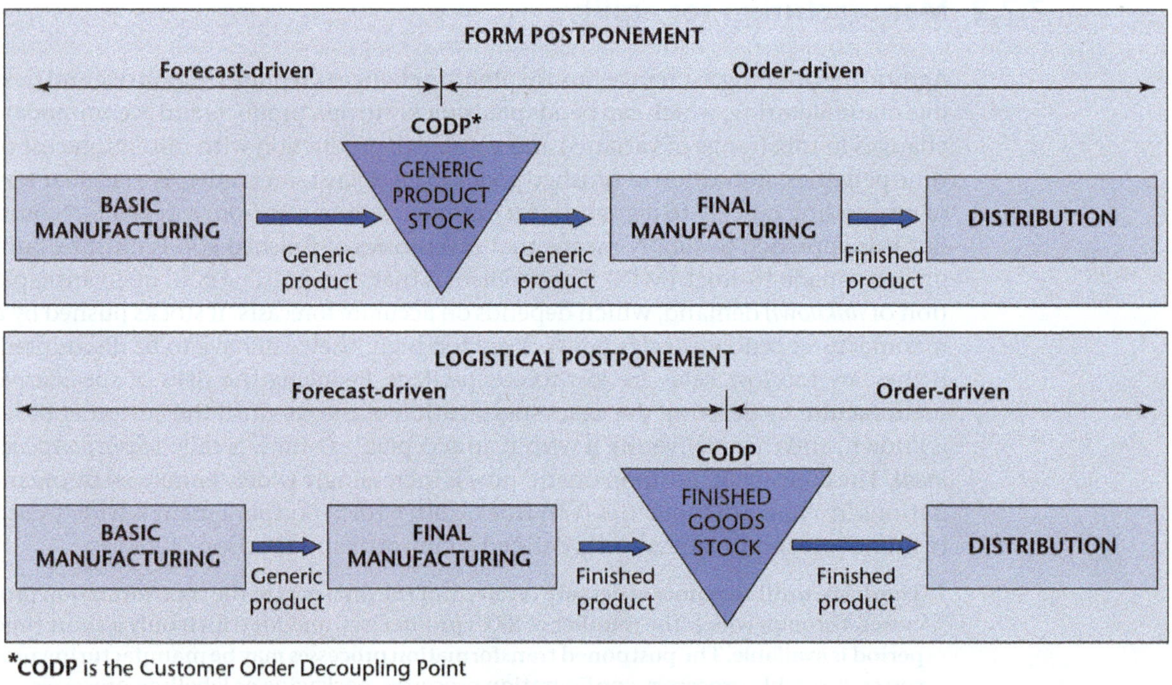

Figure 7.8 A schematic showing form and logistical postponement.
(Source: Skipworth and Harrison, 2004.)

Conceptual model for form postponement

Form postponement relies on the product being designed for the supply chain (as explained in Section 7.2.1) such that the appearance of wider customer choice can be created whilst the basic design of the product is the same. The Smart Car Case study 7.3 is an excellent example of this. The conceptual model of form postponement, shown in Figure 7.9, illustrates how it can be applied by bringing together the product/process design and the CODP.

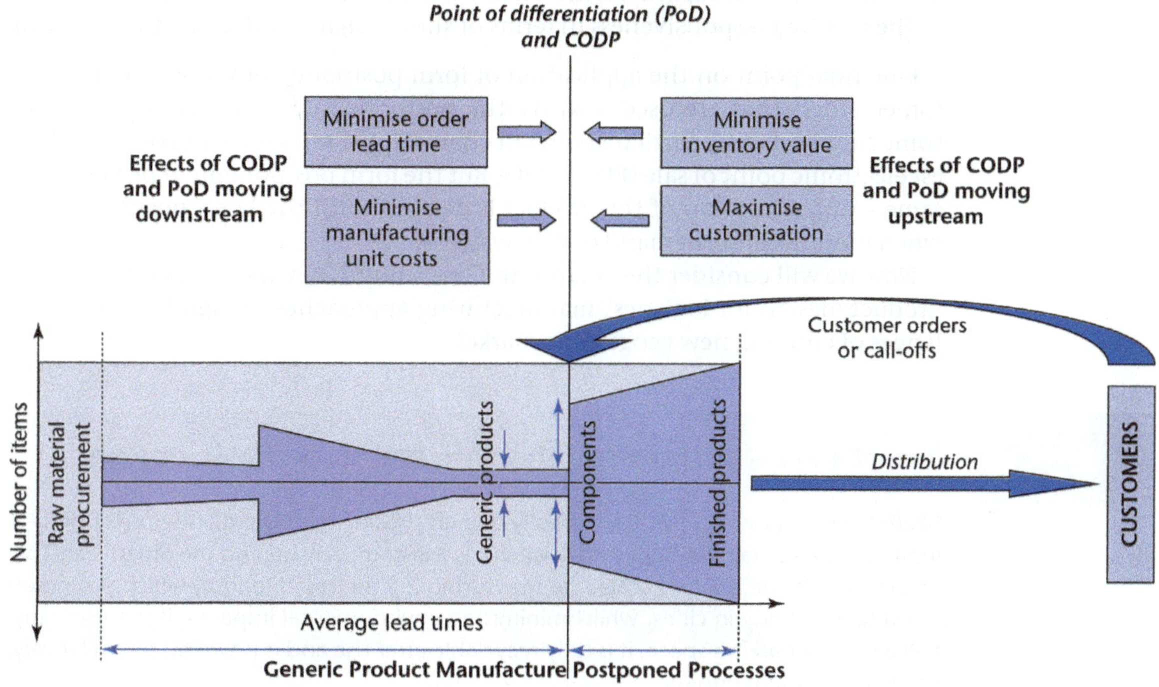

Figure 7.9 A conceptual model for form postponement.
(Source: Adapted from Skipworth and Harrison, 2004.)

The model is based upon a production variety funnel (Pude et al., 2012), which represents graphically the number of distinct parts that occur at each manufacturing stage. The vertical axis represents the number of items, the horizontal axis throughput time. The PVF is hypothetical, yet typical of FPp applications, and shows how a relatively limited range of components can be assembled into a wide range of finished products. The CODP should be located at a point of differentiation where there are relatively few generic components to be stored, reducing the risk and cost associated with inventory.

The benefits of form postponement are rooted in the fact that it mitigates the trade-offs between MTS and MTO, enabling a customised or high-variety product to be manufactured with both a short order lead time (D-time) compared to MTO and a low inventory value compared to MTS. This allows a better match between supply and demand. However, our research (Harrison and Skipworth, 2008) shows that there are many obstacles to successful application of form postponement:

- *Product design:* the extent to which it is possible to standardise the product to give only a small number of generic base products or modules. This is dependent on the demand for the different product varieties as well as the product characteristics themselves.
- *Manufacturing planning and control:* mindsets associated with MTO and MTS are inhibitors to FPp, an aspect of the lack of structural and cultural fit referred to

by Yang et al., (2004). MTO and MTS tend not to require either manufacturing planning or manufacturing processes to be responsive in the way that FPp does.

- *Postponed process capacity:* if this is insufficient it may not be possible to maintain the required responsiveness in terms of short, reliable order lead times (D-time).

One final point on the application of form postponement: it is not always customer orders that are used to drive the postponed differentiation processes. In some supply chains, particularly retail chains, it is a sales forecast based on the latest electronic point of sale (EPOS) data. But the form postponement principle is the same - differentiation of the product is delayed until the latest possible moment when more accurate demand data is available.

Now we will consider the Smart Car (Case study 7.3), which illustrates the use of product 'design for logistics', manufacturing approaches for agility and the challenges of entering new geographic markets.

CASE STUDY 7.3

Smart Cars – customisation using the same basic design

Micro Compact Car AG (MCC), a wholly owned subsidiary of Daimler-Benz (formerly a joint venture of Daimler-Benz and Swatch), is the company behind the Smart Car. The Smart City Coupé is a two-seater car measuring 2.5 metres in length, which promotes individual mobility in cities, whilst minimising environmental impact – it requires only half a normal parking space, it is fully recyclable after use and is powered by a relatively small fuel-efficient engine.

Smart Car concept

The Smart Car is a modular design based on a rigid integral body frame or safety cell (called 'TRIDION'), to which external body panels – doors, the front and rear panels – are attached. The customer can customise the product by combining two colours of the frame (black and silver) with the various colours of the external body panels plus internal trim panels and comfort features, not to mention the size and type of engine. This way the customer is given the impression of a high level of choice, although the car is the same basic design, and variation in the manufacturing process is kept to a minimum.

All the customisable parts, with the exception of the engine and the body frame, can be changed through the life of the car at the Smart Centres (the small city dealerships where the cars are sold), allowing the customer easily to repair damage to the car and refresh 'the look' like a fashion item.

Smartville and the supply chain

The Smart Car is manufactured at a purpose-built manufacturing site called 'Smartville' in Hambach (France), with 20 production buildings covering 68 hectares. The seven main module suppliers (plus a number of second-tier suppliers) designed their own modules and invested in dedicated manufacturing facilities, fully integrated with MCC's cross-shaped assembly flow line (as shown in Figure 7.10). The single-stage delivery concept allows Smart Centres to procure their cars – via the sales logistics department – directly from the manufacturing plant in Hambach instead of through a dealer or

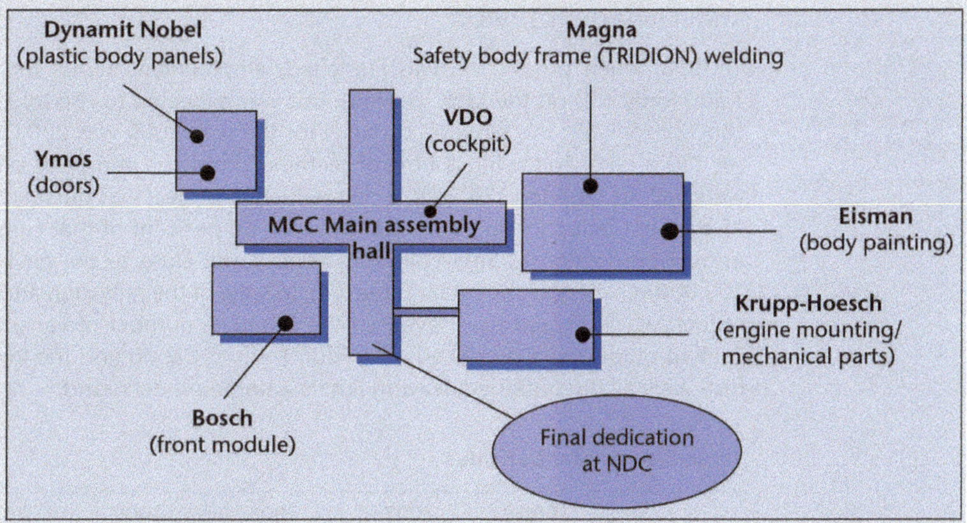

Figure 7.10 Smartville integrated manufacturing plant.

import organisation. This distribution system is very different to the tiered sales structure in the traditional automotive industry, in which national sales organisations and importers add another layer between dealers and the manufacturer. This resulted in just a two- or three-week lead time for a made to 'specific customer order' Smart Car, whilst, at the time of the Smart launch, VW had a lead time of up to six months on some models – customers could have what was in stock now, or wait!

As can be seen from Figure 7.11, the manufacturing lead time is seven days with a further week or two allowed for distribution. The order from the Smart Centre is translated into orders for the first- and second-tier suppliers, triggering manufacturing to order up the supply chain. When material has arrived, the modules are supplied in sequence for final assembly by a small number of first-tier suppliers on a one- to three-hour lead time. Final assembly takes just five hours.

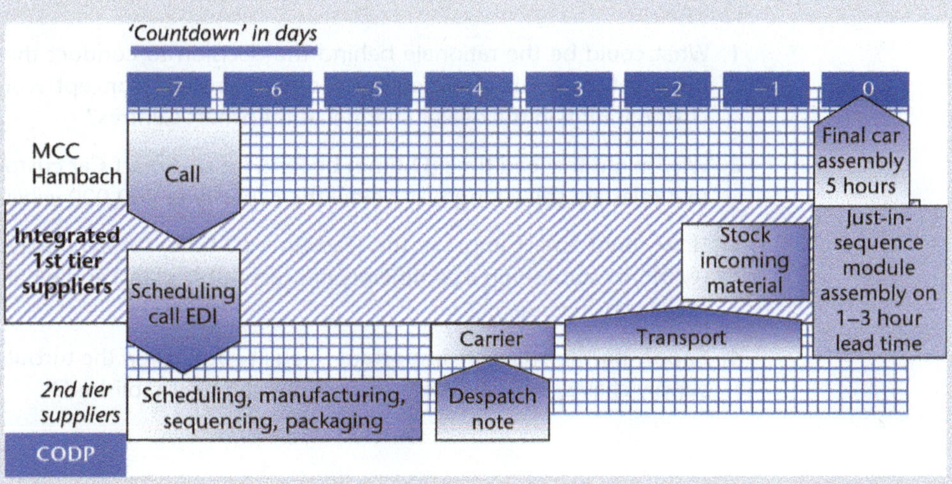

Figure 7.11 Smart Car manufacturing lead time.

Initial launch in 1998

In 1998, when production was launched, employment across the site started with 1,500 (only 650 on the MCC payroll), but was expected to rise to 2,200 as the Smart concept took off: the targeted capacity for the year 2000 was 200,000 vehicles a year (or 750 a day). Following a host of teething problems and poor sales (sales in 1999 were half the targeted 120,000), a cost reduction project was pursued in 1999, securing 15 per cent reduction in component costs – 60 per cent of that came from suppliers. Annual production at Smartville has never come close to the envisaged capacity of 200,000 vehicles (as shown by Table 7.4), in spite of the recession and the soaring price of fuel, which should have favoured the brand. A number of variants on the original ForTwo model were produced – ForFour, ForTwo Cabrio and the Roadster – however they were all discontinued, leaving Smart a single-model brand.

Table 7.4 Smart Car sales

	2006	2007	2008	2009	2010
Total	81,995	102,588	140,072	115,469	97,373

Launch into America

When launched into North America in 2008, sales peaked at about 29,000, but have since fallen from approximately 18,000 (2009) to just 9,000 in 2010. At the start of the Smart Car production it was envisaged that global capacity would be expanded by replicating the Smartville site anywhere in the world; however, sales did not justify such investment. Therefore, Smart Cars were made in Smartville (France) and shipped to America.

In March 2007 a $99 reservation programme was launched, but Smart Cars were not planned to be produced for the American market until 2008. This necessitated a long wait for customers, and many did not follow through with a purchase.

Questions

1. What could be the rationale behind the decision to conduct the final assembly at the plant in Hambach when the modular product concept would allow product customisation in the dealer channel at the Smart Centres?
2. Why might the lead time (D-time) be long for US Smart Car customers, considering that sales are still a long way below the capacity of 200,000 vehicles per year?
3. How could Smart improve the lead time (D-time) for cars delivered into the USA (without establishing a completely new assembly plant) and what are the associated supply chain issues?
4. Supply partnerships are important to agility but, given the turbulent nature of agile supply chains, what type of partnerships can be established?

3-D printing

3-D printing, also known as additive manufacturing, represents a group of technologies that create objects from the bottom-up by adding material one cross-sectional layer at a time, whereas conventional manufacturing reduces an object (e.g. steel plates) through cutting, milling and turning to deliver the end product. Printers typically utilise a moving inkjet-print head to deposit material across a build area to create a range of products and customer services. The materials which can be used include polymers, metals, sand, ceramics and composites, as well as organic substances.

The development of 3-D printing has started to challenge the design, manufacturing and flow of parts as the potential of decentralising production becomes a financially viable option. This disruptive technology provides customers with the opportunity of becoming involved with the design and manufacture of the product at the point of consumption. For example, bio-printing is allowing hospitals to provide patients with bone engineering services in-house, simplifying the medical supply chain and improving the success of surgical interventions. On the high street restaurants are also utilising 3-D printing technology, using the ChefJet printer to create customised product designs for diners.

The range of possible printers and materials has led to a multitude of shapes, sizes (from microscopic to the size of large aircraft wings) and applications. The agility of the technology has resulted in several applications for 3-D printing each with its own implications for agile manufacturing.

- *Prototyping:* the rapid production of new product and innovative designs. Firms are actively involving the customer in the design process through quickly printing new concepts which the customer can examine and provide feedback on. This allows firms to incorporate customers' comments and fine-tune ideas before committing cash to tooling (for high volume items) and capacity.
- *Spare parts (equipment and components):* after-sales service is a key part of any organisation's value stream. Providing spare parts can be costly due to the high-variety and relatively low-volume demand of items to be stored. Ensuring a good match between available inventory and demand for such items is problematic due to the unpredictable nature of the demand for spare parts. In addition, each model of product requires spare part provision for its life in use, which can be decades, for example in the case of passenger aircraft. 3-D printing enables parts to be printed to order, reducing the complexity and cost of managing spare parts inventories. The ability to take a previously digitally created object (through a system such as Computer Aided Design (CAD)) and print the item without having to create hard tools reduces the need to hold inventory. Decentralised printers provide the opportunity to deliver a localised and quick service without the need for centralised spare parts warehousing.
- *Low-volume products:* the ability to print products on demand has the potential to simplify supply chains through minimising lead times and inventories. For low-volume, high-value items 3-D printing can be used to manufacture smaller batch sizes without the need to invest in expensive hard tools such as die-casts. This not only reduces the overall cost of the supply chain but also improves the time to manufacture. 3-D printing provides an agile alternative to traditional MTS process management due to the opportunity to manufacture locally reducing P-time (see Section 5.3). Therefore, decentralising production at a cost which is not prohibitive is becoming a reality for many businesses.

- *Customised products:* 3-D printing provides the opportunity for engineering-to-order as the CODP is moved upstream allowing for high levels of customisation and perceived value by customers (Rylands et al., 2016). Each design can be unique to an individual customer and the batch size can be one, offering a truly personalised product. Further, the flexibility and agility of the technology enables businesses to decouple design and engineering activities from where actual manufacturing occurs.
- Though the technology is still relatively new for many businesses it has begun to cause disruptions in how supply chains deliver value. 3-D printing is appearing in a myriad of sectors including aerospace, automotive, food, healthcare and military. Through its ability to produce small quantities, flexibly, quickly and a relatively lower cost, businesses are actively deploying the technology to gain a competitive advantage. 3-D printing is supporting the movement of the CODP upstream to provide customised solutions. This is leading to a reduction in P-time in a manner similar to the impact of automation (see Section 5.4). However, this is not the only significant change as the technology also supports the production of more complex products with fewer components than would historically be required, leading to the lowering of inventory costs and number of suppliers. Bringing the manufacturing of previously outsourced components inhouse is displacing historical suppliers while introducing new vendors of printers and the specialist printing material (Figure 7.12).

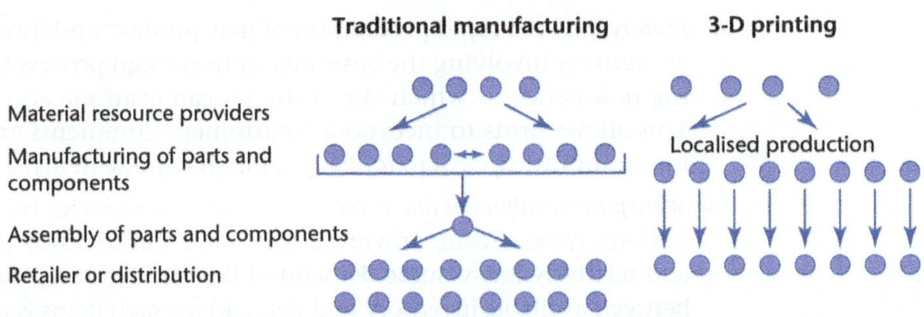

Figure 7.12 Traditional supply chain compared to the supply chain for 3-D printing with localised production.
(Source: Thomas and Gilbert, 2015.)

3-D printing provides an alternative approach to design and manufacture of products across a wide range of sectors. Most experts agree, however, that it is a complement, rather than a direct competitor, to high volume products due to the low unit costs and high output per hour of mass manufacturing.

7.2.3 Logistics for agility

Through focusing on improving customer experience and end-customer demand, logistics organisations have developed responsive and adaptable distribution networks capable of delivering small volumes quickly and reliably. Digital technologies such as barcode readers, electronic signature capture, tracking software and hardware, i.e. radio frequency identification devices (RFID) tags, and improved reporting functions, support the rapid movement and delivery of products across networks. However, digitalisation of the processes used to deliver customer value is only one aspect of the changes which are increasing the agility of logistics operators. Automation and robotics (Section 5.4.3) have also reduced the transit time through the warehouse/distribution centre, as well as the cost of labour to pick products. Likewise, improved transport routing, transport mode selection and machine learning has reduced waste in miles travelled, while improving the responsiveness of the distribution system.

Focusing upon customers and what they value has led to the establishment of a network of parcel pick-up and drop-off locations. Recognising the value of time to customers, parcel distributors have developed alternative delivery mechanisms to provide greater flexibility in terms of location and time. This has reduced the frustration experienced by customers when they are not at home to receive parcels as well as the costs associated with failed deliveries and fixed delivery time windows across individual customer delivery locations. The solutions which have been developed satisfy customers' demand for flexibility, while optimising the cost of delivery through consolidation of shipments. Distribution companies have developed new innovative approaches to storing and delivering products. Some have expanded pick-up points by forming a network of small, independent high street retailers where customers can drop off and receive parcels. In the UK, Hermes and collect plus have over 5,000 and 7,000 collection points, respectively. Others have installed specialised automated parcel storage lockers at petrol stations and large supermarkets. This removes the need for sales engineers to travel to a central location to pick up equipment as these can now be sent to local 24-hour accessible lockers. Morganti et al., (2014) report that in Germany, DHL/Deutsche Post have over 2,500 lockers while in France over 90 per cent of the population is less than a 10-minute drive (or a 10-minute walk in cities) from a locker.

These significant service and infrastructure changes, which place the customer at the centre of the supply chain, have greatly increased the responsiveness and flexibility of logistics operations. Digital and infrastructure innovation has improved the agility of logistics operators; however, organisations are also investing in different types of equipment used to deliver products. Road congestion continues to be a major source of delays and costs, especially in the last mile logistics. To overcome these barriers some businesses are looking towards the sky and investigating the use of drones.

Drones

Drones have become synonymous with military applications and as consumer toys; however, their future as practical logistics tools is beginning to show promise. For example, within the field of humanitarian logistics these remote-controlled flying machines are actively being used in the mapping of disaster sites and delivery of medicines to areas cut off by natural catastrophes. They provide unparalleled and quick access to difficult terrains, particularly in the agile responsive phase of a humanitarian crisis (see Chapter 10 for more on the stages of humanitarian logistics).

Drones have begun to be deployed within day-to-day commerce, creating the opportunity to make a positive change to society, particularly to those in rural and remote areas. Across the globe countries and businesses are developing prototype services to exploit the agility of drones. These initiatives include the following:

- In Rwanda, Zipline operates a commercial service delivering blood supplies packaged inside containers attached to biodegradable parachutes.
- Swiss Post is working with the Ticino EOC hospital group and drone manufacturer Matternet to deliver laboratory samples autonomously between two EOC hospitals in Lugano.
- Google is piloting drone food deliveries in Australia.
- DHL, with its Parcelcopter 3.0, is conducting trials in Alpine areas for transporting goods to remote or geographically challenging locations.
- Amazon has been trialling deliveries within the UK using autonomous drones to deliver packages weighing up to 2.25 kg within 30 minutes.
- Royal Mail (UK) have commenced daily drone deliveries to small islands of the coast of northern Scotland.

However, there still exists a significant gap between the publicity the technology is attracting and actual usage. Currently, several organisations are running pilots to experiment with drones. Logisticians are currently faced with many major challenges to the effective use of the technology. Regulators of airspace have yet to establish rules and legislation around the commercial use of drones. Concerns exist regarding the use of airspace and potential conflicts with aircraft. Other legislative issues which need to be addressed relate to citizens' privacy and possible surveillance use. Regardless of these issues. however, several major logistics businesses are investing heavily in drone technology (and supporting big data infrastructure) which will offer greater agility in the future to address the challenges of increasing internet sales and road congestion.

The disruptive nature of drone and 3D technologies is forcing businesses to reassess where and how they manufacture, as well as revaluating the relationships they have with customers and suppliers. The relationships and partnerships which can support changes in such a dynamic and agile environment are discussed in the next section.

7.2.4 Supply chain partnerships for agility

Relationships could be described as the critical success factor of many agile supply chains, which are dependent on a network of supply chain partners that collaborate to meet the end-customer needs by making available their resources to each other. Earlier in this chapter we compared lean and agile, indicating that fluid clusters (such as the supply networks in Section 8.6) – that are frequently reconfigured – are required in agile supply chains, whereas lean supply chains depend on long-term stable partnerships. However, herein lies a paradox: on the one hand agile supply chain relationships can be described as highly involved strategic partnerships, but on the other hand they are frequently reconfigured, which suggests a short-term relationship. This is contrary to the conventional (*stable*) strategic partnerships (described in Sections 8.3 and 8.4), which are expected to have a long duration, in part due to the investment of resource (time and effort) required to establish them and, indeed, the cost of terminating such a relationship.

Agile versus stable supply partnerships

Literature describing agile supply partnerships (high involvement, short term, HI-ST) highlights four characteristics that contribute to overcoming the apparent paradox of partnerships in an agile supply chain. They:

1. are part of a portfolio of both short-term and long-term high-involvement relationships;
2. have project-based features with a clear shared and common goal to be completed within a given time frame, e.g. large construction projects (Gadde and Dubois, 2010);
3. are developed, starting from a group of pre-qualified suppliers with whom the company is collaborating intensively on a recurrent, if not necessarily continuous, basis (Christopher et al., 2004); and
4. are supported by organisational procedures and information technology (IT) tools aimed at creating a standard platform for supply relationship management, to reduce the loss of administrative and operational efficiencies related to a supplier change (Baramichai et al., 2007).

Studying the fashion industry, which requires agility due to its short life cycles, high volatility and low predictability, Cerruti (2013) investigated the types and characteristics of supply partnerships to achieve agility. He proposed a supply partnership portfolio model, shown in Figure 7.13, which defines four types of relationships on the basis of two dimensions: degree of involvement and duration of the supply relationship.

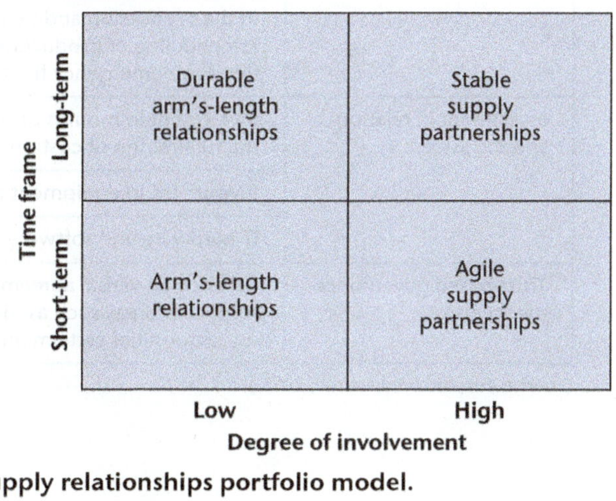

Figure 7.13 Supply relationships portfolio model.
(Source: Cerruti, 2013.)

Here, a high degree of involvement between a footwear manufacturer and its suppliers of leather and soles, is related to inter-firm knowledge-sharing routines, investment in relation-specific assets and a trust-based governance mechanism (as shown in Table 7.5). An example is the collaboration required to design a high and thin heel for women's shoes, providing an aggressive fashion look but also the required stability. The time frame of the relationship is evaluated in relation to the industry clock speed (Fine, 1998). So, for instance, in the fashion industry, the clock speed is related to the development and delivery of the seasonal fashion collections, normally two collections per year (Spring/Summer and Autumn/Winter). Therefore, Cerruti et al., (2016) considered a supply relationship with an uninterrupted sequence of purchasing orders for more than four seasons to be 'long-term'.

This matrix covers the familiar arm's-length relationships (low-involvement and short-term) and stable supply partnerships (high-involvement and long-term). In addition, it also defines two further options: durable arm's-length relationships (low-involvement and long-term) and agile supply partnerships (high-involvement and short-term). Durable arm's-length relationships are distant relationships maintained over a long period of time, which 'minimise procurement (transaction) costs; allow suppliers to maximise economies of scale, which is critical...; and maintain vigorous competition' (Dyer et al., 1998). Agile supply partnerships, whilst potentially short-lived, are not created by chance, or in an extemporary way, but are the result of deliberate investments (as to IT infrastructure, organisational procedures and/or supplier pre-qualification) aimed at acquiring future degrees of freedom.

Table 7.5 Indicators of high-involvement relationships.

Indicators	Examples specific to the footwear manufacturers
Inter-firm knowledge-sharing routine	In the collection development, the contribution to product development and industrialisation
	In the production and delivery phase, collaboration in the rescheduling of production and delivery plans related to the frequent 'emergency fighting'
Investment in relation-specific asset	Investment in moulds or other tools dedicated to the manufacturing of customised items
	Investment in equipment required for customised processes
	IT hardware and software supporting data exchange
Trust-based governance mechanism	Reliance on verbal agreement (versus formal contracts) with respect to areas such as: delivery timing; schedule replanning; or unconformities settlement

(Source: Adapted from Cerruti, 2013.)

Supply partnerships required for agile supply chains

In agile supply chains, both stable and agile supply partnerships are required, but what are the criteria for determining the suitable approach? Cerruti (2013) found that the type of strategic supply partnership (stable long-term or agile short-term) is dependent on the characteristics of the component/service (the extent to which it is impacted by the fashion look) and on the degree of turbulence an agile strategy is designed to face.

Cerruti et al., (2016) studied footwear companies, and their suppliers, in the Macerata-Fermo district, the largest footwear district in Italy. Footwear companies consider agile supply partnerships for categories of supply materials that are sensitive to the fashion trends, such as the leather upper on shoes. They can have 25–30 different leather upper suppliers every season, changing and adding them in order to get a fashion 'look' in line with the expected market trend or simply to provide more variety. These materials are difficult to be sourced in a stable way - season after season - from the same suppliers.

The use of agile supply partnerships is particularly strong in the case of footwear companies that:

- are subject to high-turbulence agility drivers: a high proportion of each seasonal collection was renewed; and
- had developed strong agile capabilities: a local, as opposed to remote, supply network and postponed purchase orders.

In an agile supply chain, strategic supply partnerships, whether agile or stable, aim to focus the distinct capabilities provided by each company on the end-customer. Nowhere do you see this done more successfully than at Li & Fung, who configure and coordinate agile supply chains.

CASE STUDY 7.4

Li & Fung – configuring the agile supply chain

Li & Fung is a Hong Kong based company that was established in the early 1900s as a mediator between Chinese-speaking sellers and English-speaking buyers. A century later it is one of the world's leading textile exporters (the largest into the USA) and generates a turnover of US$12.7 billion (2018), 70 per cent of which is from the US and European markets. Soft goods, such as apparel, account for about 70 per cent of sales, whilst hard goods (e.g. toys, footwear and beauty) make up the rest.

A global supply network

By 2012 Li & Fung had established a global network of 240 sourcing offices across 40 economies and now employs 27,000 people. This enables it to configure and coordinate a vast global supply network across Europe, USA, Asia and Southern Africa, including

15,000 regular suppliers in 60 countries (2019). It configures the entire supply chain (as shown in Figure 7.14) for its clients, which include household brands like Disney, Levi's and Reebok. Depending upon the client requirement, it begins with product design, using an in-depth understanding of consumer needs, and it finishes with delivery into the retailer. Despite this, it is known as a 'smokeless factory' since it doesn't own manufacturing facilities.

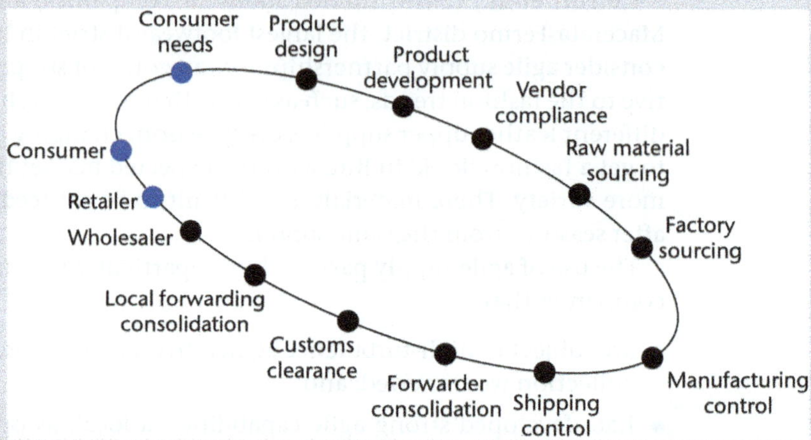

Figure 7.14 The supply chain processes that Li & Fung configure and coordinate.

Li & Fung ensures there is plenty of capacity by employing independent suppliers in parallel for the same components (e.g. yarn providers, weavers, assemblers). This has two key advantages: it allows reduction of lead times and, should unforeseen manufacturing problems occur, production can be switched quickly to another supplier.

To drive down costs, Li & Fung shifts activities to countries with low labour costs, low taxes and favourable regulations, leading to a globally dispersed supply chain, as shown in Figure 7.15, for Levi's jeans. In the past this has meant sourcing from emerging economies to supply the developed world. However, the three-year plan (2011–2013) declared that, with the emergence of consumer markets in China, and Asia in general, Li

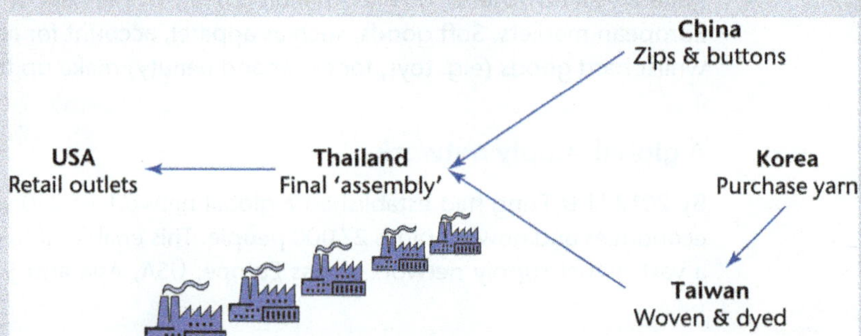

Figure 7.15 Globally dispersed manufacturing processes for Levi's jeans.

& Fung had to reverse the direction of flow for the first time in its history. The company needed to source everywhere, including the developed world, and sell to the developing world.

Supplier management

Li & Fung typically utilises between 30 and 70 per cent of a supplier's capacity to ensure that, on the one hand, they are an important customer but, on the other, the supplier is not entirely dependent on their business. Suppliers enjoy detailed performance feedback based on benchmarking across the network, giving them the opportunity to not only satisfy Li & Fung's stringent requirements but also improve their competitiveness. In any case, there is a strong incentive for suppliers to improve their performance – Li & Fung can provide ample and steady business.

Quick response is a key priority to ensure manufacturing can respond to fluctuating demand without excessive mark-downs or stock-outs. This is achieved by reserving capacity with suppliers on the basis of blanket orders and providing a detailed order breakdown (by size, style and colour) near the time of manufacture – postponed purchasing. In addition, short production runs are expected so production can be altered in tandem with market trends.

Moving forward the business faces challenges on multiple fronts. Fast-fashion brands continue to disrupt the historical structure of the retail market, along with the growth of internet firms such as Amazon and Alibaba, who all source directly. Simultaneously, global trade-war tensions have increased the tariffs on goods sourced from China, reducing the competitiveness of Li & Fung's main souring location (2018). These changes are undermining the successful business model of Li & Fung.

(Source: Based on data and information from Gupta and Radika (2005), McFarlan et al., (2012), and Faheem and Purkayastha, 2020.)

Questions

1. How does Li & Fung enable agile manufacturing?
2. To what extent does Li & Fung develop partnerships with its suppliers and are they 'agile supply partnerships'?
3. How could Li & Fung use its supply network to address the challenges created by global trade-wars?

7.2.5 Preconditions for successful agile practice

In addition to the above supply capabilities within the supply chain, there is another set of factors that need to be in place for the agile principles and practices to pay off or work at all. These are related to cross-functional alignment and enterprise-level focus on the contribution of logistics management and strategy. If revenue-generating functions (e.g. sales and marketing) in particular do not adopt at least a base-level understanding of agile principles, all efforts within logistics may be wasted. And if there is not an enterprise-wide focus on the potential value of logistics, agile efforts are not going to be recognised for what they are worth – and might not provide a compelling enough business case for the possible investment in them to be made. We propose an *enterprise-level reality check* and a *cost of complexity sanity check* before investing in agile capabilities. We also argue that service measures must put the customer first.

Enterprise-level reality check

Starting with the enterprise-wide context, most senior managers know that turning to logistics and the supply chain is a 'good call' when times get tough. Logistics probably gets mentioned most in earnings reports when cost cutting is a response offered to poor performance. In spite of its potential to contribute to cost-saving programmes, the value of logistics should not be seen as a first port of call when the bottom line needs to be improved. Agility centres on the notion of winning in the marketplace based upon service and responsiveness. Whilst such a strategy can be aimed at doing more for less, it may actually – and more importantly – be doing less to earn more. Top line improvement can flow from outperforming competitors through responsiveness to customer needs. Delivery speed and reliability can be such important sources of productivity to customers that we can earn more of their business and/or charge a premium price for the service, driving increased revenues.

In addition, in a retail supply chain the improved availability, provided by effective agile logistics processes, has the potential to increases sales. In short, an enterprise-level recognition of the contribution of logistics to increases in revenue, as well as improvements in efficiencies, is a precondition for any business case on agile practices.

Cost of complexity sanity check

The value potential of logistics can be capitalised on only if other functions comply with another key precondition: lowering the cost of complexity where differentiation has no competitive value. As much as agility principles are based on the notion that differentiation is good and 'do-able', it does not mean that revenue groups (e.g. sales and marketing) should be given carte blanche to create proliferating service, product assortments and promotions. There are limits to how much value that variety creates, and the extent to which these demands can be met without the cost of complexity spiralling out of control, even for the most agile supply chain. The key point is not to exceed the capability of the supply chain to deliver the marketing promise.

Three examples illustrate the cost of complexity:

- Product, packaging and stock-keeping-unit proliferation, leading to extremes of 80 per cent or more of products not even generating 1 per cent of revenue.
- Delivery speed is too high, resulting in increased costs for the customer because products arrive too early. This increases handling, storage and related costs.
- Promotions and special events that cause upswings in demand based on sales efforts, not on true customer demand. This in turn leads to downswings shortly thereafter.

Whilst differentiation of logistics service can generate short-term gain, the question that revenue-enhancing proposals need to answer is 'will it do so profitably?' Adding a product feature, offering special delivery service and timetables, and engaging in a special promotion might help close a deal in the market in the short term. But such deals can also create added logistics and supply chain costs that are not compensated for by the added revenue. One executive from a manufacturing company put it well:

When we showed the financial impact of certain deals our sales teams had closed, it made them realise there were certain deals we should have walked away from.

Even though it may be hard to assess economic gain or pain from product/service differentiation, reality can be checked by asking questions and pursuing actions that help to reduce non-value-added costs of complexity, such as:

- Has the organisation conducted an analysis of revenue contribution by SKU?
  - *Often a large proportion of SKUs contribute an incredibly small proportion of the revenue.* Remember, some product proliferation produces only short-term sales gains. Consider using a revenue threshold for maintaining a given SKU.
- Does the organisation have a process for reviewing the product portfolio at least annually?
  - *One-off SKU reductions do not address the ongoing tendency to proliferate SKUs over time.* There must be a limit to the number of product variations that the market can absorb? Do customers really value, or even recognise, the new flavour/colour/recipe?
- Are there hard revenue forecasts related to promotion requests that can be evaluated?
  - *Revenue upside potential is used most often to justify adding events and SKUs. Reviewing real sales impact after the event helps force discipline.*
- Is the profitability, as well as revenue contributions, reviewed at SKU level?
  - *Are added warehousing and distribution costs offset against added revenue potential?*
- Do customers *really* want fast delivery, or is reliable delivery more important, even when slower? Do customers want delivery whenever they ask for it?
  - *Understanding what the customers really value about the delivery service is crucial.*
- Are those people ordering shipments aware of the cost of rush orders and are they asked to organise shipment around real and explicit customer requests?
  - *Ticking the 'ASAP' ('as soon as possible') box on a shipment form may become standard behaviour, irrespective of customer need.*

Heineken, the brewer, offers a powerful example of the fourth (profitability) point. During a recent Christmas season it introduced a special product for promotion in the market – the magnum bottle. This seasonal promotion and product won several marketing prizes, and created a lot of buzz (or fizz, even!) in the marketplace. It was also a product that suffered from substantial added shipment, packaging and production costs because different production line set-ups, bottles, labels and boxes were needed for a very limited demand window. Was it worth the effort and focus of the responsive capabilities that were needed for a short-term gain in revenue?

Another powerful illustration of the promotions issue is a tactic that one executive calls the 'warehouse dust test':

> **We take our sales people through our warehouse when they come to us asking for new products and promotions and show them the dust levels on other promotional products and product variations that we stock. We ask them, 'Which products can be discontinued when we introduce a new product?'** *or,* **'Do we need the new product to begin with?'**

An important approach to driving improvements in customer service that the customer values is to measure it from the customer perspective.

Develop measures that put the end-customer first

All companies include customer service in some form in their performance measurement system. However, almost all operationalise this measurement internally, leading to responsiveness that is misguided and focused incorrectly, thereby limiting network integration across the supply chain. In particular, most companies measure delivery service in one or multiple ways based upon their internal definition of success. Typically, the measures focus on how reliably and quickly the company delivered against the timetable it put forward. This misses the point, as this timetable might not be aligned with end-customers' needs at all. So companies are not tracking responsiveness to these needs. It is much better to ask customers for their desired delivery window and measure execution against that customer-defined measure of success. General Electric realised this when it presented high delivery reliability scores from its own measurement to customers and received a negative reaction. Customers said performance was not as high at all by their measurement, against when they needed deliveries to take place.

GE changed its measurement set towards what it calls 'Span' measurement. Span stands for the range of delivery around customer-requested due dates. Essentially, the company now measures, across all deliveries globally, how close it was to the delivery date the customer requested when ordering. In its plastics business the company brought Span down from 30 days to just a few days within a matter of months. This means that every customer can depend upon GE delivering any product, anywhere in the globe, when they ask for it, with a maximum variation of just a few days.

The experience of GE suggests the value of several actions to improve measurement for agility:

- Share measurement dashboards with customers.
- Do not measure against your own measures of success; ask the customer what defines success for them.
- Hold all parts of the supply chain accountable against the customer-defined measure of success so that there is no escape from market sensitivity.

7.3 Combining lean and agile

As discussed earlier, there is no reason why there should be an 'either-or' approach to logistics strategy. In any case, lean approaches should be applied wherever possible, as agility always costs more. Lean and agile can be combined in three main ways, as described in Table 7.6.

Table 7.6 Three main approaches to combining lean and agile.

Hybrid strategies	Appropriate market conditions
Pareto analysis across a product range – 80:20 Use lean methods for the volume lines and agile methods for the slow movers	High levels of variety Demand is heavily skewed towards a small proportion of the product range
Decoupling point The aim is to be lean up to the decoupling point and agile beyond it, as in form postponement	Product design allows for this so the product remains generic in the early stages of manufacture, e.g. design for supply chain
Separate volatile and base demand for a given SKU Meet the forecastable element of demand using lean principles and use agile principles for the less predictable demand	Where base level of demand can be confidently predicted from past experience

(Source: Adapted from Christopher and Towill, 2001.)

Considering the three approaches, the Pareto analysis 80:20 strategy proposes using a lean approach for the SKUs accounting for, say, 80 per cent of sales and an agile approach for the remaining long tail of SKUs accounting for, say, only 20 per cent of sales. This effectively segments on the basis of demand volume only, but some SKUs, subject to high volume demand, may also be subject to high demand variability, as shown by the Kimberly-Clark Case study 2.5 in Chapter 2.

In the second approach, where a decoupling point is located when the product is still in a generic form, lean can be used up to the decoupling point and agile beyond it, as shown in Figure 7.16. Form postponement, explained in Section 7.2.2, results in this configuration. The third approach is where the predictable stable demand for an SKU is satisfied with a lean approach and the unpredictable variable demand for the same SKU is fulfilled with an agile approach.

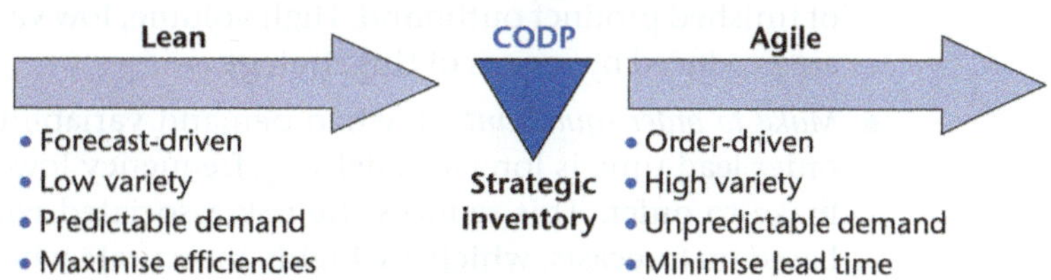

Figure 7.16 Combination of lean and agile using a customer order decoupling point (CODP).

All three of these approaches to combining lean and agile are relevant, but the application of lean and agile strategies should be driven by what the market needs. The approach to segmented supply chain strategy explained in Section 2.3 describes how supply chain strategy drivers (demand, competitive and product) can be used to determine the appropriate supply chain strategy, which may employ lean and agile approaches. Accordingly, the driver matrix in Figure 7.17 provides an example of how specific elements of the competitive profile (lead time and delivery frequency) and demand profile (demand variability) can be used to segment the SKUs and determine the appropriate segmented strategies.

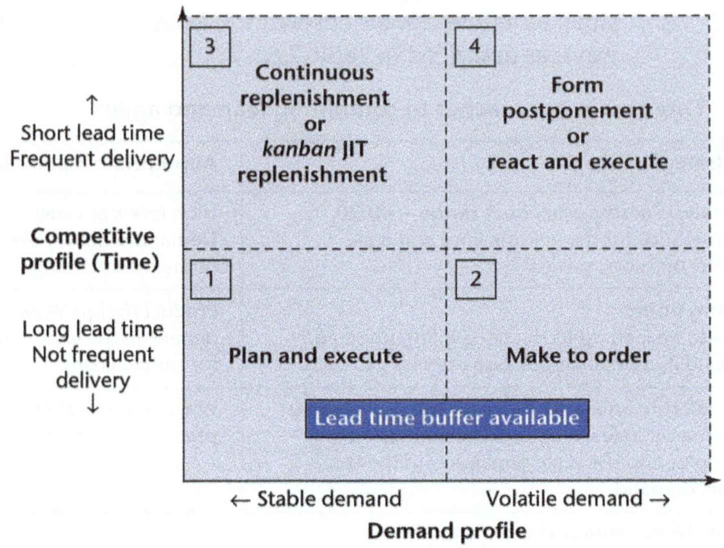

Figure 7.17 An example of a driver matrix showing four supply chain strategies.
(Source: Adapted from Christopher, 2011, p. 101.)

Supply chain strategies 1 and 3 in the diagram are lean approaches where demand is stable, whereas strategy 4 is agile where not only is demand volatile but also a short lead time is required. The four supply chain strategies are described in more detail next:

- *Plan and execute (quadrant 1):* this is the least demanding situation where demand is stable and the lead time is long. This allows a plan and execute approach where economic batch quantities are used for production and waste is minimised through the most efficient methods of production and delivery by reducing waste in the system. This strategy can be prone to excessive inventories of finished product outbound. High volume, low variety auto products typically are produced by means of this strategy.
- *Make to order (quadrant 2):* when demand variability is high (volatile), yet the order lead time is long and delivery frequency low, there is the opportunity to make to order. This reduces the risk associated with speculative manufacture based on forecasts, which are highly inaccurate when demand is volatile.
- *Continuous replenishment or kanban JIT replenishment (lean) (quadrant 3):* if we take the situation where demand is stable but lead times are short and deliveries frequent, then some type of continuous replenishment system is appropriate where deliveries are made on a regular and frequent basis, say daily, or a *kanban* pull system is operated. Both these approaches are part of a lean approach and depend on stable demand. Fast-moving consumer products are examples where continuous replenishment strategies are most often used.

- *Form postponement or react and execute (agile) (quadrant 4):* in the most challenging situation where demand is volatile and lead time is short, a react and execute approach is required, akin to an agile approach. This strategy prioritises investment in reducing lead time, and building up processes that can respond quickly to volatile demand. If, despite investment in lead-time reduction, the order lead time is still too short to allow full manufacture, the manufacture of the generic product can be conducted speculatively and the final manufacture or assembly can be postponed, as in form postponement.

CASE STUDY 7.5

Vintage Bentley Supply Chain

William Medcalf Limited (WML) renovates and rally preps 100-year-old vintage Bentleys for a global market. The small company is based in the Southeast of England and employs skilled craftspeople in the manufacture of components, refurbishment and rally preparation of cars manufactured in the 1920s. The original cars were tailor made to the requirements of the owner and are unique in terms of the design and construction of the coachwork. (The original car bodies were built by experts in the manufacture of carriages for horse-drawn vehicles).

The provenance of the cars is important to current owners; therefore, any renovations must align with the strict regulations of the Bentley owners club. These limit changes to parts like the chassis and engine. However, new owners are at liberty to upgrade and change the coachwork to suit their tastes. This provides an opportunity and challenge to WML as the business has the possibility of operating on a lean MTS approach for reoccurring parts and an agile MTO strategy for unique items designed in conjunction with the customer.

Figure 7.18 **Car chassis and engine.**

(Source: Vintage Bentley, Second in Class at Pebble Beach, 21 August 2022, William Medcalf Limited.)

WML produces and assembles many items in its own engineering shop; however, there is still a requirement to purchase parts from external suppliers and major subassemblies such as coachwork. The complexity in the supply chain requires the control and monitoring of four different supply chain strategies to meet and deliver the demanding customer requirements found in 100-year-old Bentleys. The four approaches are shown in Figure 7.19

	Make-to-stock	**Form postponement**
Short lead-time	(In-house production of regular use parts such as suspension brackets)	(Adjustment of generic items to fit car-specific requirements)
	Order-to-stock	**Engineer-to-order**
Long lead-time	(External supplier with long lead-times such as radiators)	(Subassemblies such as coach-works)
	Catalogued parts	Bespoke parts

The quadruple supply chain strategies of WML support a century-old product; however they reflect modern lean and agile practices. Balancing the different approaches requires management controls that blend forecast-driven and efficiency-driven production activities with bespoke and customer design-led items. Within the business this major challenge is met through a combination of systems to plan in-house production, form postponement of customised generic parts, supplier capacity agreements to reserve slots in long lead-time schedules and subcontractor relationship management. WML is a small business that has successfully combined lean and agile to deliver value demonstrating that these concepts are open to all organisations regardless of size.

Question

1. Which inventory management approach would be suitable for each of the quadrants and why? (Refer to Section 6.1.3.)

Deciding upon which supply chain strategy to opt for is a significant step forward for any organisation; however, it still requires skilled personnel and visionary leadership to realise the opportunity and potential that the strategy offers. Case study 7.6 provides an example of a business that has successfully deployed and nurtured a lean and agile approach to deliver value to the customer and the company.

CASE STUDY 7.6

Lean and agile leadership

DW Windsor is a service-led manufacturer of exterior lighting that delivers road and street lighting products and design services to clients globally from their world-class production facility. The business was established in the late 1970s and has continued to flourish through innovation and investing in its people. Within the assembly department of DW Windsor there are two very different sections and processes, reflecting the characteristics of the products they are manufacturing. The low-volume, high-variety agile area assembles bespoke lighting items tailored to specific client needs. The higher-volume, lower-variety lean section manufactures products which are more standardised in terms of components, assembly processes and material flows. Operating within and providing leadership of these two distinct areas is an everyday challenge for DW Windsor assembly management.

Lean and agile assembly areas

The high-volume, low-variety lean area requires employees to conduct repetitive tasks for the duration of their shift while working at a constant tempo and maintaining consistent attention to detail. The ability to produce high quality at a constant rate is critical for the productivity and delivery performance of the area. Any deviation from the standard processes could result in re-work or a customer receiving a product that does not meet the required quality standard. Failure of the assembly line to work at the constant tempo will not only result in an unbalanced line, but it could also potentially cause larger-scale problems with regard to logistics. Customer delivery failures and interruptions to material flows from suppliers delivering through JIT will occur if the assembly line does not adhere to its planned schedule.

The low-volume, high-variety agile assembly area operates with standard operating procedures (SOPs) similar to the lean area as both are required to manufacture high-quality and tested lighting products. However, the processes used to assemble MTO bespoke items are extremely varied requiring highly skilled individuals who can work independently while remaining aware of assembly times and customer deadlines. Operating in the agile area requires employees to have multiple skills, a methodical manner and the ability to adapt to sudden changes in what is required of them. Lean and agile manufacturing approaches each require a significantly different skill and personality profile in employees. Chris Gucci, production manager, encapsulates the differences as follows:

> **The skill set is not so much about training and more about the personality of the individual. An individual who had previously worked in an agile manufacturing system would potentially struggle to adapt to the lean working conditions due to the repetitive nature of the tasks. In contrast, an individual who enjoys the lean approach to working may find the agile area challenging due to the apparent 'unstructured' way people have to self-organise their assembly tasks.**

▶

The skill requirements of the team members operating in the two areas is shown in Table 7.7.

Table 7.7 Lean vs agile skills matrix.

Skill	Lean environment	Agile environment
Trained in multiple operations	✓	✓
Ability to work to standard procedures	✓	✓
Ability to deviate from standard procedures to allow for customisable options		✓
Ability to use skills and creativity to complete task to correct quality		✓
Ability to conduct repetitive tasks	✓	
Ability to work at constant tempo	✓	
Ability to problem solve		✓
Can respond quickly to changes		✓
Can work in a methodical manner	✓	✓
Highly responsible		✓
Ability to self-organise		✓

Lean and agile leaders

Each of the two assembly areas in DW Windsor has different team leaders to oversee and support the operators and processes in delivering quality products and service. The team leaders of lean and agile assembly areas have similarities as well as differences in their skill sets that reflect the characteristics of the product and process they manage. All leaders are required to be self-motivated and organised, and have the ability to assess and transfer knowledge and lead change. They are also expected to have a knowledge of lean principles to aid them in driving improvements through identifying what is value added and what is waste. Having the ability to identify problems and resolve them before they occur is another very important aspect of their roles. If a problem can be identified and resolved before reaching the respective lines, this will eliminate or reduce any downtime that might have otherwise occurred.

Within the lean environment the team leader is expected to have a knowledge of every aspect of the assembly process and be able to communicate and demonstrate this to his or her team members in a way that allows the operator to then carry out the task to the desired quality level and within the allotted time. Agile team leaders must also have the ability to flexibly move resources within their area to meet changes in demand or process complexity while maintaining performance. In order to achieve this, they must have a knowledge of all aspects of the process and be able to match team members' skills to the tasks required or to source skills from outside their teams to enable them to deliver an on-time customisable solution.

Questions

1. Why might someone operating in the agile assembly area of DW Windsor struggle to work in the lean area and how could these issues be addressed by the team leaders?
2. Combining lean and agile operations within DW Windsor has been successful. What type of relationship would you expect the supply base that supports both areas to have with each of them?
3. What inventory management approaches would you suggest for the two areas?

The vision of creating an agile supply chain is a valuable starting point but until recently it was little more than a vision. The experiences and cases presented in this section show how the vision can be realised and how the implementation of agility can be approached practically.

Summary

What is lean thinking, and how does it apply to logistics?

- Lean thinking is a philosophy that has been derived from JIT principles. It seeks perfection by gradually reducing waste from each of four areas: specifying value from the end-customer perspective; identifying the value stream through time-based mapping; making the product flow through the supply network by applying JIT principles; and letting the customer pull through application of pull scheduling.
- Longstanding approaches to material control, such as reorder point stock control, economic order and economic batch quantities (EOQ and EBQ) and material requirements planning (MRP), can be made to be far more responsive by the application of lean principles. Examples include reduction of batch sizes, reorder quantities and lead times. All of these help to reduce logistics P-times.

What is agility, and how does it compare to lean?

- Agility is a supply-chain-wide capability that aligns organisational structures, information systems, logistics processes and, in particular, mindsets. It means using market knowledge and a responsive supply chain to exploit profitable opportunities in a volatile marketplace. Agile supply is concerned with developing capabilities proactively to position a supply chain to benefit from marketplaces in which product lifecycles are shrinking, product variety is increasing and the ability to forecast demand is reducing.

- Lean thinking is concerned primarily with the elimination of waste. The order winners that are supported by this mindset are cost and quality. Agility is concerned primarily with supporting order winners of speed and flexible response. Time compression is a fundamental requirement for leanness, but only one of the enablers of agility.
- A key difference in supply strategy is that lean thinking is concerned with placing orders upstream for products that move in a regular flow.
- Agile strategy is concerned with assigning capacity so that products can be made rapidly to meet demand that is difficult to forecast.

What are the agile practices that help to underpin the agile supply chain?

- The important capabilities required for an agile supply chain are being market sensitive and network-based, and also having process integration and virtual integration, and these are necessary to meet both predictable and unpredictable demand variability. Practices to enable agility are many and span planning, product design, manufacturing and supply partnerships.
- Agile supply chains are a response to shortening product life cycles, typical of fashion products, and proliferating product variants. Crucial to achieving market sensitivity necessary for agility is the capability to develop products quickly and efficiently. Equally, once in production, the associated costs and speed are just as important. Both these goals can be achieved through product development being coordinated with supply chain design (manufacturing, sourcing and logistics).
- Agility requires responsive and flexible manufacturing, which can be adapted quickly to new products and accommodate changes in mix (range of variants) and volume of production with minimum cost or time penalties. One important approach is form postponement, which involves the delay of the differentiation manufacturing process until receipt of a customer order, thereby allowing a high variety product to be supplied on a short lead time with minimum inventory support. Another important development is 3-D printing, which offers the potential to manufacture customised items at a lower cost and more quickly than traditional manufacturing approaches.
- Agile logistics provides consumers with the opportunity to benefit from shorter lead times with deliveries tailored to their individual needs. Adaptable distribution networks are capable of delivering small volumes quickly and reliably without a prohibitive cost to the consumer. Advances in drone technology also suggest that aerial deliveries could become a regular mode of transport in the future, providing support and assistance to difficult-to-access areas as well as ensuring faster delivery of parcels in cities.
- Relationships could be described as the critical success factor of many agile supply chains, which are dependent on a network of supply chain partners that collaborate to meet the end-customer's needs by making their resources available to each other. However, whilst agile supply chain relationships can be described as highly involved strategic partnerships, they are frequently reconfigured, which suggests a short-term relationship. Agile partnerships are proposed but these

cannot be used exclusively across the supply base; stable partnerships are still required.

- Preconditions for successful agile practice include an 'enterprise-level reality check' – senior managers need to appreciate that logistics contributes to competitive advantage not just costs. A 'cost of complexity sanity check' is also a precondition to ensure, for instance, product variants are adding value and not just cost. Finally, developing measures that put the end-customer first and are developed from their perspective is essential for an agile supply chain.
- Lean and agile approaches can be combined in different ways to meet changing market needs. Building on the ideas of segmented supply chain strategy, presented in Chapter 2, it is important that lean and agile strategies are combined in order to meet changing market needs, as defined by strategy drivers – demand, competitive and product.

Discussion questions

1. Suggest order winning and order qualifying criteria for the following product environments:
   a. reprocessing nuclear fuel;
   b. upstream petroleum refining;
   c. downstream manufacture of petroleum products;
   d. high-value automotive products, such as Range Rover or BMW 5 series.
2. To what extent would lean and agile mindsets contribute to the support of such products in the marketplace?
3. What matters more: value to the customer or value to the shareholder? Refer to Section 3.7 when formulating your response. How does this question impact on the philosophy of lean thinking?
4. What is meant by the term *overproduction*? Why do you think this has been described as the biggest waste of all?
5. Explain the difference between surge and base demands. Multi Electronique SA (ME) produces a range of electrical connectors for the automotive industry. Currently, the six production lines at its factory in Toulouse are fully loaded, operating a three-shift system for five days per week. One of ME's major customers wants to place an order that would add loading equivalent to a seventh production line, but only for the summer months (May to September). Sales are keen to accept the new order, but it would need to be taken at prices that are no higher than for current business. Suggest options for how ME might manage this order if they accepted it.
6. Refer back to Figure 2.2 in Chapter 2: it shows a Pareto curve for the sales per SKU of a book stockist. A small number of 'hot sellers' constitute most of the sales, whilst there is a lengthy tail of slow-selling lines and new introductions. The operations people are pressing for the 'tail' to be chopped in half, arguing that it adds cost, not value, to the business. They argue that each order is taken at fixed cost, regardless of size. Sales order processing and pick and dispatch from the warehouse are examples of such fixed costs. 'Instead, we should focus on the core of the business: 90 per cent of our business comes from just 10 per cent of the titles,' the operations

director argues. 'We could chop our costs in half and lose only 5–7 per cent of the business. Think of the effect on margin!' Sales, on the other hand, are reluctant to give up any of the titles, arguing that it is customer choice that drives the business. 'We have built up this business on the strength of our product range,' the sales director argues. 'Retailers come to us because we are a one-stop shop. If we haven't got it in stock, we get it.' Explain the above in terms of a lean versus agile debate, using the concepts of market winners and qualifiers and benefiting from small volumes.

References

Abernathy, W.J. and Utterback, J.M. (1978) 'Patterns of industrial automation', *Technology Review*, vol. 80, no. 7, pp. 40–7.

Baramichai, M., Zimmers, E.W. Jr and Marangos, C.A. (2007) 'Agile supply chain transformation matrix: an integrated tool for creating an agile enterprise', *Supply Chain Management*, vol. 12, no. 5, pp. 334–48.

Boothroyd, G., Dewhurst, P. and Knight, W. (1994) *Product Design for Manufacture and Assembly*. New York: Marcel Dekker.

Cerruti, C., Mena, C., Skipworth, H. and Tavoletti, E. (2016) 'Characterizing agile supply partnerships in the fashion industry', *International Journal of Operations & Production Management*, vol. 36 no. 8, pp. 923–47.

Cerruti, C. (2013) 'Agile supply partnerships: the paradox of high-involvement and short-term supply relationships in the Macerata-Fermo footwear district', PhD thesis, Cranfield School of Management.

Choi, T.Y., Netland, T.H., Sanders, N., Sodhi, M.S. and Wagner, S.M. (2023) 'Just-in-time for supply chains in turbulent times'. *Production and Operations Management*. vol. 32, pp. 2331–40.

Christopher, M. (2016) *Logistics and Supply Chain Management*, 5th edn. Harlow: Financial Times Prentice Hall.

Christopher, M., Lowson, R. and Peck, H. (2004) 'Creating agile supply chains in the fashion industry', *International Journal of Retail & Distribution Management*, vol. 32, pp. 367–76.

Christopher, M. and Towill, D. (2001) 'An integrated model for the design of agile supply chains', *International Journal of Physical Distribution & Logistics Management*, vol. 31, no. 4, pp. 235–46.

Delbridge, R. and Oliver, N. (1991), 'Just-in-time or just the same? Developments in the auto industry: the retailers view', *International Journal of Retail & Distribution Management*, vol. 19, no. 2, pp 20–60.

Dyer, J.H., Cho, D.S. and Chu, W. (1998) 'Strategic supplier segmentation: The next "best practice" in supply chain management', *California Management Review*, vol. 40, no. 2, pp. 57–77.

Ellram, L., Tate, W. and Carter, R. (2008) 'Applying 3DCE to Environmentally Responsible Manufacturing Practices', *Journal of Cleaner Production*, vol. 16, iss. 15, pp. 1620–31.

Erixon G. (1996) 'Design for modularity', in Huang, G.Q. (ed.) *Design for X: Concurrent Engineering Imperatives*, pp. 356–79. London: Chapman & Hall.

Fine, C.H. (1998) *Clockspeed: Winning Industry Control in the Age of Temporary Advantage*. Reading, MA: Perseus Books.

Gadde, L.E. and Dubois, A. (2010). 'Partnering in the construction industry – problems and opportunities', *Journal of Purchasing & Supply Management*, vol. 16, no. 4, pp. 254–63.

Gao, S., Jin, R. and Lu, W. (2020) Design for manufacture and assembly in construction: A review, *Building Research & Information*, vol 48, no. 5, pp. 538–50.

Gupta, V. and Radhika, A.N. (2005) *Li & Fung: The Global Value Chain Configurator*, Case Centre, available from https://www.thecasecentre.org/educators/products/view?id=62324

Harrison, A. and Skipworth, H. (2008) 'Implications of form postponement to manufacturing: a cross-case comparison', *International Journal of Production Management*, vol. 46, no. 1, pp. 173–95.

van Hoek, R. (2001) 'The rediscovery of postponement: A literature review and directions for research', *Journal of Operations Management*, vol. 19, no. 2, pp. 161–84.

van Hoek, R., Harrison, A. and Christopher, M. (2001) 'Measuring agile capabilities in the supply chain', *International Journal of Operations Management*, vol. 21, no. 1, pp. 126–47.

Holweg, M. and Miemczyk, J. (2003) 'Delivering the "3-day car" – the strategic implications for automotive logistics operations', *Journal of Purchasing & Supply Management*, vol. 9, no. 2, pp. 63–7.

Jahre, M. and Refsland-Fougner, A.-K. (2005) 'Logistics – the missing link in branding – Bacalhau da Noruega vs. Bacalhau Superior', ISL – Logistics Conference Proceedings 2005, Lisbon.

Krafcik, J.F. and MacDuffie, J.P. (1989) *Explaining High Performance Manufacturing: The International Automotive Assembly Plant Study*. International Motor Vehicle Program. Cambridge, MA: MIT.

Lee, H.L. (1993) 'Design for supply chain management: concept and examples', in Sarin, R. (ed.) *Perspectives in Operations Management*, pp. 835–47. Boston, MA: Kluwer Academic Publishers.

Lee, H.L. (1995) 'Product universality and design for supply chain management', *Production Planning and Control*, vol. 6, no. 3, pp. 270–7.

Lee, H.L. and Tang, C.S. (1998) 'Variability reduction through operations reversal', *Management Science*, vol. 44, no. 2, pp. 162–72.

McFarlan, F.W., Shih-ta Chen, M. and Chi-Ho Wong, K. (2012) *Li & Fung 2012*, Case Centre, available from https://www.thecasecentre.org/educators/products/view?id=107008

Mason-Jones, R., Naylor, R. and Towill, D.R. (1999) 'Lean, agile or leagile: matching your supply chain to the market place', *International Journal of Production Research*, vol. 38, no. 17, pp. 4061–70.

Morganti, E., Dablanc, L. and Fortin, F. (2014) 'Final deliveries for online shopping: the deployment of pickup point networks in urban and suburban areas', *Research in Transportation Business & Management*, vol. 11, pp. 23–31.

Pine II, B.J. (1993) *Mass Customisation, the New Frontier in Business Competition*. Boston, MA: Harvard Business School Press.

Porter, M.E. (1985) *Competitive Advantage: Creating and Sustaining Superior Performance*. New York: Free Press.

Pude, G.C., Naik, G.R. and Naik, P.G. (2012) 'Application of value stream mapping tools for process improvement a case study in foundry, *IOSR Journal of Mechanical and Civil Engineering*, vol. 3, pp.7–12.

Rungtusanatham, M. and Forza, C. (2005) 'Coordinating product design, process design, and supply chain design decisions', *Journal of Operations Management*, vol. 23, nos 3–4, pp. 257–65.

Rylands, B., Böhme, T., Gorkin III, R., Fan, J. and Birtchnell, T. (2016) 'The adoption process and impact of additive manufacturing on manufacturing systems', *Journal of Manufacturing Technology Management*, vol. 27, no. 7, pp. 969–89.

Shingo, S. (1988) *Non-Stock Production*. Cambridge: Productivity Press.

Skipworth, H. and Harrison, A. (2004) 'Implications of form postponement to manufacturing: a case study', *International Journal of Production Research*, vol. 42, no. 1, pp. 2063–81.

Thomas, D.S. and Gilbert, S.W. (2015) *Costs and Cost Effectiveness of Additive Manufacturing*, NIST Special Publication 1176, p. 12.

Ulrich, K.T. (1994) 'Fundamentals of Product Modularity', in Dasu, S. (ed.) *Management of Design: Engineering and Management Perspectives*, pp. 219–29. Boston, MA: Kluwer Academic Publishers.

Womack, J. and Jones, D. (2003) *Lean Thinking*, 2nd edn. New York: Simon & Schuster.

Yang, B., Burns, N. and Backhouse, C. (2004) 'Postponement: a review and an integrated framework', *International Journal of Operations and Production Management*, vol. 41, pp. 2075–90.

Zhang, D.Z. and Sharifi, H. (2000) 'A methodology for achieving agility in manufacturing organisations', *International Journal of Operations & Production Management*, vol. 20, no. 4, pp. 496–512.

Zhang, D.Z. and Sharifi, H. (2007) 'Towards theory building in agile manufacturing strategy – a taxonomical approach', *IEEE Transactions on Engineering Management*, vol. 54, no. 2, pp. 351–70.

Suggested further reading

Goldman, S., Nagel, R. and Preiss, K. (1995) *Agile Competitors and Virtual Organisations*. New York: Van Nostrand Reinhard.

Peeters, K. and van Ooijen, H. (2020) Hybrid make-to-stock and make-to-order systems: a taxonomic review, *International Journal of Production Research*, vol. 58, no. 15, pp. 4659–88.

Womack, J.P., Jones, D.T. and Roos, D. (2007) *The Machine that Changed the World: The story of lean production–Toyota's secret weapon in the global car wars that is now revolutionizing world industry*. Simon and Schuster.

Samuel, D., Found, P. and Williams, S.J. (2015) 'How did the publication of the book *The Machine That Changed The World* change management thinking? Exploring 25 years of lean literature', *International Journal of Operations & Production Management*, vol. 35, no. 10, pp. 1386–1407.

Stark, A., Ferm, K., Hanson, R., Johansson, M., Khajavi, S., Medbo, L., Öhman, M. and Holmström, J. (2023) 'Hybrid digital manufacturing: Capturing the value of digitalization', *Journal of Operations Management*, vol. 69, no. 6, pp. 890–910.

Part Three

WORKING TOGETHER

In a supply network, no firm is an island that stands on its own. Nor does it compete on its own. A focal firm depends on its network partners for components to assemble, for products to sell, for the movement of goods, and so on. Whilst Part Two focused on the central logistics task of achieving responsiveness to customer demand, most firms cannot achieve this without the support of their network partners. Complete vertical integration of an industry is unusual today – although 'vertical retailers', such as Zara, have developed a similar strategy. Functional specialisation of suppliers on those parts of the value proposition in which they excel, coupled with integration into the supply network, is more common.

This is becoming especially relevant today. Some manufacturing firms, for example in the electronics and automotive industries, add only 10–20 per cent of total added value internally. The rest is created in the supply base – by commodity suppliers, by co-designers and co-manufacturers, by main suppliers and by their supply partners. Chapter 8 offers approaches to integration and collaboration in the supply chain, and Chapter 9 offers insights into sourcing and supply management.

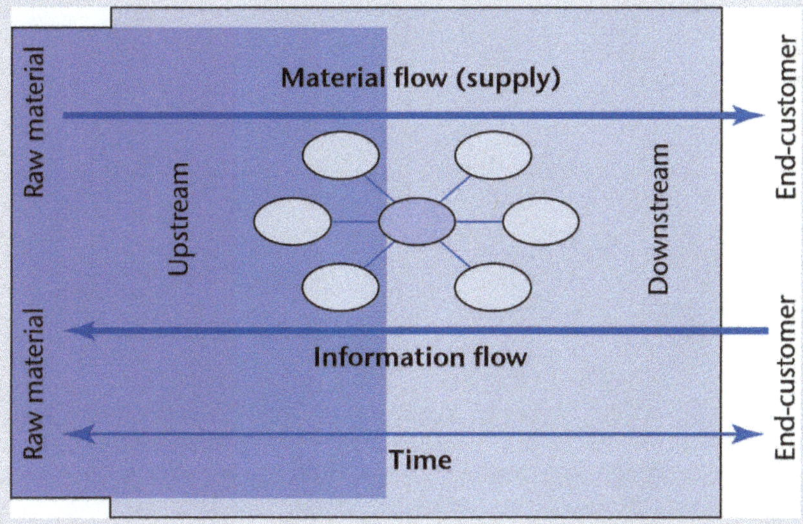

CHAPTER 8

Integrating the supply chain

Objectives

The intended objectives of this chapter are to:

- **explain the need to coordinate processes both within a company and between companies;**
- **introduce a range of options for buyer–supplier relationships;**
- **understand how the appropriate buyer–supplier relationship can be selected;**
- **describe the implications of establishing strategic partnerships.**

By the end of this chapter, you should be able to understand:

- **the benefits of collaboration within supply chains;**
- **the range of alternative inter-company relationships;**
- **the benefits and challenges of operating strategic partnerships;**
- **ways of approaching strategic partnership implementation.**

Introduction

A number of alternative supply chain structures have emerged, based upon networks and the degree of inter-firm **collaboration**. A well-known view is that of Cooper and Gardner (1993), which is further developed by Lambert et al., (1996) and Enz and Lambert (2023), who distinguish a 'spectrum' of possible supply relationships, ranging from:

- *Arm's length*: where the relationship is purely transactional and is conducted through the marketplace with price as its foundation. A detailed contract specifies the responsibilities of both parties including terms and conditions. Undue familiarity is avoided, and neither party is controlled by the other. Divorce is a readily available option when the contract finishes.
- *Through partnerships:* this requires coordination in terms of establishing 'rules of the road' whereby partners can work together. This is the key step to integrating the supply chain. Partnerships also require collaboration, which goes beyond integration by including long-term commitments to technology sharing and to closely integrated planning and control systems. The two firms

become interdependent, that is, they adapt to each other and develop common governance processes. Individual contracts are still in evidence but embedded within a broader relationship of mutual trust. Outline specifications are more common, but there is 'an incentive to do more than is expected'.

- *To vertical integration:* where the relationship is cemented through ownership. Vertical integration can extend for one or more tiers and its direction may be upstream, downstream or both.

Optimising the supply chain process inevitably leads to a growing interdependence amongst supply chain partners, and collaborative behaviour becomes more in evidence. However, collaborative relationships are not appropriate for all buyer–supplier relationships, as indicated by Kraljic's (1983) purchase portfolio matrix (described in Section 9.3). For some materials where supply risk is low, because many qualified suppliers are available, and buyer power is high (termed leverage items by Kraljic) an arm's length relationship is more appropriate.

Lambert's partnership model (1996), recently validated for current times by Enz and Lambert (2023), is based on the principle that more collaboration is not necessarily better and that what's important is the appropriateness of the relationship. It is possible to 'over manage' relationships by investing more resources (employee's time, information systems, etc.) than the value the relationship can generate. The model aims to guard against this possibility, or for that matter the reverse – under-managed relationships – by assessing two key factors: drivers and facilitators.

Many factors may impact the establishment of the most appropriate supplier relationship. For instance, centralised purchasing decisions also may impact greatly on supplier relationships. Whilst operations and logistics are developing supplier relationship management, purchasing may replace existing suppliers with new ones with whom there is no current relationship. And whilst centralisation lowered purchasing costs overall, manufacturing and logistics costs were increased (Pagell, 2004). Purchasing may be measured on the visible reductions in piece part prices, but the invisible costs of longer transport times, extra inventories and poor delivery reliability go unchallenged.

The overall aim of this chapter is to explore the need for integrating supply chain processes, approaches to **integration (internal and external)** and then to review different types of supply relationship, the impact on the firms involved, and the situations where a given type of relationship is most appropriate for the company's competitive position.

Key issues

This chapter addresses five key issues:

1. **Integration in the supply chain**: the benefits of internal and external coordination and how it might be achieved.
2. **Electronic integration in the supply chain**: the different ways of electronically integrating, and three key technologies – **electronic data interchange (EDI)**, **radio frequency identification devices (RFID)** and blockchain.
3. **Choosing the right supply relationships:** which relationship is appropriate in different circumstances and how transaction cost economics (TCE) informs this.

4. **Strategic partnerships in the supply chain:** different levels of collaboration, how strategic partnerships can be implemented and what type of partnering is appropriate, as well as barriers to their implementation.
5. **Supplier networks:** the development of Italian districts and Chinese industrial areas.

8.1 Integration in the supply chain

***Key issue:* How can we integrate internally, externally and electronically?**

What drives integration in the supply chain? Procter & Gamble's desire is to design the supply chain to meet the needs of end-customers, starting from point of sale and working backwards to deliver the right product, in the right place, at the right time, of the right quality. The following are four principles of Procter & Gamble's supply chain strategy:

- Produce every product that needs to be produced every day through short cycle production.
- Communicate with suppliers in real time – suppliers with whom we have built long-term relationships and with whom we have integrated systems.
- Draw demand data from the point nearest to the end-customer – in this case, the retail cash register.
- Collaboration between all supply chain partners using a multifunctional approach (commercial and supply chain working together) and aligned metrics focusing on delivering to the end-customer.

All of these principles involve integration – both internal and external. 'Integration' in the context of the supply chain is concerned with *coordination and synchronisation of* material and information flows both upstream and downstream.

Evidence that improved integration (both upstream and downstream) leads to improved performance for the supply chain as a whole has been found by survey research for firms in fabricated metal products, machinery and equipment manufacturing (Frohlich and Westbrook, 2001). Integration was measured across eight variables, four concerned with business processes and four with information systems as shown in Figure 8.1:

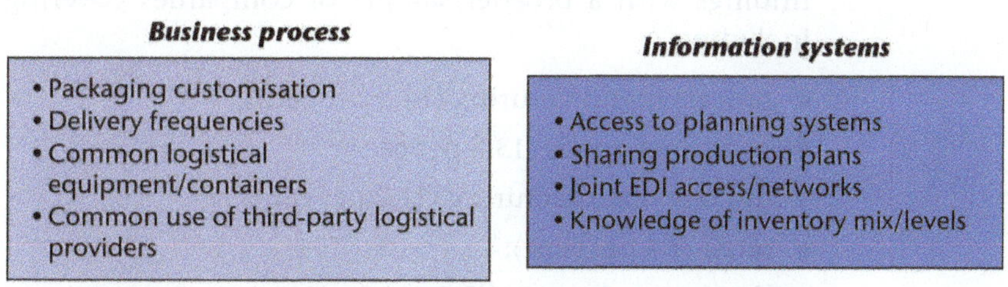

Figure 8.1 Practices with which integration was measured.

(Source: Adapted from Frohlich and Westbrook, 2001.)

The authors coined the term '**arcs of integration**' (our version of which is shown in Figure 8.2) which indicates both:

- *the direction of integration:* upstream with suppliers and/or downstream with customers; and
- *the degree of integration:* the extent to which the integration practices are evident across either the supplier or customer base.

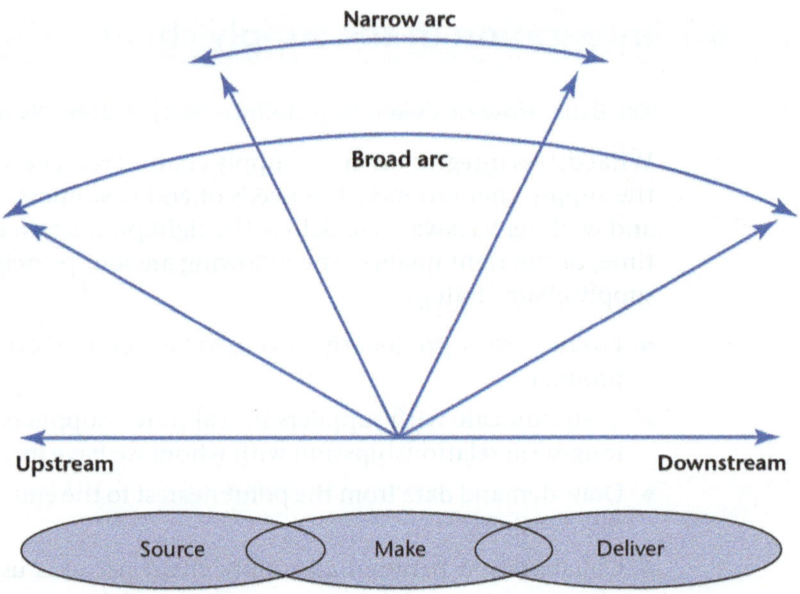

Figure 8.2 Arcs of integration.
(Source: Adapted from Frohlich and Westbrook, 2001.)

This landmark study indicated that supply chain performance was positively proportional to 'the breadth' of the arc and the 'balance' of the arc. In other words, high levels of integration with, say, customers do not lead to high levels of business performance if integration with suppliers is neglected. The arc of integration also supports the view that the more integrative processes and systems are established with a greater proportion of customers/suppliers, the better the supply chain performance.

More recently, Schoenherr and Swink (2012) conducted a global survey of 403 supply chain professionals, which confirmed Frohlich and Westbrook's (2001) findings with a broader sample of companies covering 27 different industries: including

- process manufacturing (14.3 per cent);
- consumer goods (13.8 per cent);
- discrete manufacturing (11.2 per cent);
- retail (7.4 per cent);
- third-party logistics (5.9 per cent);
- wholesale and distribution (5.7 per cent);

- high tech (5.2 per cent);
- aerospace and defence (4.3 per cent); and
- chemicals (4.0 per cent).

Further, 64 per cent of the firms were involved in manufacturing, while the remaining 36 per cent were involved in distribution or retail activities, so the arcs of integration findings are shown to apply across the end-to-end supply chain.

8.1.1 Internal integration: function to function

Another survey – this time of over 300 organisations in the USA – probed integration between marketing and logistics functions within a focal firm (Stank et al., 1999). As we discussed in Section 6.1.2, sales and operations planning (S&OP) can improve integration between these functions. Consistent with this idea, Stank et al., (1999) found that more frequent integrative behaviour between marketing and logistics resulted in better performance and better interdepartmental effectiveness. This may seem obvious, but the improvements in performance included cycle time reduction, better in-stock performance, increased product availability levels and improvements in order-to-delivery lead times. This is, no doubt, due to the successful resolution of conflicting objectives, which were discussed in Section 2.3.1, where similar enablers to alignment between marketing and supply chain management are considered.

Stank et al., (1999) found that firms with higher internal integration demonstrated higher relative logistics performance compared with less integrated firms. There was no difference between 'high' and 'low' integration firms on basic service; that is, consistent delivery on request data and advance notification of delays and shortages. However, on the 'higher value' service elements, such as delivery reliability, there was a significant difference. High-integration firms had higher performance in terms of meeting customer needs, accommodating special customer requests and new product introductions. This resulted in an enhanced customer perception of the organisations. Similar conclusions are arrived at by Windahl and Lakemond (2006), especially where the firm is developing integrated products and services such as 'power for life'.

A study of Spanish food manufacturers by Gimenez (2006) shows that the highest levels of external integration are achieved by firms that have already achieved the highest levels of internal integration between logistics, production and marketing. The implications of this research are that firms should continue to work at improving internal integration. For example, functional barriers between purchasing, manufacturing and distribution may lead to the following scenarios:

- Purchasing buys castings on the basis of low price, but the supplier has a poor record for delivery reliability and quality. Manufacturing is faced with uncertain deliveries and high reject rates.
- Manufacturing aims to keep machine and labour productivity high, so batch sizes are kept high. Distribution is faced with poor availability, especially of class B and C parts.

- Distribution wants to maintain a fast throughput warehousing operation, so resists carrying out any post-manufacturing operations. Manufacturing is faced with the additional complexity of customising products.

Internal integration is the key starting point for broader integration across the supply chain. As Robert Lynch said (cited in Kirby, 2003: 69), 'For some reason alliance professionals find it easier to create alliances with their major competitors than with other divisions in their own companies. We don't deal with our own internal integration. How can we integrate externally if we can't do it internally?'

Activity 8.1

Taking your business (or one well-known to you) as an example, how well do the internal functions integrate? Consider the purchasing–manufacturing–distribution example above and develop a scenario for the company, using the company's names for the functions concerned. What impact does your scenario have on material flow?

Alignment between supply chain management and the rest of the business

Key functions that form parts of the supply chain or impact supply chain performance need to align around priorities, opportunities and approaches. The fact that this is often not the case impedes supply chain efforts and might be what stands between 'great plan' and 'great success'.

Figure 8.3 shows a chart from van Hoek and Mitchell (2006) that demonstrates the challenge of internal alignment. This chart captures findings from an internal survey of a globally operating manufacturing company (repeated in many other companies with similar results). The survey included existing supply chain priorities and initiatives (as shown down the y-axis). The supply chain team and peers in other functions – in particular, sales – were surveyed. They were asked for their opinion about the relative importance of these priorities and the current performance on them. The difference between importance and performance is considered to be an indication of the opportunity for improvement.

Figure 8.3 shows how opportunity scores of respondents from sales contrasts with those from supply chain. When bars point to the right, sales sees a greater priority; when bars point to the left, the supply chain sees a greater priority. Taken together, the chart tells a shocking story of misalignment. Not least, when looking at the smallest bar in the centre of the graph, it appears that there is one and only one area where supply chain and sales more or less agree – the area of internal alignment. An interpretation of this is that the only thing we agree upon is that we do not agree on anything, and that we need to align better. Another obvious area of misalignment is that sales is asking for improved transportation management and delivery services. But sales is asking for less focus on the enablers of improved delivery service, such as forecasting accuracy. The chart reveals the painful challenge many supply chain managers face on a day-to-day basis: complaints about shipments but little support for its improvement efforts that are critically dependent on support from other functions.

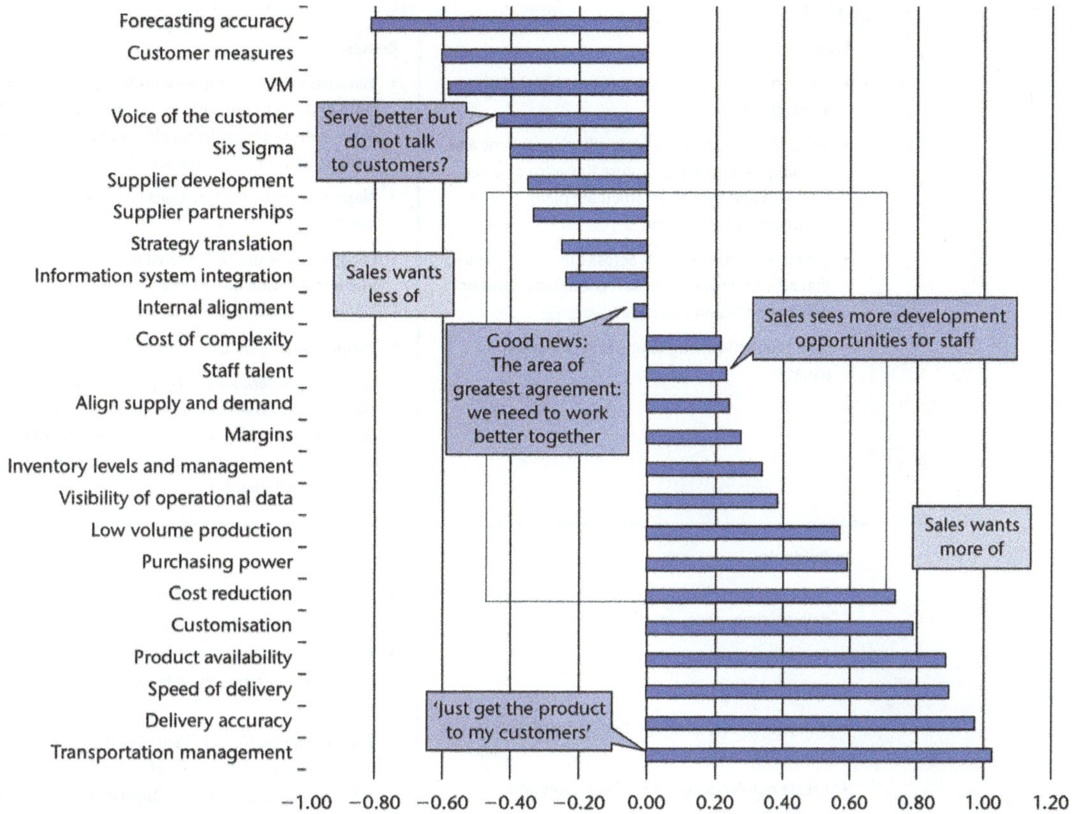

Figure 8.3 Misalignment between supply chain and sales.
(Source: van Hoek and Mitchell, 2006.)

CASE STUDY 8.1

Internal alignment at Alfa Laval

Many basic improvements were identified when the supply chain executive team from Alfa Laval examined the alignment throughout the company, as illustrated in Figure 8.4, Four areas of alignment improvement initiatives were highlighted: interactions with peers from other functions; interactions with their bosses and the board; interactions with their teams; and their own day-to-day behaviour. Examples of actions defined by the team are shown in Figure 8.4, which they termed their 'alignment compass'.

Two important aspects received a great deal of attention – improving the initiative planning process, and improving communication and training in supply chain and operations. Considering the former, it was surprising for the supply chain executive team to see that peers in other functions did not appreciate many of the strategic initiatives within the supply chain function. The realisation dawned that this would make these initiatives at best very difficult to implement and at worst impossible. The team decided that the initiative planning process needed to be improved by introducing pilots in cross-functional efforts for supply chain initiatives currently ongoing and that for future initiatives the planning process could be improved by capturing the voice of the organisation at the start. Key aspects identified included initial discussions with key

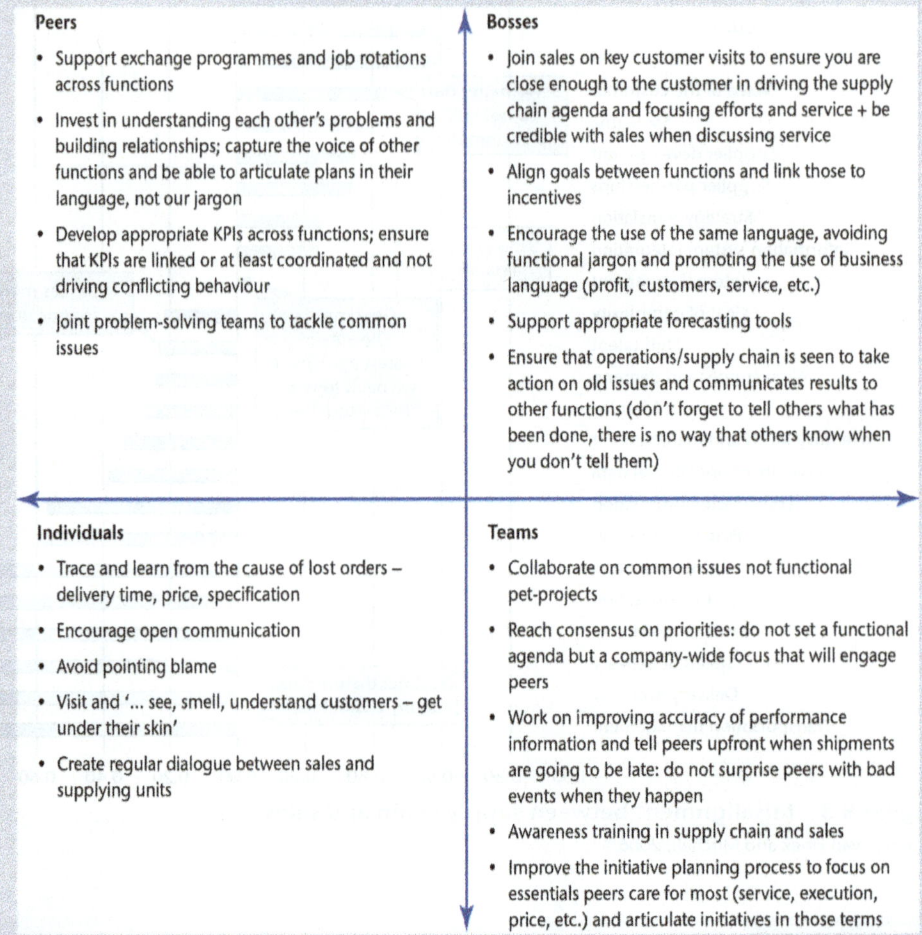

Figure 8.4 Alfa Laval's alignment compass.

peers to ensure engagement, time and resource commitment, and the effective focusing of initiatives.

In the improving communication and training area it was concluded that the rationale for supply chain initiatives was not clearly communicated at the start, and that the lack of clear justification for initiatives – why are they important? – led to a lack of commitment amongst peers to supporting the initiatives. Specific improved communication tactics included:

- avoiding the use of jargon and technical language;
- promoting the use of a shared business language that communicates initiatives in terms of their cross functional output objectives and in terms of benefits in relation to priorities in other functions;
- using training in other functions as a channel for communication;
- communicating the rationale for initiatives from the start, and frequently updating peers on progress and, more importantly, results against cross functional output objectives.

A key point is that these communication improvements are meant to be personal in nature and not the responsibility of an internal communications department. They should be included in the personal toolkit of supply chain managers to increase the probability of initiative success through effective cross-functional management and, most importantly, the supply chain manager's personal effectiveness. It was found that driving success in these areas will require training, coaching and possible 'tag teaming' with peers – or even job rotation.

(Source: Based on van Hoek and Mitchell, 2006.)

Questions

1. Can you provide examples of how functional agendas might clash, leading to challenges in supply chain initiatives?
2. Can you suggest additional integrative mechanisms along the axes of the alignment compass?

The Alfa Laval case demonstrates that effective communication between supply chain and other functions is a key challenge in ensuring cross-functional alignment around important business goals. Travis Perkins plc developed a simple, but effective, approach to this, as illustrated by Case study 8.2.

CASE STUDY 8.2

The 'language of profit' at Travis Perkins plc

Following the 2008 economic downturn, Travis Perkins (TP), the UK's leading building materials supplier, encountered substantial supply chain disruptions. A 30% plunge in demand, combined with supplier delivery reductions, resulted in diminished product availability and surplus inventory. TP's supply chain management (SCM) team faced an uphill battle convincing operations and senior management, preoccupied with cost-cutting, to prioritise supply chain enhancements. A major impediment was the impenetrable technical language of SCM, frequently leading to confusion.

To bridge this communication gap, TP crafted a 'language of profit', reframing SCM concerns in accessible financial terms. This strategy effectively illuminated the financial repercussions of losses in supply chain performance, highlighting both lost revenue and inflated costs.

Case in point: instead of presenting uninspiring availability percentages, TP computed the monetary impact of stock-outs, using a straightforward formula: 'lost sales = stock-out days × average demand × sales price'. By concentrating on the 30 SKUs with the greatest lost sales, TP furnished branch teams with a clear action plan and empowered them to address the most critical issues. Furthermore, this approach enabled TP to convey the 'cost of missed opportunity' directly to supplier managing directors, encouraging their collaboration.

▶

In a similar vein, TP quantified the expense associated with excessive vehicle idling, uncovering a staggering £900,000 in annual wasted expenditure. This stark financial revelation spurred management intervention and fostered healthy competition among branches to minimise idling.

By adopting the 'language of profit', TP successfully united its entire organisation—from branch personnel to senior leadership and even external suppliers—behind supply chain improvement endeavours. This shared financial vocabulary proved essential for catalysing action and showcasing the financial value of effective SCM.

(Based on Robin Proctor, Travis Perkins plc, 2013, updated from the Travis Perkins website, 2018.)

Question

1. Identify other supply chain challenges that companies might face and how they could be translated into the 'language of profit' to align other functions around important business goals.

Alignment between supply chain management and new product development

In addition to improving internal alignment with sales, new product development is a key peer function that deserves internal alignment focus. In Section 7.2.1 we considered product design for agility from the product designer's perspective. However, it is pointed out often that the impact of the supply chain on new product development (NPD) and new product introduction is important in areas such as:

- shipping products to market fast enough (before product launch dates);
- ensuring sufficient inventory at the launch date; and
- ensuring a flow of parts and components for new product manufacturing.

Examples of how this presents itself in practice are provided by Nike and Reckitt Benckiser (van Hoek and Chapman, 2006). At Nike – as in most fashion companies – it is important to ensure that all key accounts have sufficient stock available at the start of each of the four seasons in a year when a rush for products begins. That means ensuring supply of several thousand SKUs from multiple suppliers globally, through the distribution channel to all customers on time simultaneously. Missing the launch date disappoints customers and affects overall product revenue. Equally, when a new blockbuster video game is introduced in the market, one-third or more of the entire sales take place within the first 24 hours of the product becoming available, with people lining up in front of stores before a midnight release. Obviously, in this example, it is also crucial to ensure sufficient supply to stores in order to avoid lost sales, and disappointed customers and accounts. In conclusion, new product development and the supply chain is another key area where internal alignment must be targeted.

Like many companies, Reckitt Benckiser, a consumer products company, found forecasts for new products to be one area where misalignment between supply chain and NPD was particularly costly and challenging. A major challenge with new products is that there is less historical reference data to use as a base number for forecasting and there are more uncertainties to contend with around such important issues as an exact launch date, and supply volumes. Misalignment was found to be costly because poor forecasts led to limited product availability, disappointed customers and lots of firefighting and last-minute fixes. Several reasons were found for the underperformance of the forecasting process. These included tendencies to average out forecasts when functions do not agree, delayed response due to lack of group consensus, and even forecasts that become available late as a result of forecasting being given a low priority for too long.

In order to address these shortcomings and contribute to supply chain readiness, Reckitt Benckiser created a new role in the supply chain team – a new product introduction forecasting manager. This manager is dedicated to working with functions involved in the NPD process specifically to drive alignment around the forecast. The manager flags forecasting differences between functions, spots possible challenges in assumptions and works across functions to arrive at a more accurate forecast. Next, the forecasting manager supports the translation of the forecast into a supply chain capacity plan and forms a natural spotlight in the organisation for avoiding bottlenecks.

With supply chain readiness for NPD improved and with fewer execution issues and less firefighting, the supply chain team has manoeuvred itself into a better position. It is less likely to be distracted by last-minute crises and more likely to be considered a useful member of the NPD team that can make valuable contributions based upon the capability it has to offer.

Activity 8.2

Assume for a moment that you are a supply chain manager invited into a new product development team meeting. What questions would you ask of the team to ensure you can prepare your supply chain for effective product launch?

8.1.2 External integration: company to company

If significant improvements can be achieved by internal integration, potential for the benefits of external integration could be even higher. Analysis of the supply chain often shows that production lead time is measured usually in weeks rather than days. This is caused by excessive inventories of raw materials, packaging materials and intermediate products being held upstream of the final point of manufacture. Not only does this represent a cost burden, it also increases the P-time of the supply chain as a whole.

The Japanese concept of *heijunka* seeks coordination of material movements between different processes in the **supply network**. *Heijunka* is often referred to as 'levelled scheduling', which involves distributing volume and mix evenly over a given time period. Output of each major process in the supply chain therefore matches end-customer demand as closely as possible throughout that time period (Harrison, 2005).

In today's world of increasingly volatile demand patterns, level schedules may not be possible to achieve, at least not for all products at all times. In this case transparency of information upstream and downstream is essential for synchronisation to work. In this section we will cover the following three approaches developed to improve coordination between suppliers and customers, such that service levels are improved and inventories reduced, particularly when demand is highly variable.

- Collaborative planning, forecasting and replenishment (CPFR);
- Vendor-managed inventory (VMI);
- Just-in-time 2 (JIT2) or supplier in plant.

Approaches specific to retail, such as Efficient Consumer Response (ECR) and Quick Response (QR), are covered in Chapter 6.

Collaborative planning, forecasting and replenishment (CPFR)

Collaborative planning, forecasting and replenishment (CPFR) is aimed at improving collaboration between buyer and supplier so that customer service is improved whilst inventory management is made more efficient. The trade-off between customer service and inventory is thereby altered (Oliveira and Barratt, 2001).

The CPFR movement originated in 1995. It was the initiative of five companies: Walmart, Warner-Lambert, Benchmarking Partners, and two software companies, SAP and Manugistics. The goal was to develop a business model to forecast and replenish inventory collaboratively. An initial pilot was tested between Walmart and Warner-Lambert using the Listerine mouthwash product and focusing on stocks kept in the retail outlets. The concept and process were tested initially by exchanging pieces of paper. This generated clear visibility of the process and later the internet was used for this information exchange.

With Voluntary Inter-industry Commerce Standards Association (VICS) support, organisations including Procter & Gamble, Kmart and Kimberly-Clark undertook pilots to test the idea of sharing information to improve inventory handling. One of the pilots in the UK grocery sector is described in Case study 8.3.

CASE STUDY 8.3

CPFR trials in the UK grocery sector

CPFR pilots have been a popular diversion in the UK grocery sector. Often, they show – as in this case – that considerable opportunities for improvement exist, but that the problems of scaling up the pilot are too great. The scenario for this pilot, researched by one of our Master's students, Alexander Oliveira, was a manufacturer that supplied a major grocery retailer in the UK. Figure 8.5 shows the typical demand series for one of the ten products in the study, all of which were in the high-volume ambient category. Total sales through the till (EPOS) for a given week were really quite stable. Whilst there is apparent high demand variation, most of this is due to predictable behaviour such as that due to different store opening hours. The day-to-day demand for this product actually was relatively stable over the course of a year. Figure 8.5 places the pilot in context. The manufacturer's national distribution centre (NDC) supplied one of the retailer's regional distribution centres (RDCs), which in turn served 10 stores in the pilot (it served a lot more stores in total – about 80).

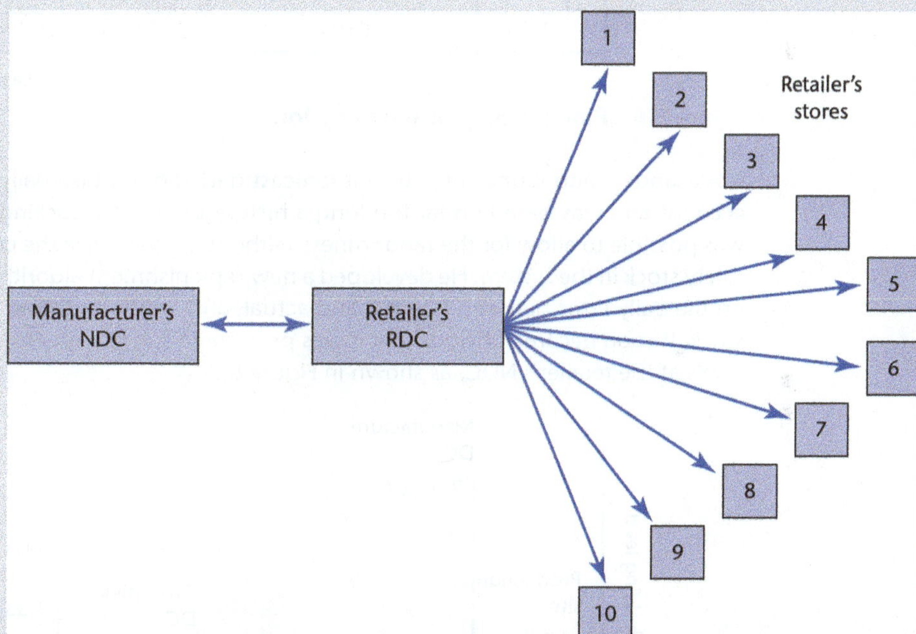

Figure 8.5 A collaborative planning pilot.

The starting situation that Alexander found was that forecasting methods were based on a history of the last two to three months. Whilst this gave the correct day-to-day pattern, it was insensitive to actual demand during a given week. As can be seen in Figure 8.6, the actual demand pattern varies from day to day across the series due to a proportion of randomness in the pattern. The replenishment cycle was unresponsive because daily deliveries were based on forecasts. This resulted in high safety stocks and poor on-shelf availability. Figure 8.6 provides an inventory profile across the supply chain. The sum of the vertical (average days of stock) and horizontal (average lead time in days) gives the total time for a new batch of product to progress from manufacturing site to shelf of a massive four to five weeks!

Alexander coordinated the provision of forecast data from both manufacturer and supplier. Both forecasts were posted on a website, and he was asked to provide instructions as to how much product the manufacturer should supply each day. Stock for the ten stores was 'ring fenced' at the retailer's RDC – that is, it could not be supplied to any other than the ten stores in the pilot.

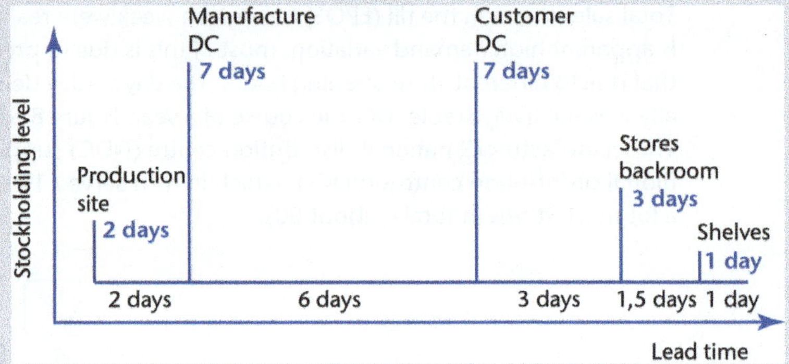

Figure 8.6 Pipeline map at start of pilot.

Alexander soon found that current forecast data did not take daily fluctuations into account and was based on far too long a history period. By tracking daily demand, it was possible to allow for the randomness without anything like the current quantity of safety stock in the system. He developed a new replenishment algorithm that was based on the daily error between forecast and actual, and which added an extra day's buffer stock. It soon became obvious that it was possible to run the system on far lower stock levels at the retailer's NDC, as shown in Figure 8.7.

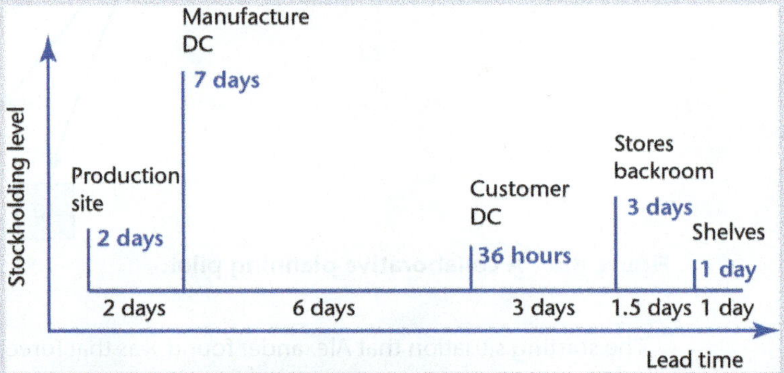

Figure 8.7 Pipeline map at end of pilot.

Alexander's work had succeeded in reducing the stock level at the NDC from seven days to three days (72 hours). In spite of the huge potential savings, the retailer did not go ahead with scaling up the pilot. This can be attributed to several factors. First, many other improvement initiatives were under way. The CPFR initiative would have needed further scarce resources. Second, scaling up would have required a different operating routine at all NDCs and the supporting IT infrastructure would need to have been changed. Third, what worked with one relatively efficient manufacturer may not have worked with others. Nevertheless, Alexander came up with the following five enablers for CPFR implementation (Barratt and Oliveira, 2002):

1. *Define single point of contact for each trading partner:* to ensure that information is neither lost nor deteriorates during the exchange.
2. Define motive (short medium and long term) behind collaborating, to balance out the collaborative objectives over time.
3. Expand the scope and complexity of collaborative projects to ensure a critical mass.
4. Information sharing must be continuous to ensure transparency required for collaborative planning.
5. Growing trust over time through resolving small issues in the CPFR process makes partners develop confidence in each other and believe that the long-term goal is attainable.

Questions

1. Suppose that the retailer's total sales were €20 billion, and that the 10 SKUs together accounted for 0.4 per cent of these sales. Calculate the approximate savings in inventory to the retailer.
2. Do you consider that the reasons given for not scaling up the pilot are valid?
3. Would there be any benefits to the manufacturer?

Having shown that the CPFR concept can have bottom-line impact on their businesses, companies are looking to expand the programmes from the handful of items involved in the pilots to the hundreds or thousands of items covered in most trading relationships. This has been a challenge for all organisations.

When implementing CPFR, a significant amount of time and effort is required up-front to negotiate specific items such as goals and objectives, frequency of updates to plan, exception criteria and key performance measures. The result is a published document defining the relevant issues for each organisation that has been jointly developed and agreed. Exception criteria include the thresholds for the difference in forecasts between the retailer and manufacturer, for a given SKU, and the actions that will be taken to establish an agreed forecast. For example, if the difference in the two forecasts is more than 5 per cent then a specific algorithm may be used to establish a single forecast number (which goes beyond a simple average), or the planners from each of the organisations may be required to manually agree a forecast figure for the SKU in question.

A nine-step business model was published by VICS (*VICS CPFR Guidelines*, 1999). This 'road map' offers organisations a structured approach to CPFR implementation, based on the experiences of buyer and supplier companies involved in the CPFR pilots. The model is as follows with examples of what each step might cover:

1. Develop front-end agreement, covering objectives and resources.
2. Create joint business plans: partnership strategies from individual corporate plans and a joint calendar for planning activities and exception criteria.

3. Create individual sales forecasts: retailer, based on EPOS data and promotions, and manufacturer, based on market knowledge.
4. Identify exceptions to sales forecasts according to the pre-established exception thresholds.
5. Resolve/collaborate on exception items using the pre-defined algorithm or manual collaborative approach between planners.
6. Create order forecast (retailer and manufacturer).
7. Identify exceptions to order forecast according to the pre-established exception thresholds.
8. Resolve/collaborate on exception items using the pre-defined methods.
9. Generate orders.

In summary, CPFR focuses on the process of forecasting supply and demand by synchronising various plans and projections from both the supplier and the customer. CPFR requires extensive support in the form of internet-based products, which can result in major changes to the key business processes. An academic survey of the success of CPFR (Oliveira and Barratt, 2001) found a significant correlation between companies with high information systems capabilities and the success of CPFR projects. The firms with high levels of CPFR implementation use information systems capable of providing timely, accurate, user-friendly and interfunctional information in real time.

Skjoett-Larsen et al., (2003) propose that CPFR should be seen as a general approach to integrating supply chain processes, and not as a rigid, step-by-step model as proposed by VICS. In keeping with this view, Lapide (2010) states that, 'CPFR ideas have been effectively executed, but not as we expected using the standard processes developed more than 14 years ago at the peak of the publicity!' An example of an adapted CPFR approach applied with great success can be found at O2 Communications Company as described in Case study 8.4.

CASE STUDY 8.4

Successful CPFR at O2

In the UK, Telefonica's O2 brand delivers mobile network services and handsets through its retail network. O2's supply chain team prioritises close supplier collaboration, guided by the principles of British Standard BS11000. Central to this partnership is a weekly Collaborative Planning, Forecasting, and Replenishment (CPFR) cycle. This process analyses actual product received (intake) against supplier projections, leveraging a jointly agreed-upon forecast and tailored replenishment factors (like safety stock and lead times) to create a future intake schedule.

To facilitate this collaboration, O2 worked with a software developer to build a complete software solution incorporating a Supplier Collaboration Hub (SCH). This web-based platform enables real-time exchange of sales information, forecasts, and mutually accepted supply schedules, providing three primary advantages:

1. Transparency: Suppliers gain direct insight into upcoming delivery requirements based on real-time sales and projected demand.
2. Responsiveness: Suppliers can input their anticipated delivery capacity, allowing the system to immediately simulate the effects of any potential supply gaps.
3. Pre-emptive Action: Early awareness of potential shortfalls empowers proactive intervention, mitigating the impact on the end consumer.

Even with a 50% rise in average unit cost and a product portfolio that has more than doubled, the SCH has empowered O2 to maintain 95% handset availability while effectively managing inventory expansion.

(Source: Based on Nicky McGroarty, O2, 2017.)

Benefits of CPFR

Attaran and Attaran (2007) claim that most companies and industries can benefit from CPFR and they report cases of success in Walmart, Procter & Gamble, Heineken USA, Dell Computers and Coca-Cola. Further, they insist that companies that experience variation in demand, those that buy or sell a product on a periodic basis and those that deal in highly differentiated or branded products will benefit the most. Nestlé UK states that the advantages of collaborative systems are significant, and lists the following benefits:

- There is improved availability of product to the consumer, and hence more sales.
- Total service is improved, total costs are reduced (including inventory, waste and resources), and capacities can be reduced owing to the reductions in uncertainty.
- Processes that span two or more companies become far more integrated and hence simple, standard, speedy and certain.
- Information is communicated quickly, in a more structured way, and is transparent across the supply chain to all authorised users. All users know where to find up-to-date information.
- An audit trail can be provided to say when information was amended.
- Email prompts can update users of variance and progress, and can confirm authorisations.
- The data in the system can be used for monitoring and evaluation purposes.
- The process can be completed in a quick timescale, at a lower total cost.
- All trading partners become more committed to the shared plans and objectives. Changes are made with more care and are immediately visible to all.

Many of these benefits are being experienced by those implementing the CPFR philosophy. Walmart and Sara Lee experienced sales increases of 45 per cent and a decline in weeks-on-hand inventory of 23 per cent. The benefits experienced by Procter & Gamble and its retail partners include a reduction in replenishment cycle time of 20 per cent. The increased visibility of the supply chain resulted in a reduction of in-store availability from 99 to 88 per cent being detected with sufficient lead time to respond. This saved three to four days of stock-outs for the retailer. Forecast accuracy improvements of 20 per cent have also been experienced.

Vendor-managed inventory (VMI)

Vendor-managed inventory (VMI) is an approach to inventory and order fulfilment whereby the supplier, not the customer, is responsible for managing and replenishing inventory. The advantage is that a large element of uncertainty in the supply chain is removed through shared information. The need for safety stock can thereby be dramatically reduced. In practice, the basis on which decisions will be made is agreed between the supplier and customer beforehand (e.g. availability levels, replenishment frequency and/or quantity), and is based on the customer's sales information. Under VMI, the supplier assumes responsibility for monitoring sales and inventory, and uses this information to trigger replenishment orders. In effect, suppliers take over the task of stock replenishment.

The inventory is managed – although not necessarily owned – by the vendor, and is typically located at the customer's organisation, although it may also be located at a 3PL. This is another parameter that will be determined before establishing VMI and illustrates how broadly VMI applications may vary. In fact there are many different types of VMI according to different variations of inventory location (at vendor, 3PL or customer) and ownership, as shown in Figure 8.8. For instance, one type of VMI is called VMI-Consignment (VMI & CS); the inventory is owned by the supplier and located on the customer's side (Ben-Daya et al., 2013). In this situation, only when the goods are used or sold will the supplier invoice the customer (Dong and Xu, 2002). The inventory could be owned by the supplier but assigned to the customer, and the customer contracted to purchase it eventually. This is particularly appropriate when the inventory is customised and therefore specific to a certain customer.

VMI was first developed in the USA in the mid-1980s when two leading fast-moving consumer goods (FMCG) companies, Procter & Gamble and Walmart, put the theory into practice to resolve the problem of stock-out or excessive inventory (Yao et al., 2007). Since then other companies have implemented VMI including

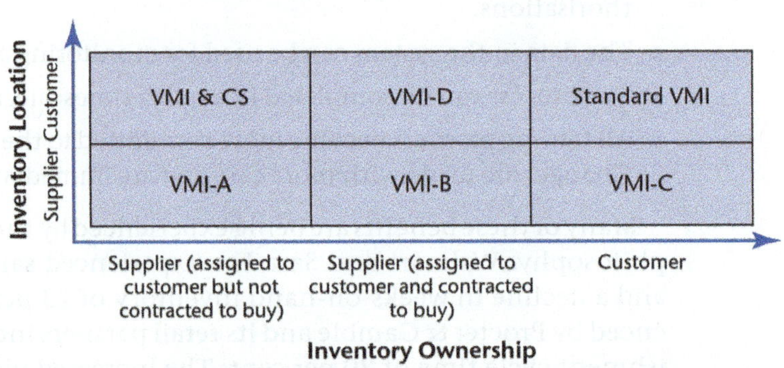

Figure 8.8 Variations of VMI based on inventory location and ownership.
(Source: Adapted from Shen and Skipworth, 2014.)

JC Penney, Herman Miller, Campbell's Soup, Barilla SpA, Shell Chemical, General Electric and Intel (Fry et al., 2001; Bichescu and Fry, 2009).

How VMI works

The supplier tracks its customers' product sales and inventory levels, sending goods only when stocks run low. The decision to supply is taken by the supplier, not the customer, as is the case traditionally. The supplier takes this decision based on the ability of the current level of inventory to satisfy prevailing market demand, whilst factoring in the lead time to resupply. The smooth running of VMI depends on a sound business system. It also requires effective teamwork between the customer and the supplier. In order for both parties to gain full benefit from the system, appropriate performance measures need to be used. The top priority measure is that of product availability at the customer. It is in both parties' interests to maximise product availability, avoiding lost sales in the short term and building customer buying habits in the long term. By emphasising the supplier's responsibility for maximising product availability, VMI aims to achieve this with minimum inventories. In order to combine both of these apparently conflicting goals, it is necessary for the supplier to have access to real-time demand data at the customer.

Internet-based applications for sharing demand data are increasingly popular as illustrated by O2 in Case study 8.4. Customer demand and inventory data are often processed through software packages to automate the application of decision rules and to identify stock lines that need replenishment.

Potential benefits

The immediate benefit to a supplier engaged in VMI is access to data on:

- customer sales;
- inventory levels at the customer.

The immediate benefit to the customer, on the other hand, is a reduction of the inbound inventory on its site and a possible reduction of its associated working capital.

The assumption is that the supplier can use this data to provide better control of the supply chain and so deliver benefits for both the customer and itself.

Having the supplier take the decision on replenishment aims to minimise the impact of *demand amplification*, presuming the supplier does have sight of the customer's sales and forecasting information. This critical problem erodes customer service (availability), loses sales and increases inventory levels and costs. The ability to dampen demand amplification caused by infrequent, large orders from customers is key to the success of VMI. The surplus capacity and excess finished goods held by suppliers to counteract such variation can then be reduced.

In the longer term, suppliers should integrate demand information into their organisation and develop the capability to drive production with it. This helps to replace the traditional push scheduling, based on forecasts and buffer stocks, with pull scheduling, based on meeting known demand quickly out of manufacturing. Also, the more the supplier is able to integrate with the customer through VMI the higher the switching costs are for the customer, improving the security of the supplier's position.

Activity 8.3

There are a number of different ways in which the use of VMI can benefit the supplier and the customer. Make a list of those benefits you think exist under the headings of 'supplier benefits' and 'customer benefits' and be clear upon what conditions these benefits depend, for instance inventory location and ownership.

Potential problems in setting up a VMI system

Other than the practical difficulties of setting up a VMI system, a number of problems can prevent the attainment of the above benefits. Six of them are listed next.

- *Unwillingness to share data:* Customers may be unwilling to share their marketing plans and product range strategies with suppliers/manufacturers. This is particularly true in the UK grocery sector, where supermarkets have strong own brands that compete with those of the manufacturers.
- Customers continue to be the owners of information on actual demand passing through their tills. An inability to forward this information, whether due to reluctance or to procedural and technical problems, will prevent suppliers from responding effectively, leading to the need for higher safety stocks and increasing the risk of stock-outs.
- *Seasonal products:* The benefits of VMI are quickly eroded in fashion and seasonal products, especially apparel. VMI in these cases can involve suppliers making to stock based on a pre-season forecast with little scope for manufacturing in season. Small quantities are delivered from this stock to the retailers over the season. Naturally, the forecast is regularly at odds with actual demand, so products will be understocked or overstocked frequently. In effect, all that has happened is that the burden of owning inventory and disposing of excesses has been moved onto the supplier.
- *Investment and restructuring costs:* Adopting a VMI approach incurs a high investment by the customer and supplier. Setting up the processes and procedures for undertaking this new way of working takes time and effort. The customer will need to close its materials management function if it is to make cost savings, whilst the supplier will need to develop the capability to take over this task.
- *Customer vulnerability:* The process of outsourcing materials management to suppliers makes the customer more dependent on them.
- *Lack of standard procedures:* The practicalities of the processes and procedures that underpin VMI may not be transferable from one customer to another. Customers may ask for different tagging methods or bespoke labelling. With many industrial products there is no barcode standard.
- *System maintenance:* Errors creep into inventory records due to incorrect part counts, mislabelling, damage, loss and theft. These records need to be maintained through manual methods such as stock counts.

Despite the potential problems in establishing VMI the benefits are such that there are widespread applications between manufacturers and retailers and also between manufacturers and their suppliers.

Just-in-time 2 (JIT2) or supplier in plant

As mentioned in Section 8.1.2, where demand patterns are variable and unpredictable transparency of information upstream and downstream is essential for synchronisation of material flows. For example, between a supplier and manufacturer, the supplier must be able to access the customer's forward production schedules, and the customer must be able to see into the supplier's 'stockroom'. A supplier-in-plant approach achieves these high levels of transparency by placing a supplier employee in the customer's purchasing office and allowing him or her to participate in the customer's production planning, plan material replenishment from his or her own company and even place orders with his or her own company. An excellent example of this approach can be found at Bose and is described in Case study 8.5.

CASE STUDY 8.5

Bose Corporation put 'supplier in plant'

The Bose Corporation, a USA-based manufacturer of hi-fi equipment (as shown in Figure 8.9) developed the JIT2 concept in the early 1990s. Bose recognised that, if the traditional buyer–supplier relationships were to be made more effective, more people would be required in its organisation. However, budget constraints meant that no additional people could be employed in this role. This acted as a driver to develop the JIT2 concept.

Figure 8.9 **Bose's speaker system.**

A logical extension of the just-in-time concept, described in Chapter 6, is to place customer and supplier processes closer together. The JIT2 approach goes a stage further by eliminating the buyer and the salesperson from the customer–supplier relationship, thus fostering increased communication between the parties. The principle is simple:

a supplier employee who resides full time in the customer's purchasing office replaces the buyer and supplier. This *supplier in plant* is empowered to use the customer's scheduling system to place orders with his or her own company. In addition, the supplier in plant does the material planning for the materials supplied by his or her company.

The supplier in plant is also part of the production planning process, so production is planned concurrently with the supplier organisation. This form of integration streamlines the supply process by removing the multi-level planner–buyer–salesman–supplier plant process by making this the responsibility of one individual. This dramatically reduces the demand uncertainty experienced by the supplier organisations. The benefits of this streamlining have also resulted in major business improvements for Bose. These include:

- 50 per cent improvement in terms of on-time deliveries, damage and shortages;
- 6 per cent reduction in material costs;
- 26 per cent improvement in equipment utilisation;
- major reductions in inventory holdings.

The Bose supplier-in-plant concept demonstrates how collaboration and integration can benefit the supply chain. The supplier in plant can, to a large degree, be superseded by today's electronic integration techniques.

Questions

1. What are the opportunities for the JIT2 supplier-in-plant principle in your chosen company?
2. Could the principle help to improve integration, either by a company representative working in the customer's organisation, or by representatives from major suppliers working in your chosen company?

We will now move on to consider electronic integration which can be seen as an enabler of other forms of integration, such as CPFR and VMI. It also supports the establishment of closer customer–supplier relationships, which will be discussed later in this chapter.

8.2 Electronic integration

Achieving visibility throughout the supply chain is of paramount importance in the search for competitive advantage. The exponential development of internet technology, together with the increased power of the personal computer, has transformed business-to-consumer (B2C) relationships, as discussed in Section 2.1.3. Equally it offers organisations a relatively cheap means of integrating information systems across the supply chain in business-to-business (B2B) relationships as illustrated by the O2 Case study 8.4.

The internet provides a platform-independent communications highway that can be used as a cross-company interface to enable electronic commerce. Thereby, it fosters operationally efficient, connected and cooperative relationships amongst manufacturers, suppliers and distributors. Using the internet can provide an easy and cost-effective answer that is available to all partners in a network. Trading partners can integrate electronically in three ways:

- information sharing;
- transactional; and
- collaborative planning (covered in the previous section).

Information sharing: the electronic sharing or exchange of information

Trading partners are given access to a system with shared information. Often, however, one partner transmits shared information to another. The information is sent on a 'for your information' basis; the recipient uses the data as it stands, and no feedback is given. Shared information may include product descriptions and pricing, promotional calendars, inventory levels, shipment tracking and tracing. This type of arrangement supports only independent planning by each partner. Uncertainty is reduced by each partner becoming aware of other partners' activities. However, trading partners do not have the opportunity to comment on or change the plan in any way.

We develop the concept of information sharing by means of a case study in *continuous replenishment* (CR). Continuous replenishment logistics is a pioneering approach to using developments in IT to supply demand quickly from the manufacturer. Using electronic point of sale (EPOS) data to track customer demand through the till, CR shares data from retailer to supplier. The aim is for the supplier to replace quickly what has been sold today, so that stock availability on the shelf is maintained at the retailer. Case study 8.6 gives a view of where fashion logistics is heading.

CASE STUDY 8.6

Continuous replenishment in the apparel industry

Global 'vertical' supply strategies in the apparel industry aim to emulate retailers such as Zara, which sources everything from set manufacturing plants that are situated within the same geographic region as most of its retail outlets. Setting up a similar operation in the US would be problematic – for a start, there is not much left of the apparel manufacturing base because it went overseas long ago for cost reasons. Competitive pressures are constantly increasing – a significant percentage of the industry is fashion-driven – and fashion changes continuously. Thus, time-to-market is increasingly important. Kumar and Arbi (2008) note:

> **Turnaround time is important for US fashion retailers intending to compete with Europe's low-cost fashion providers, including H&M and Zara. Both European stores have created production models that deliver inexpensive fashion apparel in weeks, rather than months. Zara designs, produces and delivers a garment in 15 days to US stores according to a 2005 profile by Harvard Business School's Working Knowledge. For American apparel chains, Central America is a potential outsourcing destination, with lower production costs than the USA, falling tariffs and approximately 21 days to get designs made and delivered, 43 days if American material is used.**

The internet has further impacted the importance of competing on turnaround time. Chaudhry and Hodge (2012) observe that:

The resulting shortening of product lifecycles has been further exacerbated by the ubiquitous use of the internet which equips the consumer with information about competing products, special offerings and the prices.

Retailers, both 'bricks-and-mortar' and online, drive the industry and – in a fragmented and very competitive marketplace – they are moving quickly to address its longstanding logistics problems. Increasingly, they are turning to suppliers to respond faster to better quality information, including the use of systems such as Product Lifecycle Management (PLM). Kurt Salmon Associates (Rubman and del Corrado, 2009), consultants to the industry, have highlighted that many retailers have embraced the concept of integrating retailer PLM and supplier sourcing systems, including JC Penney, Guess Inc and Men's Warehouse. Real-time collaboration is essential to driving product development in the industry. Also a shorter product development lead time enables the delay of design, material selection and colour decisions to maximise the on-trend opportunity.

Mark Harrop (2017), a long-standing apparel industry observer and MD of WhichPLM, remembers that in the late 1990s, his company provided a complete design and development platform that would allow brands and retailers to share key product data with their extended supply chains. However, the internet was still fairly primitive, and in many non-Western regions remained a barrier to supply chain connectivity for some time. Still, today, almost two decades later, Harrop finds it frustrating to see that a significant percentage of the PLM's customers do not make use of their solution's ability to power end-to-end collaboration, and instead revert to emailing PDFs of technical specifications back and forth. He believes it to be a matter of mindset:

Retailers must embrace the idea that sharing information with their supply chain partners is the only possible way they can take part in this future. . . and communicate in real-time.

Kuhel (2002) proposes an apparel supply chain of the future that is based on continuous replenishment, which we have adapted. Let us assume a designer and retailer of fashion apparel is situated in the north-eastern USA. A new range has been designed, and early sales are encouraging. These early sales figures are used to refine forecasts quickly, and to prime the logistics pipeline with a flow of product that matches expected demand. After this, it is essential to regulate the flow of finished goods to match actual demand. This is how it is done.

As soon as an item is purchased, the retailer collates the electronic point of sale (EPOS) data from its stores or on-line, and sends the data upstream. The 'pull' signal (Chapter 6) goes back all the way to the yarn manufacturer. Figure 8.10 represents the path that a garment might take from concept to delivery. Six stages are involved.

1. *Planning:* apparel retailer determines design for a product, evaluates costing with the supplier and then sends demand data and forecast upstream. These signals set the supply chain in motion. Later, once the product has gone to market, a web-based link from the retailer's EPOS/online system to the manufacturer triggers replenishment responses.

2. *Raw material:* suppliers respond to demand signals via phone, fax, email or integrated Internet based system. Raw cotton is compressed into bales, and fitted with radio frequency identification device (RFID) tags to specify source and type.
3. *Fabric:* manufacturers weave and ship product in response to demand from the retailer. Inventory/shipment tracking starts here. In-transit data is passed downstream via the internet or integrated system workflow.
4. *Assembly:* fabrics and trims come together at the final assembly plant, which in this example is situated in the Caribbean. (Manufacturers situated within short shipping times of the USA are favoured over Far East suppliers.) The plant has an ERP system that processes orders received electronically. Finished goods are assembled and barcoded by store prior to dispatch. All suppliers to the apparel retailer use compatible or integrated systems.
5. *Distribution:* the product is shipped by container to the retailer's national distribution centre (NDC). Here, store orders are cross-docked using the barcode to identify the destination store. They are then forwarded to regional distribution centres (RDCs) that serve 50–100 stores and on-line retail.
6. *Retail:* as items are purchased, EPOS/on-line triggers replenishment responses.

(Sources: Kuhel, 2002; updated by Harrison, 2005; updated by Dr Mark Baker, 2018.)

Questions

1. Summarise the 'current state' problems that are typical of the apparel industry, and their implications for supply chain integration.
2. Identify potential barriers to executing the proposed apparel 'supply chain of the future'.

Transactional: the electronic execution of transactions

This is usually found in business-to-business (B2B) e-commerce, with the trading partners focusing on the automation of business transactions such as purchase orders, invoices, order and advanced shipment notices, load tendering and acknowledgements, and freight invoices and payments. These transactions involve the electronic transmission of a fixed-format document with predefined data and information fields as described in Section 8.2.1 Electronic data interchange (EDI). More recently the blockchain has emerged, allowing more secure and traceable transactions between supply chain members. This will be covered in Section 8.2.3.

8.2.1 Electronic data interchange (EDI)

Electronic data interchange (EDI) enables standardised electronic business messages to replace manual paper-based processes, such as customer order schedules, purchase orders and invoices. In the past EDI was plagued with issues relating to computer system incompatibility between companies which often caused the data being transmitted to be corrupted. For example, in the case of an automotive component supplier, customer order schedules being sent from a main automotive assembler were being corrupted such that due dates were altered, causing problems with the delivery service. Now, of course, EDI systems operate on the internet and are therefore platform independent, allowing much greater accessibility and easier use.

Further, the EDIFACT (Electronic Data Interchange for Administration, Commerce and Transport) standard provides an internationally agreed message format, directories and guidelines for multi-country and multi-industry EDI communications, thus allowing standardised EDI communications across a global supply chain. However, as described in Case study 8.8, about a blockchain pilot in the shipping industry, EDI systems still rely on companies collecting information and often rekeying information between non-integrated systems, leading to human error and data inaccuracies which are replicated across the supply chain. Blockchains (described in Section 8.2.3), on the other hand, enable the visibility of validated data across a network of supply chain members with no rekeying required, thus improving the accuracy of the data.

The UK grocery sector is at the forefront of EDI technology, having been using it for more than 35 years. A joint study between Global Standards (GS1) and Cranfield University (Adnan-Ariffin and Coussins, 2010) reported:

> **Our research of the UK's top 15 grocery retailers covering 90 per cent of the sector has found that the sector saves £650 million per year in costs by using EDI instead of manual paper-based processes for its orders, invoices and des-patch advices. . . Around 85 per cent of UK grocery retailers use EDI for purchase orders and invoices compared with 27 per cent outside the grocery sector.**

This demonstrates that the grocery sector is far ahead of other sectors in terms of EDI implementation and is enjoying the savings that EDI can bring.

EDI has also been routinely used across automotive supply chains between component manufacturers, sub-assemblers and the main automotive assemblers to improve coordination and synchronisation of material flow by transmitting call-off and delivery schedules. More recently, EDI is being used to improve integration of vehicle manufacturers with their hundreds of dealerships that sell the vehicles and parts to the end-customers. EDI can improve demand visibility from the perspective of the manufacturers in terms of customer orders and improve supply visibility for the end-customer (the consumer) in terms of specifications, stock availability, prices and delivery information. Typically the data sourced from either the manufacturer or the dealerships is not transferred in real time but instead is batched and held for overnight processing so there is up to a 24-hour delay on data transmission. However, this is of little consequence when the order lead time for cars is typically measured in weeks or months, rather than days. These types of system can improve the accuracy of vehicle specifications and the tracking of deliveries such that they are timely from a customer perspective.

According to IBM (2024):

> **EDI is alive and well and will remain critical to business for many years to come. However, the true future lies in using and evolving B2B integration alongside disruptive technologies such as IoT, blockchain and AI, to deliver innovative levels of multi-party supply chain collaboration.**

A challenge for EDI implementations across numerous companies remains the diversity in information systems with which EDI must interface, creating the need for significant time and effort to enable the integration of the systems and the accurate and automatic transfer of data fields.

8.2.2 Radio frequency identification devices (RFIDs)

A radio frequency identification device (RFID) is a product-tracking technology that is applied widely in supply chains today (Angeles, 2005). An RFID, often called a *tag*, can be attached to a piece of merchandise and informs a reader about the nature and location of what it is attached to. Figure 8.10 shows how the reader can relay this information to a management system that can create a picture of what merchandise is where, at a level of detail that has not been possible previously.

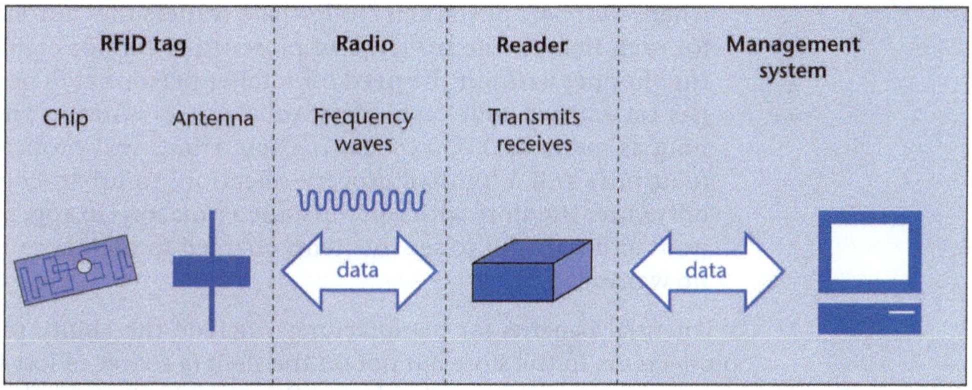

Figure 8.10 An RFID system.

An active tag has a power source; a passive tag does not. Active tags use a battery, have a limited life and cost far more. The *antenna* is a device that uses radio waves to read and/or write data to the tags. The reader manages the interface between antenna and management system. A big advantage of RFID technology over barcodes is that the tag does not have to be directly in the line of sight of the reader. Tags can be detected remotely by readers because the radio waves can pass through many materials (see, for example, www.ems-rfid.com). Trials have been conducted across a range of frequencies – 125 kHz to 2.45 GHz for chip-based tags – but standards are still being debated in many sectors. The management system enables data from tags to be collected and sorted for the purposes of management information and action.

The key piece of information held on a tag is the *electronic product code* (EPC, the standards for which were developed by the Auto-ID Centre). This 'number plate' is unique to each tag. The unique number can then be linked to information about the product to which it is attached, for example about when and where the product was made, where its components came from and shelf-life details. Some tags may hold this additional information on board. However, the intention is that most tags will hold only the EPC, and additional information will be stored remotely, on a database linked to the management system.

Readers tell us *what* the product is and *where* it is located in the supply chain. The management system compiles this information and allows us to know *how many* products are present at that location for each time bucket. This translates into dynamic data that allows us to know rates of consumption, and stock data at a given point in time – together with what needs to be done. One can already envision that such data will enable supply chain planning and control to be transformed.

Product tagging allows for several interesting applications including:

- tracking products throughout the distribution pipeline ('asset tracking') to provide continuous quantities and position by SKU in the supply chain;
- tracking products through back of store to the shelf;
- intelligent shelves, whereby 'sweeping' of product by thieves from shelves in store shows up automatically and raises alarm signals;
- registering sales without involving a cashier: a fancied future state is one where shoppers push their trolley past readers that automatically read EPCs for each item in the trolley, and present the bill for credit card payment to the shopper without the need for retailer personnel to be involved. Amazon has established four cashierless Amazon Go stores in the US, and is planning as many as 3,000 by 2021. These stores will provide freshly prepared foodstuffs and a 'limited grocery selection' to urban consumers who need only enter the store with a pre-installed Amazon Go app, grab the goods they want and walk out to see the items charged to their account. No queues and no waiting.

Potential benefits for manufacturers include the ability to understand when products are in the store but not on the shelf (a source of lost sales that manufacturers cannot control) and reducing the opportunities for theft. Retailer benefits include ability to track products in the pipeline against delivery schedules, automation of the checkout process and ability to expand customer information on buying patterns.

Technically, products can be tracked all the way to the customer's home and into it. However, when Benetton planned to track products after the sale, with an eye on returns, it was met with customer resistance on grounds of invasion of privacy. This caused Benetton to delay plans for rolling out this idea. The other major hurdle to implementation is the price of the tags. Price/margin levels in most consumer packaged-goods mean that the cost of tags needs to be low enough to be affordable at the individual product level. Walmart launched a case tagging programme but experienced a lack of supplier cooperation to the extent that it was abandoned, as described in the following Case study.

Beyond product-level tagging in retail channels, many other applications are already in place at case level or raw material level (see Case study 8.6 on continuous replenishment in the apparel industry), and in higher-value goods such as automotive parts.

CASE STUDY 8.7

RFID case tagging at Walmart

In 2003 Walmart began a programme implementing RFID, which turned out to be far more challenging than expected and reveals the many issue in the retail sector. Problems began shortly after the announcement in June 2003 of the initiative to tag cases and pallets. This announcement was made at a meeting of the VICS (Voluntary Interindustry Commerce Solutions) retail data standards organisation, which merged with GS1 US (Global Standards One) in 2012. Walmart suppliers raised concerns about the costs of RFID tags and the process of applying the tags to the cases, which they realised would need to be completed in their distribution centres. Many suppliers also made it clear that they did not understand what the benefit was for them. Leading manufacturers such as Procter & Gamble, who themselves were actively engaged in RFID programmes, were of the view that the benefit varied greatly depending upon the product category. This contrasted sharply with Walmart's universal approach where one-size-fits-all and the objective was to tag all products from every supplier.

Walmart continued to press on with their RFID programme for many years but many suppliers simply refused to apply the tags and eventually in early 2009 the Walmart case tagging project was terminated. This appeared to be triggered by a press release from P&G stating that they had 'validated' the benefits of RFID in merchandising and promotional displays, and on the basis of their findings were ending their pilot programme with Walmart for those displays. This suggests that Walmart had not responded to the information generated and not improved in-store execution.

So, the question arises, did the Walmart programme progress the application of RFID in the supply chain or did it hinder progress?

It is widely acknowledged by those in the industry that the Walmart programme did advance the technology significantly, but many of the RFID technology investors in that period lost.

On the contrary, many retailers and manufacturers were watching and waiting to see the outcome of the Walmart programme. In the US at least, no other retailer has initiated a case tagging programme since. This is despite the fact that, as mentioned earlier, manufacturers such as P&G and Kimberly-Clark believed there was real benefit for both manufacturers and retailers for *some* products and *some* applications, if the programmes were executed appropriately.

Walmart has explored a so-called 'item-level' tagging programme that began in 2010, and other retailers, such as first Macy's and more recently Target, have announced plans to tag every item in their stores. Many other retailers are also aspiring to item-level RFID initiatives.

It is probable that when these programmes reach critical mass in terms of the level of items tagged and reader infrastructure rollouts and, most importantly, show the mutual benefits, retailers will return to case-level tagging – and most likely with much better results.

If retailers approach 100 per cent inventory accuracy in their stores enabled by item-level tagging, its unlikely that they'll tolerate lower levels of accuracy up the supply chain.

(Source: Based on Gilmore, D. (2017) 'Supply Chain Comment: Did Walmart's Failed Case Tagging Program Set RFID Back or Move it Forward?', Supply Chain Digest, 19th April 2017.)

Questions:

1. Identify and discuss the benefits of RFID tagging to manufacturers and retailers?
2. P&G highlight that RFID is of real value to *some* products and *some* applications. What do you think they mean by that? Which products and which applications?

8.2.3 Blockchain

Blockchain is the technology which supports bitcoin and was proposed in 2008 as a solution to the double-spend problem. Double-spend results from digital currency used in one transaction being copied to fund more transactions. Blockchain technology is a combination of transaction consensus across a peer-to-peer distributed network and cryptography, which ensures that each transaction is verified and cannot (theoretically) be altered once consensus has been reached (Nakamoto, 2008).

According to Lindsey Gallacher (2017), who completed a Master's thesis at Cranfield School of Management on blockchain technology for supply chains:

> **due to blockchain's fundamental characteristics of security, immutability, transparency and distributed configuration, its potential to promote visibility and enhance efficiency end to end in the supply chain has been recognised.**

Suggested applications are wide ranging and include: procurement, from supplier selection and performance to payment; converting manual to digitised or automated processes; reducing transaction and dispute resolution cycle times; disintermediation; trade finance; asset management; reducing fraudulent activities and counterfeit products; and provision of provenance.

However, despite the envisaged potential, due to the immaturity of the technology there are currently few, if any, full-scale deployments in a commercial context and therefore the benefits are largely unproven. In 2018, IBM was working with a number of big companies on plans to implement blockchain technology. Walmart, for instance, is planning to use blockchain to trace the origin of the leafy green foods sold in its stores in response to food safety scares including E. coli outbreaks in lettuce. IBM was also working with the world's largest container shipping firm, A.P. Moller-Maersk, to create an industry-wide trading platform designed to speed up trade and save billions of dollars. However, few details are released of these ventures so we present here, in Case study 8.8, a case of a small-scale blockchain application from the shipping industry.

CASE STUDY 8.8

Marine Transport International and Agility Science pilot of Container Streams distributed ledger

Marine Transport International (MTI), together with Agility Science (AS), developed the aptly named Container Streams distributed ledger technology, based on open source with an MIT permission licence.

According to Jody Cleworth, CEO of MTI:

> **The creation of a cyber physical world, representing physical assets in real time, is one of the greatest appeals of the distributed ledger system.**

A distributed ledger allows physical assets to be represented digitally. All contributors to the ledger – supply chain partners – share a 'single version of the truth'. This single version is also programmable through smart contracts, creating added value.

Many shippers or distributors are currently left dealing with multiple forms of communication as they try to manage the different milestones for the shipping and logistics industries. The EDIFACT (Electronic Data Interchange for Administration, Commerce and Transport) standard provides an internationally agreed message format, directories and guidelines for multi-country and multi-industry EDI communications. However, today's EDIFACT systems are submission-led by users who collect and often rekey information into various systems, often multiple times. This can result in inaccurate information being replicated across the supply chain.

Container Streams distributed ledger technology can operate with all kinds of existing systems (legacy systems, blockchain systems, shipping portals, weighbridges, etc.) and messaging protocols (EDIFACT, email, API) thus allowing the sharing and streaming of data between supply chain members. Smart contracts can be programmed, allowing the automation of processes which are currently performed by operators as part of their day-to-day activities.

The development of Container Streams was inspired by the implementation of a new regulation in 2016 by the International Maritime Organization (IMO) aimed at improving safety aboard container ships by putting in place reporting requirements that ensure a proper weight balancing of containers as they are being loaded onto vessels. The intention was to prevent accidents due to improper loading, and to avoid the loss of lives at sea. Practically speaking, this new regulation, called SOLAS VGM (Safety of Lives at Sea – Verified Gross Mass), requires an EDI data transmission of the weight of each container to the shipping line prior to the container's arrival at the loading port. This ensures that the port can plan the loading sequence of containers in advance and be certain that the overall load balance of the vessel is within a tolerable safety range.

Given the amount of data necessary because of this impending regulation, Container Streams distributed ledger technology was developed as a solution for digital weight reporting. For the pilot, Container Streams assembled data streams from weighbridges (or connected devices) in real time at Parry & Evans, a recycling business. More than 44 different data points were collected that were relevant for the ongoing journey of the container. These data points include, but are not limited to, container weight and size, type, number, shipping line, hauler, commodity and its description. In addition, all associated paperwork, including any regulatory and customs clearance documentation, could be captured.

When this data met the ledger and a smart contract, the SOLAS VGM application was used to create the view in the ledger and present the data to the port authorities (at Felixstowe and Rotterdam) and shipper (Prism Recycling). This created a streamlined, visible and verified data flow between all actors required to report and send the data.

The benefits observed from the container stream pilot are as follows:

- There is increased visibility of container weights, enabling the completion of the Verified Gross Mass (VGM) required for containers and preventing overweight containers, which increases health and safety in the maritime and haulage industry.
- Data exists on the ledger, aiding completion of customs clearance and SI forms.
- It is easy to track the movement of containers in real time, enabling shipping companies to provide customers with better tracking data on products.

(Source: Based on Martyn Walker and Jodi Cleworth, 2018*.)

Questions

1. Discuss the advantages of the Container Stream distributed ledger technology compared to simple EDI communications between the supply chain members.

2. From the perspective of the various supply chain members involved what issues might you envisage with the use of Container Stream distributed ledger technology and how might they be overcome?

How do blockchains work?

Blockchain's' functionality is enabled by a peer-to-peer transaction network which is decentralised or distributed in configuration and supports peer-to-peer transactions. The distributed nature (secured by cryptography) enables the network to operate without an intermediary. There are three network configurations as illustrated in Figure 8.11:

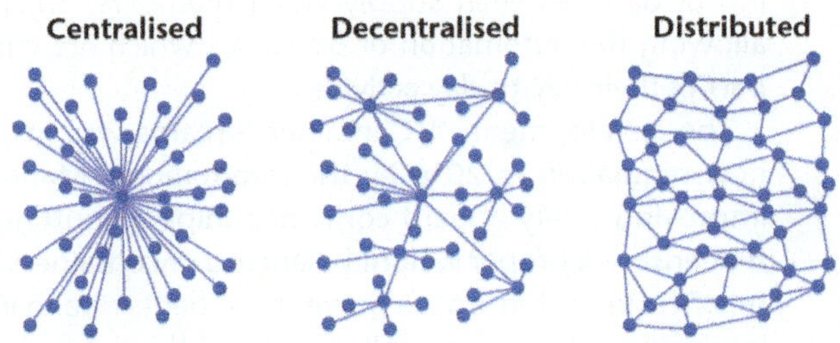

Figure 8.11 Network configurations.
(Source: Walport, 2015.)

- Truly public blockchains, such as Bitcoin, are distributed in nature.
- Consortium and permissioned networks as might be used for a company or supply chain, are placed towards the middle of the spectrum (to reflect the relative increase in centralised control).
- Centralised ledgers which are similar to database technologies currently in place.

Public keys, rather than personal information, are the basis of identity on public blockchains. Each member of a blockchain has a public and private key which together can be used to encrypt and decrypt data. Asymmetric cryptography ensures that while a public key can be generated from a private key this process cannot work the other way round. For this reason, private keys must be kept secure; otherwise the data could be compromised.

Digitally signed transactions not yet on the blockchain are grouped together sequentially to form a block and are released to the network for validation. Once this is complete the block is attached to the last block in the chain, providing a time-stamp of its addition. Thus, each blockchain member has an identical copy of the ledger.

The benefits of blockchains for supply chains

Gallacher (2017) identified the following benefits of blockchain technology in supply chains, for which there is consensus amongst researchers:

- *Trust:* blockchain can create trust in the supply chain through the technology and associated data management processes. However, while this is beneficial among supply chain partners that have little or no established relationship, it may be said that trusting blockchain is effectively asking people to trust the system rather than each other, and within established, mature relationships this could have a detrimental effect on the existing trust.

- *Security:* it is expected that blockchain will increase data security and reduce fraud in general, especially thanks to the resilience and redundancy provided by the distributed or decentralised nature of the networks.
- *Transparency and provenance:* blockchain can provide transparency and traceability that ensures provenance throughout the supply chain, although a challenging aspect of providing end-to-end transparency and provenance is the provision of digital representation at the local level at each handover point in the entire supply chain.
- *Efficiency* (cost and operational): direct cost savings from expediting transaction cycle times and working capital being released quickly back into the system following dispute resolution (facilitated by the transparency and immutability of ownership and location of goods or services). Operational efficiencies are expected to result from transparency and coupling physical goods, digital representation and documentation as they flow through.
- *Change:* blockchain will continue to bring about change, notably with regard to new processes and potential business models; the way businesses and supply chain partners collaborate; skill sets required and organisational change.

Given the immaturity of the blockchain technology it is not surprising that there is a resistance to change in terms of:

- a new type of relationship (increased data sharing) with supply chain partners and consortium members (who may also be competitors);
- moving away from legacy systems and processes;
- educating people to perform new roles to enable successful transformation and widespread adoption;
- uncertainty regarding which processes should be migrated to the blockchain and how this transformation will occur.

With the benefits envisaged in terms of security and visibility in a world where risk factors, whether geopolitical, economic or relating to natural disasters, are increasing, it is hard to imagine that blockchain will not be adopted on a commercial scale.

8.3 Choosing the right supply relationships

***Key issues:* What types of supply relationships can be adopted? How can each type of relationship be tailored to different types of product?**

There are many possible types of relationship in the supply chain and these can be viewed in the form of a continuum. This can range from *arm's length*, where the relationship is conducted through the marketplace with price as its foundation, to *vertical integration*, where the relationship is cemented through ownership. **Vertical integration** can *extend* for one or more tiers and its *direction* may be upstream, downstream or both. A continuum of relationship options is shown in Figure 8.12. Each of these relationship styles has motivating factors that drive development

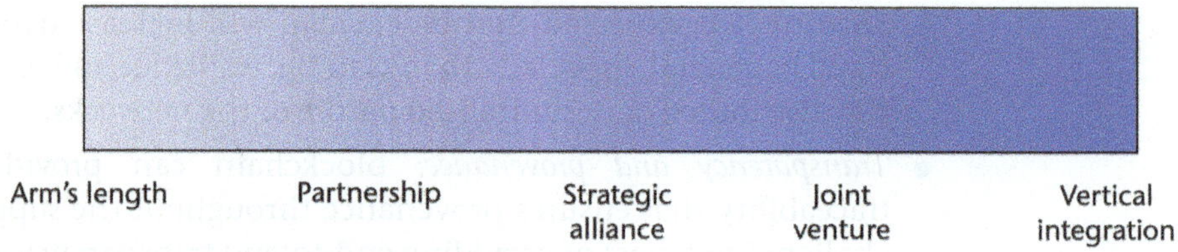

Figure 8.12 Relationship styles continuum.
(Source: Adapted from Cooper and Gardiner, 1993.)

and that govern the operating environment. The duration, breadth, strength and closeness of the relationship vary from case to case and over time.

A focal firm is unlikely to have the same type of relationship with all of its customers and suppliers. The firm may adopt a range of styles: choosing which type of relationship to adopt in a given supply chain situation is an important strategic issue. **Kraljic's purchase portfolio matrix** (described in Section 9.3) segments supply items on the basis of supplier risk and the buyer's strength (or power) in the relationship, and this can help to determine the appropriate relationship with suppliers. For example, grocery retailers often adopt an arm's-length style for 'own brand' goods, such as kitchen paper, where there are many available suppliers and buyer power is high-termed *leverage items* by Kraljic. To obtain lowest price solutions, grocery retailers use online auctions (Smart and Harrison, 2003). Strategic alliances are used often for relationships that do not strictly fall under the umbrella of buyer–supplier relationships. For example, the alliance between Tesco Express and Esso fuel stations was used to develop the station forecourts.

Companies tend to deal with a large number of suppliers, even after the **supply base** has been rationalised (which is described in Section 9.2). Treating them all in the same way fails to recognise that some have different needs from others. Differentiating the role of suppliers and applying appropriate practices towards them allows a focal firm to target purchasing and supply chain management resources to better effect.

Historically, a popular view is that Japanese companies consider all of their tier 1 suppliers as partners. This is not really true: for example, Japanese automotive manufacturers do not regard all of their suppliers as equal. In fact amongst the typical 100–200 tier 1 suppliers to an OEM, only about a dozen will enjoy partnership status. Typically, these elite few tend to be large organisations. For example, the partner module suppliers in the Smart Car Case study 7.3) are responsible for managing their portion of the inbound supply chain and also have developed sophisticated marketing, product development and logistics capabilities.

The extent to which companies have undertaken restructuring of their supply chain through selection of lead suppliers, whilst demoting the majority to tier 2, is exceptional. Even in the early 1990s, two-thirds of companies were reported to be reducing their supplier base. Anecdotal accounts of the reductions abound. For example, Sun Microsystems was reported to have consolidated the top 85 per cent of its purchasing spend from across 100 suppliers in 1990 to just 20 a few years later.

Case study 8.9 explains some of the dynamics in automotive inbound supply chains, and the changing roles and responsibilities of suppliers.

CASE STUDY 8.9

Automotive supply chains: a range of inbound logistics solutions

Automotive assemblers and their inbound supply chains have developed many solutions to orchestrate the manufacturing and delivery of the thousands of parts that go to make up a vehicle. The many potential inbound logistics solutions are summarised in Figure 8.13.

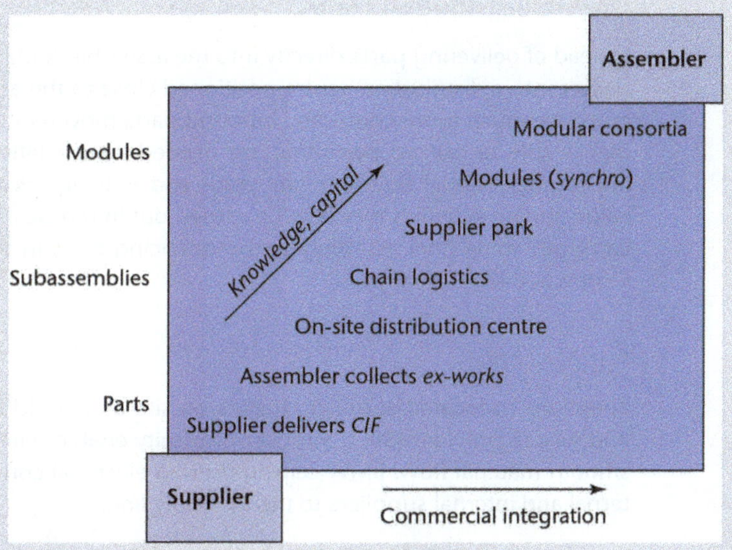

Figure 8.13 Evolving inbound supply relationships.

Changes are of increasing value to the vehicle assemblers, where the complexity of the logistics operation has been greatly downsized by reducing the number of tier 1 suppliers and broadening their responsibilities. Yet the ability of the assemblers to customise their finished products has increased. Quality consistency is expected at 50 ppm, whilst demanding price reduction targets are the norm.

Supplier delivers CIF (carriage, insurance and freight)

The supplier delivers the ordered parts to the assembler's factory, and includes the distribution costs in the piece part price.

Assembler collects ex-works

The assembler subcontracts the process of parts collection from a number of suppliers visited on a daily frequency. Parts are taken to a consolidation centre, where they are decanted into trailers destined for different assembly plants. An example is the Ford operation run by Exel at Birmingham in the UK. Parts collections are made from the Midlands region of the UK, and dispatched to 22 Ford plants around Europe.

Automotive supplier community

This is a dedicated co-location of suppliers in the region of dedicated vehicle manufacturers. The big difference from all the other integration types is that deliveries are made to more than one vehicle assembly plant. An example for more than one OEM plant is the BMW Innovation Estate in Wackersdorf where several suppliers provide parts for four BMW sites.

On-site distribution centre

Instead of delivering parts directly into the assembler's plant, the logistics partner may deliver into a distribution centre positioned close to the assembler's plant. The advantages are much more controlled inbound parts movements into the plant. The assembler is able to call up parts that are needed for a relatively short time period, thus improving material flow into the plant and reducing vehicle congestion. Additional value-adding activities may also be carried out in the DC. Thus, for example, suppliers carry out some final assembly and sequencing tasks in the new Integrated Logistics Centre at BMW, Cowley.

Supply centres

These are co-located supplier clusters on site and could be part invested by the VM and service provider (3PL). Supplier proximity enables late module configuration with smooth material flow. BMW Leipzig uses an electrical conveyor system to connect external and internal suppliers to the assembly line.

Chain logistics

Here the objective is to increase the *speed* of the inbound supply chain. If not planned and managed, drivers' hours regulations across Europe can lead to waste as the supply chain stops to allow for rests. The higher the speed of inbound supply, the lower the stock that needs to be held at the assembly plant. A useful further advantage is that the higher the speed, the less packaging and fewer containers are needed in the supply chain. An example of chain logistics is the ALUK operation that supports the Toyota plant at Burnaston in the UK. Parts movements from a supplier in southern Spain are planned in four-hour stages, where the full trailer is swapped for an empty one in a similar fashion to the Pony Express in the days of the Wild West!

Supplier park

A supplier park is a cluster of suppliers located outside but close to a final assembly plant; popular with JIS suppliers and associated with new assembly plants linked to supplier by conveyor belts, tunnels or bridges. (JIS = just-in-sequence: the capability to supply a module in accordance with the drumbeat requirements of an assembler.) Major tier 1 subassembly manufacturers are positioned on a supplier park close to the assembly hall. Major subassemblies are then sequenced into the assembly hall in response to a 'drumbeat' (based on the master schedule – see Chapter 6), which identifies the precise specification of the next body to be dropped onto the trim and final assembly track. Suppliers then have a finite amount of time to complete assembly and deliver to the point of use on the track. An example here is the Exel operation at the VW–Seat plant at Martorell near Barcelona, where material movements on the supplier park are specified and orchestrated by means of Exel's IT systems.

Modules

The VW–Seat plant at Martorell demonstrates a further advance in logistics thinking. Instead of delivering a large number of subassemblies, why not get the tier 1 suppliers to coordinate all the parts needed to produce a complete module that then simply can be bolted onto the car? Product variety can be increased by customisation of the modules. The advantages are illustrated in Figure 8.14.

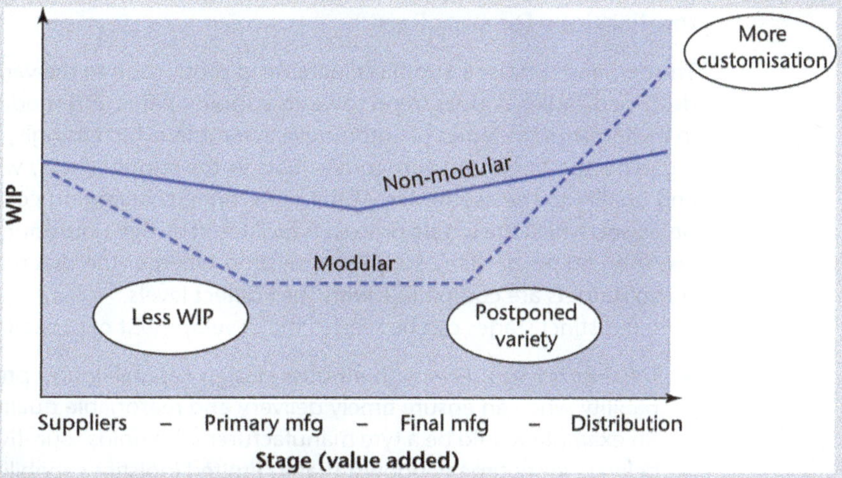

Figure 8.14 Modularisation: doing more with less.

Modular designs offer less WIP and a considerably downsized process for the assembler, and greater variety for the customer. Downsizing of the assembly process means that it is shorter, and can be positioned closer to customer demand. Complexity can then be added later in the pipeline between customer order and delivery of the specified car into the customer's hands – a concept called *postponed variety*. The term *synchronous supply* has been used to describe the delivery of modules not just at the correct quality and correct time, but on a real-time basis with the assembler and with the added challenge of zero safety stock. The condominium approach goes a step further in integration. In this case the suppliers reside and operate under the same roof as the vehicle manufacturers. Due to outsourcing and the lean management, VMs often do not need adjacent space at the final assembly track and can thus offer their factory space to suppliers. Suppliers then assemble their own modules inside the assembly area. An example for the condominium is the Ford Industrial Complex at Camacari in Brazil.

Modular consortia

This is the highest possible integration step for suppliers in the automotive industry. The whole assembly operation is divided into separate modules, with a supplier responsible for each. Therefore, the suppliers not only assemble the modules, but they also perform part of the final vehicle assembly.

The VW bus and truck plant in Brazil is an experiment in the further development of the modular concept. The truck assembly operation has been divided into seven modules, with a supplier responsible for each. All the direct workers are on the supplier's payroll, and the supplier not only assembles the module, but also performs final assembly of the vehicle. The assembler's task has been downsized to engineering, design, supervision and administration. The Mercedes plant at Hambach in France, which produces the micro compact Smart Car, divides the vehicle into five main modules. Seven suppliers are fully integrated into the final assembly plant, whilst 16 non-integrated suppliers deliver submodules and parts. The whole information system – which supports manufacturing, logistics and distribution – is outsourced to Accenture.

Implications for suppliers

The demands on tier 1 suppliers increase in proportion to the various logistics solutions described earlier. A clear trend towards supplier parks and modularisation can be seen in the logistics strategies of automotive assemblers. Increasingly, tier 1 suppliers are being expected to control subsequent tiers in the supply chain, whilst ensuring delivery and quality to the assembler. At the same time, challenging cost reduction targets are being set, whilst the whole process is facilitated by tier 1 outbound defect levels that are less than 50 ppm. Many suppliers question whether the draconian demands for 'cost down' targets are compatible with such defect levels.

Four distinct stages can be seen in the development of capabilities by tier 1 suppliers:

- *Tier 1 basic:* suppliers with inhouse design capability and project management capability who can ensure timely delivery and reasonable quality reliability (50 ppm). An example would be a tyre manufacturer who holds four–five days' stock and who delivers to set time windows: that is, limited logistics capability.
- *Tier 1 synchro:* suppliers who provide all of the basic capabilities, but with virtually no safety stock. Additional capabilities for the supplier are synchro logistics and IT expertise, which is closely integrated with the assembler, greater flexibility and more secure emergency procedures. They operate through 'clone' plants that are situated on supplier parks no more than 10 minutes' travel time from the assembler's production line.
- *Tier 0.5:* full service providers, who integrate component manufacturing through supply chain management to achieve the optimum design of a given module. They carry out pre-emptive market research and develop innovative designs through shelf engineering (designs that are prepared proactively in advance of need and placed 'on the shelf', thus saving time in the event that the need does arise). They are partners in major cost reduction projects at each model change, and in continuous improvement projects in between.
- *Tier 0:* the highest possible integration. In addition to tier 0.5 responsibilities, the tier 0 supplier is responsible for a vehicle manufacturer's main assembly operations divided into separate modules, with a tier 0 supplier responsible for each. Therefore, the supplier performs final VM module assembly operations. Final VM assembly line work retention is a matter of the VM's strategic choice but it could be performed by the tier 0, as exhibited online by supplier Magna for BMW.

There is a substantial passing of risk from the assembler to the tier 1 supplier at each stage. Increasingly, the supplier takes responsibility for designing and developing new products of increasing complexity in advance of new model programmes. And there is no guarantee that the supplier will get the work, because competitive tenders are issued for each new model. This forces suppliers to keep primary manufacturing and core business at a 'home' location, and to construct low-cost, late-configuration 'postponement' plants near the OEM's assembly hall to enable synchro deliveries. The decision by BMW to switch R50 (Mini) assembly from Longbridge to Cowley left a number of suppliers with £2 million synchro assembly units in the wrong place.

The strategic dilemma for tier 1 suppliers who currently supply the assemblers directly is whether to expand into system integrators (tier 0.5), or to become indirect suppliers to such organisations. Siegfried Wolf of Magna International described the tier 0.5 transition as follows:

> **To become part of this new tier, companies will require a worldwide presence, global sourcing, programme management, technology, JIT and JIS know-how and specialist production knowledge. They will also require a high level of R&D spend.**

So, after tier 0.5, where do the competitive challenges lie? Tier 2 suppliers still will be largely low-overhead, product-based companies that have limited service capability. Price pressure will continue to be severe, and return on sales often little above break-even. Tier 2 suppliers often cannot afford expensive inspection and test resources, so defect levels will continue to be relatively high, often in the range 1,000–2,000 ppm (i.e. 1–2 per cent). This will present major challenges for tier 0.5 suppliers, who must also guarantee delivery reliability to the assembly track, and a module that fits perfectly at all times.

As an example of tier 0.5 evolution, the joint venture between Canada's Magna Inter national and Japan's Calsonic Kansei ('Magna Kansei') produces the complete fascia ('cockpit module') for the Nissan Micra at a new facility close to Nissan's Washington plant in north-east England. Sales of the joint venture have almost trebled as it assumes responsibility for all of the components and subassemblies that make up the module. Calsonic Kansei designed, developed and tested the Micra fascia from a Nissan-engineered concept design. Co-location of supplier engineers at the Nissan development HQ in Atsugi City meant that Nissan product development teams supervised the design and development process. Magna Kansei assumes responsibility for parts it makes itself, for sourcing externally made parts, and for final module assembly and shipment JIS to the Nissan plant. There are 32 tier 2 suppliers: 18 are *imposed*, where Nissan sets the price and commercial details. The rest are *nominated* by Magna Kansei. This effectively limits the amount of integration that can take place at the design stage. Imposed suppliers that have been selected mainly on price act as barriers for improvement of quality capability.

(Sources: Harrison, 2000, 2004; Bennett and Klug, 2009.)

Questions

1. Summarise the advantages and risks to suppliers who want to achieve tier 0.5 status.
2. Consider the differences that can be seen between the logistics conditions of the supplier integration models discussed above. Comment on the geographic proximity, shared investment, asset specificity, IT-system integration and transport costs connected with the above models in a drive towards a 'tier zero' status for progressive suppliers and their vehicle manufacturers.

8.3.1 The transaction cost economics (TCE) view of relationships

Transaction cost economics (TCE) (Coase, 1937; Williamson, 1975, 1983) is a term that has often been used to explain supply chain management phenomena, particularly those related to 'the boundary decisions of companies, such as outsourcing, insourcing and relationship termination. The theory focuses on finding the governance structures (i.e. relationship structures) that will minimise transaction costs (Williamson, 1975; Zhao et al., 2004). According to Williamson (1985, 2008) governance structures involve the choice of managing operations and their associated costs through one of three different ways:

- a firm's internal hierarchy, in other words within the company, or vertical integration;
- open markets, where the relationship is on the basis of a short-term, arm's-length contract, with typically many suppliers per part; or
- long-term contracts (which Williamson termed hybrids), where the relationship is more involved, goes beyond the individual transactions and can be termed a strategic partnership.

So what does TCE say about the conditions under which these different types of relationship incur the minimum transaction costs and therefore may be deemed most appropriate?

TCE predicts that outsourcing, as in the open-market, arm's-length relationship, will prevail for low-frequency transactions, with few transaction-specific investments and characterised by a low level of uncertainty (Williamson, 2002).

Much of the explanatory power of TCE turns on asset specificity (Williamson 1975, 1985), which refers to relationship-specific investments that cannot be easily internalised or redeployed to another relationship. When buying firms work closely with vendors they tend to invest in relationship-specific assets, both physical (e.g. IT and equipment) and human (e.g. skills, knowledge and relationships). These kinds of relationship, often called **partnerships** (Lambert et al., 1996) or simply hybrids, involve significant inter-company asset co-specialisation, as further explained in Section 8.3.3. Research has shown that this kind of relationship can bring the benefits of hierarchies (i.e. asset specialisation and control) without its limitations (e.g. higher costs and reduced flexibility) and can ultimately lead to lower transaction costs (Dyer, 1996). These benefits motivate firms to maintain relationships as the benefits would be lost in the event of termination.

On the other hand, Williamson (1983) also argues that long-term relationships involving high investments in relationship-specific assets create bilateral dependency, as managers fear losing their investments or wasting efforts in trying to redeploy their assets, which effectively become the economic equivalent of hostages. In these cases, the higher the investment, the greater the motivation to maintain the relationship, creating lock-in situations (Caniels and Gelderman, 2005).

The other key factor highlighted by TCE that drives transaction costs and thus the selection of relationship type is uncertainty. Williamson (2008) argues that as uncertainty and associated disturbances increase, the additional transaction costs incurred through the necessary cooperative adaptation mean that internalising the activities becomes more attractive. Ellram et al., (2008) define uncertainty as the degree of volatility and unpredictability in the supply market (e.g. the exchange rate) and it has been suggested that this would remove some of the advantages of outsourcing. Therefore, in a situation of high uncertainty it would appear preferable to conduct the activity inhouse rather than to outsource.

We now look more closely at the long-term partnership that Williamson termed a hybrid.

8.4 Strategic partnerships in the supply chain

Key issues: **What are partnerships and their advantages? How can they be implemented and what are the barriers to their implementation?**

So far, we have used the term 'partners' in a supply chain to apply to all firms that are involved in a given network. Here, we review the added value that '**strategic partnerships**' may bring, assuming the conventional idea that these are long-term, rather than the short-term agile partnerships (discussed in Section 7.2.4). Generally, strategic partnerships are cooperative relationships that have been characterised as being based upon:

- the sharing of information;
- trust and openness;
- coordination and planning;
- mutual benefits and sharing of risks;
- a recognition of mutual interdependence;
- shared goals;
- compatibility of corporate philosophies.

8.4.1 Economic justification for partnerships

Entering into a partnership with a company, to whatever extent, implies a transition away from the rules of the open marketplace and towards alternatives, such as the long-term contract or partnership structure as described by TCE in Section 8.3.1. These different structures must demonstrate benefits; otherwise they will not deliver competitive advantage.

Open market relationships are typified by short-term contracts, arm's-length relations, little joint development and many suppliers per part, but these are contrasted by other supplier relationships. Long-term contract or partnership relationships, for example, are evident in the 'lean' model of supply. The Japanese tend to infuse their transactions with the non-economic qualities of commitment and trust. These characteristics are important in successful partnerships. Whilst this may increase initial investment costs and risks, it appears that these 'non-economic qualities' and other relationship specific assets described by TCE help to secure other economic and strategic advantages that are difficult to achieve through the open market system as explained by TCE (Section 8.3.1).

8.4.2 Advantages of partnerships

Within partnerships, savings come in the form of reduced negotiations and drawing up of separate contracts, reduced monitoring of supplier soundness, including supply quality, and increased productivity. These are accompanied by strategic advantages of shortened lead times and product cycles, and conditions amenable to longer-term investment.

These advantages, however, need to be set against the problems that can be associated with the introduction of commitment and trust which are explained in Section 8.4.5.

Activity 8.4

Consider the reasons why a company would wish to enter into a partnership with a customer or supplier. List the advantages and disadvantages you can think of.

8.4.3 Implementing strategic partnerships

A strategic partner is a company with whom a focal firm has decided to develop a long-term, collaborative relationship. 'Collaboration' may be the ultimate objective of a number of phases through which a supply relationship may evolve. A transition route from open-market negotiation to collaboration is shown in Figure 8.15.

Obligational aspects of the relationship increase from cooperation to collaboration. Coordination can be defined in terms of establishing 'rules of the road' whereby partners can work together. This is the key step to integrating the supply chain. Collaboration goes beyond integration by including long-term commitments to technology sharing and to closely integrated planning and control systems. The two firms become interdependent, that is, they adapt to each other and develop common logistics governance processes.

British Standard BS 11000 provides a framework for collaborative business relationships, to help business entities develop and manage their interactions with other organisations for maximum benefit to all. Using an 8-stage approach, the framework is designed to enable organisations of any size and sector to apply best practice principles to their own way of working, to get the most out of their business relationships. In March 2017 the International Standard was released – ISO44001.

And here it is important to offer a word of warning. It is apparent from our research (Koulikoff-Souviron and Harrison, 2007) that strategic partnerships are very demanding and resource intensive. So, it is necessary to determine where is

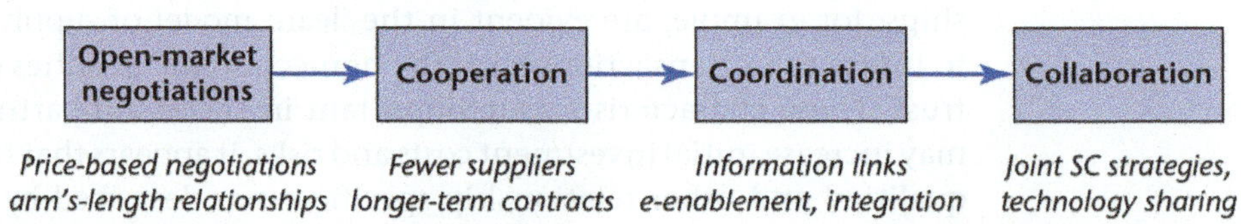

Figure 8.15 The transition from open-market negotiations to collaboration.
(Source: Adapted from Speckman et al., 1998.)

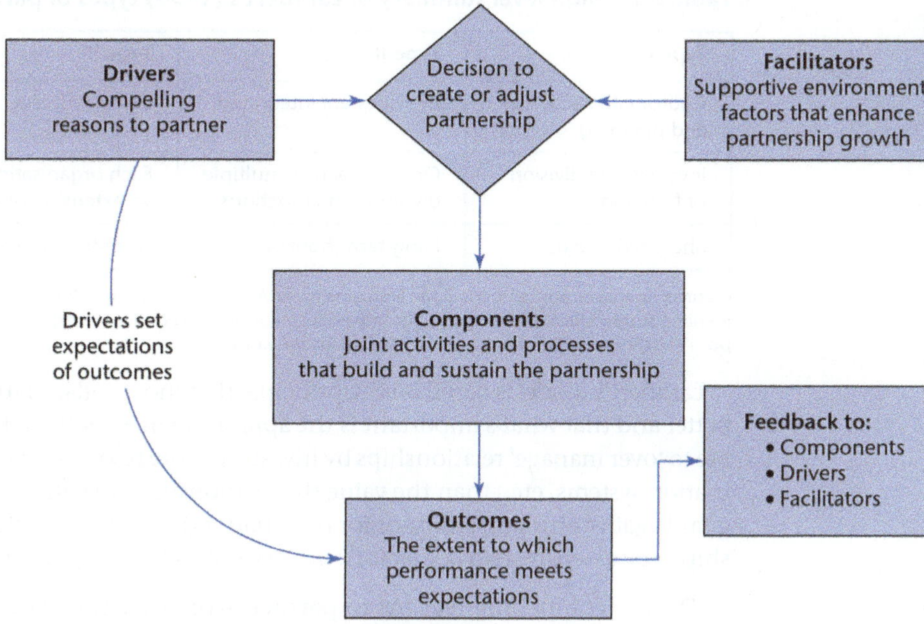

Figure 8.16 Lambert's Partnership model.

(Source: Lambert, D.M., Emmelhainz, M.A. and Gardner, J.T. (1996) 'Developing and implementing supply chain partnerships', The International Journal of Logistics Management, vol. 7, no. 2, pp. 1–17. for more information see: www.scm-institute.org. Reproduced by kind permission of Professor Doug Lambert.)

the most appropriate point along the route in Figure 8.16 for a given supply relationship. There is no point in pursuing a partnership just because it is 'more to the right'. In some cases, as stated earlier, an arm's-length relationship based on open-market negotiations will be most appropriate. Lambert's partnership model offers a framework which can be used to determine when a partnership is appropriate and what level of involvement across different operations might be most effective.

8.4.4 Lambert's partnership model

Douglas Lambert established a partnership model (1996), shown in Figure 8.17, which defines three levels of partnership (similar to those previously shown in Figure 8.16) from type I to type III, representing increasing levels of collaboration, as illustrated in Figure 8.17 and summarised in Table 8.1.

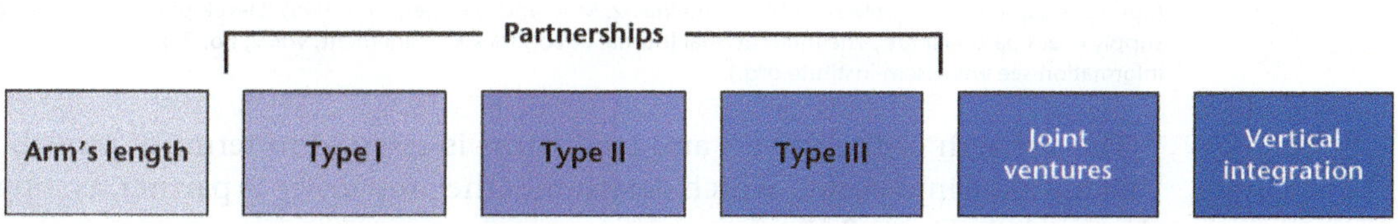

Figure 8.17 Three types of partnership.

(Source: Lambert, D.M., Emmelhainz, M.A. and Gardner, J.T. (1996) 'Developing and implementing supply chain partnerships', The International Journal of Logistics Management, vol. 7, no. 2, pp. 1–17. for more information see: www.scm-institute.org. Reproduced by kind permission of Professor Doug Lambert.)

Table 8.1 High level summary of Lambert's (1996) types of partnerships.

Type I	Type II	Type III
Coordinated activities and planning	Activities are integrated	Significant level of integration
Involves one division or function	Operates across multiple divisions and functions	Each organisation views the other as an extension of itself
Short-term focus	Long-term horizon	Long-term horizon with no end date

(Source: Adapted from Lambert, D.M., Emmelhainz, M.A. and Gardner, J.T. (1996) 'Developing and implementing supply chain partnerships', The International Journal of Logistics Management, vol. 7, no. 2, pp. 1–17. (For more information see www.scm-institute.org.)

Lambert's model is based on the principle that more collaboration is not necessarily better and that what's important is the appropriateness of the relationship. It is possible to 'over manage' relationships by investing more resources (employee's time, information systems, etc.) than the value the relationship can generate. The model aims to guard against this possibility, or for that matter the reverse – under-managed relationships – by assessing two key factors: drivers and facilitators, as outlined in Table 8.2.

- *Drivers:* compelling reasons to partner, which are the expected benefits from a closer relationship.
- *Facilitators:* supportive environmental factors that enhance partnership growth by increasing the likelihood of its success.

Table 8.2 Drivers and facilitators from Lambert's partnership model (1996).

Drivers	Facilitators
Probability that the relationship will substantially reduce *channel costs* or *improve asset utilisation*	Probability that the two organisations will *mesh smoothly* in terms of *culture* and *business*
Probability that the relationship will substantially improve *customer service level as measured by the customer*	Probability that the *management philosophy and techniques* of the two companies will match smoothly
Probability that the relationship will lead to *substantial marketing advantage*	Probability that both parties have the *skills and predisposition* needed for mutual relationship building
Probability that the relationship will result *in profit growth or reduced variability in profit*	Probability that the parties are *similar* in terms of various important factors (e.g. relative size in terms of sales, technological sophistication) that will affect the success of the relationship

(Source: Adapted from Lambert, D.M., Emmelhainz, M.A. and Gardner, J.T. (1996) 'Developing and implementing supply chain partnerships', The International Journal of Logistics Management, vol. 7, no. 2, pp. 1–17. (For more information see www.scm-institute.org.)

The strength of the drivers and facilitators is assessed in terms of probabilities that translate into points, which determines the propensity to partner, as shown in the matrix in Figure 8.18.

Crucial to the success of the partnership model is that it is applied through a two-day workshop where cross-functional, multi-level teams from each of the potentially partnering organisations attend. Another powerful aspect is that the drivers (which effectively represent each organisation's expected benefits from

Facilitator points \ Driver points	8–11 points	12–15 points	16–24 points
5–11 points	Arm's length	Type I	Type II
12–15 points	Type I	Type II	Type III
16–25 points	Type II	Type III	Type III

Figure 8.18 Propensity to partner matrix.

(Source: Lambert, D.M., Emmelhainz, M.A. and Gardner, J.T. (1996) 'Developing and implementing supply chain partnerships', The International Journal of Logistics Management, vol. 7, no. 2, pp. 1–17. for more information see: www.scm-institute.org. Reproduced by kind permission of Professor Doug Lambert.)

the relationship) are identified and scored selfishly and independently by the two companies, to ensure that neither company is inhibited. Ultimately, however, the lowest score is used to type the relationship because this is what will drive the level to which partnering is possible.

Once the relationship is 'typed' – the target relationship is identified – then the current relationship is assessed against eight components, such as planning and communication, and an action plan is jointly established to move the relationship towards the appropriate level.

The Lambert model has been tested on hundreds of companies since it was established in 1996, such as McDonald's, The Coca-Cola Company, Mars, Cargill, and 3M, many of whom have applied it to a number of their more strategic relationships. Despite this, the partnership model remains unchanged and has proven to be an enduring approach to improving partnerships, such that they deliver more value to both companies. Indeed, Enz and Lambert (2023) studied 31 relationships and analysed how the management components were implemented in each relationship compared to the recommendations in the Lambert Partnership Model. They found that managers did not differentiate types of partnerships, which led to over-resourcing relationships with low potential and under-resourcing those with the highest potential for creating value. The research reinforces the need for a formal structure like the Lambert Partnership Model to establish joint goals for a relationship and guide management in implementation.

We now consider the barriers to developing partnerships in the first place.

8.4.5 Barriers to developing strategic partnerships

The transition from multiple sourcing and arm's-length negotiation of short-term, purchase-price-allocated contracts to a partnership based on cooperation, collaboration, trust and commitment requires a supply chain process to be put in place, which needs designing, developing, optimising and managing. A key step in achieving this is to ensure that supplier development and purchasing teams are fully involved in the changes.

Failure to do this often leads to purchasing executives undertaking behaviour incompatible with fostering successful strategic partnerships. Whilst many are familiar with – and voice support for – partnerships, in practice their approach and practices are not supportive. Barriers that have been identified include the following:

- There is an inappropriate use of *power* over the supply chain partner.
- Buyers focus on their own company's *self-interest*, often because they are incentivised to do so.
- There is a focus on the *negative implications* of entering into partnership.
- Whilst buyers value trust, commitment and reliability, they continue to be *opportunistic* and seek gains at their partner's expense.
- *Price* is viewed as the key attribute in supplier selection.

These barriers, which are explained next, show that the decision criteria used by buyers retain a legacy of the traditional approach where the choice of lowest price remains the most defining characteristic. Unless such behaviour is changed, it prevents supply chain relationships from developing beyond a crude application of commercial power, where the free market is used to instil discipline and promote a supply base in which it is assumed that the fit survive. An explanation of the barriers follows.

Power

The ability of one member in the supply chain to control another member at a different level can be detrimental to the overall supply network, and it can provide a source of conflict. Conflict is associated clearly with power, arising when one organisation impedes the achievement of the goals of another. For example, in retailing, shelf space is a key resource that has potentially conflicting implications for the retailer and for its suppliers. The retailer looks for maximum return on space and contribution to its image, whilst the supplier seeks maximum shelf space, trial for new products and preference over competitors.

Focus on negative implications of partnership

Buyers consider the benefits gained through heightened dependence on a smaller number of suppliers less favourably, and tend to highlight the risks. Buyers also consistently view the cost-saving aspects of supply chain management as more important than the revenue-enhancing benefits.

Opportunism

A key issue that prevents partnerships from enduring appears to be the gap between the strategic requirements of long-term partnerships and tactical-level manoeuvring – in particular, opportunism. It is a problem to resolve this, given that the dimensions that characterise close working relationships also provide both opportunity and increased incentive for opportunistic behaviour. This is caused when partners cannot easily obtain similar benefits outside the relationship and when specialised investments have been made. Buyers often assume that suppliers will take advantage if they become too important, and as such act to prevent this. The consequences for the partnership relationship come second in their considerations.

Self-interest

Companies face difficulties in establishing and maintaining supply chain partnerships. Even in the automotive industry, often considered the supply chain exemplar, companies keen to implement single sourcing continue to multisource, particularly for non-critical items and commodity items. They rarely enter into collaboration, even when the customer is dependent on the supplier - that is, when the product is strategically important and alternatives are limited - and instead set their self-interest higher than the need to act according to common best interest.

Focus on price

The focus on price may be due in some part to buyers having trouble valuing matters such as know-how, technological capability, a particular style of production or a spirit of innovation, and therefore being unable to price them accurately. Their concern that suppliers may act opportunistically tends to lead them to avoid entering into areas where these factors prevail. Significantly, one of the key areas that feature these traits is that of design and development. It seems that, in this area, buyers find it extremely difficult to measure designer performance or the amount of productive time spent during design, and therefore feel the need to guard against high bids from suppliers.

8.5 Supplier networks

***Key issues:* What are supplier networks and how can they be manifested?**

Supplier networks can be formal or informal groups of companies whose common interest is that they all supply a particular customer, or support an entire industry. Two such networks are considered here:

- Italian districts;
- Chinese industrial areas.

8.5.1 Italian districts

One way of organising supply networks has been popularised and led by industrial districts in Italy (Becattini, 2002). Porter (1990) commented on the strengths of the Italian ceramic tile 'cluster' in the Sassuolo district in his *Competitive Advantage of Nations*. Producers benefited from 'a highly developed set of suppliers, support industries, services and infrastructure', and the geographic concentration of firms in the district 'supercharged the whole process'. Districts are characterised by hundreds or even thousands of small, family-owned firms with a handful of employees working single shifts. The great majority of firms are led by entrepreneurs who are craftsmen, often relying on the most basic planning and control tools. Concern currently focuses on the ability of districts to adapt to changes in global competition, as Case study 8.10 explores.

CASE STUDY 8.10

Supply chain internationalisation in the Marche shoe district

The National Association of Italian Footwear Manufacturers (Assocalzaturifici – http://www.assocalzaturifici.it) explains, 'The success of the footwear sector in Italy is linked to an enterprising spirit and to the structure of the sector. The structure is a "web" of raw material suppliers, tanneries, components, accessories, machinery manufacturers, model makers and designers. This has resulted in a territorial - of firms and the formation of shoe manufacturing districts such as Marche, Tuscany, Venetia and Lombardy. The leading position of the Italian shoe industry is due to superior product quality and high levels of innovation and the fact that 85 per cent of its production is exported.' The Marche shoe district is the largest concentration of producers of shoes and accessories in Europe, spanning between the Provinces of Macerata and Fermo. There are more than 2,500 shoe firms, almost 500 shoe components firms and more than 100 leather firms employing almost 50,000 workers, with combined sales of almost €3 billion. The district is export-orientated, with more than 80 per cent of production going abroad – mainly to Germany, the USA, Russia and increasingly to Asia, including China.

District firms are mostly small family businesses with fewer than 20 employees, but there are also a few larger firms with internationally recognised brands. The district leader, Della Valle Group, produces high-quality shoes and bags, matching a classic style design with comfort and a sporty look. Traded on the Milan Stock Exchange, it has sales close to €1 billion (not only in footwear and not only in the Marche district), and has developed strong international brands – such as Tod's, Hogan and Fay, plus a growing network of directly owned stores. Leading positions in specific market niches are occupied by Fornari (focused on trendy female teenager shoes with its brands Fornarina and Akibiki), by Falc (specialising in children's top-quality shoes under Falcotto and Naturino brand names) and by Santoni (focused on top-quality handmade shoes with prices up to €1,500). Top fashion firms such as Prada, Dolce & Gabbana and Hugo Boss have signed licensing agreements with Macerata district firms for the production of their shoe collections. Figure 8.19 shows two products from the Santoni website.

The shoe district has developed as an integrated supply network, offering the vast and competitive range of components and equipment required for making shoes – from leather processing to soles moulding or laser cutting. Logistics is simplified by the geographical concentration of firms in the district and the personal knowledge and trust that characterises relationships amongst district entrepreneurs. Flexibility by the small firms' supply network enables the ups or downs of fashions to be met.

Since the 1990s, however, the district network has had to come to terms with an outsourcing trend to low labour-cost countries that is always a threat to mature and labour-intensive industries in developed economies. As a result, production of low-cost shoes has been outsourced almost fully, first to Eastern Europe and then to the Far East. In low-price product ranges, district companies retain only high-value activities of design, marketing and distribution in the Macerata district.

Figure 8.19 Italian style from the Santoni Collection.
(Source: gpriccardi/Adobe Stock Photo.)

Outsourcing has also affected the core district products in medium- to high-quality footwear. Here, however, foreign partners are involved in only less complex tasks to preserve Italian style and quality. The result is an increasingly widespread network. Processed leather is brought into the district after initial processing in Asia (mainly India and China). The leather is then checked, cut and prepared to be sent to Eastern Europe for further processing (mainly to Romania and the Balkans area for sewing and hemming). Prepared leather is returned to the district for finishing and assembly. Such partial outsourcing – called *outward processing traffic* – preserves the high-quality standards of district shoes whilst cutting down on costs. The shoe manufacturers' offshoring has triggered the international expansion of the largest shoe component manufacturers who have been following their 'industrial customers'. For instance, Finproject – the largest sole producers of the district – opened production plants in Romania, India and Mexico, and has established a logistics and commercial company to trade with China.

This makes logistics a critical activity. Transportation costs per unit have increased, and responsiveness has been put at risk. This is of particular concern to a business that is linked to fashion, where season collections and sales campaign deadlines cannot be missed. Whilst offshore sourcing has led to significantly longer lead times, increasing inventories and lot sizes are not an effective answer. Most district firms offer differentiated products based on fashion trends, and therefore would face a high risk of mark-downs at the end of season. Therefore, firms normally order only 25–30 per cent of requirements for a seasonal collection from their suppliers on the basis of forecasts, and these are mainly carry-over models and 'classic' leather. Orders for the rest of the collection are made in line with incoming orders from fashion fairs, distributors and boutiques.

Most of the companies are finding that their new international network (including a sales network that is extending progressively towards Asia) is becoming too complex to be managed without appropriate IT systems. Therefore many companies are adopting an ERP system as well as specific applications (especially for the tracking the progress of their suppliers). Leading district firms are tackling logistics issues through increased information processing capabilities and through advanced services from logistics service providers. In order to manage a production network spanning from nearby district suppliers to Eastern Europe (mainly for shoes) and China (for clothing), Fornari has installed SAP–AFS (Apparel and Footwear Solution). This new ERP system has allowed the company to improve visibility over production planning and tighten control over suppliers. Fornari has outsourced outbound logistics, and is considering a logistics platform to handle information exchange for district subcontractors and foreign suppliers to reduce costs, an RFID system to improve responsiveness to European customers and a logistics network to support its strong selling presence in China.

However, most district companies are not large enough to become attractive propositions for IT or logistics service providers. Whilst they can't afford to lose outsourcing opportunities, these small firms risk being unable to manage the more complex networks that result. Moreover, most district entrepreneurs do not fully support the potential advantages of sharing outsourced services. Since they lack the accounting tools for getting a complete picture of logistic costs, they do not perceive logistics as a competitive weapon. They care only about emergencies when a rush order is required or when a planned delivery is late, but dealing with such emergencies becomes more difficult when distant foreign partners are involved.

Developing the infrastructure, the skills and the mindsets, in order to manage such a radical change in international supply chain management, is probably the biggest challenge district companies will face in the next 5–10 years.

(Source: Professor Corrado Cerruti, University of Rome Tor Vergata, updated 2018.)

Questions

1. Analyse the strengths and weaknesses of the Italian shoe district logistics model.
2. Discuss the implications for the Italian shoe district of outsourcing elements of shoe production to Asia.

8.5.2 Chinese industrial areas

Manufacturing of goods has been extensively offshored to low-cost countries such as China, and trade between China and Europe has increased dramatically in the past 30 years. According to the European Commission (European Commission, 2024) China is the EU's second largest trading partner for goods after the United States, with bilateral trade reaching €739 billion in 2023. China is the EU's third-largest partner for exports and the biggest for imports.

In order to keep pace with these burgeoning trade flows, China has developed massive industrial areas. But 'one of the unique characteristics of industrial policy in China is that it involves government intervention at all levels, from the political elite all the way down to village leaders' (Liu, 2005). Government intervention has created another way of organising supply partnerships by means of industrial areas. First was Shenzhen in Guangdong Province (1980s), then Pudong of Shanghai (1990s). Tianjin was included in China's 11th Five-Year Programme (2006–10) as part of the country's effort to boost regional development of the Bohai Gulf Region in particular and the north-east and north-west of China.

More recently, the 14th Chinese Five-Year Plan (2021–2025) highlights "high-quality green development and emphasizes innovation as the core of modern development, relying on the dual circulation strategy as the growth paradigm coupled with reforms to increase living standards. Building on the achievements of the 13th Plan, it aims to reduce the carbon intensity of the economy and peak carbon dioxide emissions before 2030".

Summary

What are the benefits of integration in the supply chain?

- Integration in the supply chain is developed through improved coordination upstream and downstream. Coordination is concerned with establishing the 'rules of the road', whereby material and information flows work in practice.
- Research has shown that improved coordination between marketing and logistics results in better performance in areas such as cycle times, inventories, product availability and order-to-delivery lead times. Internal integration is the essential precursor to external integration.
- Improved responsiveness from supply chains is facilitated by integrated processes (including joint strategy determination) and synchronisation (coordinated flow facilitated by transparency of information upstream and downstream).
- JIT2 aims to achieve inter-company collaboration manually by placing customer and supplier together as supplier in plant.
- Benefits of electronic collaboration listed by Nestlé UK include improved availability of product to the consumer and hence more sales. The total service is improved, total costs are reduced (including inventory, waste and resources), and capacities can be reduced owing to the reductions in uncertainty achieved. In addition, processes that span two or more companies become far more integrated and, hence, simple, standard, speedy and certain. Trading partners become more committed to the shared plans and objectives.
- Electronic collaboration can be undertaken in three ways: transactional (the transmission of fixed-format documents with predefined data and information fields); information sharing (a one-way process of providing access to information such as product description and pricing, sales information, inventory and promotional calendars); and collaborative planning (electronic collaboration at strategic, operational and tactical levels).
- The closest supply relationships exhibit both 'together' and 'separate' tensions. Separation, especially during periods when the relationship is under pressure as a result of logistics failures, demands continuous remedial work. Research in the auto industry indicates that heavy downward cost pressures on suppliers limit the progress at which relationships deepen.

What are the different types of relationships in the supply chain?

- Supply chain relationships can vary from arm's length at one extreme (characterised by a focus on price, and by few points of contact between the organisations concerned), to vertical integration at the other (characterised by integration of processes and by contacts at all levels).
- The choice of the appropriate relationship is helped by recognising that some suppliers are more strategic than others. One way to segment the supplier base is to use the purchase portfolio index, and to divide suppliers according to strategic, bottleneck, non-critical and leverage characteristics.

- Partnerships may create more value, and have been described using seven factors: the sharing of information, trust and openness, coordination and planning, mutual benefits and sharing of risks, a recognition of mutual interdependence, shared goals, and compatibility of corporate philosophies.
- Three stages of the development of partnerships have been defined: cooperation, coordination and collaboration. The move towards collaborative partnerships is characterised by increases in the time horizon and the scope of activities involved.
- Lambert et al., (1996) established an enduring partnership model which determines the appropriate level of partnering (collaboration) on the basis of an assessment of drivers and facilitators. So the extent to which the partnership can deliver benefits drives the extent to which the partners should invest resource in working collaboratively.

How can closer supply chain relationships be implemented?

- Supply base consolidation seeks to reduce the suppliers with whom an organisation deals directly to a smaller number of strategic suppliers. Rationalisation involves re-tiering the supply chain so that other suppliers are placed under a lead supplier, or 'tier 1' supplier.
- Barriers to implementation of strategic partnerships include the inappropriate use of power, self-interest, a focus on negative implications, opportunism, and a preoccupation with price.
- Districts are a distinctly Italian solution to competitive advantage that involve the clustering of numerous SMEs in a focused network with close geographic distances between partners. Again, flexibility to respond to globalisation issues is proving to be a challenge.
- Industrial areas have supported China's extraordinary economic growth over the last 20–30 years. They have been developed by long-term, detailed government planning and financing. Binhai New Area exhibits many textbook features – such as clustering of firms around the state-of-the art port and airport. There are challenges, too, including better third-party logistics, development of the shipment centre and supporting services.

Discussion questions

1. Consider the use of partnerships with customers to improve competitiveness. Discuss this within a group scenario using the following guidelines:
   a. Make a list of companies in your chosen company's industry known to undertake supplier development. This should include all its customers and other companies that are potential customers.
   b. Make a list of all the types of development and improvement that your chosen company would like help with.
   c. Assemble these lists along the two sides of a grid, following the example shown in Figure 8.20. Mark on the grid where each of the companies is able to provide the necessary help.

d. Examine the grid you have constructed and identify the following:
   - issues that require help that current customers provide;
   - issues that require help that only potential customers provide;
   - issues that require help that no one provides;
   - customers (current or potential) that provide a great deal of help;
   - customers (current or potential) that provide little or no help.

e. Use these five criteria as the basis for identifying companies that should be valuable in ensuring your company's long-term success. These companies are the ones that should be considered as likely partners.

f. Having identified the likely partners, identify the difficulties in establishing partnerships and the problems in maintaining them.

g. Conclude with the actions that you would undertake to overcome the problems associated with partnerships in order to achieve their advantages.

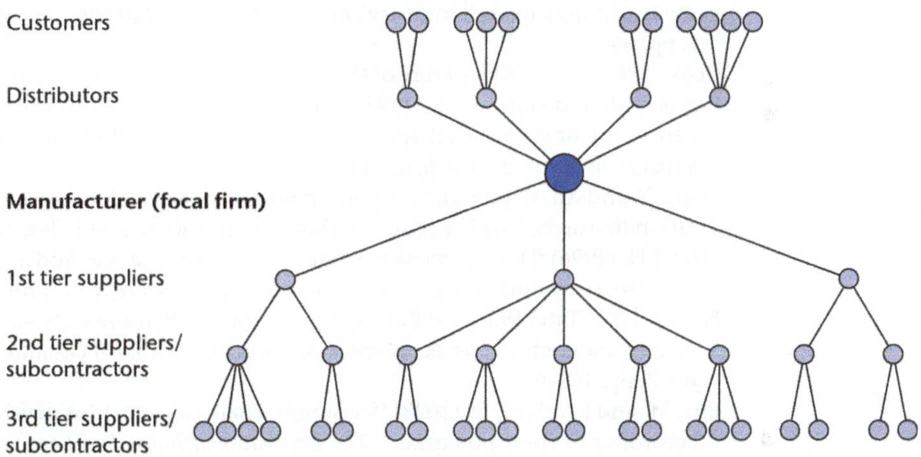

Figure 8.20 A supplier development grid.

2. 'Supply chain relationships don't mean anything. At the end of the day, it depends entirely on who has the most power. It's the big boys in the supply chain who decide just how much of a relationship there's going to be.'

   Discuss the implications of this statement.

References

Adnan-Ariffin, S. and Coussins, O. (2010) 'EDI Cost Savings Report: Cutting costs and paper with electronic transactions in the supply chain', GS1 and Cranfield School of Management.

Aitken, J. (1998) 'Integration of the Supply Chain: The Effect of Inter-organisational Interactions between Purchasing-Sales-Logistics', PhD thesis, Cranfield School of Management.

Angeles, R. (2005) 'RFID technologies: supply chain applications and implementation -issues', *Information Systems Management*, vol. 22, no. 1, pp. 51–65.

Attaran, M. and Attaran, S. (2007), 'Collaborative supply chain management: the most promising practice for building efficient and sustainable supply chains', *Business Process Management Journal*, vol. 13, no. 3, pp. 390–404.

Barratt, M. and Oliveira, A. (2002) 'Supply chain collaboration: exploring the early initiatives', *Supply Chain Planning*, vol. 4, no. 1, pp. 16–28.

Becattini, G. (2002) 'Industrial sectors and industrial districts: tools for industrial analysis', *European Planning Studies*, vol. 10, no. 4, pp. 483–93.

Ben-Daya, M., Hassini, E., Hariga, M. and AlDurgam, M.M. (2013) 'Consignment and vendor managed inventory in single-vendor multiple buyers supply chains', *International Journal of Production Research*, vol. 51, no. 5, pp. 1347–65.

Bennett, D. and Klug, F. (2009) *Automotive Supplier Integration from Automotive Supplier Community to Modular Consortium*, Proceedings of the 14th Annual Logistics Research Network Conference, 9–11 September, Cardiff.

Bichescu B.C. and Fry M.J. (2009), 'Vendor-managed inventory and the effect of channel power', OR Spectrum, Heidelberg, vol. 31, no. 1, pp. 195–228.

Caniels, M.C. and Gelderman, C.J. (2005) 'Purchasing strategies in the Kraljic matrix – a power and dependence perspective', *Journal of Purchasing and Supply Management*, vol. 11, no. 2, pp. 141–55.

Chaudhry, H. and Hodge, G. (2012) 'Postponement and supply chain structure: cases from the textile and apparel industry', *Journal of Fashion Marketing and Management*, vol. 16, no. 1, pp. 64–80.

Coase, R.H., (1937) 'The nature of the firm', *Economica*, vol. 4, no. 16, pp. 386–405.

Cooper, M. and Gardner, J. (1993) 'Building good business relationships – more than just partnering or strategic alliances', *International Journal of Physical Distribution and Logistics Management*, vol. 23, no. 6, pp. 14–26.

Dong, Y. and Xu, K. (2002), 'A supply chain model of vendor managed inventory', Transportation Research, Part E, *Logistics & Transportation Review*, vol. 38E, no. 2, pp. 75–95.

Dyer, J.H. (1996) 'Does governance matter? Keiretsu alliances and asset specificity as sources of Japanese competitive advantage', *Organization Science*, vol. 7, no. 6, pp. 649–66.

Ellram, L.M., Tate, W.L. and Billington, C. (2008) 'Offshore outsourcing of professional services: A transaction cost economics perspective', *Journal of Operations Management*, vol. 26, no. 2, pp. 148–63.

Enz, M. and Lambert, D. (2023) 'Are supply chain partnerships developed and implemented according to their potential?', *The International Journal of Logistics Management*, https://www.emerald.com/insight/0957-4093.htm

European Commission (2024) 'China EU trade relations with China. Facts, figures and latest developments', https://policy.trade.ec.europa.eu/eu-trade-relationships-country-and-region/countries-and-regions/china_en#:~:text=China%20is%20the%20EU's%20second,and%20the%20biggest%20for%20imports

Frohlich, M. and Westbrook, R. (2001) 'Arcs of integration: an international study of supply chain strategies', *Journal of Operations Management*, vol. 19, no. 2, pp. 185–200.

Fry, M.J., Kapuscinski, R. and Olsen, T.L. (2001) 'Coordinating production and delivery under a (z, Z)-type vendor-managed inventory contract', *Manufacturing & Service Operations Management*, vol. 3, no. 2, pp. 151–73.

Gallacher, L. (2017) 'Understanding the Potential Value of Blockchain Technology for the Supply Chain', Master's thesis, Cranfield University.

Gilmore, D. (2017) 'Supply chain comment: did Walmart's failed case tagging program set RFID back or move it forward?', *Supply Chain Digest*, 19th April 2017.

Gimenez, C. (2006) 'Logistics integration processes in the food industry', *International Journal of Physical Distribution and Logistics Management*, vol. 36, no. 3, pp. 231–49.

Harrison, A.S. (2000) 'Perestroika in automotive inbound', *Supply Chain Practice*, vol. 2, no. 3, pp. 28–39.

Harrison, A.S. (2004) 'Outsourcing in the automotive industry: the elusive goal of tier 0.5', *Manufacturing Engineer*, Feb/Mar, pp. 42–5.

Harrison, A. (2005) 'Levelled scheduling', in Slack, N. (ed.) *Blackwell Encyclopedic Dictionary of Operations Management*, 2nd edn, pp. 151–2. Oxford: Blackwell.

Harrop, M. (2017) 'The future of supply chain transparency: PLM meets the IoT and blockchain', *WhichPLM*, 20 October 2017.

van Hoek, R. and Chapman, P. (2006), 'From tinkering around the edge to enhancing revenue growth: supply chain – new product development alignment', *Supply Chain Management: An International Journal*, vol. 11, no. 5, pp. 385–9.

van Hoek, R. and Mitchell, A. (2006) 'Why supply chain efforts fail; the crisis of misalignment', *International Journal of Logistics, Research and Applications*, vol. 9, no. 3, pp. 269–81.

Holweg, M. and Miemczyk, J. (2002) 'Logistics in the "three day car" age: assessing the responsiveness of vehicle distribution logistics in the UK', *International Journal of Physical Distribution and Logistics Management*, vol. 32, no. 10, pp. 829–50.

Hunter, L., Beaumont, P. and Sinclair, D. (1996) 'A "partnership" route to human resource management?', *Journal of Management Studies*, vol. 33, no. 2, pp. 235–57.

IBM (2024) 'The Future of EDI', accessed on 30th August, 2024 at https://www.ibm.com/watson/supply-chain/resources/future-of-edi/#:~:text=EDI%20is%20alive%20and%20well,multi%2Dparty%20supply%20chain%20collaboration.

Kirby, J. (2003) 'Supply chain challenges: building relationships', *Harvard Business Review*, July, pp. 65–73.

Koulikoff-Souviron, M. and Harrison, A. (2007) 'The pervasive human resource picture in interdependent supply relationships', *International Journal of Operations and Production Management*, vol. 27, no. 1, pp. 8–27.

Kraljic, P. (1983) 'Purchasing must become supply management', *Harvard Business Review*, vol. 61, no. 5, 109–17.

Kuhel, J. (2002) 'Clothes call', *Supply Chain Technology News*, vol. 4, no. 2, pp. 18–21.

Kumar, S. and Arbi, A.S. (2008) 'Outsourcing strategies for apparel manufacture: a case study', *Journal of Manufacturing Technology Management*, vol. 19, no. 1, pp. 73–91.

Lambert, D.M., Emmelhainz, M.A. and Gardner, J.T. (1996) 'Developing and implementing supply chain partnerships', *The International Journal of Logistics Management*, vol. 7, no. 2, pp. 1–17. (For more information see www.scm-institute.org)

Lamming, R. (1993) *Beyond Partnership*. Hemel Hempstead: Prentice Hall.

Lapide, L. (2010) A History of CPFR, *Journal of Business Forecasting*, Winter.

Liu, L. (2005) *China's Industrial Policies and the Global Business Revolution – the Case of the Domestic Appliance Industry*. Abingdon: Routledge.

Nakamoto, S. (2008) 'Bitcoin: a peer-to-peer electronic cash system', at https://bitcoin.org/bitcoin.pdf

Oliveira, A. and Barratt, M. (2001) 'Exploring the experience of collaborative planning initiatives', *International Journal of Physical Distribution and Logistics Management*, vol. 31, no. 4, pp. 266–89.

Pagell, M. (2004) 'Understanding the factors that enable and inhibit the integration of operations, purchasing and logistics', *Journal of Operations Management*, vol. 22, no. 5, pp. 459–87.

Porter, M. (1990) *The Competitive Advantage of Nations*. London and Basingstoke: Macmillan.

Rubery, J., Carroll, M., Cooke F., Grugulis, I. and Earnshaw, J. (2004) 'Human resource management and the permeable organisation: the case of the multi-client call centre', *Journal of Management Studies*, vol. 41, no. 7, pp. 1199–222.

Rubman, J. and del Corrado (2009) 'Creating Competitive Advantage through Integrated PLM and Sourcing System', Kurt Salmon Associates, at www.kurtsalmon.com

Schoenherr, T. and Swink, M. (2012) 'Revisiting the arcs of integration: Cross-validations and extensions', *Journal of Operations Management*, 30, pp. 99–115.

Shen, Y. (2014) 'Develop a vendor managed inventory strategy', MSc thesis, Cranfield University.

Shen, Y. and Skipworth, H. (2014) 'Develop a vendor managed inventory strategy', MSc Thesis, Cranfield University.

Skjoett-Larsen, T., Therne, C. and Andersen, C. (2003), 'Supply chain collaboration: theoretical perspective and empirical evidence, *International Journal of Physical Distribution and Logistics Management*, vol. 33, no. 6, pp. 53–49.

Smart, A. and Harrison, A. (2003) 'On-line reverse auctions and their role in buyer–supplier relationships', *Journal of Purchasing and Supply Management*, vol. 9, pp. 257–68.

Speckman, R.E., Kamauff, J.W. and Myhr, N. (1998) 'An empirical investigation into supply chain management', *International Journal of Physical Distribution and Logistics Management*, vol. 28, no. 8, pp. 630–50.

Stank, T.P., Daughtery, P.J. and Ellinger, A.E. (1999) 'Marketing/logistics integration and firm performance', *The International Journal of Logistics Management*, vol. 10, no. 1, pp. 11–24.

Walport, M. (2015) 'Distributed ledger technology: beyond block chain'. Available at: https://www.gov.uk/government/uploads/system/uploads/attachment_data/file/492972/gs-16-1-distributed-ledger-technology.pdf (accessed: 27 June 2017).

Windahl, C. and Lakemond, M. (2006) 'Developing integrated solutions: the importance of relationships within the network', *Industrial Marketing Management*, vol. 35, no. 7, pp. 816–18.

Williamson, O.E., (1975) Markets and Hierarchies: *Economics and Antitrust Implications*, The Free Press, New York.

Williamson, O.E. (1983) 'Credible commitments: using hostages to support exchange', *American Economic Review*, vol. 73, no. 4, pp. 519–38.

Williamson, O.E. (1985) *The Economic Institutions of Capitalism*. New York: Free Press.

Williamson, O.E. (2002) 'The theory of the firm as governance structure: from choice to contract', *Journal of Economic Perspectives*, vol. 16, no. 3, pp. 171–95.

Williamson, O.E. (2008) 'Outsourcing: transaction cost economics and supply chain management', *Journal of Supply Chain Management*, vol. 44, no. 2, pp. 5–16.

Yao, Y., Evers, P.T. and Dresner, M.E. (2007) 'Supply chain integration in vendor-managed inventory', *Decision Support Systems*, vol. 43, no. 2, pp. 663–74.

Zhao, H., Luo, Y. and Suh, T. (2004) 'Transaction cost determinants and ownership-based entry mode choice: a meta-analytical review', *Journal of International Business Studies*, vol. 35, no. 6, pp. 524–44.

Suggested further reading

Brown, S. and Cousins, P. (2004) 'Supply and operations: parallel paths and integrated strategies', *British Journal of Management*, vol. 15, no. 4, pp. 302–20.

Cousins, P., Handfield, R., Lawson, B. and Petersen, K. (2006) 'Creating supply chain relational capital: the impact of formal and informal socialisation processes', *Journal of Operations Management*, vol. 24, no. 6, pp. 851–63.

Das, T.K. and Teng, B.-S. (1998) 'Between trust and control: developing confidence in partner co-operation in alliances', *Academy of Management Review*, vol. 23, no. 3, pp. 491–513.

Fawcett, S. and Magnan, G. (2002) 'The rhetoric and reality of supply chain integration', *International Journal of Physical Distribution and Logistics Management*, vol. 32, no. 5, pp. 339–62.

Fernie, J. and Sparks, L. (eds) (2004) *Logistics and Retail Management*, 2nd edn. London: Kogan Page.

Li, S., Ragu-Nathan, B., Ragu-Nathan, T. and Subba Rao, S. (2006) 'The impact of supply chain management practices on competitive advantage and organisational performance', *Omega*, vol. 43, no. 2, pp. 107–24.

Ploetner, O. and Ehret, M. (2006) 'From relationships to partnerships – new forms of cooperation between buyer and seller', *Industrial Marketing Management*, vol. 335, no. 1, pp. 4–9.

Randall, G. and Seth, A. (2005) *Supermarket Wars: Global Strategies for Food Retailers*. Basingstoke: Palgrave Macmillan.

Scarborough, H. (2000) 'The HR implications of supply chain relationships', *Human Resource*

CHAPTER 9

Sourcing and procurement

Objectives

The objectives of this chapter are to explain:

- Value contributions that procurement can make to the supply chain;
- What procurement does or the basic procurement processes of strategic sourcing, supplier relationship management and operational ordering and buying;
- Four operating principles for engaging with procurement teams to capture supply market value:
  a. align internally before turning attention externally
  b. involve procurement early and develop category strategies
  c. focus on total cost of ownership, not just price
  d. after the contract has been signed, the harder work of supplier relationship management begins.
- The role that procurement can play in building a more sustainable supply chain.

By the end of this chapter, you should be able to understand:

- the three core procurement processes;
- the drivers of procurement value and how to engage with procurement teams to capture maximum value;
- how to approach the management of the supply base;
- the role of procurement in improving social and environmental sustainability.

Introduction

Supply management, enshrined in Kraljic's (1983) formative article 'Purchasing must become supply management', is concerned with inbound logistics (Figure 1.2) and addresses the broad task of coordinating the inbound flow of materials – including supplier selection, risk management, and material planning and control. 'Procurement', or 'purchasing', focuses on the upstream part of the supply chain and on interfaces with suppliers in particular.

Sourcing is concerned with the strategic decision of whether to obtain parts or services internally (within the company) or externally. If externally, then the next decision is which supplier to source from. Reflecting the literature, we use the terms 'supply management', 'procurement' and 'sourcing' interchangeably. Procurement is essentially a functional domain of the supply chain, just like manufacturing or distribution. The operational focus of procurement is to ensure that supplies of goods and services are in place so that a company can produce its product and/or service and ship it to the end-customer. Tactically, procurement also contributes to basic value drivers - such as price competitiveness and service levels. Strategically, procurement holds the potential to accelerate innovation, and drive step changes in costs and performance levels. Ever since the call from Kraljic to approach procurement strategically the function there has been growing recognition of its importance. If you consider that companies can spend half or more of their sales revenue on external spend with suppliers (Mena et al., 2021) it is understandable that companies cannot afford to ignore procurement as a critical enabler of business success. Supply disruptions during the COVID-19 pandemic and beyond only further reinforced the importance of managing key suppliers and supplies well (van Hoek, 2021).

Key issues

This chapter addresses four key issues:

1. **What does procurement do?** the core roles of the procurement function and how they drive value.
2. **Key drivers of procurement effectiveness and engagement with procurement teams:** business alignment, early involvement of procurement, total costs and value focus.
3. **Managing the supply base:** preferred suppliers, policies per segment, vendor rating – leading to 'customer of choice' status.
4. **The role of procurement in sustainability:** concrete ways to enact sustainable supply chain programs.

9.1 What does procurement do?

Key issue: The core roles of procurement and how they drive value

If the purpose of the procurement process is to help ensure 'supply' in the 'supply chain', how is that achieved? Essentially there are three core processes to consider, as shown in Figure 9.1. The **strategic sourcing** process focuses on identifying and selecting suppliers against business needs. After this process, the suppliers have been contracted, but they have *not yet delivered* the physical goods. For this, we have the operational process in which supplies are ordered and received, and suppliers are paid for their services. The supplier relationships management process focuses on the ongoing management of most important suppliers, after contracting and beyond the day to day ordering.

Figure 9.1 Procurement strategic sourcing, ordering cycle and managing supplier relations.

In Figure 9.1 the procurement core processes are shown as interlinked circular processes. On the right are the **operational procurement** activities that focus on placing orders, receiving goods and paying invoices. Aligning procurement processes with suppliers can be valuable, linking ordering systems on the 'buy' side with shipment systems on the 'supply' side. Managerial integration can create even greater benefits. This type of integration takes time, effort and investment and, as a result, it cannot be achieved with all suppliers. So companies contract with selected suppliers and agree upon product and service catalogues (see 'contracting' in the middle of Figure 9.1) so that – in the operational process – not every purchase needs to be treated as a new one. Buyers can order from selected and pre-qualified suppliers so that they do not have to find fresh sources and negotiate new commercial terms for every order.

Aligning contract and catalogue management effectively means that the left cog in Figure 9.1 is needed – strategic sourcing. Suppliers are selected and contracted for longer-term relationships in a particular area of spend. But, prior to that, the company's need for procured products and services is assessed in depth, its current spend with suppliers in each area of spend is assessed, the supplier market is studied, and a strategy to meet business needs by means of a procurement strategy is developed. Typically, this strategy is developed by a team of buyers, but includes business users and stakeholders such as manufacturing. Often, senior management is asked to sponsor and sign off on strategies. In short, there is a lot that happens before procurement action even begins, such as **tendering** for **framework agreements**. Development of a strategy for a given category of spend might lead to the conclusion that the category would be better made inhouse, and so should not be tendered at all. The result of the strategic sourcing process typically is the appointment of suppliers whose contracts are used in tactical procurement (production planning, project sourcing, etc.) and operational procurement (in the ordering cycle). Based upon tactical and operational experiences with contracted suppliers, performance is often evaluated and rated. Vendor ratings can then be used as the basis for supplier development and relationship management in the third core processes (section 9.3 will go into greater detail).

Figure 9.1 can be used to assess the maturity of a procurement function. If procurement is mostly focused on 'procure and pay' and 'operational' activities, then its buyers are more tactical in nature. If a company allocates staff and time to activities more to the left, it can be expected to see greater returns on its efforts and have the opportunity to align procurement more deeply with strategies and drivers of customer value.

Figure 9.2 offers an indication of staff time allocation in different processes, by maturity level. Staff in a less mature organisation will mostly focus on the operational procurement activities and allocate little time to strategic sourcing and supplier relationship activities. Whereas staff in more mature procurement organisations should not be allocating too much time on ordering, pricing orders and tracing shipments and payments and more time on sourcing and supplier relationships respectively. If that is the case, it is likely that operational processes are not running smoothly enough, leading to the escalation of many operational issues and/or staff is not strategic enough in capability or positioning to deliver procurement value. It is common today for professional procurement organisations to have a heavy focus on strategic sourcing, over the ordering cycle, and aspire to over time migrate towards a greater focus on **supplier relationship management**, in addition to strategic sourcing.

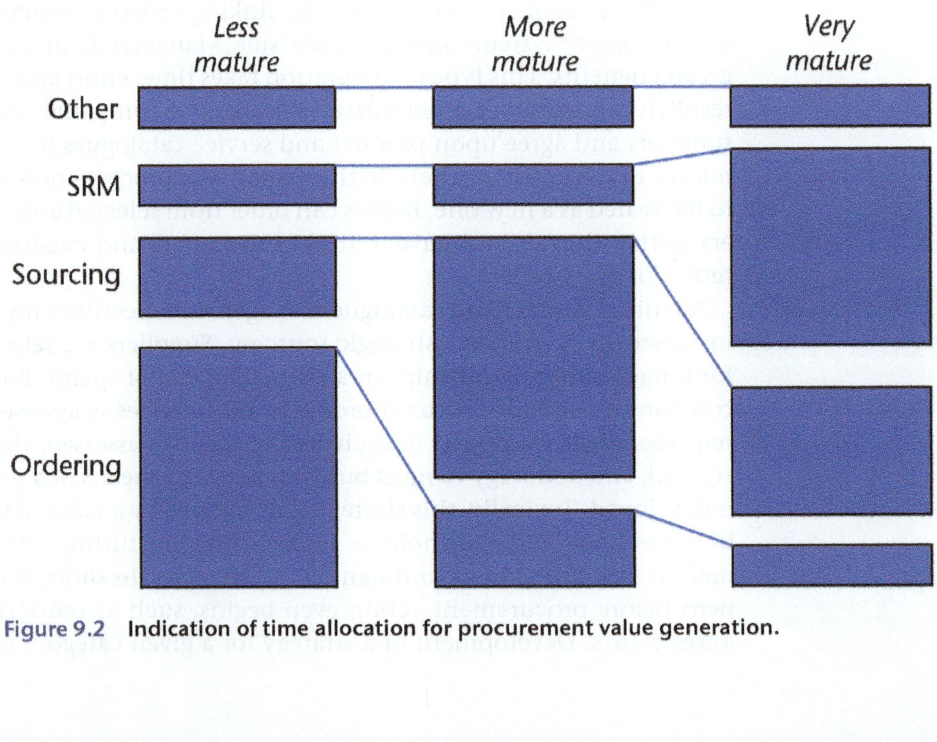

Figure 9.2 Indication of time allocation for procurement value generation.

CASE STUDY 9.1

The evolution of the procurement function at Moet Hennessy (based upon van Hoek et al., 2023)

Moet Hennessy is the wine and spirits division of the LVMH group. The company has external spend of about $4bn per year across a wide range of categories of spend, from bottles and ingredients to marketing and transportation (see Figure 9.3). Moet Hennessy's global procurement team of over 100 buyers around the world supports so-called 'maisons' (including Moet & Chandon, Hennessy and Glenmorangie), see Figure 9.4.

The company's chief procurement officer Dominique Lebigot's perspective on the evolution of procurement is that in the 1980s procurement's focus may have by and large been on operationally ensuring supplies and beginning to drive cost savings from negotiations and strategic sourcing efforts. Since then, however, procurement's scope has evolved and expanded to include a focus on productivity, service levels, innovation and corporate social responsibility considerations. Simply because a lot of the environmental and social impact of the company's supply chain originates from the supply-base, the procurement team has assumed a key role in focusing on sustainability in the supply chain. In addition to that, procurement is engaging around innovation and growth in supplier relationships. Through this focus on supplier relationships the company aims to not only ensure supply and help manage costs, the company also targets the acceleration of innovation and revenue growth as a result of that.

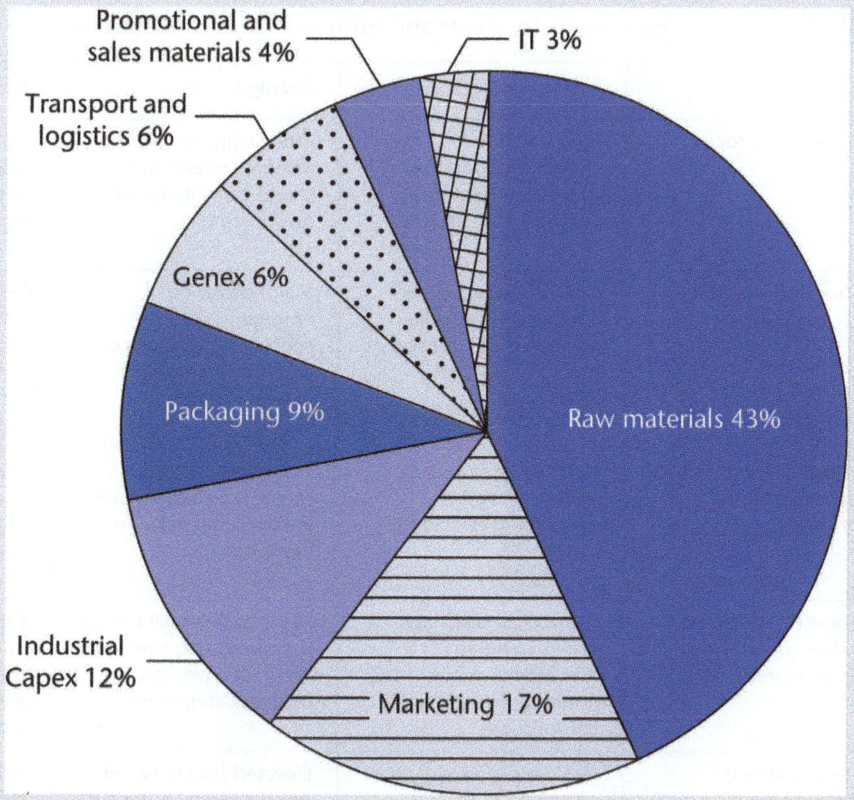

Figure 9.3 Procurement spend breakdown of Moet Hennessy.
(Source: Adapted from Moet Hennessy – Dominique Lebigot.)

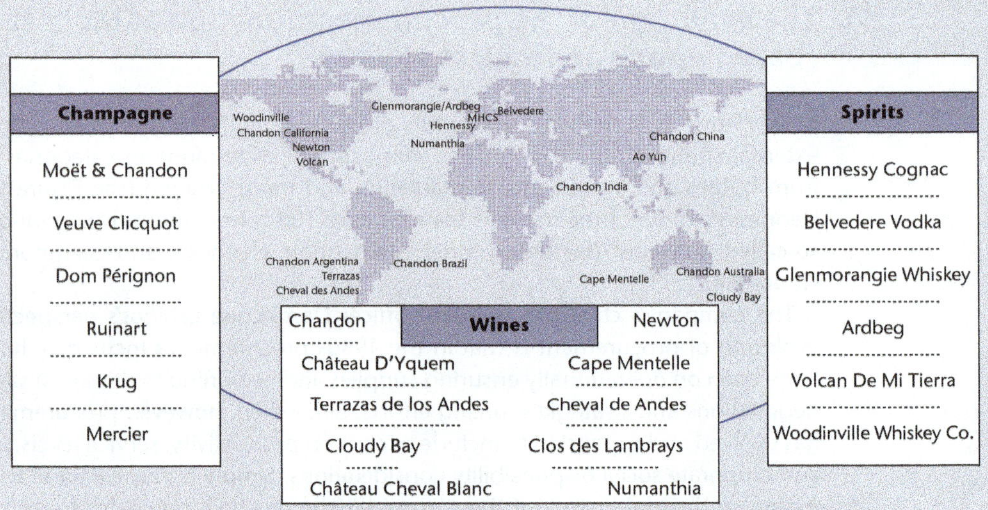

Figure 9.4 The maisons supported by Moet Hennessy's procurement team.
(Source: Adapted from Moet Hennessy – Dominique Lebigot.)

Table 9.1 offers a simplified description of what procurement departments in different stages of maturity look like by describing relative focus on procurement subprocesses.

Table 9.1 Procurement maturity levels and business value contributions.

	Less advanced	**Average**	**Best practice**
Operations focus	Procurement as a more clerical function that processes order forms and purchase admin	Automating to reduce resource needs and create capacity to focus on sourcing	Machine-like set up that can be integrated in a shared service environment, sometimes outside of procurement
Sourcing agenda	One-off negotiations with existing suppliers, no strategy or consistent focus, hardly any tendering	Major driver of emergence of procurement, focus on penetrating pools of external spend	Few areas of external spend untouched, most sourcing projects updated several times already and more focus on relationships with suppliers
Supplier relationship management practice	Hardly any; imposing their process for interacting, back-office centric	Initial steps after tenders, perhaps some limited feedback and catch ups	Major rebalance in resourcing and talent mix, top2tops, joint action planning, etc. to capture premium access
Top KPIs/business value contributions of procurement	Number of purchase orders handled and other volume metrics, order process compliance	Move to financial benefit measurement; savings, contract coverage, business alignment	Expansion into value and multidimensional metrics: cost effectiveness and TCO, innovation, sustainability
How visible is procurement?	Not too prominent One-off negotiations	Elevated profile based upon savings, potential tenders, framework agreements	Relationship meetings, focus beyond the contract and on working together for the long run

9.2 Key drivers of procurement effectiveness – how to engage with the procurement team

Key issues: **What are the key drivers of procurement effectiveness? How can business alignment, early involvement of procurement in product design and a total cost approach drive effectiveness of procurement?**

Every supply chain organisation engages with procurement teams, whether they are housed in the supply chain organisation or outside of it. Depending upon the drivers of customer value and industry structure, procurement has different contributions to make towards a supply chain's competitiveness. The best-known is to ensure cost-efficient supply of goods and services. This driver is particularly valuable in:

- narrow margin industries;
- price-sensitive markets;
- companies that have a high procured value ratio, meaning that the value of procured goods and services is high in comparison to revenue generated.

In such environments a high share of total costs is managed in the procurement process.

Figure 9.5 shows an example of such an operating environment. A company with €1.1 billion in revenues buys in €754 million. So, in this example, procured goods and services amount to almost 70 per cent of revenues. After investments, other costs and salaries, the company makes a narrow 2.5 per cent or €28 million in profit. If procurement is able to lower prices on all the procured goods and services by only 5 per cent, it will more than double profits.

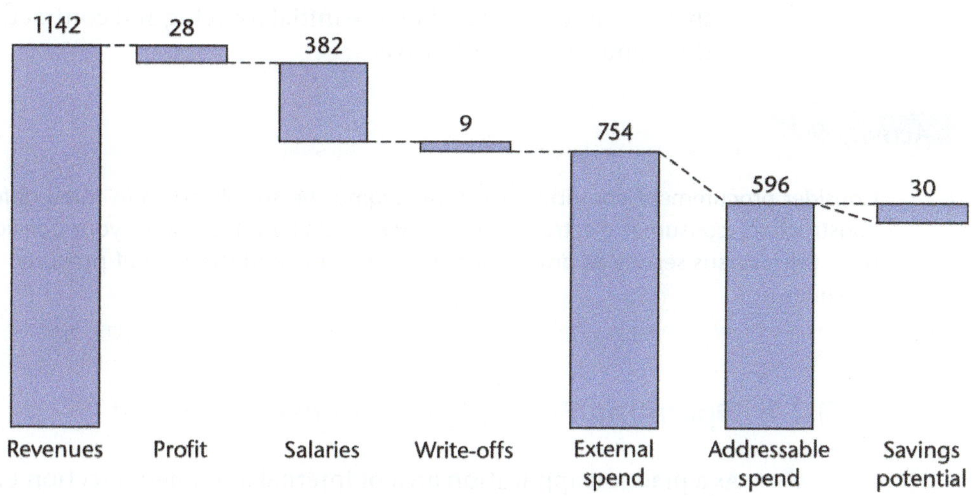

Figure 9.5 'Waterfall' of revenue, purchasing spend and profit.

But viewing procurement as essentially a function to drive down costs ignores its enormous strategic potential. As Cousins and Speckman (2003) say:

> **To view procurement as a cost savings activity only is to sentence one's company to competitive failure.**

While cost savings are still the most widely used performance indicator for procurement (Mena et al., 2021), cost savings are not the only contribution that procurement can make towards competitiveness of a supply chain. Case study 9.1 illustrates a broader set of performance contributions. Ensuring reliable delivery of supply helps ensure that production schedules are met and customer deliveries are not at risk. Also, JIT delivery needs to be negotiated and implemented with suppliers. In lean operating environments this reliability is of high value for seamless process execution. In more agile environments (Section 7.2), responsiveness of the supply base is of particular value and, again, capable suppliers need to be selected. Also, avoiding risks of discontinued supply and supplier bankruptcies or supply interruptions are amongst the contributions that procurement can make to supply chain performance. Innovations and contributions to step changes in services and service levels are achieved more easily through close supplier relations.

It is for these reasons that it is commonly recommended that four operating principles should be followed in the engagement with procurement teams:

- Align with procurement internally around its broader strategic role within the company before turning to supplier relations.
- Involve procurement early and fully in supply chain design and development, not just when a contract needs to be drawn up about prices for a supplier already selected, so that a category strategy can be developed.
- Focus on total costs of ownership or customer value sought, not solely on price.
- Do not consider the procurement job done when a supplier contract is signed; this moment marks the start of the supplier relationship management work that arguably is harder than the initial sourcing and contracting work, and more time- and resource-intensive.

Activity 9.1

Consider procurement contributions to managing the supply chain in three different sectors: construction, consumer electronics and grocery retailing. Include in your consideration margins, price versus service as drivers of customer value, and the ratio of procured value against revenues.

9.2.1 Operating Principle I: Business alignment

As a practical application area of internal alignment (Section 8.1.1), the first operating principle touches upon the work that an organisation needs to do internally, before it turns to the supply base. Procurement operates in a complex internal stakeholder environment and given procurement's focus on – and dominant role in – supplying, these upfront steps often are ignored or not focused on sufficiently.

The downside of that is that procurement might be sourcing supplies that are not fully right for business needs, running the risk of focusing on the wrong supplies, wasting supplier time and credibility internally, as well as company credibility in the supply market.

So, if procurement's role is to assure the inbound flow of materials, it is important for procurement professionals to be aligned closely with their peers in the supply chain. Likewise supply chain and business teams are advised to engage with procurement teams to ensure that sourcing strategies are business-centric and can be implemented fully. Without that it will be hard to know exactly what to buy and what opportunities in the supply market are most valid for consideration. Achieving this alignment takes consistent effort, much of it on the part of procurement professionals themselves.

How is alignment achieved in procurement? It is achieved at a number of stages, times and levels. Business plan alignment is achieved around the annual business planning and review cycle at a senior level between business unit management and procurement leadership. Alignment around specific business objectives that need to be addressed can be achieved through cross-functional operation of a project team. Coordination around specific contracts can be regulated by ordering policies and authorisations that specify that orders over a certain value need to be co-signed by procurement.

Achieving alignment requires of procurement and supply chain professionals alike:

- The ability to identify potential levers for alignment and to spot business needs.
- A willingness to see functional expertise as a price of entry, not a differentiator. Peers expect procurement and supply chain professionals to be knowledgeable about procurement and supply chain – and this is not a likely subject of conversation: business needs are.
- A service focus to centre the effort on peer needs, not procurement desire to drive value.
- A flexibility in articulating the agenda differently, depending upon business needs, and creativity to find a way to stick to the agenda, despite different business needs.
- The ability to 'sell' ideas through participation rather than through the use of authority or position (using these is a sign of reluctance to engage).
- To stand strong on business values, such as: 'customers first, positions last'; 'improvement forever, complacency never'; 'value centricity, position focus eccentricity,' to help keep the discussion focused.

Ways to achieve alignment include:

- Embedding/stationing key procurement staff in the businesses to make them part of the business 'fabric'.
- Using metrics of the business to evaluate performance.
- Studying business plans and business training material.
- Interviewing executives, getting invited to business meetings to understand the agenda of priorities and issues.

Markers of aligned procurement organisations include:

- A strong business partner focus amongst staff.
- Incentives and performance indicators that are not solely financial – such as cost savings based on PPV (purchase price variance – the 'standard cost' that has been budgeted and then used as a measure of procurement's performance) as his ignores other performance measures such as those based on quality and delivery reliability.
- Results that are not claimed by procurement, but procurement contributions are referenced in business results (annual reports, for example).
- Procedures and authorisations that exist, but are hardly referenced, due to seamless working relationships in which peers acknowledge each other's role and have clarity about roles and responsibilities.

Procurement professionals typically use stakeholder mapping as a technique for **business alignment**. A stakeholder map lists key internal stakeholders in a strategic sourcing project. This can involve for example:

- Budget holders whose spend is impacted,
- Senior executives that can sponsor and guide the project,
- Operational managers that use the product or service being sourced,
- Colleagues in support functions such as IT or HR that may be impacted by the project.

The stakeholder map captures not only roles and responsibilities of key colleagues, it also considers their information needs and ability to impact project results.

The purpose of stakeholder mapping is to identify key stakeholder to align with and to identify alignment approaches specific to the stakeholder. These might include approaches for gaining support to the project, seeking project-team participation and active or passive communication about the project.

Activity 9.2

Consider this example stakeholder map, consider what the description of a CEO and of a user of purchased services procurement might be.

Stake-holder name	Role	Involvement in procure-ment	Degree of impact (low–high)	Stake-holder goals	Commu-nication preferences	Stake-holder concerns	Agreed upon pri-orities and focus areas
	CEO						
	User of purchased services						

9.2.2 Operating Principle II: Involve procurement early to develop strategies for procurement categories

Principle II calls for involvement of procurement early and fully in supply chain projects, supply chain design and right across the product lifecycle, from design through to disposal. This broad-based involvement allows procurement to adopt a long-term, strategic role and to seek innovative opportunities to leverage supplier market value.

When approaching the procurement of goods and services in a particular category or area of the supplier market strategically, the company can be much smarter about how to approach the supplier market. Procurement already will be knowledgeable about supply market opportunities against business needs and will have benchmarked its approaches against competition.

A procurement strategy is typically focused on a category of products or services and so is often referred to as a *category strategy*. Categories could range from health and beauty products in retail, to surfacing products in the construction sector. Chapter headings of a strategy document for a procurement category typically include:

- The specification of supply chain stakeholders engaged in the development of the strategy for the purpose of properly specifying business needs and aligning business stakeholders;
- An overview of current procured value and existing supply base;
- An analysis of the supply market and supply market trends (what are the major suppliers, what are their strategies, how interesting are we as a customer?);
- Intelligence about competitor approaches and benchmark performance in the category;
- Consideration of the need to buy versus the opportunity to in-source; should we procure at all and, if we do, how will suppliers connect into our supply chain processes?;
- Total cost of ownership considerations (see following section).
- Supply-facing strategic options and relevant performance indicators for this category; taking in all of the above, how should we approach the supply base, including relationship considerations? Do we want to negotiate or form a partnership, for example?;
- Implementation and communication plans that focus on engaging the user base in the business and along the supply chain during and after the procurement project.

The availability of strategies for procurement categories, rather than the more limited procurement role in buying, is a key indicator of a company's procurement maturity. Early, timely and full involvement of procurement teams in supply chain projects ensures time to develop such a strategy and in turn enables greater returns on the project.

9.2.3 Operating Principle III: Total cost of ownership, not just price

Because savings are such a predominant traditional focus of procurement, it is understandable that negotiating lower prices is a captive domain for procurement professionals. Whilst price is an important aspect of the value exchange with the supplier, it might be a limited focus (see segmented supply chain strategy in Section 2.3). Price is typically the order winner in commoditised markets, where products and services are easily exchangeable. But delivery speed and reliability, product quality and innovation are more often the order winners in other markets. So, when squeezing prices relentlessly, service levels may drop in order to compensate for the price discounts. In Section 1.4, we reviewed the trade-off between cost and time: more of one means less of the other. It is for this reason that it is wiser to analyse total cost of ownership before negotiating price.

The total cost of ownership (TCO) concept acknowledges that price might only be the tip of the iceberg of cost drivers. Figure 9.6 displays this graphically. For example, price matters when buying a car. But so do maintenance costs, warranty, durability of the car, how quickly you can take delivery, the running costs (fuel, oil) and related costs (insurance, taxes). Beyond the initial purchase price there are costs that occur over time, during the lifecycle of the product, such as warranty. TCO is the equivalent to inbound logistics that cost-to-serve (CTS, Section 3.5.2) is to outbound logistics.

Figure 9.6 Total cost of ownership – initial purchase price might be only a fraction.
(Source: Jurgen Ziewe/Shutterstock.)

The objective of TCO is to get below the price of a purchase and to identify how much it costs a company over the product lifecycle. This includes pre-purchase costs, such as supplier evaluation and quality assurance.

The TCO situation can change over time. Figure 9.7 compares costs of products A and B: product A has a lower purchase price but higher maintenance costs. As a result, over time product A is more expensive than product B. If the purchase had been made with the intention to use the product for > 5 years, it would be advisable to purchase product B over product A.

Figure 9.8 compares costs of product C and D over time. Product C again has a lower initial purchase price, but that price does not include shipping and packaging. The price of product D *does* include shipping and packaging – making it a cheaper product once at the factory (total delivered costs).

Whilst it may be difficult to quantify total costs fully, simply *considering* total costs before buying provides an advantage in procurement. For example, service terms could be more important than price for a particular supply, and the category strategy would show this. Alternatively, it could be that technological edge is more of a differentiator between competitors, so this should be reflected in the search criteria for suppliers. Table 9.2 lists cost items for different cost areas over the product life cycle, and Activity 9.2 invites you to apply these.

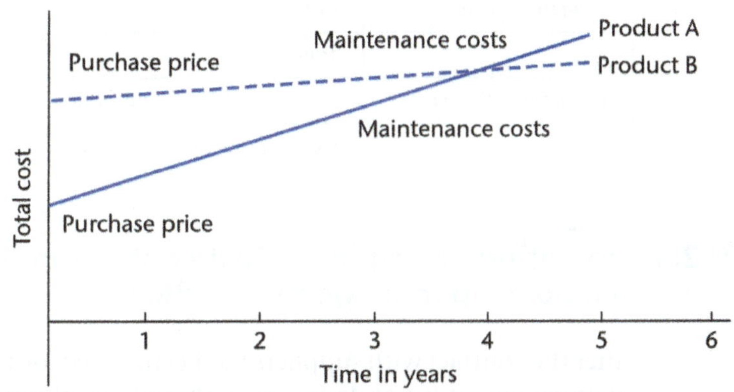

Figure 9.7 Cost of ownership over time for product A and product B.

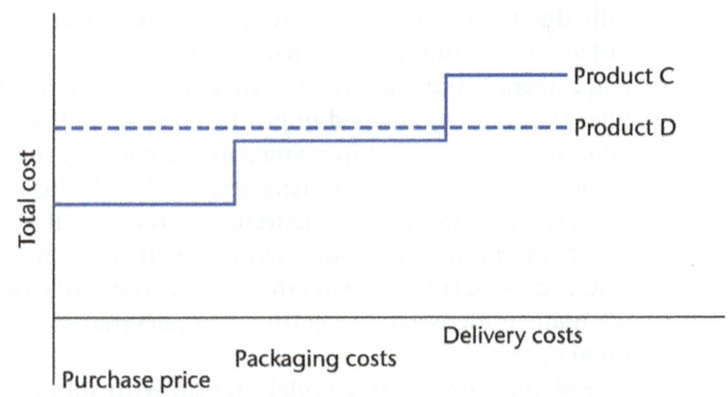

Figure 9.8 Cost of ownership over time for product C and product D.

Activity 9.3

Using the TCO checklist in Table 9.2, consider the purchase of: (1) a computer; and (2) a newspaper. List which cost factors might be relevant in the respective purchases and compare your views for the two.

Table 9.2 Drivers of total cost of ownership (TCO).

Cost area	Cost item	Applicable? Yes/No, how?
Purchase price	Price	
Delivery service	Shipping	
	Packaging	
	Extra charge for express shipping	
	Taxes and duties	
Warranty	Repairs	
	Service	
Operating costs	Insurance	
	Training	
Implementation costs	Phasing out existing product	
	Disposing of existing product	

9.2.4 Operating Principle IV: Post contracting comes supplier relationship management (SRM)

After the contract with suppliers has been signed for a particular category, the work of procurement is not done – even though, traditionally, that is what might have been the approach. When a contract has been signed, it still needs to be implemented. A lot of contracts that have been closed have never been implemented fully due to lack of business support, lack of leadership with the new supplier(s), or lack of alignment with business needs. So, again, without business alignment and category strategies, contracting could be a wasted effort. But a contracted supplier that is not managed might be equally ineffective. Without implementation and supplier relationship management, many of the contracted benefits evaporate before they are realised during the contract's duration. So, if not managed past contract agreement, the procurement process will probably generate limited value. There are improvement opportunities in supplier relationships well beyond the initial contracting. This relates also to the SKF case (Case study 9.2) where the company is focused on selecting suppliers that have a process for finding improvement opportunities.

SRM aims for ongoing collaboration with suppliers so that a company can not only help contracted suppliers implement contracts effectively. SRM also aims to ensure that the company achieves 'performance to contract' and continuous improvement over time (Mena et al., 2012). The effective ongoing management of critical supplier relationships may, over time, also enable a focal company to benefit from supplier innovation capabilities as referenced in Case study 9.2. It is important for supply chain and business teams to engage with procurement in the management of these critical relationships, just as it is important to engage with customers. Considering how much of a company's revenue is spend with suppliers it makes a lot of sense to engage with procurement in supplier relationship management, not just in the strategic sourcing and contracting of suppliers.

CASE STUDY 9.2

SKF supplier screens

SKF is a manufacturing company based in Sweden that produces a wide range of industrial parts and equipment. The company has undergone a multi-year effort to centre its sourcing more on TCO. In the company's experience, TCO has an impact on the evaluation of suppliers. SKF looks for 10 things when engaging with suppliers:

- a process to find cost-saving opportunities;
- a team able to implement programmes to achieve promised savings;
- a tool that measures expected/actual cost-saving initiatives;
- a culture that embraces value initiatives;
- a willingness to enter into agreements that focus on value created;
- ongoing pipeline of innovative, problem-solving solutions;
- well recognised in the industry for best practices;
- a log of applied solutions with resulting financial impact;
- a proven record of buying on TCO as opposed to price;
- value propositions with 'hard' monetary impact, not soft benefits.

These screens clearly demonstrate a focus far beyond price alone. They also show a focus on ongoing improvements, delivery and collaboration across companies to achieve success. This provides a good segue into the next operating principle: ongoing **supplier relationship management (SRM)**.

9.3 Managing the supply base

Key issues: **How can you segment your suppliers and what are the implications for preferred supplier selection? How do you rate your vendors? What is the impact of sustainable supply chain management (SSCM)?**

The basic steps to supplier relationship management are:

1. Reducing the supply base.
2. Segmenting the supply base.
3. Establishing policies per supply market segment.
4. Implementing vendor rating and improvement planning.

5. Assigning executive ownership to most important suppliers to foster relationship potential.
6. Managing towards a customer of choice status.

9.3.1 Reducing the supply base

Paradoxically, the first step to managing the supply base for value through relationships is to exclude the majority of suppliers. The rationale for this action is the inability of a company to allocate development resources to suppliers when there are simply too many of them.

One of the steps to prepare for reduction of the supply base is to collect the list across business units and operating entities, together with the amount of annual spend and which parts of the organisation are buying from which suppliers. This information also proves valuable in strategic sourcing efforts because it is helpful to have this information available in advance of developing a category strategy. Based on this spend information, the opportunity to rationalise much of the supply base may be revealed. For example, it may reveal that different business units within a company are buying from the same suppliers under different contractual terms, or that a number of different suppliers are used for non-critical items without anybody ever considering to contract a few with better terms. It also tends to reveal that the majority of spend is concentrated with a few suppliers, and that the remaining suppliers are high in number, low in spend. The few suppliers with whom a lot of business is done are obvious candidates for relationship management; others may not provide returns on the substantial investments involved.

CASE STUDY 9.3

Tail spend management at AIAC

A Canadian manufacturing company, part of the AIAC group, engaged in an effort to more strategically source and manage its critical supplier relationships. In addition to running sourcing projects across its largest categories of spend, the company also targeted its so-called tail spend for optimisation. Tail spend is external spend with suppliers below a threshold. It is minor spend with, typically, many suppliers with whom the company does not have the bandwidth to develop a relationships management approach, or even develop a category strategy. Elements considered in the programme included:

- Analyse and categorise data using pareto analysis – tail spend ranged in the several million dollars across several hundred of suppliers. Spend could be grouped into categories of spend that could be rationalised.
- A lot of the smaller spend is scattered across multiple suppliers that offer overlapping services and products, making it unnecessary to retain relationships with all suppliers. Sometimes there were also agreements with suppliers in place that were simply not used by selected buyers.
- A change in policy can enable the shortening of the supplier list; booking business travel through a travel management system for example can remove a long list of hotels from the supplier list.

- Pre-populated catalogues can also be used to avoid proliferation or orders and payment channels such as the use of company credit cards (p-cards) to enable removal of suppliers from the list.
- Consortium buying was also considered. By buying small spend categories through specialist consortiums, greater leverage can be achieved without the need to maintain direct relationships with all suppliers.
- Finally, AI chatbot technology can be used to negotiate with tail spend suppliers who buyers typically have little time to negotiate with (see: van Hoek et al., 2022).

The project did not only provide insight into a large group of suppliers that previously had gone largely unmanaged, It also introduced simplification of its supply-base, drove additional savings and provided the opportunity for buyers to focus more on most important supplier relationships.

9.3.2 Segmenting the supply base

Not all suppliers are created equal. There are large and small suppliers by spend; suppliers that do business with multiple parts of a company; suppliers that have been contracted through a strategic sourcing effort – and those that are not. Therefore, it is advisable to segment the supply base, just as we segment markets and customers (Section 2.2). In the best-case scenario, supplier segmentation should align with market segmentation, based on the notion that supply chains should be organised from the customer back, across the businesses and companies involved.

Basic segmentation criteria tend to include:

- the amount of spend with the supplier; and
- criticality of supplies for the smooth operation of the supply chain and for delivery to the customer.

Activity 9.4

Supplier segmentation is the supplier-facing version of customer segmentation in a B2B market. So a salesperson meeting with a procurement person is like two different parts of the business meeting each other, creating a match or a mismatch. Consider the conversation between a salesperson visiting a client considered to be a non-core 'cash cow' (customers who can be depended on for steady, dependable cash flow with little opportunity for growth), whilst the procurement person is considering the customer in terms of forming a strategic relationship. Also consider the reverse situation.

The widely used *purchase portfolio matrix* (Kraljic, 1983), one version of which is presented in Figure 9.9, is based on the notion that a company will seek to maximise purchasing power when it can. This approach assumes that the key factors that affect the relationship are the strength of the buying company in the buyer–supplier relationship, and the number of suppliers able and willing to supply a product in the short term.

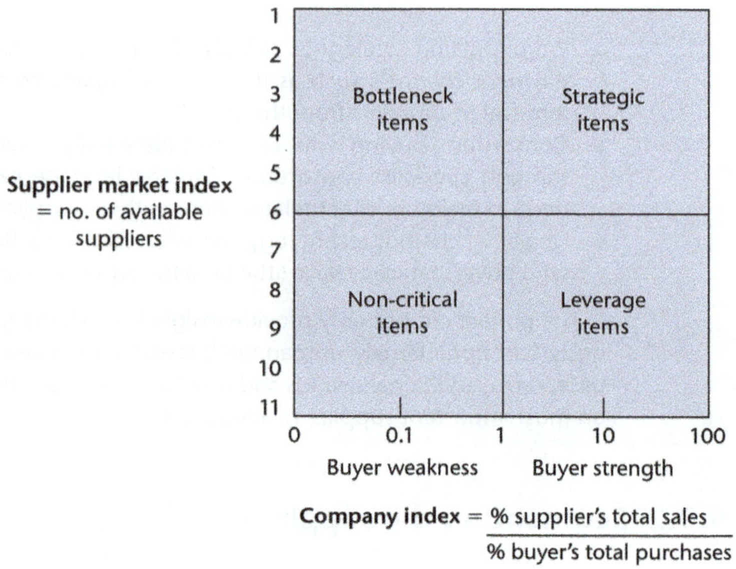

Figure 9.9 Purchase portfolio matrix.

Strategic items

Strategic items are those for which the buyer has strength but there are few available suppliers. In this situation, procurement should use its power strategically to draw suppliers into a relationship that ensures supply in the long term.

Bottleneck items

Where the buyer has little power and there are few alternatives, then these items are termed *bottlenecks*. The aim of purchasing in this situation is to reduce dependence on these items through diversification to find additional suppliers, seek substitute products and work with design teams to ensure that bottleneck items are avoided in new products where possible.

Non-critical items

Tail spend can be found in this segment; suppliers with minor spend on which there is little dependency. These suppliers typically earn little prioritisation and in fact are prime target for rationalisation.

Leverage items

Where there are a large number of available suppliers and the buyer has high spending power, then the buyer will be able to exercise this power to reduce prices and push for preferential treatment. Naturally, care should be taken not to antagonise suppliers just in case these favourable market conditions change.

This approach to segmentation is heavily weighted towards the buyer's viewpoint. However, it applies to many firms today and it makes clear that supplier need to work on their relative strategic importance to a company in order to strengthen their position in a supply relationship.

A major value of the Kraljic framework is that it helps procurement professionals 'to move commodities and suppliers around specific segments in the portfolio in such a way that the dependence on specific suppliers is reduced' (Gelderman and van Weele, 2002). Thereby, it is possible for positions to be changed *within* the matrix – either by suppliers or commodities. For example, some bottleneck items (such as maintenance, repair and overhaul – MRO) might be migrated into the leverage segment by simplifying the specification – or making it more generic and so allowing pooling of demand between different product groups. Figure 9.10 shows such possible migration routes from 'bottleneck' to 'leverage'. Such migrations and more strategic supply relationships help in the implementation of *target pricing*, whereby marketing in a company establishes the price of a product that will support the target market share. Target price less margin leaves the *target cost*, which is then used to establish prices for suppliers (as well as design and manufacturing target costs). Target pricing encourages more collaborative partnerships, and less adversarial relationships (Section 8.4).

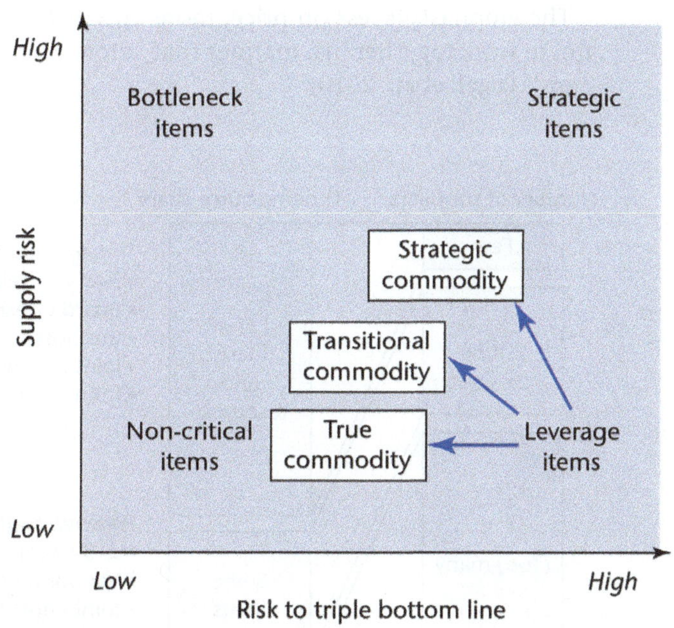

Figure 9.10 Migration of bottleneck items.

Activity 9.5

Selecting a company of your choice, use a copy of the purchase portfolio matrix (Figure 9.9) and plot on it the names of its top 10 customers and top 10 suppliers. Which position would your chosen company prefer to be in? Suggest actions that would improve the situation.

But in what may be a departure from the original Kraljic framework, the impact of sustainable supply chain management (SSCM) has apparently been to distort the familiar relationships. By changing the axes of the matrix to risk to the triple bottom line (TBL, Section 1.3.2) Pagell et al. (2010) created modified segments (Figure 9.11). 'Price' becomes subordinated to 'TBL risk', with all three values – environmental, social and economic – at stake. Some segments remained relatively unchanged – bottleneck and non-critical items are in the same positions when TBL risk is low. In the strategic segment, risks have been expanded to encompass all three TBL values. The biggest change was in leverage items. In SSCM, companies are dividing leverage items into three subsegments:

True commodities: retain the characteristics of the 'traditional' leverage items: suppliers would have an impact on only a single value of the TBL.

Strategic commodities: are recognised for their potential ability to be leveraged in terms of their long-term competitive advantage. Instead of using buyer power, small numbers of selected suppliers were being given long-term contracts and premium prices to invest in new product development.

Transitional commodities: initially these may be regarded as strategic commodities. But by working to reduce TBL risk, it may be possible to convert them over time into true commodities.

The emphasis is less on price, more on *supply-base continuity*. Partners in SSCM aim to work together in a manner that 'allows them to thrive, invest, innovate and grow' (Pagell et al., 2010).

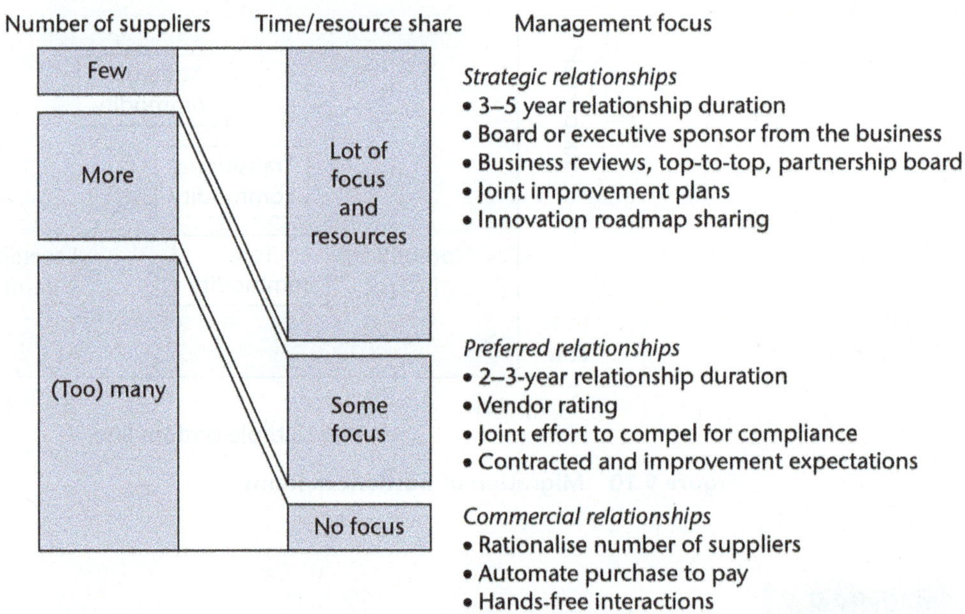

Figure 9.11 The sustainable purchasing portfolio matrix.

CASE STUDY 9.4

The criticality of supplier relationship for Rolls Royce

Rolls Royce, the UK-based manufacturer of plane engines, works with highly specialised and dedicated supplier relationships. An engine features about 48,000 parts and many of those are engineered and designed to the specific engine. All suppliers are certified and closely audited for safety regulatory requirements. Many of these parts are sourced from one supplier only and the supplier may run a dedicated operation and production line for those parts.

Because of the importance of these suppliers Rolls Royce shares detailed production forecasts and plans with suppliers, and during the COVID-19 pandemic the company worked with suppliers through multiple updates of the forecast and sought to keep supply-lines open. Switching suppliers in case of supplier closures would take 12–18 months for engineering, certification etc. and would effectively risk shutting down Rolls Royce production for that time.

Based upon van Hoek and Loseby (2021).

9.3.3 Establishing policies per supplier segment

If suppliers are segmented as a reflection of how they are not all similar, the obvious next step is to agree upon, and implement, policies that reflect the differing nature of relationships with suppliers in different segments. These tend to be centred around the amount of time and resources allocated to the relationship (for example, from limited resourcing in the commercial segment to extensive resourcing in the strategic segment) and the degree to which the relationships are embedded and stewarded inside the company.

Typical policy considerations are shown in Figure 9.12. After this step, we move from preparing for supplier relationship success by weeding out select relationships and establishing the relationship framework. This helps to implement differentiated levels of resource towards capturing relationship value. These efforts are of increasing selectivity and commitment.

Criteria	Sub-criteria	Effective weight	Criteria score	Subtotal
Quality	Customer reject Factory audit	0.171 0.075	8 7	1.368 0.525
Responsive	Urgent delivery Quality problem	0.13 0.18	9 9	0.117 0.162
Discipline	Honesty Procedural compliance	0.024 0.012	7 6	0.168 0.072
Delivery		0.336	7	2.352
Financial		0.067	9	0.603
Management	Attitude Business skill	0.038 0.010	7 9	0.266 0.09
Tech. capability	Tech. prob. solving Product ranges	0.068 0.016	9 9	0.612 0.144
Facility	Machinery Infrastructure Layout	0.102 0.02 0.03	9	0.918 0.18 0.27
Total vendor rating				7.847

Figure 9.12 Supplier segments and policy considerations.

Preferred suppliers

Suppliers that win contracts as part of a strategic sourcing project tend to be considered as *preferred suppliers*. These are favoured over non-contracted suppliers, and with the implementation of these contracts the suppliers get support and stewardship from the customer. Often, their success is a target for a procurement professional, and contract usage is measured as a key performance indicator. These suppliers are kept closer, and the relationship receives attention. But time and resources are not committed by the customer to the extent allocated to strategic relationships.

Strategic relationships

A very small number of suppliers can become of strategic importance to the fundamental success of a company, and to the performance of the supply chain. The single most important characteristic of such relationships is that there can be very few. Unfortunately, partnership-type terminology is one of the most inflated business terms. The term is used often by sales personnel to try to establish an appearance of commitment, whereas the real commitment for these types of relationships is simply unaffordable and uneconomical to spread too thinly.

CASE STUDY 9.5

Mars, a sweet treat for a good listener

Mars, the manufacturer of confectionery and pet food, has been on a multi-year journey towards supplier relationship management.

The key first step taken by the company was to conduct a survey in order to capture 'the voice of the supplier'. This proved a very worthwhile exercise, providing the company with a large quantity of feedback from its suppliers. It also gave the company a number of clear pointers 'on how it could change for the better its existing interaction with its most important suppliers, thus creating more value for Mars without necessarily incurring higher costs'.

Feedback from the suppliers included statements such as: 'Interaction with Mars about the business is limited, especially compared to other companies'; 'Mars is surprisingly quiet about its growth plans'; 'We did at least three presentations but none of the actions have gone forward. We did not receive any feedback on our unsuccessful proposals.'

These statements clearly reveal a desire among suppliers to know more so they can do more for Mars. They represent a clear call for sharing, transparency and open channels of communication, something of a departure from the traditional procurement practices of negotiating and closed tender processes, and so requiring a reset of the toolkit.

Mars has learned some valuable lessons in the course of this project:

- It takes time to build relationships and realise value (in particular because the supplier may not be used to this type of collaborative behaviour from procurement.
- It takes resources.
- Procurement foundations must be strong.
- A buying firm typically has more work to do to prepare for proper SRM than the suppliers do.
- SRM is a business program, not a procurement to-do, because if procurement were doing this independently of the business great improvements might be identified but not adopted by the business.

9.3.4 Vendor rating

Vendor rating is a measurement effort focused on supplier performance. Basic spot checks on delivery reliability (correct quantities and times) are used typically for commercial suppliers. Broader-based measures are needed for strategic and preferred relationships, as shown in Figure 9.12. Vendor rating is not 'measuring for the sake of measuring': it is measuring for the sake of *jointly improving* both supplier and customer processes. In the best cases, vendor rating results are used as a basis for a standing discussion of joint improvement opportunities between a supplier and customer team of stakeholders. Joint action plans are developed and progress is evaluated; joint improvement projects and teams may be involved. The supplier is asked explicitly to offer improvement suggestions to the customer, and performance challenges are owned jointly, not just reported to the supplier with a one-sided assignment to 'fix them'. In short, vendor rating is a mechanism to develop and advance the relationship, and to centre relationship management on business-relevant improvement opportunities, structurally and consistently. The vendor rating results are discussed on a regular basis and use an agreed set of metrics to provide structure and consistency in focus and commitment.

The steps involved in setting up a vendor rating system are:

1. *Select the team:* vendor rating is best undertaken by a cross-functional team of stakeholders who have various interests in a given commodity from design through to logistics. The process is not exclusive to the procurement function – vendor rating works better when there are business peers of procurement professionals involved in the dialogue to represent a broad internal client base. Often, performance data are partially collected, based upon qualitative input from users, and improvement suggestions should not come from procurement alone. So, as in strategic sourcing, business engagement and alignment is important preparation for vendor rating effectiveness.
2. *Establish the rating criteria:* the actual set of metrics used is a tool, and there is some sophistication that goes into its design. For example, the metrics categories may be consistent across categories but with different weighting between the categories, depending upon the category strategy. Also, metrics should be consistent between suppliers in the same category to allow for comparison between suppliers. The metrics categories typically include price, delivery reliability and quality, with innovation and process improvement as possible extras. Delivery tends to be reliability more than operational in nature: an on time in full (OTIF) measure, for example, that can be extracted from the company's ERP system. Quality and innovation may be more subjective in nature.
3. *Determine the effective weighting:* this establishes the team's view of the relative importance of each criterion. This may be achieved by asking members to undertake a paired comparison of the criteria that have been defined in step 2.
4. *Score each supplier's performance:* team members are asked to rate the criteria for each supplier. To minimise the risk of bias, a set of rating guidelines is established for each criterion, and a scale agreed – for example, from 1 = poor to 10 = excellent.

An example of the output of a vendor rating for a supplier is shown in Figure 9.13.

Sharing performance feedback may occasionally be considered risky or as giving up negotiation leverage when the supplier performance is good. That would be true if negotiation leverage is all that matters, but in preferred supplier relationships that is not at all the case. These are the relationships in which good performance is celebrated and shared as a joint success. Essentially, the customer wants the supplier to do well. Additionally, with a continuous improvement focus, no performance is perfect, so there is always work to be done and the performance bar is always rising. Figure 9.13 shows the output for three areas – price, quality and delivery reliability. Whilst supplier A scores very positively on price, it shows weaker performance on delivery reliability, prompting supplier and customer to work on forecasting processes collaboratively.

Beyond vendor rating, there are advanced levels of business involvement in supplier relationship management when it gets to more exclusive relationships, as we explain next.

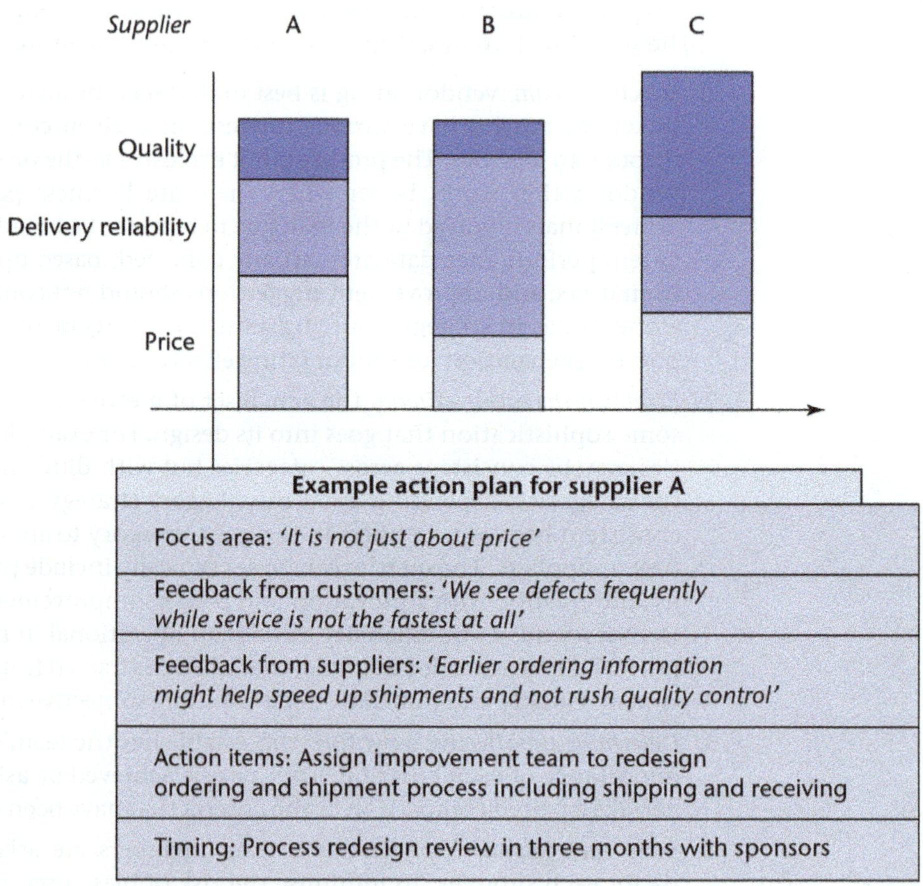

Figure 9.13 Vendor rating example.

Emission split in Scopes 1, 2 and 3 upstream for selected industries (CO_2e, 2019)

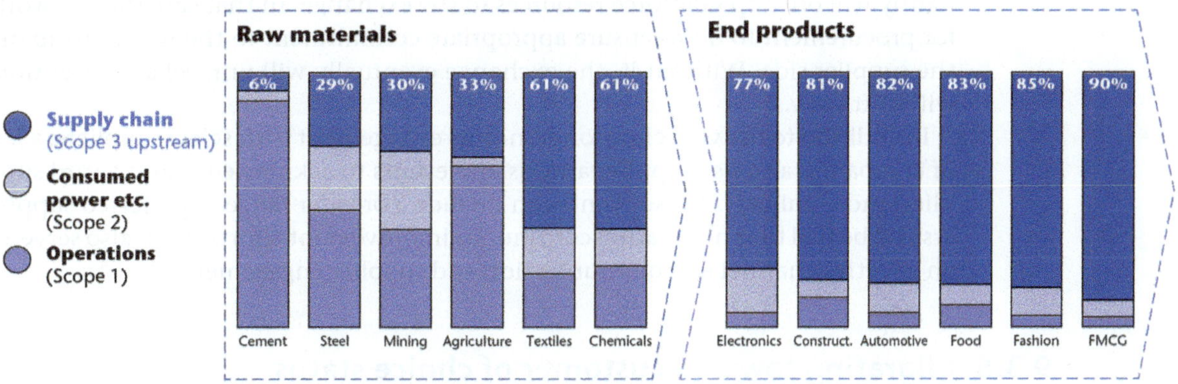

Note: Top companies selected based on number of reported Scope 3 upstream categories and Industry fit:
FMCG = fast-moving consumer goods

Figure 9.14 Example vendor rating report and action planning.

9.3.5 Executive ownership of supply relationships

The rationale behind executive ownership is that there is so much value to be gained from select supplier relationships that it should not be left to procurement alone to manage them - and that it is worth the involvement of senior executives from across business units that use supplier services and goods. Typically, companies will shortlist their most important suppliers and invite senior executives of business units that are prominent users of the suppliers on the list to assume ownership of between one and three supplier relationships.

The role of an *executive owner* of the relationship includes:

- hosting two or three top-to-top meetings with peers from the supplier to discuss the relationship and business opportunities;
- serving as a steward of the supplier inside the organisation;
- serving as an escalation point for usage and performance issues with the supplier;
- serving as a sponsor of joint improvement projects and ensuring proper resource allocation towards these projects.

Procurement may do most of the detailed work to support the executive owner but should not seek to take over the relationship. Rather, procurement should seek to enable the relationship. If it is hard in a business to find executives who are willing to take on ownership of a few supplier relationships, the value of suppliers is not being properly recognised within the company. In such cases, procurement has some internal marketing to do. Alternatively, it may be that executives already have suppliers that they regularly interact with, but on a more informal basis. Here, procurement needs to infuse the systematic selection of the shortlist and rigour into the way that relationships are managed. The value that can be derived from this should provide the incentive. Finally, it may be that the supplier predominantly will offer up salesforce resources to the exchange. In that case there is work for procurement to do to ensure appropriate commitment to the relationship on the supplier side. Without it, the exchange eventually will unravel and attention will shift away.

In addition to the very close 'one-on-one' engagement with select suppliers, a lot of companies also use supplier awards and events to acknowledge and award suppliers more publicly. These events can include a broader range of preferred suppliers and be tied to vendor rating continuous improvement efforts. They also serve as an effective channel for communication and supplier engagement.

9.3.6 Migrating towards customer of choice status

A final stage in implementing and rolling out supplier relationship management is more of an aspirational stage that is not yet fully achieved by many companies. In this stage all the investment in preparing to focus on a select few suppliers and the resource allocation geared towards selected suppliers, begins to pay off at an advanced level of supplier privileges. Supplier relationship management in many respects is 'reverse marketing' – it is the marketing of a company to its suppliers, seeking to acquire preferred status as a customer.

Think back to Activity 9.3 on segmentation: does this not have a lot to do with 'selling' the supplier? Again, this goes well beyond the traditional approach of procurement as the function that drives prices down through tough negotiations. This has everything to do with unleashing the full power of business-aligned procurement – with business engagement, ownership and involvement at multiple levels, from category strategy development, through strategic sourcing, through segmentation and strategic relationship ownership. The purpose of seeking **customer of choice** status is to acquire a level of support from suppliers, not just in price points or shipment conditions but wholly and fully that is preferred to competition. In search of this goal, supplier relationship management might pay off as a competitive differentiator. This obviously requires an organisation's ability to achieve a status with its supplier, making it worthy of such investment.

Customer of choice status entails several benefits, including:

- first access to innovations and R&D;
- customised solutions on a technology, process, service and product level hardwired into company supply chain processes;
- best account management staff allocated to the account;
- supplier wanting to do more than is needed;
- all senior executive ownership met with equal level engagement, both in seniority, resource allocation, account management support and time commitment.

The Tips box offers a set of tips and suggestions for supplier relationship management.

***Tips*: For effective supplier relationship management**

1. Supplier relationship management is a process, not a one-off activity.
2. We need to align internally before looking outward, but often look outside first.
3. Again, this is also not just about price: do not set all measures in a one-sided way but have the discussion about which measures to use as a basic level engagement with suppliers, ending up with joint and shared scorecards.
4. Procurement challenges suppliers but should steward them internally.
5. Don't try to do it on your own: the more sponsors and business interactions the better (including for vendor rating).
6. If you do not know how suppliers are graded, the supplier might, as suppliers very often conduct customer satisfaction surveys.
7. Measuring is less important than joint action planning; also share relative positions of a supplier against its competition to drive up performance.
8. Any feedback conversation is an improvement opportunity to drive progress.

9.4 Procurement's key role in sustainable supply chain management

***Key issue:* Understanding the role of procurement in sustainable supply chain management**

Sustainable supply chain management as a topic marbles its way through this textbook and it will feature in the next chapter about the future prominently again. Before we can conclude our review of procurement processes and business value contributions of procurement this section considers the role of procurement in sustainable supply chain management.

In its annual state of sustainable supply chain report CSCMP (2023) points out how corporate buyers are key drivers behind sustainable supply chain programs and how they have grown in importance as a driver. What that means is that procurement professionals are factoring sustainability into their core processes and are asking suppliers to engage in the topic and their company's sustainable supply chain program.

9.4.1 Why procurement has a key role to play

According to the Carbon Disclosure Project (a not-for-profit organisation that aims to support transparency about carbon emissions), the majority of carbon emissions in many industries are in scope 3. Scope 1 emissions are those caused by a company's internal operations. Scope 2 emissions are those caused in the generation of power consumed by the company. Scope 3 are emissions caused in the supply chain. Needless to say, if a company is serious about substantial carbon emission reductions it will have to turn to procurement to help reduce emissions that come with the supplies bought from suppliers.

For social sustainability procurement equally has a key role to play. Social scandals around working conditions that haunted Nike and Apple originated from suppliers that worked for Nike and Apple. So, ensuring social sustainability crucially depends upon procurement's ability to export standards into the supply base.

9.4.2 The role of procurement in sustainability

Key to procurement's role in sustainability is that procurement can grow business value generation throughout its core processes. These provide ways for procurement to make sustainability very concrete.

In strategic sourcing procurement can factor questions about sustainability into its evaluation of supplier capability. Sustainability contributions can be part of what gets contracted also. In supplier relationship management sustainability can be factored into supplier segmentation as discussed in Section 9.3.2, and sustainability can inform continuous improvement efforts. In the ordering cycle procurement professionals can request compliance of suppliers with its supplier code of conduct (SCOC). Additionally, the pattern of ordering can support carbon reduction efforts. Consolidating orders into a single shipment and ordering from near and local sources help reduce carbon emissions.

Activity 9.6

Considering the three core procurement processes (strategic sourcing, supplier relationship management and the ordering cycle), what steps can procurement teams take to contribute towards a more sustainable supply chain? Think for example of supplier selection (which questions to ask?), ordering patterns (which standards to set) and continuous improvement with suppliers (how to include in vendor rating?).

9.5 What does top procurement talent look like?

Obviously, talent needs vary by supply chain segment, and within the procurement segment it varies by subprocess. If savings are very important, then negotiating skills are important. For strategic sourcing seeking to unleash contributions to supply chain competitiveness, a lot more skills are needed. Whereas, traditionally, negotiating skills are emphasised in procurement, the list of skill requirements has grown long and far beyond that. Skill requirements include:

- *Strategic thinking:* in order to approach supply markets more smartly and with company strategic priorities in mind.
- *Entrepreneurial focus:* to be able to spot opportunities in the supply market against end-market needs.

- *Creativity and solution orientation:* to be able to find ways around supply market constraints and barriers.
- *Communication skills:* to engage internally and build bridges to suppliers.
- *Quality and improvement focus:* to continue to improve the performance of the supply base over time.
- *Relationship skills:* not to 'wheel and deal' but to develop joint ongoing improvement focus with suppliers and grow those relationships over time.
- *Stewardship skills:* to represent suppliers internally and ensure they achieve proper alignment with the business.
- *Consultative skills:* to engage with the business and ensure proper articulation of business needs for suppliers to fulfil.
- *Service posture:* towards business partners who specify and order, and towards suppliers who actually do the majority of the work. Whilst it is fine to report results, procurement talent should not seek the spotlight over suppliers and its internal customers.

In short, this profile is suited ideally to Master's graduates in the supply chain domain. Often, procurement roles are much sought after, even if just for a few years, due to the opportunity to make a clear and visible impact on large parts of the business. Procurement results are clear and often targeted in investment updates, merger and acquisition plans, budgets and business plans. So, procurement allows for demonstrable impact with senior exposure, which in turn makes it an even more relevant milestone along the career path of future CEOs.

Summary

What is the role of procurement in the supply chain?

- Procurement is the upstream part of the supply chain that faces suppliers. Given the amount of value procured by most companies, procurement plays a key role, not only in helping manage the company bottom line, but also in ensuring critical supplies, delivery service and product quality.
- Essentially, most companies and supply chains are critically dependent on supplies and suppliers for customer service and performance. It is therefore recommended that procurement is involved early and fully, so that strategies can be developed per product category, strategies that appreciate total cost of ownership, not just purchase price.
- Supplier relationships should be managed proactively with segments, performance measurement and management, policies per segment and executive ownership for key relationships.
- Procurement has concrete and important contributions to make to a company's sustainable supply chain efforts. The talent profile required for effectiveness in procurement is that of (future) top leaders of the company. The ability to demonstrate high-level, concrete business impact within procurement makes it a function much sought out by aspiring and ambitious talent.

Discussion questions

1. List 'before' and 'after' descriptions for procurement as a function and the professionals within that function when considering what procurement came from (staff order processor negotiating discounts after supplier selection was made by others) and how it is described in this chapter when it comes to:
   a. business alignment and business involvement;
   b. stage and degree of involvement of procurement in supply chain design and strategy;
   c. amount of time devoted to strategy discussion;
   d. link between category strategy, supplier segmentation, and vendor rating, and company and supply chain strategic priorities;
   e. calibre of staff in the function (defined as having the potential to migrate to other parts of the business, potentially make CEO one day and have a visible impact on company and supply chain performance, both on a day-to-day basis as well as in terms of progressing strategy).
2. Please also offer descriptions/examples of what these differences look like.
3. Brainstorm when is a good time to involve procurement in example supply chain projects such as the building of a new warehouse, the introduction of new product and the revision of customer service terms. What are possible contributions to these projects that procurement can make and how can procurement be involved?

References

CSCMP (2023) The state of sustainable supply program, Oakbrook, IL.

Cousins, P. and Speckman, R. (2003) 'Strategic supply and the management of inter- and intra-organisational relationships', *Journal of Purchasing and Supply Management*, vol. 9, no. 1, pp. 19–29.

Gelderman, C. and van Weele, A. (2002) 'Strategic direction through purchasing portfolio management: a case study', *Journal of Supply Chain Management*, vol. 38, no. 2, pp. 30–8.

van Hoek, R. (2021) 'Larger, counter-intuitive and lasting – The PSM role in responding to the COVID-19 pandemic, exploring opportunities for theoretical and actionable advances', *Journal of Purchasing and Supply Management*, vol. 27, Issue 3, 10068, ISSN 1478–4092.

van Hoek, R. and Loseby, D. (2021), 'Beyond COVID-19 supply chain heroism, no dust settling yet – lessons learned at Rolls Royce about advancing risk management thinking', *International Journal of Operations & Production Management*, vol. 41, no. 10, pp. 1579–92.

van Hoek, R. DeWitt, M., Lacity, M. and Johnson, T. (2022) 'How Walmart automated supplier negotiations', *Harvard Business Review online*, Nov. 08.

van Hoek, R., Lebigot, D., Bagot, A. and Sexton, S. (2023) 'Insight from industry: Moet Hennessy's development of an innovative supplier diversity program in the wine and beverage industry', *Supply Chain Management*, vol. ahead-of-print, no. ahead-of-print. https://doi.org/10.1108/SCM-01-2023-0041

Kraljic, P. (1983) 'Purchasing must become supply management', *Harvard Business Review*, September/October, pp. 109–17.

Mena, C., van Hoek, R. and Christopher, M. (2021) *Leading Procurement Strategy*, Kogan Page, UK.

Pagell, M., Wu, Z. and Wasserman, M. (2010) 'Thinking differently about purchasing portfolios: an assessment of sustainable sourcing', *Journal of Supply Chain Management: A Global Review of Purchasing & Supply*, vol. 46, no. 1, pp. 57–73.

Part Four

CHANGING THE FUTURE

The final part of this book takes a somewhat different approach. It takes the lessons learned in the previous nine chapters and considers how future changes can be expected. The rationale for these changes is based on earlier lessons combined with current leading-edge thinking on logistics and supply chain. Chapter 10 considers the impact on logistics and supply chain management of the future of factors such as sustainability, humanitarian logistics, digitisation and technology, and the creation of supply chain managers of the future. We hope that this will provide input to the process of taking the lessons learned in this book off the page and putting them into practice to create improvements in tomorrow's supply chains.

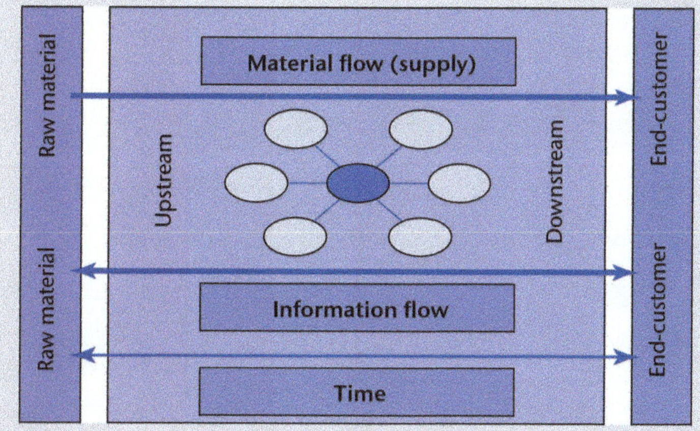

CHAPTER 10

Logistics future challenges and opportunities

Objectives

The intended objectives of this chapter are to:

- **consider major changes that are impacting supply chain strategies (the 'what');**
- **identify how management of the supply chains of the future will be affected by the advance and changes in technology, sustainability and humanitarian aspects of logistics and supply chain;**
- **list key issues in managing the transition towards future state supply chains (the 'how'), including requirements for supply chain managers of the future.**

By the end of this chapter you should be able to understand:

- **key issues that will affect the way supply chains of the future will be structured;**
- **improved ways in which supply chains may compete in the marketplace;**
- **ways of approaching implementation in major change areas, including through the development of leaders of the future.**

Introduction

We are looking at an exciting future for logistics and the supply chain in general, and the managers in it, in particular CEOs, are well aware of this. As Figure 10.1 shows, the 2024 Annual PWC CEO survey featured supply chain on the list of change priority areas. New requests from the board for supply chain to help achieve pillars of future strategic success and competitive differentiation are supercharging logistics and supply chain managers – it is a good time to study this field.

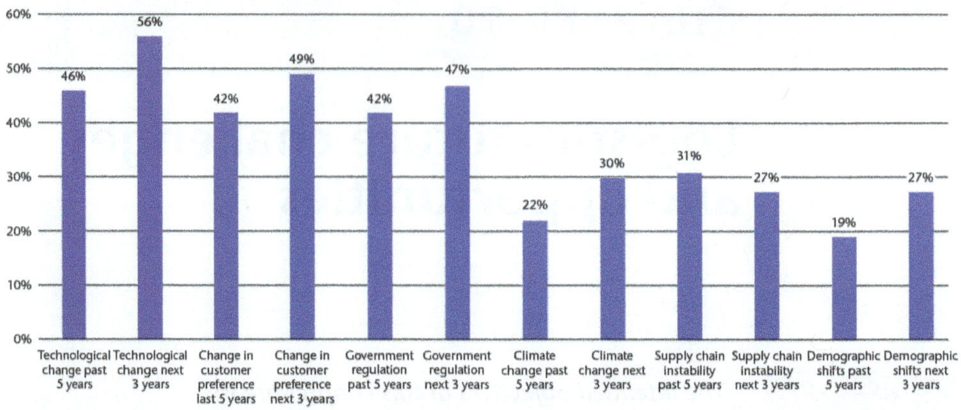

Figure 10.1 Impetus for change according to global CEOs.

(Source: Adapted from PwC's 27th Annual Global CEO Survey (2024), retrieved from: www.ceosurvey.com.)

Activity 10.1

Considering the change area priorities for CEOs, from the PwC survey featured in Figure 10.1, how might these impact the supply chain of the future? What is the relationship between these change priorities and the need for greater supply chain stability?

Everything you have learned in the book so far offers you crucial basics to travel on the journey towards supply chain management becoming a key enabler of advancements of the firm's competitive position. The question becomes: what is it that we will be working on in the next few years as we strive to further deliver on the promise of supply chain management? There is not one single answer to this question. If one thing should be clear from the cases and examples offered in this book so far, it is that there are multiple answers, depending upon markets, company maturity and strategy. No two supply chains are alike, and companies often participate in multiple supply chains. Furthermore, there are multiple scenarios and initiative areas on which both practice and research should focus. There is, accordingly, plenty of scope for progress, in terms of both basics and the more innovative areas. The difference between 'satisfactory' companies and supply chain managers and 'excellent' companies and supply chain managers will be in the degree of executing concepts, such as those covered in this book, and implementing them for real. In this chapter we offer both key areas where work is to be done, even for the best companies, as well as levers to develop for successful supply chain managers of the future. So, in this chapter, we look both at the 'what' and the 'how' of supply chains of the future.

Key issues **This chapter addresses five key issues:**

1. **Technology change – technological innovations and digitisation:** technological enablement of supply chains of the future from source to ship, from make to store.
2. **Pulling the chain in the right direction:** how do we manage sustainable supply chains in the future and 'put our money where our mouth is'?
3. **Chained to a bigger cause:** what is the role of logistics in humanitarian efforts?
4. **The critical link in the chain – or supply chain managers and the future of work:** the major influences on creating supply chain managers of the future and the rapidly migrating talent profile needed for success.
5. **Changing chains:** practical lessons on how the massive changes needed to create the supply chain of the future can be managed and achieved.

10.1 Digitalisation of the supply chain and tech enablement

***Key issue:* Technological advancements enable new supply chain capability and performance levels**

Technology has historically enabled performance and capability enhancement along the supply chain. The invention of the modern railway connects villages to ports and ports to factories. Intermodel connected road and rail transportation in an efficient and environmentally friendly manner, and barcodes help revolutionalise not just store check-out (its original use case) but also inventory management, tracking and tracing and material handling.

Across every stage of the supply chain newer technologies continue to advance practice and capability in the supply chain. In **last mile delivery** drones, automatic guided vehicles have made their introduction. In transportation **electric trucks** are being introduced as a more environmentally friendly mode. In production, robotics and **3D printing** increase productivity and reduce inventory levels. By being able to print parts less inventory has to be on hand and local production becomes a less costly proposition. Table 10.1 lists technology applications and supply chain performance enhancements supported by **digitalisation**. It is key to note that technology plays an enabling role in the supply chain. It is not as much about what the technology can do as it is about what you can do with technology. As Table 10.1 clarifies, technology can have a multitude of beneficial impacts on supply chain capability, from productivity improvements to service enhancement, from risk reduction to responsiveness.

Table 10.1 Newer technologies along the supply chain and supply chain contributions.

Supply chain stage	Newer technology options	Supply chain capability contributions
Plan	AI input, including risk monitors, informing (re-)forecasting	Improved accuracy and ability to respond to demand variations and changes
Source	Rapid supplier search, AI chatbot for negotiations, risk monitoring platforms	Productivity, greater spend coverage and resilience and innovation acceleration, improved visibility into the supply base, including tier 2 and 3
Make	Robotics, 3D printing of parts	Productivity advances that enable manufacturing closer to the customer, contributing to responsiveness gains. 3D printing reduces parts inventory and enables efficient local production of parts
Store	**Lights out warehouses*** with robotics for pallet handling, sorting, packing and handling, blockchain for product tracing and tagging	Productivity, reduced reliance on scarce labour and improved working conditions
Deliver	Drones and AGV in last mile, electric trucks in inbound transportation	Enhanced delivery speed and service to consumers, avoiding driver shortage

*Fully automated warehouses that operate without human intervention, using robotics for tasks like pallet handling and sorting, improving productivity and reducing labour dependency.

What is key for technology adoption are a few key decision-making items (see Mena et al., 2021):

- Starting not with the technology but with the problem we would like to solve with possible help of technology;
- Thinking through what new capability technology can add over existing capabilities and technologies; and
- Thinking through how to fit technology in with existing technology.

In addition to those considerations for the mindful adoption of technology, the careful approach of adoption and roll out is critical. Switching over warehousing systems or transportation management systems poorly can lead to massive service disruptions and loss of revenue and customer satisfaction. Equally so, engagement of leadership, supply chain managers, cross functional peers and often suppliers is crucial. There are several barriers that need to be bridged (see van Hoek, 2024) including:

- Education of users and training of suppliers
- Articulation of a business case for the change and engaging leadership around this case
- Securing investment and organisational engagement
- Investment in technology infrastructure and IT support

It is likely that technological advancements will continue at a rapid pace across the supply chain. For managers this requires a lifelong learning approach. It does not require technological expertise, rather it requires the ability to consider technology as an enabler, in specific ways, for specific supply chain challenges, and a careful roll out and adoption approach.

CASE STUDY 10.1

Walmart automates supplier negotiations

Walmart International, the retailer with operations in South Africa, India, China, Canada, Mexico and Latin America, has adopted Pactum's AI chatbot technology for supplier negotiations. Buyers will select suppliers and develop negotiations scripts with variables that can be negotiated and items that can be traded. The bot reaches out to suppliers and negotiates over chat. This technology grows procurement productivity through taking over negotiations from suppliers, enabling them to focus on more important negotiations or relationships. The technology also grows the amount of supplier spend negotiated, with resulting savings, by negotiating with suppliers that Walmart buyers might not have bandwidth for. Like in an in-person negotiation the bot provides opportunities for the supplier to gain from the negotiation as it explores value opportunities for both parties.

(Source: Based on van Hoek et al. (2022).)

CASE STUDY 10.2

Siemens accelerates response to supply disruptions

Siemens from Germany uses Scoutbee's rapid supply search AI technology that enables the company to develop a long list of alternative suppliers for existing products using web scraping. This functionality is particularly valuable when faced with supply chain disruptions. During disruptions a common response is to search for alternative sources and available inventory. What the rapid supply search enables is accelerated identification of alternative sources and more information about these suppliers quickly, enabling the buyer to rapidly turn to the evaluation of those sources, ahead of competitors that are likely also searching for supply options.

(Source: Based on van Hoek and Lacity (2023).)

10.2 Pulling the chain in the right direction, in the right manner

***Key issue:* Environmentally and socially responsible organisations gain advantage and enable sustainability by innovating supply chain practices.**

The CSCMP (2023) Annual State of Sustainable Supply Chain report shows how customers (both consumers and corporate buyers), investors and current and prospective employees are recognised as drivers behind sustainable supply chain programmes. This indicates how in addition to compliance with legislation, sustainability is also good for competition in financial, customer and talent markets.

10.2.1 A growing agenda

As Table 10.2 illustrates sustainable supply chain management has evolved from a focus on being a good (enough) corporate citizen that complies with laws and avoid negative reputational effects from poor environmental or labour practices like pollution, unsafe and improper working conditions. This focus originated

Table 10.2 Progression of sustainable supply chain management.

From	*Via*	To
Corporate social responsibility	*Focus*	Sustainable supply chain management
Compliance	*Objective*	Competitive advantage and sustainability
Reputation	*Priorities*	Market access and futureproof supply chain
Partial; reversed logistics or sourcing	*Scope*	Supply chain-wide engagement, from upstream suppliers to downstream consumers, environmental, social and governance
Tier 1 suppliers	*Supply-line*	Tier 1–3 suppliers
Reducing waste, emissions and impact on environment, ensuring compliance and minimum standards	*Outcomes*	Gaining value from waste, circular and regenerative

from the fact that NGOs, communities and media started publicising poor business practices, often of tier 1 suppliers of major brands such as Nike, Apple and Disney. It drove a response in parts of the supply chain; improved labour standards for tier 1 suppliers, reversed logistics to reduce landfilling and start recycling and it led to a reduction in negative impacts of the supply chain.

More modern approaches to sustainable supply chain management focus not just on complying with the law but also on achieving competitive advantage in financial, customer and talent markets through new capability development and the creation of a more sustainable supply chain. For these efforts no part of the supply chain is excused, and the focus is on environmental and social sustainability, as well as on supply chain governance that supports a roll out of programmes not just to tier 1 suppliers but also to their suppliers. The latter is both important and challenging. It implies impacting business with whom no direct trading relationships exist and with business that may not be known or directly visible for a company. As a result it is crucial to approach sustainable supply chain management in collaboration with suppliers, and they with their suppliers in turn. In addition to reducing the negative impact on sustainability, creating a more circular supply chain that can be regenerative becomes the longer-term outcomes.

10.2.2 Environmental sustainability

Section 9.4.1 clarified that the majority of carbon emissions of a business originate from the supply chain in the vast majority of industries. Equally so, wasteful production practices upstream in the supply chain rightly reflect poorly upon downstream companies that ordered those products made. As companies progress on the spectrum of Table 10.2 their focus on environmental sustainability will change, and Table 10.3 offers guidance and tips for doing just that.

A more basic approach to the topic is to articulate and publish commitments to longer-term reduction targets, such as 50 per cent emission reduction against the 2020 baseline by 2030. Walmart did that years ago with its project Gigaton. The objective of Gigaton, set in 2017, was to remove a gigaton of CO_2 emissions from Walmart's supply chain by 2030. The company achieved this goal six years early because it did more than commit to a longer-term target. Walmart developed a reporting methodology and platform and actively engaged with over 5,000 suppliers to set goals and report progress annually. The company offers guidance, tools and active supplier recognition and reward, and progressed into a leadership approach that includes science-based targets (SBT's) reported annually. It also seeks to not just reduce but also target regeneration. That is the ability to leave the world in a better place than it was found. The 17 United Nations Sustainable Development Goals (UN SDGs) provide rich domain for regenerative supply chain contributions; the bottom of Table 10.3 offers tips for how to enable progress. The Bayer case study (10.3) offers real-world illustration of most of these tips.

Activity 10.2

Pull up the 17 UNSDGs and brainstorm how supply chain management can impact each of the 17 goals across sourcing, producing, storing and shipping operations.

Table 10.3 Progressing environmental sustainability in the supply chain.

	Company actions
Minimum standards approach	Articulate and publish commitments, set long-term reduction targets
Leader approach	Science-based targets with detailed public disclosure annually
	Articulate UN SDG contributions and seek circularity and regeneration
How to's/tips	• Assign C-level ownership • Train staff, suppliers and supply chain partners • Embed progress in personal target setting • Assume a lifecycle costing approach over operating cost approach • Engage industry partners and professional associations • Adopt a continuous improvement mindset and focus • Be transparent, including about challenges, and welcome innovative input • Consider how technology can support

CASE STUDY 10.3

Bayer Sustainability Program

Bayer, the Germany headquartered life sciences company that operates in the pharmaceutical, biomedical and crop sciences industries, exemplifies many of the tips from Table 10.4. The company is 20 years into its journey to improve sustainability of its business, and it has assigned lead executive ownership to no other than its CEO. It has made sustainability targets a mandatory component of all personal targets for managers in the company, meaning that managers' pay for performance and performance evaluations are partly based on their concrete contributions to company progress.

The company has set science-based targets and articulated internal and supplier codes of conduct that define minimum standards and support compliance with these via training, including for suppliers. It supports both industry consortia such as the Pharmaceutical Supply Chain Initiative, devoted to a more sustainable pharmaceuticals supply chain, as well as more generic professional associations such as Ecovadis. Ecovadis provides certification of sustainability capabilities and Bayer encourages suppliers to get certified. Ecovadis certification comes with suggestions for improvement and Bayer encourages just that over time.

(Source: Based on van Hoek and Udesen (2024).)

10.2.3 Social sustainability

In addition to environmental impact, supply chains also have a demonstrable impact on social sustainability. Part of the roots of corporate social responsibility social sustainability focuses on workers and communities in which a company operates. A minimum standard is to ensure compliance with labour laws in the various regions of operation. Safe, fair and ethical working conditions (including working hours and fair pay) are among those. And companies can include those requirements not only in their own code of conduct but also in their supplier code of conduct. This can enable more supply chain-wide adherence to standards. Ensuring that communities in which a company operates are positively impacted is another area of opportunity. In a more minimum standard approach this can be done through charitable efforts and community events.

A more ambitions approach is to target impact beyond minimum standards and aspiring economic inclusion of people and communities as a source of value generation and innovation. Supply diversity and inclusion is an example initiative that can do just that. Rather than just buying from suppliers with compliant labour practices, it seeks to commission suppliers with diverse (women, minority, ...) ownership or management in the supply chain. Doing so enables not just economic inclusion of minorities, but it can also drive real added business value. Inviting diverse suppliers into the supply chain may bring different and new perspectives, capabilities and talent into the chain. This can propel innovative efforts. Equally so it is a way for a company to 'put its money where its mouth is' a lot more clearly and very concretely when compared to community events or charitable donations.

Table 10.4 Progressing social sustainability in the supply chain

	Company actions
Minimum standards approach	Assurance of compliance with legal requirements in regions of operation and commitment to people in the supply chain and communities of operation
Leader approach	Setting higher standards including for economic inclusion as a source of innovation and value generation
How to's/tips	• Incorporate minimum standards from internal code of conduct into supplier code of conduct in order to 'hold hands' in the supply chain • Don't put it all on suppliers/avoid the risk of bluewashing • Factor into supply chain design (where to operate, where to source from) • Include in direct supplier engagement but also promote tier 2 and 3 efforts (e.g. tier 1 supplier diversity and indirect supplier diversity or diverse supplier spend from tier 1 suppliers)

10.3 Chained to a bigger cause

Section 10.3 is co-authored by Dr Iana Shaheen of the University of Arkansas
Key issue: **Logistics and supply chain capabilities enable response to humanitarian disasters and challenges**

In recent years, the frequency and severity of natural disasters have significantly increased, driven by factors such as climate change and urban expansion into vulnerable areas. This increase in disasters emphasises the growing importance of humanitarian logistics. An effective logistical response to these disasters is vital in saving lives, but before considering **humanitarian logistics** strategies, we need to first consider its definition. Kembro et al. (2024, p. 10) define it as:

> **The logistics and supply chain management focusing on the preparation for, response to, and recovery from a humanitarian crisis, with the aim of saving lives and alleviating the suffering of affected populations.**

Humanitarian logistics differs significantly from commercial logistics, primarily in its focus and operational environment. While commercial logistics is mostly concentrated on profit maximisation and efficiency, which ensures a stable demand and supply chain, humanitarian logistics prioritises rapid, flexible responses to unpredictable demand fluctuations caused by emergencies and focuses on saving lives (Holguín-Veras et al., 2012). Humanitarian efforts often deal with sudden, volatile demand spikes and operate in challenging conditions without the structured supply chains typical in commercial settings.

In humanitarian logistics, the identification of the true customer is complex, as donors contribute both funds and goods, while beneficiaries, who receive the aid, do not directly pay for these products, leading to a unique business model where the end-user and the investor are different.

There are two main business models of humanitarian logistics: emergency aid and developmental aid. Emergency aid logistics focuses on immediate relief to support populations affected by sudden crises or disasters. It emphasises rapid response to save lives and alleviate suffering in the short term. This requires a highly flexible and responsive supply chain, often characterised by pre-positioned supplies to ensure quick deployment. In contrast, developmental aid logistics is concentrated on long-term improvements in vulnerable communities. It aims to promote sustainable development through the methodical and strategic distribution of resources necessary for projects like education, healthcare and infrastructure. The supply chains in developmental aid are planned over longer periods, requiring robust coordination with local stakeholders, and often integrating efforts to enhance local logistical capacities.

Kovács and Spens (2007) review literature on the different phases of disaster response, a type of emergency aid logistics, and define three phases:

- preparedness (or preparation) before the disaster;
- immediate response after the disaster;
- reconstruction (or recovery), which happens over a longer period of time.

10.3.1 Preparedness phase

Preparedness is used to enable the immediate response to be more effective and thus reduce the severity of the disaster outcome. This phase is crucial, as here the physical network, IT systems and the bases for collaboration are developed (Kovács and Spens, 2007). Network design is very important for shortening response times, for instance, 'Pre-positioning critical relief supplies in strategic locations around the world is a strategy recently implemented by some humanitarian relief organisations to improve their capacities in delivering sufficient relief aid within a relatively short timeframe' (Balcik and Beamon, 2008; pp. 102).

Another important aspect of preparedness is collaboration and coordination amongst all the actors involved in humanitarian emergencies, such as donors, aid agencies, other non-government organisations (NGOs), governments, military and logistics providers (for example Balcik et al., 2010). Tomasini and Van Wassenhove (2009) identify two perspectives of coordination in humanitarian logistics: the former is geographic and differentiates between the international, national and field levels, and the latter links different types of coordination to the disaster life cycle, according to the objectives and stakeholders involved.

10.3.2 Immediate response phase

The immediate response phase has two consecutive objectives: the first is to activate the 'silent' network, or temporary networks, as defined by Jahre et al. (2009). The linkages with feasible donors, suppliers, other NGOs and so on, are created in the preparedness phase but are activated only when the catastrophic event happens. To do this, a contingency team is shaped, whose main aim is to create proper channels of both information and material flow.

The second objective is to restore, in the shortest time possible, the basic services and delivery of goods to reach the highest possible number of beneficiaries. As Kovács and Spens (2007) mention, the immediate response links humanitarian demand, supply and fulfilment management, operating under a shortage of resources and information. As highlighted by Van Wassenhove (2006, p. 480), 'At the start, it is speed at any cost and the first 72 hours are crucial.'

10.3.3 Reconstruction phase

The *reconstruction* phase aims to address the problem from a long-term perspective. The effects of a disaster can be enduring and have dire consequences for the population involved. Unfortunately, this phase is often neglected, due to the shortage of funds (Kovács and Spens, 2007). Cozzolino et al. (2012) observe that the immediate response and reconstruction phases require two different strategies, as shown in Figure 10.2.

On the one hand, the immediate response is about speed and flexibility – having sufficient capacity and resources available quickly – while cost is not the key priority. These requirements can be matched with the agile supply chain strategy (as described in Chapter 7). The aim of the reconstruction phase is to create a constant and efficient supply flow, where lower costs are required. Clearly, this requires a lean supply chain, as described in Chapter 7.

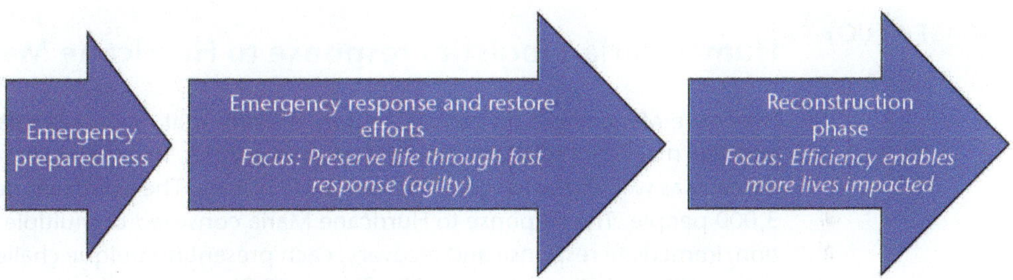

Figure 10.2 Humanitarian logistics phases and the related strategies.
(Source: Adapted from Cozzolino, A., Rossi, S. and Conforti, A. (2012) 'Agile and lean principles in the humanitarian supply chain: the case of the United Nations World Food Programme', Journal of Humanitarian Logistics and Supply Chain Management, vol. 2, no. 1, pp. 16–33.)

10.3.4 Future challenges

The importance of efficient, effective and equitable humanitarian logistics response is continuing to grow as the world faces an increasing number of complex developmental and emergency situations. Looking ahead, the future of humanitarian logistics needs to be formed by several key aspects:

- *Lean and agile practices.* The United Nations World Food Programme (WFP) demonstrates effective integration of agile and lean principles in humanitarian logistics. For example, during WFP operations in Darfur, Sudan, rapid response capabilities and strategic long-term planning maximised resource efficiency and aid impact (Cozzolino et al., 2012).
- *Sustainability.* For example, the 'State of Logistics and Supply Chain in the Humanitarian Context 2023' report discusses environmental sustainability as a key component in supply chain development within humanitarian sector (HELP

Logistics, 2023). The report highlights that incorporating sustainable practices is not only beneficial for the environment but also enhances the efficiency and effectiveness of humanitarian responses.

- *Last mile delivery.* During the Cyclone Idai in Mozambique in 2019, humanitarian stakeholders were faced with a major challenge to deliver aid to remote and inaccessible areas. These organisations utilised drones and other innovative technologies to ensure that food, water and medical supplies reached victims in the most isolated regions. This example emphasises the importance of improving 'last mile' logistics in humanitarian efforts.
- *Community engagement.* In the United States, local community groups play a significant role in supporting first responders with logistics activities during disasters. They provide essential aid and resources to enhance the effectiveness of emergency responses and foster greater resilience within the community.
- *The focus of developmental.* In the long-term response to the Rohingya refugee crisis, developmental aid has played a crucial role in supporting displaced populations across the region. This included sustained logistical support for basic needs, education and employment opportunities. Recent unstable political situations across the globe have led to an increase in the number of refugees, highlighting the importance of logistics in development aid beyond immediate disaster response.

CASE STUDY 10.4

Humanitarian logistics response to Hurricane Maria

Hurricane Maria was a powerful Category 4 storm that made a landfall on Puerto Rico and the main United States on 16 September 2017. The Hurricane caused immense damage as well as the longest blackout in US history. The estimated death toll was over 3,000 people. The response to Hurricane Maria consisted of multiple phases: preparation, immediate response and recovery, each presenting unique challenges and requiring specific logistics operations (see Figure 10.3).

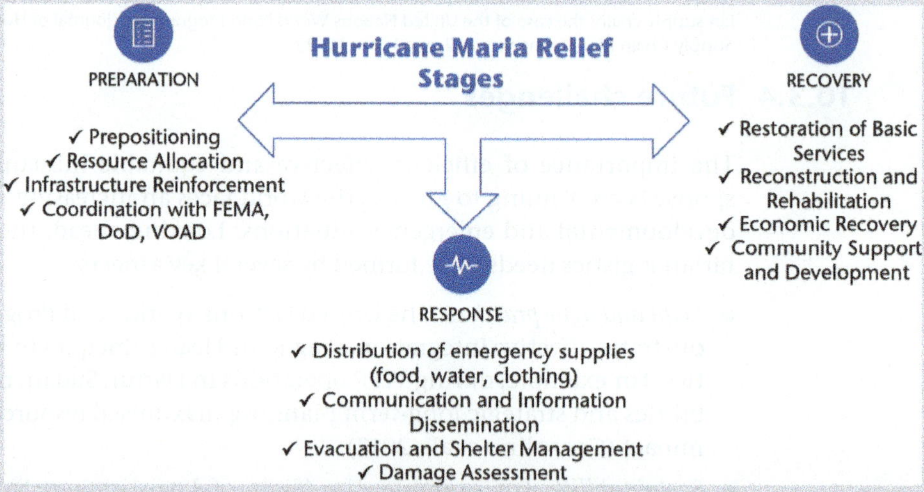

Figure 10.3 Humanitarian logistics activities during and after Hurricane Maria.
(Source: Dr. Iana Shaheen of the University of Arkansas.)

Preparation phase

In preparation for Hurricane Maria, agencies such as Federal Emergency Management Agency (FEMA) and VOAD (National Voluntary Organizations Active in Disaster) were already stretched thin due to the recent impacts of Hurricane Irma (August 30th, 2017). Despite efforts, significant gaps remained, particularly in pre-positioning supplies which are crucial for a rapid response. Prior to the landfall, FEMA mobilised resources including the dispatch of 3,000 staff members and preparation of over 274,000 meals as well as essential equipment (e.g., generators and cots) to ensure quick distribution after the landfall. The Department of Defense (DoD) also supported logistical operations by placing ships, the USS Kearsarge and USS Oak Hill, near the potentially affected areas, so that they can perform search and rescue operations, medical evacuations and provide substantial logistical support.

Response phase

Immediately following the hurricane, FEMA reported the destruction of 80 per cent of the power transmission lines on the island, which affected all 3.4 million residents. This created significant challenges of organisation operating in the response phase. With the power grid down, generators became essential for operating everything from water pumps to hospitals. However, FEMA and DoD were facing logistical challenges to deliver the necessary fuel because the infrastructure was significantly damaged. Emergency logistics operations included the DoD and FEMA coordinating the delivery of over 4 million meals and 6 million litres of water. The logistical response was delayed due to the following factors:

1. Airport damage. Many airports in Puerto Rico were significantly damaged, which limited their operational capacity. The damage affected the number of flights that could bring in relief supplies and personnel from the US. For example, only military and relief flights were initially allowed at some airports, delaying the broader distribution of aid.
2. Road blockages. Most of the island roads were blocked by extensive debris and fallen trees or flooded. This significantly delayed the distribution of aid from ports and airports to affected communities, complicating the 'last mile' logistics.
3. Power outages. The hurricane destroyed the power grid, leaving most of the island without electricity for an extended period. The power outage affected critical facilities, (e.g. hospitals and water treatment plants), it and disrupted communication and coordination efforts necessary for an effective and efficient response.
4. Port limitations. Ports were critical for bringing large volumes of relief supplies into the affected areas. However, many ports experienced significant damage, and operational restrictions had to be imposed, which slowed down the offloading of supplies and equipment needed for both immediate relief and rebuilding efforts.

Recovery phase

The recovery phase was long and slow due to the extensive infrastructure damage. Satellite technology was used to assess and visualise the recovery of electricity across Puerto Rico, indicating a significant inequality in recovery rates between urban and rural areas. The longest power outages, lasting over six months, occurred predominantly in rural municipalities, impacting low-income neighbourhoods the hardest.

Questions

1. Discuss the key issues that delayed the logistics efforts in both the response and recovery phases.
2. Discuss the 'last mile' distribution challenges faced during response to Hurricane Maria. How are these challenges similar to or different from those encountered in commercial logistics?
3. How do the coordination mechanisms between different logistics stakeholders in humanitarian logistics (like FEMA, DoD and VOAD – local agencies) vary from the coordination process in a typical commercial supply chain? Consider aspects such as communication, lean practices, resource sharing and objective alignment.

10.4 The critical link in the chain

***Key issue:* What are the changing needs and requirements that apply to the most effective supply chain managers?**

Ultimately, the purpose of this book is to support the development of effective supply chain managers; people are the single most important key to any success in supply chains. As mentioned in Chapter 4, the World Bank points at a skill shortage in the profession. It should be noted that today's and tomorrow's supply chain managers look very different from the supply chain staff of the recent past. There are several key capabilities that will make or break supply chain managers of the near future:

- These managers need to be effective at interfacing with customers. This is new because, in the past, supply chain staff used to be almost completely internally and operationally focused. Sales monopolised the customer, leaving supply chain managers short of 'supply chain relevant' customer insight.
- Functional knowledge is a base requirement (this used to be a differentiator, now it is a qualifier).
- They need to have strong interpersonal skills (van Hoek et al., 2002). Supply chain staff used to be technical and operational in background and training. They were heavily focused internally, without the ability to align peers around efforts and priorities, and unable to engage businesspeople in their efforts.
- They need to have general management and strategic management capabilities and skills. Hence, they should no longer be solely operationally focused and boxed in, which makes them unable to integrate and be seen as contributing to corporate strategic goals.
- They need to be able to develop and foster relationships internally and externally (as opposed to being focused on only running an operation).
- They need to be able to translate supply chain efforts and jargon into business language that their peers can respond to and relate to their own day-to-day efforts.

- They need to have a service ethic that does not include always saying 'yes'. Traditionally, supply chain people have been very good at either saying 'no' to special requests, or saying 'yes' all the time. They therefore need to manage trade-offs in operations, while finding creative ways to serve the customer and becoming an essential part of the business organisation (chain wrapped around the heart) and being considered key business partners.
- They need to be 'businesspeople' that help build and grow the business and use the supply chain as a tool – not the purpose – in doing so. Creativity, innovative approaches to business problems and entrepreneurial approaches to leveraging supply chain capabilities and practices to the benefit of the customer are key.

This will help supply chain managers avoid traditional pitfalls such as:

- Being unable to align the organisation around supply chain opportunities;
- Lacking crucial *voice of the customer* (VoC) insights to achieve success with final customers (VoC processes aim to go beyond customer satisfaction measurement by crafting a more comprehensive, cross-functional exchange with selected customers);
- Being only operationally focused, with limited insight into strategic business goals;
- Taking initiatives in an effort to help peers, but not succeeding due to the points listed above;
- Being great at supply chain concepts, but weak at solving customer problems and becoming a partner that is mission critical for supply chain partners.

Activity 10.3

1. Consider what personal development courses are key for a supply chain student to follow, in addition to supply chain programmes.
2. Find an example of a recent supply chain job advertisement at a management level, critique it for competency requirements and propose how it might be modified to fit the future challenges in the area.

Finally, we have a few pointers for the supply chain managers of the future:

- Traditional logistics people are often seen as being best at saying 'no', often because of initiative overload. Avoid saying 'no' for technical reasons, but ask about the business need that a request serves.
- One way to select what initiatives to support is to avoid being caught out by those without clear business and cross-functional involvement, ownership, sponsorship and goal sharing.
- Do not rely on technology as a 'be all and end all'. Most of the tough supply chain challenges can at best be supported by technology, but mostly they involve people and processes – and management of change skills.
- Traditional supply chain people often spend a lot of time taking calls about problems, fighting fires and being the hero of the day. But this can distract from working on structural solutions that will prevent those problem

calls from happening to begin with. So stop fixing things and start solving problems.

- Traditional logistics people were born and raised in areas of functional expertise and have built their careers around those skills. This leads to communication and business alignment issues. Supply chain management is a cross-functional job. So stop being a functional expert and start being a business general manager.
- Think growth, not just cost containment. The supply chain is often called on first to deliver savings and operational synergies – most often in tough times and during mergers. While the supply chain has a key role to play here, an emphasis on cost containment underestimates the contribution of the supply chain to growth and keeps it in a negative box – insulated from the happy times during periods of growth!
- Put the end-customer first – as ally and, ultimately, as judge.

10.5 Changing chains

***Key issue:* How do we actually make the transition to supply chain effectiveness happen?**

Based upon the experiences of having worked with and for many companies and the detailed study of companies in different industries, countries, stages of development and parts of the supply (detailed in van Hoek et al., 2010), it appears that there are some big lessons about changing supply chains that are being learned today. Most textbooks and research on supply chains pay too much attention to the technical aspects of management, leaving change management largely uncovered and unstudied. We have found that there are some clear pointers in making change happen in a supply chain. Whilst this list is not exhaustive, we intend it to be informative and useful.

Leaders and companies that make change happen in supply chains over and over again experience the following:

1. *Prepare for the (longer) run:* major supply chain change efforts tend to take longer than initially planned and longer than might be anticipated up front. And there are typically no shortcuts to true implementation of the plan (no matter what consultants and vendors might say).
2. *Plan to re-plan:* most major supply chain change efforts end up being executed differently than initially planned and the change programmes are often revised along the way in order to be able to respond to changed circumstances or additional change issues found along the change journey.
3. *A voyage of discovery:* there is real learning as you go along. As change programmes evolve and progress, managers learn about new changes and behavioural challenges – and how to incorporate them into the change programme.
4. *The boardroom pitch is only the start of the test:* after pitching successfully to senior management and gaining their buy-in, middle management and staff across the

organisation need to be engaged in the effort to give the programme a chance for real implementation. Additionally, given the learning that needs to happen along the way and the extended time period, real reconfiguration and implementation changes require (senior) management commitment, which needs to be earned repeatedly. So, in short, boardroom support helps launch the change but is not merely sufficient when it comes to making the change actually happen.

5. *Integrative but not integral:* change programmes in supply chains often focus on different parts of the supply chain. Whilst they all require integrative actions to ensure business alignment and cross-functional peer support, they often do not address the whole supply chain. Often it might be one part of the supply chain taking the lead – logistics or procurement, for example – and that is fine: the supply chain is big and comprehensive enough for many strides forward, some even simultaneous.
6. *Internal customers are a proxy for end-customers:* customer service first is key in all good supply chain efforts but not all parts of the supply chain have direct access to the customer, let alone the end-customer. For those, often more upstream, segments of the supply chain, internal customers might be focused on as a proxy for end-customers. Just like external integration requires internal alignment as a basis, focusing on internal service is a good foundation for external service capability: good service ethos also runs everywhere in your blood, not just when in front of a customer.
7. *Inside first:* many supply chain reconfigurations start internally to the company before they impact other segments of the supply chain externally, following the lessons on internal alignment.
8. *IT integration:* this was also a hot topic in the early 1990s, but it appears to still be hard to achieve and is not easily enabled but rather a source of a lot of work. It is important to keep that in mind, and not to assume that technology makes it easy to change broken processes. Technology cannot change broken processes or poor alignment without the hard managerial change work to support it.
9. *Benchmarks and best practices open eyes and help change programmes to stay on track:* external benchmarks are useful to set direction, make the case for change and audit progress on the change journey using externally verifiable standards.
10. *Cross-functionality:* is key to engaging relevant stakeholders in the supply chain, although not all functions and businesses need to engage. Rather than full supply chain integration, the concept of selective integration is key and specific to company and context. This also helps make change management more focused and perhaps doable.
11. *Consistent cross-functionality:* is a key characteristic of supply chain reconfiguration. Together with the complexity of the change process we suggest this is a marker of effective supply chain change management.
12. *Training and communication:* these are well-known levers. Training staff and management are key enablers of change effectiveness and readiness. Communications – to remind and reinforce across the organisation – are useful tactics as long as they are updated with the change journey adjustments and learnings during the change journey.

10.6 A great function to be in

***Key issue:* The future of supply chain has a lot to offer to the students of this text.**

As a final section, we wanted to offer a reflection on how much the future of supply chain has to offer for aspiring talent. Just consider:

- a growing CEO and board interest;
- opportunities to impact international operations and flows, with many echelons and parties in the supply chain;
- a focus on topics of growing importance such as sustainability, innovation and collaboration;
- an ability to touch many parts of the business and peer functions;
- a large change management agenda that requires the development of general management skills and capabilities.

All in all, not a bad stop on a career journey for future business leaders and CEOs and certainly a functional domain where an influx of new talent is very welcome!

Summary

What does the supply chain of the future look like?

- *Technology enabled:* technologies will further enable new levels of supply chain capability development and performance improvement along the supply chain. From drones to AI, from robotics to AGVs, technologies will continue to emerge and develop for the consideration of supply chain managers building and developing supply chains of the future.
- *Pulling the chain:* supply chains will play a growing role moving business, society and industry towards a more environmental and socially sustainable future. A key will be for supply chain managers to move beyond articulating commitment and long-term ambitions and turning ambition into demonstrable action and delivered results.
- *A greater cause:* Unleashing corporate supply chain capabilities in response to humanitarian disasters can serve a greater good and improve and accelerate emergency readiness, response and recovery efforts.
- *Critical link in the chain:* The development of a 'new breed' of supply chain managers that will help realise all of the above is a critical pathway from today to tomorrow and a very worthy focus of leadership.
- *Changing chains:* The capability to make the change actually happen for real is what stands between potential and results delivered and provides a litmus test for supply chain managers. The lessons from this book can inform and support efforts but there are no universal solutions in the supply chain and that, in many ways, is why supply chain is such an exciting place to be.

We hope the readers of this book will have picked up insights and lessons that they can use on their journey to create supply chains of the future. In our experience of working for many different companies in different industries and countries, and based upon our research from across the past decades, we are convinced about one thing: most of the progress in supply chain management is still 'up for grabs'. Both at the basic and more advanced levels, most companies still have only started on the journey of opportunity and possibility. Actually, making the change happen will be the characteristic that sets leaders apart in our field. We wish readers the best in making change happen and in working for a better supply chain of the future.

Discussion questions

1. We started out in Chapter 1 by defining supply chain management as 'Planning and controlling all of the business processes that link together partners in a supply chain in order to serve the needs of the end-customer'. How will leading-edge developments covered in this chapter contribute to this vision?
2. Suggest how the change areas discussed in this chapter apply to our model of the supply network (Figure 1.2) and to the integration of demand and supply.

References

Balcik, B. and Beamon, B.M. (2008) 'Facility location in humanitarian relief', *International Journal of Logistics - Research and Application*, vol. 11, no. 2, pp. 101–22.

Balcik, B., Beamon, B.M., Krejci, C.C., Muramatsu, K.M. and Ramirez, M. (2010) 'Coordination in humanitarian relief chains: practices, challenges and opportunities', *International Journal of Production Economics*, vol. 126, no. 2, pp. 22–34.

Cozzolino, A., Rossi, S. and Conforti, A. (2012) 'Agile and lean principles in the humanitarian supply chain: the case of the United Nations World Food Programme', *Journal of Humanitarian Logistics and Supply Chain Management*, vol. 2, no. 1, pp. 16–33.

CSCMP (2023) Third annual state of sustainable supply chain report, Oak Brook, IL, CSCMP.

HELP Logistics (2023) State of Logistics and Supply Chain in the Humanitarian Context 2023 https://www.help-logistics.org/fileadmin/user_upload/Dateien_HELP/documents/report/State_of_Logistics_Report__March_2024.pdf

van Hoek, R. (2024) 'From Compliance to Impact – Perspectives on how to develop a supplier diversity program that is less narrowly scoped and more wholeheartedly adopted', *Journal of Purchasing and Supply Management*, forthcoming.

van Hoek, R., Chatham, R. and Wilding, R.D. (2002) 'People in supply chains: the critical dimension', *Supply Chain Management, An International Journal*, vol. 7, no. 3, pp. 119–25.

van Hoek, R., DeWitt, M., Lacity, M. and Johnson, T. (2022) 'How Walmart is automating supplier negotiations', *Harvard Business Review*; https://hbr.org/2022/11/how-walmart-automated-supplier-negotiations

van Hoek, R., Johnson, M., Godsell, J. and Birtwistle, A. (2010) 'Changing chains: three case studies of the change management needed to reconfigure European supply chains', *International Journal of Logistics Management*, vol. 21, no. 2, pp. 10–15.

van Hoek, R. and Lacity, M. (2023) 'How global companies use AI to prevent supply chain disruptions', *Havard Business Review*; https://hbr.org/2023/11/how-global-companies-use-ai-to-prevent-supply-chain-disruptions

van Hoek, R. and Udesen, T. (2024) 'Developing a benchmark for supplier code of conducts – lessons learned from Bayer's journey towards sustainable procurement and research opportunities', *Benchmarking: An International Journal*, vol. 31, no. 4, pp. 1163–80.

Holguín-Veras, J., Jaller, M., van Wassenhove, L., Pérez, N. and Wachtendorf, T. (2012) 'On the unique features of post-disaster humanitarian logistics', *Journal of Operations Management*, vol. 30, no. 7–8, pp. 494–506.

Jahre, M., Jensen, L. and Listou, T. (2009) 'Theory development in humanitarian logistics: a framework and three cases', *Management Research News*, vol. 32, no. 11, pp. 1008–23.

Kembro, J., Kunz, N., Frennesson, L. and Vega, D. (2024) 'Revisiting the definition of humanitarian logistics', *Journal of Business Logistics*, vol. 45, no. 2: e12376.

Kovács, G. and Spens, K. (2007) 'Humanitarian logistics in disaster relief operations', *International Journal of Physical Distribution and Logistics Management*, vol. 37, no. 2, pp. 99–114.

Kovács, G. and Spens, K. (2009) 'Identifying challenges in humanitarian logistics', *International Journal of Physical Distribution and Logistics Management*, vol. 39, no. 6, pp. 506–28.

Tomasini, R. and van Wassenhove, L. (2009) *Humanitarian Logistics*, INSEAD Business Press. London: Palgrave Macmillan.

van Wassenhove, L.N. (2006) 'Blackett memorial lecture humanitarian aid logistics: supply chain management in high gear', *Journal of the Operation Research Society*, vol. 57, no. 5, pp. 475–89.

Glossary

3

3D printing A manufacturing process that creates a physical object from a digital design by layering material, allowing for on-demand production and reducing the need for large inventories of parts.

A

activity-based costing (ABC) A process-based alternative to allocating overheads, which allows better decisions to be made.

agile supply chain A supply chain designed to be flexible and responsive to unpredictable and volatile market demands. It leverages speed and adaptive capabilities to meet customer needs swiftly.

Agility The capacity of a supply chain to rapidly respond to changes in demand or market conditions, ensuring flexibility and speed.

arcs of integration A concept introduced by Frohlich and Westbrook that illustrates the direction (upstream with suppliers and/or downstream with customers) and the degree (extent across supplier or customer base) of integration. High breadth and balance in the arc lead to improved supply chain performance.

B

Big Data Large and complex data sets that require advanced methods and technologies for analysis. Big Data analytics can provide valuable insights into consumer behaviour and enhance decision-making in supply chain management.

bullwhip effect A phenomenon in supply chain management where small fluctuations in demand at the retail level cause increasingly larger fluctuations in demand at the wholesale, distributor, manufacturer and raw material supplier levels. This often results in inefficiencies such as high inventory levels and poor customer service.

business alignment The process of ensuring that procurement strategies and activities are aligned with the broader business objectives and goals. This involves engaging stakeholders and obtaining executive sponsorship for procurement initiatives.

business to business A transaction or relationship between two businesses, often involving products or services used in production or operations.

business to consumer A transaction or relationship between a business and individual consumers, focusing on selling products or services directly to the end-user.

C

capacity planning The process of determining the production capacity needed by an organisation to meet changing demands for its products. Capacity planning involves long-term strategic decisions about how much capacity is needed and when to increase it.

carbon costing is a cost applied to carbon pollution to encourage polluters to reduce the amount of Green House Gas (GHGs) emissions they emit into the atmosphere – it's a way of shifting the cost of damage back to those who are responsible!

collaboration In the context of supply chains, this involves long-term commitments between partners for technology sharing and closely integrated planning and control systems. Collaboration goes beyond mere integration.

competitive criteria The standards by which supply chains compete in the marketplace, often including factors such as cost, quality, time, dependability, agility and sustainability.

cost–time profile (CTP) A graph that plots cumulative time against cumulative cost for a set of discrete activities, which together form a process or a supply chain.

cost to serve (CTS) The cost of the administrative, commercial and logistics activities related to customer service delivery, as measured through ABC methodology.

customer of choice A status achieved by a buyer organisation when suppliers prioritise them over others due to strong relationships, reliable transactions and mutual benefits. This can lead to better service and preferential terms.

customer order decoupling point (CODP) The point in the supply chain where the product is customised to meet a specific customer's order. Upstream from this point, activities are based on forecasts and downstream activities are based on actual demand.

customer value The customer-perceived benefit gained from a product/service compared with the cost of purchase. In order to measure customer value, we need to understand what *aspects* of a product or service a customer values.

cycle times The time required to complete a cycle of operation from start to finish. In supply chains, this can refer to production cycles, shipping cycles, or order fulfilment cycles.

D

demand management The process of forecasting and managing customer demand to ensure that products are delivered to meet customer needs efficiently. This includes aligning capacity and resources to match demand.

demand variability The degree of fluctuation in customer demand over time. High demand variability can challenge supply chain management and necessitate responsive strategies.

dependability A supply chain's ability to consistently deliver products or services as promised, meeting or exceeding customer expectations for reliability.

digitalisation The use of digital technologies to change a business model, resulting in new revenue and value-producing opportunities. In supply chains, this includes the adoption of technologies like AI, blockchain and IoT to enhance efficiency and transparency.

direct costs Cost that can be tied to specific products. The most obvious examples are direct labour and direct materials. Thus, we can allocate exactly the cost of bought-in parts to the products into which they are built.

Dotcom stores Dedicated distribution centres for processing online orders, often characterised by optimised layouts and efficient picking processes not open to the public.

D-time Delivery time, or the time the customer is willing to wait for a product after placing an order. A mismatch between P-time and D-time can lead to customer dissatisfaction and lost sales.

E

efficient consumer response (ECR) A strategy aimed at improving the supply chain to respond to consumer demand more efficiently. ECR focuses on better collaboration and information sharing between retailers and manufacturers.

electric trucks Vehicles powered by electric engines used in transportation to reduce carbon emissions and improve environmental sustainability in supply chain operations.

electronic data interchange (EDI) A technology used for the electronic integration of the supply chain, allowing for the automated exchange of business documents in a standardised format between supply chain partners.

end-customer The final consumer or business that purchases and uses the finished product. End-customers are central to the supply chain as their purchasing behaviour initiates the flow of materials and drives supply chain activities.

end-customer demand The primary driver of supply chain activities, representing the needs and preferences of final consumers who determine the flow of products through the network.

enterprise resource planning (ERP) An integrated management system that focuses on automating the back-office functions of an organisation. It integrates various business processes such as finance, HR, manufacturing and supply chain management into a single system.

F

financial risks The uncertainties related to financial exposures, such as currency fluctuations, credit risk and economic downturns, which can impact the supply chain's cost structure.

forecast accuracy The precision of predicting future demand, which is critical for maintaining optimal inventory levels and meeting customer needs without overproduction or stockouts.

framework agreements Long-term agreements with suppliers that set out the terms and conditions for the supply of goods or services over a period of time. They provide a structure for future transactions without the need for repeated negotiations.

Fresh food depots A specialised warehouse facility equipped with multiple temperature zones to store and distribute perishable goods efficiently.

Friend shoring When production is sent only to countries deemed to be trusted political allies by the government of the home country.

G

geopolitical risk Risks arising from political or geographical events and circumstances, including natural disasters, wars, terrorism and pandemics, that could disrupt supply chains.

H

humanitarian logistics The process of planning, implementing and controlling the efficient flow and storage of goods and materials to alleviate the suffering of vulnerable populations, particularly during crises and disasters.

I

independent demand Demand for an item that is not influenced by the demand for any other item. Such demand is typically forecasted based on market conditions.

indirect costs are whatever is left over after direct costs have been allocated. Indirect costs are also called 'overheads' and include everything from the managing director's salary to the rent rates paid for the distribution centre - anything that cannot be allocated directly to a given product.

Information flow The exchange of data and communication necessary to coordinate and optimise activities within the supply chain, including demand forecasts, order processing, and inventory management.

integration (internal and external) The coordination and synchronisation of material and information flows within a company (internal) and between companies (external) to enhance supply chain performance.

J

just-in-time (JIT) A production strategy that strives to improve business return on investment by reducing in-process inventory and associated carrying costs. JIT is part of lean manufacturing and focuses on producing only what is needed, when it is needed.

K

Kraljic's purchase portfolio matrix A strategic tool used to determine the appropriate supplier relationship based on supply risk and purchasing power. It helps identify situations where an arm's length relationship or a more integrated partnership is appropriate.

L

last mile delivery The final step in the delivery process, where goods are transported from a transportation hub to the final delivery destination, often focusing on speed and efficiency enhancements through technologies like drones and AGVs (Automatic Guided Vehicles).

lead time The total time taken from the initiation of a process to its completion. In supply chain management, it typically refers to the time between placing an order and receiving the product.

lean thinking A management philosophy focused on reducing waste and improving efficiency through continuous improvement. It involves identifying and eliminating non-value-adding activities in the supply chain.

logistics The detailed coordination and implementation of complex operations involving the movement, storage, and flow of goods, services and information from origin to consumption.

logistics strategy A long-term plan that aligns logistics capabilities with business objectives, emphasising efficiency, customer service and competitive advantage.

M

manufacturing planning and control (MPC) A comprehensive approach to managing production processes, involving the coordination of resources, materials and information to meet customer demands efficiently and effectively.

marketing strategy A plan that integrates an organisation's marketing goals into a cohesive whole. It focuses on anticipating, identifying and satisfying customer requirements profitably, and aligning with supply chain strategies to enhance customer satisfaction and operational efficiencies.

material flow The physical movement of products and raw materials from suppliers to manufacturers, warehouses, and ultimately to customers.

N

nearshoring The repatriation of production activities from a lower lower-cost country, such as China, to another lower lower-cost country, such as Poland, that is nearby a major market such as Europe.

O

offshoring When production is sent to another country, typically overseas; it is often driven by cost minimisation objectives including access to low-cost labour and raw materials.

operational procurement The day-to-day activities involved in ordering, receiving and paying for goods and services. It includes managing purchase orders, tracking shipments and handling invoices.

operational risks Risks that originate from internal processes, people and systems within a company, potentially leading to disruptions in operations.

P

P:D ratios The ratio of production time to delivery time. A critical metric for assessing the alignment of supply chain processes with customer expectations.

partnerships A key step in supply chain integration, where partners work together under agreed 'rules of the road' and establish mutual trust, often with shared technology and governance processes.

product variety The range of different products or variants offered by a company. While it enhances customer choice, increased product variety often leads to higher production costs and longer lead times due to complex inventory and supply chain requirements.

P-time Production time, or the time required to produce and distribute a product through the supply chain.

pull scheduling A lean manufacturing principle where production is based on customer demand rather than pushing products to the market. It ensures that each process step only produces what is required by the next step, reducing waste and inventory.

Q

quick response (QR) A strategy in retailing where suppliers and retailers use technology to respond more quickly to shifts in consumer demand, thereby reducing inventory levels and improving service levels.

R

radio frequency identification devices (RFID) A technology facilitating electronic integration in supply chains by using electromagnetic fields to automatically identify and track tags attached to objects.

reshoring (or backshoring) Repatriating production from a previously offshored location to the home country.

S

safety stock Extra inventory held to mitigate the risk of stockouts due to demand variability and supply chain uncertainties. Reducing lead times can decrease reliance on safety stock.

sales and operations planning (S&OP) An integrated business management process that helps ensure that all parts of an organisation are aligned with the demand and supply plans. It involves forecasting and planning to balance demand and supply effectively.

segmented supply chain strategy A strategy that combines elements of both lean and agile methodologies to cater to different market segments. It balances efficiency with responsiveness to meet varying customer demands effectively.

seven wastes The seven categories of waste identified in lean thinking: overproduction, waiting, transporting, inappropriate processing, unnecessary inventory, unnecessary motions and defects. These are targeted for elimination to improve process efficiency.

strategic partnerships High-level collaborations in supply chains that involve shared resources and long-term agreements to achieve mutual benefits and competitive advantages. These partnerships require careful implementation and management.

strategic sourcing A methodical approach to procurement that focuses on building long-term relationships with suppliers and selecting them based on strategic business needs. It emphasises cost efficiency, quality, and innovation.

supplier relationship management Supplier relationship management (SRM) The ongoing process of managing and optimising a company's interactions with its suppliers. It involves evaluating supplier performance, fostering collaboration, and developing long-term partnerships.

supplier relationship management (SRM) The ongoing process of managing and optimising a company's interactions with its suppliers. It involves evaluating supplier performance, fostering collaboration and developing long-term partnerships.

supply base The network of suppliers that contribute components, commodities and other inputs to a focal firm's product or service offerings. Significant value is often added at this level in industries such as electronics and automotive.

supply chain mapping The process of visualising and documenting the entire supply network to identify potential risk points and enhance risk management.

Supply chain resilience The adaptive capability of a supply chain to prepare for unexpected events, respond effectively and recover swiftly with minimal impact on operations.

supply chain risk The potential adverse effects that uncertainties can have on the supply chain's operations, affecting its performance in terms of quality, cost and speed, as well as reputational standing.

supply chain risk management A systematic approach involving supply chain mapping, risk identification, risk evaluation and risk mitigation to manage potential risks across the supply network.

supply chains A network of interconnected entities—suppliers, manufacturers, distributors and retailers—that collaborate to produce and deliver products or services to end customers.

supply chain sustainability The integration of eco-friendly, socially responsible, and economically viable practices into supply chain operations and strategy.

supply network A complex web of interconnected businesses and processes that contribute to the production and delivery of goods and services, highlighting the interdependence of different firms within the network.

T

technological risks Risks arising from technological failures, cybersecurity threats or obsolescence that can disrupt supply chain operations and data integrity.

tendering The formal process of soliciting bids from suppliers for goods or services.

tier 1 customers Direct customers of a focal firm, usually businesses that purchase goods for resale or for further processing.

time-based process mapping A strategic tool for creating visibility of time constraints and flow across the supply chain. This mapping identifies bottlenecks and inefficiencies, enabling organisations to streamline processes and eliminate waste.

triple bottom line An accounting framework that evaluates a company's performance based on three dimensions: environmental sustainability, social responsibility, and economic profitability.

V

value stream A set of actions (both value and non-value-added) that are required to bring a product or service from conception through to delivery to the end-customer. Value stream mapping is a tool used to visualise and understand the flow of materials and information.

vendor rating A system for evaluating and scoring suppliers based on various performance metrics, such as quality, delivery and cost. This helps in identifying preferred suppliers and managing supplier relationships effectively.

vertical integration A form of supply chain relationship where ownership unites multiple stages of production or distribution within a single company, either upstream, downstream or both.

virtual integration A practice in agile supply chains that involves using information technology and partnerships to achieve efficiencies and responsiveness without owning all of the assets or stages in the supply chain.

Index

Note: "**Bold**" page numbers refer to Glossary